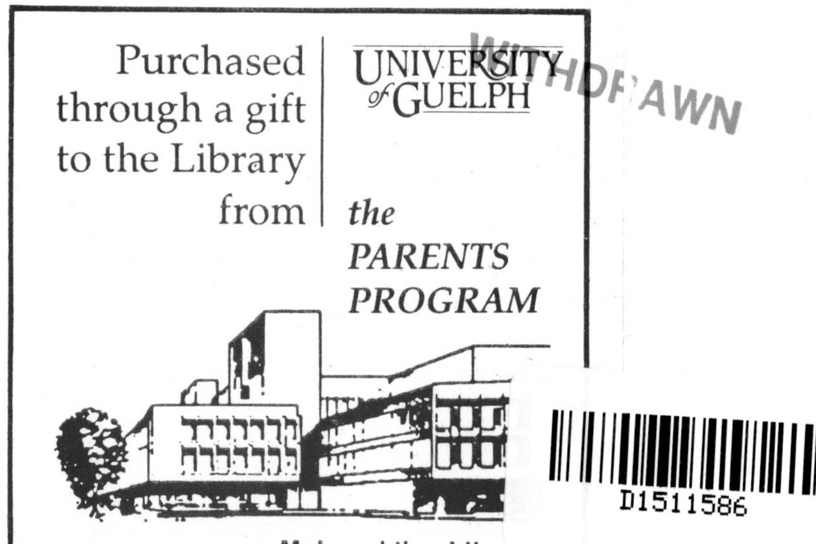
Purchased
through a gift
to the Library
from
UNIVERSITY
of GUELPH
the
PARENTS
PROGRAM
WITHDRAWN
D1511586
McLaughlin Library

Developments in Environmental Modelling, 18

Introduction to Environmental Management

Developments in Environmental Modelling

1. ENERGY AND ECOLOGICAL MODELLING edited by W.J. Mitsch, R.W. Bossermann and J.M. Klopatek, 1981

2. WATER MANAGEMENT MODELS IN PRACTICE: A CASE STUDY OF THE ASWAN HIGH DAM by D. Whittington and G. Guariso, 1983

3. NUMERICAL ECOLOGY by L. Legendre and P. Legendre, 1983

4A. APPLICATION OF ECOLOGICAL MODELLING IN ENVIRONMENTAL MANAGEMENT PART A edited by S.E. Jørgensen, 1983

4.B APPLICATION OF ECOLOGICAL MODELLING IN ENVIRONMENTAL MANAGEMENT PART B edited by S.E. Jørgensen and W.J. Mitsch, 1983

5. ANALYSIS OF ECOLOGICAL SYSTEMS: STATE-OF-THE-ART IN ECOLOGICAL MODELLING edited by W.K. Lauenroth, G.V. Skogerboe and M. Flug, 1983

6. MODELLING THE FATE AND EFFECT OF TOXIC SUBSTANCES IN THE ENVIRONMENT edited by S.E. Jørgensen, 1984

7. MATHEMATICAL MODELS IN BIOLOGICAL WASTE WATER TREATMENT edited by S.E. Jørgensen and M.J. Gromiec, 1985

8. FRESHWATER ECOSYSTEMS: MODELLING AND SIMULATION by M. Straškraba and A.H. Gnauck, 1985

9. FUNDAMENTALS OF ECOLOGICAL MODELLING by S.E. Jørgensen, 1986

10. AGRICULTURAL NONPOINT SOURCE POLLUTION: MODEL SELECTION AND APPLICATION edited by A. Giorgini and F. Zingales, 1986

11. MATHEMATICAL MODELLING OF ENVIRONMENTAL AND ECOLOGICAL SYSTEMS edited by J.B. Shukla, T.G. Hallam and V. Capasso, 1987

12. WETLAND MODELLING edited by W.J. Mitsch, M. Straškraba and S.E. Jørgensen, 1988

13. ADVANCES IN ENVIRONMENTAL MODELLING edited by A. Marani, 1988

14. MATHEMATICAL SUBMODELS IN WATER QUALITY SYSTEMS edited by S.E. Jørgensen and M.J. Gromiec, 1989

15. ENVIRONMENTAL MODELS: EMISSIONS AND CONSEQUENCES edited by J. Fenhann, H. Larsen, G.A. Mackenzie and B. Rasmussen, 1990

16. MODELLING IN ECOTOXICOLOGY edited by S.E. Jørgensen, 1990

17. MODELLING IN ENVIRONMENTAL CHEMISTRY edited by S.E. Jørgensen, 1991

Developments in Environmental Modelling, 18

Introduction to Environmental Management

Edited by

P.E. Hansen

Department of Mathematics and Physics, Royal Veterinary and Agricultural University, Thorvaldsenvej 40, DK-1871, Frederiksberg C, Denmark

S.E. Jørgensen

Langkaer Vaenge 9, DK-3500 Vaerløse, Copenhagen, Denmark

ELSEVIER
Amsterdam — London — New York — Tokyo 1991

ELSEVIER SCIENCE PUBLISHERS B.V.
Sara Burgerhartstraat 25
P.O. Box 211, 1000 AE Amsterdam, The Netherlands

Distributors for the United States and Canada:

ELSEVIER SCIENCE PUBLISHING COMPANY INC.
655, Avenue of the Americas
New York, NY 10010, U.S.A.

Library of Congress Cataloging-in-Publication Data

Introduction to environmental management / edited by P.E. Hansen, S.E. Jørgensen.
p. cm. -- (Developments in environmental modelling ; 18)
Includes bibliographical references and index.
ISBN 0-444-88469-6 (hardback : acid-free-paper). -- ISBN 0-444-88532-3 (pbk. : acid-free-paper)
1. Environmenal protection. 2. Agriculture--Environmental aspects. I. Hansen, P. E. II. Jørgensen, Sven Erik, 1934- III. Series.
TD170.I584 1990
363.7--dc20 91-14791
CIP

ISBN 0-444-88469-6

This book is printed on acid-free paper.

Printed in The Netherlands

EDITORS' PREFACE

This volume grew out of a course in environmental management, launched at the Royal Veterinary and Agricultural University in Copenhagen in 1971 and held every year since then. Among the many persons who have contributed to the creation and maintenance of this course and of the Danish lecture notes for it, let us mention just two: the late Prof. Niels Haarløv for his inspiring enthusiasm in the initial phase, the 1970's, and Assoc. Prof. Marta Willems for her unselfish and conscientious contribution in the 1980's.

Two circumstances have left their stamp on the book. Firstly, it was written for a course which was, and still is, intended to give an *overview* of environmental management in a broad sense, not to go deep into any specific area. Secondly, to some extent *agriculture* is its home ground - had it been conceived at, say, a technical university, the weight attributed to the various subjects might have been different. It is our hope that versatility has neither led to shallowness nor been disfigured by a lack of balance.

Since the book will still have as an important purpose to serve as a textbook for the RVAU course mentioned above, and since some of its chapters had to be dominated by Danish matters, one may ask (and some did ask) if it could not just as well have been published once again in *Danish* - why did it have to come out in English? It is our belief that this question sticks too much to the past. A specific environmental problem may be local or national, but the entire area is rapidly becoming more and more influenced by international considerations, and this must inevitably be reflected in teaching, especially at university level. Though the book can hardly stand alone as a textbook for a similar course in another country, we believe it may serve as a relevant reference and source of information for teachers in the area, in particular (but not exclusively) in the EC countries. Besides, it is hoped that the book will induce contacts between the authors - most of whom are from the RVAU, while the rest work at Danish environmental institutions or other universities - and their colleagues abroad.

Undoubtedly, the book will be found to have some shortcomings. Let us mention a few of those that we are aware of.

The order in which the various subjects are treated is debatable, and it is certainly not necessary to read the book linearly, nor do we suggest that a course should go through the subjects this way. The rough idea was that Chapters 2 - 7 present the relevant basic

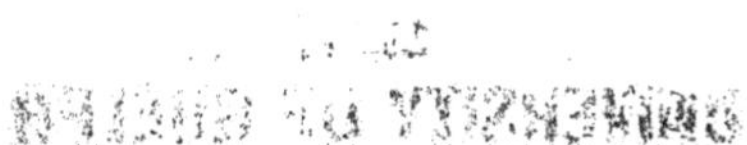

disciplines in and close to *natural science,* Chapters 8 - 10 do the same for *social science,* and finally Chapters 11 - 13 treat a discipline (ecology) and two subjects which are more *specific* to the field of environmental science.

Due to circumstances out of our control, we did not succeed in providing, as originally intended, a chapter on *noise*, nor one on the environmental aspects of various *forms of agriculture* (including 'ecological agriculture'). Besides, as explained by Prof. Wulff in Chapter 10, the treatment of Danish environmental law does not go as much into the detail of the actual legislation as might be expected, for the simple reason that this legislation is at present (spring 1991) about to be changed, yet no final bill has been passed. Should this book achieve a second edition, we hope to be able to supply these requirements.

The various chapters are characterized more by their authors and subjects than by the mild attempt of standardization on our side. Note that the *references* are listed at the end of each chapter, because they are, to a large extent, relevant to one chapter only. Papers in a *Scandinavian* language (Danish, Swedish, Norwegian) are indicated, both in the text and in the reference lists, by an asterisk, e.g., Petersen (1985*).

Finally we want to thank all those who have contributed to the realization of this volume or who have otherwise been helpful. Among these, let us mention Fritz Ingerslev, Helle Kürstein, Lene Duvier, Svend Tage Jakobsen, Børge Bundgaard, the late Jørgen Hyttel, and the staff at Elsevier, Amsterdam. See also the 'Acknowledgment' notes added by some of the authors at the end of their chapter. We encourage readers to communicate to us all errors and misprints they find, and all criticisms and points of view they might come up with. This will be of great value to us in connection with a possible reedition in the future.

Copenhagen, April 1991

Poul Einer Hansen
Sven Erik Jørgensen

CONTENTS

Chapter 6.3 ECOLOGICAL ASPECTS OF INSECT PEST CONTROL
Jørgen Eilenberg, Holger Philipsen and Leif Øgaard

Chapter 6.4 ECOLOGICAL ASPECTS OF CHEMICAL WEED CONTROL
Jens Carl Streibig

Chapter 7 GENE-TECHNOLOGY

Ebba Lund

Chapter 8 COUNTRYSIDE PLANNING

Jørgen Primdahl

LIST OF CONTRIBUTORS

AUTHORS

B. Bügel Mogensen, Department of Environmental Chemistry,
National Environmental Research Institute, Mørkhøj Bygade 26 H, DK-2860 Søborg.

J. Eilenberg, Department of Ecology and Molecular Biology, RVAU.

A. Helweg, Institute of Weed Control (Danish Research Service
for Soil and Plant Science), Flakkebjerg, DK-4200 Slagelse.

S.E. Jørgensen, Department of Chemistry,
National School of Pharmacy, Universitetsparken 2, DK-2100 Copenhagen Ø.

L. Kamp Nielsen, Freshwater-Biological Laboratory
(Copenhagen University), Helsingørsgade 51, DK-3400 Hillerød.

S. Kjeldsen-Kragh, Department of Economics and Natural Resources, RVAU.

E. Lund, Department of Veterinary Microbiology, RVAU.

H. Philipsen, Department of Ecology and Molecular Biology, RVAU.

J. Primdahl, Department of Economics and Natural Resources, RVAU.

K. Rasmussen, Department of Chemistry, RVAU.

H. Saxe, Department of Terrestrian Ecology,
National Environmental Research Institute, Vejlsøvej 11, DK-8600 Silkeborg.

S. Storgaard Jørgensen, Department of Chemistry, RVAU.

J.C. Streibig, Department of Agricultural Sciences, RVAU.

H. Wulff, Department of Economics and Natural Resources, RVAU.

L. Øgaard, Department of Ecology and Molecular Biology, RVAU.

EDITORS

P.E. Hansen, Department of Mathematics and Physics, RVAU.

S.E. Jørgensen, Department of Chemistry,
National School of Pharmacy, Universitetsparken 2, DK-2100 Copenhagen Ø.

All addresses are in Denmark. RVAU = The Royal Veterinary
and Agricultural University, Bülowsvej 13, DK-1870 Frederiksberg C.

1 INTRODUCTION

SVEN ERIK JØRGENSEN

1.1 MULTIDISCIPLINARY CHALLENGE

Environmental management has three 'legs' on which to stand. Firstly, it must take into consideration the *environment* - that is, the ecosystem - and attempt to provide management which will maintain a reasonable, close-to-the-natural balance for this system; secondly, it must reflect on the best attainable long-term conditions for *human society*, including its social-economic conditions; and finally, it must determine which solutions are technically and economically *feasible* and which are not.

The problems of environmental management are related to the *emissions of energy and mass* from human society. Such emissions have been taking place ever since the time of the earliest human settlements. Now, however, they have reached such levels that not only is nature affected in its vital processes, but the very existence of life on earth seems endangered. This is why we refer to these emissions as *pollution*, and why we are concerned about their effects on nature: if we cannot eliminate pollution, how can we at least reduce it, and how can we support nature in absorbing the part that is unavoidable?

Environmental management must draw upon many disciplines and professions.

The consideration of the natural balance of ecosystems requires a good knowledge of *ecology*, particularly of systems ecology where the properties of the *entire* ecosystem are in focus. Also *zoology* and *botany* are essential biological prerequisites, as well as general *microbiology*.

As the emissions, besides energy, from human society consist of various chemical compounds, *chemistry* becomes crucial for a solid understanding of *environmental* management. This has given rise to a sub-discipline: environmental chemistry. In this context, we are particularly interested in what are, to use a self-explanatory term, called *biogeochemical reactions*.

Various physical processes determine the transport of energy and pollutants in the ecosystem. In other words, we also need to include *physics* in our considerations.

The pollution problems originate from the human societies, and if this dominant species, *homo sapiens*, were to disappear from the earth, then all pollution problems would also disappear. It is our desire to maintain the human societies on earth and, to a reasonable extent, keep them an integrated part of nature. These societies must therefore be understood and must be taken into account in the context of environmental management strategies. This implies that *social-economic* factors and *legislation* will also have to be included in environmental management.

When we turn to the search for solutions of environmental problems, still further disciplines have to be drawn upon.

Environmental technology is concerned with technical methods of avoiding or reducing the various harmful effects of emissions. It is mainly based upon chemical engineering, but also requires - as do almost all technological disciplines - assistance from process regulation, mechanical and electrical engineering and, recently, computer engineering.

The striving towards pollution abatement during the 'Seventies and 'Eighties has clearly shown that environmental technology and legislation, even when they are at their best, cannot by themselves solve the pollution problems. It is necessary to integrate what is termed *ecotechnology* in the management strategy. Ecotechnology has emerged as a new discipline during the 1980s. It had indeed been applied even earlier, but it is only now that it has become acknowledged and accepted as a discipline in its own right, with a full scientific explanation of its fundamental concepts and principles (Mitsch and Jørgensen, 1989).

Ecotechnology is defined as the design of human society within its natural environment, for the benefit of both. As is the case with the older technological disciplines, ecological engineering and ecotechnology have been supplied with a basis within the theory of science.

The principles of ecology and environmental science have been developed during the twentieth century, particularly in the last twenty years. The time is now ripe for the application of these principles. Furthermore, tools such as *ecological modelling* have also been developed, and with the advent of high-speed computers, such modelling has been refined and may offer the possibility of quantifying even complex ecosystems, and showing how they operate as a whole.

Since environmental management involves so many different disciplines, it is not possible for one person to cover all its aspects. Sound environmental management thus requires *interdisciplinary cooperation* in a team whose members represent a variety of views, such as the scientific, the social-economic and the tecnological - not to mention the political - points of view.

To give a complete coverage of the knowledge from all the background disciplines needed in environmental management would be an enormous task, and in one volume one should not expect more than a summary. This book, therefore, should first of all be regarded as a multidisciplinary *introduction* to the most important aspects of environmental management.

As this book is written mainly by authors with a scientific background, and mainly for students with an applied science (e.g., agriculture) as their major subject, scientific/agricultural viewpoints and disciplines tend to dominate. However, as environmental legislation marks out the limits of environmental management, one important chapter has been devoted to this topic.

On the other hand, the social-economic aspect is covered only rudimentarily in the book. Besides being touched on in several other chapters, this aspect is however the main theme in Chapter 9, Environmental Economics and, from another point of view, in Chapter 12, Environmental Impact Assessment.

As mentioned above and also indicated in the title, this book is merely an introduction to the topic. On the other hand, it could be argued that such an introduction should be an obligatory part of the curriculum in all higher education related to environmental issues, such as the studies of engineering (all branches), chemistry, biology, agriculture, forestry, veterinary medicine, law, economy, and social science.

For those desirous of working professionally with environmental issues from a natural-sciences point of view, it would be necessary to go more deeply into such topics as environmental technology, ecotoxicology, environmental legislation and ecotechnology.

1.2 THE ENVIRONMENTAL FIELDS

A summary of the assembly of environmental fields was given above, but it seems appropriate at this point to treat this subject in more detail, that is: to propose definitions of the various fields, to specify the topics they cover, and to mention in which chapters of this book they are dealt with.

The scientific basis for the various environmental fields is termed *environmental science.* It integrates all those parts of science which are needed to understand environmental issues and to solve the problems involved. Biology (particularly ecology) and chemistry are the two disciplines from which environmental science extracts its most basic material and fundamental knowledge. But environmental science must draw also on geology, geography, physics, meteorology, economy, law and social science.

Environmental science must not be regarded as a kind of stew, prepared by mixing small bits of all the above disciplines. Environmental science is more than the sum of its components from other sciences: it is a synthesis, an integration of these components which gives a *new* understanding of our relations to the environment in which we live: how does it function, and how much do we depend on it?

In this process, it is important to keep a *macroscopic* view and not get lost in the analysis of details. Of course, analytical results are needed, for instance, concerning pollutants, when one is trying to solve a specificenvironmental problem. But the environment is so complex and has so many interacting components that it is impossible to survey all its details. Yet it is feasible to *understand* how the ecosystems are working as systems or unities, and how these systems, consequently, are affected by pollutants. Environmental science is the recurring theme through all parts of this book, and it affects even the chapter on environmental law.

As already mentioned, *ecology* is the sub-discipline of biology which is the most important for environmental science. It is most conveniently defined by means of a classification of

	Basic division:						
Taxonomic division:	Morpho-logy	Physio-logy	Gene-tics	Molecul. biology	Eco-logy	Evolu-tion	etc.
Bacteriology	×	×	×	×	×	×	
Ornithology	×	×	×	×	×	×	.
Zoology	×	×	×	×	×	×	.
Botany	×	×	×	×	×	×	.
Entomology	×	×	×	×	×	×	.
Phycology	×	×	×	×	×	×	.
Mycology	×	×	×	×	×	×	.
etc.			. . . . .				

Figure 1.1. Division of biology.

biological fields based upon the *size* of the system, see Fig. 1.1. Ecology is concerned with all the macroscopic processes of the ecosystems, with their mass/energy balances and transfers, and with the interactions of the various components. Chapter 11 is devoted to presenting the ecological considerations that are relevant to environmental management.

Environmental technology is the technology that aims at eliminating or reducing the harmful effects of the emissions from human societies.

Probably, the most important tasks of *environmental engineering* are how to *quantify* emissions and their effects, and how to select the proper environmental technology to solve the problems caused thereby.

Environmental engineering must not be confounded with *sanitary engineering*, an autonomous technical discipline for more than 60 years. Sanitary engineering focuses on sewage systems, water supplies and sewage treatment. Environmental engineering covers the treatment of solid waste and the various air pollution problems. Moreover, it considers not only sewage water and water supplies, but also industrial waste water; on the other hand the construction and maintenance of sewage systems are *not* included in environmental engineering.

Environmental engineering and technology are touched upon in several chapters of this book. Particularly relevant are the chapters on air pollution and on water resources.

Ecotoxicology deals with the effects of toxic substances on the environment, from organism level to ecosystem level. This discipline is mainly represented in the chapters on *pesticides*.

One of the most difficult problems in environmental management is how to quantify the impacts of *immissions*. Ecosystems are so complex and have so many interacting components that a survey of the total effects of the immissions is hard to provide. A tool to obtain such a survey is *environmental modelling*, and the last chapter of the book is devoted to a presentation thereof.

The systematic collection of knowledge of effects, without taking the interactions into consideration (as is done in models), is termed EIA, Environmental Impact Assessment. This methodology is presented in Chapter 12.

1.3 ENVIRONMENTAL MANAGEMENT

The relations between environmental management and the various fields mentioned in Section 1.2 are illustrated in Fig. 1.2.

Environmental legislation (2) may cooperate with environmental technology (3) to regulate emissions (1), or with ecotechnology to reduce impact (5). Both combinations result from environmental management, (4) and (6).

Impact is assessed by means of EIA and/or modelling, see (7) and (8) in Fig. 1.2. Emissions and impact are related to each other (9), and environmental management attempts to determine how low the emission should be to ensure an acceptable impact (10).

To omit emission completely ('zero discharge') is not feasible. Yet, by a combination of careful environmental technology, ecotechnology and environmental legislation, we may attempt to build up the kind of environmental management that will be able to maintain our environment in a close-to-ecological balance.

Obviously, this environmental management will become rather complicated. But it should not come as a surprise that a complex problem concerning a complex system requires a complex solution.

Good environmental management must make use of a wide spectrum of solutions simultaneously. One of the reasons for this is that all ecosystems are different and perform differently, and this is true even for different ecosystems representing the same types of lakes, forests, savannahs, etc.

Also, a wide spectrum of environmental technologies is needed. No universal technology is at hand: every pollution situation is different from all others. The chemical composition of the emission is different; the environment is different; the neighbouring emissions are different; therefore we need an individual solution which will most often be different too, from case to case.

The fortunate thing is that environmental technology and ecotechnology have by now reached such a standard that we do have a wide spectrum of possibilities at our disposal.

It is a challenge to find a good environmental management solution to an environmental problem. But as resources allocated to environmental problems are usually limited, it is of great importance to examine the problem carefully and consider various solutions before a final management decision is taken. In addition, this practice ensures economy for the solution of other problems.

As already mentioned a 'zero discharge' situation is unrealistic. There being more than five billion people on earth, we cannot expect our environment not to be affected. But there is a great difference between damaging the ecological balance and only influencing it slightly.

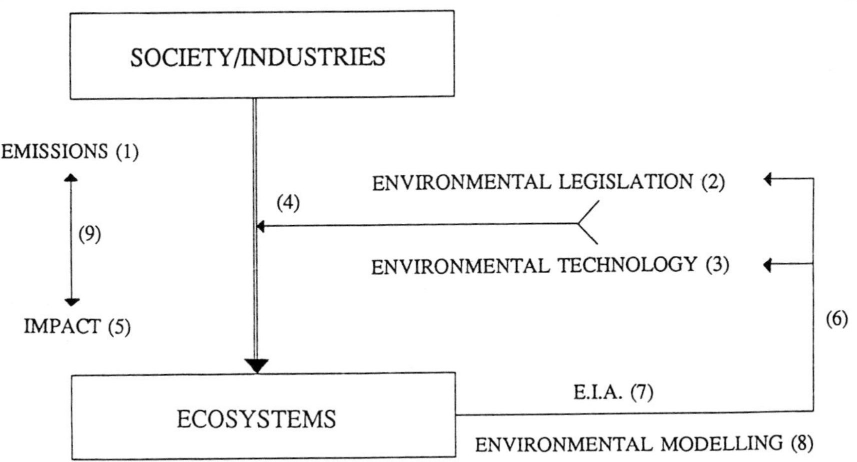

Figure 1.2. Environmental management: relations to other fields.

It is important in this context to emphasize that certain ecosystems are crucial and must at all costs be maintained undisturbed, or almost undisturbed, whereas for certain other ecosystems it may be acceptable that they be influenced by human activity to a greater extent. This is exemplified and discussed in more detail in Chapter 4, Water Pollution.

Such a distinction between ecosystems leads to a management which requires *planning*. A planning of all human activities under consideration, thereby keeping their effect on our environment under control, is a key to a more comprehensive solution of the environmental crisis that we are facing towards the end of the 20th century. Unfortunately, there are numerous examples of poor planning which have damaged the environment severely, even without any profit being gained by anybody. And there are even more examples of poor environmental planning that have led to a short-term profit but a long-term economic disaster.

As this review has tried to clarify, environmental management must play on many strings:

1) *Planning* of all human activities regarding their effects on the environment.

2) Development of an unambiguous and comprehensive *environmental legislation*, and equally important: the enforcement of this legislation.

3) Use of a wide spectrum of *environmental technology and ecotechnology*, and the combination thereof.

4) Further development of '*new and alternative technology*', which most often implies a technology with little or no pollution involved. Ecological agriculture and integrated agriculture are examples of such technologies.

5) Use of *recycling* of raw materials and waste materials to the greatest possible extent. Recycling is an attractive method of solving pollution problems: what is recycled is not emitted, and at the same time resources are saved.

6) Use of knowledge about the *interdependency* between society and the ecosystems, and about how all parts of the system interfere with each other. Such knowledge is important because a solution to one problem may cause even greater problems somewhere else in our society or in the environment. This adds to the difficulty of environmental management and prompts the manager to apply a macroscopic view.

1.4 THE ENVIRONMENTAL CRISIS

Up to the end of the 1960's nobody was concerned with environmental problems. Since then the situation has radically changed: we have witnessed - and we have become painfully conscious of - an explosion of problems that constitute a real environmental crisis.

Various factors have caused these sudden changes which have forced new ways of thinking in the philosophy of science, regarding the relation man-nature and the relation technology-society.

We shall attempt to point out the various factors that have caused these changes. The most important among the observed lines of development and changes of direction are listed below, including the changes in the sciences and in society caused by the environmental crisis.

(1) *The population growth* is a major factor. The pollution is largely proportional to the population, assuming a certain technological level. For some time, the population growth has

been faster than exponential, i.e., the doubling time has been decreasing. At present it is about 35 years, i.e., the expected number of people in 2025 is more than 10 billion. Up to now, it has not been possible to ensure a fair standard of living for the global population: at least 40 % of the present population do not get sufficient food, either in quantity or quality, or do not have satisfactory housing.

(2) *The standard of living* in the developed countries has increased more rapidly than ever before in History. Roughly estimated, this increase corresponds to a doubling of the production during the last 35 years, and thereby also to a doubling of the level of pollution.

(3) *The technological development* has changed the production methods and the life style dramatically, particularly in the developed countries. Labor has become more expensive compared with raw materials, and the production tends to base itself on the 'throw away' concept, to save labor. Furthermore, many of the new products that have been developed to facilitate life in the developed countries cause more pollution. A few examples: cadmium batteries; pesticides; various types of ready-made food.

It has been estimated (Jørgensen and Johnsen, 1989) that each of the factors (1), (2) and (3) has caused a doubling of the pollution level during the last 35 years, i.e. together they have led to a 2x2x2 = 8 times higher pollution level today than that of about 1955: a quite significant change.

(4) Fortunately, the dramatic increase in the pollution level has started to *change society's attitude* towards nature. Many countries have established a Ministry of the Environment and an environmental legislation and administration. It has been realized that the level of pollution cannot continue to go on rising.

After World War Two, the rapidly growing new technologies led mankind think that man was the 'Master of the Universe'. Today we are coming to realize that we must follow the laws of nature as do all other creatures, and consider ourselves as what we are: a part of nature. We have learned that we depend on the environment, and that our very existence is threatened if we disregard nature.

It is a sorry fact of life that it takes a long time before a majority comes to realize this, and before the new attitude has induced an efficient policy. Consistent environmental legislation is necessary, but not sufficient: it costs money to transform it into action, and this money must be taken from other activities. Besides, the growth of population, production and technology continues steadily, and in spite of increasing investments in environmental technology, the pollution level is still increasing.

(5) Thirty-five years ago, the general opinion was that technology would provide the answer to any major problem of mankind whatsoever. We believed that we were in just the initial phase of an industrial revolution which would eventually solve all the problems of mankind. But suddenly this revolution was called off and replaced by the environmental crisis, and we had to realize that 'the trees do not reach to the sky'.

The lesson was that *a technological development must be coordinated with nature*: otherwise it will not be realized. Today we are more sceptical as to what technology can do for us.

Even the environmental problems cannot be solved by environmental technology alone: we also need ecologically sound planning, ecotechnology and alternative technology. A new, 'clean' technology is slowly emerging and will, provided we know how to control the development, replace the old one. However, this development needs to be strongly promoted in the nearest future - if not, the survival of homo sapiens on earth is literally endangered.

(6) Nature has surprised us many times, and in relation to the environmental problems we have often been caught napping. On the one hand, nature has a large buffer capacity - on the other, it also accumulates and biomagnifies pollutants.

Through our attempts to solve the environmental problems we have learned that *nature is much more complex* than we once imagined. Ecology has come into focus, and we have witnessed a rapid development of ecological science which has shed further light on the complexity of the living nature.

Other sciences have also contributed to this understanding. Physics, for instance, has discovered hundreds of new elementary particles during the last decades and has exposed the complicated nature of the nuclear forces. The idea of finding one universal form or 'world equation' for all types of forces has been dropped.

The common trend towards an acknowledgement of the enormous complexity in nature has made science more humble. Nature possesses so many details and so many interrelations that we can never hope for a complete description of it, even if we analyse all the components and all their possible interactions. In other words, we cannot attain the goals of science through *reductionism,* but must supplement analysis with synthesis and apply a *holistic* view.

Table 1.1. Estimated environmental stress indices for pollutants now and in the future.

	Now	Year 2000-2030
Heavy metals	90	130
Radioactive wastes	35	120
Carbon dioxide	75	75
Solid wastes	35	120
Waterborne industrial wastes	35	80
Oil spills	40	70
Sulfur dioxide and sulfates	20	70
Waste heat	5	70
Nitrogen oxides	20	36
Litter	20	40
Pesticides	30	130
Hydrocarbons in air	10	20
Photochemical oxidants	15	20
Carbon monoxide	10	15
Organic sewage	20	40
Suspended particulates	20	90
Chemical fertilizers	30	50
Noise	5	15

This shift in science - some scientists speak about a *shift of paradigm* - has been caused partly by the environmental crisis. And without this shift it would hardly be possible to produce the scientific basis for a solution of the environmental problems that we face.

1.5 CLASSIFICATION OF POLLUTION PROBLEMS AND ABATEMENT

It is obvious that the selection of a proper environmental management strategy depends on the character of the pollution problem considered and of the abatement methods at hand. Therefore, a classification is presented which refers to the various chapters of the present book.

A pollutant can be defined as any material or any set of conditions which has created a stress or an unfavourable alteration of an individual, a population, a community or an ecosystem, beyond the point found under normal environmental conditions (Cloud, 1971). The range of tolerance to stress varies considerably with the type of organism and with the type of pollutant (Berry, 1974).

To determine whether an effect is unfavourable or not may be a difficult and often highly subjective process. Table 1.1 shows a list of some major pollutants and an estimate of the environmental stress they are causing, now and in the future. Each figure in the table is an environmental stress index computed as the product of three weight factors: (1) persistance (ranging from 1 to 5), (2) geographical range (from 1, only of local interest, to 5, the pollutant is a global problem), and (3) complexity of interactions and effects (from 1 to 9). The highest possible index is therefore 225.

It is important to recognize that there are both natural and man-generated pollutants. Of course, the fact that nature is polluting does not justify the extra addition of such pollutants by man, as this might result in the threshold level being reached.

In general, pollutants can be classified into two groups:

1. non-threshold or gradual agents, which are potentially harmful in almost any amount, and
2. threshold agents, which have a harmful effect only when present in concentrations above (or below) some threshold level.

When a threshold agent is acting, each increase in concentration will take it closer to the limit of tolerance until finally, as the last straw that broke the camel's back, the threshold is exceeded.

Non-threshold agents include various types of radiation, many man-made organic chemicals not found in nature, and some heavy metals, such as mercury, lead and cadmium. Theoretically, there is no safe level for such an agent; however, the degree of damage at very low trace levels may be considered negligible or worth the risk when compared with the benefits accrued by using the products or processes in question.

Threshold agents include various nutrients, such as phosphorus, nitrogen, silica, carbon, vitamins and minerals (calcium, iron, zinc, etc.). When added or taken in excess, such agents may overstimulate the organism or the ecosystem, thereby damaging the ecological balance. Examples are the eutrophication of lakes, streams and estuaries by fertilizer run-off or municipal waste water.

In addition, an organism's sensitivity to a particular pollutant varies from one stage of its life cycle to another. For example, threshold limits are often lower in the juvenile stage than in the adult stage where body defense mechanisms have been fully developed. This is the case for chlorinated hydrocarbons, such as DDT, and heavy metals - both of which include some of the most harmful pollutants.

The threshold level and the type and extent of damage vary widely with different organisms and stresses. For some pollutants, the threshold may be quite high, while for others it can be as low as 1 part per million (1 ppm) or even 1 part per billion (1 ppb).

The threshold level is closely related to the concentration found in nature under normal environmental conditions. Even uncontaminated parts of the ecosphere contain almost all elements, although some of them only in very small concentrations.

Pollutants can also be characterized by their longevity in organisms and in ecosystems. Degradable pollutants are broken down naturally into more harmless components, provided the system is not overloaded. By contrast, non-degradable pollutants or persistent pollutants are broken down very slowly (or not at all), and the intermediate components are often as toxic as the pollutant itself.

Knowledge of the degradability of the various components is of great importance to environmental management, since the concentration of a pollutant in the environment is a function not only of input and output, but also of the processes which take place. These processes must of course be taken into account whenever the concentrations of the pollutant are being computed. An instance of such considerations is found in Chapter 6.2, on the degradation of pesticides; it is demonstrated that the decomposition rate is an important parameter for the evaluation, comparison and selection of pesticides.

A pollution problem caused by a threshold agent does not depend on the polluting compound only, but also on the *sphere* to which it is emitted. The four spheres: the lithosphere, the atmosphere, the hydrosphere and the biosphere, have different compositions and give rise to different environmental responses and processes. As an example, acceptable concentrations of heavy metals are significantly higher in the lithosphere than in the hydrosphere, because the natural concentrations are higher in the lithosphere, and because it has a greater ability to bind heavy metals in harmless forms (by adsorption and ion exchange).

Similarly, the technology required to solve a pollution problem depends on the nature of the problem: whether it concerns waste water, air pollution or solid waste. A widely applied classification of pollution problems is therefore based upon the four spheres.

Table 1.2. Classification of pollution problems, with examples of agents.

Sphere	Threshold agent	Non-threshold agent
Lithosphere	Nitrogen	DDT
Hydrosphere	Organic matter	Mercury
Atmosphere	Carbon Dioxide	Carbon Monoxide
Biosphere	Sodium	Cadmium, Insecticides

The classification according to sphere may be combined with the threshold/non-threshold classification, as illustrated in Table 1.2 where examples of all the elements of the classification matrix are given.

Chapters 2-5 of this book are devoted to the pollution problems related to three of the four spheres: the lithosphere (Chapter 2), the atmosphere (Chapter 3) and the hydrosphere (Chapters 4 and 5). All four chapters treat pollution both by threshold and by non-threshold agents; by comparison of the standards established for these three types of pollution, it becomes clear that the characteristics of the spheres are reflected in these standards. Abatement strategies for threshold and for non-threshold agents are also presented in all four chapters. In the case of the former, a mass balance is often a good start; in the case of the latter, the toxic level is the first obvious question to be asked.

In principle, environmental management is concerned with the effects of pollutants on the biosphere. The crucial question is: "What will be the final concentrations in various biota of the compound or element considered, and what effects will result from this?" It is, therefore, not possible to distinguish between pollution of the biosphere and pollution in general. The examples listed in Table 1.2 for the three other spheres cannot be separated from corresponding cases of pollution of the biosphere, and *vice versa*. However, the examples in the table concern components which effect the biosphere rather directly, while the emission is indirect. By contrast, Chapter 7 treats a pollution problem related, to some extent, to direct emission into the biosphere, viz. the emission of artificial genes.

REFERENCES

Berry, J.W., 1974. Chemical Villains: A Biology of Pollution. Mosby Publ., St. Louis, USA.

Cloud, P.E., Jr., 1971. Resources, population, and quality of life. In: S.F. Singer (ed.): Is There an Optimum Level of Pollution? McGraw-Hill, New York.

Jørgensen, S.E., and Johnsen, I., 1989. Principles of Environmental Science and Technology. Studies in Environmental Science, vol. 33. Elsevier, Amsterdam, 627 pp.

Mitsch, W., and Jørgensen, S.E., 1989. Ecological Engineering. An Introduction to Ecotechnology. John Wiley, New York.

2 SOIL POLLUTION

SØREN STORGAARD JØRGENSEN AND KJELD RASMUSSEN

2.1 INTRODUCTION

The soil, or pedosphere, constitutes the upper layer of loose material of the solid earth. The soil is the natural habitat for terrestrial plants. Due to the processes of soil formation, most soils have, in the undisturbed natural state, a horizontally layered structure. A clear boundary between the soil as such and the underlying parent material, the subsoil, is rarely observed. The soil depth may be quite variable, ranging from 10-20 cm to more than one m. In cultivated soils the layer structure has commonly been disturbed by cultivation. The soil depth is then often taken - as is the case in this text - as the depth of the plough layer, 15-30 cm.

The science of *edaphology* is concerned with the soil as the growth medium for plants, whereas *pedology* characterizes the soil as a geological phenomenon, taking into account its composition, formation and classification.

The soil supports a large diversity of plants in a natural ecosystem and is the site for production of food and fibre for human use on agricultural lands and in natural and cultivated forests. The soil functions as a filter for water which passes through it and in turn becomes a drinking-water resource in groundwater or streams. Surface and underground water runoff from soils greatly influences a variety of aquatic ecosystems. The soil is also the natural habitat for numerous populations of microorganisms which decompose dead plant material and other organic compounds and thus maintain a number of natural cycles of chemical elements.

The soil receives a large proportion of the wastes and potential pollutants that are produced by modern society, be they of domestic, agricultural, or industrial origin. Such pollutants may be added directly to the soil, or they may be introduced via the atmosphere, e.g., 'acid rain' or lead from car exhausts.

A large part of the waste materials added, both natural organic compounds such as, e.g., contagious material, and some artificial organic compounds such as, e.g., certain pesticides, is decomposed by the soil microorganisms. Other man-made organic compounds alien to the soil environment may persist in the soil for a long time. Chemical elements such as, e.g., plant nutrients or toxic metals applied in excessive amounts cannot be destroyed in the soil at all. Such elements may be concentrated in the soil, or they may be leached into the groundwater or streams. Soil acidification caused by 'acid rain' may considerably alter the ability of a soil to retain the chemical elements needed.

This chapter deals mainly with soil pollution caused by excesses of plant nutrients and toxic elements distributed over large areas. Point-source pollution, for example from sanitary landfills or chemical deposits, is only mentioned briefly.

For the environmental management of the soil resource, soil properties and the hydrological conditions are of great importance and these will be dealt with first.

2.2 SOIL CONSTITUENTS AND PHYSICO-CHEMICAL PROCESSES

Although generally true in a qualitative sense, many of the following statements are quantitatively characteristic for soils of the temperate humid regions only, the soils of Denmark being typical.

A unit volume of soil in its natural state consists of roughly 50% solid particles and 50% pore space. The pore space is filled with soil solution and air in highly variable proportions, determined mainly by the weather and soil texture (particle-size distribution). The solid particles are either inorganic material, mainly silicates, or organic material. In natural soils, the ratio between inorganic and organic material varies considerably, a typical agricultural soil contains 2%-5% organic matter by weight.

The soil silicate minerals consist of primary minerals, such as quartz (SiO_2), and secondary minerals such as layer silicate clay minerals. The clay minerals are present in very small particles, belonging to the clay fraction (particle size < 2µm). They constitute from a few to more than 20% of the inorganic material. Important non-silicate inorganic soil constituents are iron and aluminium oxides and hydrous oxides. These are also found in the clay fraction and may constitute 2%-5% of the inorganic material of this fraction.

Box 2.1. Conversion factors.

One dm^3 of a typical mineral soil in its natural state contains approximately 1.3 kg of dry soil. Thus 1 dm^2 corresponds to 3.0 kg of soil to a depth of 23 cm or

$$3.0 \times 10^{-3} \times 10^{6} \times \frac{\text{kg} \times \text{t} \times \text{dm}^2}{\text{dm}^2 \times \text{kg} \times \text{ha}} = 3000 \text{ t ha}^{-1} \text{ to 23 cm depth.}$$

If the content of some compound is expressed on a dry-soil basis, then the following conversion factors may be applied:

$$\text{t ha}^{-1} \text{ to 23 cm depth} = \% \times 30$$
$$\text{kg ha}^{-1} \text{ to 23 cm depth} = \text{mg kg}^{-1} \times 3.0 \text{ ,} \qquad \text{or}$$

$$\text{t ha}^{-1} = \% \times \text{depth in cm} \times 1.3 \text{ ,}$$
$$\text{kg ha}^{-1} = \text{mg kg}^{-1} \times \text{depth in dm} \times 1.3 \text{ .}$$

One milliequivalent (meq) equals one millimole of a monovalent ion or ½ millimole of a divalent ion etc. It then follows that

$$\text{kg ha}^{-1} = 13 \times (\text{meq/100g}) \times (\text{molar weight}) \times (\text{depth in dm}) \times (\text{valency})^{-1} \text{ .}$$

The agricultural area of Denmark is slightly less than 3×10^6 ha. If the total national load of some compound is considered distributed evenly over that area, then the overall average load is approximately

$$\text{kg ha}^{-1} = \frac{1}{3} \times (\text{national load in 1000 t}) \text{ .}$$

Table 2.1. Specific surface area and cation exchange capacity (CEC) values for common soil minerals. After Talibudeen (1981). Values for entire soils are given for comparison.

Mineral type	Surface area m^2g^{-1}	CEC meq $100g^{-1}$
Allophanes (poorly crystalline aluminium silicates)	500 - 700	50 - 100
Hydrous oxides of aluminium and iron (pH 8)	25 - 40	0.5 - 1
Kaolinites	10 - 20	2 - 6
Clay micas	90 - 130	20 - 40
Smectites	750 - 800	60 - 120
Vermiculites	750 - 800	120 - 200
Loamy soil		15 - 25
Sandy soil		2 - 10

2.2.1 Cation Exchange and Adsorption Properties

The silicate clay minerals and the humus are responsible for the cation-exchange properties of soils. Due to their small particle size and layer-lattice crystallographic structure, pure layer silicate clay minerals have cation-exchange capacities (CEC) of up to more than 100 milliequivalents (meq) per 100 g dry material, as illustrated in Table 2.1. Humic materials may have even higher exchange capacities (up to 400 meq per 100 g). The cation-exchange capacity of humus depends much more on its origin and composition and the pH (it increases with increasing pH) than does that of clay minerals. Most soils in Northern Europe have contents of clay minerals and humus such that their CEC ranges between 5 and 25 meq/100 g. The exchangeable cations are dominated by calcium and to a lesser extent magnesium in near-neutral soils, and by hydrogen and aluminium in acid soils.

A CEC of 20 meq/100 g corresponds to a content of 10-15 tons of Ca in the plough layer of one hectare if the exchange complex is completely saturated with Ca. (See also Box 2.1).

In the soil, chemical equilibrium will be attained between dissolved cations in the soil solution and cations adsorbed by the clay and humus cation exchange complex. If an excess of cations is added to the soil, e.g., with fertilizer or as a pollutant, some of these cations will be adsorbed by the exchange complex, but this is followed by the release of an equivalent amount of other cations from the complex. The released ions may be leached from the soil together with an equivalent amount of anions.

The soil organic matter consists of plant and microorganism debris in various stages of decomposition, including a fairly stable end product with high molecular weight which is called humus.

The binding strength of cations to the adsorbing components of soil varies. This means that various cations are prone to leaching to a different degree. Specific examples will be given later in this chapter. For most elements exchangeable cations are available for uptake by plants.

Anionic compounds in the soil such as phosphates, $H_2PO_4^-$ and HPO_4^{2-}, may be adsorbed by iron and aluminium oxides. Other anions, such as nitrate, NO_3^-, are not retained by ion exchange or other adsorption processes.

2.2.2 Water in Soils

The constituents of the clay fraction, clay silicates, oxides and humus, also determine the water-holding capacity of the soil. Typically, loam soils may have a water-holding capacity to 1 m depth corresponding to about 250 mm of precipitation, whereas sandy soils may hold only about one fourth of this amount.

The amount of water percolating and thus the leaching of dissolved material is determined by precipitation, evapotranspiration, depth of the groundwater table, and water-holding capacity. A high water-holding capacity increases evapotranspiration, and thus decreases the leaching rate. In some areas of East Denmark, the net leach-ing rate corresponds to not more than about 100 mm per year, whereas the western part of the country, having a high rainfall and sandy soils with low water-holding capacity, may have a leaching rate corresponding to 350-450 mm per year.

2.2.3 Soil Acidification

Soil acidification is defined as a decrease in soil acid neutralization capacity (v. Breemen et al., 1983). As a result of biological processes a number of acids are formed in soils, the quantitatively most important one being carbonic acid. If the soil contains an excess of calcium carbonate this will gradually be dissolved according to the following reaction:

$$CO_2 + H_2O + CaCO_3 \rightarrow Ca^{2+} + 2\ HCO_3^-$$

and calcium and hydrogen carbonate ions will be leached from soils of the humid regions. However, the soil pH will stay around 7.5-8 until all calcium carbonate has been removed.

In calcium-carbonate-free soils, hydrogen ions released from carbonic acid will react with the cation-exchange complex and release metal ions such as calcium and magnesium, accompanied by a gradual decrease in pH. Under such soils, the groundwater contains dissolved calcium, magnesium and hydrogen-carbonate ions. The rather weak acid carbonic acid cannot cause the soil pH to drop below about 4.5. In natural soils even lower values may be observed due to the action of certain organic acids that are stronger acids than carbonic acid. Under such soils, the groundwater becomes acid and contains dissolved aluminium, iron, and manganese and very little calcium and magnesium. However, pH values lower than about 3.8 are rarely found in natural soils of the temperate regions because solid aluminium compounds act as buffers in this pH region.

```
      -  ___________  -                          -  ___________  -
Mg2+  - | clay or   | -  Ca2+               Mg2+ - | clay or   | -  Ca2+
      - | humus     | -        + 2H+  ->         - | humus     | -  H+     + Ca2+
Ca2+  - | particle  | -  Ca2+               Ca2+ - | particle  | -  H+
         -----------                                -----------
```

Figure 2.1. Schematic ion exchange process illustrating the exchange of adsorbed calcium ions with hydrogen ions from the soil solution.

In cultivated soils which are fertilized and harvested, a further production of carbonic and other acids will take place. This accelerates soil acidification and leaching of metal ions. In agricultural practice these effects are counteracted by liming at regular intervals. Drainage of moors and bogs, cultivation of old grassland, and clear-felling of forests induce oxidation of organic matter and thus increase the production of acids, particularly carbonic acid in the soil. However, oxidation of organic matter is not the most important reason for the very acid waters (pH 4 or lower) which may appear when certain water-logged areas are drained. Such soils often contain iron pyrite, FeS_2, formed under anaerobic conditions. With the access of air after drainage this compound is oxidized to sulfuric acid and soluble iron sulfates:

$$2FeS_2 + 7\frac{1}{2}O_2 + H_2O \rightarrow 2Fe^{3+} + 2H^+ + 4SO_4^{2-}$$

Hydrolysis of the iron sulfate releases more sulfuric acid and produces iron oxides:

$$Fe_2(SO_4)_3 + (x+3)H_2O \rightarrow Fe_2O_3,xH_2O + 6H^+ + 3SO_4^{2-}$$

The iron oxides eventually precipitate as ochre (Vækst, 1984*; Madsen and Jensen, 1988*).

Atmospheric pollution resulting from the burning of fossil fuels, e.g., in coal-fired power stations and car engines, may produce 'acid rain' containing strong acids such as sulfuric and nitric acids. Upon reaching the soil, these acids accelerate soil acidification and produce more intensive leaching of cations than the processes already mentioned. (See also Section 2.6).

2.2.4 Natural Leaching Processes in Eastern and Western Denmark

The differences in natural leaching processes may be illustrated by a comparison between Eastern and Western Denmark. The natural leaching processes have not progressed equally far in these two parts of the country. The loamy soils of Eastern Denmark were developed on glacial deposits from the last (Weichsel) glaciation. When the ice melted away, about 10,000 years ago, the glacial deposits often contained 20%-30% of calcium carbonate. At the present day, calcium carbonate has been leached from the upper layers of these deposits but is still present below the root zone, and the groundwater still contains calcium and hydrogen carbonate ions and only very little dissolved iron. Travertine is typical as a natural spring deposit, and the ionic composition of streams of this area illustrates this situation.

The sandy surface layers of South-West Jutland are geologically much older (nearly 100,000 years). The youngest of these layers were formed by glacial streams during the last glaciation, the oldest are from the previous (Saale) glaciation or shortly after it finished. These deposits do not contain calcium carbonate. The groundwater contains little calcium, and spring deposits are iron and manganese compounds (bog iron ore).

The sandy soils of West Denmark thus have a lower content of plant nutrients than the richer soils of East Denmark. They have a low cation-exchange capacity, a low water-holding capacity, and there is a larger excess rainfall than in the eastern part of the country. All this means that leaching is much more pronounced in the West than in the East. Also the groundwater table is present at a high level which means that a polluting agent appears much more rapidly in the groundwater in this part of the country. On the other hand, a specific polluting agent will be more diluted than in East Denmark.

Table 2.2. Contents of some plant nutrients extractable with boiling nitric acid in 44 characteristic Danish agricultural soils (Tjell and Hovmand, 1978).

Element	Content, mg kg^{-1}		coefficient of
	Median	Mean	variation, %
Ca	2480	2600	45
Mg	740	1035	75
Mn	232	268	57
Cu	8	13	103

2.3 PLANT NUTRIENTS IN SOILS. AMOUNTS AND CHEMICAL PROPERTIES

By convention, plant nutrient elements are classified as macro- and micronutrients according to the amounts required by growing plants. Micronutrients are those which are consumed by an agricultural crop in amounts less than one kg per hectare per year. Macronutrients are nitrogen, phosphorus, sulfur, calcium, magnesium and potassium. Hydrogen, oxygen and carbon are normally not counted. Essential micronutrients include manganese, copper, zinc, iron, molybdenum, and boron. Some elements (e.g., cobalt, vanadium, nickel) are essential for certain plants only, while the probable essentiality of others is still under discussion. Fig. 2.2 shows the distribution of biological and non-biological elements in the periodic table of the elements.

A natural fertile soil contains all essential nutrients but in highly variable amounts, depending mainly on the mineralogical composition and the geological and pedological history of the soil. The total content of most essential nutrients may be divided between a large pool which is resistant to leaching and not available to plants, and a small part which is exposed to leaching and is plant available. Some examples are given in Tables 2.2 and 2.3.

IA	IIA	IIIA	IVA	VA	VIA	VIIA	VIII	VIII	VIII	IB	IIB	IIIB	IVB	VB	VIB	VIIB	0
H																	He
Li	Be											B	C	N	O	F	Ne
Na	Mg											Al	Si	P	S	Cl	Ar
K	Ca	Sc	Ti	V	Cr	Mn	Fe	Co	Ni	Cu	Zn	Ga	Ge	As	Se	Br	Kr
Rb	Sr	Y	Zr	Nb	Mo	Tc	Ru	Rh	Pd	Ag	Cd†	In	Sn	Sb	Te	I	Xe
Cs	Ba	La	Hf	Ta	W	Re	Os	Ir	Pt	Au	Hg†	Tl	Pb†	Bi	Po	At	Rn
Fr	Ra	Ac	Th	Pa	U												

Figure 2.2. Periodic table of the elements, indicating biological importance. ○: Bulk biological elements. □: Trace elements believed to be essential for plants or animals (man). Dotted □: Possibly essential. †: Toxic trace elements only (animals, including man).

Table 2.3. Typical values for the contents of some plant nutrient elements and probable nutrient pools in characteristic Danish agricultural soils. The extractable amounts given include the mobilizable fraction (cation exchangeable) except for nitrogen and sulfur, where the extractable amounts include only nitrate, NO_3^-, ammonium, NH_4^+, and sulfate, SO_4^{2-}.

Element	kg ha^{-1}, 25 cm depth total	extractable	Extractant	Mobilizable fraction in	Resistant fraction mainly in
N	5000	5-50	Water	Organic matter	Humus
S	800	10	Water	Organic matter	Humus
P	1000	100	0.5 M $NaHCO_3$	Organic matter, absorbed, $Ca_3(PO_4)_2$	Humus, $Ca_3(PO_4)_2$
K	30000	200	1 M NH_4Ac	Clay minerals	Feldspars
Ca	12500	5000	1 M NH_4Cl	Clay minerals, $CaCO_3$	Feldspars
Mg	3500	250	1 M NH_4Cl	Clay minerals	Mica
Mn	1000	10	0.5 M $Mg(NO_3)_2$	(Hydrous) oxides	Oxides, feldspars
Cu	50	10	0.02 M EDTA	Organic matter complexes	Humus, oxides, silicates
B	8	2	Water	(Hydrous) oxides (?)	Humus, oxides silicates

The nitrogen and sulfur pools are found mainly in the soil organic matter; phosphorus partly in organic matter and partly in minerals; calcium, magnesium and potassium as major constituents of primary soil minerals; and most micronutrients (and other trace elements) as 'contaminants' substituting for macro-element atoms in the crystal lattices of primary and secondary soil minerals.

2.3.1 Soil Chemistry of Calcium, Magnesium, and Potassium

Labile calcium, magnesium and potassium occur in soils as Ca^{2+}, Mg^{2+} and K^+ only. Unless other cations, such as H^+, are entering the soil, leaching of these elements is prevented because they are held by the cation exchange complex.

The unavailable pool of the three elements mentioned is found in primary minerals, such as felspars (K, Ca), and as structural elements in micas and clay minerals (K, Mg). Calcium and magnesium also occur in carbonates from which they can be released by acids as weak as carbonic acid. The labile part of the three elements is present as dissolved ions (very little) and adsorbed by the ion exchange complex. In arable soils of the temperate regions, normally about 80%-90% of the exchangeable metallic ions is calcium. Calcium and magnesium may be exchanged with, e.g., hydrogen ions and taken up by plants or leached. Calcium deficiency in plants is rare in agriculture, whereas magnesium and particularly potassium have to be applied in fertilizers. Calcium, and to a lesser extent magnesium, may be leached into the groundwater where it does no harm except producing a larger degree of water 'hardness'. Potassium may become 'fixed' in a semi-labile state in clay minerals, from whence it may be leached only by the action of acids, and it is thus retained as a reserve plant nutrient.

2.3.2 Soil Chemistry of Some Micronutrients

Labile and plant-available copper, zinc, iron and manganese are found as the cations Cu^{2+}, Zn^{2+}, Fe^{2+}, and Mn^{2+}, respectively, adsorbed by the exchange complex and thus protected against rapid leaching. Molybdenum and boron are found as anions, mainly MoO_4^{2-} and HBO_3^{2-}. Further to their occurrence as substitutions in the crystal lattices of primary and clay minerals, pools of these elements may be found in organic matter (Cu), as free oxides (Fe, Mn), or adsorbed on oxide surfaces (Mo, B).

The soil pH is an important parameter for determining the mobility and plant availability of most micronutrients. At high pH, the above-mentioned elements, except Mo and B, will all be precipitated as insoluble oxides and/or complex-bound by soil organic matter (Cu, Zn). Iron and, particularly important, manganese become oxidized and subsequently precipitated under aerobic conditions. Manganese added as plant-available Mn^{2+} may thus be oxidized and precipitated as Mn(IV) hydrous oxide, increasing the total manganese content of the soil even if the plants still show a manganese deficiency.

Borate, HBO_3^{2-} and molybdate, MoO_4^{2-} are strongly retained by iron and aluminium oxides and to a lesser extent by clay minerals. These ions are even less prone to leaching than cations adsorbed by the ion exchange complex.

2.3.3 Soil Chemistry of Nitrogen, Phosphorus, and Sulfur

Nitrogen, phosphorus and sulfur are not constituents of the silicate minerals of soils. The total contents of most soils are less than 0.1% of both phosphorus and sulfur. Total nitrogen contents of 0.1% to 0.2% are common in agricultural soils. More than 95% of the nitrogen and sulfur is found in organic compounds in the soil.

Of the total phosphate content, typically about half is present in organic compounds. The other half is found in slightly soluble inorganic phosphates such as calcium and (in acid soils) aluminium and iron phosphates, and as adsorbed phosphates.

Nitrogen is a unique element in the sense that it is the plant nutrient which is taken up in the largest amounts by plants, and normally present in the same soil ecosystem in several chemical forms. In a specific ecosystem there is a dynamic equilibrium between the various forms of nitrogen. This is illustrated in Fig. 2.3.

A typical agricultural soil contains 5-10 tons of nitrogen per hectare in organic compounds, either as more or less decomposed plant residues or humic material. Living plants will take up nitrogen from the soil solution as ammonium, NH_4^+ or, more commonly, as nitrate, NO_3^-. Organic nitrogen in the soil thus only becomes available to plants after decomposition of organic matter to ammonium and nitrate by microorganisms. In a neutral and aerobic soil at temperatures above 4-5 °C, ammonium will immediately become oxidized, via nitrite, NO_2^-, to nitrate. The same holds for ammonium and ammonia, added as a fertilizer.

Organic nitrogen compounds in soils are only slightly soluble and are thus not leached. Ammonium compounds are soluble but the ammonium ion is retained by the cation exchange complex and thus protected against leaching. Nitrate compounds are soluble and the nitrate ion is not retained. Nitrate is thus the nitrogen species most exposed to loss by leaching. Under anaerobic conditions, in a water-logged soil, nitrate undergoes denitrification, being reduced by certain microorganisms to gaseous dinitrogen, N_2, or dinitrogen oxide, N_2O, which is then lost to the atmosphere. Chemical denitrification, e.g., by iron(II) or organic matter, is also possible. Some nitrogen is lost to the atmosphere as gaseous ammonia, NH_3 from soil or from animal manure or compost.

Gaseous dinitrogen, N_2, can be assimilated by biological nitrogen fixation, either by free-living soil microorganisms or, more importantly, by microorganisms in symbiosis with leguminous plants.

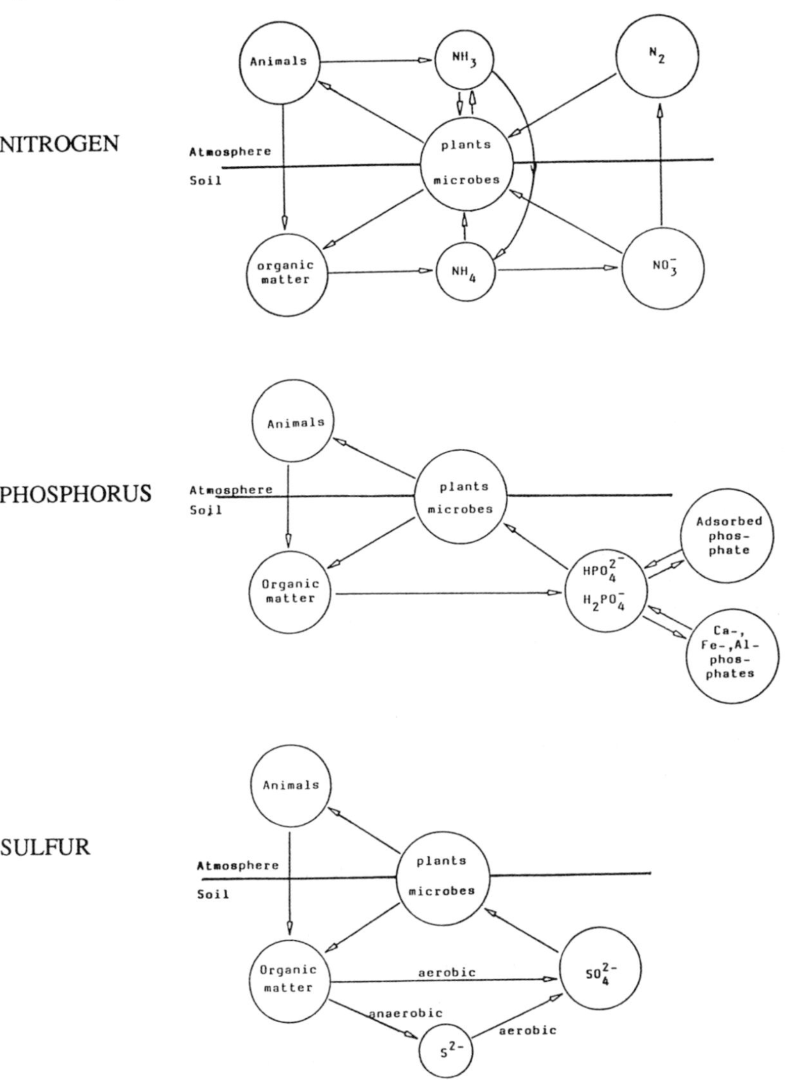

Figure 2.3. Simplified flow-diagrams for nitrogen, phosphorus and sulfur transformations in the soil-biosphere system. Only pools and pathways are indicated. Amounts and turnover rates may vary considerably. External turnover is not shown.

Table 2.4. Nutrient balance for an average Danish agricultural soil. - Source: Elm Andersen (1980*).

	kg ha^{-1} yr^{-1}					g ha^{-1} yr^{-1}				
Element	P	K	Ca	Mg	S	Mn	Cu	Zn	Mo	B
Added:										
Precipitation	0	3	9	3	15	100	18	150	?	30
Animal waste	22	58	27	9	13	550	150	450	2	55
Fertilizer+lime	20	54	240	5	21	207	311	45	1	81
Total	42	115	267	17	49	857	479	645	3	166
Removed:										
Crops	18	80	18	9	15	400	30	250	3	60
Leaching	0	2	254	16	56	72	6	88	?	18
Total	18	82	272	25	71	472	26	338	3	78
Increase	24	35	-5	-8	-22	385	443	307	0	88

The leaching of nitrate becomes intense when the following conditions are present simultaneously:

1. A high content of easily decomposable organic matter
2. A high soil temperature
3. A high biological activity
4. No plants available for nitrate uptake
5. An excess of precipitation and thus a downward water movement

In a temperate, humid climate such conditions may prevail after harvesting a grain crop in August. It is thus recommended to sow catchcrops in order to reduce nitrate leaching. Long-season crops, e.g., root crops and well-managed grassland crops, suffer less nitrate leaching.

The nitrate balance of a soil depends only very little on the soil's total nitrogen balance. The nitrogen balance is mainly determined by the organic-matter balance. The total nitrogen content is increased when the content of organic matter is increased, e.g., by maintaining a permanent grassland crop or by annual additions of large amounts of compost or animal manure. The content of organic matter and nitrogen is lowered with a continuously grain-producing form of agriculture without animals.

Phosphorus and sulfur transformations in soils are illustrated in Fig. 2.3, together with nitrogen transformations. As for nitrogen, the sulfur balance and to some extent that of phosphorus are linked to the organic-matter balance.

Under normal conditions, phosphorus only appears as phosphate groups in organic compounds or as inorganic phosphate ions and does not enter into redox reactions in soils.

Phosphate ions formed by mineralization of organic phosphates are adsorbed by iron and aluminium oxides or are precipitated as insoluble calcium phosphates (neutral/alkaline soils) or as iron or aluminium phosphates (acid soils). Thus, phosphate is normally protected against leaching.

Organic sulfur-containing compounds are decomposed by microbial action, forming sulfate, SO_4^{2-}, under normal aerobic conditions. Sulfate forms only soluble compounds in the soil and will be leached if not taken up by plants or microorganisms. Under anaerobic conditions, sulfide, S^{2-}, may be formed and precipitated as iron sulfides. This happens in water-logged areas in swamps and shallow-water coastal areas.

2.4 NUTRIENT BALANCES, ILLUSTRATED BY THE CASE OF DANISH AGRICULTURAL SOILS

An agricultural soil receives plant nutrients in fertilizers and animal wastes, with rain water (as aerosols originating from the ocean and as atmospheric pollutants) and directly from the atmosphere. Nutrients are removed in crops, lost with drainage water and in some cases volatilized into the atmosphere.

2.4.1 Elements Other Than Nitrogen

Up to around 1980, the production structure of Danish agriculture was rather uniform throughout the country, making it reasonable to calculate an average nutrient balance for the total agricultural area of the country. Such calculations, based on area, fertilizer and feedstuff import statistics, crop yields and crop analyses, etc. have been performed for a number of plant nutrients except nitrogen (Elm Andersen, 1980*).The main results are shown in Table 2.4. Even with a uniform agricultural structure the average figures given must conceal rather large variations between regions and between individual farms. Also, there is some variation between crops, annual grass and root crops removing a considerably larger amount of plant nutrients than, e.g., grain crops. Permanent grassland was not common in Danish agriculture in this century prior to 1980.

The figures show that for the nutrients investigated the largest inputs are from fertilizers and animal manure (and from limestone in the case of calcium). However, for some elements the amounts received by precipitation are not insignificant. In the western part of the country, some elements, such as magnesium and sulfur, from the North Sea are carried inland as liquid aerosols. Nutrients are mainly removed in crops. Large amounts of sulfur are leached as soluble sulfates. Particularly large amounts of calcium are lost by leaching, calcium being the predominant ion held by the ion-exchange complex and being released by the action of acids produced in the soil or received by precipitation.

For phosphorus and potassium and all micronutrients, the balance is positive. Statistics also show that the annual amounts of phosphorus and potassium added in fertilizers and animal manure have changed but little since the early 1960's. More than twice the amount of phosphorus was added than was removed in crops at the end of the 1970's, and calculations show that since the start of phosphate fertilization in the beginning of this century an average of about one ton of phosphorus per hectare has been accumulated in Danish agricultural soils. Even so, phosphate leaching from the soils is still quite low (Rebsdorf and Thyssen, 1987*).

A more recent (1985) phosphate balance for Danish agriculture shows the following figures (Miljøstyrelsen, 1988*):

Added, kg ha^{-1}		Removed, kg ha^{-1}	
Animal waste	17.5	Crops	22
Atmospheric	0.2	Leaching	0.2-0.4

It seems that the fraction taken up by crops is increasing and that leaching is quite low. However, if the amount leached reaches a lake or watercourse, its phosphate content may be of some importance, cf. Chapter 4.

In very intensively exploited agricultural areas in the Netherlands, phosphorus concentrations corresponding to about 100 mg l^{-1} and a loss by leaching of about 3-8 kg ha^{-1} y^{-1} have been observed (Petersen et al., 1987). Such amounts may cause serious eutrophication of water.

The nutrient balance is positive for all micronutrients investigated. However, the excesses are not considered to be environmentally harmful, apart from copper in localized areas receiving large amounts of pig slurry, as pig feed has a high content of added copper (up to 100 ppm), and similarly, where a copper solution is used as a foot disinfectant for cattle. Zinc and molybdenum are not normally used in fertilizers in Denmark. Toxic elements such as mercury, cadmium and lead are dealt with later in this chapter.

2.4.2 Nitrogen Balance

Using a similar approach to that for the other nutrients, several attempts have been made to calculate an average nitrogen balance for Danish agriculture. However, since nitrogen appears in so many chemical forms, and since several of the transformation processes are quantitatively incompletely known, the resulting balance sheet may not give a very precise picture. Setting up a balance sheet for a country as a whole is considered meaningful only for a country with uniform topography and climate and where nearly the whole rural area is arable agricultural land. Denmark is probably unique in this respect.

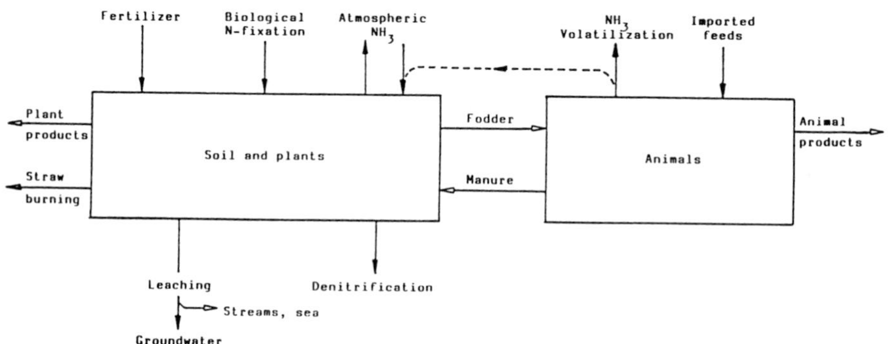

Figure 2.4. Flow diagram for over-all nitrogen turnover in the plant and animal production system of Danish agriculture.

Table 2.5. Estimated average nitrogen balances of Danish agriculture, including an estimate of the effect of restrictive measures aimed at a reduction of the loss of nitrogen.

Year	1950	1985	199?
Input, kg ha^{-1}:			
Fertilizer	20	135	110
Imported feeds	12	57	57
Precipitation + atmospheric deposition (NH_3)	5	20	18
Biological N-fixation	50	10	10
Total input	87	222	195
Output, kg ha^{-1}:			
Sold plant products	6	25	25
Sold animal products	10	33	33
Burning of straw	0	2	0
Denitrification	15	35	35
NH_3-volatilization	25	45	35
Leaching loss	31	82	67
Total output	87	222	195

Since 1980, a considerable effort has been put into the calculation of nitrogen balance sheets for Danish agriculture past and present. This has been done mainly in order to elucidate the possible connection between the increasing consumption of fertilizer nitrogen and nitrogen in animal foods, and the increasing content of nitrate in groundwaters and streams and - more recently - oxygen depletion in sea waters.

The pathways considered are shown in Fig. 2.4, and Table 2.5 shows average balances estimated for Denmark as a whole around 1950, in 1985 and in 199?, indicating the estimated effect of some restrictive measures introduced in order to reduce nitrogen consumption without reducing the agricultural production (see later). The figures are based on various sources (Schrøder, 1984*; Jørgensen and Lassen, 1984*; SJVF, 1986; Rude, 1987; and Laursen, 1988*).

It should be noticed that these figures illustrate a net balance for plant plus animal production. In a balance sheet for plant production alone, 'imported feeds' on the input side should be substituted with animal manure, about 110 kg N annually per hectare in 1985 (65 kg N in 1950). On the output side there should be added fodder-plant production, about 50 kg N annually per hectare (1950, and 1985). The large average amount of 110 kg ha^{-1} yr^{-1} of nitrogen in animal manure is important in a pollution context. As shown later, it is by improved management of manure that the largest reduction in ammonia volatilization and nitrate leaching can realistically be obtained.

All balance sheets have been estimated on the implicit assumption that, on the average, there is no net loss or gain in the large pool of organic nitrogen in the soil. This assumption which can be tested only under specific, local conditions, adds a further uncertainty thereto.

The consumption of fertilizer nitrogen has increased by a factor of more than six during 35 years. The consumption topped in 1984 at 145 kg N per ha. The present consumption is higher than in most European countries; only the Netherlands has a higher consumption (228 kg N per ha in 1983). Nitrogen in imported feeds has also increased considerably and so has deposition with rain and from the atmosphere. The last figure should be compared with ammonia volatilization from agriculture which stems partly from animal manure and to a lesser extent from ammonia evaporating directly from plants and from liquid ammonia used as a fertilizer. At present, the amount lost by ammonia volatilization is about twice the amount deposited from the atmosphere, indicating that a large part is deposited outside agricultural areas, mainly in the sea.

The estimates of biological nitrogen fixation cannot be very precise. Fixation by free-living microorganisms probably amounts to only a few kg N ha^{-1} yr^{-1}, but microorganisms in symbiosis with leguminous crops are able to fix large amounts (100-200 kg N ha^{-1} yr^{-1}). This accounts for the large estimate in 1950 (Table 2.5) because at that time mixed grass-clover pastures were common in Danish agriculture. This is no longer the case, but grain legumes, mainly peas, are becoming increasingly popular (4%-5% of the agricultural area in 1988).

The nitrogen content of agricultural products has been calculated from production statistics and representative analyses. Even so, the various published estimates differ considerably, and the figures in Table 2.5 must be taken with some caution. However, the estimate of the loss by denitrification may be much more imprecise. Denitrification varies considerably from one year to another and from one field to another. Denitrification requires a certain temperature, anaerobic conditions and the simultaneous presence of nitrate and easily oxidizable organic matter (or Fe(II)). Denitrification losses are believed to be considerably higher in clay and loam soils than in sandy soils.

The leaching losses reported in Table 2.5 have been calculated in order to make up the balance and must be quite uncertain. Even so, it is probably true that leaching of nitrate has increased by a factor of about two from 1950 to 1985 - and it was not insignificant in 1950. Also, nitrate leaching can be reduced only slightly if agricultural production has to be maintained at the same level and with the same production structure of Danish agriculture (Rude, 1987).

Nitrate leaching occurs when there is downward water movement in the soil, and more nitrate is being added or formed by mineralization of organic matter (this happens when the temperature is higher than about 4 °C) than can be taken up by the crop.

2.5 NITROGEN POLLUTION

Nitrogen pollution occurs in the form of nitrate in drainage and groundwaters and as ammonia evaporating to the atmosphere (see Fig. 2.4).

2.5.1 Extent of the Problem

The extent of nitrogen pollution is influenced by several parameters:

1. Fertilization
   a. amount
   b. type (commercial fertilizer or animal manure)

2. Type of crops
3. Microbial activity in the soil
4. Climate (rainfall)
5. Soil properties (texture)

Although slight losses of nitrate and ammonia do occur from an unfertilized soil-plant ecosystem, nitrogen pollution problems are serious only in an agricultural practice with intensive use of fertilizers and/or animal manure.

Fertilizers are used in order to maintain a high agricultural production. However, according to the generally confirmed corollary of dimishing returns, with increasing crop yields, the proportion of added nutrient which is lost is also increasing. This is demonstrated in Table 2.6 and indicates that waste and pollution are two sides of the same thing.

As a matter of good agricultural practice, commercial nitrogeneous fertilizer can be applied at a rate such that virtually all its nitrogen is taken up by the plants during the growing season. Thus, the loss of nitrogen by leaching during the growing season is very small. Recent investigations indicate that ammonia may evaporate directly from the plants at high rates of nitrogen application and at certain development stages of plants.

From animal manure in the form of liquid or solid manure or of slurry, not all the nitrogen can be taken up by plants during the growing season. The nitrogen in animal manure occurs as organic nitrogen compounds and as ammonia/ammonium ions, NH_3/NH_4^+, the composition ranging from less than 10% organic nitrogen in liquid manure, to 30%-40% in slurry, and even about 70% organic N in solid cattle manure.

This means that some ammonia is lost by volatilization during storage and distribution in the field, particularly from liquid manure and slurry. The actual amount lost depends on the handling practice. In the soil, the inorganic nitrogen can be taken up by plants or leached, but organic nitrogen only after mineralization, i.e., after transformation by microbial action into ammonium and further to nitrate. This process takes place continuously in the soil, and the most intensively when the soil is warm and humid. In a temperate climate, nitrogen mineralization is not finished within one year, and often a fertilizer effect (after-effect) is seen in second-year crops. The efficient use of animal manure as a fertilizer thus depends on a delicate balance: The manure should be stored and brought into the field and mixed into the soil without delay, so as to reduce losses by ammonia volatilization. Once in the soil, a crop should be available in order to take up the inorganic nitrogen present and continuously being released by mineralization.

As a consequence, manure is less effective as a source of nitrogen for plants than is commercial fertilizer. In Danish agricultural practice, the following utilization factors relative to nitrogen in commercial fertilizer are typical (first-year effect only):

Spring barley, slurry distributed in November of the previous year (because the tank was full)	0.15
Same, distributed in March, injected into the soil	0.35
Sugarbeet, slurry distributed in March	0.65
Sugarbeet, solid manure distributed in March	0.40

Table 2.6. Local field experiments with nitrogen fertilization of spring barley. Average of 784 trials on loamy soils and 467 trials on sandy soils, 1975-84. Nitrogen in grains was calculated assuming a nitrogen content of 1.55%. 'Utilization' means: nitrogen in grains as percentage of nitrogen in fertilizer. - Source: Bennetzen (1985).

N in fertilizer kg ha^{-1}	Grain yield 100 kg ha^{-1}	N in grains kg ha^{-1}	Utilization %
	Loamy soils		
0	32.3	50	*
40	41.7	65	*
80	46.4	72	90
120	47.7	74	62
160	48.4	75	47
	Sandy soils		
0	23.3	36	*
40	32.1	50	*
80	37.4	58	73
120	39.7	62	52
160	40.5	63	39

It is well-known that crops with a long growth period (root crops, grassland) 'pay better' for manure than do crops with a short one (spring grains). Even so, there is always a considerable loss of nitrogen when large doses of manure are used. This eventually ends up by polluting the ground or surface waters. The problem has become serious in many industrialized countries because animal production now takes place in very large units.

Whether using commercial fertilizer or manure, the leaching loss of nitrogen during the growing season is low, even at rather high dose rates. This is because of plant uptake and because of the low water run-off during this period. After crop harvest, mineralization of organic nitrogen continues, both from crop residues and from manure and soil organic matter. Experiments with N-labelled nitrogen have shown that only about 3% of fertilizer nitrogen was leached during the first year after application. This indicates that crop residues are incorporated in the large pool of organic material in the soil, and nitrogen is released at a similar rate as from this pool (Kjellerup and Kofoed, 1983*).

2.5.2 Nitrogen in Drainage and Groundwaters

During the last 2-3 decades there has been a steady increase in the concentration of nitrate in Danish groundwaters, as is the case in several other European countries. The highest concentrations are observed in western Denmark with its sandy soils and high rainfall. In some areas, more than one fourth of the drinking water has nitrate concentrations above the guidance limit of 25 mg NO_3^- per liter, 5%-8% exceeds the maximum permissible limit of 50 mg NO_3^- per liter. In the eastern part of the country with loamy soils and lower rainfall, nitrate concentrations are still low, and increasing concentrations are only seen locally. But there are indications that the difference between east and west is due to the nitrate reaching the groundwater more slowly in the eastern loamy soils, rather than because of effective nitrate reduction (Overgaard, 1986).

Leaching of nitrate from the root zone increases with increasing fertilizer application, cf. Table 2.6. An amount of 20-60 kg N per ha annually is not uncommon from fields which are fertilized for optimal agricultural production. Leaching is most intense from sandy soils, where most of the leachate reaches the groundwater and only 0%-30% goes into drainage water. In loam and clay soils, most of the leachate goes into the drainage water and much less into the groundwater. Nitrate concentrations in the leachate vary considerably with fertilization, time of year, crop, rainfall, and whether the soil is sand, loam or clay. The drinking-water limit of 50 mg NO_3^- per liter can easily be exceeded.

2.5.3 Preventive Measures

In order to reduce nitrogen pollution, mainly from agricultural activities, the following legislation has been enacted in Denmark:

- each farm should have crop rotation and fertilization plans prepared on the basis of acknowledged standards for N and P fertilization for optimal agricultural production,
- 65% of the area of each farm should be grown with 'green fields', i.e., crops with a long growth season, such as winter grains, grassland or root crops. Spring grains combined with catch crops are also counted as 'green fields'.

Furthermore, the following legislation has been enacted specifically in order to reduce the pollution of surface and ground waters with nitrate and ammonium from animal manure:

- only manure from not more than 2.3 'animal units' (each unit corresponding to, e.g., one milk cow or 8 growing pigs) may be applied per ha per year,
- animal farms should have storage capacity for at least 9 months' manure production,
- slurry tanks and other storage facilities should be leak free: liquid manure and slurry may be distributed on bare soil only if it can be mixed into the soil within 12 hours.
- during the period from harvest (August-September) to the first of November, liquid manure and slurry may not be distributed on bare soil unless a winter crop is sown.

These rules are intended not only to reduce nitrogen (and phophorus) pollution, but also to obtain maximum recirculation of the plant nutrients in animal manure.

2.6 NATURAL AND ANTHROPOGENIC SOIL ACIDIFICATION

Acidity (hydrogen ions) is formed in all natural soils by the respiration processes of plant roots and microorganisms and under some circumstances as a result of ion uptake by plant roots. Hydrogen ions are also formed by oxidation of ammonia and ammonium salts such as ammonium nitrate added as fertilizer or originating from the decomposition of organic material:

$$NH_3 + 2O_2 \rightarrow H^+ + NO_3^- + H_2O$$

$$NH_4NO_3 + 2O_2 \rightarrow 2H^+ + 2NO_3^- + H_2O$$

Table 2.7. Estimated acid load on an average Danish agricultural soil 1981. Above the dotted line: carbonic acid, below: nitric and sulfuric acids. 1 keq = 1000 eq H^+. - Source: Hovmand and Petersen (1984).

	$keq\ ha^{-1}\ yr^{-1}$
Root respiration	4.50
H^+-exchange by plant ion uptake (net)	0.80
Nitrification	>2.10
Atmospheric deposition of rain and particulates (0.29 + 0.03)	0.32
Gas deposition of SO_2 and NO_x(0.65 + 0.20)	0.85
Total	>8.60

Furthermore, hydrogen ions are formed by oxidation and hydrolysis of sulfur and nitrogen oxides from the atmosphere ('acid rain'):

$$SO_2 + \frac{1}{2}O_2 + H_2O \rightarrow 2H^+ + SO_4^{2-}$$

$$2\ NO_x + (5\text{-}2x)O + H_2O \rightarrow 2H^+ + 2NO_3^-$$

Table 2.7 gives an estimate of the total annual production of hydrogen ions in a Danish agricultural soil around 1981.

A total of 10 keq H^+ ha^{-1} yr^{-1} corresponds to the introduction of about one ton of lime ($CaCO_3$) ha^{-1} yr^{-1} in order to maintain a pH-value around neutrality (pH 7). The contribution from acid rain corresponds to about 10%-20% of this (see Petersen, 1986).

The amount of nitrogen that gives rise to soil acidification corresponds to the amount of ammonia or ammonium that is oxidized according to the processes illustrated and then leached as nitrate. The amount shown in Table 2.7 is probably too low as it corresponds to 2.10 x 14 = 29.4 kg N ha^{-1} yr^{-1}, whereas the loss by leaching according to Table 2.5 is about 80 kg ha^{-1} yr^{-1}. Half of this might reach the groundwater. Under vulnerable sandy soils in the western part of Denmark, a decreasing pH in groundwaters has been observed, and this is considered to be a result of excessive nitrogen leaching (Overgaard, 1986).

In an uncultivated soil, acid production will be much smaller than in an agricultural soil, and much less nitrate is formed by nitrification. The atmospheric fall-out is of course the same as on a cultivated soil. The soil pH in an uncultivated soil is normally lower, about 4 - 4.5.

As to the effects of hydrogen ions that are added to or produced in a soil, it is important to distinguish between the weak acid, carbonic acid, i.e.

$$CO_2 + H_2O \rightarrow H_2CO_3 \rightarrow H^+ + HCO_3^- \qquad pK\ 6.3\ ,$$

organic acids of intermediate strength, i.e.

$$RCOOH \rightarrow RCOO^- + H^+ \qquad pK\ 2 - 4\ ,$$

and the strong nitric and sulfuric acids

$$HNO_3 \rightarrow H^+ + NO_3^- ,$$

$$H_2SO_4 \rightarrow 2H^+ + SO_4^{2-} .$$

Carbonic acid is formed by respiration and ion uptake processes and cannot produce a soil pH lower than about 4.5. Nitric and sulfuric acids formed as illustrated above can reduce the soil pH to about 3, being lowest when the soil humidity is low and the acid concentration consequently high. Organic acids of intermediate acid strength may be present in naturally acid sandy soils and give rise to pH-values between 3.5 and 4.

In soils with a reasonably high clay content, the pH will rarely decrease below 4 because clay minerals and aluminium oxides act as a buffer and neutralize hydrogen ions. However, in this process aluminium ions are released which are toxic to plants and may be transported downwards together with nitrate and sulfate ions and thus acidifying deeper soil layers.

The toxic effect of dissolved aluminium ions on roots is considered a contributory cause of the dieback of forests in several Central European countries. It is uncertain whether such forest dieback is occurring in Denmark. Slight acidification of drain water, groundwater and lakes has been observed in the western part of Denmark.

2.7 TOXIC ELEMENTS ('HEAVY METALS') IN SOILS

Trace elements are taken up by plants and animals, including man, in very small amounts ('traces'). Some of them are essential plant nutrients, such as the micronutrients already described. Others are essential nutrients for animals and man, and some again are taken up without apparently being essential for either plants or animals. A few elements are toxic, even in trace concentrations, for plants and/or animals. However, most essential trace elements are needed in very small concentrations only, and are toxic in higher concentrations. For these elements, both deficiency and toxicity symptoms are known. Such elements must be supplied in amounts which lie between the limits of deficiency and toxicity. A number of trace elements can be concentrated through the food chain.

The designation 'heavy metal' was originally a purely chemical category including only the metallic elements with a specific gravity of more than 7.0 g cm^{-3} in the free state. According to this definition, heavy metals include:

1. essential elements with no toxic effects, such as iron (Fe),
2. trace elements which are essential in low concentrations and toxic in higher concentrations, such as copper (Cu), zinc (Zn), nickel (Ni), and several others.
3. toxic trace elements, such as cadmium (Cd), mercury (Hg), and lead (Pb).

Nowadays, in an environmental context, the term 'heavy metal' is often used as a designation for an element with toxic effects, including the above-mentioned but also light metals, such as aluminium (Al), and even non-metallic elements with some toxicity, such as arsenic (As) and selenium (Se).

The risk of a specific trace element appearing in toxic or deficient concentrations in the soil depends on geochemical and biological conditions and on the technology employed.

Table 2.8. Typical concentrations of selected heavy metal elements in waters, soil, and biological material - Sources: a.o. Bowen (1979).

Metal	Sea water µg kg^{-1}	Rain µg kg^{-1}	Soil mg kg^{-1}	Plant dry matter mg kg^{-1}	Muscle dry matter mg kg^{-1}
Pb	0.5	30	20	2	0.3
Hg	0.3	< 0.1	0.02-0.1	0.02	0.2
Cd	0.1	0.3	0.2	0.2	0.5
Ni	0.5	1	10	0.5	1
Cr	0.3	-	20	0.5	0.05
Zn	5	-	40	20	240
Cu	0.3	-	20	5	10

Table 2.9. Typical concentrations of selected heavy metal elements in soil and crop (area basis) and in animal manure and sewage sludge (maximum permissible concentration in sewage sludge in Denmark after 1995, if distributed on agricultural land).

Metal	Soil kg ha^{-1}	Crop g ha^{-1}	Solid manure, dry matter mg kg^{-1}	Sewage sludge dry matter mg kg^{-1}
Pb	50	10	3	120
Hg	0.3	0.1	?	1.2
Cd	0.6	1	1	1.2
Ni	30	2.5	4	45
Cr	60	2.5	4	100
Zn	120	100	-	4000
Cu	60	25	-	1000

Problems will be most serious for elements which are active in the lowest concentrations and where the gap between the deficiency and toxicity limits is narrow.

Chemical and ecological aspects of heavy metals in soils are discussed, e.g., in the monography by Alloway (1990).

2.7.1 Element Sources in an Industrial Society

Modern technology results in a change in the biosphere and in the soil also with respect to trace elements. These changes are of different natures and have different causes.

In modern intensive agriculture, fertilizers are used as 'pure' chemical compounds (or mixtures of pure compounds) so that selected plant nutrients are added to the soil in order to make up for the loss in harvested crops. However, trace elements not added are also removed by crops, thereby depleting the soil for, e.g., elements that are not essential for plants but are essential for animals and man eating the crops. The products of intensive agriculture may thus be deficient in certain trace elements essential to man.

A different kind of problem originates from the need of modern industry to use large amounts of fossil resources. This implies that large amounts of (maybe toxic) trace elements are liberated from geological deposits and enter biochemical cycles in critical concentrations. Such elements appear as pollutants in air, water or food and are spread by wind and water. Even so, the most serious pollution is local, close to emitting industry or a busy motorway (lead).

Also the large consumption of fossil fuels brings trace elements into circulation, and so does the production of waste material in industry and in private households. The deposition of such waste on soils may introduce unacceptable amounts of toxic trace elements into soils, plants and food chains. This will be dealt with later in this chapter.

2.7.2 Lead, Mercury, Cadmium, and Nickel

Lead, mercury, and cadmium are known as toxic elements only. Nickel is now considered essential at least for some plants and animals and is probably less toxic than the other three. The four elements, and especially cadmium, are those which call for the most serious concern with regard to pollution of agricultural soils at present. Chromium (Cr) and vanadium (V) are suspect, but less is known about these elements than is the case for the other four, both with regard to toxicity and their abundance in soils. Estimated average contents in Danish soils are shown in Table 2.8 together with contents in other environments and biological materials. In Table 2.9, soil contents are calculated on an area basis and compared with the contents in crops and animal manure and with permissible concentrations in sewage sludge applied to agricultural land. It is seen that only a very small part of the soil content is taken up by an annual crop.

Lead pollution of soils originates mainly from atmospheric fall-out the source of which is lead added to automobile fuel. This emission source is rapidly declining, in Denmark, e.g., from around 900 t yr^{-1} on a national basis in 1976 to just over 100 t yr^{-1} in 1989, and a further decline is expected. This is reflected in the content of lead in dust collected by domestic vacuum cleaners, declining from an average of 240 mg kg^{-1} in 1979 to 9 mg kg^{-1} in 1989 (Jensen and Jensen, 1990[*]). Much smaller amounts come from fertilizers, animal manure and from sewage sludge applied to agricultural land. A large amount of metallic lead (about 800 t yr^{-1} on a national basis in 1984) is introduced into Danish soils as lead pellets from shotgun ammunition used either for sports and training purposes on specific shooting ranges (about one third) or for hunting, distributed over the total rural area. Of course this metallic lead is much less reactive than the lead added in gaseous or aerosol form, but in slightly acid soils such pellets may be transformed into dissolved lead in a few hundred years (Jørgensen and Willems, 1987). The annual amount of lead added to the soil in lead pellets is declining because of the gradual introduction of steel pellet ammunition.

Mercury in soils originates mainly from the atmosphere. A smaller part comes from fertilizers and sludge and from seed treated with mercury containing fungicides (now prohibited in Denmark). It should be noted that a larger amount of mercury now appears to evaporate from soils (as volatile organic mercury compounds) than is added from the atmosphere (Department of the Environment, 1987).

Table 2.10. Estimated lead, cadmium, and mercury balances for Danish soils (whole country) about 1985. - Various sources.

Element	Pb	Cd	Hg
Content, t	50,000	2000	< 1000
Added, t yr^{-1}:			
Atmospheric	200	9	2
Fertilizer	< 100	< 3	0.15
Ammunition	800	-	-
Total added	< 1100	< 12	~ 2
Removed, t yr^{-1}:			
Crops	5	0.6	0.8
Leaching	1	1	0.3
Atmospheric	0	0	2.4
Total removed	6	1.6	3.5
Increase, t yr^{-1}	1000	10	-1.5
Increase, %	0.7	0.5	-0.15

Cadmium in soils originates to some extent from the atmosphere but mainly from phosphate fertilizers because the phosphate minerals used for fertilizer manufacture always contain cadmium. However, the cadmium content depends on the geological origin of the mineral. Igneous phosphates, such as those from the Kola peninsula in the Soviet Union and from South Africa, have a low cadmium content, whereas sedimentary phosphates from the USA and Africa north of the Sahara have high and variable cadmium contents.

An estimated balance for lead, mercury and cadmium in Danish agricultural soils is shown in Table 2.10. The total turnover is small compared with the figures for micronutrients shown in Table 2.4. Leaching is considered negligible on the average but might take place in some highly polluted acid soils. For lead and cadmium, there is a slight increase in the average soil content, whereas it seems that Danish soils are losing mercury. Compared, as is done here, to the total amounts, the increase is not alarming, but it should be kept in mind that an increase is an addition to the plant-available pool which is probably only a small part of the total amount.

Cadmium is the heavy element which gives rise to the most serious concern with regard to toxic elements in Danish soils at the present time. The origin and balance for nickel are incompletely known at present.

The toxicities of lead, cadmium and mercury are different. The relative toxicity may be illustrated by the PTWI (Provisional tolerable weekly intake) values proposed by the WHO in mg per kg body weight for an adult person per week:

Pb	0.0500
Cd	0.0075
Hg	0.0050, including
Methyl-Hg	0.0033

The behaviour of these elements in the soil follows the same pattern as that of the metallic plant nutrients already described earlier in this chapter. Processes and soil-plant equilibria are illustrated in Fig. 2.5. Cadmium is more mobile in the soil than lead and mercury, mainly because it forms weaker complexes with soil-organic matter than do lead and mercury and especially copper (Christensen, 1989). Mercury is unique in its ability to form volatile organic compounds (methyl mercury). These elements are all more labile and plant available in acid soils, Fig. 2.6.

Plants take up a polluting metallic element from the soil but the same amount or more may be taken up through the leaves directly from the atmosphere or as aerosol.

2.8 AGRICULTURAL USE OF NON-AGRICULTURAL WASTES

Many of the waste products of modern society are of biological and thus of agricultural origin. Such wastes should be returned to the soil both for ecological reasons for recirculation in order to avoid the depletion of plant nutrients and other biological components, and in order to avoid large deposits of biological waste. However, application to agricultural land requires that toxic material such as the elements described above and non-degradable industrial products (plastics, hazardous chemicals) are not present in unacceptable amounts.

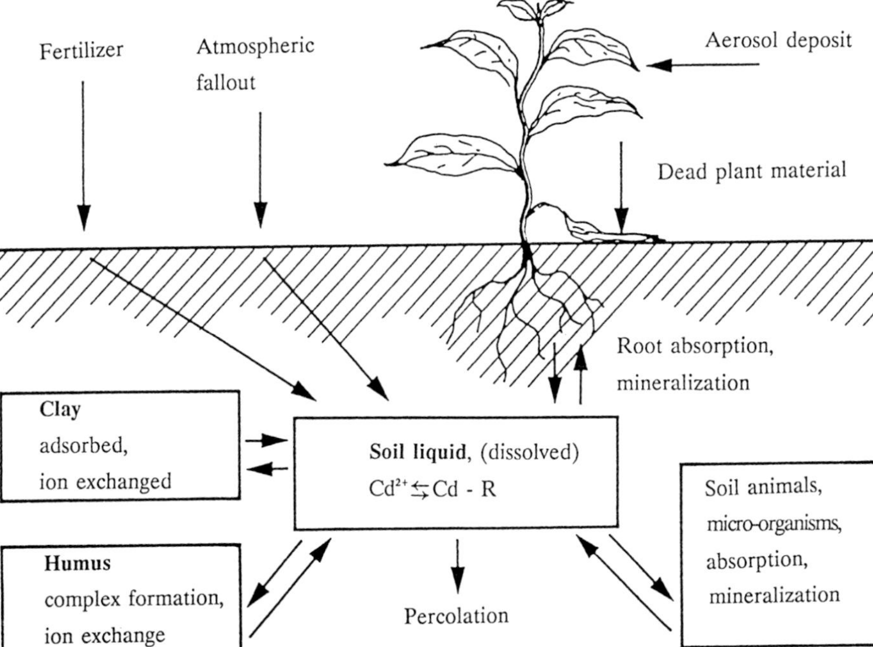

Figure 2.5. Simplified picture of trace-metal behaviour in the soil-plant ecosystem. - Source: Miljøstyrelsen (1980) (modified).

2.8.1 Sewage Sludge

Sewage sludge originates from mechanical-biological(-chemical) treatment of municipal waste water (see Chapter 5). The annual production in Denmark (1986) of sewage sludge corresponds to about 150,000 t of dry matter, i.e., about 30 kg per person on an average. About one fourth of this is incinerated, one fourth is deposited in sanitary landfills, and half of it is applied to agricultural soils where it has some fertilizing effect (N and P) and to some degree acts as a soil conditioner (organic material).

By incineration, sludge ash is produced which weighs about 10% of the sludge dry matter. The ash does not contain nitrogen but has a high content of phosphate. The heavy metals of the sludge are concentrated in the ash where they are less prone to leaching and uptake by plants than in the sludge. Sludge ash is at present deposited in special landfills.

The environmental problems which are encountered when using sewage sludge on agricultural land are its possible content of germs and parasites (see Chapters 4 and 5) and toxic elements such as heavy metals. Rules regarding treatment procedures for reducing infection risks, and maximum permissible limits for the contents of plant nutrients and certain heavy-metal elements are now enacted in Denmark. These rules cover sewage sludge as well as other biological-matter products (see the following section).

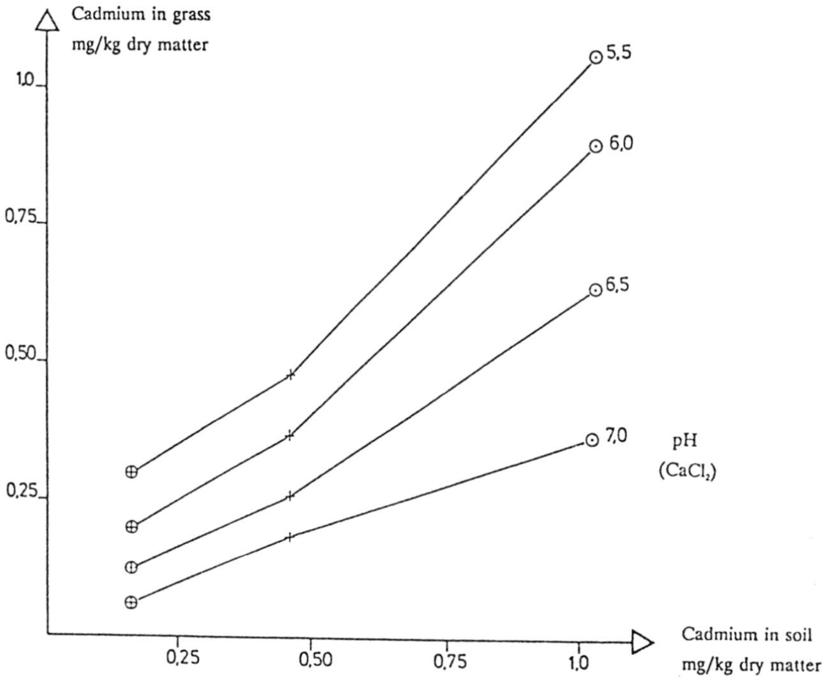

Figure 2.6. Cadmium uptake in rye grass, as influenced by soil pH and cadmium concentrations in a sandy loam soil. - Source: Miljøstyrelsen (1980*).

2.8.2 Compost

Private households and certain industries, e.g., within food processing and pharmaceutical production, give rise to large amounts of biological wastes. For ecological reasons, such wastes should be returned to the soil instead of being incinerated or dumped in landfills. In order to facilitate handling and further decomposition in the soil, such wastes are often composted.

Composting can be described as partial decomposition of a heterogeneous mixture of biological origin by a mixed microbial population in a warm humid environment. If the process is carried out aerobically, the temperature typically rises to 70-75 °C, about half the amount of dry matter is decomposed accompanied by a loss of carbon dioxide and ammonia, and the final pH is between 8 and 9. In anaerobic composting, the temperature rises to only 30-35 °C, decomposition is less pronounced, and reduced, often evil-smelling compounds are produced. The final pH is low, often below 5, and little ammonia is volatilized.

Aerobic composting is normally preferred in order to obtain a product which is free of pathogens (because of the high temperature) and convenient to handle. Composting can be technically difficult, and the composition and the quality of the product depend on the composition of the starting material and on the actual composting procedure. Non-biological material, such as paper and cardboard, plastics, glass, metals, and chemicals should not be present. Household wastes should be separated, preferably at the source.

The organic matter of aerobic compost is similar to soil organic matter, or humus. Compost contains all the plant nutrients of the starting material, except some ammonia lost by volatilization. It also contains some pollutants present in the starting material, such as heavy metals. For the use of compost on agricultural land, similar limits for heavy-metal contents should apply as for sewage sludge.

The following common rules for agricultural use of sewage sludge, composts, and biological wastes from certain industries are enacted in Denmark:

- the amount of material applied per ha per year (including animal manure) must not exceed 10 ton of dry matter, 250 kg of total nitrogen, and 40 kg of total phosphorus;
- the heavy-metal contents given in Table 2.11 must not be exceeded. Contents may be calculated on the basis of dry matter or phosphorus;
- soils receiving such materials must not have metal concentrations exceeding the following values (mg per kg dry matter, soluble in strong acids):

cadmium	0.5
mercury	0.5
lead	40
nickel	15
chromium	30
zinc	100
copper	40

- sewage sludge and separated municipal waste must be composted (55°C for a minimum of 2 weeks, not to be used for crops that are eaten raw) and/or heat treated (70°C for a minimum of 1 hour).

Table 2.11. Maximum permissible concentrations of heavy metals in sewage sludge (municipal and certain food processing industries) and in separated household waste of biological origin. Danish legislation.

	1990 - 1995		After 1995	
	mg per kg dry matter	mg per kg total P	mg per kg dry matter	mg per kg total P
Cd	1.2	320	0.8	200
Hg	1.2	320	0.8	200
Pb	120	15,000	120	10,000
Ni	45	4,000	30	2,500
Cr	100	*	100	*
Zn	4,000	*	4,000	*
Cu	1,000	*	1,000	*

The overall purpose of imposing maximum limits for, e.g., heavy metals is to reduce the circulation of such compounds in ecological cycles and food chains, rather than reducing the content in a specific product such as, e.g., compost and sludge.

2.8.3 Fly Ash and Desulfurization Products

Energy production in coal-fired power stations also results in waste products. The coal used typically contains about 10% mineral components or ashes. About 75% of this is collected in flue-gas filters and is called fly ash. Even in a small country like Denmark, this amounts to about one million tons per year. A large proportion of this is used as a raw material for the production of cement and concrete, and as filling material in road and dam constructions.

The distribution of fly ash on agricultural land has been considered as it has some liming effect and it contains a number of plant nutrients. However, as it also contains a number of harmful elements, cadmium being the most suspect, dumping at special landfill sites is preferred to spreading on agricultural land.

In some procedures for sulfur-dioxide removal this compound is absorbed by a dispersion of lime in water, the resulting product being calcium sulfite, $CaSO_3$. This compound can be oxidized by air to calcium sulfate, $CaSO_4$. Calcium and sulfate are plant nutrients, but calcium sulfite is toxic to plants. Cadmium can be present as a trace impurity, especially if the desulfurization product is mixed with fly ash before leaving the power station.

In other procedures, SO_2 is neutralized with ammonia. After oxidation, ammonium sulfate is produced which can be used as a fertilizer (Gissel Nielsen and Bertelsen, 1988*).

2.9 POLLUTION CAUSED BY RADIOACTIVE FALL-OUT

Background radioactivity in the soil-plant ecosystem arises from cosmic radiation, naturally occurring radionuclides, and from man-made radionuclides. On the whole, the predominant part of the total radioactivity originates from natural sources.

Soil Pollution

Widespread radionuclide pollution of agricultural soils can arise mainly from nuclear explosions in the atmosphere and from leaks or accidents at nuclear installations for military purposes or energy production. The effect of radionuclide fall-out is determined by isotopic composition, chemical form, and distribution in space and time. The long-lived isotopes originating from the atmospheric bomb tests in the 1950's were mainly strontium-90 (half-life 28.1 yr) and cesium-137 (half-life 30.1 yr), and they were distributed all over the globe via the stratosphere. The long-lived isotopes originating from the Chernobyl accident in 1986 were dominated by cesium-137 only, and the distribution was largely determined by wind direction and speed immediately after the accident.

The chemical forms of the isotopes vary considerably depending on the source. This affects important properties, such as plant uptake and chemical binding in soils (e.g., Livens and Rimmer, 1988). Although extensive field studies are - fortunately - not available, it may be assumed that radioisotopes behave chemically and biologically in much the same way as their corresponding stable isotopes. However, stable isotopes do not always exist (Plutonium).

REFERENCES

Alloway, B.J. (ed.), 1990. Heavy Metals in Soils. Blackie, London, 339 pp.

Bennetzen, F., 1985*. Oversigt over Landsforsøgene. Forsøg og undersøgelser i de landøkonomiske foreninger 1984. (Review of Danish field experiments 1984). Copenhagen, p. 79.

Bowen, H.J.M., 1979. Environmental Chemistry of the Elements. Academic Press, London, 227 pp.

van Breemen, N., Mulder, J., and Driscoll, C.T., 1983. Acidification and alkalinization of soils. Plant and Soil 75: 283-308.

Christensen, T., 1987. Cadmium soil sorption at low concentrations. Water, Air, and Soil Pollution 34: 293-303, 305-314.

Elm Andersen, C., 1980*. Dyrkningsfaktorer og planternes kemiske sammensætning (Cultivation factors and the chemical composition of plants). Agric. Vet. Res. Council, Copenhagen, 261 pp.

Gissel Nielsen, G. and Bertelsen, F., 1988*. Afsvovlingsprodukter - hvad gør de ved miljøet? (Desulfurization products and the environment). Miljøværn 20: 1-8. See also papers by the same authors in Environmental Geochemistry and Health, 1987-1989.

Hovmand, M. and Petersen, L., 1984*. Forsuringsprojektet: Jordforsuring. (The Acidification Project: Soil Acidification). Miljøstyrelsen (National Agency of Environmental Protection), Copenhagen, 1-89.

Jensen, L.T. and Jensen, H., 1990*. Bly i støvsugerposer. (Lead in vacuum cleaner dust). Dansk Kemi 5: 174-175.

Jørgensen, S.S. and Lassen, R., 1984*. Om udnyttelsen af kvælstof i dansk landbrug. (The utilization of nitrogen in Danish agriculture). Ugeskr. f. Jordbr. 129: 689-692.

Jørgensen, S.S. and Willems, M., 1987. The fate of lead in soils: The transportation of lead pellets in shooting-range soils. Ambio 16: 11-15.

Kjellerup, V. and Kofoed, A.D., 1983*. Kvælstofgødskningens indflydelse på udvaskning af plantenæringsstoffer fra jorden. (The influence of nitrogen fertilization on the leaching of plant nutrients from the soil). Tidsskr. f. Planteavl 87: 1-22.

Laursen, B., 1988*. Landbrugets kvælstofudledning. (Nitrogen pollution from agriculture). Ugeskr. f. Jordbr. 133: 352-359, 1069-1073.

Livens, F.R. and Rimmer, D.L., 1988. Physico-chemical controls on artificial radionuclides in soil. Soil Use and Management 4: 63-69. Also other papers in the same issue (p. 69-90).

Madsen, H.B. and Jensen, N.H., 1988*. Potentially acid sulfate soils in relation to land forms and geology. Catena 15: 137-145.

Miljøstyrelsen (National Agency of Environmental Protection), 1980*. Cadmiumforurening. (Cadmium Pollution). Copenhagen, 90 pp.

Miljøstyrelsen (National Agency of Environmental Protection), 1987*. Kviksølvredegørelse. (Mercury - Review of Use and Pollution). Redegørelse No. 5. Copenhagen, 104 pp.

Miljøstyrelsen (National Agency of Environmental Protection), 1988*. Fosfor - kilder og virkninger (Phosphorus - Sources and Effects). Copenhagen, 120 pp.

Overgaard, K., 1966. Report on Project No. 76. Miljøstyrelsen (National Agency of Environmental Protection), Copenhagen, 123 pp.

Petersen, L., 1986. Effects of acid deposition on soil and the sensitivity of the soil to acidification. Experientia 42: 340-344.

Petersen, R.C., Madsen, B.L., Wilzbach, M.A., Magadza, C.H.D., Paarlberg, A., Kullberg, A., and Cummins, K.W., 1987. Stream management: Emerging global similarities. Ambio 16: 166-79.

Rebsdorf, Aa. and Thyssen, N., 1987*. Udvaskning af fosfor fra naturarealer og landbrugsjord. (Leaching of phosphor from uncultivated areas and from agriculture). Ugeskr. f. Jordbr. 132: 1093-1096.

Rude, S., 1987*. Vandmiljøplanen og landbruget. (The 'Water and Environment' Plan and Danish agriculture). Inst. Agric. Economics. Rep. No. 34. Copenhagen, 68 pp.

Schrøder, H., 1984*. Udviklingen i kvælstoftabene fra dansk landbrug. (Nitrogen loss from Danish agriculture). Ugeskr. f. Jordbr. 129: 611-616.

SJVF (Danish Agricultural and Veterinary Research Council), 1986. Evaluation Report. Copenhagen, 69 pp.

Talibudeen, O., 1981. Cation exchange in soils. In: D.J. Greenland and M.H.B. Hayes (eds.): The Chemistry of Soil Processes. John Wiley, Chichester, 115-177.

Tjell, J.C. and Hovmand, M.F., 1978. Metal concentrations in Danish arable soils. Acta Agric. Scand., 28: 81-89.

Vækst (Journal of Hedeselskabet = The Danish Land Development Service), 1984*. Special issue, on ochre. 105(5): 1-25.

3 AIR POLLUTION

HENRIK SAXE

3.1 INTRODUCTION

3.1.1 The Problem

A most tangible predicament of our days results from conflicting interests between the desire for a healthy, safe and attractive physical, chemical and biological environment on the one hand, and a high material standard of living on the other. The price of the latter is rapid consumption of the limited global resources of raw materials and fossil energy, and the resulting pollution. In the future, our raw materials will be of increasingly lower grade or recycled, both of which will demand even more energy. Abatement of pollution, e.g., by using smoke filters on chimney stacks, only creates more solid wastes, the deposition of which is already becoming a global problem. If these problems are not properly balanced, they will inevitably result in a series of global disasters, some say, second only to that of a full-scale nuclear war.

We therefore need to change our present attitude to the environment most radically. This chapter will demonstrate that air pollution is the major menace of global environmental disasters, as exemplified by recent large-scale problems such as the unprecedented forest decline, the increasing greenhouse effect, and the depletion of the Antarctic ozone layer. If we go on demanding 'irrefutable proofs' or rely on warnings from sophisticated computer models rather than on common sense, we could irrevocably lose control of our environment, just as we are beginning to understand it.

Several types of pollution by organic substances are not described in this chapter, since they are mostly a local indoor problem at many work places, and in this connection considered to be of minor importance.

3.1.2 The Historical Perspective

Air pollution has only been a global problem for a century and a half, i.e., since the beginning of the industrial revolution. It has, however, been a local problem in Europe for millennia, as indicated, for example, by the ancient Roman poets Horace and Seneca. A passage in Homer's Odyssey (750 B.C.) about the effect of smoke on metal spears and swords indicates that the destructive qualities of 'smoke' have been known even longer.

By the end of the Middle Ages, London was the paradigm of a polluted metropolis. In 1306, Edward the First proclaimed a law against the use of pulverized coal in melting furnaces. (Try it, and you might lose your head!) Elizabeth the First (1533-1603) proclaimed a law against the burning of coal in London whenever the parliament was in session. But even though air pollution had been known and described for centuries, actual scientific research on its effects did not commence until the late 19th century, coinciding with the industrial revolution and a wide range of new problems introduced with the enormous escalation of air pollution.

Table 3.1. Contents of 'clean' air.

Element	Concentration		Turn-over time	
constant content				
nitrogen, N_2	78.08	vol %	10^6	years
oxygen, O_2	20.95	vol %	5000	years
argon, A	0.93	vol %		
neon, N	18.2	ppm		
helium, He	5.2	ppm		
krypton, Kr	1.1	ppm		
variable content				
carbon dioxide, CO_2	275	ppm	5	years
methane, CH_4	0.7	ppm	5	years
hydrogen H_2	0.5	ppm	7	years
nitrous oxide, N_2O	285	ppb	very	stable
ozone (nearest Earth)	30	ppb	25	years
very variable content				
carbon monoxide, CO	0.1	ppm	6	months
nitrogen dioxide, NO_2	1	ppb	10	days
ammonia, NH_3	1	ppb	5	days
sulfur dioxide, SO_2	0.3	ppb	2	days
hydrogen sulfide, H_2S	0.2	ppb	2	days
hydrocarbons	25	$\mu g\ m^{-3}$	2	days

3.1.3 The Definition

We shall define air pollution as *any change in the 'clean', pre-industrial atmosphere caused by either natural catastrophes (e.g., volcanic eruptions) or by anthropogenic (man-made) activities*. The typical constituents of this 'clean' air are given in Table 3.1.

3.1.4 Specific Air Pollutants

Some air pollutants are among the elements already present in clean air (Table 3.1), but contained at *elevated concentrations* in polluted air, while others (all man-made) are completely new to the atmosphere of the Earth. An overview of the most common air pollutants is given in Table 3.2. Since their existence and concentrations differ with the environment and with time (Anonymous, 1987a), their prevalence in the environment will be discussed in succeeding sections.

3.2 UNITS OF CONCENTRATION

Concentrations of gaseous air pollutants are expressed either as mass-per-unit-volume (e.g. $\mu g\ m^{-3}$) or as volume-per-unit-volume. The latter is expressed either as parts per million (ppm, ppmv or μl^{-1}) or parts per billion (US: 10^{-9} l l^{-1}; ppb). It would be better to use mass-per-unit--mass, in line with standard SI measurements of substances in solids or liquids, e.g. as $\mu g\ g^{-1}$, but this is, however, rarely practiced, since a gram of gas is difficult to visualize.

Table 3.2. Constituents of air pollution, classified as dry deposition, wet deposition, and particulates.

Dry deposition (gases)	Wet deposition (rain, fog, snow)	Particulates (dry or wet)
CO_2, CO, hydrocarbons: C_2H_4		
SO_2, H_2S	$H_2SO_4 \rightarrow H^+ + SO_4^{2-}$	carbon
$NO_x = NO + NO_2$	$HNO_3 \rightarrow H^+ + NO_3^-$	metals
HNO_3, NH_3	NH_4^+	+ gases
photooxidants: O_3, PAN, etc.	$HCl \rightarrow H^+ + Cl^-$	+ liquids
free radicals: $O^·$, $OH^·$, etc.		
HF; 'heavy metals'; CFC (freons), BFC; organic solvents; bacteria, virus, etc.		

Mass-per-unit-volume and volume-per-unit-volume are converted by the following formulae (Unsworth and Ormrod, 1982):

$$\mu g\ m^{-3} = \frac{ppb \times M \times 10^3}{V_o} \times \frac{T_o}{T} \times \frac{P}{P_o}, \qquad ppb = \frac{\mu g\ m^{-3} \times V_o \times 10^{-3}}{M} \times \frac{P_o}{P} \times \frac{T}{T_o}\ .$$

V_o is the molar volume of an ideal gas, equivalent to 22.4 x 10^{-3} m^{-3} mol^{-1} at standard temperature (273°K) and pressure (1 atm or 101.3 KPa). For any other conditions, appropriate corrections must be made.

The major point to be drawn from these formulae is that a mass-per-unit-volume expression does not allow an immediate comparison of one pollutant with a different one in terms of numbers of molecules; an atmosphere containing 1 ppmv SO_2 contains the same number of pollutant molecules as one containing 1 ppmv O_3 or NO_2 because the molecular weight and the volume of gas containing one gram molecule has already been taken into account. A volume-per-unit-volume expression is therefore most often preferred.

Particulates and aerosols cannot be measured in ppm or ppb, and mass per unit volume measurements must also be qualified by the ranges of the particle sizes or the droplet diameters.

3.3 SOURCES AND EMISSION

Anthropogenic outdoor air pollution comes from many sources, as indicated for some of the major species in Table 3.3 and Fig. 3.1.

In cities, a large and increasing proportion of the generated NO_x ($NO + NO_2$) comes from transport. The figure for London was 51% in 1976 and 59% in 1984. Data for Munich (Rüdiger, 1987) are shown in Fig. 3.1. The recent EEC directive on car emissions (Section 3.23.2) is an attempt to change this development.

The emission of sulfur dioxide and particulates has been reduced in recent years, due to restrictive regulations, while the emission of nitrogen oxides has gone up (Fig. 3.2).

Table 3.3. Sources of generated atmospheric pollution in England. (Wellburn, 1988).

Operation	Particulates (%)	SO_2 (%)	NO_x (%)	CO (%)	Hydrocarbons (%)
Power and heat	47.9	74.9	53.2	2.2	2.3
Transport	6.5	2.3	42.7	76.7	59.7
Refuse disposal	5.3	0.3	2.9	9.4	5.9
Other operations	40.2	22.4	1.1	11.1	16.6
Solvent evaporation	-	-	-	-	15.4

The production of volatile organics and photochemical oxidants (mainly resulting from hydrocarbons and nitrogen oxides) has increased.

Sources (and the development in emissions and concentrations) of other gaseous pollutants such as CO_2, CH_4, N_2O, O_3 and CFC's are given in Section 3.21.

3.3.1 Particulates

Air pollution by particulates was reviewed by Shaw (1987). Particles are classsified by size into three fractions: *coarse* particles (>2 µm), frequently produced in mechanical processes such as wind erosion, or in the metal industry, etc.; *fine* particles (0.1 - 2 µm), most of them man-made; and *condensation nuclei* (<0.1 µm) produced during the cooling of flue gases inside chimney stacks and immediately after. The condensation nuclei may grow to become fine particles, but once the gas is diluted in the atmosphere, the growth of particles stops, or is even reversed by evaporation. The latter are the *primary particles*.

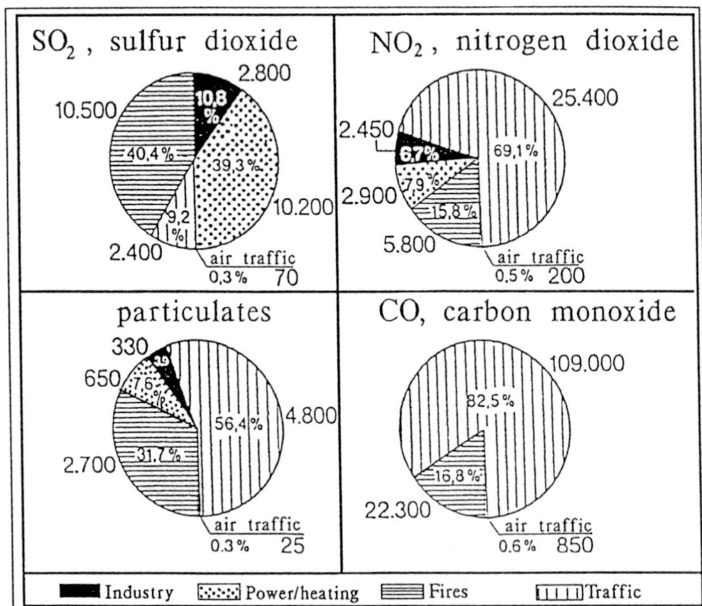

Figure 3.1. Sources of generated air pollution in Munich. - Source: Rüdiger (1987).

After emission, some of the flue gases are converted to compounds with a lower vapour pressure, e.g., SO_2 to H_2SO_4 and NO_2 to HNO_3. These are then substrates for the formation of *secondary particles*. As an example we have the formation of ammonium nitrate particles:

$$HNO_3(gas) \leftrightarrow NH_3(gas) \leftrightarrow NH_4NO_3^{\cdot}(solid)$$

This balance is valid at *low* relative humidity and ambient temperatures. Higher humidity pushes the balance to the right, but above 62% RH at 25°C the ammonium nitrate particle becomes hygroscopic, producing a suspension of ammonium nitrate, and ammonium- and nitrate ions:

$$NH_4NO_3 \text{ (solid)} \overset{H_2O}{\leftrightarrow} NH_4^+ \text{ (aqueous)} + NO_3^- \text{ (aqeous)}$$

When particles are *hygroscopic* and take up water, they become heavier and are deposited more rapidly. Their increasing volume affects the refraction of light, reducing atmospheric visibility. Most important, however, they provide surfaces of available water for other processes in atmospheric chemistry. The production of both primary and secondary particles depends upon thermodynamic parameters.

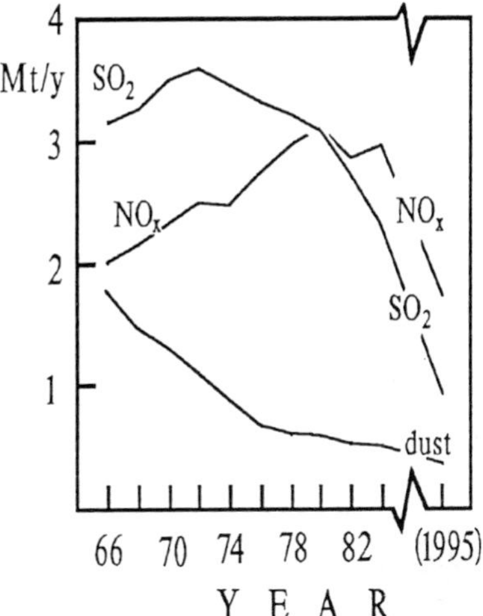

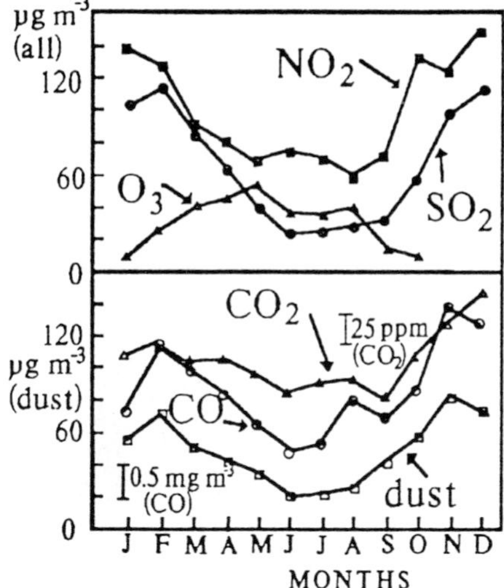

Figure 3.2. Two graphical illustrations, after Lahman (Anonymous, 1987a). - Left: Restrictive legislation has cleaned up SO_2 and dust in Europe and North America, while NO_x are expected to be gradually diminished in the 1990's. Photo-oxidants are increasing due to increasing concentrations of nitrogen oxides and hydrocarbons. - Right: Annual cycles of air pollutants. CO is measured in mg m^{-3},O_2 in ppm, and the rest in mg m^{-3}.

Analyses of dust from environmental aerosol samplers reveal elevated levels of many elements in city areas, especially lead, chromium, manganese, silver, zinc, iron, cobalt, aluminum, cadmium and molybdenum, as compared to rural sites. Ratios between individual elements reflect their possible sources. Pb:Br (lead to bromine) is used to identify the source of airborne lead; when the lead is mainly from vehicle exhausts, the ratio is about 2.6. A V:N ratio (vanadium to nickel) of about 2 suggests that the emissions originate from burning fuel oil, while a lower ratio suggests other industrial processes, usually metallurgical processes involving nickel. A Cl:Na ratio (chlorine to sodium) of 1.8 is characteristic of *natural* sources of the elements such as sea spray, while a higher ratio indicates other potential emitters of chlorine such as coal-burning and chemical industries.

3.3.2 Gases

Some power-plant *fuels* discharge less pollutants when burned than others. The emission from natural gas, for instance, is typically free of sulfur dioxide and low in particulates, while SO_2 from coal and oil depends on the quality of the fuel (400-3000 ppm measured in the stack). Emission of CO occurs only when burning peat and natural gas (2000-5000 ppm and 100 ppm), while HCl is only emitted from coal-burning plants (80 ppm).

Use of *lead-free* petrol in transport gives a higher emission of *carcinogenic PAHs* (polyaromatic hydrocarbons) which, however, do not accumulate in the environment as does the ‘heavy metal’ they relieve. It is not normally possible to distinguish contributions by individual industrial sources from others.

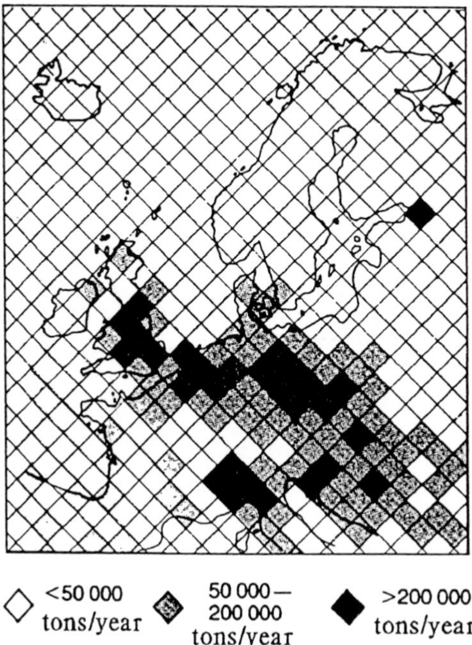

Figure 3.3. Origin of European sulfur-dioxide emission. - Source: Fenger (1985).

Most of the SO_2 (Fig. 3.3) and NO_x emissions in Europe originate in Central Europe, the BeNeLux-countries and England. The profoundly improved SO_2 emission control in Western Europe during the last two decades has gradually moved the predominant SO_2 emission eastward, whereas the increasing traffic in Western Europe has moved the predominant NO_x emission westward. The recent directive concerning mandatory catalyzers for motorcars (Section 3.23.2) within the EEC, and the even stronger legislation in several EFTA countries, will again move the predominant NO_x emission eastward. In Western Europe, England has long been considered 'the dirty land', but luckily the Westernly wind from the Atlantic is predominantly clean.

3.4 CONCENTRATIONS IN THE ENVIRONMENT

Anthropogenic air pollutants can be found everywhere, but of course their average concentrations depend on the location. Of all man-made sulfur dioxide, 93% is emitted in the Northern Hemisphere, and of this 20% over Europe, which covers only 1% of the Earth's surface (Moss, 1978).

3.4.1 Concentration Cycles

Average concentrations of individual air pollutants are not in themselves an adequate measure for the situation. The concentration of each pollutant cycles in annual, weekly and diurnal patterns, and its effect when deposited on living and dead material depends on a vast number of interacting environmental and biological factors, besides the ex-posure pattern. While materials react mostly to the long-term *average* concentrations, living organisms also react to the *peak values*. As an example a recent WHO health study has linked the main adverse effects of nitrogen oxides on human health to exposure to high concentrations for short periods of time. For this reason, a new EEC directive on NO_x emission requires hourly rather than daily readings when monitoring this gas.

Examples of *annual cycles* (based on monthly average of daily averages) of SO_2, NO_x, O_3, CO, CO_2, and suspended particulates are given in Fig. 3.2.

The concentrations of sulfur dioxide and nitrogen oxides are higher in the winter due to greater production of heat and lower absorbtion by vegetation. The concentration of ozone is highest in the summer, due to the higher solar ultra-violet radiation. Also, ozone is higher in rural sites than in cities, where it reacts with NO.

Fig. 3.4 gives *24-hour cycles* (based on hourly averages of continous readings) of SO_2, NO_x, and O_3. Nitrogen oxides are the first to increase in the morning (NO before NO_2), due to morning traffic. Sulfur dioxide rises later, when many industries use more power than during the night. In the winter there is a second SO_2-peak during the evening (heating). Ozone increases early in the afternoon, during and after the peak of solar radiation.

3.4.2 Mean Concentrations and Percentiles

SO_2, NO_2 and O_3 concentrations in the average European *rural* areas range from 2-13 ppb SO_2, 2-15 ppb NO_2, and 25-70 ppb O_3 as monthly averages (Eliassen et al., 1988).

Table 3.4. Different ways of giving concentration, µg m^{-3}. Example from West Berlin, 1985. - Source: Anonymous (1987a).

	SO_2	NO_2	O_2	CO	dust
Annual mean concentration	65	77	16	2400	86
Monthly max. mean	188	99	33	3800	143
Daily max. mean	406	175	65	6600	311
30-minutes max. mean	-	308	101	14000	-
98% percentile	256	175	-	8000	226

Daily and hourly values, and concentrations in urban areas, are 10-50 ppb higher for the first two gases, while ozone concentrations, as just mentioned, are lower in the cities than in the countryside.

For the purpose of using information on pollutant concentration to evaluate injuries, it is important to know both short- and long-term average values and short- and long-term peak values of the predominant pollutants.

Alternatively, concentrations may be given as *percentile* values. A 99% percentile value of, say, 60 ppb indicates that the concentration did not surpass 60 ppb during 99% of the monitoring period. Two or three percentile concentrations, e.g., at the 50%, 90% and 99% levels, may be more informative than average concentrations over several durations.

Table 3.4 illustrates the different results when indicating the concentration by either annual means, monthly means, 24-h means, 30-min means or 98% percentiles.

The WHO listed the general air-pollution situation in major cities. The top-ten reads: Tel Aviv, Sao Paulo, Frankfurt, Chicago, Sidney, New York, London, Copenhagen, West Berlin and Osaka. However, since different methods were employed in monitoring the pollutants, and several polluted cities were not listed, such data should be used with care.

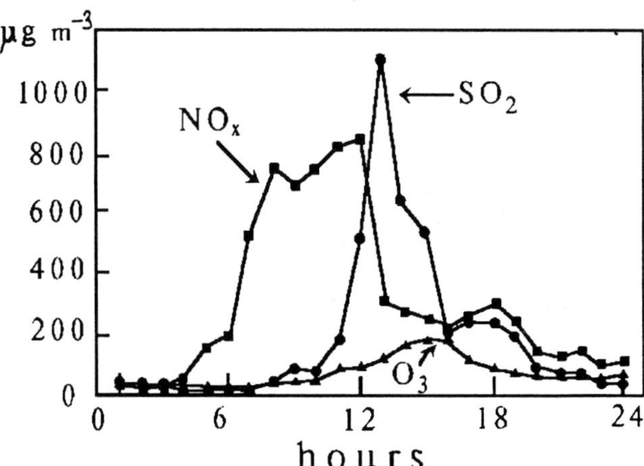

Figure 3.4. 24-h cycles of air pollution in London. - Source: Anonymous (1987a).

3.5 TRANSMISSION

The fate of air pollutants emitted to the atmosphere can be described by three processes (Fig. 3.5): *transmission* (dispersion and long range transport), *chemical transformations* and *deposition.*

3.5.1 Dispersion

Pollutants released into the atmosphere will primarily follow the movements of the air in a so-called *plume* (Fig. 3.6). However, fine and coarse *particles* with a mobility several orders lower than that of gases are excepted from this rule. While the diffusion coefficients for gases are in the range of 10^0-10^{-1}, those of fine particles are 10^{-5}-10^{-7}, and for coarse particles 10^{-8}-10^{-9}. The particulates, therefore, are rapidly lost from the plume.

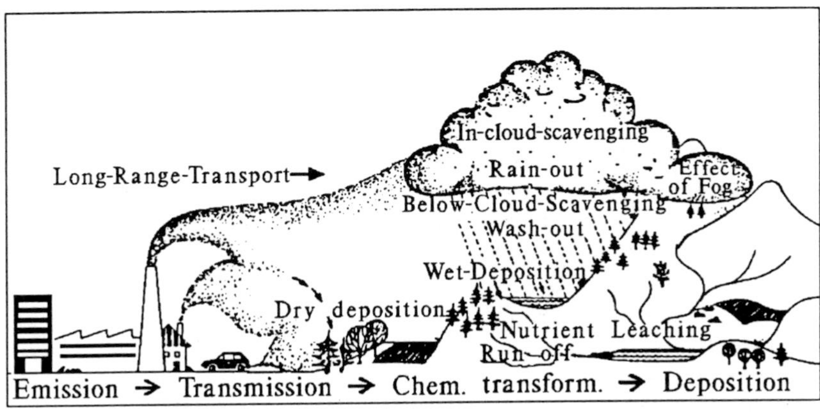

Figure 3.5. Transmission, chemical transformation, and deposition of emitted air pollutants. - Source: Wellburn (1988).

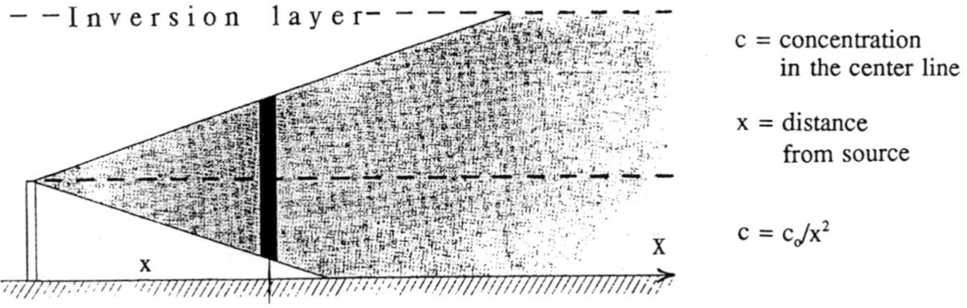

Figure 3.6. Dispersion of a plume. The concentration c of air pollutants falls off with the square of the distance x from the emission point of the stack until vertical dispersion is hindered by solid objects or by an inversion layer. - Source: Fenger (1985).

Due to turbulence, the gaseous pollutants (and condensation nuclei) spread in vertical and horizontal directions within the plume, increasing its cross-section, but reducing pollutant concentrations with distance from the source and the center of the plume. The downward dispersion is limited by the Earth's surface while upward dispersion may be limited by a thermal inversion layer (Fig. 3.6), depending on the meteorological conditions. From there on, the pollution spreads only horizontally, with slower dilution.

The vertical temperature distribution has a great impact on the stability of the air, and therefore on the dispersion of air pollutants. When a volume of air, visualized in Fig. 3.7 by plumes, stochastically moves upward, it will expand, due to falling pressure with increasing height; this expansion makes the temperature of the volume of air drop approximately 1°C/100 m, as indicated by the dotted lines in Fig. 3.7. If the temperature in the surrounding air also falls 1°C/100 m, as indicated by the full lines in Fig. 3.7, we have the *neutral* situation shown in the top figure (a). Below (b) is the situation where the air temperature falls faster than 1°C/100 m. Our volume of air will be surrounded by colder and therefore heavier air - and will proceed to rise. If the air temperature falls more slowly than 1°C/100 m (c), it becomes difficult for our volume of air to rise. In the extreme case (d), where the surrounding temperature rises sharply at a certain height, an *inversion-layer* forms at this level.

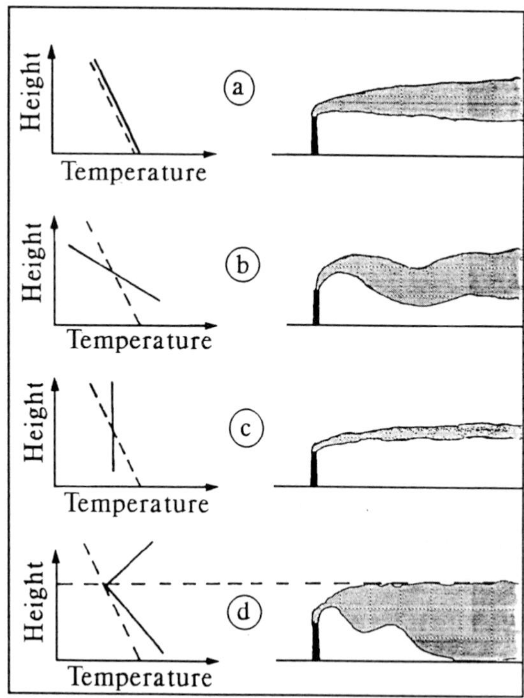

Figure 3.7. Impact of vertical temperature distribution on dispersion of emitted air pollutants, cf. text. - Source: Fenger (1985).

Fig. 3.8 illustrates this meterological situation, called a *thermal inversion*, where a blanket of hot air sits on top of colder air, so that the pollution from cars, chimneys and stacks cannot rise and disperse in the atmosphere. Under such conditions the air we breathe is a menace to our health. There have been incidents in West German cities where people were recommended not to drive their cars, and even to stay indoors. But, out of 14 incidents of 'smog alarm' during thermal inversions in Berlin from 1980-1987, eight were provoked by fires, four by high levels of long-range transport of air pollutants and only two by traffic. Sulfur dioxide and nitrogen dioxide reached 24-h values of up to 0.90 and 0.19 mg m^3, while 30-min values reached 2.30 and 0.33 mg m^3 respectively.

With a very low chimney, as with a private house, a turbulence around the house may drive the smoke down, creating a local problem.

When the height of a stack is increased, the maximal resulting concentration at the Earth's surface is generally diminished by the square of this increase. But once the plume reaches and is limited by the Earth's surface and a thermal layer, the pollution disperses only horizontally, and concentrations are no longer dependent on the height of the source.

The *temperature* of the smoke contributes to the 'effective height' of a stack through a 'thermal lift'; the plume from a typical 130 m power-plant stack is thus lifted to 200 m at normal wind speed. This is the reason why a wet-process smoke purification which significantly cools the smoke temperature (thus decreasing the 'effective height' of the stack), may not give a reduction in pollution as measured locally.

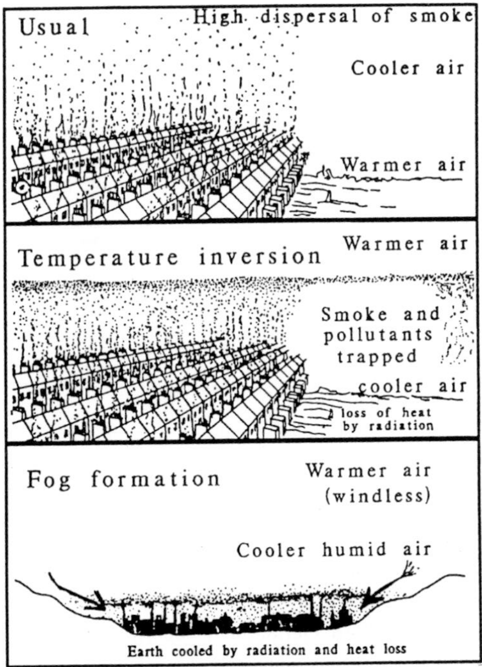

Figure 3.8. Thermal inversion. - Source: Mellanby (1980).

3.5.2 Long-Range Transport

A typical wind speed of 5 m s^{-1} equals over 400 km per 24 h. Since many air pollutants have a turn-over time in the atmosphere of several days (Table 3.1) they are transported over considerable distances.

The days are gone when local air-pollution problems could be solved by building taller stacks. Local sources have become abundant, and the background levels too high. This was recognized by the International Stockholm Conference on the Environment back in 1972, stating as 'Principle no. 21' that *all countries have an obligation to ensure that activities within their jurisdiction or control do not cause environmental injuries in other countries.*

Today, nearly two decades later, we all realize the importance of this principle. Air pollution does not respect borders or political systems; it is truly an *international* problem.

Computer models are used to describe long-range transport of air pollution. Simple models based on plumes are reliable only under local, *stationary* conditions. When the direction and speed of the wind, the thermal conditions or the roughness of the landscape changes, more complicated models must be used. This is the case in countries like Denmark, where power plants are typically located along the coastline.

In Western Europe, the long-range transport of air pollutants has been monitored by the EMEP programme. Considering the importance of long-range transport of air pollutants, a Danish jest that future Danish investments in pollution abatement would be better spent if donated to abate East European pollution, no longer makes anyone laugh.

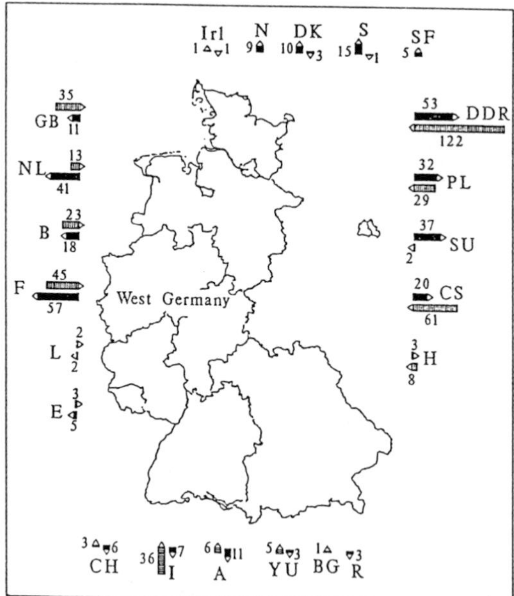

Figure 3.9. Sulfur balance for West Germany, 1986. Import (striped arrows) and export (black arrows) are both given in kilo tons. Import exceeds export by 14% = 50 Kt for one year. - Source: Lahman (Anonymous, 1987a).

3.5.3 Two Examples of Import/Export of Air Pollutants

Scandinavia. Danish sources of emission are responsible for only 1/4 of all sulfur and 1/5 of all nitrogen deposited in Denmark, and for only 10-15% of all sulfur and 18% of all nitrogen deposited on the sensitive South Scandinavian areas. Therefore, even rigorous reductions in Danish emissions will by themselves only contribute a little to a reversal of the current acidification in the southern parts of Sweden and Norway. International reductions in both East and West are essential to alleviate the Scandinavian problem.

Germany. Fig. 3.9 illustrates the SO_2 import/export situation for West Germany in relation to other European countries. West Germany has a net import of sulfur: 399 - 349 = 50 kilo t per year. This reflects the higher level of air pollution in Eastern than in Western Europe.

3.6 CHEMICAL TRANSFORMATIONS

Meteorological and chemical circumstances determine the effects of emitted air pollutants. We all know of episodes called *smog* (smoke and fog), once a common event in London; and 'photochemical smog', typical for the Los Angeles area. Both situations build up because the emitted air pollutants cannot escape, rather than because of chemical reactions that only proceed at high concentrations; the reactions are the same at lower pollutant concentrations.

In the chemical transformations of air pollutants, we distinguish between *homogeneous* and *heterogeneous* reactions.

3.6.1 Homogeneous Reactions and Photochemistry

Homogeneous reactions are *gas-gas reactions,* in particular involving O_3, NO_x and volatile hydrocarbons, frequently energized by solar UV rays. The photochemistry generates short-living, very reactive radicals (e.g., O• and OH•), as well as longer living molecules (e.g., PANs = peroxyacyl nitrates), which take part in the long-range transport of air pollutants.

At the high temperatures of industrial processes and motor vehicles, atmospheric O_2 and N_2 combine to form NO. This reacts with O_3 and volatile hydrocarbons (R-) in the complex photochemical reactions of the so-called 'photochemical oxidant pool', producing several reactive oxidants which make up the *photochemical smog.*

One important conclusion from our present knowledge of reactions in the photochemical oxidant pool is that a reduction in one component may lead to either an increase or a decline of other components. A reduction in, for instance, the atmospheric NO_x concentration, may give either an increase or a decline in ambient O_3, depending on the hydrocarbon concentration. The most important components to reduce, if photochemical smog is to be controlled in urban areas, seem to be the volatile hydrocarbons.

3.6.2 Heterogeneous Reactions, Acid Rain

Heterogeneous reactions involve both gases and particulates (or raindrops). The frequency of collisions between particles and gas molecules is low compared to gas-gas interactions, because of the previously mentioned low diffusion rates of particles and because of their low numbers (10^2-10^4 molecules cm^{-3}) relative to gas molecules (10^{-11}-10^{-12} cm^{-3}). But due to special properties of particles, several important reactions are of the heterogeneous type. The formation of *acid rain* is an example of heterogeneous atmospheric reactions.

In the formation of acid rain, there is interaction between molecules in the gas- and the particle- (or raindrop-) bound aqueous phase (hydration). For sulfur dioxide, we have:

$$SO_2 + H_2O \rightarrow H_2SO_3 \leftrightarrow H^+ + HSO_3^- \leftrightarrow 2\,H^+ + SO_3^{2-}$$

Carbonic acid is formed from carbon dioxide in the same manner. Sulfuric acid, however, is formed through photooxidation:

$$SO_2 \xrightarrow{h\nu<390} SO_2^{\cdot} \xrightarrow{SO_2(\rightarrow SO)} SO_3 \xrightarrow{H_2O} H_2SO_4 \leftrightarrow 2\,H^+ + SO_2^{2-}$$

Nitric acid is formed from a reaction between NO_2 and the atomic $O\cdot$ or the $OH\cdot$ radical:

$$NO_2 \xrightarrow{O\cdot} NO_3 \xrightarrow{NO_2} N_2O_5 \xrightarrow{H_2O} 2\,HNO_3 \rightarrow 2\,NO_3^- + 2\,H^+ ,$$

$$NO_2 \xrightarrow{OH\cdot} HNO_3 \leftrightarrow NO_3^- + H^+ .$$

Here we have both gas-gas and gas-particle reactions involved, so that the complete process involves both homogeneous and heterogeneous reaction steps.

Hydrochloric acid is formed when NaCl (ocean spray) comes in contact with a strong acid:

$$NaCl + H_2SO_4 \rightarrow NaHSO_4 + HCl ,$$

$$NaCl + HNO_3 \rightarrow NaNO_3 + HCl .$$

In all cases, we get protons, i.e., the acidity of the acid rain. The negatively charged nutrient anions (SO_4, NO_3, etc.) play an important role in the indirect effects of acid rain.

The equilibrium between the two phases is described for weak electrolytes by *Henry's law*, which maintains that the ratio between the vapour pressure of a gas and its concentration in the aqueous phase is constant. Based on this constant, gases may be classified according to their water solubility, which in turn determines the composition of the acid deposition. HNO_3 and H_2SO_4 are associated with either hygroscopic particles or drops of water.

Ammonia, which is very water soluble, can neutralize the acidity in rain and particulates. In intensively managed agricultural countries like Denmark and Holland this mechanism, or alkaline dust from the fields, tends to neutralize the acid deposition. For this reason, acidification should not be evaluated by SO_2 and NO_x emissions alone:

$$NH_3\,(gas) + (2\,H^+, SO_4^{2-}) \rightarrow NH_4^+\,(aq) + HSO_4^-\,(aq) .$$

3.7 DEPOSITION

Sooner or later, all air pollution will be *deposited* on the surface of the Earth (including forests, fields, roads, cars, buildings etc.), either in the original chemical form or following physico-chemical transformations.

Deposition is classified as *dry deposition* or *wet deposition.* Wet deposition occurs as 'rain out' (Fig. 3.5), when supersaturated aqueous vapour in clouds condenses on particles which grow and are drawn down by gravity; and as 'wash out', when rain drops collide with particles or take up pollutant gases while falling to the ground. In the high air pollution concentrations of cities, 'wash out' is the typical process, while in the country, 'rain out' is most common.

Environmental factors (e.g., wind speed), as well as the shape and the quality of the receiving surface, determine the velocity of deposition. A forest, for instance, has a large specific surface compared to a desert, and a coniferous forest has a larger one than a deciduous forest. The concentration of acids (dissociated as H^+, SO^{2-} and NO_3^{-}) in rain falling in the open is therefore less than in the throughfall in a forest, particularly in a coniferous forest. Furthermore, a humid surface absorbs water-soluble gasses such as sulfur dioxide several times faster than a dry surface.

The dry deposition contributes as much to the acidification of the environment as the acid rain. The primary gases of the dry deposition may be directly absorbed by the target and oxidized either before or after they are taken into the organism. However, pollutants with a low water solubility (e.g., O_3 and NO) typically react before they even meet the organism.

3.8 UPTAKE

When a gas, a particle or a raindrop has been deposited on the surface of building materials, it elicits its effects. For living organisms, however, the external effects are of little consequence. To have an effect on plant or animal life, the air pollutants have to be taken into the organism. The primary route of pollutant uptake is through the mouth and into the lungs and stomach of higher animals, or through the stomatal opening and into the intercellular air space and mesophyll cells of leaves in higher plants. Plants may also take up pollutants through their roots.

The Swedish example of SO_2 uptake in conifers, see Table 3.5, demonstrates that uptake is not linearly proportional to either atmospheric concentration or to deposition. The example demonstrates how the uptake in a plant may depend on physical and biological factors.

A pollutant which has passed through the mouth or stomates damages important functions in *membranes,* including their permeability. If the pollutant or its reaction products pass through the cellular membrane (in plants, after passing the cellulose cell wall) and enters the cells, further damage occurs. This is discussed in detail later.

Fig. 3.10 shows the pathways of a gaseous air pollutant into a dry leaf with open stomates.

Molecules outside the *'boundary layer'* of a leaf essentially migrate by convection and turbulence. Inside the boundary layer, which is defined as a perfectly still layer of air surrounding the leaf (or any surface), within which all molecular movement is conveyed by *passive diffusion,* the net molecular movement is slow, depending on the diffusion coefficient for the gas in question. The resistance to molecular movement through the boundary layer (R_a) is the first resistance that any gaseous pollutant encounters. The thickness of the boundary layer, and thus its resistance, is mainly a function of wind speed and -direction, and of epidermal trichome ('hair') density and size.

Table 3.5. Pollutant uptake in Swedish conifers depends on physical and biological factors. When the plant is covered by snow it may never receive any pollutants, whatever the atmospheric concentration. A broadleaf tree is even more protected, as it does not have leaves during the winter period. When the leaf is wet, the strong sink effect of the wet surface draws most of the sulfur dioxide into solution on the surface. When the stomates are closed, the SO_2 flux into the plant is near zero. Of the sulfur dioxide deposited, only 30% gets inside the plant and threatens growth. Since most of the sulfur-dioxide pollution occurs in winter, even less than 30% of the average annual exposure quantity ever penetrates the leaves.

Situation at leaf surface		time of the year		
Snow cover				20%
No snow cover				80%
	Closed stomata:		45%	
	wet surface, rain	9%		
	wet surface, dew	10%		
	dry surface	26%		
	Open stomata:		35%	
	wet surface, rain	3%		
	wet surface, dew	2%		
	dry surface	30% !		

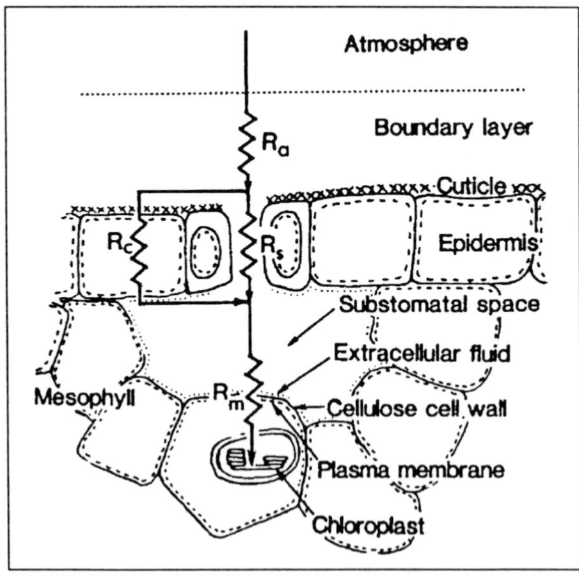

Figure 3.10. Likely access routes for gaseous air pollutants into a plant leaf. "R" denotes various types of resistance met by a pollutant molecule during uptake (described in the text). - Source: Wellburn (1988).

When the pollutant molecule reaches the leaf surface, it may enter by two routes: either through the stomates, which have the lowest resistance (R_s), or through the epidermal cells (R_c). These two pathways (resistances coupled in parallel) are coupled in series with the external boundary-layer resistance and an internal resistance (R_m). The internal resistance is a series of resistances. *First*, there is a resistance to passive diffusion through the internal air spaces of the leaf onward to the mesophyll cell surfaces. Here the gas may affect both the cellulose walls and the outer cell membrane (plasmalemma). If these are the ultimate targets, the internal resistance is identical with only the resistance of the internal air spaces. *Next*, there is the passage through the cell wall, through the plasmalemma, and through the cytoplasm, toward other ultimate targets, e.g. the chloroplast membranes. *Finally*, the restricted turn-over of the molecule is often referred to as the *biochemical resistance*.

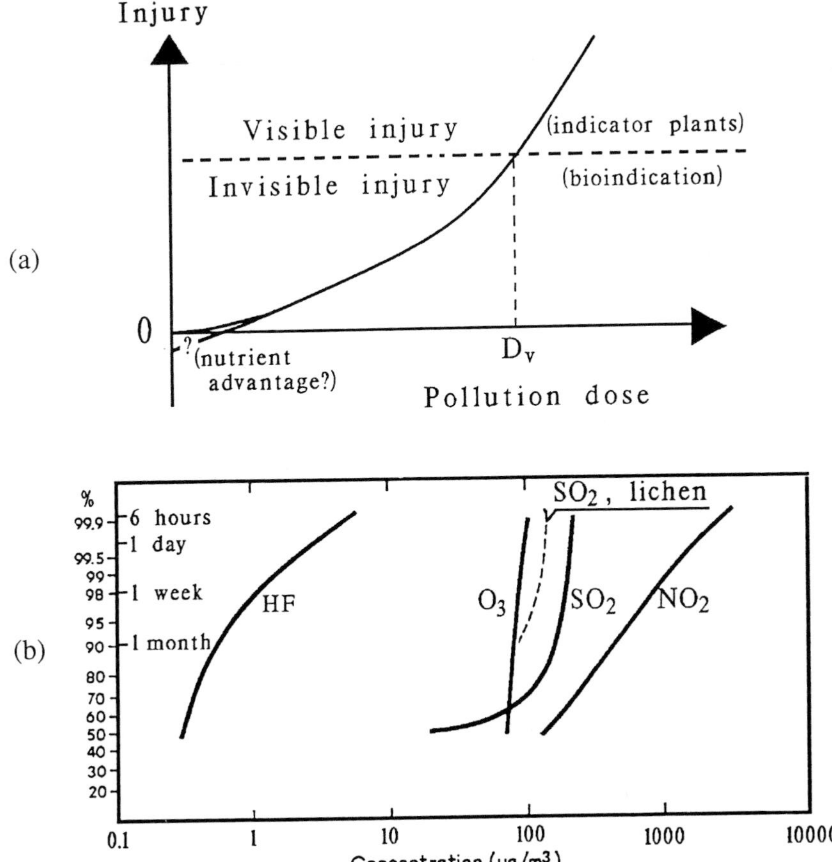

Figure 3.11. Visible and invisible injury. (a) General dose-response relationship of air pollution and plant response. (b) Threshold concentrations of some air pollutants plotted on log-normal distribution paper (Moseholm, 1988).

3.9 THRESHOLD DOSES FOR EFFECTS

For plants and animals we may distinguish between *visible* and *invisible* injuries, and between *quantitative* and *qualitative* injuries. Several types of threshold levels have been established experimentally.

For humans we know much less about threshold doses, since very few experiments can be carried out safely. A recent publication by the WHO (Anonymous, 1987c), contains guidelines (occurrence, effects and threshold doses) for Europe, on 15 inorganic substances, several of which we deal with in this chapter, and 12 organic substances not described in this chapter (except for PAHs, see Section 3.16.2).

3.9.1 The Principle of Visible and Invisible Injuries

As indicated by the theoretical graph in Fig. 3.11 (a), increasing pollutant stress increases damage to living organisms, except maybe at very low levels (Section 3.12.1).

Up to a certain exposure dose (D_v), which depends on the pollutant, the exposure concentration and -time, as well as on the plant species and cultivar, there is no visible injury. This, however, does not mean that doses below D_v do not cause any effects, but they are invisible. Examples of invisible injuries (or stimulations) are changes in transpiration, photosynthesis or enzyme activities. Physiological and biochemical measurement of invisible injury (or stimulations), called *bioindication,* may give early warning of pollutant stress that in the long term develops into visible injury.

Doses above D_v, which induce visible injury (e.g., scorching of leaves, reduction in measurable growth or changes in root:shoot ratios), may be detected at an early stage by the use of sensitive plants, *bioindicator plants* (Posthumous, 1982). The best known example is the use of tobacco (*Nicotiana tabacum* L. *cv.* Bel W_3) as an early warning of ozone, which induces necrotic speckles on the upper surface of the leaves.

Taking the average of a large number of plants, Fig. 3.11 (b) shows threshold concentrations as a logarithmic function of exposure time for hydrogen fluoride, ozone, sulfur dioxide and nitrogen dioxide. The threshold is defined as the concentration below which no visible injury will occur in dicotyledons (and lichens).

Clearly, *hydrogen fluoride* (e.g. from ceramics production) is the most phytotoxic of the gases. It is, however, not very widely distributed. *Ozone* is very aggressive with a threshold value below 100 µg m^{-3}, relatively independent of exposure time, whereas *sulfur dioxide* is remarkably aggressive at low concentrations over a long time. This was not expected from early short-term studies. Lichens (*Hypogymnia physodes*) are more sensitive to sulfur dioxide than dicotyledons, and have therefore been used as bioindicator plants for sulfur dioxide. *Nitrogen dioxide* is relatively non-phytotoxic by itself, though it significantly increases the phytotoxicity of sulfur dioxide during combined exposures (which is always the case in the ambient environment).

3.9.2 Quantitative and Qualitative Injuries

Whether an injury is visible or invisible, it may be measured both quantitatively and qualitatively. The *quantity* is of major interest when using the biomass of the product, e.g., for paper, timber or fibers. But the *quality* of these products is also important, and it is of major interest when we are dealing with food plants. It is then the basis of our health.

In commercial trade, however, the quantitative and the qualitative measures are combined in an *economic* index, which is what merchants primarily care about. Unfortunately, this index often emphasizes the quantity and appearance of food products above their purity and nutritional quality; hence the success of present day 'chemical' agriculture.

3.10 EFFECTS OF CARBON MONOXIDE

Second to carbon dioxide, *carbon monoxide*, CO, is the most widely distributed and abundant atmospheric pollutant of the troposphere (i.e., the atmosphere below 15 km.). Emissions of carbon monoxide caused by man exceed those of all other pollutants combined (excluding CO_2), being more than 600 Mt (1 Mt = 10^6 tons) per annum. About 5% of that produced by the activities of man arises from the surface of the oceans and another 5% arises from a variety of natural processes such as volcanoes, electrical storms, 'marsh gas' from rotting vegetation and a variety of other biological sources.

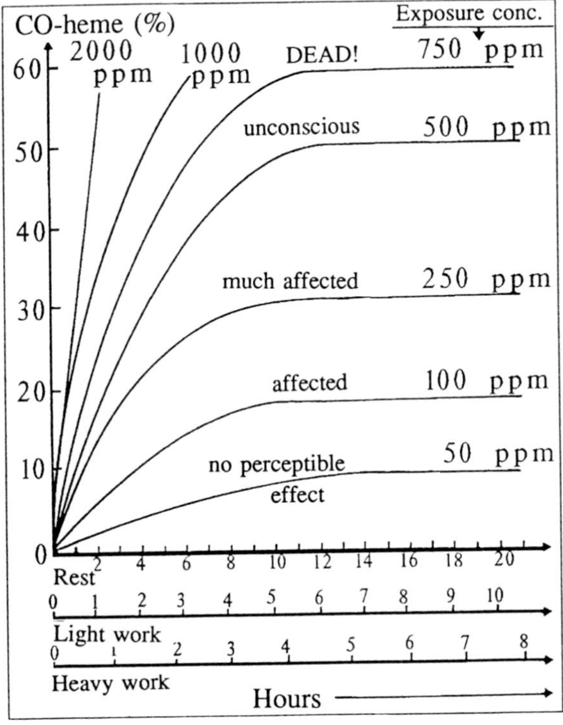

Figure 3.12. The effects of carbon monoxide on man depend on his activity. - Source: Saxe and Andersen (1986).

While the oceans are the major sink for carbon dioxide, carbon monoxide is mainly removed in the troposphere by reaction with the hydroxyl radical ($OH^{\cdot}$), and by soil microbes in numerous biological mechanisms. Removal is most efficient in natural, tropical soils. Only when the northern forest soils have warmed sufficiently, can they supplement the steady uptake of carbon monoxide by tropical forest soils. Agricultural processes appear to select against those microbes that are the most efficient in carbon-monoxide removal. If tropical soils are cultivated and northern forest soils are damaged by 'acid rain', then the overall levels of CO, and thereby CO_2, may rise and enhance the 'greenhouse effect' (Section 3.21).

Carbon monoxide is not toxic to plants (Bennett and Hill 1973). As a global estimate it has been estimated that plants take up one quarter of that of soil (Wellburn 1988). Indeed CO is one of the few air pollutants (apart from HS) to which plants are less sensitive than man.

Carbon monoxide is a *very toxic* gas for man and animals, even in quite low concentrations. It binds to the haemoglobin molecule in blood with a 300 times higher affinity than oxygen. The transport of oxygen with the blood is thus strongly inhibited. The first symptoms of poisoning are headache and dizziness. The effect increases with the *activity* of the person (Fig. 3.12). But fortunately, CO-binding is easily *reversible*, and after a few hours in fresh air the CO-heme percentage falls back to normal (0.5%), even after it has been as high as 10%-20%. Carbon monoxide does not cause chronic injury.

Urban concentrations may reach 50 ppm in rush hours, and as high as 150 ppm in tunnels and garages. The CO produced by a single cigarette (Section 3.19.2) reacts immediately with haemoglobin in the lung tissue, boosting the CO-heme to about 10%.

3.11 EFFECTS OF CARBON DIOXIDE

Carbon dioxide, CO_2, is a *prerequisite for life* on Earth as we know it today. This is partly because CO_2 together with water, minerals and light is the substrate of primary production (photosynthesis) in the oceans and in limnetic and terrestrial ecosystems; and partly because it raises the temperature at the surface of the Earth.

The latter effect, however, is currently getting out of control. The role of carbon dioxide in the so-called '*greenhouse effect*' (Section 3.21) has therefore made CO_2 a serious air pollutant, the most ubiquitous and abundant, and maybe the most alarming of them all!

3.12 EFFECTS OF SULFUR DIOXIDE

Together with smoke and dust, sulfur dioxide is among the earliest and most abundant man-made air pollutants. But in Western Europe and North America the atmospheric SO_2 concentration is at present diminishing (Fig. 3.2).

3.12.1 Vegetation: Invisible and Visible Injuries

Several studies have demonstrated that plants in cities grow at a reduced rate compared with those growing in rural sites. A combination of different air pollutants, mainly O_3, SO_2 and NO_x and their reaction products, is thought to be responsible. But even plants in rural sites are adversely affected by air pollution, though in some cases they may benefit. Sulfur dioxide and nitrogen oxides have a special position among air pollutants, since sulfur and nitrogen are among the essential plant nutrients, and this is why both harmful and beneficial effects of these pollutants are conceivable (Fig. 3.11). In this section, we consider invisible and visible effects of sulfur dioxide on vegetation.

Studies of the effects of sulfur dioxide on plants were first initiated in the late nineteenth century. The existing literature is therefore voluminous, and has frequently been reviewed. The concise review by Hällgren (1978) on physiological and biochemical effects of sulfur dioxide on plants still applies, though more recent reviews by Unsworth and Ormrod (1982), Koziol and Whatley (1984), Treshow (1984), Ormrod (1986), Hutchinson and Meema (1987), Schulte-Holstede et al. (1988), Heck et al. (1988), Wellburn (1988) and Darrall (1989) are recommended for more current information on the effects of SO_2 and several other (wet or dry deposited) air pollutants on vegetation.

Stomatal mechanisms. The opening and closing of stomatal pores in leaves made waterpr-oof by a thick outer cuticle was a prerequisite for the development of higher land plants. The cuticle prevents improvident loss of precious water, while the regulated pores allow the essential gas exchange, uptake of carbon dioxide and output of oxygen, with a minimal loss of water vapour. Stomates are usually closed during the night, when most plants do not need gas exchange, since there is no light to drive photosynthesis. Some plants (CAM plants), however, have to take up carbon dioxide by night and store it for photosynthetic use during the day, when stomates are closed, to avoid loss of water in extremely hot and dry climates.

The loss of water through stomata depends upon stomatal opening, leaf- and air temperature, relative humidity, wind exposure, surface structure of the leaves, and availability of water in the soil. To understand how air pollutants damage plants through effects on stomata, one must understand the basic stomatal mechanisms.

An optimal balance between loss of water vapour and exchange of CO_2 and O_2 has established itself for all plants and climates through millennia of natural selection. All effects - changing the stomatal mechanisms are therefore injurious to the plants.

The stomatal opening is defined by two *guard cells*, and the aperture is regulated by *active* and *passive* mechanisms (Jarvis and Mansfield, 1981).

The *active* mechanism is an energy-requiring K^+-pump, which controls the *turgor pressure* in the guard cells relative to their surrounding cells in the epidermis, the outermost cell layer of the leaf. When the relative guard cell turgor is high, the pore is open. The active mechanism is affected by light, carbon dioxide, temperature and gaseous pollutants.

The *passive* mechanism involves changes in cell turgor caused by drought, relative humidity, temperature and gaseous pollutants.

SO_2-injury to transpiration (stomata). Stomates are affected by lower concentrations of SO_2 than those which induce visible injuries. It may therefore be used as an early warning that a pollutant is about to damage the plant.

Low SO_2 concentrations (30-280 µg m^{-3}) typically open the pores, especially in young plants, at high relative humidity and with ample water and nutrients in the soil. With higher SO_2 concentrations (above 280 µg m^{-3}), or with concurrent exposure to low NO_2 or O_3

concentrations, the stomata close. Acid rain (produced by sulfur dioxide and nitrogen dioxide) may also provoke stomatal closure, but typically at pH below 3.5, which occurs only rarely in nature.

The *opening* by *low* SO_2 concentrations is caused by a 'perforation' of the membrane structure of the epidermal cells surrounding the guard cells. The surrounding epidermal cells are affected by sulfur dioxide sooner than the guard cells, because the cuticle inside the leaf is thicker on the latter, so sulfur dioxide attacks the plasmalemma of the surrounding cells sooner. The opening reaction thus works through the passive mechanism.

A *closing* by *higher* sulfur dioxide doses is partly caused by the same passive mechanism, only now, the SO_2 'perforation' simultaneously affects the guard cells. However, the *active* mechanism is also involved, since high sulfur dioxide concentrations only close stomates under *aerobic* conditions, indicating an energy demand. Besides, the phytohormone ABA (abscisic acid), which influences the active stomatal mechanism, is affected by sulfur dioxide. Finally, sulfur dioxide affects photosynthesis, thereby changing the intercellular carbon dioxide concentration, which governs the active mechanism.

Experimental evidence indicates that grasses, which are *resistant* to sulfur dioxide, possess fast-responding stomates, so that closure works as a negative feedback mechanism on further pollutant uptake. The same plants, however, also demonstrated a rapid metabolizing of *sulfite*, a toxic by-product (explained later) of sulfur dioxide. Thus, several mechanisms work in parallel in protecting the resistant grass species and cultivars.

Mechanisms of photosynthesis. To understand the injury to photosynthetic mechanisms, elementary knowledge of the basic processes is needed (Fig. 3.13).

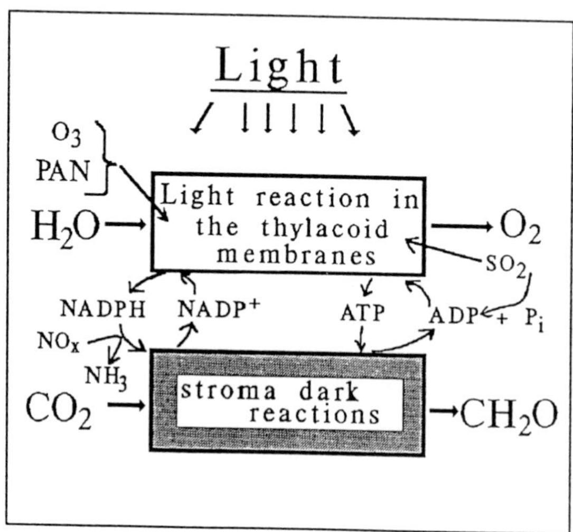

Figure 3.13. Gross chemistry of photosynthesis, turning carbon dioxide and water into sugars and oxygen. NADPH, reduced nicotine-amide-dinucleotide-phosphate; ATP, adenosine-tri-phosphate; CH_2O, sugars; P_i, ortho-phosphate. Possible sites of air pollution are given for SO_2, NO_x and photochemical oxidants.

The light- and dark processes of photosynthesis in higher plants are situated in the *chloroplasts*, which are organelles with a double unit membrane envelope. Inside the envelope, there is a ramified membrane net forming connected sacs called *thylakoids*, the photosynthetic membranes. Chlorophyll and other light-absorbing molecules are embedded in the thylakoid membranes.

When light is absorbed, the energy is translated into an active flow of electrons (e^-) and protons (H^+) across the membrane. A steep proton gradient is built up, with high H^+ concentrations inside the sacs (Fig. 3.14). There is consequently a passive flow of protons out of the sacs through special pores, which are connected with an enzyme (ATPase), which harvests the energy of the H^+ flux in the chemical bonds of the ATP molecule (photophosphorylation). At the same time, the process splits water, supplying 'reducing power' (NADPH + H^+) with an output of oxygen.

Both the energy and the reducing power are needed by the *Calvin cycle* of the dark processes, which is a series of chemical transformations that take place outside the sacs in the so-called *stroma*. The Calvin cycle captures carbon dioxide and converts it to sugars, while ATP and NADPH are turned back into ADP and NADP. Animals and some plant tissues (e.g., roots) which lack photosynthesis, are dependent on this 'primary production' and oxygen for their survival (both for energy and for building blocks in their organisms).

SO_2-injury to photosynthesis. Sulfur dioxide injures photosynthesis in at least two *direct* ways: (1) it affects thylakoid electron transport, and thereby the production of ATP and NADPH, and (2) it competes with ortho-phosphate during photophosphorylation.

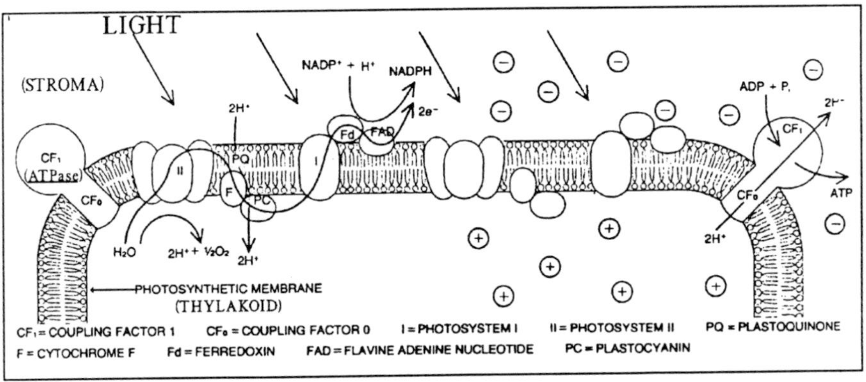

Figure 3.14. Mechanisms of electron transport in thylakoid membranes. The mechanism of photosynthesis harvests light energy in chemical bonds of ATP and reducing equivalents in NADPH (cf. Fig. 3.13). - Source: Miller (1979).

Sulfur dioxide also injures photosynthesis in several *indirect* ways: (1) The sulfite produced by SO_2 breaks bisulfide bonds:

$$SO_3^{2-} + RS\text{-}SR \leftrightarrow RS^- + RS\text{-}SO_3^- ,$$

whereby it changes the structure of proteins and membranes, e.g., the apo-protein of chlorophyll, and the structure (and thus the function) of thylakoid- and plasma membranes. (2) Until it is turned into sulfate (primarily by oxidation in the chloroplasts), sulfite inhibits metabolic processes. Remaining sulfite and its oxidized product are eventually reduced (primarily in the chloroplast) and incorporated in the normal sulfur metabolism of the plant. (3) The acidity produced by sulfur dioxide turns chlorophyll into inactive pheophytin. (4) Sulfur dioxide inhibits superoxide dismutase (SOD). When SOD becomes less efficient in removing superoxide ($\cdot O_2^-$), this very aggressive radical, which is naturally produced during illumination of chloroplasts, rapidly breaks down the light-absorbing pigments: chlorophylls and carotenoids. (5) Finally, the sulfur dioxide-induced closure of stomates inhibits carbon-dioxide uptake and thereby photosynthesis.

Though several SO_2 effects on photosynthesis work on the light processes, sulfur dioxide has also been reported to inhibit important enzyme activities in the Calvin cycle. It mainly affects ribulose-1,5-bis-phosphate carboxylase (the CO_2-assimilating enzyme), phosphoenol pyruvate carboxylase and malate dehydrogenase.

Other invisible SO_2-injuries to vegetation. Sulfur dioxide injures structural proteins, enzymes and membranes other than those involved in photosynthesis, by some of the same mechanisms mentioned above.

In some studies, SO_2 inhibits *phloem loading* (Noyes 1980), affecting the transport of sugars from the leaves to the roots, at lower concentrations than those that inhibit photosynthesis.

On a more subtle level, sulfur dioxide even affects plant hormones (reviewed by Meyer et al., 1987). It may also strike at other stages of the plant's life cycle, for example through effects on *pollen* (reviewed by Wolters and Martens, 1987). Sulfur dioxide and other pollutants also affect microorganisms interacting with plants, as well as *adaptation* and processes of *selection* in all organisms.

Visible SO_2 injuries to vegetation. All the mentioned *invisible* injuries may, in time or with increased concentration or combined with environmental stress, e.g., by concurrent exposure to other gaseous pollutants, develop into *visible* injuries: scorching of leaves, reduction of growth, and changes in root:shoot ratios. The expression of the visible injury depends on the pollutant gas and exposure concentration (Fig. 3.11), species and cultivar, as well as on several environmental factors. Visible symptoms of sulfur dioxide and other pollutants are further described in Section 3.20.2.

In order to protect sensitive plants from direct effects of sulfur dioxide (in the presence of ambient nitrogen dioxide and ozone), the WHO recommends (Anonymous, 1987c) that SO_2 should not exceed 30 $\mu g\ m^{-3}$ as an annual average, nor 100 $\mu g\ m^{-3}$ as a maximum 4-h means. Since sulfur as a nutrient affects the balance of sensitive ecosystems, the given guidelines may not be sufficient to protect them.

Beneficial effects of SO_2 on vegetation. If sulfur dioxide has not been oxidized in the atmosphere to sulphate before reaching the vegetation, most of it will be oxidized when it encounters water on the outside or on the inside of leaves, in the lungs, or in the soil. Higher plants and the algae are capable of using their photosynthetic electron flow to reduce sulfate to sulphydryl groups (-SH) needed for the synthesis of sulfur containing amino acids by a process known as *'assimilatory photosynthetic sulfur reduction'* (Wellburn, 1988). Low concentrations of sulfur dioxide may, therefore, be beneficial to plants growing in sulfur-deficient soil, even when the soil accumulates none of the sulfur.

Meadow grass growing in soil with a sub-optimal sulfur content can experience increased growth and reduced specific transpiration, when exposed to only 50 $\mu g\ m^{-3}$ sulfur dioxide. Meadow grass growing in soil with optimal sulfur content is not affected by this SO_2 concentration.

Sulfur dioxide is reported to significantly improve plant production in the vast central agricultural areas in the U.S.A.. The (over)fertilized European agriculture, however, does not experience a similar advantage.

3.12.2 Human Health

Inhalation experiments with sulfur dioxide have demonstrated a wide range in sensitivity to this gas. *Asthmatic* sufferers tend to be particularly sensitive, but hyper-sensitivity occurs also in a less predictable manner among other individuals (Waller, 1987).

Possibly the most famous health-effects study that has been reported is one that followed *the great London smog* of December 1952, in which 4000 premature deaths were associated with extraordinarily high sulfur-dioxide and smoke concentrations occurring over a period of four days (Fig. 3.15). The incident resulted in the so-called *Clean Air Act* in England in 1957, which together with later legislation has effectively dealt with the problem.

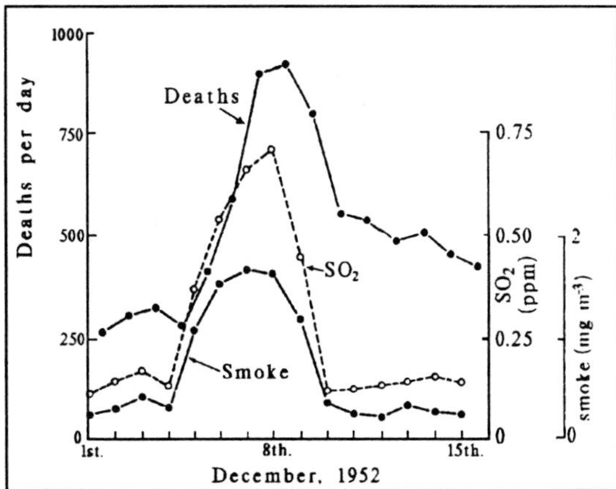

Figure 3.15. Death and pollution levels in the smog of 5-9 December 1952 in London. The graphs show the increase in the number of deaths in this period and the current rise in the amount of SO_2 and smoke in the air. - Source: Mellanby (1980).

Since then, there has been a number of other studies relating exposure to peak concentrations of sulfur dioxide to the incidence of *bronchitis*, but other than these, little has been reported on the adverse health effects caused by this pollutant, especially during the post-coal-smoke era, since the end of the 1960's.

Most studies nowadays concentrate on possible long-term effects of low levels of pollutants. One aspect is, whether people who were exposed to high air-pollutant concentrations during their early childhood carry residual effects into their later years. Studies of cohorts of children born in the 1950's have indicated a small adverse effect on lung function and on the prevalence of respiratory symptoms related to childhood exposure.

The long-term effects of exposure, even to the severe pollution of past decades, seem to be very readily swamped by the effects of *smoking*, if and when that habit is taken up, so most of the investigations really need to be confined to life-long non-smokers, and even then 'passive' exposure to environmental tobacco smoke indoors may prove more important than that due to true urban air pollutants.

WHO guidelines (Anonymous, 1987c) recommend a maximum 1-h value of 350 $\mu g\ m^{-3}$ SO_2 (0.125 ppm), with a 500 $\mu g\ m^{-3}$ SO_2 (0.180 ppm) maximum 10-min value to ensure protection of human health in short-term exposures. In long-term protection the limit is 50 $\mu g\ m^{-3}$ SO_2 (0.018 ppm). These values are relevant when combined with effects of (only) SO_2 and particulate matter (see Section 3.16.2).

3.12.3 Erosion of Buildings and Art Objects

Sulfur dioxide (and acid rain) erode stone and metal materials.

The main mineral constituents of building stones, that are significantly affected by atmospheric pollution, are *calcium carbonate* and *magnesium carbonate*. *Limestone* consists essentially of calcium carbonate with negligible amounts of magnesium carbonate. Magnesian limestones consist of calcium carbonate together with relatively large amounts of magnesium carbonate; they are essentially *dolomite*, which is a double carbonate of calcium and magnesium.

Another class of stone affected by air pollution is *sandstone*. This consists essentially of fragments of quartz bound together, amongst other things, by material which is limestone or dolomitic in character.

Sulfur dioxide causes the most important of all air pollutant effects: wet and dry deposition of sulfur dioxide followed by chemical reactions and dissolution of the products in rain water, and direct dissolution of the stone in acidic rainwater, and transfer of reaction products into the body of the stone.

Several chemical reactions have been proposed to describe the erosion of limestone, although the details of the processes and the circumstances of their occurrence are still poorly understood. The main reactions are:

$$CaCO_3 + SO_2 + O_2 \rightarrow 2\ CaSO_4 + 4\ CO_2 + 2\ H_2O\ ,$$

$$CaCO_3 + SO_2 + O_2 \rightarrow CaSO_4 + CO_2\ ,$$

$$CaCO_3 \cdot MgCO_3 + 2\ SO_2 + O_2 \rightarrow CaSO_4 + MgSO_4 + 2\ CO_2\ .$$

Calcium sulfate is sparingly soluble in water, and on evaporation the dihydrate, *gypsum* ($CaSO_4 \cdot 2\,H_2O$) is formed. The soluble reaction products can undergo cycles of solution and recrystallication within the stone pores, giving rise to effects on the stone long after the initial exposure. Such effects make it difficult to relate currently observed decay phenomena to current levels of pollution.

Ammonia, carbon dioxide and nitrogen dioxide may also play a part in the erosion process. But air pollution is only one of a number of factors which are involved in the erosion of stone, and it has often been blamed for effects that can be traced to other causes. These include stone porosity, meteorology (e.g., wind speed), relative humidity, and level and frequency of precipitation.

Rates of erosion of stone buildings have been measured to range from 0.05-1.2 mm per year, with a typical average of 0.1 mm.

Sulfur dioxide and acids oxidize *metals*. The main effect is caused by gaseous air pollutants rather than by acids. It is a major problem for automobiles, metal constructions in buildings (e.g., bridges), and art.

Erosions reduce the value of both applied materials and of art objects. In Denmark, erosion by air pollution has been estimated to induce damage to buildings and other applied materials amounting to 15 US$ per inhabitant per year, and damage to art objects of an equivalent sum. The damage to art, however, does not immediately translate into necessary expenses and is, therefore, rarely 'appraised', though such art may be difficult or impossible to replace.

3.13 EFFECTS OF OXIDES OF NITROGEN

Atmospheres that are polluted with nitrogen oxides contain both nitric oxide (NO) and nitrogen dioxide (NO_2), together often referred to as NO_x. However, the quantitatively dominant nitrogen oxide in the atmosphere, produced by denitrification processes, is *dinitrogen oxide* (N_2O), which normally occurs at levels around 500 µg m^{-3}. But this gas is inert and insoluble in water, though highly lipid soluble (used in anaesthesia, laughing gas), and is normally not included when the abbreviation NO_x is used to denote air pollution. While dinitrogen oxide does not play a significant role in the context of tropospheric pollution, it contributes to ozone depletion in the stratosphere through photochemical reactions (Section 3.22), and thus with time to global warming (Section 3.21.4).

3.13.1 Vegetation

Recent reviews on the effects of NO and NO_2 on plants were published by Anonymous (1987c), Rajagopal and Saxe (1988), and Wellburn (1988).

Deposition of NO_x onto *plants* is a major component of NO_x dry deposition on all natural surfaces. Like sulfur, nitrogen is a plant nutrient, and the nitrogen oxides that have not been oxidized to nitrate in the atmosphere before reaching the vegetation or the soil, will be oxidized at that point. Higher plants and the algae are capable of incorporating nitrogen oxides taken up by their leaves in the basic N-metabolism. Nitrogen deposition thus plays a major ecological role.

Low concentrations of nitrogen oxides may be beneficial to plants growing in nitrogen-deficient soil, even when the soil accumulates none of the nitrogen. Nitrogen oxides enrich plant production in certain agricultural areas, as mentioned for sulfur dioxide. However, such stimulation will not always be desirable in nature, since susceptibility to insect attack or environmental stress such as frost may be increased at the same time (Anonymous, 1987c).

Nitrogen dioxide is more toxic (or beneficial) to most plants than NO, mostly because it is much more water-soluble, and therefore more easily taken up by and dispersed in the plant. Typically, though, nitrogen dioxide causes less foliar injury than sulfur dioxide, and most of its effects are seen only as 'more-than-additive' effects in combination with sulfur dioxide or other pollutants.

As for other pollutants, the plant response to nitrogen oxides depends on species and cultivar as well as on dosage. From exposure experiments, we know that concentrations lower than 0.1 ppm for several weeks may either stimulate or inhibit growth. Higher doses typically diminish the dry weight as well as other growth parameters. Actual *visible* symptoms of nitrogen oxides at these or higher levels, however, are rare. A particular environment with high NO_x concentrations is greenhouses, with a carbon-dioxide-enriched atmosphere produced by *in situ* hydrocarbon combustion. But even here, several months of 1 ppm NO exposure only caused visible symptoms in one out of several plant species (Rajagopal and Saxe, 1988).

Damaging effects of NO_2+SO_2 in combination at similar level have been established both for short-term and long-term treatments. Injury occurs at concentrations above 0.02-0.07 ppm. Studies so far, however, have been performed only on a few plant species, but there is evidence that environmental conditions can greatly alter the response to NO_2+SO_2. Concentrations that are damaging in winter, for example, may have little effect or may even promote growth in the summer. Recent experiments, in which ozone was added to mixtures of nitrogen dioxide and sulfur dioxide, suggest that the threshold for injury may be as low as 0.015 ppm NO_2 when there are similar amounts of SO_2 (0.015 ppm) and O_3 (0.03 ppm).

Nitrite formed in the plant due to NO_x absorption is toxic, but rapidly removed by *nitrite reductase*. SO_2 and O_3, however, inhibit this enzyme, which is regarded as the main reason for increased harmful effects of NO_2 in conjunction with SO_2 and O_3. Another reason is the formation of *free radicals*. Finally, the reduction of nitrite in the chloroplasts 'steals' reducing power from the normal processes of photosynthesis (Fig. 3.13).

In order to protect sensitive plants from direct effects of nitrogen dioxide (in the presence of ambient SO_2 and O_3, the WHO guidelines recommended that NO_2 should not exceed 30 $\mu g\ m^{-3}$ as a yearly average of 24-h mean values, or 95 $\mu g\ m^{-3}$ as a maximum 4-h means (Anonymous, 1987c). Since nitrogen is a nutrient, any N-deposition will affect ecosystems, changing in particular the more sensitive ones through gradual eutrophication. To avoid this, the total N-deposition should not exceed 3 $g\ m^{-2}$ per year.

3.13.2 Human Health

Morrow (1984) and Anonymous (1987c) recently reviewed over 130 studies of NO_x toxicology.

Acute and subacute toxicity studies with nitrogen dioxide and animals have led to a 1-h exposure LD50 estimate (LD50: lethal dose for 50% of tested individuals) for humans of 174 ppm NO_2. Other studies indicate that intermittent nitrogen dioxide exposures with short-term peak levels may be more toxic than continuous NO_2 exposures. Bronchitis and pneumonia contribute to subacute mortality. Many subacute effects tend to be persistent, and some are progressive. Acute NO_x effects seem to include lipid peroxidation and antioxidants in the role(s) of protectants. Studies with acute levels, however, are of limited relevance to ambient air quality.

Chronic exposures of mice, rats, guinea pigs, and dogs to nitrogen dioxide at urban levels (mostly below 1 ppm NO_2 have been carried out for from one week to several years. These studies show evidence of multiple diseases of the lungs and spleen. From animal experiments it has been estimated that humans exposed to 0.1 ppm NO_2 form 3.6 mg (carcinogenic) nitrite each day, which enters the blood, is oxidized to nitrate and subsequently excreted in the urine. There is evidence that NO could be more toxic than NO_2. Though nitrogen oxides have not been found to induce cancer, there is evidence that they facilitate metastases (the spreading of tumors).

Studies on effects of chronic exposures of humans to ambient levels of nitrogen dioxide give conflicting results. Children suffer the most, but most reports consider the small reductions in pulmonary performance to be of little medical significance. There are several reports, however, of respiratory disorders in children exposed to domestic NO_x sources: gas cookers and -heaters and tobacco-smoking parents. Little is known of nitrogen dioxide interaction with human lung tissue *in vivo*, but lipid peroxidation is a popular theory.

Effects of nitrogen dioxide in interaction with other oxidants have recently attracted increasing interest. Effects of nitrogen oxides on humans are discussed further in Section 3.19.

WHO guidelines (Anonymous, 1987c) recommend NO_2 levels of 400 $\mu g\ m^{-3}$ (0.21 ppm) and 150 $\mu g\ m^{-3}$ (0.08 ppm) as 1-h and 24-h maximum mean values in the protection of human health.

3.13.3 Erosion of Materials

The erosion of stone and metal materials by HNO_3 and other products of NO_x is analogous to that described for sulfur dioxide and its reaction products (Section 3.12.3).

3.14 EFFECTS OF OZONE AND OTHER PHOTOOXIDANTS

Photochemical oxidants in the troposphere are secondary air pollutants formed under the influence of sunlight by complex photochemical reactions in air which contains nitrogen oxides and reactive hydrocarbons as precursors (Section 3.21.5). Some ozone, however, may originate as influx from the stratosphere.

3.14.1 Deterioration of Materials

Ozone is a reactive gas with respect to *organic molecules* (Wellburn 1988), rather than to stone and metals. We shall examine its effect on materials, be they part of plants, animals or useful materials, before considering consequences for living organisms.

Any double bond in hydrocarbons is likely to be highly sensitive to chain-breaking and cross-linking reactions initiated by ozone. This produces *peroxyl radicals* by peroxydation and secondary *ozonides*, which can be photochemically excited to produce more free radicals in the same way that the photochemical smog chain reactions are propagated in the atmosphere. The only difference is that they occur on the surface of materials that are being attacked, causing loss of tensile strength of and damage to the saturated components. Natural polymers like rubber, cotton, cellulose or leather, as well as paints, elastomers (mainly used in tyre manufacture), plastics, nylon and fabric dyes, are all degraded.

The global economic costs of annual damage to materials due to ozone, and of efforts to protect against it, are huge and constitute over 30% of that caused by all forms of atmospheric pollution to non-living (organic and inorganic) materials.

Most materials in biological tissues are in close proximity to water. This changes quite considerably the characteristics of ozone attack upon unsaturated carbon compounds. Instead of free radicals, hydrated forms of ozone may form hydrogen peroxide and aldehydes, by a process called *ozonolysis*. This process does not evolve free radicals, except for ozone reactions in alkaline solutions or with hydrogen peroxide, which may form hydroxyl radicals:

$$O_3 + H_2O \rightarrow 2\ OH\cdot + O_2\ ,$$

$$O_3 + H_2O_2 \rightarrow HO_2\cdot + OH\cdot + O_2\ .$$

However, hydrogen peroxide is very quickly removed by *catalase* within living biological systems:

$$2\ H_2O_2 \rightarrow 2\ H_2O + O_2\ .$$

Peroxyacyl nitrates or PANs are capable of oxidizing similar compounds to those sensitive to ozone, but little research has been carried out to follow this damage.

3.14.2 Vegetation

Visible injury. Photochemical oxidants, especially ozone, visibly damage the leaves and needles of sensitive plants. For reviews, see Guderian (1985), Prinz (1988), Wellburn (1988).

The biological activity of photochemical oxidants was clearly manifested for the first time during the early 1940's, when vegetation injury was observed in the Los Angeles Basin in the United States. Since that time, as a consequence of the increasing emissions of photochemical oxidant precursors, the photochemical oxidants have become the most important air pollutants in North America, accounting for over 90% of the damage to agricultural vegetation (Adams et al. 1986), affecting natural vegetation (Duchelle et al., 1983), and defined by some schools of thought as the *major factor* in the 'European type' of *novel* forest decline (Prinz et al., 1987). The first observations of ozone and PAN (peroxyacetyl nitrate) injury to vegetation in Europe were made in 1963 in West Germany. In other parts of the world also, for example South and Central America, Asia and Australia, photochemical oxidants threaten vegetation, including both the economic and the ecological performance of plant life.

Visible expressions, such as leaf-yellowing, necrosis, defoliation and premature senescence (old age), may become apparent. Characteristic ozone symptoms, such as *chlorotic* and *necrotic flecking*, have been observed in Europe in vines, potatoes, peas, beans and spinach.

Clover species are among the most sensitive native plants in relation to ozone. With Bel W_3 tobacco being used as a biological indicator plant, ozone effects have been observed in many countries of the European region, as far north as Sweden. A further description of visible symptoms of ozone is given in Section 3.20.2. Band-forming necrosis on the abaxial leaf surface of the small stinging nettle is used as a biological indicator for PAN.

Invisible injury. In addition to the visible, morphological effects, chronic and subtle effects on physiological processes, such as photosynthesis, transpiration and translocation of photosynthates, may inhibit the production and distribution of carbohydrates in plants, decreasing the vitality of both leaves and roots and reducing growth and crop production. *Gaseous* ozone works largely by disrupting membrane integrity (unsaturated regions of fatty acids), while ozone in aqueous solution works on both membranes and enzymes, which in turn affects metabolic processes. *Plasmalemma*, the cell membrane, becomes leaky to certain important cations, like potassium, and is more damaged than other membranes, such as the envelopes of mitochondria or chloroplasts. The *sulphydryl groups* of the S-containing amino acids cysteine and methionine are oxidized to disulfide bridges or to sulfonate residues, whilst the pyrrol ring of tryptophane is opened up to form N-formylkynurenine. These reactions alter the activity of most enzymes.

The free radicals (the hydroxyl radical, monatomic oxygen, hydrogen peroxide and the superoxide radical), produced when ozone meets the aqueous phase in plants, are mainly responsible for the cellular effects of ozone (Thompson et al., 1987).

Ozone destroys NADH and NADPH, while PAN only oxidizes these compounds to their natural counterparts, NAD^+ and $NadP^+$ (Fig. 3.13, Section 3.12.1).

As for other air pollutants, plants affected by photooxidants have reduced resistance to fungi, bacteria, viruses and insects, and also to climatic stresses (frost or drought). Oxidants may also affect the quality of plant material used as food or fodder.

Photooxidants are among the most toxic air pollutants of plants. In order to protect sensitive plants from direct effects of photochemical oxidants, the WHO guidelines (Anonymous, 1987c) recommend that PAN should never exceed 300 $\mu g\ m^{-3}$ (0.070 ppm) as 1 hour means, and 80 $\mu g\ m^{-3}$ (0.018 ppm) for 8 hours. Ozone should never exceed 200 $\mu g\ m^{-3}$ (0.1 ppm) for 1 hour, 65 $\mu g\ m^{-3}$ (0.033 ppm) for 24 hours and 60 $\mu g\ m^{-3}$ (0.030 ppm) for the growing season (100 days).

3.14.3 Human Health

There is no doubt that in some cities around the world, and notably in Los Angeles ('Smog City'), traffic pollutants have for many years provided the main contribution to air pollution, and possible risks to human health have principally been associated with the photochemical complex formed when volatile hydrocarbons interact with oxides of nitrogen (Waller, 1987). While the more obvious eye-irritant effects are linked with trace constituents such as PAN, there could be respiratory effects from the ozone present in the mixture.

This is something one did not expect to find in European cities (at least in the North), because of the lower sunlight intensity and higher levels of smoke (which rapidly breaks down ozone). However, with the latter removed by improved legislation, and with increased traffic, photochemical pollution did begin to show up in cities like London during the 1970's.

The most notable episodes in several European cities occurred during the unusually warm and sunny summer of 1976, when the ozone concentration was about 0.2 ppm for several hours and on many days in succession. Though these ozone levels were of similar magnitude to those in Los Angeles, other attributes of the mixture were missing, in particular the eye-irritant effects. There was at the time, however, a sharp increase in deaths in cities like London, but this was linked with high temperatures rather than with pollution. In contrast to the experience of the cold, dark impenetrable gloom of the old London fogs, the population at large generally enjoyed the exceptional spell of warm, sunny weather.

In Menzel's (1984) review of the toxicity of ozone in man and animals, a wide variety of biochemical and physiological changes were noted. There is considerable evidence for a free-radical-mediated or lipid-peroxide-mediated toxicity in lung tissue. Ciliated cells of the upper airways are mainly affected, as is also the case with medium levels of nitrogen oxides found in indoor pollution (Section 3.19). Epidemiological studies, however, fail to detect increased respiratory infections in humans due to ozone. It is an interesting observation, though, that biochemical changes in the blood of Californian residents compared to those of Canadians exposed to similar test exposures of ozone showed a difference, indicating that the Californians had acquired some tolerance to ozone.

Ozone appears to be a weak *mutagen* and to produce chromosomal abnormalities, and it often strikes in combination with other pollutants with a similar effect.

Photooxidants are ubiquitous air pollutants, and are concluded to be among the most toxic to man, with a special problem in the indoor environment (Section 3.19.3).

The WHO recommends 150-200 μg m^{-3} (0.75-0.1 ppm) as a 1-h mean value of ozone never to be exceeded, with an 8-h guideline of 100-120 μg m^{-3} (0.05-0.06 ppm) ozone for an ideal margin of protection (Anonymous, 1987c).

3.14.4 Reduction in Visibility

Reduction in summertime visibility can be caused by the atmospheric *aerosols* formed by photochemical activity. Measurements of the optical scattering coefficient over central London during June-August have related this to the occurrence of photochemical processes. Ozone concentrations reached record levels for a UK city on 27 June 1976 (max. 1-h mean 212 ppb), following the usual diurnal pattern with aerosol formation and growth, as measured by the scattering, lagging some hours behind the peak ozone concentration.

The summertime visibility data for Heathrow in England underwent steady deterioration over the period 1962-73. After 1973, a sharp improvement was evident; this may, however, have been due to a decrease in aerosol sulfate formation as a consequence of a decrease in oil consumption immediately after the 1973 oil crisis, and a decrease in the sulfur content of the oil. A decrease in volatile hydrocarbons may likewise play a role.

3.15 EFFECTS OF ACIDIFICATION

Acid precipitation (rain, snow, clouds/fog) causes acidification of terrestrial and aquatic (mostly freshwater) ecosystems and corrodes building materials (Section 3.12.3). These injuries are caused by the oxidation products of NO_x and SO_2, respectively aqueous HNO_3 and aqueous H_2SO_4, though over half of the acid deposition (as previously mentioned) arrives as - *dry* deposition (SO_2, NO_x, gaseous HNO_3) to be oxidized *in situ*. Hauhs & Wright (1988) reviewed the effects of acid deposition on soil and water acidification, and its reversibility. Direct and indirect effects of acidic deposition were reviewed by Linthurst (1984). The critical loads for sulfur and nitrogen for terrestrial and aquatic systems was reviewed by Nilsson and Grennfelt (1988). Recent bibliographies on acid rain and the environment were given by Farmer (1984) and Grayson (1988).

3.15.1 Terrestrial Ecosystems

Regions with acidified surface waters, such as southernmost Norway and the Adirondack Mountains of New York, are characterized by acid soils and bedrock and soils highly resistant to chemical weathering. Acid deposition has caused major changes in these ecosystems.

The acid-base status of soils is controlled by a number of key factors such as base saturation, weathering of silicate minerals, aluminum mobilization, CO_2 dissolution and S- and N-dynamics, as well as atmospheric deposition.

Fig. 3.16 gives a schematic view of key processes governing acidification of soil and water.

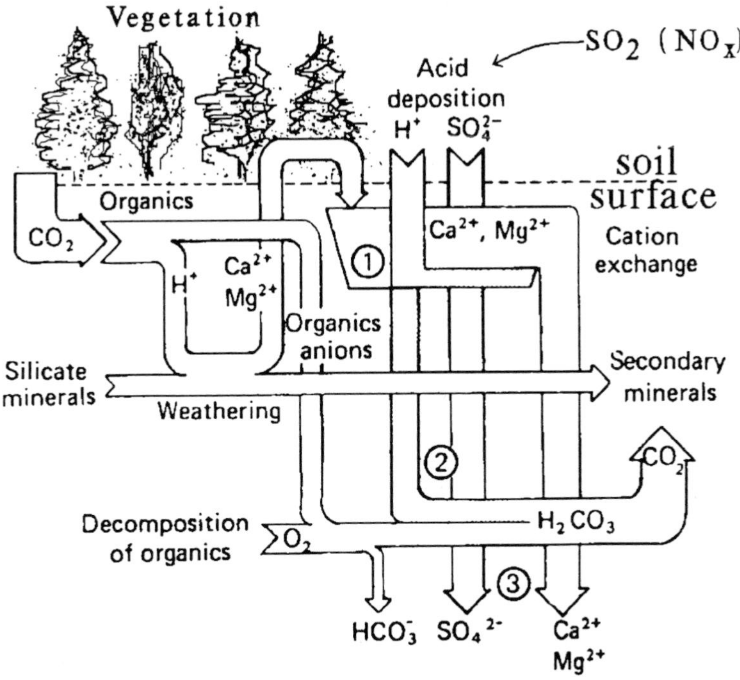

Figure 3.16. Schematic view of key processes governing acidification of soil and water. - Source (modified): Hauhs and Wright (1988).

Weathering of silicate minerals into secondary minerals is a natural process, providing the ultimate source of basic cations (Mg^{2+}, Ca^{2+}) which serve as nutrients for the plants. The weathering rate sets the upper limit for the long-term net proton supply that can be neutralized. Soils with low rates of silicate weathering rates are widespread on the granitic bedrock of Scandinavia. These soils are acid and have low base saturation. Cations not taken up by plants, temporarily bind to (negatively charged) clay minerals.

Decaying flora and fauna release protons (H^+) and basic inorganic cations, while the organic anions, not being able to bind to the clay minerals, are washed deeper into the soil and decomposed by aerobic microorganisms into HCO_3^- H_2CO_3 and CO_2.

Acid deposition, mainly from industrial pollution, brings H^+, SO_4^{2-} and NO_3^- to the soil. Because the protons are smaller cations than the nutrient cations, they are more forcefully attracted to the negatively charged clay minerals, where they displace the Ca^{2+} and Mg^{2+} cations. If these cations and the deposited NO_3^- are not immediately taken up by plant roots, they are washed deeper into the soil together with the deposited SO_4^{2-}, and are eventually lost for future plant growth. The acidification of the top soil increases the solubility and mobility of aluminum, manganese and iron, raising their level of availability to toxic concentrations. This may harm mycorrhiza (symbiotic soil fungi) and fine roots of all plants. All the processes caused by acid deposition effects on the soil-ecosystem diminish plant uptake of water and of nutrient cations and anions. This constituted an early hypothesis for novel forest decline which is treated in detail in Section 3.20.4.

The visible symptoms in plants, caused indirectly by the effects of acid rain on the soil, are partly symptoms of specific mineral deficiencies, e.g., of Mg^{2+} or Ca^{2+}, and partly symptoms of specific mineral poisoning, e.g., by aluminum or manganese.

There are few direct effects of acid rain on vegetation (Evans, 1984a,b; Herrick, 1986). Some sensitive cultivars of soybeans in simulated treatments and scorching of apple leaves after repeated evaporation and sublimation of acid rain are among the rare examples.

3.15.2 Aquatic Ecosystems

Acidification of surface waters and loss of fish populations have occurred in a number of regions in Europe and North America. The regional distribution of acid surface waters provides strong empirical evidence for a causal link to acid deposition. Laboratory and field experiments and simple soil-chemistry models demonstrate that the input of mobile, strong-acid anions to sensitive, naturally acid soils is sufficient to initiate the transfer of acidity from the soil to surface waters. Thus the link between acid deposition on catchment soils and water acidification has been established both at the empirical and the process-oriented level.

With the combined dry and wet deposition during winter being collected in snow and ice, the sudden melting during the first days of spring causes an *'acid push'*, when acid water collects into rivers and lakes. Because this acutely acidic, aluminum-rich water typically eliminates fish populations in lakes (e.g., brown trout and perch) by recruitment failure, elimination of a population may lag many years after a chronic acidification has been observed. It may take as much as a 60% decrease in acid deposition to reverse lake acidification (Hauhs and Wright, 1988). A thorough description of the effects of the acidification of aquatic ecosystems (including plants, fish, insects and microorganisms) does not, however, belong in this chapter.

3.15.3 Human Health

There are no direct effects of acid precipitation on human health. Indirect effects of acid rain, however, could be harmful to the population over a longer time period through changes in water quality. Since a linkage between high-nitrate water supplies and the occurrence of stomach cancer is suggested, the European Community has taken the precaution of legislating for a maximum nitrate level in public water supplies of 50 mg l^{-1}. Levels in drinking water in the Netherlands, Denmark and the UK are already approaching, or in certain places exceeding, that value, and methods are being evaluated to treat and remove nitrate from such supplies efficiently. The most favoured remedy involves a combination of ion exchange to replace nitrate with bicarbonate and using microbial denitrification to reduce the exchanged nitrate to nitrogen. However, by far the largest contamination of natural waters by nitrate arises from excess run-off from fields which have been treated with artificial fertilizers.

The most likely hazard from alterations to public water supplies by acidic precipitation, however, may be a general increase in the level of *aluminum* leached from soils in certain water-catchment areas. Regions on calciferous bedrock (e.g., Denmark and the Northwestern Germany) suffer only minor changes. There has been an increase in the number of cases of a rare bone-wasting disease (osteomalacia) in areas where aluminum levels in water supplies are 1000-2000 ppm. Another disease attributed to the availability of aluminum in natural waters is Alzheimer's disease, a senile dementia that occurs much earlier in life than is normally the case, and the sufferers die about 10 years after the onset of the condition. In parts of Scandinavia it is now standard practice to remove aluminum from water used for kidney dialysis treatment and for making up baby food. In some cases, treatment of entire drinking-water supplies is now being introduced.

Even *food quality* may deteriorate due to acidified soils and waters, since the living organisms that we harvest from these systems accumulate increased amounts of aluminum and heavy metals with reduced rates of important nutrients. Most agricultural products, however, are not affected, since the farmer controls the soil pH in his fields.

3.15.4 Erosion of Materials

Acid rain erodes stone and metal materials because of its acidity. The predominant mechanisms have already been described in Section 3.12.3.

3.16 EFFECTS OF PARTICULATES

Particulates have existed in the Earth's atmosphere as long as the Earth itself. Volcanic activity, earthquakes, dust storms and fires have intermittently propelled smoke and dust into the atmosphere. In the past centuries, man has added significantly to the natural load of particulates in the atmosphere (Sections 3.3.1 and 3.5.1). However, particulates are relatively heavy air pollutants and remain suspended in the air for only a short time.

3.16.1 Vegetation

The main direct effect of particulates on plants is a repression of physiological activities: *gas exchange* is obstructed when particulates (with rain becoming 'mud') block stomata, and - *photosynthesis* is reduced when dust and smoke deposited on leaves diminish the light reaching the chloroplasts. With photosynthesis, respiration and transpiration impaired, the plants become weakened and may die. Other balances, such as insect or fungal relationships, may also be upset.

Chemical leaching from the dust can dissolve the cuticle of the leaf, causing desiccation. If the dust contains heavy metals, such as nickel, manganese, boron, zinc, and copper, accumulation of these toxic compounds in the soil and subsequent uptake by vegetation cause injury. Particulates deposited from the atmosphere, however, also bring a number of trace elements to the plants and soil that are beneficial to the ecosystems as a whole.

3.16.2 Human health

The relation between 'smoke' (and sulfur dioxide) and bronchitis was mentioned in Section 3.12.2. But there are other effects of some specific types of smoke and dust.

Diesel exhaust and PAHs. Rural/urban differences in lung cancer rates show for some diseases a higher mortality rate for people living in and immediately around large cities. One possible factor under intensive study is the PAHs (polyaromatic hydrocarbons) associated with diesel smoke. Over 500 types of PAHs have been identified in the atmosphere, of which benz-pyrene (BaP) is the best known. Very high PAH concentrations can occur in work places, typically from 1 to 5 ng m^{-3} BaP, but concentrations above 10 µg m^{-3} BaP have been found in some aluminum-smelting industries. In the developing countries, the BaP exposure averages about 4 µg m^{-3} during cooking with biomass fuels.

A major complication when investigating traffic pollutants is that they are emitted within the breathing zone, so that a distance of a few meters is liable to make a substantial difference in exposure. The exact exposure of individuals to traffic pollution is thus much more difficult to assess than that to pollutants transported over longer distances.

Cernansky (1983) has reviewed the effects on humans of diesel exhaust. The quoted effects include nausea, headache, coughing and irritation of eyes, nose and throat. Gasoline engines produce less odors and irritants than diesel engines, and this will be even more pronounced when catalytic converters reduce unburned hydrocarbons from the gasoline engines in Europe, as has been the case in the U.S. for a decade. Converters for diesel engines have not yet been devised. Diesel exhaust is believed to be the most important air pollutant in causing human cancer.

Owing to its carcinogenicity, no safe level of PAHs can be recommended. The United States Environmental Protection Agency (EPA) has estimated a lifetime cancer risk of 9 per 100,000 exposed people per ng m^{-3} PAH over a lifetime.

Lead and other 'heavy metals'. An estimated 80%-90% of the lead in ambient air is derived from the combustion of leaded petrol (alkyl-lead additives). Lead affects *haem biosynthesis, the nervous system and blood pressure*. There have been several investigations into the effects of environmental exposure to lead on blood-lead levels, with the objective of checking the effectiveness of current pollution-control measures. Preliminary results indicate a decrease in human blood-lead levels with time, although it is too early to see the full significance of reducing the lead content of petrol.

The WHO recommends a guideline of 0.5-1.0 μg m^{-3} lead, which means that 98% of the general population will be maintained below a blood lead level of 0.2 μg m^{-3} (Anonymous, 1987c). Since this guideline is not sufficient to protect *children*, other initiatives are necessary.

Effects of other heavy metals (e.g., cadmium, chromium, mercury, nickel and vanadium) contained in particulates and inhaled by man and animals are also of consequence to our health. For a further description, the reader is referred to Anonymous (1987c).

Arsenic. Arsenic in the air is present mainly in particulate form as inorganic arsenic. It is released to the atmosphere from both natural and anthropogenic sources. The principal natural source is volcanic activity. Man-made emissions arise from the smelting of metals, the combustion of fuels, especially of low-grade brown coal, and the use of pesticides (Anonymous, 1987c). Global natural emissions have been estimated to be 7,900 tons per year, whereas anthropogenic emissions are about three times higher. Rural air contains 1-10 ng m^{-3} and urban air up to 1 μg m^{-3} arsenic.

Because arsenic is *carcinogenic* and there is no known safe threshold, no safe level for it can be recommended. At an air concentration of 1 μg m^{-3} arsenic, a conservative estimate of the lifetime risk is as high as 3 deaths in a thousand.

Asbestos. Another factor that may cause lung disease is asbestos (Anonymous, 1987c). Asbestos is used everywhere: filters, fire protection, building materials, brake linings, etc. An English study clearly illustrates that mortality from pleural mesothelioma was high in areas of known extensive usage of asbestos in the relevant past. When the microscopic, needle shaped fibers of asbestos are inhaled, they fasten deep in the lung alveoli. Twenty to fifty percent of townspeople bear benign tumours induced by such asbestos fibers. Since asbestos does not break down or move away, the benign tumours may in time develop into a sweeping epidemic of malicious lung cancer. The period of incubation is thought to be 20-30 years, or approximately the time that asbestos has been used on a large scale.

Though exposure to airborne asbestos concentrations is more of a problem in indoor situations than in the general environment, appreciation of the dangers that can arise from the handling of asbestos based building materials has led to more stringent controls with respect to building construction and demolition. Where once construction and demolition would take place without much concern over airborne asbestos fibre concentrations, today special measures are required to be taken to contain the asbestos, and monitoring is carried out as a further check to see that the controls are being implemented effectively.

Asbestos is a proven human carcinogen for which no safe level can be proposed. No threshold is known to exist. Exposure should therefore be kept as low as possible.

3.16.3 Soiling of Surfaces

Possibly the most widespread source of surface soiling nowadays arises from emissions from diesel vehicles. Also associated with vehicles is the soiling nuisance associated with the fall-out of resuspended road dust. Dust nuisance can also arise from improperly controlled activities such as demolition, road works, land filling, handling and processing of dusty products (e.g., cement, road stone coating and flour milling).

The high optical absorbance and fineness of diesel smoke particles (90% below 1 μg m^{-3} a median diameter of 0.1-0.2 μg m^{-3}) together with their oily nature, all point to a greater soiling potential on a unit mass basis for diesel smoke than for other common airborne particulates. The blackness of diesel particles is three times that of smoke from coal combustion. The small size of the diesel particles means impacts over long distances.

Road dust and dust from sources such as cement works is very coarse and impacts over much smaller distances than diesel exhaust particles. Measurements of the size distribution of dust deposited on to a horizontal glossy surface in central London was found to be typically in the range of 20-100 μg m^{-3} diameter.

The coarse types of dust are thus of major importance in soiling horizontal glossy surfaces. Considerable costs are paid every year for polishing the enormous window surfaces of modern cities.

3.17 EFFECTS OF RADIATION

Radioactive isotopes, which occur as gases and particulates, are the most recent components of anthropogenic air pollution. Though natural (background) radiation and radiation related with accidents are hazards, the real hazard to life on Earth would be the excessive radiation which would result from even a 'limited' nuclear war.

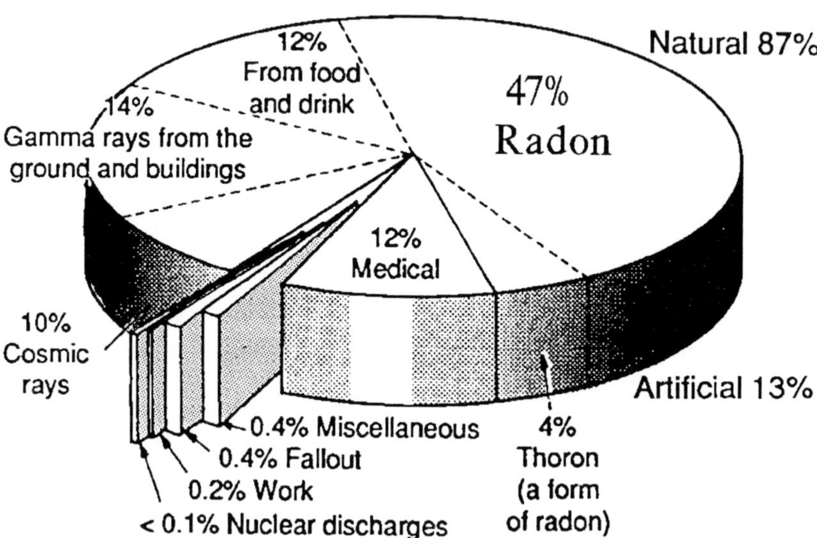

Figure 3.17. Sources of radiation in the environment. - Source: Anonymous (1989).

When nuclear power plants function as they are meant to do, they improve emissions with respect to CO_2, SO_2, NO_x, particulates, and even radiation, as compared with coal-fired power plants. The real risks with nuclear power plants are therefore related to accidents, attacks by terrorist groups (stealing material for producing nuclear weapons), and war-time use of nuclear weapons. Radioactive fallout from a war-time nuclear attack increases by 10-100 times when 'successfully' targeted on a nuclear power plant. If a nuclear war does not wipe out civilization by radiation, its climatic effects will ('Nuclear winter', Turco et al., 1984).

Following the *Chernobyl nuclear accident* in the USSR in April 1986, there has been a continuing interest in information on radiation levels to which the general public is being exposed. Poor communication between nations, and between Government departments responsible for monitoring radioactivity and local authorities, has led to suspicion and fears in some quarters that important information is being withheld. On the positive side, the Chernobyl accident has incited the launch of several new monitoring programmes and has led to new political agreements between nations regarding cooperation and exchange of information in case of future nuclear accidents.

Since natural rock contains and emits traces of radioactive isotopes far exceeding the trace amounts released by peace-time nuclear activities (Fig. 3.17), it is frequently argued that the latter are of no consequence to human health. But since radiation causes cancer, with no guideline for a safe threshold exposure, any increase in radioactivity is unsatisfactory, especially with long-life isotopes.

Exposure to natural isotopes seeping from hard rock into houses (mostly the radioactive noble gases *radon-222* and *radon-220*, members of the uranium-238 and thorium-232 decay chains) should be kept at a minimum. About half the radiation received today by man comes from radon seeping into our houses. The increased insulation of houses (lowered air-change) has accentuated this problem. It is estimated that 2,500 people die each year from lung cancer caused by radon (Anonymous, 1989). Preliminary tests in the U.S.A. have shown dangerous levels of the invisible, odorless gas in 54% of 130 schools checked by the EPA. Worst area in the tests: Nashville, where the risk in some schools equals that of smoking more than four packs of cigarettes a day!

The WHO recommends that simple remedial measures should be considered for buildings with radon-daughter concentrations of more than 100 Bq m^{-3} EER (equilibrium equivalent radon) as an annual average. Remedial action in buildings with radon-daughter concentrations higher than 400 Bq m^{-3} EER as an annual average should be considered without delay (Anonymous, 1987c).

3.18 EFFECTS OF COMBINED POLLUTANTS

In the sections on effects of single gases there was frequently mention of the effects of *combinations* of pollutants. Typically, air pollutants cause more severe effects when found together. In nature air pollutants always work in concert, also with some other stress factors, e.g., drought, frost, storm and insect or pathogen attacks. Wellburn (1988) recently reviewed 'interactions': synergistic and more-than-additive effects, contribution of stress, mechanisms of pollutant interactions, and effects of pollutant 'cocktails' on plants and humans.

Table 3.6. Ratio between indoor and outdoor concentrations of pollutants originating from outdoors. - Source: Fenger (1985).

pollutant	concentration ratio
CO	0.2
NO_x	0.2
O_3	0.7
SO_2	0.3
fine dust	0.3
lead	0.8

It is impossible to list all the effects of all possible combinations of all pollutants and environmental stress factors, and it is likewise unthinkable to establish truly reliable guidelines for complete protection of life on Earth. Legislators, therefore, have to be very scrupulous when recommending guidelines for individual pollutants and, whenever 'priorities force them', to introduce a new factor (like an increased load of oxidant, a new pesticide, or a new gene engineered organism) into our complex scene of 'modern life'. Most of these new factors were not even given a thought until they revealed themselves by surprising effects, e.g., the unpredicted decay of stratospheric ozone over Antarctica (Section 3.22.3).

3.19 INDOOR AIR POLLUTION

A major purpose of air-pollution abatement is to protect human health. Like this chapter, most air-quality studies deal with outdoor air pollution, though modern man spends most of his time indoors, especially in the cities and during the winter. Some special aspects of indoor air pollution other than radiation will therefore be briefly touched upon in the present section. Broader reviews were given by Spengler and Sexton (1983) and Nero (1988).

Our efforts to conserve energy have decreased the exchange between indoor and outdoor air. Air pollution originating from outside sources is reduced inside our houses in both peak values and mean concentrations. This is due to the duration of the air-change and absorption in building materials, furniture, carpets, pot plants and others. Table 3.6 shows ratios between outdoor air pollutants measured outdoors and indoors.

The low air change, however, also means that pollution sources inside the houses are of increased importance. Fungi, bacteria, household dust and mites may be a special problem in houses with wall-to-wall carpets with respect to *allergies* and other illnesses.

3.19.1 Open Fires

A more general problem arises from gas kitchens, gas-heating systems and open fires which give off high levels of nitrogen oxides, primarily NO which gradually turns into NO_2. NO is produced from the natural content in the air of O_2 and N_2 which combine at temperatures above a few hundred °C. The NO_x concentration in a kitchen with a gas cooker has been found to reach 0.12 ppm in the summer and 0.20 ppm in the winter, when windows are rarely opened. For comparison, the NO_x concentration in a busy street during the rush-hour is about 0.10-0.20 ppm, mostly as nitrogen dioxide.

A 'cosy' open fire gives off complex pollutants, such as *dioxines* and heavy metals, when plastics, painted or impregnated wood, or coloured magazines and pamphlets are burned in order to save oil, coal or natural gas. Most people associate prestige with large fireplaces, which, when open, use up too much wood too quickly. If closed, they give prolonged incineration and pollute the room less, but are no longer so cosy. With a low oxygen supply they burn incompletely, with maximum pollution being emitted to the outdoor environment.

Even a *candle* produces nitrogen oxides, soot particles and hydrocarbons. The NO_x concentration in our drawing-rooms when the candles on a Christmas tree are lighted reaches 1.2 ppm. When the goose or the steak is ready in the gas oven, and all of the family have danced around the Christmas tree singing carols, the cilia in their respiratory systems, which normally take care of removing dust and bacteria, are paralyzed (even at 0.7-1.0 ppm). And the more we dance and sing, the more we breathe, and the worse the effect becomes. Children and asthmatics suffer the most. Fortunately, Christmas Eve offers other facets of real quality and joy that keep our minds off the itching eyes or an annoying cough.

3.19.2 Tobacco-smoking

The smoking of tobacco is practiced worldwide by hundred of millions of people (Anonymous, 1987c). In 1982, 6.2 million tons of tobacco were produced; annual per capita consumption in the U.S.A. was more than 3,500 cigarettes. While smoking in the industrialized countries is on its way down, cigarette smoking in the developing countries is increasing, and many cigarettes and other products, e.g., 'bidis', have very high tar and nicotine contents.

Tobacco-smoking has proved to be a truly devastating habit as regards the health of both active and 'passive' smokers (Crawford, 1988), interacting with other trends of modern civilization, such as 'stress', unbalanced food habits (too much sugar, fat and alcohol), urban air pollution and too little sleep. The most toxic component in tobacco smoke is the PAHs (polyaromatic hydrocarbons), e.g., benzpyrenes (Section 3.16.2), in tobacco tar which are extremely carcinogenic. The content of benzpyrenes in the tar depends partially on the variety and growth conditions of the tobacco, and the uptake thereof on how it is smoked (inhalation, filters, etc.). Smokers are also exposed to extreme concentrations of toxic gases, e.g., CO (Section 3.10) and NO_x (Section 3.13.2). It is uncertain whether the *nicotine*, which is the stimulating and habit-forming component in tobacco smoking, is harmful in the concentrations at which it is taken up.

Of the various forms of the disease, *lung cancer* is the most important cause of death in the world, with an estimated total of deaths in excess of one million annually. Tobacco-smoking, primarily cigarettes, causes 90% of all lung cancers; risk of this disease is proportional to the number of cigarettes smoked. When smokers stop smoking, their risk of cancer stops increasing, but it does not decrease. Therefore, the earlier the age at initiation of smoking, the greater the individual risk on a life-time basis.

Tobacco-smoking also causes bladder cancer, cancer of the renal pelvis, oral and pharyngeal types of cancer, cancer of the pancreas and other types. Tobacco-smoking is therefore the most dangerous of all 'air pollutants' to man.

3.19.3 Indoor Ozone

Problems due to ozone pollution indoors are not appreciated by most people, and the situation could get worse. In the past there was some appreciation by those working with specialized equipment, such as X-ray machines, ultraviolet lamps, xenon-arc lighting and other high-voltage generating equipment that one of the many associated hazards was the release of *ozone* due to the ionizing influence of the electrical discharges involved. Perhaps the most hazardous task involving exposure to ozone over long periods has been *electric and torch welding*, which is often carried out in restricted spaces.

However, the advent of *photocopiers*, as well as *laser printers* for our personal computers, with their huge popularity and their installation throughout many places of work not originally designed for such equipment, has brought about more instances of unacceptable ozone levels indoors. Such machines are usually placed in semi-isolated or poorly ventilated corners or in small side-rooms, accentuating the problem.

The recommended working level for ozone indoors during a 40-h working week of below 0.1 ppm ozone is probably too high. Indoor levels below 0.05 ppm would be more desirable, though outdoor levels frequently exceed this concentration.

High-risk groups include children, the aged, individuals with pre-existing respiratory or immune-system diseases, people with coronary heart disease and those with the glucose-6-p-hosphate dehydrogenase deficiency syndrome. Short exposures to high or intermittent ozone levels cause proportionally more harm than long exposures to low levels. Ozone may also work *synergistically* when other pollutants are present.

3.20 FOREST DECLINE

European forests are ecosystems planned and planted by man and are usually *monocultures*, i.e., much less complex than natural ecosystems. Forests in other parts of the world, e.g., the U.S.A., are often self-propagated and more like natural ecosystems.

We must distinguish between three categories of forest decline: natural forest decline, smoke-induced forest decline and novel forest decline.

3.20.1 Natural Forest Decline

Stand-level dieback in forests is by no means a new phenomenon (Mueller-Dombois, 1987), even for dieback not caused by fire or flooding. The traditional explanation for this natural decline of trees and stands has been a *biotic* agent, either an insect pest or a fungal or bacterial disease. Biotic agents can be either natural or man-induced. A stand-level dieback caused by a disease organism should be considered natural when the pathogen can be regarded as part of the ecosystem's indigenous biota. The dieback should not be considered natural when it is caused by introduced pests.

Long-term, subtle *climatic change* has also been suggested as a cause of stand-level dieback. Pollen-spectrum records provide many examples of tree-species declines associated with climatic change. Table 3.7 gives a historical overview of forest decline in Europe. (German: 'Waldsterben').

Table 3.7. Forest decline record for Europe.

Year	Geographical area	Tree species
1449-50	Nürnberger Reichswald	Pine
1477	Nürnberger Reichswald	Pine
1726	Nürnberger Reichswald	Pine
1872-76	Southern Germany	Fir, spruce, pine
1904-06	Sachsen	Spruce
1911-14	Solling	Spruce, even young trees
1931-34	E Preussen, Sachsen, Schles	Spruce
1947-50	SW Germany	Spruce, fir, oak, beech
1959-60	NW Europe	Spruce, pine, beech, oak, larch
1976-??	Western Europe	*All* forest tree species

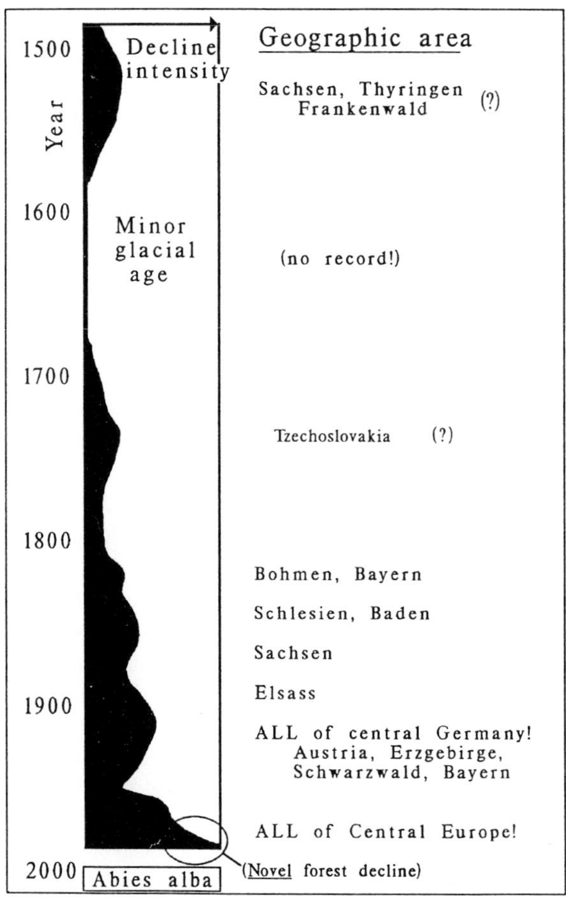

Figure 3.18. Historic record of German 'Tannensterben'. - Source: Larsen (1986a).

The increased forest decline in this century has been caused by *smoke damage* on top of the ever-present natural decline, while the greatly accelerated decline since 1976 is caused by *novel* decline effects in addition to the two former types.

Fig. 3.18 gives the history of dieback of a very sensitive species, namely the German 'national tree', the Silver Fir, *Abies alba.* (German: 'Tannensterben').

Silver Fir is the forest tree by far the most sensitive to decline in Europe, with a serious increase in dieback during this century (due to smoke damage) and particularly since the early 1970's (due to novel decline).

The apparently rare occurrence of decline of this species during the seventeenth century was due either to a generally lower temperature ('the little ice age'), or to a series of wars in this period that left little opportunity for recording forest health.

German foresters have tried for centuries to uncover the reason for the unique sensitivity of Silver Fir, and great interest was aroused when a professor in Göttingen (Larsen, 1986a,b) claimed to have found the explanation, one which very clearly illustrates the complexity of forest-decline syndromes. He claimed that the main predisposing factor (Fig. 3.21) for the decline of Silver Fir is an *insufficient genetic variation* which causes a lack of adaptability. The reason for this reduced variation and adaptability is suggested to date back to the last glacial period, when today's dominant Silver Fir provenance in Europe only survived as a very limited refugial population.

The limited genetic variation and adaptability permanently predispose Silver Fir to many types of stress, such as frost, drought, pollution and other abiotic and biotic stresses. So smoke damage and novel decline only intensify the dieback of Silver Fir, while the underlying reason for the decline is 'natural'.

3.20.2 Smoke-induced Forest Decline

It is an established fact that air pollution from nearby smelters, or other industrial emissions, can cause stand-level mortality of trees by toxification, though the tree response is modulated by a range of environmental and genetical factors (Smith, 1981; Kozlowski and Constantinidou, 1986a,b).

The main air pollutants responsible for smoke-induced forest decline (German: 'Rauchschäden') are *sulfur dioxide* and *nitrogen oxides*, with hydrogen fluoride playing a geographically limited role, and photochemical oxidants playing only a minor role, except in California.

Smoke-induced forest decline today is most widespread in Eastern Europe and in Asia. In heavy industrialized regions, e.g. around the Chinese cities of Chunqing and Chengdu, vast areas of pine forests have been killed by SO_2 (and NO_x) concentrations often exceeding 1 ppm for prolonged periods. Chinese coal is among the highest in the world in sulfur content, with up to 10% sulfur.

Visible symptoms of air pollution on trees. Several visible symptoms of air pollutants on annuals have been described in Sections 3.12.1, 3.13.1, 3.14.1 and 3.15.1. The present section supplements this characterization, with a focus on visible symptoms on trees caused by air pollutants. Symptoms on broad-leaved species, however, are more or less the same as for annuals. An illustrated review of visible symptoms of air pollutants in trees was given by Davis (1973), while a recent, several-hundred-pages long colour atlas by Hartmann et al.

(1988) reflects the complexity of several types of damage to trees. Recognizing the cause of damage from a visible symptom requires a specialist. One has to be able to distinguish symptoms caused by air pollution from those caused by normal environmental stress: frost, drought, insects, fungi, bacteria, virus, mineral deficiencies and toxicity, and from causes of unknown origin such as novel decline.

Trees appear to be most sensitive to *sulfur dioxide* in early summer, when leaves are expanding. Young leaves on *conifers* are therefore mainly damaged rather than previous years' needles. *Acute* sulfur-dioxide injury to conifers usually appears as a reddish-brown discoloration of the needle tips. Depending upon the severity of the exposure, the discoloration may progress towards the needle base. Bands may appear on the needle when successive fumigations are involved, each band representing a distinct fumigation. *Chronic* sulfur-dioxide injury may also involve some tipburn, but is mainly observed as a general yellowing of needles, with premature defoliation of older needles.

On *broad-leaved* species, sulfur-dioxide injury appears as areas of injured tissues located between green veins. The injured tissues may appear yellow, if the damage is light. If it is severe, however, the interveinal areas will turn ivory to tan as the tissues die. The cells and tissues adjacent to the veins remain alive, yielding the characteristic pattern.

Symptoms of nitrogen oxides alone are rarely seen, since NO_x always occurs together with SO_2 and tend to intensify the visible symptoms of the latter.

Ozone has been responsible for several decades of widespread injury and mortality of Ponderosa pine in the mountains east of Los Angeles. Ozone has also been implicated in the chlorotic dwarf and the emergence of tipburn disease of eastern white pine in the U.S.A., perhaps in some cases interacting with sulfur dioxide. *Conifers* appear to be most susceptible to ozone in the late spring or early summer, just before or soon after the leaves have matured. *Acute* ozone injury to conifers usually appears as death of the needle tips, or sometimes of the entire needles. In less severe cases, chlorotic mottle is observed. A mottle results where small patches of injured tissue, turning yellow or brown, alternate with green, healthy patches of tissue; this symptom is a useful diagnostic tool. As with most pollutants, premature defoliation may also occur, giving the tree a tufted appearance. Most pines are susceptible, while spruces and firs are relatively resistant.

On *broadleaved* trees, ozone symptoms appear as 'flecks' or 'stipples' of dead white-to-tan or pigmented reddish-purple tissue on the upper leaf surface. Individual spots of this type are usually less than three millimeters in diameter. Usually only the palisade (upper mesophyll) cells are affected, as can be determined by examining microscopic sections. In severe cases the injury may extend through the leaf to the lower surface. Leaves that have recently matured appear to be most sensitive.

Fluorides from the manufacture of steel, aluminum, glass, fiberglass, tile, brick, pottery and P-fertilizer have caused dramatic destruction of vegetation. Fluoride symptoms on *conifer* needles usually consist of tip necrosis, with the injury progressing toward the needle base in severe cases. The injured tissue is at first yellow, then tan, and finally turns reddish-brown. Needles are most sensitive in the spring, and preceeding years' needles are quite resistant to discoloration, though they may abscise prematurely. In general, pines are particularly susceptible to fluoride injury.

Table 3.8. System of classification of trees according to health, as recommended by the European Community. (*): If 26-60% of the existing needles (leaves) are yellowed, then one class higher, above 60% two classes higher. (**): If 25% of the needles are yellowed, then one class higher. Optional parameters, which may be included during classification, are: crown deformation, trunk condition, annual terminal shoot length, age of oldest needles, fall of healthy twigs, extra twigs, and others. - Source: Wellburn (1988).

Class	Needle (or leaf) loss, %	Description
0	1 - 10 (*)	Healthy
1	11 - 25 (**)	Slightly damaged
2	26 - 60 (**)	Medium to seriously
3	61 - 99	Dying
4	100	Dying

In *broad-leaved* trees, fluorides are taken into the leaves and are transported to the leaf tips and margins. As the concentration of fluoride in these tissues builds up to toxic levels, cells and tissues begin to suffer injury. The leaf tips and margins fade in colour and as the injury progresses, these areas become reddish-brown and the tissues die. A sharply defined, narrow, reddish-brown band or line often separates the injured from the healthy tissues. If successive exposures occur, additional narrow dark lines may form, giving the injured leaf a wavy, zonate appearance. Most hardwoods are at least intermediately resistant to fluorides.

Ammonia from urban areas or from intensive animal or poultry husbandry or from mink farming damages plant species. The symptoms include interveinal bleaching of oak leaves - very much like sulfur dioxide injury - brown, irregular-shaped lesions on certain weed species, and marginal chlorosis in mild cases. Old spruce needles may become black, while younger needles turn reddish-yellow.

3.20.3 Novel Forest Decline

Novel (or recent) forest decline (German: 'Neuartiger Waldschäden') appears in at least two continents: Europe and North America. It is, however, probably not the same phenomenon that dominates forest decline on the two continents, or even in different regions thereof, but it may always be *defined* by: (a) displaying symptoms different from natural or smoke-induced forest decline, (b) occurring over large geographical areas, and (c) affecting several or all forest tree species at the same time, though to a varying degree.

This as yet unexplained phenomenon was first noted in West Germany in the early 1970's. Several authors have recently thoroughly reviewed novel forest decline (Blank, 1985; Hinrichsen, 1986; Klein and Perkins, 1987; Prinz, 1987; Prinz et al., 1987; Moseholm, Andersen and Johnsen, 1988).

***Symptoms and classification of damage*.** The general symptoms of novel forest decline in Europe are *premature* yellowing and loss of previous years' foliage. The novel decline, in fact, is quantified on this basis, on a 0-4 classification (Table 3.8).

The *visible* symptoms in each injury-class of the seven most common European forest tree species are illustrated in a seven-language EEC booklet with instructive colour plates (Bauer, 1985), while additional illustrations are given by Hartmann et al. (1988). Needle yellowing and loss of needles progresses in the '*European* novel decline' from the inside of the crown outward, and from the bottom up.

Europe. Novel forest decline has become one of the most controversial ecological issues in Europe for many years.

It has been most thoroughly studied in West Germany. An increase in the rate of needle yellowing and loss of needles *from the inside of the crown outward, and from the bottom up*, was observed in *Silver Fir* from the early 1970's, at high altitudes (above 7-800 m) in the Southern part of West Germany in the Black- and the Bavarian forests: traditionally clean-air regions. After the dry summer of 1976, the named symptoms were observed to be widespread amongst other species such as Norway Spruce, Scots Pine and Common Beech.

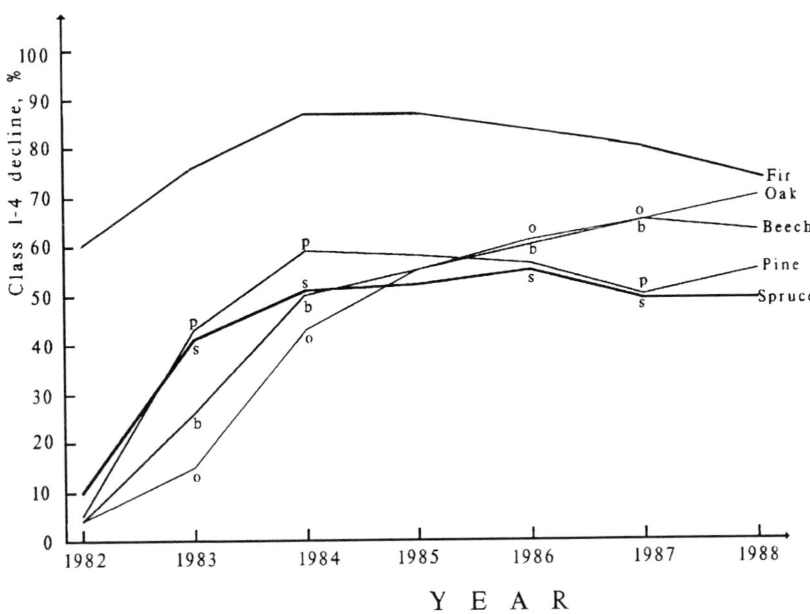

Figure 3.19. Development 1982-88 in Class 1-4 decline of selected forest trees, representing 87% of West Germany's 7.4 million ha forests. Norway spruce covers 39%, pine 20%, beech 17%, oak 9%, silver fir 2%. Class 4 (dead trees) never exceed a few percent, but of course, they are removed annually from the intensively managed West German forests, i.e., new trees are entering this class every year. The line density indicates the quantitative importance of each species.

It was several years, however, before a programme for a large-scale forest survey was designed and carried out. But since 1982 detailed reports, based on nation-wide assessments of the development, have been issued annually for each state and for the whole republic by the German 'Bundesministerium für Ernährung, Landwirtschaft und Forsten'. Short extracts of these reports were published by Anonymous (1983); Breloh and Kirch (1984); Breloh and Dieterle (1985); Lehringer (1986); Anonymous (1987b); and Ladwig (1988). Some of the essential data are summarized in Fig. 3.19.

A major part of the total forest decline in West Germany today is of the novel type, though smoke-induced decline (predominantly on the borders with Eastern Europe) and natural decline (as demonstrated for Silver fir) also play their part.

Moseholm et al. (1988) reviewed information on forest damage in other European countries, indicating the West German problem to be a widespread European problem. However, development in European forest decline during the 1980's has been estimated by different survey techniques in different countries and in different years. It is thus our conservative estimate that novel forest decline in Europe peaked already in the mid-1980's.

The apparent increase in forest decline between 1985 and 1988 illustrated in Fig. 3.20 was reported by a respected German magazine (Anonymous, 1988e), based on decline data by the EEC-method. The illustrated small decline intervals make arbitrary variations visible, and absolute differences between regions give a false picture of forest decline, since the observed decline included effects of climate, soil and genotype, which vary with the regions.

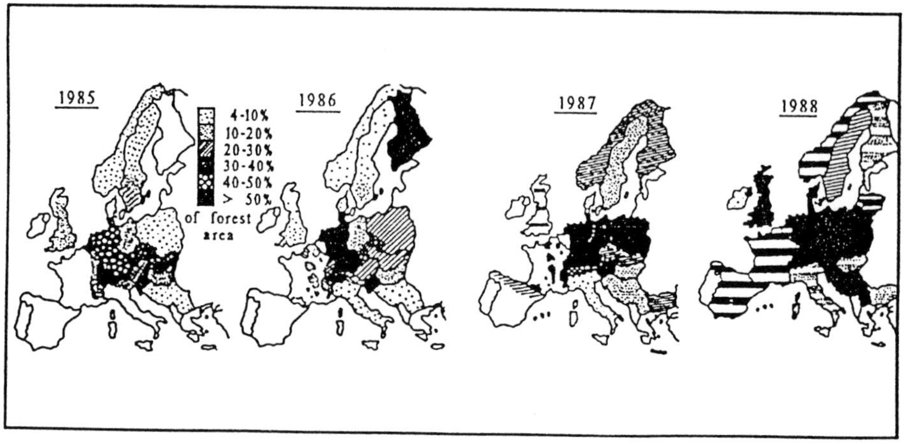

Figure 3.20. This may be a map of the development in recognition of forest decline for 1985-88, rather than of a real development in decline symptoms. The development of decline in Germany is not consistent with this map! - Source: Anonymous (1988e).

In Denmark, for example, a steady improvement in the health of forests was observed from 1984-1988 using the so called 'X+Y-method'. Novel decline was not officially recognized until 1987 (Bjørnskov, 1988*), even though 50% of the forest trees were affected (using the EC-method) just south of the border in Schleswig-Holstein (Anonymous, 1988c,e). With the EC-method the overall health of Danish forests improved from 1987-1988, in contrast to the impression one may get from Fig. 3.20.

North America. In the U.S.A., serious forest decline is frequently observed along the 1500 km Eastern mountain range of the *Appalachian mountains*, from Camels Hump, White Face Mountain and Mount Washington in the North to Mount Mitchell in the South. Decline is also evident in the San Bernadino Mountains of California, mostly affecting Ponderosa and Jeffrey pines. In Canada vast areas of sugar maple plantation declined seriously in the early and mid-1980's, due to causes unknown.

The *novel* decline on the Appalachian Camels Hump (Vermont) dates back to 1965 (Vogelmann et al., 1988), and is thus prior to the advent of European novel decline. But as in Europe, the forest decline in the Appalachians is a blend of natural, smoke-induced and novel decline, though sometimes one type is completely dominant above the others. In the montane forest ecosystems, on *Camels Hump*, which at altitudes above 850 m are dominated by red spruce *(Picea rubens)*, white birch *(Betula papyrifera)*, and balsam fir *(Abies balsamea)*, only red spruce *(Picea rubens)* show the *European* leaf-yellowing syndrome of novel decline. But as in Europe, rapid changes occurred in the growth of all three species from 1979-1986. The conifers were affected since 1965, the broadleaf trees only since 1979.

Liedeker et al. (1988) studied red spruce *(Picea rubens)* and (the European) Norway spruce *(Picea abies)* growing together on three other locations in the Northern Appalachians under the best conditions possible and being protected from adverse environmental stresses. They found symptoms of all degrees of 'European novel decline' on both species, with no major symptomatic evidence of either biotic or abiotic diseases: needle loss and yellowing progressed from the inside of the crown outward, and from the bottom up. The distinct yellow spotting on the upper surfaces of the foliage and its correlation to needle age, previously reported for Norway spruce in Europe, was observed on both spruce types studied by Liedeker et al. (1988). Their report, therefore, represents immaculate cases of the European type of novel decline in the U.S.A.

In less protected sites, the loss in biomass increment is associated with the more frequently observed 'American novel decline' syndrome: Apical dieback, where *needle loss progresses from the outside of the crown inward, and from the top down.* An analysis of climate and competition as contributors to decline of red spruce in high-elevation Appalachian forests revealed that competition did not explain the decline, while climate only explained a part of it (McLaughlin et al., 1987). Natural decline, therefore, cannot as yet explain the decline which began in the U.S.A. during the early 1960's, a decline unprecedented within the available tree-ring record of surviving trees over the past 200 years. This decline is, therefore, considered as (American) novel decline.

A common cause of decline is *insect* attacks, though these may also be secondary events. The top and slopes of Mount Mitchell, the highest mountain (2034 m) in the Appalachians, are covered with *dead* and *dying* trees. Visitors frequently believe that these trees were killed by novel decline and 'the acid rain', and do not recognize the much more subtle symptoms of novel decline. The Fraser fir *(Abies fraseri)* on Mount Mitchell was killed by the balsam wooly aphid *(Adaleges piceae)*. This latter pest was introduced into New England and Southeastern Canada from Europe in about 1900. Hence, the decline is not natural. Once established at Mt. Mitchell (1956), it spread southward along the Blue Ridge Parkway, and has at present infested thousands of hectars of forest, killing over 300,000 Fraser fir trees in the Mt. Mitchell area alone. Aphids may have already seriously damaged a tree before there is any visible evidence. Usually, the first highly visible sign of infestation is the appearance of yellow foliage; at this stage the tree is already dying. The infestation may have been active for 2 or 3 years. Later this yellow foliage turns a deep reddish-brown or rust colour. After this stage, the needles are shed, leaving the gray snags standing.

Some authors (Woodman, 1987) find no conclusive evidence that acid deposition (SO_2, NO_x and acid rain) or other regionally dispersed pollutants affect the productivity of North American forests. Hence, they do not believe that air pollution explains novel decline in the Appalachians. Others (Anderson et al., 1988) find clear symptoms of *ozone* tip burn, and chlorotic mottling on eastern white pine, which may explain at least part of the American-type novel decline. Plantations had higher percentages of trees affected than did natural stands. Stands with symptomatic trees were most common on southwest aspects, but there were no correlations with elevation and percent slope. Ozone is the predominant phytotoxic air contaminant in the eastern United States.

In conclusion, the American forest decline includes symptoms of *European type* novel decline, as well as of acute ozone damage, which, together with a harsh climate, explains most of the *American type* novel decline. Natural factors seem to be of greater importance in the overall decline in the U.S.A., than is recognized in Europe.

3.20.4 Causes of European Novel Decline, and 'the Ecological View'

Since we have distinguished symptoms of novel decline in Europe from those of natural decline, as well as air-pollution or smoke-induced decline, we have to ask ourselves: 'what indeed *does* cause novel forest decline in Europe'? The best answer we can give today is 'nothing in particular': it is a combination of multiple conditions.

There have been well over a hundred suggestions of single triggering factors. Hinrichsen (1986) refers to six major schools of thought on novel forest decline: 1) Soil acidification and aluminum toxicity, 2) ozone injury, 3) magnesium deficiency, 4) excess nitrogen, 5) growth-altering organic chemicals, and 6) general stress: the ecological view.

Soil acidification and aluminum toxicity. The most popular initial hypothesis was based on a suggestion that wet and dry acid deposition affect the soil by destroying its buffering system. This would lead to leaching of nutrients and mobilization of toxic aluminum ions (Section 3.15.1), which would damage the mycorrhiza and the fine root system of the tree, and thereby its stability in storms and its ability to take up water and nutrients, eventually resulting in its death (Ulrich & Pankrath, 1983). *Ulrich's hypothesis* has been extensively criticized, mainly on grounds that damage to trees occurs on a variety of soils, including those in calcareous areas with characteristics markedly different from those found in the Solling Mountains where Ulrich developed his hypothesis. His hypothesis cannot explain either the temporal or the geographical development of the novel decline syndrome, and it was therefore discarded already in 1982 as the universal explanation for novel decline.

The ozone hypothesis. Based on extensive field observations and measurements of ozone and sulfur-dioxide concentrations in West Germany, the suggestion that ozone (and other photooxidants) may be involved in novel decline has particularly been advocated by Prinz (1987). Ozone has been found to cause yellowing and browning of needles in laboratory studies. Ozone damages cell membranes (Section 3.14.2), resulting in an increased leaching of ions by acid fog and acid rain. Ozone also causes damage to chlorophyll, and thus reduction in carbohydrate production and root growth. This leads to a smaller uptake of water and nutrients, and reduced stability in storms.

The paucity of historic data on ambient ozone and other air pollutants, however, makes it impossible to say if this hypothesis can explain the temporal development of novel decline. Symptoms induced by *short-term* ozone in the laboratory do not correspond with symptoms of *European*-type novel decline in nature, but rather with the *American* type. *Long-term* exposure to ozone, however, has recently been demonstrated to induce the symptoms of novel decline in Norway spruce.

Magnesium deficiency. This hypothesis, founded on foliar and chemical analysis in spruce stands at high elevations, advocates that the yellowing of spruce foliage is due to extreme magnesium deficiency. Acid deposition adds nitrogen to the ecosystem, but leaches out magnesium and calcium from needles and the soil (Section 3.15.1). The leaching from foliage is presumably accelerated by episodic ozone or frost damage to cuticles and cell membranes.

Excess nitrogen. This hypothesis is the result of cumulative research since the mid-1960's, and is based on the premise that with the onset of the industrial revolution forest ecosystems have received excessive doses of the 16 elements considered essential for all plant growth. All elements can be taken up by trees through their foliage and roots.

In particular, the atmospheric deposition of nitrogen over wide areas has increased dramatically since the Second World War and could be causing the novel forest decline in Europe, as well as other effects on ecosystems (Nihlgård, 1985; Skeffington and Wilson, 1988). Excess nitrogen is known to cause: increased growth and hence a relative deficiency in other elements, inhibition of mycorrhiza, increased frost sensitivity, increased susceptibility to root-disease fungi, changes in root:shoot ratios, and altered patterns of nitrogen metabolism. The hypothesis, however, seems speculative and lacks firm field evidence.

Organic chemicals. It is postulated that among the thousands of organic compounds produced every year in Europe and North America, a few of them, singly or in combination, may produce at least some of the novel decline symptoms. Ethylene and aniline are examples of such compounds. The hypothesis lacks field evidence, which, due to the low concentrations in question, is very hard to obtain.

The ecological view. Like cancer, novel forest decline will probably have to be understood as a disease syndrome, induced by multiple factors involving several predisposing, several triggering, and several secondary factors (Klein and Perkins, 1988). In recent years, therefore, in explaining the novel decline syndrome the different schools of thought have more or less joined forces in a common, composite theory: *the ecological view.* This combines the knowledge of foresters, plant physiologists, plant pathologists, entomologists and ecologists (Lange, 1983; Tigerstedt et al., 1985; Larsen, 1987[*]).

Larsen (1987[*]) gives an excellent overview of this concept of the total forest decline, using a thermodynamic analogue (Fig. 3.21).

3.21 THE GREENHOUSE EFFECT

3.21.1 The Normal and the Enhanced Greenhouse Effect

The Earth's climate is constantly changing. As indicated in Fig. 3.22, climatic change is determined by a complex interplay between physical, chemical and biological processes: the influence of continental drift, variations in solar intensity, volcanism, the impact of meteors and comets, changes in the Earth's orbital parameters, ice accumulation and depletion, variations in oceanic circulations and chemistry, changes in terrestrial and aquatic life, and changes in atmospheric composition and circulation. Recent reviews have been given by Bolin et al. (1986); Harrington (1987); Anonymous (1988b); Pearman (1988); Fenger and Laut (1989[*]), and Houghton and Woodwell (1989).

Ecosystem stability

STATE (Thermodynamic analogue)	FACTORS
Stable	Stability factors: 1. The best choice of tree species and provenance in relation to local growth conditions 2. The most ecological forest management
Labile	Predisposing factors. 1. Wrong choice of tree species or provenance 2. Wrong type of forest management 3. Changes in climate and soil conditions 4. Introduction of 'new' pests 5. Changes in air quality (air pollution)
Degeneration	Primary provoking factors: 1. Climate extremes (frost, draught, storm) 2. Large scale insect and fungi attack 3. Air pollution extremes (SO_2, O_3, salt, etc.)
Destruction	Secondary factors: 1. Insects (bark beetles) 2. Fungi (heart-rot and honey fungus) 3. Decline of mycorrhiza

Figure 3.21. A stable ecosystem is secured by several stabilizing factors. Predisposing factors make the ecosystem labile and sensitive to the triggering factors. Degenerated ecosystems are easy victims for the secondary factors, causing the irrevocable end of the ecosystem. - Source: Larsen (1987).

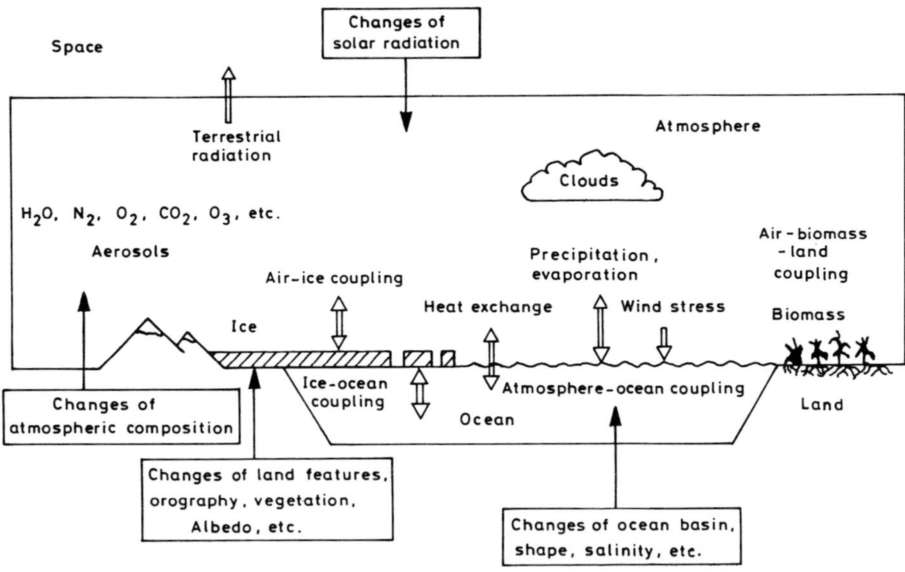

Figure 3.22. Schematic illustration of the components of the coupled atmosphere-ocean-ice-Earth climatic system. The full arrows are examples of external forcing processes eventually leading to changes in climate. The open arrows are examples of internal processes. - Source: Anonymous (1988a).

Despite the above-named influences, many of them large, and despite changes in the radiant intensity of the sunlight over the past 4.5 x 10^9 years, the average temperature of the Earth's surface has remained remarkably constant, hovering near 15°C. This implies the presence of strong negative feedbacks reacting to any major environmental change. Lovelock (1979, 1988) interprets this in his 'Gaia theory' as a 'conscious' behaviour on the part of the Earth. During the past century, however, man's influence on his environment has been increasing at an unprecedented rate, so even a 'Gaia effect' may be of no avail.

The average temperature of the planet is the result of a balance between absorbed solar radiation and outgoing long-wave (infrared) radiation, i.e. heat. The incident short-wave (visible, but not ultraviolet) solar radiation easily penetrates the atmosphere, heating the surface of the Earth. A major part of the incident energy is subsequently reflected with an increased average wave length. But because the atmosphere, mainly due to the presence of water vapour, clouds and carbon dioxide, absorbs a significant fraction of the long-wave radiation emitted from the Earth's surface, it returns part of the energy back to the surface, raising the average temperature to about +15°C.

This influence of the atmosphere, often referred to as the 'greenhouse effect', is a *natural* process, which is essential for life on Earth as we know it at present. An important factor in this balance is the reflectivity *(albedo)* of the planet. Without an atmosphere, and assuming the present value of the albedo (approx. 0.30), the average temperature of the Earth's surface would be a freezing -20°C.

The problem we are facing today is that we have caused the blanket to thicken during the last century by increasing the concentrations of gases like CO_2, CH_4, N_2, halocarbons (mainly chlorofluorocarbons, CFCs), and tropospheric ozone (Anonymous, 1988a). Since all these gases (and others) have the absorption properties described above, they increase the temperature of the Earth's surface; therefore, they are known as 'greenhouse gases'.

3.21.2 Carbon Dioxide, CO_2

Continuous carbon-dioxide measurements in the atmosphere for the last 30 years show a gradual increase from 315 ppm in 1958 to about 350 in 1988 (Fig. 3.24, left part).

Ice-core analyses of the carbon dioxide content have determined the preindustrial level to be 270-280 ppm. In addition to the steady increase, the carbon dioxide concentration variates with season, altitude and latitude.

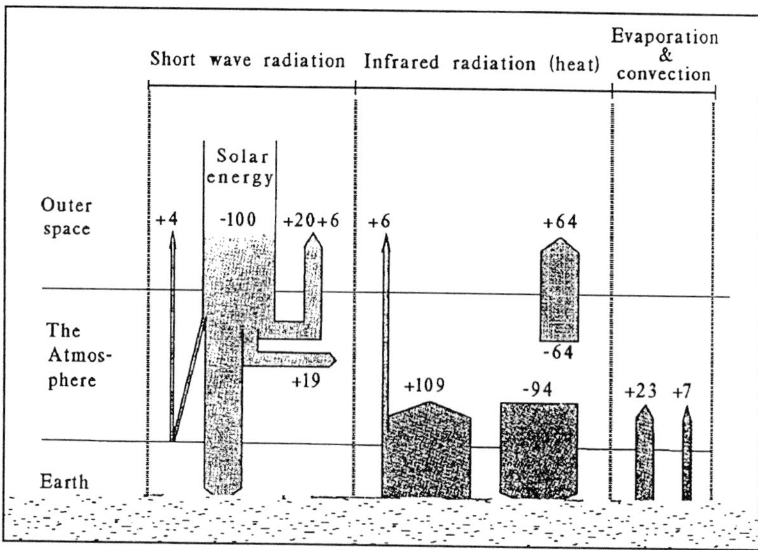

Figure 3.23. Energy balance on the Earth and in the atmosphere, expressed in percent of total solar energy entering (1340 watt m²). Solar radiation is of relatively short wavelength, with a maximum around 0.5 μm, and 51% of the energy is absorbed by the Earth; the rest of the solar energy is either reflected to outer space (30%), from the atmosphere (6%), from clouds (20%), or from the surface of the Earth (4%), or it is absorbed in the atmosphere (19% net), in ozone (3%), carbon dioxide (2%) and water vapor (14%). The energy absorption creates heat and reemission of long-wave radiation. The Earth emits 115%, most of which (94%) is reflected back to Earth. 70% net heat radiation is reemitted to outer space. Finally, heat of evaporation (23%) and convection (7%) transfer energy from the Earth's surface back to space. - Source: Fenger (1985).

The observed increase in atmospheric CO_2 concentration is mainly due to the burning of fossil fuels (coal, oil and gas). During the past two centuries, however, clear-cutting of forests and cultivation of land have also contributed substantially to the increase. The present global emission of carbon dioxide due to the fossil fuel is about 5,500 Mt per year measured as carbon (1 Mt = 10^6 tons). Deforestation, and other land-use changes, lead to an emission of 1,000-2,000 Mt per year. Since the annual accumulation in the atmosphere is only about 3,000 Mt, more than half of the amounts emitted must end up somewhere else, most of it probably in the oceans.

Future levels of carbon dioxide in the atmosphere can be estimated based on assumptions on future fossil fuel use. Our somewhat limited understanding of the global carbon cycle, in particular the exchange of carbon dioxide between the atmosphere and the oceans and between the atmosphere and vegetation, contributes to making such estimates uncertain. At present, CO_2 increases by almost 2 ppm per year, but in a hundred years it may increase by 4 ppm per year.

If the emission of carbon dioxide stopped, it could take several hundred years before the concentration in the atmosphere returned to its pre-industrial value.

3.21.3 Methane, CH_4

Measurements of CH_4 in air bubbles trapped in ice from Greenland and Antarctica indicate that the atmospheric concentration of CH_4 has more than doubled over the last 300 years, to the present level of 1.7 ppm (Figure 3.24, right part).

The methane concentration increases a little less than 1% per year, with an estimated lifetime in the atmosphere of 8-10 years. Biogenic and abiogenic sources are of approximately the same magnitude, including animal husbandry, rice cultivation, biomass burning, fossil-fuel use, car emissions, and waste dumps. These anthropogenic activities, coupled with the photochemical reactions in the troposphere, are mainly responsible for the present increase in the CH_4 content of the atmosphere.

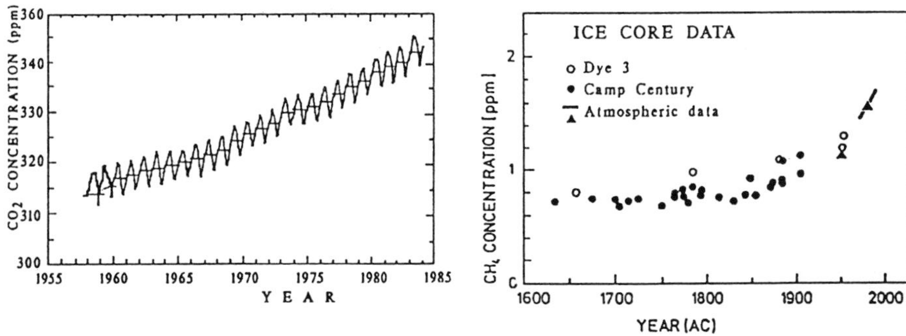

Figure 3.24. Atmospheric content of CO_2 (data from Mauna Loa, Hawaii) and of CH_4 (historic record from air bubbles trapped in ice). - Source: Anonymous (1988a).

The peat bogs of the Siberian tundra may hold the key to the world's future under the influence of the greenhouse effect (Pearce, 1989a,b). The problem is that there may be no researchers present to record the first crucial phase. Climate models predict that the frozen tundras of Canada and Siberia will warm up more than other parts of the planet in the coming decades. As the frozen bogs melt, they may release huge amounts of methane trapped in the permafrost.

Methane is the second most important greenhouse gas after carbon dioxide and permafrost is a major trap for methane created by organisms in wetlands such as the peat bogs of the tundra. Release of this gas would accelerate global warming.

3.21.4 Nitrous oxide, N_2O

Direct atmospheric measurements over the 1980's have shown that the N_2O concentration increases at a rate of just below 1% per year. At present (1988) it is 307 ppb. Analysis of polar-ice cores indicate the pre-industrial level to be 285 ppb. Nitrous oxide is emitted from natural soils, fertilizers and cultivated land, ocean- and freshwater ecosystems and biomass- and fossil-fuel burning. The increase of the latter is the main cause of the increase during the last century. There has been some recent concern that the use of catalytic converters in cars (installed to reduce emission of CO, NO_x and hydrocarbons) and combustion of coal in fluidized beds (a combustion method with reduced emission of SO_2 and NO_x) leads to substantial increases in N_2 production. It is not yet known whether the magnitude of these extra N_2O emissions is large enough as compared to other anthropogenic emissions of N_2O to be significant. The matter clearly needs further investigation.

3.21.5 Tropospheric ozone, O_3

Less than 10% of the total amount of ozone is found in the *troposphere*, the lowest level of the Earth's atmosphere, up to 15 kilometers. But the ozone in the troposphere is today about 100% higher than a hundred years ago, a menace increasing by approximately 1% per year over extended areas of the Northern hemisphere, with higher increases over industrialized continents, and no increase in the Southern hemisphere. Ozone has a relatively short lifetime in the lower troposphere, and its production mainly depends on the abundance of photochemical reactions with CO, NO_x, CH_4 and hydrocarbons. All of these are known to increase only on the *Northern* hemisphere, just as several of the greenhouse gases are more abundant on the Northern than on the Southern hemisphere, in particular the short-lived gases.

3.21.6 Stratospheric ozone, O_3

Although it is present at concentrations of only a few parts per million, ozone is most abundant in a level of the Earth's atmosphere known as the *stratosphere*, between 15 and 50 kilometers up. The present depletion of ozone in the stratosphere will influence the climate mainly by altering the temperature structure and thereby also the dynamics of the stratosphere. It is difficult to predict how such changes will affect the climate at the Earth's surface.

A more direct effect of stratospheric ozone depletion is an increase in UV-light penetrating down to the surface. This would add a small amount to the heating produced by increased concentrations of greenhouse gases.

A further discussion of the impact of CFC's and other trace gases on the depletion of the stratospheric ozone 'layer' is continued in Section 3.22.

3.21.7 Halocarbons, CFC-11, CFC-12 and others

Measurements of the global distributions and trends of the main halocarbons, CFC-11 ($CFCl_3$), CFC-12 (CF_2Cl_3), CCl_4 and CH_3CCl_3, have been carried out since 1978. Their average atmospheric concentration is 0.2 ppb with an increase of 4% per year and an average lifetime in the atmosphere of 75 years.

The CFC's or *freon* gases are used in *refrigerators* because of their useful physical properties with regard to evaporation and condensation. They are useful propellants in spray cans, used as inflater gases in insulation materials, and for cleaning of electronic chips, because of their chemical inertness. The latter property is the very reason that CFC's represent a problem for the stratospheric ozone (discussed later), since they do not break down in the troposphere.

Since carbon dioxide is a major natural component of the atmosphere, much of the radiation that it can absorb is already absorbed, and a further increase in its concentration will give only a relatively small additional greenhouse effect. On the other hand, the purely artificial CFC gases absorb at wavelengths where the undisturbed atmosphere would be transparent. This explains why one molecule of, e.g., CFC-11 will be more than ten thousand times as effective as a greenhouse gas as an additional molecule of CO_2.

The long-term impact of a trace gas on the ozone layer and on climate depends not only on the amounts emitted, but also on its atmospheric lifetime, since the accumulation in the atmosphere is proportional to its chemical lifetime. The above-named halocarbons are of anthropogenic origin, and, except for CCl_4, they have mainly been released to the atmosphere during the last two to three decades. For this reason, their atmospheric concentrations are far from equilibrium. In 1987, it was internationally agreed at a conference in Montreal that emissions were to be diminished by 20% in 1994 and by one half by 1999. But if the Montreal Protocol is not improved, the atmospheric CFC concentrations will continue to increase for the next few decades (Fig. 3.28).

3.21.8 The Relative Importance of Individual Greenhouse Gases

By taking into account both the absorption efficiency per molecule and the accumulation rate of the various gases in the atmosphere, one can estimate the relative importance of the different greenhouse gases. Fig. 3.25 shows the expected temperature increase during the coming 50 years due to various trace gases. It is noteworthy that carbon dioxide alone contributes only half of the total expected effect, and that the CFCs alone actually contribute almost 50% of the CO_2 effect. Of course, these projections depend on assumptions of the magnitude of future releases of these gases. For example, CFC emissions have been assumed to continue to increase at the present rate, in contradiction to the Montreal agreement.

3.21.9 The Enhanced Greenhouse Effect Changes Global Climate

Climate models suggest that the global mean surface temperature should have increased by 0.4-1.1°C due to the presently experienced increase in greenhouse gases. The observed temperature increase during the last 100 years is reasonably consistent with such calculations.

During the so-called *El Niño* years (e.g., 1986-87), when the directions of equatorial winds are reversed, it is normal to have average annual global temperatures above the mean, while temperatures in anti-El Niño years are below it. 1988 was an anti-El Niño year, but the first half of the year was the warmest period on record (Fig. 3.27), i.e., at least since 1861, which was the year of the first reliable record. Any remaining doubts as to whether the present global heating is a natural part of the normal short- and long-term cycling of global temperature (Fig. 3.26 A,B,C), or is indeed caused by the enhanced greenhouse effect, were consequently eliminated by most scientists during 1988 (Houghton and Woodwell, 1989).

The four warmest average annual global temperatures ever measured were all in the 1980's (Fig. 3.27). This unusual warmth is most evident in the southern hemisphere, where seven of the eight warmest years on record occurred within this decade. The arctic area experienced the warmest climate in the late 1930's and early 1940's.

Towards the middle of the next century, the temperature is estimated to increase by 1.5-4.5°C. Such an increase, if realized, will make the Earth's surface warmer than it has been for at least 5,000 years. The temperature is generally expected to increase the most near the poles and during the winter, though it is not yet possible to make detailed prediction about the future climate in specific regions of the globe. If elevated temperatures are sustained for several decades, it is probable that the sea levels will rise, eventually creating severe problems in many coastal areas.

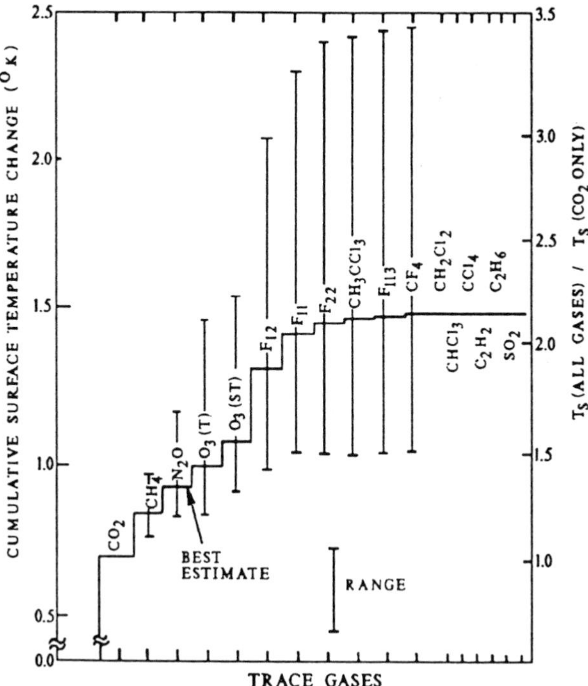

Figure 3.25. Cumulative equilibrium surface warming resulting from the WHO trace-gas scenario. - Source: Anonymous (1988a).

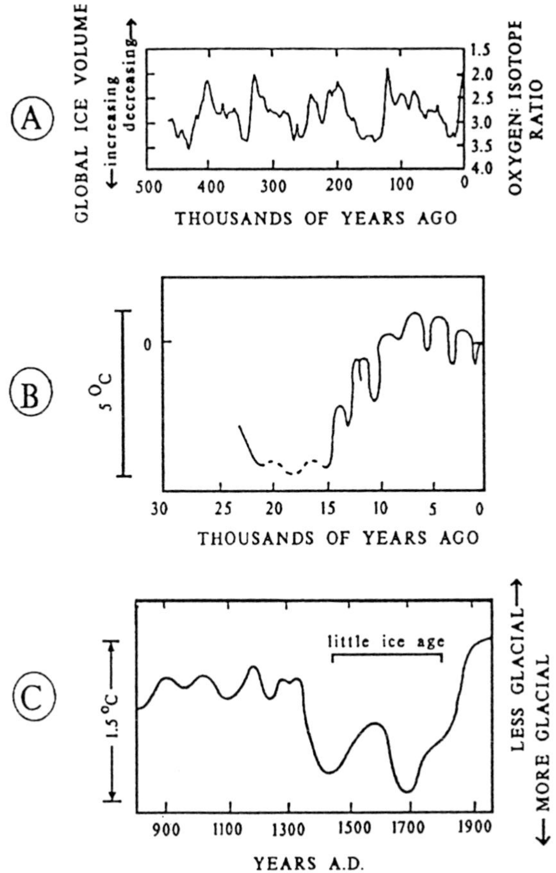

Figure 3.26. A: Climate of the last half million years deduced from measurements of oxygen isotope ratios in plankton shells which relate to ice volume. B: Climate of the past 25,000 years as estimated from changes in tree rings, fluctuations in glaciers and shifts in vegetation patterns as recorded in pollen spectra. C: Climate of the last 1000 years estimated from evidence relating to East European winters. - Source: Anonymous (1988a).

The changes in temperature and rainfall are likely to have a very significant impact on agriculture and forestry; in some areas beneficial, in most others adverse (Parry et al., 1988). As an example, a 3°C higher annual average temperature would in itself increase forest production in Scandinavia by a third. However, effects through changes in soil moisture may be more important to plant production than a global change in temperature. With a doubling of 'CO_2 equivalents' (including all greenhouse gases), soil moisture is predicted to be reduced in the order of 50% in the mid-latitudes (North America, Africa, Central Europe), but increased in northern latitudes (Canada, Scandinavia) and the southern hemisphere. This would have devastating consequences for the vast grain-producing areas in North America, where the bad harvest in 1988 may have been just a preview. Changes in average temperature and rainfall may not be as important as the predicted increase in extreme climatic conditions induced by the greenhouse effect.

3.21.10 Other Anthropogenic Effects on Global Climate

Human activity may also influence the regional and global climate by increasing the load of particulate matter in the atmosphere. This is brought about mainly by emissions of SO_2 that subsequently oxidizes to sulfate particles. Another anthropogenic influence can come from changes in the albedo of the Earth's surface by clear-cutting of forest.

The climatic consequences of increased concentrations of aerosol particles, however, are difficult to quantify. In principle, the scattering of light by such particles will tend to reduce the intensity of the sunlight reaching the surface, thereby leading to a cooler climate. On the other hand, if the particulates contain elemental carbon (soot), they will also absorb sunlight. In cases with an aerosol occurring over a reflecting surface, e.g., ice, snow or desert, the absorbtion will tend to heat the lower atmosphere and also the Earth's surface. It seems likely, however, that the direct net effect of anthropogenic aerosols on climate is a *cooling*. This cooling is most probably smaller in magnitude than the heating effect due to greenhouse gases, at least as an average over the globe.

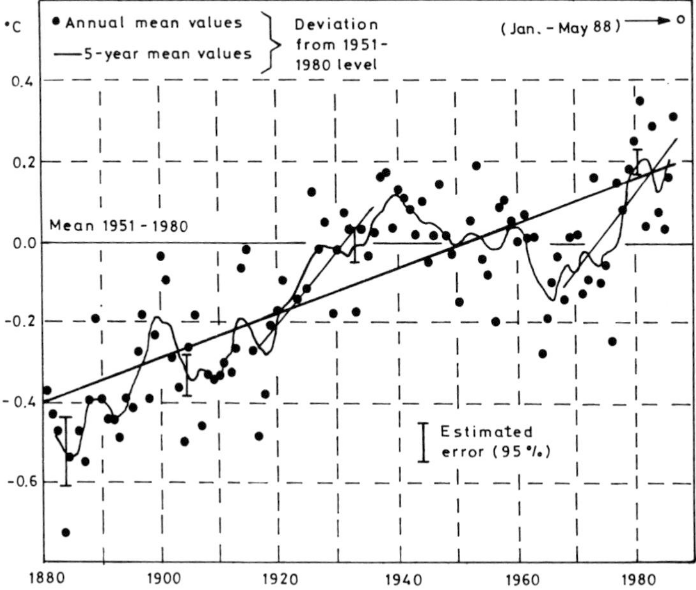

Figure 3.27. Changes in global mean temperature in the last century. Data adopted from NASA. - Source: Dansgaard (1988).

Another important effect of aerosols on climate may work through a change in the physical properties of clouds. A higher concentration of aerosol particles, that can act as 'cloud condensation nuclei', will cause the clouds to contain a larger number of cloud droplets. This, in turn, will make a cloud brighter and thereby increase the amount of sunlight that is reflected back to space. This effect has been demonstrated for individual plumes from ships, but the magnitude of the overall effect has not yet been established.

3.21.11 Can We Reduce the Changes in Climate?

Several of the greenhouse gases (CO_2, N_2, CFCs) have effective lifetimes in the atmosphere in the order of 100 years or more. This implies that even if all anthropogenic emissions were stopped immediately, it would take hundreds of years before the atmospheric concentrations returned to normal.

In the case of carbon dioxide it is possible to reduce the concentration *actively*, e.g., by planting more trees. The amount of carbon dioxide that can be withdrawn from the atmosphere in this way, however, is quite small, and the effect is also limited to the time during which the new forests actually increase their biomass. The tropical rain forests are in equilibrium, and since the total carbon in those rapidly cycling ecosystems only represent a few years of production, the clearing of tropical rain forests, fortunately, means less to the global CO_2 balance than would the clearing of temperate forests. But there is, of course, a multitude of other reasons why the rain forests should be conserved.

The future emissions of greenhouse gases depend on what we choose to do. Emissions of CFCs are likely to be strongly reduced in the near future, because of their serious impact on the ozone 'layer'. This can be done without any major economic sacrifices. A reduction of the emissions of CH_4 and N_2O will require control of both combustion processes and agricultural practices. Carbon-dioxide emission, being directly linked to the total use of fossil fuels and thereby the energy policy in general, is by far the most fundamental problem. 'Cleaning' is not technically nor economically feasible.

Although all use of fossil fuels results in emission of carbon dioxide, the emission per produced energy unit is almost twice as high for coal as for natural gas, with oil in between the two.

Nuclear power and renewable sources of energy (mainly wind- and solar power and biogas) do not add carbon dioxide to the atmosphere. However, since nuclear and renewable energy represents only a small part of the global energy supply, even a doubling of the global nuclear and renewable-energy programs would be insufficient to reduce the threat of a climatic change. The most effective way of reducing carbon-dioxide emissions at the present time is probably *investment in energy conservation.*

At a meeting in Toronto in June 1988 on policy implications of the changing atmosphere, it was recommended that the global carbon-dioxide emission be substantially reduced by the year 2005. It was estimated that half of the decrease could be achieved by more efficient energy use and the other half by alternative energy supply systems.

Climatic change is clearly a *global* problem that has to be dealt with internationally. The UNEP, WHO, IASA and ICSU are among the active international organizations performing and coordinating work in the general area of changing global climate.

3.22 THE STRATOSPHERIC OZONE 'LAYER'

3.22.1 Origin

A continuous process of photodissociation of oxygen creates *stratospheric* ozone (O_3), mainly high above the equator. Here, solar radiation of very short wavelengths penetrates the atmosphere most deeply, though (for the present) it is so strongly absorbed that it never reaches the ground. Winds within the stratosphere then carry the ozone around the Earth to maintain the ozone 'layer'.

Short-wave (< 243 nm) solar UV light is energetic enough to break up the oxygen molecule, which consists of two atoms strongly bound together, to produce free oxygen radicals, a particularly active form of oxygen. To form ozone, a further molecule of oxygen combines with an oxygen radical. The process is stable only when a third body is present, the most common one being a molecule of nitrogen, to take away some of the energy produced by the reaction:

$$O_2 \rightarrow 2\,O \xrightarrow{+\,2\,O_2\,(N_2)} 2\,O_3\,.$$

At the very top of the atmosphere there is a lot of radiation but very little air, so there is not much ozone. At the Earth's surface there is a lot of air, but little radiation, so not much ozone is formed there either. The ozone is at maximum concentration at around 23 kilometers.

Over 90% of the atmospheric ozone is located in the stratosphere (15-50 km), though in concentrations of only a few ppm. While the even lower concentrations of ozone (30-80 ppb) at the Earth's surface are harmful to the health of man, animals, plants and to several materials (Section 3.14), the stratospheric ozone layer beneficially *screens* all life on Earth from harmful effects of the sun's ultraviolet radiation.

3.22.2 Predictions of Deterioration

In the early 1970's, scientists at the University of California and the University of Michigan in the U.S.A. suggested that certain long-lived compounds containing chlorine (man-made chlorofluorocarbons, CFC's), would escape to the stratosphere. To some extent this also goes for bromidefluorocarbons (BFC's) and for N_2O. Under the higher stratospheric UV-radiation CFC's decompose, releasing free chlorine, which supposedly increases the normal rate of destruction of ozone. The chlorine atom reacts with ozone in a catalytic cycle, which effectively removes two molecules of ozone without consuming chlorine. Since CFCs are also active as greenhouse gases (Section 3.21), much interest has focused on these compounds during the last decade. Because of their long chemical lifetime in the atmosphere (they are added five times faster than they decompose), they accumulate at a far from steady-state rate.

Nearly all CFC (84%) is emitted in the industrialized world, but China's plan for a refrigerator in each house may change this, if substitutes for CFCs are not soon found.

Other chemicals may play an important role in stratospheric ozone decline. Recent information on *halons* (chlorobromofluorocarbons) used in fire extinguishers indicate this product to be 10-1000 times as active as CFCs.

3.22.3 Antarctica

In 1987, alarming news attained worldwide attention: "Above the Antarctic, the ozone layer is shattered" (Farman, 1987; Stolarski, 1988).

Scientists had for many years measured the Antarctic ozone with instruments on the ground and aboard balloons and satellites. The *British Antarctic Survey* had studied the ozone layer since 1957. In 1982 they noticed strange depletions in the layer above the Antarctic. However, ozone levels are notorious for bouncing about, the instrumentation was rather old, and an American satellite viewing the Antarctic continent from 800 kilometers up had not spotted anything amiss. But with new instruments on the ground, it became certain by 1984 that something dramatic was happening above Antarctica.

Prior to this, atmospheric chemists thought that they were getting somewhere with their understanding of ozone. Observations and models agreed that changes were less than 1% per year. However, over Antarctica the depletion suddenly became more than 50% for an extended period of 30-40 days.

In 1987, for the first time, measurements were made from aeroplanes in a joint action between the British and the American. They found that year to be the worst one on record for the ozone layer. One week in October, the layer was only 125 Dobson units, or half as thick as at the same time of the year in the mid-1970's. The Dobson unit, named after an eminent Oxford professor, provides a convenient way of expressing what the total thickness of the ozone layer would be at sea-level pressure. One Dobson unit is equal to a 10^{-5} m-deep layer of undiluted ozone at standard temperature and pressure.

Scientists have speculated in recent years about the cause of the depletion of the Antarctic stratospheric ozone in early spring. Many researchers thought that it was the consequence of burdening the stratosphere with a host of man-made compounds containing chlorine. American scientists ran the first National Ozone Experiment from their McMurdo Base in Antarctica in 1986, and their findings were consistent with these views. The findings were not consistent, however, with two other theories - those based on the solar cycle and a mechanism of upwelling air. In March 1988, a 100-man scientific committee finally concluded, based on the 1987 experiments, that it was indeed the release of CFC's into the atmosphere by humans that caused a 'hole' to open up in the ozone layer over Antarctica each spring (Farman, 1987; Isaksen, 1988).

3.22.4 The Arctic Region

Fortunately, the Arctic is unlikely to be as badly affected as the Antarctic, because the air at the northern polar region is warmer and less stable. It is in cold and stable conditions that an extensive ozone hole can form. But scientists have very little information about the air above the Arctic. They do know, however, that over the past decade there has been a decrease of at least 6% in levels of ozone in the Arctic stratosphere during January and February. Recent findings by NASA and the National Oceanic and Atmospheric Administration (NOAA), which revealed levels of chlorine compounds in the Arctic that were higher than normal, indicate that the problem may be getting worse.

Starting on New Year's day 1989, more than 200 scientists from the US and Europe joined forces in an effort to determine the extent of ozone depletion in the stratosphere above the

Arctic (Anderson, 1988). The project, involving two aircraft flying 26 flights during 6 weeks, balloons and extensive observations from the ground, was by far the largest attempt made to study the state of the ozone layer in the northern hemisphere systematically. It was of special interest to look for evidence for ozone depletion over populated areas of northern Europe, since researchers have reported an ozone hole, linked to the Antarctic hole, over southern Australia and New Zealand. Preliminary results (Pearce and Anderson, 1989) indicate that the chemistry that destroyed more than 50% of the ozone layer above Antarctica is also at work above the Arctic. But there are as yet no data to suggest that ozone is actually being destroyed in the Arctic.

3.22.5 High Northern Latitudes

Total-ozone measurements with ground-based Dobson instruments were carried out at *high* northern latitudes (Scandinavia, Northern Canada and Iceland), to follow trends before and after the latest solar cycle maximum in 1979 (Isaksen and Rohde, 1988). Two types of satellite observations, which had indicated a large ozone depletion over high northern latitudes in the same period, were proved to be wrong (drift in satellite instrumentation). A small depletion of a few percent in the winter-time total ozone in the mid- and high latitudes of the northern hemisphere was, however, verified as having occurred since 1970.

But an assessment of the possible CFC-induced breakdown of stratospheric ozone with ground- or satellite-based Dobson instrumentation is greatly complicated over industrialized regions (e.g., Europe and the U.S.A.), where tropospheric (0-15 km) ozone (less than 10% of total ozone) has greatly increased over the last decades. The observed 30-50% increase in tropospheric ozone over Europe during the latest three decades, for instance, could contribute to total ozone by an order of 2%-3%. Such an increase could mask simultaneous decreases in the stratosphere, which would otherwise have been observed by satellite- or ground-based instruments that observe *total* ozone.

Dobson observations in Scandinavia, as well as global satellite observations, indicate that total ozone increased during 1987 and 1988 at northern latitudes. This could be connected with the above-mentioned rises in tropospheric ozone resulting from industrial activities. The observed increase could also be a result of the UV effect from 11-year solar-cycle variations, but due to the large year-to-year variation in total ozone caused by meteorological processes, it will take several years to confirm this theory.

However, if the small, but consistent winter-time depletion of total ozone at northern latitudes since 1970 (except in 1987-88), which could not be attributed to known natural variations like the solar cycle, was indeed caused by CFC's (as is proved for Antarctica), it will sooner or later reach unacceptable levels, unless legislation changes CFC emissions. All data sets agree that most of the observed long-term depletion occurs in the upper stratosphere (40-45 km), precisely where CFC's are expected to have their largest effect.

The recent depletion was even 2 or 3 times greater (0.4%-0.8% per year) than can be explained by current models. A possible explanation for this is that current models do not include the particular chemical reactions that are believed to cause the Antarctic ozone 'hole', and that such processes may also occur in the high northern and the Arctic regions, although at a less pronounced rate. The previously mentioned Montreal Protocol was based on such erroneous models.

3.22.6 Effects of Depletion of Total Ozone

The depletion of stratospheric ozone over Antarctica does not in itself represent a *direct* threat to our civilization or to life on Earth. But if the same mechanisms of ozone depletion are also found to be active over the Arctic and northern latitude regions, and if the depletion keeps increasing every year, we do have cause to worry. The joking advice by former president of the United States, Ronald Reagan that "we will simply use broad-brimmed hats and sun glasses", will not suffice.

At a UNEP meeting in the Hague in October 1988, a 4% reduction in the total ozone layer over populated areas in Europe since the mid-1970's was quoted as having caused a 12% increase in human *skin cancer*. The deeper atmospheric penetration of shorter wavelengths of solar UV radiation will also profoundly alter tropospheric chemistry, and thus the air we breathe, in unpredictable ways.

3.22.7 The Future of the Ozone Layer?

The future global average ozone depletion was estimated by Isaksen and Rohde (1988), see Fig. 3.28. In case a , where we have no effective restrictions in ozone emissions, drastic reductions will occur in the ozone column during the next century. Cases b and c , based on EPA estimates following the Montreal Protocol (including or excluding bromine chemistry), demonstrate the Montreal agreement to be insufficient to control future ozone depletion. Case d assumes that all use of Freon-11 (CFC-11), Freon-12 and Freon-13 is *immediately* replaced by Freon-22, which has a much shorter atmospheric life-time, and which is mainly being oxidized in the stratosphere.

None of the cases, however, include the processes behind the dramatic ozone depletion already observed over the Antarctic. We still know too little to include these in our models.

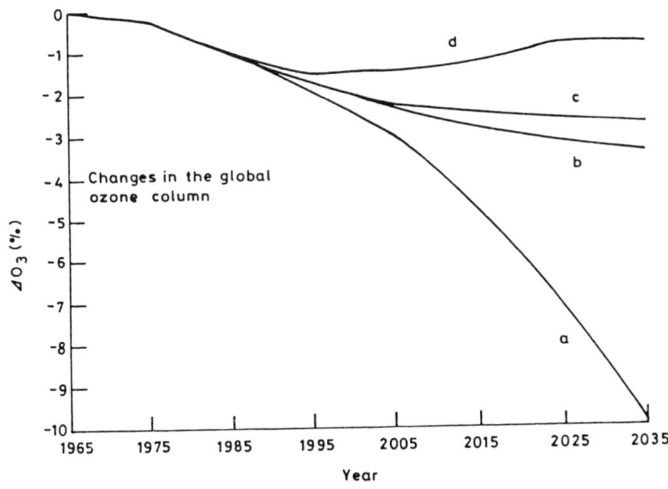

Figure 3.28. Ozone scenario; a: No restrictions, b: According to the Montreal protocol, and no regulations for Br-halocarbons, c: do., and Br banned, d: CFC-11, CFC-12 and CFC-13 also banned. - Source: Isaksen and Rohde (1988).

Because of the time it takes for the halocarbons to be transported to the stratosphere, and because of substantial amounts of CFC bound up in plastic foams and in use as refrigerants, and because of the inertia of technological change, it will at best take 10-20 years before the *increase* in CFC depletion of stratospheric ozone is terminated. And even then the Antarctic hole is predicted to persist for centuries.

It was considerations like these that made the Hague UNEP meeting in October 1988 decide that the Montreal Protocol needed rapid improvement. In March 1989, the EEC countries agreed upon stopping all CFC production before the turn of the century. There is also an urgent need to study the present and potential future biological effects of large ozone depletions like those now occurring in the Antarctic. One cannot rule out the possibility that an ozone depletion comparable to this could also develop over the north polar region, or indeed at any latitude. The fact that the recent discovery of the Antarctic ozone hole came as a complete surprise to the scientific community should serve as a warning.

3.23 NATIONAL AND INTERNATIONAL REGULATIONS, AND ABATEMENT

As early as 1909, the American Gifford Pinchot, at an international conference in the Hague, proposed the need for international cooperation regarding the use and conservation of materials (Plum, 1984*). But the two world wars delayed the matter, and little was done during the rapidly escalating pollution of the 1950's and 1960's. So the historic starting point of international cooperation on the environment came to be the previously mentioned *Stockholm Conference* in 1972 (Section 3.5.2). The conference was only partly a success, but has since been followed up by much stronger initiatives and decisions.

Today, most countries have their own set of regulations to manage air-pollution problems. Larger regions like the EEC have provisional orders common to all member states. On an even larger scale, the UN recommends principles and guidelines, e.g., the WHO's "Air Quality Guidelines for Europe" (Anonymous, 1987c). Stern (1982) reviewed the history of air-pollution legislation in the U.S.A.

3.23.1 National Regulations

National and international regulations were summarized for several countries (Denmark, England, France, Holland, Japan, Norway, Poland, Sweden, U.S.A., West Germany, East Germany, and the EEC) by Anonymous (1984*). In most of the countries studied, legislation appeared to be based solely on national considerations, with no regard to the questions of *trans-boundary* air pollution.

The quoted study found fundamental differences in the overall strategies adopted. Countries such as Denmark, England, France, E. Germany and Poland made extensive use of high stacks as a means for achieving an acceptable local air quality. On the other hand, installations in the U.S.A. were required, in principle, to comply with prescribed air-quality standards using stacks the heights of which were determined independently of emission rates. Holland, Sweden and W. Germany represented a mixture of these two approaches, requiring the use of the most advanced technology, after which the stack height was calculated on the basis of the acceptable contribution to the pollution load in the surrounding area.

Table 3.9. Selected European emission standards. - Source: Anonymous (1984).

Country	Pollutant	Emission standard
Holland, Sweden, West Germany:	SO_2	0.15 - 0.23 g/MJ
	NO_x(as NO_2)	0.27 - 0.31 g/MJ
	Particles:	0.02 g/MJ
Denmark, England, France:	SO_2	0.80 g/MJ
	NO_x(as NO_2)	0.45 g/MJ

Table 3.10. Selected air quality standards in the U.S.A. (μg m^{-3}). Primary standards are not valid in big cities, and there are no clear rules for secondary standards. TSP: total suspended particulates. - Source: Anonymous (1984).

Air-pollutant	Measuring time	Primary standard	Secondary standard
SO_2	3 hours	-	1,300
	24 hours	365	-
	1 year	80	-
NO_2	1 year	100	100
TSP	24 hours	260	150
	1 year	75	60
Lead	3 months	1.5	1.5

Table 3.11. Recent air quality standards in Denmark (μg m^{-3}), 1986-87.

Air-pollutant	Measuring time	Maximum conc.	Method of calculation
SO_2	1 year	80	median of 24 h during a year
	winter	130	median of 24 h during a winter
	24 hours	250	98% percentile of all days in a year
TSP	1 year	150	arithmetic mean of all 24 h mean values during a year
	24 hours	300	95% percentile of all 24 h mean values during a year
NO_2	1 year	200	98% fractile of all mean hour values over a year

Emission standards. Of the 11 countries mentioned above, all but East Germany and Poland applied *emission standards*, dictating the permissible emissions of SO_2, NO_2 and particulates from given installations (Table 3.9), and typically setting limits for sulfur contents in different types of fuels.

Air-quality standards. In addition to the above emission standards, all of the mentioned 11 countries except England and France applied *air-quality standards*, indicating the maximal concentrations of SO_2, NO_2, particulates and often many other substances, permitted in the air. In the U.S.A., the "National Ambient Air Quality Standards" sets a good example of strict air-quality standards (Table 3.10).

The legislation, however, keeps improving. As an example, we give the most recent Danish air-quality standards for SO_2, particulate (1986), and NO_2 (1987) in Table 3.11.

3.23.2 International Regulations

Power plants. In 1988, the EEC finally approved a motion put forward in 1983 regarding a 60% reduction in sulfur-dioxide emission and a 40% reduction in NO_x emissions from large boilers (> 50 MW). These reductions, however, turned out to be unrealistic as a *general* requirement, since some countries had newer power plants than others, and some had turned to nuclear power. Each member country thus had its own reduction requirements. In Denmark the SO_2+NO_x reductions are to be a 34%+3% decrease before 1993, a 56%+35% decrease before 1998, and 67%+35% decrease before 2003 (as compared to 1980 levels). A 35% reduction in sulfur dioxide has already (1989) been realized through improved national regulations for maximum sulfur content in fuel oil (1%), gas oil (0.2%) and coal (0.9%), and increased use of natural gas. It is a Danish goal to reduce NO_2 emissions by as much as 50% before 2005.

Automobiles. Denmark wanted 3-way-catalyzers (Gould 1989) on cars of all sizes (US standard), while the EEC majority wanted medium and small cars (2.0 l) to have only simple catalyzers (which are less efficient). After the right to veto was waived in 1988, the EEC went ahead and realized their plans from October 1989 (some countries only from 1990, and England only from the mid-90's). Denmark retained the demand for stricter standards, though a Parliamentary election delayed plans by another year (October 1990). Western European countries outside the EEC have already introduced 3-way-catalyzers on all cars. A 3-way--catalyzer removes most of the CO, NO_x and hydrocarbons emitted from petrol engines, but emissions of carbon dioxide are increased, and mileage may go down.

As yet, there are no technical solutions for cleaning the exhaust from *diesel* engines (Gould, 1989).

3.23.3 Abatement

Indoor and outdoor air pollution should primarily be abated *at the source*, i.e., by a low content of pollutants (sulfur, lead, etc.) in the fuel, by choosing the best method of combustion, by filtering emissions, by diluting emissions and by removing the pollutant from the environment.

Removing pollutants during production. The burning of coal produces ashes, and smoke filtering produces products rich in sulfur. The ashes are mostly used in the production of cement and concrete, or for land fills, roads or dams. The sulfur may either be caught in a wet process with chalk and used as gypsum in the building industry, or recycled for the chemical industry. NO_x (and NH_4) may be removed by the fluid-bed technique or selectively catalyzed to NK and water.

Removing pollutants from the environment. Ambient air pollution levels may be diminished by planting more forests. This would also help in protecting our resources of clean groundwater, and help stop the present growth of desert areas and arid climates.

Even indoors, foliage plants could help us in removing air pollutants in factories, offices and in energy-efficient homes (Wolverton et al., 1984).

3.24 WILL AND ETHICS

Cut to the bone, the problems with air pollution are related 'only' to will and ethics. 'Good ethics' demand that we leave this earth with all of its beauty and diverse life-forms to our children the way we received it from our ancestors (or better).

For two thousand years the paradigm of *humanity-over-power* has fought the dominant paradigm of *power-over-humanity*. Only if we let the former paradigm win in our civilization and in our personal lives can we solve our problems with pollution.

'Green movements' in European politics, and recent grass-root movements in the U.S.A. (Devan and Sessions, 1985) give reason for hope. But we have to do more than legislate for a clean world, we have to *live* it.

REFERENCES

Adams, R.M., Hamilton, S.A. and McCarl, B.A., 1986. The benefits of pollution control: The case of ozone and U.S. agriculture. Amer. J. Agric. Econ., 68: 886-893.

Andersen, I., 1988. First-footers to seek Arctic ozone hole. New Scientist 24/31 Dec: 4.

Anderson, R.L., Brown, H.D., Chevone, B.I. and McCartney, T.C., 1988. Occurrence of air pollution symptoms (needle tip necrosis and chlorotic mottling) on Eastern white pine in the Southern Appalachian Mountains. Plant Disease, 72: 130-132.

Anonymous, 1983. Ergebnisse der Waldschadenserhebung 1983. Allgemeine Forst Zeitschrift 38: 1381-1412.

Anonymous, 1984*. Forsuringsprojektet: Udenlandske regler og standarder. (Acidification: Foreign regulations and standards). Miljøstyrelsen, Strandgade 29, 1401 Copenhagen K.

Anonymous, 1987a. Air Pollution Control in European Metropoli. International Conference proceedings. 30/9-2/10 1987, Berlin.

Anonymous, 1987b. Ergebnisse der Waldschadenserhebung 1987 in der Bundesrepublik Deutschland. Allgemeine Forst Zeitschrift, 42: 1279.

Anonymous, 1987c. Air quality guidelines for Europe. WHO Regional Publication, European Series No. 23. Regional Office for Europe, Copenhagen.

Anonymous, 1988a. Report from the ozone and climate contact committee to Nordic Council of Ministers "Ämbetsmannakommittén". Nordic Council of Ministers, Store Strandstræde 18, Copenhagen, Denmark.

Anonymous, 1988b. Global change, IGBP report no. 4. The international geosphere-biosphere programme: A study of global change. IGBP secretariat, Royal Swedish Academy of Sciences, Box 50005, S-104 05 Stockholm, Sweden.

Anonymous, 1988c. Waldschadenserhebung 1988. Bundesministerium für Ernährung, Land wirtschaft und Forsten, the FRG.

Anonymous, 1988d. The 1987 forest damage survey in Europe. Report summary from the Economic Commission for Europe 6th. session of the Executive body for the convention on long-range transboundary air pollution. Sofia 31/10-4/11 1988.

Anonymous, 1988e. Zur Entwicklung der Waldschäden in Europa. Allgemeine Forst Zeitschrift, 43(39): 1056-1057.

Anonymous, 1989. Radiation agency notes the rising menace of radon. New Scient., 1656:31.

Bauer, F., 1985. Diagnosis and classification of new types of damage affecting forests. Special edition, Commission of the EC/ DG VI, F3 Forests and Silviculture, Brussels.

Bennett, J.H. and Hill, C., 1973. Inhibition of apparent photosynthesis by air pollutants. Journal of Environmental Quality, 2: 526-530.

Bjørnskov, L., 1989*. De danske skoves sundhedstilstand, resultater af overvågningen i 1988. (The health of Danish forests: Survey results). Skov- og Naturstyrelsen.

Blank, L.W., 1985. A new type of forest decline in Germany. Nature 314: 311-314.

Bolin, B., Döös, B. R., Jäger, J. and Warrick, R. A. (eds.),, 1986. The greenhouse effect, climatic change and ecosystems. SCOPE Report no. 29. John Wiley & Sons, Chichester.

Breloh, von P. and Dieterle, G., 1985. Ergebnisse der Waldschadenserhebung 1985. Allgemeine Forst Zeitschrift, 40: 1377-1394.

Breloh, von P. and Kirch, C., 1984. Waldschäden in der Bundesrepublik Deutschland. Allgemeine Forst Zeitschrift, 39: 1265-1301.

Cernansky, N. P., 1983. Diesel Exhaust Odour and Irritants: A Review. Journal of the Air Pollution Control Association, 33(2): 97-104.

Crawford, W.A., 1988. On air pollution, environmental tobacco smoking, radon, and lung cancer. JAPCA, 38: 1386-1391.

Dansgaard, W., 1988*. Sidste nyt om klimaændringen. (Latest news of the climatic changes). Naturens verden, 1988: 368-369.

Darrall, N.M., 1989. The effects of air pollutants on the physiological processes in plants. Plant, Cell and Environment, 12: 1-30.

Davis, D.D., 1973. Air pollution damages trees. U.S. Dept. of Agric. Forest Service NE Area, State and Private Forestry, 6816 Market Street, Upper Darby, Pennsylvania 19082, U.S.A..

Devall, B. and Sessions, G., 1985. Deep Ecology - Living as if nature mattered. Bibbs M. Smith, Inc. Utah, U.S.A.

Duchelle, S.F., Skelly, J.M., Sharick, T.L., Chevone, B.I., Yang, Y.-S. and Nellessen, J.E. (1983. Effects of ozone on the productivity of natural vegetation in a high meadow of the Shenandoah national park of Virginia. - J. Environ. Manag., 17: 299-308.

Eliassen, A., Hov, Ø., Iversen, T., Saltbones, J. and Simpson, D., 1988. Estimates of airborne transboundary transport of sulphur and nitrogen over Europe. EMEP/MSC-W, Report 1/88, Aug. 1988. The Norwegian Meteorological Institute, West (MSC-W) of EMEP.

Emanuel, W. R., Shugart, H. H., and Stevenson, M. P., 1985. Climatic change and the broad-scale distribution of terrestrial ecosystem complexes. Climatic Change 7: 29-43.

Evans, L.S., 1984a. Acidic precipitation effects on terrestrial vegetation. Annual Review of Phytopathology, 22: 397-420.

Evans, L.S., 1984b. Botanical aspects of acidic precipitation. Botanical Review, 50: 449-490.

Farman, J., 1987. What hope for the ozone layer now? New Scientist, 1586: 50-54.

Farmer, P., 1984. Acid rain and the environment 1980-84: a select bibliography. Letchworth. Information bibliographies series: 3.

Fenger, J., 1985*. Luftforurening, en introduktion. (Air pollution: an introduction). Teknisk Forlag A/S, Denmark.

Fenger, J. and Laut, P., 1989*. Drivhuseffekten. Global luftforurening og klimaændringer. (The greenhouse effect. Global air pollution and climatic change). (Preliminary report).

Gould, R., 1989. The exhausting options of modern vehicles. New Scientist, 1664: 42-47.

Grayson, L., 1988. Acid rain and the environment 1984-88: a select bibliography.

Guderian, R., 1985. Air Pollution by Photochemical Oxidants. Formation, Transport, Control, and Effects on Plants. Springer-Verlag, Berlin.

Harrington, J. B., 1987. Climatic change: A review of causes. Canadian J. Forest Res. 17, 1313-1339.

Hartmann, G., Nienhaus, F. and Butin, H., 1988. Farbatlas Waldschäden, Diagnose von Baumkrankheiten. Eugen Ulmer GmbH & Co., Stuttgart.

Hauhs, M. and Wright, R. F., 1988. Acid deposition: reversibility of soil and water acidification - a review. Commiss. of the EC/Air Pollution Res. Report 11. EUR 11633.

Heck, W. W., Taylor, O. C. and Tingey, D. T., 1988. Assessment of Crop Loss from Air Pollution. Elsevier Science Publishers Ltd., England.

Herrick, C.N., 1986. The National Acid Precipitation Assessment Program, Annual Report. NAPAP, 722 Jackson Place, NW, Washington, DC 20503, U.S.A.

Hinrichsen, D., 1986. Multiple pollutants and forest decline. Ambio, 15: 258-265.

Houghton, R.A. and Woodwell, G.M., 1989. Global climatic change. Scientific American, 260(4): 18-26.

Hutchinson, T. C. and Meema, K. M., 1987. Effects of Atmospheric Pollutants on Forests, Wetlands and Agricultural Ecosystems. NATO ASI Series G: Ecological Sciences, Vol. 16. NATO Adv. Res. Workshop at Toronto, May 12-17, 1985. Springer Verlag, Berlin.

Hällgren, J.-E., 1978. Physiological and biochemical effects of sulfur dioxide on plants. In: J.O. Nriagu (ed.): Sulfur in the Environment, part II: Ecological Impacts. John Wiley & Sons, Chichester.

Isaksen, I. S. A. and Rohde, H., 1988. Discussion paper prepared for the UNEP meeting on the ozone depletion issue. The Hague 17-18 October, 1988.

Jarvis, P. G. and Mansfield, T. A., 1981. Stomatal Physiology. Society for Experimental Biology, Seminar Series, 8. Cambridge University Press, Cambridge.

Klein, R.M. and Perkins, T.D., 1987. Cascades of causes and effects of forest decline. Ambio, 16: 86-93.

Klein, R.M. and Perkins, T.D., 1988. Primary and secondary causes and consequences of contemporary forest decline. Botanical Review, 54: 1-43.

Koziol, M. J. and Whatley, F. R., 1984. Gaseous Air Pollutants and Plant Metabolism. Papers from an International Meeting held in Oxford, August 2-5, 1982. Cambridge Univ. Press.

Kozlowski, T.T. and Constantinidou, H.A., 1986a. Responses of woody plants to environmental pollution. 1.Sources and types of pollutants and plant responses. Forestry Abstr. 47:5-51.

Kozlowski, T.T. and Constantinidou, H.A., 1986b. Environmental pollution and tree growth. 2.Factors affecting responses to pollution and alleviation of pollution effects. Forestry Abstr., 47: 105-132.

Ladwig, S., 1988. Zustand des Waldes in der Bundesrepublik Deutschland 1988. Allgemeine Forst Zeitschrift, 43: 1382-1390.

Lange, O.L., Nobel, P.S., Osmond, C.B. and Ziegler, H. (eds.), 1983. Physiological Plant Ecology IV, Ecosystem Processes: Mineral Cycling, Productivity and Man's Influence. Springer-Verlag, Berlin.

Larsen, B., 1986a. Das Tannensterben: Eine neue Hypotese zur Klärung des Hintergrundes dieser rätselhaften Komplexkrankenheit der Weisstanne (*Abies alba* Mill.). Forstw. Cbl., 105: 381-396.

Larsen, B., 1986b. Die geographische Variation der Weisstanne (*Abies alba* Mill.). Wachstumsentwicklung und Frostresistenz. Forstw. Cbl., 105: 396-406.

Larsen, B., 1987*. Skovenes sundhedstilstand - økologisk stabilitet. (The health of the forests - ecological stability). Skoven, 8: 276-279.

Lehringer, S., 1986. Ergebnisse der Waldschadenserhebung 1986 in der Bundesrepublik Deutschland. Allgemeine Forst Zeitschrift, 41: 1320-1321.

Liedeker, H., Schütt, P. and Klein, R.M., 1988. Symptoms of forest decline (Waldsterben) on Norway and red spruce. A morphological comparison in Vermont. European Journal of Forest Pathology, 18: 13-25.

Linthurst, R.A. (ed.), 1984. Direct and indirect effects of acidic deposition on vegetation. Acid Precipitation Series, vol. 5. Butterworth Publishers, London.

Lovelock, J.E., 1979. Gaia - A New Look at Life on Earth. Oxford Univ. Press, 157 pp.

Lovelock, J.E., 1988. The ages of Gaia, a bibliography of our living Earth. W.W. Norton & Co., New York.

McLaughlin, S.B., Downing, D.J., Blasing, T.J., Cook, E.R. and Adams, H.S., 1987. An analysis of climate and competition as contributors to decline of red spruce in high elevation Appalachian forests of the Eastern United States. Oecologia, 72: 487-501.

Mellanby, K., 1980. The biology of pollution, 2nd. edition. Studies in Biology no. 38. Edward Arnold Publishers Ltd., London.

Menzel, D.B., 1984. Ozone: an overview of its toxicity in man and animals. Journal of Toxicology and Environmental Health, 13(2/3): 183-204.

Meyer, A., Müller, P. and Sembdner, G., 1987. Air Pollution and Plant Hormones. Biochem. Physiol. Pflanzen, 182: 1-21.

Miller, K.R., 1979. The photosynthetic membrane. Scientific American, March 1978: 104-123.

Morrow, P.E., 1984. Toxicological data on NO<MV>x<D>: an overview. Journal of Toxicology and Environmental Health, 13(2/3): 205-227.

Moseholm, L., Andersen, B., and Johnsen, I., 1988. Acid Deposition and Novel Forest Decline in Central and Northern Europe. Final Report, Dec. 1986. Nordic Council of Ministers, Copenhagen.

Moss, M.R., 1978. Sources of sulfur in the environment, the global cycle. In: J.O. Nriagu (ed.): Sulfur in the Environment, I. The Atmospheric Cycle. J. Wiley & Sons, New York.

Mueller-Dombois, D., 1987. Natural dieback in forests. BioScience, 37: 575-583.

Nero, A.V. Jr., 1988. Controlling indoor air pollution. Scientific American, 258(5): 24-31.
Nihlgård, B., 1985. The ammonium hypothesis - an additional explanation to the forest dieback in Europe. Ambio, 14: 2-8.
Nilsson, J. and Grennfelt, P., 1988. Critical Loads for Sulphur and Nitrogen. Report from a workshop held at Skokloster, Sweden, 19-24 March, 1988. The Nordic Council of Ministers. Miljørapport 1988:15. NORD 1988:97.
Novikoff, A.B. and Holtzman, E., 1970. Cells and Organelles. Holt, Rinehart & Winston, New York.
Noyes, D.N., 1980. The comparative effects of sulfur dioxide on photosynthesis and translocation in beans. Physiological Plant Pathology, 16: 73-79.
Ormrod, D.P., 1986. Gaseous air pollution and horticultural crop production. Horticultural Reviews, Vol. 8. AVI Publishing Co.
Parry, M.L., Carter, T.R. and Konijn, N.T., 1988. The impact of climatic variations on agriculture. I: Assessment in cool temperate and cold regions. Kluwer Publ., Wageningen.
Pearce, F., 1989a. Methane locked in permafrost may hold key to global warming. New Scient., 1654: 28.
Pearce, F., 1989b. Methane: the hidden greenhouse gas. New Scientist, 1663: 37-41.
Pearce, F. and Anderson, I., 1989. Is there an ozone hole over the north pole? New Scient., 1653: 32.
Pearman, G.I. (ed.),, 1988. Greenhouse; planning for climate change. CSIRO/Brill, Leiden.
Plum, N. M., 1984*. Økologisk Håndbog. Vækst, velfærd, og økologi. (Ecological handbook. Growth, welfare and ecology). 2. ed. Christian Ejlers' Forlag, Copenhagen.
Posthumus, A.C., 1982) Biological Indicators of air pollution. In: M.H. Unsworth and D.P. Ormrod (eds.): Effects of Gaseous Air Pollution in Agriculture and Horticulture, pp. 27-42. Butterworth Scientific, London.
Prinz, B., 1987. Causes of forest damage in Europe: Major hypothesis and factors. Environment, 29(9): 10-37.
Prinz, B., 1988. Ozone effects on vegetation. In: I.S.A. Isaksen (ed.): Tropospheric Ozone, pp. 161-184. D. Reidel Publishing Co., Berlin.
Prinz, B., Krause, G.H.M., and Jung, K.-D., 1987. Development and causes of novel forest decline in Germany. In: T.C. Hutchinson and K.M. Meema (eds.): Effects of atmospheric pollutants on forests, wetlands and agricultural ecosystems, pp. 1-24. Springer Verlag, Berlin.
Rajagopal, R. and Saxe, H., 1988. Perspectives in Environmental Botany, 2: 25-71.
Rüdiger, S., 1987. Bericht für die Konferenz zur Luftreinhaltung in Europäischen Grossstädten. In: Air Pollution Control in European Metropoli, Int. Conf. in Berlin, 30/9-2/10 1987.
Saxe, H. and Andersen, A.S., 1986*. Luftforurening. (Air pollution). In: Miljøforvaltning, 4. ed., pp. 275-310. DSR Forlag, RVAU, Copenhagen.
Schulte-Holstede, S., Darrall, N.M., Blank, L.W. and Wellburn, A.R., 1988. Air Pollution and Plant Metabolism. Proc. 2nd Int. Symp. on Air Pollution and Plant Metabolism in Munich, 6-9 April, 1987. Elsevier Appl. Sci, London.
Shaw, R.W., 1987. Air pollution by particles. Scientific American, 257(2): 84-91.
Skeffington, R.A. and Wilson, E.J., 1988. Excess nitrogen deposition: Issues for

consideration. Environmental Pollution, 54: 159-184.

Smith, W.H., 1981. Air Pollution and Forests. Springer Verlag, New York.

Spengler, J.D. and Sexton, K., 1983. Indoor Air Pollution: A Public Health Perspective. Science, 221(4605): 9-17.

Stern, A.C., 1982. History of air pollution legislation in the United States. Journal of the Air Pollution Control Association, 32: 44-61.

Stolarski, R.S., 1988. The Antarctic ozone hole. Scientific American, 258(1): 20-26.

Thompson, J.E., Legge, R.L. and Barber, R.F., 1987. The role of free radicals in senescence and wounding. Tansley Review no. 8. New Phytologist, 105:317-344.

Tigerstedt, M.A., Puttonen, P. and Koski, V. (eds.), 1985. Crop Physiology of Forest Trees. Proc. Int. Conf.: Managing Forest Trees as Cultivated Plants, Finland, 23-28/7 1984.

Treshow, M., 1984. Air Pollution and Plant Life. John Wiley & Sons, Chichester.

Turco, R.P., Ackerman, T.P., Pollack, J.B. and Sagan, C., 1984. The climatic effects of nuclear war. Scientific American, 251(2): 23-33.

Ulrich, B. and Pankrath, J. (eds.), 1983. Effects of accumulation of air pollutants in forest ecosystems. D. Reidel Pub. Co., Dordrecht, FRG.

Unsworth, M.H. and Ormrod, D.P., 1982. Effects of Gaseous Air Pollution in Agriculture. Butterworth Scientific, London.

Vogelmann, H.W., Perkins, T.D., Badger, G.J. and Klein, R.M., 1988. A 21-year record of forest decline on Camels Hump, Vermont, U.S.A. Eur. J. Forest Pathology, 18: 240-249.

Waller, R.E., 1987. Urban air pollution and health, the changing scene. In: Air Pollution Control in European Metropoli. Proc. Int. Conf. 30/9-2/10 1987, Berlin.

Wellburn, A., 1988. Air pollution and acid rain: the biological impact. Longman Scientific & Technical, England. 274 pp.

Wolters, J.H.B. and Martens, M.J.M., 1987. Effects of Air Pollutants on Pollen. The Botanical Review, 53: 372-414.

Wolverton, B.C., McDonald, R.C. and Watkins, E.A., Jr., 1984. Econ. Botany, 38: 224-228.

Woodman, J.N., 1987. Pollution-induced injury in North American forests: facts and suspicions. Tree Physiology, 3: 1-15.

ACKNOWLEDGMENTS

The production of this chapter was made possible through support from The National Forest and Nature Agency and from The Danish Agricultural and Veterinary Research Council. For proof-reading I sincerely thank I. Møller, R. Rajagopal and B. Saxe.

4 WATER POLLUTION

LARS KAMP NIELSEN

4.1 THE MANAGEMENT OF SURFACE WATERS

Water is a universal solvent and it transports dissolved and particulate matter at all levels, from inside the cell to organisms, from ecosystems to continents and oceans. Due to its abundance - water is the most abundant chemical compound on earth - and its properties, water is very extensively used by mankind. But the different uses affect both the quality and the quantity of the available water and the management of water pollution, and water resources play an important role in both national and international politics.

Examples of the various uses of water and their effects are listed in Table 4.1. Practically all these uses create conflicts with each other, and historically there are many examples of wars with a background in a conflict on access to the use of water for one or more of the listed uses - 'rivals' means 'those who share a river'. To solve these conflicts in a peaceful manner various strategies and measures can be implemented. The principles involved in the most important among these strategies are listed in Table 4.2.

The selection of strategy involves considerations of: effectiveness in relation to the environment, administrative complexity and costs, conflicts with legislative practice in adjacent areas, consequences for planning and localization, and many other possible problems. In practice the management of water pollution is most often a compromise with elements from all the various strategies, and the measures are laid down in several different legislations (cf. Chapter 10).

Table 4.1. The utilization of surface waters and the potential pollution consequences.

Utilization	Potential problems
Drinking water and irrigation	Reduced flow and reduced water level in dry periods. Concentration of polluting substances.
Fishing	Change in biological structure. Damage to benthic flora and fauna. Increased resuspension by trawling.
Hydroelectric power	Increased amplitudes in water flow and water level. Reduced migration of fish. Changes in sedimentation pattern.
Navigation	Oil spills. Disturbance of fish and birds.
Aquaculture	Pollution with organic matter, nutrients and antibiotics. Introduction of diseases among the natural fish populations.
Recipient of waste water	Pollution with organic matter, nutrients and toxic substances.
Cooling	Temperature increase. Increased turnover of biotic and abiotic components. Changes in biological structure.
Recreation	Disturbance of fauna and destruction of littoral plant communities. Pollution from littering.

Table 4.2. Strategies for the management of water pollution.

Strategy		Measures
'Zero discharge'		Ban on import and use.
Source-oriented:	Quota assessment	Legislation (possibility for tradeable quotas).
	Percentage reduction of emission	Legislation with time schedules.
	Best available technology	Negotiable planning. Taxes and/or subsidies.
Recipient-oriented:	Recipient quality planning	Planning and legislation.
	Percentage reduction of immission	Legislation with time schedules.

In Denmark the pollution of surface water and groundwater is regulated by the following pieces of legislation:

Environmental Protection Act,
Watercourse Act,
Nature Conservation Act,
Action Plan for the Aquatic Environment.

These laws and plans of action are supplemented with a great number of statutes, statutory orders, circulars, and guidelines. The overall principle of Danish legislation in the area is the Recipient Quality Planning (Fig. 4.1), by which the regional authorities, the *county councils*, set the quality standard for each water body - stream, lake or coastal water. This is done on the basis of (1) studies of the prerequisites and the possibilities of the recipient, (2) socio-economic consequence analysis, and (3) a public hearing.

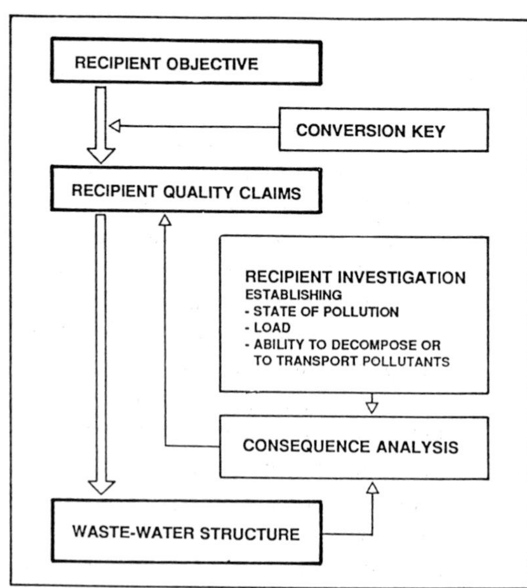

Figure 4.1. The recipient-planning process. - After Anonymous (1983*).

Table 4.3. The objective system. - After Anonymous (1983*).

Objective	Extended (A)	General (B)	Reduced (C)
Water-courses	Watercourses covered by particular scientific interests	Watercourses with - spawning and fry grounds for salmonids (B_1) - salmonid water (B_2) - cyprinid water (B_3)	Watercourses essentially influenced by (C_1): - waste water - groundwater extraction - other physical interventions Watercourses influenced by ochre (C_2)
Lakes	Lakes covered by particular scientific interests (A_1) Lakes with: - bathing-water areas (A_2) - unfiltered water for public supply (A_3)	Lakes with a natural and diverse animal and plant life	Lakes influenced by (C_1): - waste water - groundwater extraction - other physical interventions Lakes with a loading from agriculture (C_2)
Coastal waters	Coastal waters covered by particular scientific interests such as: - marine botany/zoology - water-bird area - seal area Coastal waters covered by fishery interests such as: - fry grounds - pound-net fishery - other fishery - oyster and mussel catch - storing of live fish Coastal waters used for bathing Coastal waters with a natural oxygen depletion	Coastal waters where the fauna and the flora have been influenced only slightly, and where the hygienic conditions are good	Recipient coastal waters: - waste-water outlet nearby - power-plant nearby - grazing areas nearby - loaded by agriculture - fish-farming area - refuse dump Coastal waters used by the shipping trade in connection with: - commercial harbour - laying-up area Coastal waters used for the extraction of raw materials such as: - boulders - sand and pebble gravel - shells Coastal waters included by temporary or permanent construction

The recipient quality plan serves as a framework within which the local authorities, the *municipal councils*, are responsible for the development of a master plan for sewage treatment, sewer structure and point-source emissions from industry in the total catchment area of the recipient. The recipient-quality standards are translated into water-quality parameters, and a control programme shared by the two authorities is set up before implementation of the plan. An amendment of the Environmental Protection Act in 1983 linked the recipient quality planning more closely to the general physical planning, together with the other regional planning acts.

The recipient quality objectives are in principle a compromise between the natural preconditions of the considered body of water and the requirements from other sectorial plans. The objectives can be, for example, water for drinking, irrigation and cooling; recreational demands and nature conservation; research and reference uses; or commercial interests such as navigation, agriculture, fishing and mining. The term 'recipient' emphasizes the interests in using the water body as a receiver of pollutants.

The quality objectives are divided into 3 categories:

a) extended criteria,
b) general criteria,
c) reduced criteria.

The criteria for the various categories for each type of surface water are shown in Table 4.3. As an overall objective the aim of the planning is that most recipients should be placed in categories a) and b) and very few in category c); but especially the diffuse and uncontrollable discharges from agriculture, the difficulties in the surveillance and control in open marine areas and the complicated and time-consuming planning procedure in relation to rapidly increasing pollution problems have necessitated supplementary action plans.

In theory, the recipient planning is a policy with a high planning potential and a high degree of public participation through a decentralized interaction between the users of water. And, very important for a sustainable exploitation of the water resources, the procedure allows for a frequent revision of the criteria and of the connected planning.

For many of the users of water almost the only important characteristic of water is its *quantity*, e.g., for navigation, cooling, irrigation, hydropower and as a recipient and conveyor of pollutants. For other uses the *quality* is very important, e.g., for drinking, fishing, and recreation. The quality requirements are generally met when the recipient has a natural flora and fauna, and fewer conflicts between the various users occur when rivers, lakes and coastal waters are in a sound ecological balance.

4.2 AQUATIC ECOLOGY

As reflected in the recipient quality criteria, the ecological balance is an overall quality parameter satisfying most of the requirements for the use of surface waters, and biological indicators are widely used as planning and control parameters. Due to the qualifications needed for identification and quantification of organisms, the biological parameters are often substituted by or supplemented with relevant physical and chemical parameters, but the relevance of these must be based on sound basic and applied ecological research.

A balanced aquatic ecosystem consists of autotrophic and heterotrophic organisms in a structural and functionally stable relationship with the surrounding abiotic environment.

In terrestrial ecosystems the physical organization of the autotrophs is important, since water is a major controlling factor for the primary production. A great proportion of the photosynthetic energy is devoted to structures and mechanisms for the conservation and storage of water. Other important factors for terrestrial production are temperature, nutrients, and herbivory.

In aquatic ecosystems, less energy is devoted to the physical structure and the controlling or limiting factors appear in a somewhat different order of priority: water transparency, nutrients, temperature and herbivory. The much smaller investment in structure leads to a much faster turnover rate of the primary producers in aquatic ecosystems compared to terrestric systems.

A stable ecosystem requires a balance between production and decomposition of organic matter, and since oxygen is needed for an efficient decomposition, but is produced by the primary production only, the oxygen regime expresses the balance between the autotrophic and heterotrophic components.

In terrestrial ecosystems the balance itself has no feedback control on the ecosystem due to the buffering by the vast oxygen reserve in the atmosphere. But in the aquatic environment including waterlogged soils, the oxygen easily goes into a deficit due to the low solubility in water (10 mg O_2 l^{-1} at 15°C) and the slow diffusion rate of oxygen in water (10 000 times slower than in air).

Since oxygen is the ultimate controlling factor of the ecological balance in aquatic systems, most of the important water pollution problems refer to the balance between internal production of organic matter and external loading with organic materials on the one hand and the consumption of oxygen and the air-water equilibrium on the other. Other impacts such as physical disturbances, toxic substances and exploitations of abiotic and biotic resources affect the structures and functions of the ecosystem and thereby also the oxygen balance. Consequently, prerequisites for the management and control of water pollution are studies on (1) the loading and transport of organic matter, nutrients and toxic substances, (2) the metabolization and fate of these substances and (3) the structural and functional relationships between and within biotic and abiotic compartments.

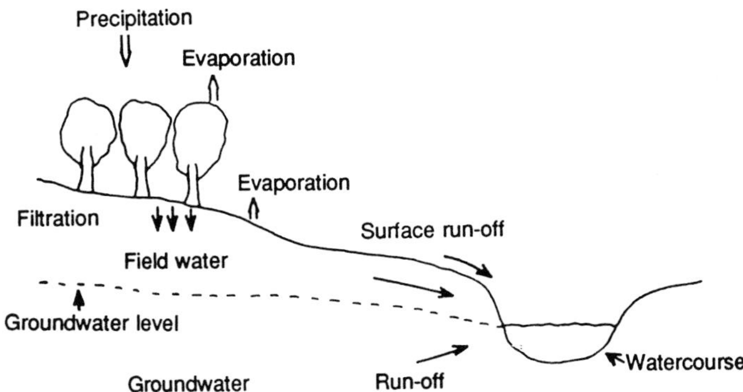

Figure 4.2. Water exchange between atmosphere, soil, and watercourses. The precipitation surplus from the soil is transported as run-off to the watercourse, with contributions from the surface, from fields and from groundwater. - After Jensen et al. (1988*).

Table 4.4. Characteristic waterflow data from Danish watercourses. Figures are specific waterflow in l sec^{-1} km^{-2}. - After Moth Iversen et al. (1989*).

Watercourse	Period	Max.	Median max.	Mean	Median min.	Min.
Jutland:						
Ribe Å, Staunager	1933-1970	69	37	11.6	3.7	2.5
Skjern Å, Ålergård	1924-1970	80	35	13.5	7.5	4.0
Gudenå, Åstedbro	1917-1970	127	37	11.6	4.4	2.7
Uggerby Å, Åstedbro	1917-1970	146	50	10.1	2.5	1.3
Fyn:						
Brende Å, Årup	1919-1970	82	45	7.9	0.3	0.01
Sealand:						
Tryggevælde Å, Lille Linde	1917-1970	126	62	6.6	0.3	0.02
Harrested Å, Møllebro	1921-1970	119	49	5.7	0.3	0.00
Værbækken, Falkensten	1928-1970	233	52	4.9	0.0	0.00
Bornholm:						
Bagå, Sorthat	1920-1970	250	92	7.4	0.6	0.2

4.2.1 The Hydrological Cycle

The major conveyor of dissolved and particulate matter to and within aquatic ecosystems is water, and a properly estimated water balance is needed in all water pollution studies. As described in Chapter 5 one third of the precipitation is left for river discharge on a global scale. The excess precipitation discharges to the streams by surface run-off, bypass from the field storage, by drainage pipes or as seepage from the groundwater (Fig. 4.2).

Within rather small distances, variations in specific run-off (mm yr^{-1} = 0.0327 l km^{-2} sec^{-1}) occur due to variations in precipitation, evaporation and infiltration capacity (Table 4.4).

Soil composition, vegetation cover, microclimate, slope, and field storage influence both the evaporation loss and the distribution between the run-off mechanisms.

The amplitudes in annual variations (Fig. 4.3) reflect the various run-off patterns: In drainage areas with high infiltration capacities (sandy soils) and low storage capacities, the evaporation loss is low and groundwater seepage is the dominant run-off. The run-off is buffered by the groundwater reservoir and the seasonal variations are small. In clayish moraine soils with steeper slopes the infiltration is low and the evaporation is high, resulting in a relatively low run-off, but with high amplitudes due to the dominance of surface and bypass discharges.

4.3 WATERCOURSES

Streams start as springs, small groundwater-fed channels or outlets from lakes. Moving down an ideal stream the slope and the velocity decrease and change the stream from an eroding to a depositing watercourse, reflected in a change from a stony bottom to a fine-grained sediment (Fig. 4.4).

For a constant specific run-off, the discharge volume and water depth are increasing and they buffer the temperature changes. If the stream starts as a groundwater-fed well, the temperature regime develops as shown in Fig. 4.5.

The current velocity $\bar{v}$ in a channel-shaped stream is given by:

$$\bar{v} = \frac{1}{n} R^{2/3} s^{1/2}, \tag{4.1}$$

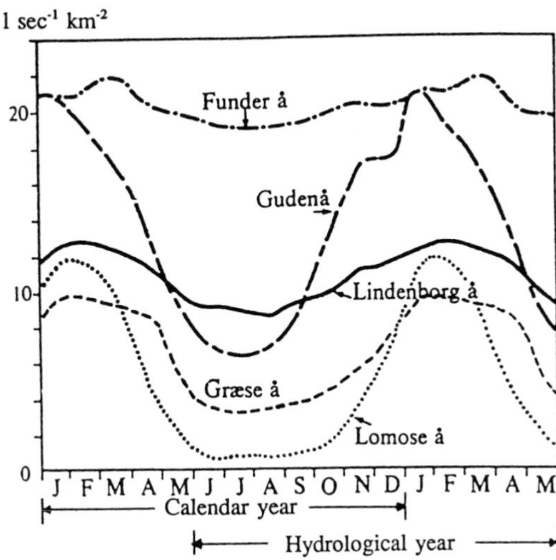

Figure 4.3. Normal annual variations in run-off for five Danish watercourses. After Anonymous (1990*).

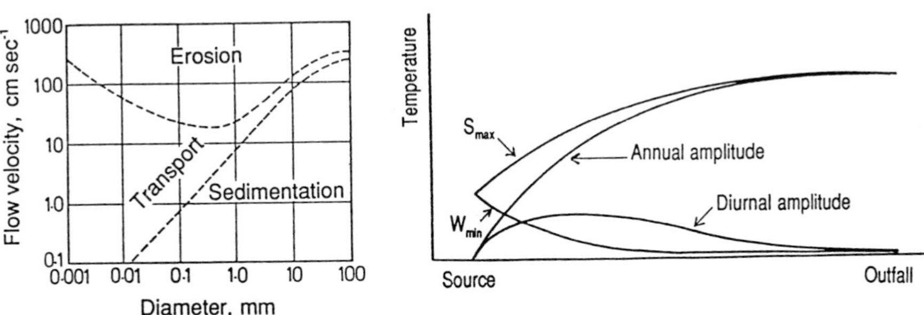

Figure 4.4. (Left) Inorganic particles: The relation between flow velocity and erosion/sedimentation. - Source: Moth Iversen et al. (1990*).

Figure 4.5. (Right) Course of maximal summer temperature (S_{max}), minimal winter temperature (W_{min}), and annual and diurnal temperature amplitudes downstream in an ideal watercourse. - Source: Moth Iversen et al. (1990*).

where n is a friction constant (Manning number, or rouhgness), s is the slope, and R is the hydraulic radius of a cross section, in relation to the 'wet' perimeter. For a rectangular profile the latter quantity is given by:

$$R = \frac{d \times w}{2d + w}, \tag{4.2}$$

where d is the average depth and w is the average width. The velocity can be measured with a calibrated propeller ('Ott-propeller') at several points of a cross section and an average can be calculated. The discharge Q is found by multiplying the average current velocity $\bar{v}$ by the cross-section area A , i.e., $Q = \bar{v} \times A$. A better measure with respect to transport is the transport velocity, which is estimated as the transport velocity of a dye tracer.

Often a continuous registration of the discharge is needed. For a given stream section an empirical relation exists between the water level H and the discharge Q . The water level can be recorded automatically by a hydrometric station, and by use of the Q/H-relation the discharge can be estimated. However, in streams where the water level is raised due to growth of macrophytes, which reduces the current velocity and thereby increases the cross section, the Q/H-relation has to be modified for the various degrees of vegetation cover (Fig. 4.6).

The average current velocity changes over the year with changes in discharge and the resulting increases in hydraulic radius and slope.

Most autotrophic organisms and most invertebrates in streams live at solid surfaces and only for short periods do they move freely in the water. Consequently, the very local current becomes important for the supply of nutrients, food particles and oxygen. The current decreases, the closer are solid surfaces and the water-air interface (Fig. 4.7). The vertical transport is normally not a problem, since the water movement changes from laminar (unidirectional) to turbulent flow already at velocities above 1 mm s^{-1}.

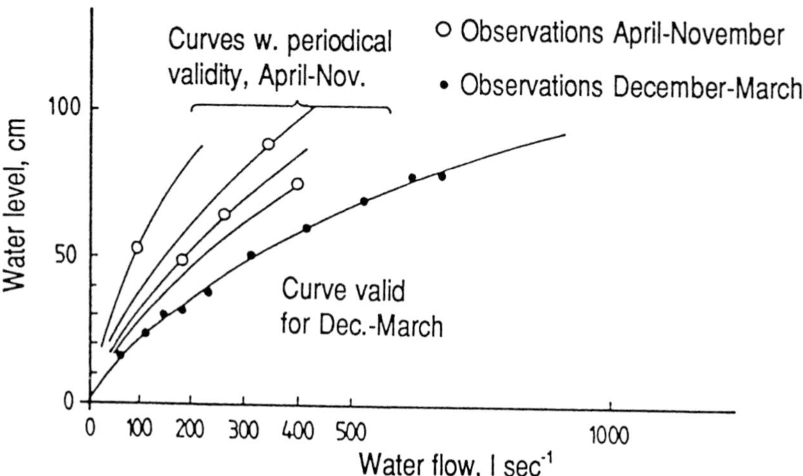

Figure 4.6. The relation between water level and flow-rate in a watercourse with no macrophytes in winter. - After Moth Iversen et al. (1990*).

As in most terrestrial ecosystems, direct grazing of plants (herbivory) only plays a minor role in the energy balance in streams. Most of the energy input comes from external sources in the form of dead organic matter, or it is derived from upstream sections (allochthonous input). Only a minor part is produced at the site in the stream (autochthonous input). The allochthonous matter is divided into Coarse Particulate Organic Matter (CPOM) with particle diameters > 1 mm and Fine Particulate Organic Matter (FPOM) with diameters < 1 mm; the latter is further divided into material of terrestrial origin (FPOM 1) and material of upstream origin (FPOM 2). The relative import of the various particle fractions along an ideal stream is shown in Fig. 4.8. Even if the stream is surrounded by forest along all its stretches, the import decreases downstream, since the import is determined by the ratio of the bank length to the stream-surface area.

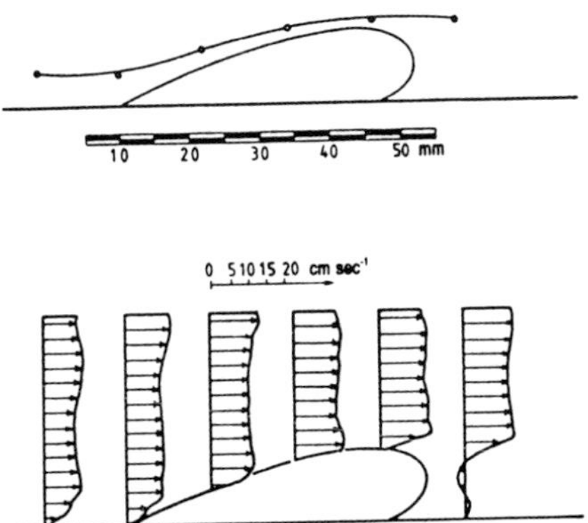

Figure 4.7. Flow conditions around a stone, as measured in an experiment. Arrows indicate flow direction and flow velocity. Above: position and thickness of the boundary surface. - After Moth Iversen et al. (1990*).

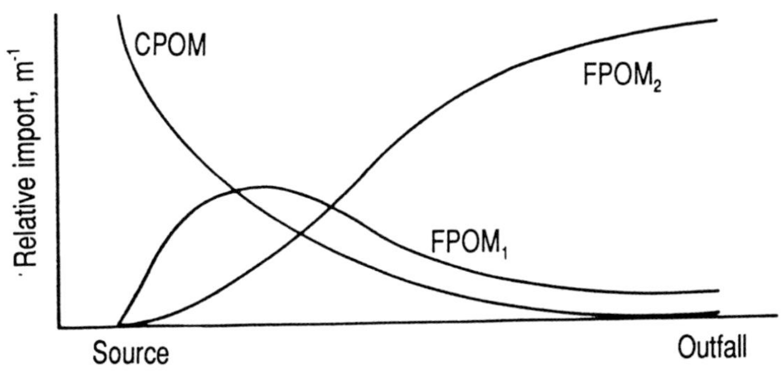

Figure 4.8. Relative import of allochthont, i.e., particulate organic matter, down along the ideal watercourse. CPOM = crude particles of organic matter (leaves, branches, etc.); $FPOM_1$ = fine particles from terrestrial CPOM; $FPOM_2$ = fine particles from algae and macrophytes produced upstream. - Source: Moth Iversen et al. (1990*).

4.3.1 The Autotrophic Components

The relative importance of the various autotrophic components downstream in an ideal watercourse is shown in Fig. 4.9. Along the upper parts with high current velocities, only attached vegetation is important, and the relation between microbenthic algae and macrophytes is determined by the penetration of light. In the upper reaches, and in early summer even in the lower ones, the microbenthic algae are dominant. But in the competition for light, the rooted macrophytes win later in the summer, shading out the microbenthic algae. In the lower stretches of big rivers the development of free floating phytoplankton is possible, provided there are sources such as lakes or stagnant river sections.

The microbenthic algae serve as food for many invertebrates and some vertebrates: snails, mayfly larvae, and fish (chichlids). The macrophytes are not directly so important as food items, but they have many indirect effects on the energy balance: decrease of current velocity and increase of sedimentation, forming substrate for biofilms and invertebrates, providing both concealment and shelter for fish and ousting the microbenthic algae by shading. As previously pointed out, light is the most important controlling factor of the autotrophic components, but nutrients can play a role in the competition within both microbenthos and macrophytes. For instance, many observations suggest that a mass occurrence of filamentous macroalgae such as *Cladophora* is a result of increased phosphorus loading.

4.3.2 The Heterotrophic Components

The current velocity and the supply of food and oxygen determine directly and indirectly the abundance and distribution of invertebrates and fish in water courses. The unidirectional flow restricts the fauna to substrate-attached invertebrates and strong, swimming fish species.

The adaptations to running water include: form resistance (being flat, having claws, building heavy shelters), physiologically conforming respiration (oxygen-concentration-dependent respiration) and a dominance of species utilizing allochthonous food import.

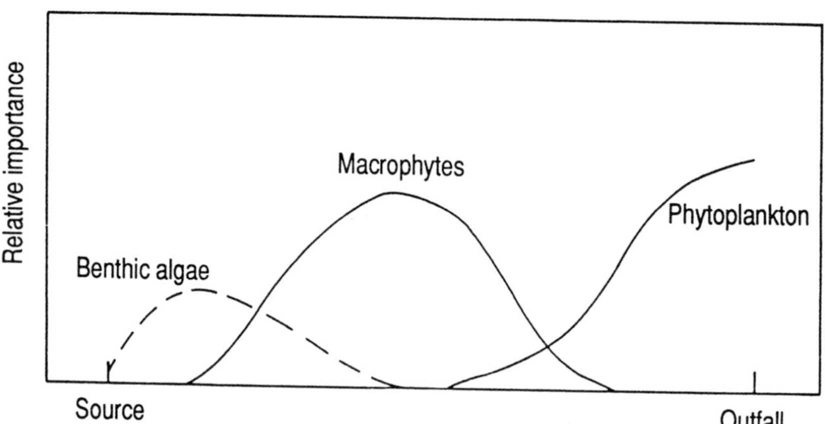

Figure 4.9. Relative importance of autotrophic organisms for the transformation of energy in the ideal watercourse. - Source: Moth Iversen et al. (1990*).

Figure 4.10 shows the important feeding types downstream an ideal watercourse. In the upper reaches, where the dominant organic material is CPOM and FPOM 1 from the surroundings and microbenthic algae (cf. Figs. 4.8 and 4.9), the dominant fauna is shredders (1), which fragmentize the coarse particles and produce fine particles for the filter feeders (3); together with these two feeding types the scrapers (2) are important, scraping off the microbenthic algae; and hierarchically above all these consumers, the carnivores (5) live. In such small streams the substrate is coarse and the current velocity high, allowing trout to spawn and their eggs to develop, buried in the gravel.

Further downstream the shading of trees decreases, and the microbenthic algae increase in importance, and so do the scrapers. The accumulating sediments stimulate the detritivorous invertebrates (4). In this zone the adult trouts thrive, together with other salmonid fishes.

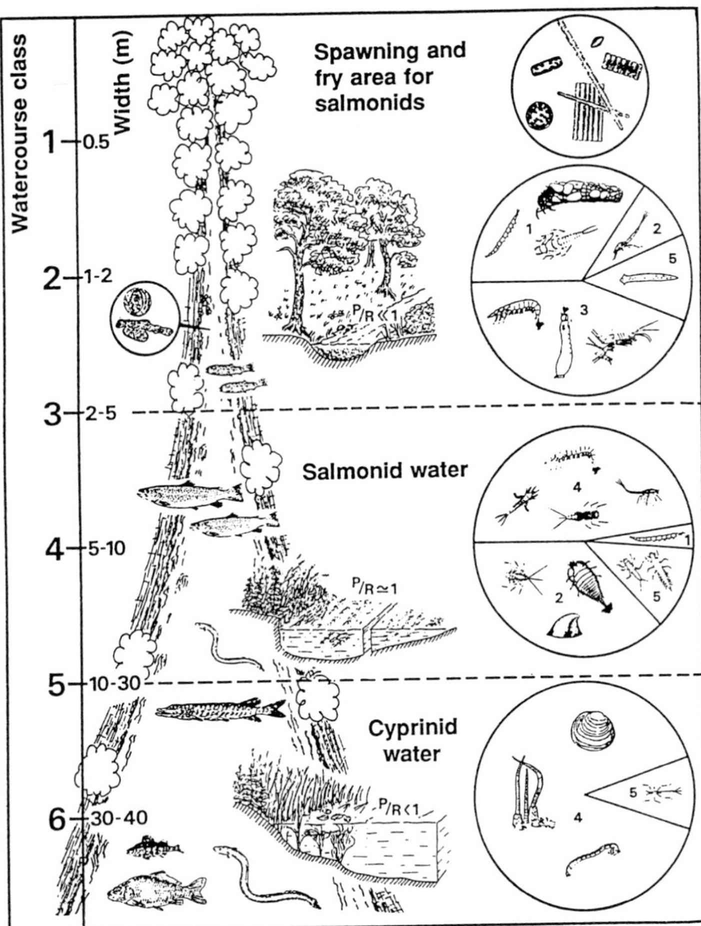

Figure 4.10. Course of the flora and fauna downstream in an ideal watercourse. - After Anonymous (1990*).

Table 4.5. Biomass B (g org. matter m^{-2}) and production P (g org. matter m^{-2} $year^{-1}$) of the invertebrate fauna in three different watercourses. The figures are distributed over functional feeding categories. - For detailed references, see Moth Iversen et al. (1990*).

	Rold Kilde DK		Suså 1979/80 DK (Vetterslev)		River Thames GB	
	P	B	P	B	P	B
primary consumers:						
tearers	5.3	2.3	1.9	0.4	-	-
scrapers	0.13	0.04	31.7	0.6	2.8	2.8
sediment eaters	2.6	0.9	33.5	5.1	4.3	0.6
filtrators, passive	< 0.01	< 0.01	25.6	1.5	-	-
filtrators, active	-	-	0.8	0.8	21.4	44.7
total:	8.0	3.2	93.5	8.4	28.5	48.1
predators, total:	0.9	0.4	5.3	1.2	0.4	0.2

In the lower reaches the sediment accumulation increases further, and the oxygen becomes scarcer, reflected in a decreased photosynthesis/respiration ratio. The detritivores become dominant and the frequently high biomass also stimulates specialized carnivores. The fish fauna will be dominated by carp fishes which can tolerate lower oxygen concentrations.

Table 4.5 shows the quantitative distribution of biomass and production for the various feeding types in three watercourses. The life cycles in the upper reaches are long (2-3 years) due to low summer temperatures and low-quality food for the shredders. In the mid reaches the life cycles are short during summer (a few weeks), favoured by high temperatures and high-quality food from biofilms on macrophytes. In the lower reaches the food supply from accumulated sediments is more constant, the life cycles are again longer, and the growth is slower.

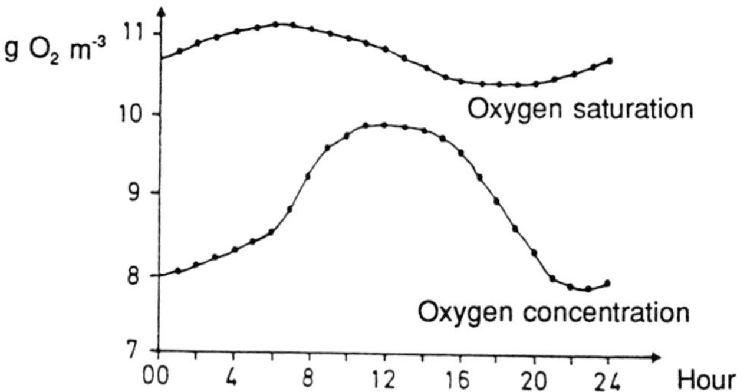

Figure 4.11. Diurnal variation in concentration of dissolved oxygen and in oxygen saturation (estimated theoretically at the temperatures measured). Data from the Danish river Gryde Å. After Anonymous (1986*).

4.3.3 The Oxygen Balance

The balance between oxygen production and oxygen consumption regulates, together with reaeration, the oxygen concentration in streams. An oxygen balance is a valuable tool for the description of the energy metabolism and how the pollution with organic matter affects the oxygen regime and thereby the ecological balance. The change in oxygen concentration over time for a given stream is estimated by measuring the concentration in the upstream endpoint and the concentration in the downstream terminal point a residence time later:

$$\frac{dC}{dt} = \frac{C_1 - C_2}{t_W} \quad \text{g } O_2 \text{ m}^{-3} \text{ time}^{-1} , \tag{4.3}$$

where C_1 is the oxygen concentration in g O_2 m^{-3} at the upstream terminal point, C_2 is the concentration at the downstream terminal point, and t_w is the residence time.

This net change is the sum of the oxygen provided by the autotrophic gross production and reaeration, subtracting the sum of oxygen-consuming processes such as plant respiration, bacterial respiration, vertebrate and invertebrate respiration, nitrification, and chemical oxidation. Since gross photosynthesis changes with insolation, the oxygen concentration shows a characteristic diurnal variation (Fig. 4.11).

The reaeration depends on temperature and the concentration gradient:

$$\frac{dC}{dt} = K_2(20°C) \times 1.024^{(temp(t) - 20)} \times (C_m(t) - C(t)) , \tag{4.4}$$

where K_2 is the reaeration constant at 20°C, temp(t) is the temperature, $C_m(t)$ is the saturation concentration for oxygen, and $C(t)$ is the actual concentration of oxygen. For some Danish streams the following relation holds between K_2 and the hydraulic parameters:

$$K_2(20°C) = 37406 \, \bar{v}^{0.846} \, \bar{d}^{-0.672} \, s^{1.154} , \tag{4.5}$$

where $\bar{v}$ is the average current velocity (m s^{-1}), $\bar{d}$ is the average water depth, and s is the slope (m m^{-1}). The value of K_2 in Danish streams ranges from 1 to 10 d^{-1}.

In big rivers and outlets from lakes, where phytoplankton is the dominating autotrophic component, the fate of oxygen can be simplified in the classical *Streeter-Phelps* equation:

$$\frac{dC}{dt} = K_1L - K_2(C_m(t) - C(t)) , \tag{4.6}$$

where L is the concentration of degradable organic matter, and K_1 is the first-order degradation constant for L . This simple equation has the advantage that a loading with organic material can be directly incorporated in the oxygen balance, but in small macrophyte-dominated streams the oxygen consumption by the sediment and the production and consumption of oxygen by the macrophytes dominate the oxygen balance, as seen in the example from the Danish Suså river (Table 4.6).

Descriptive models for the diurnal variation are relatively simple to establish, provided the sediment composition and macrophyte biomass are constant over time. Predictive models for entire seasons or years are complicated and they require the prediction of hydraulic parameters, sediment transport or accumulation, and many other parameters.

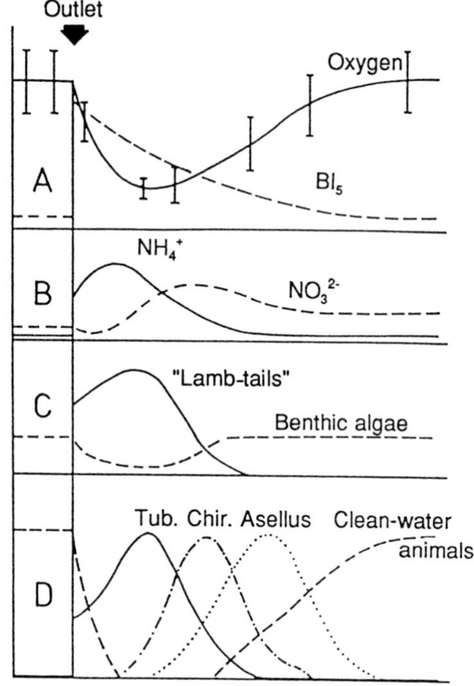

Figure 4.12. The effect of an outlet of municipal waste water in a small, fast-flowing brook in summer. A: Mean concentrations of oxygen and BI_5, and diurnal variation of the oxygen concentration. B: Mean concentrations of ammonium and nitrate. C: Biomasses of 'lamb-tails' and benthic algae. D: Relative densities of various groups of invertebrates (Tub. = *Tubificidae*; Chir. = *Chironomus* sp.). - Source: Moth Iversen et al. (1990*).

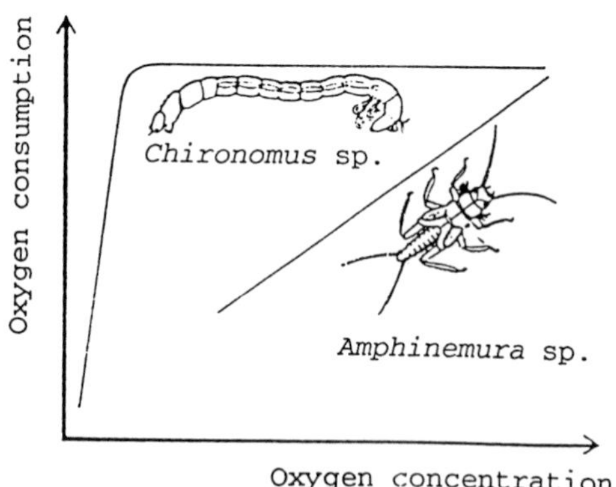

Figure 4.13. The gnat *Chironomus* sp. lives in polluted watercourses; the stone fly *Amphinemura* sp. lives in clean watercourses. The figure shows oxygen uptake as a function of oxygen concentration for the two insects. - After Moth Iversen et al. (1990*).

Table 4.6. Oxygen consumption in two Danish watercourses, distributed over sediment, water, and macrophytes. The degree of macrophyte coverage was estimated on a scale ranging from 0.0 to 1.0. - After Moth Iversen et al. (1990*).

	Oxygen consumption in the watercourse mg O_2 m^{-2} h^{-1}	% of total oxygen consumption			Macrophyte-coverage degree
		sediment	water	macroph.	
Suså, at Pindsobro					
July 26	830	45	1	54	0.5
August 15	300	78	3	19	0.2
August 30	310	65	2	33	0.2
September 27	120	99	1	0	0.0
Sneslev Lilleå					
August 10	350	34	2	64	0.6
August 30	240	53	2	45	0.4
October 13	300	53	1	46	0.3

4.3.4 Effects of Organic Pollution

The effect of the discharge of degradable organic material into a stream depends on the amount in relation to the flow in the stream, and on the biological structure of the stream. Also the time pattern of the discharge plays a role - the biological community can more readily tolerate a short pulse of pollutants than a continuous discharge with a lower concentration.

For an ideal watercourse with a discharge of municipal sewage in its upper reaches, the changes downstream in concentration of biologically degradable organic matter expressed as the so-called BOD (Biological Oxygen Demand) decreases exponentially and the oxygen concentration shows a minimum at some distance downstream of the outlet (Fig. 4.12). Ammonia nitrogen from the mineralization of organic nitrogen has a maximum, but it is nitrified, and an increased nitrate concentration thus appears further downstream (B). The microbial flora downstream of the discharge is dominated by feather-like or lambtail-like colonies of bacteria, fungi and protozoans with the bacteria *Sphaerotilus* dominant. Further downstream microbenthic algae take over (C). The macroinvertebrate fauna shows a characteristic succession pattern with species with the lowest demands for oxygen showing a maximum, where the oxygen has its minimum concentration. Moving downstream, species with higher demands for oxygen take over (D).

The most pollution-tolerant species are often coloured red, since they contain haemoglobin and, therefore, can maintain their oxygen uptake at lower oxygen tensions compared to cleanwater species (Fig. 4.13). Downstream of an organic-matter discharge we often find high densities of macroinvertebrates due to the high amount of food. The organic matter is consumed by microorganisms and invertebrates, and together with the normally occurring dilution, a 'self-purification' process allows the natural fauna to reestablish itself at some distance downstream.

Table 4.7. Saprobic index: Examples of the indicator value G, the distribution of the 10 points over pollution degrees, and the average value of the index s. - After Moth Iversen and Lindegaard (1988*).

		G	I	II	III	IV	s
Pollution indicator	*Eristalis*	5				10	4.0
	Psychoda	5				10	4.0
Pollution dominants	*Tubificidae*	4		1	3	6	3.5
	Chironomus	5		1	5	4	3.3
	Asellus	5		2	8		2.8
Clean-water animals	*Gammarus*	3	4	5	1		1.7
	Leuctra	2	3	5	2		1.9
	Protonemura	5	9	1			1.1
	Ephemera	3	5	4	1		1.6
Indifferent forms	*Corixa*	1	2	6	2		2.0
	Platambus	1	2	7	1		1.9

Streams are very dynamic systems with significant diurnal and seasonal variations in current velocity, temperature and oxygen concentrations. Therefore, the surveillance of the ecological state is difficult and costly if only chemical and physical parameters are measured, and a short pulse of pollutants from a point source can easily escape detection. An integrated measure for the total impact of pollutants is provided by the qualitative and quantitative composition of the biological communities. The selection of organisms for biological monitoring of pollution must include the following considerations: What parameters influence the various organisms? What are their life cycles? How long must a period of impact be, to be reflected in their abundance? Are the organisms easy and fast to identify? What are the purposes of the analysis? What are the costs?

Originally, ciliates were used as indicator organisms, but they are difficult to identify and have a short life cycle. In Eastern Europe benthic algae are used, but since they are very sensitive to incident light, their use is limited to shade-free localities. Fish are not well suited, on account of their mobility. In most of Western Europe macroinvertebrates are used for the surveillance of watercourses, and together with physical and chemical parameters, macroinvertebrate indices form the background for both planning, control and restoration of watercourses.

4.3.5 Biological Indices

At the start of the century Kolkwitz and Marsson developed a classification scheme for the pollution state of rivers based on observations that certain organisms appeared at the same degree of pollution - some were found only in unpolluted rivers, others were found only in strongly polluted waters. In its present form this so-called *saprobic system* identifies four degrees of pollution:

oligosaprobic (I),
b-mesosaprobic (II),
a-mesosaprobic (III),
polysaprobic (IV).

Each species found is given an average saprobic value, s, by distributing 10 points over the four pollution degrees; species with a broad distribution have their 10 points distributed evenly over all the degrees, while species with an ecologically narrow distribution might have all their 10 points in one or two degrees. The average value of s is found by multiplying the number of points from each degree by 1, 2, 3, and 4, respectively, and dividing the sum by 10. To allocate a higher weight to species with a narrow ecological distribution, each species is given an indicator value ranking from 1 to 5. Finally, the relative abundance of each species is calculated, and the saprobic value S for the sampling site can be estimated:

$$S = \frac{\Sigma\ (H \times s \times G)}{\Sigma\ (H \times G)}\ , \qquad (4.7)$$

where H is the relative number of individuals, s is the average saprobic value of each of the species, and G is the indicator value for the species. Examples of the G-value, the distribution of the 10 points and the resulting s-value are given in Table 4.7.

However, simplified versions of the saprobic system are often used, based only on smell, view and a semi-quantitative classification of macroinvertebrates as pollution indicators, pollution-dominant organisms or clean-water organisms.

The monitoring of streams based on biological indices such as the saprobic index depends on the persons performing the sampling and the accuracy of identification, and may thus vary considerably (Fig. 4.14). The saprobic system is also very sensitive to the current velocity, which means that at a given BOD-concentration a much lower degree is achieved at high current velocities (Fig. 4.15).

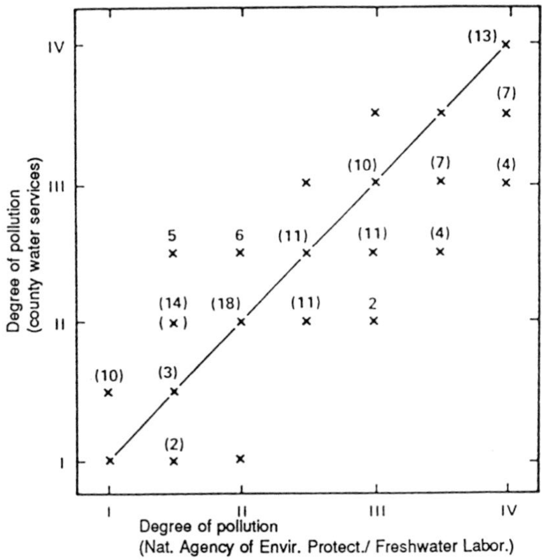

Figure 4.14. Degree of pollution of 14 watercourses in Jutland. Values assessed by local county water services are plotted against values assessed by the National Agency for Environmental Protection. - After Moth Iversen and Lindegaard (1988*).

Table 4.8. The Trent index, originally developed for the River Trent in England, represents a method of classification of watercourse pollution which is considerably simpler than the calculation of the saprobic index. - After Moth Iversen and Lindegaard (1983*).

		Total number of groups present				
		0-1	2-5	6-10	11-15	>16
				index		
Plecoptera nymphs present	several groups	-	7	8	9	10
	only one group	-	6	7	8	9
Ephemeroptera nymphs present	several groups*	-	6	7	8	9
	only one group*	-	5	6	7	8
Trichoptera larvae present	several groups**	-	5	6	7	8
	only one group**	4	4	5	6	7
Gammarus present	none of the above	3	4	5	6	7
Asellus present	none of the above	2	3	4	5	6
Tubificids and/or red midge larvae	none of the above	1	2	3	4	-
None of the above	possibly: organisms such as *Eristalis*	0	1	2	-	-

* except for *Baëtis rhodani* ** including *Baëtis rhodani*

The following systematic entities are considered as groups:

Each genus of Tricladida (flatworm)
Oligochaeta (worms) except the Naididae family
Each genus of Hirudinea (leeches)
Each genus of Mollusca (snails, mussels)
Each genus of Malacostraca (giant crayfish)
Each genus of Ephemeroptera (Mayflies) except *Baëtis rhodani*
Each genus of Plecoptera (stone flies)
Baëtis rhodani (Mayfly)
Each family of Trichoptera (caddis fly)
Each genus of Neuroptera and Megaloptera (net-veined wings)
The family Chironomidae (midge larvae) except *Chironomus* sp.
Chironomus sp.
The family Simuliidae (black flies)
Each family of other Diptera (two-winged) and of Helodidae
Each genus of Elminthidae (clawed bugs)
Each family of other Coleoptera (bugs)
Hydracarina (water mites)

A much faster method than the one based on the saprobic system is the *Trent Index*, originally developed for the river Trent in England. It is based on easily identifiable species or systematic groups (genera or families) and it requires in principle only the separation into different groups, not necessarily the identification of the group. The groups are ranked, with the cleanwater species such as stoneflies and mayflies in the upper end and the pollution-dominant species and pollution-indicator species such as tubificids and *Eristalis* in the lower end. The index value is simply found by moving down through the scheme (see Table 4.8).

Variations of the Trent Index include *Chandler's Index*, assessing the sensitivity to pollution and the relative abundance of each group on a scale from 1 to 100; and the *Viborg Index* which is specially adopted for Danish streams and uses negative values for some groups and only considers Gammarus if there are more than 10 individuals per sample.

Generally, pollution will cause stress on ecosystems, and the *diversity* will decrease. The diversity can be expressed simply by number of taxa or species, but the occurrence of a single individual will have too much importance, and since the number of individuals is a function of sample size and sample number, a great number of samples has to be investigated to register all taxa or species. To overcome this problem the *Shannon-Weaver Index* (also called the Shannon Index, see Table 11.3, C) can be used:

$$H = -\Sigma(P_i \times \log_2 P_i) , \tag{4.8}$$

where P_i is the relative abundance of the i'th species, i.e., $P_i = n_i/N$, where n_i is the number of the species i, and $N = \Sigma n_i$ is the total number of individuals in the sample.

4.3.6 Ochre Pollution

In many soils pyrite (FeS_2) and siderite ($FeCO_3$) are found. Pyrite is formed in anaerobic sediments where sulphate is reduced in the presence of iron, for instance, when seawater meets freshwater under anoxic conditions, as during glacial eras. When the groundwater level is lowered by draining or by water abstraction from lignite- and gravel pits, or for irrigation and drinking purposes, the soil becomes oxidized, and *ochre*, $Fe(OH)_3$, can be formed:

$$FeS_2 + 3½\ O_2 + H_2O \rightarrow Fe^{2+} + 2\ SO_4^{2-} + H^+ , \tag{4.9}$$

and further:

$$Fe^{2+} + ¼\ O_2 + H^+ \rightarrow Fe^{3+} + ½\ H_2O . \tag{4.10}$$

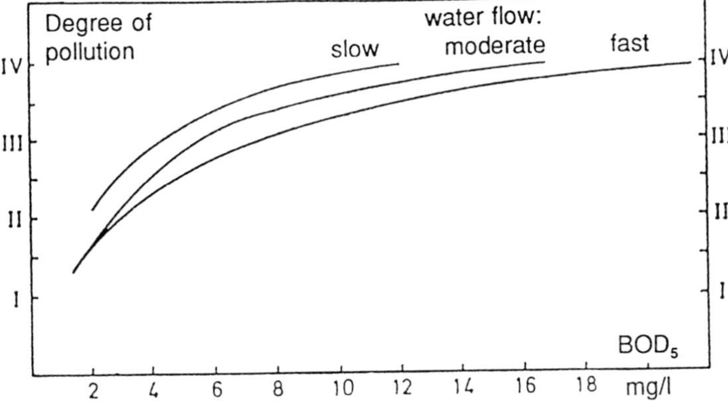

Figure 4.15. The relation between degree of pollution (ranging from I to IV) and average concentration of BOD_5 (= BI_5) in watercourses with slow, moderate, and fast water flow. - After Anonymous (1986*).

Table 4.9. Assessment of the water consumption in Denmark and of the future requirements for irrigation. Figures are in million m^3 $year^{-1}$. After Moth Iversen et al. (1990*).

	1970	1977	Required for irrigation Normal year	Dry year
Total water consumption	720	1210		
Fields and gardening	25	330		
Fields (excl. gardening)			1374	2526

The Fe^{2+} ion is stable if pH < 3, but already at pH 3.5-4 a microbial oxidation can take place, and at pH above 4-5 also a chemical oxidation occurs, and precipitation of ochre is observed:

$$Fe^{3+} + 3\ H_2O \rightarrow Fe(OH)_3 + 3\ H^+ . \tag{4.11}$$

For every mol of pyrite oxidized, four moles of H^+ are formed, and consequently the water becomes acidic; pH-values as low as 1-2 can be found in drains from lignite pits.

Ochre has a serious impact on the receiving streams. It precipitates on the respiratory organs of invertebrates and on the gills of fish. It inhibits the penetration of light, and especially the microbenthic algae suffer. And the very fine ochre particles reduces the porosity of the sediments and prevents the transport of oxygen down into the sediment, destroying bottom-living organisms and eggs from salmonid fishes. The direct toxic effects of Fe^{2+} cannot be distinguished from the indirect effects of ochre precipitation, but the diversity in the recipient is likely to decrease (Fig. 4.16).

It is possible to precipitate the iron with lime ($Ca(OH)_2$) in basins before it reaches the stream, but the process is costly, and only up to 95% of the Fe^{2+} ions are oxidized.

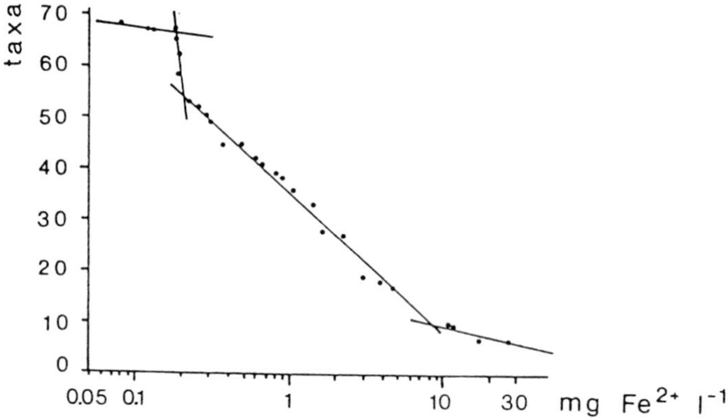

Figure 4.16. The relation between number of invertebrate taxa and average Fe^{2+} concentration found in an investigation of the Danish Vidå river. - Source: Rasmussen and Lindegaard (1988).

Table 4.10. Estimate of accessible groundwater resources in Denmark considering, a.o., waterflow in the streams, consumption, and remaining resources, regionally and nationally. - After Anonymous (1990*).

County/region	Available volume (10^6 m^3)	Consumption (10^6 m^3)	Difference (10^6 m^3)
Copenhagen region	90	197	-107
West Sealand	82	52	30
Storstrøm	83	52	31
Bornholm	18	6	12
Fyn	84	79	5
South Jutland	187	111	76
Ribe	206	109	97
Vejle	171	140	31
Ringkjøbing	331	82	249
Århus	173	102	71
Viborg	196	64	132
North Jutland	226	163	63
Denmark, total	1847	1157	690

Table 4.11. Quality objectives for Danish watercourses. - Source: Anonymous (1990*).

		Purpose	Description	Maximal degree of pollution
Stringent objective	A	Area of particular scientific interest	Particular natural conditions should be protected	II *
General objectives	B_1	Spawning and fry-growth ground for salmonids	To be of use as a spawning and fry-growth ground for trout and other salmonids, including hatching and fry-breeding in fish farms	II
	B_2	Salmonid water	To be of use as a growth and residence ground, including trout breeding in fish farms	II
	B_3	Cyprinid water	To be of use as a growth and residence ground for eel, perch, pike, and cyprinids	II (II-III)
Modified objectives	C	For abstraction of drinking water only		II-III
	D	Influenced by wastewater		II-III
	E	Influenced by ground-water utilization		II-III
	F	Influenced by ochre		

* The pollution-degree limit is established for each individual watercourse

4.3.7 Water Abstraction

In Denmark, the total freshwater consumption in 1970 was about 720 million m^3 (Table 4.9), corresponding to a rainfall of about 17 mm per year. In 1990 it had increased to about 1200 million m^3, corresponding to about 30 mm per year, i.e., about 10% of the excess precipitation. But if we consider the available groundwater reserve and the need by the watercourses in relation to the consumption (Table 4.10), many regions show a critically large exploitation.

The water abstraction for households and industry is constant over the year, and to some extent it returns to the streams. On the other hand, the abstraction for irrigation takes place in the critical period where the discharge is at its minimum, and due to the increased evaporation the water is not returned to the watercourses.

An example (Suså river, Fig. 4.17) shows that the effect of abstraction decreases with the distance of the well from the river. It was predicted that an optimal irrigation of 7% of the drainage area would reduce the river discharge by 25-30% in the critical summer period.

The reduced discharge increases light penetration and growth of macrophytes, and the reduced current velocity reduces the mechanical erosion of these plants and their associated biofilm. The accumulation of organic sediments will increase, and so will plant respiration, resulting in longer and more frequent periods of critically low oxygen concentrations.

4.3.8 Regulation and Maintenance of Streams

The annual variations in discharge create problems for the agricultural use of the open land. In rainy seasons and after melting of snow, flooding of the riparian surroundings prevents the farmers from draining and working in the fields and may damage the crops. Channelling of the streams, and constructing floodways in severe cases, are methods to minimize flooding.

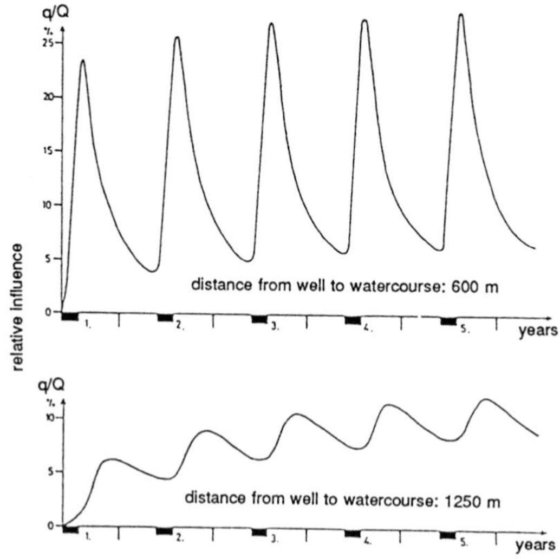

Figure 4.17. Simulations of the hydrological effect on a watercourse of 2 months' extraction of groundwater for irrigation. Q = yield of pumping (m^3 h^{-1}); q = reduction in waterflow (m^3 h^{-1}); i.e., q/Q measures the *relative* influence. - After Moth Iversen et al. (1990*).

Table 4.12. Overview of relative change in the degree (°) of pollution at various testing stations for Danish watercourses. - Source: Anonymous (1984*).

County	Number of stations	Years compared	Improvement (%) ≥1°	Improvement (%) ½°	No change (%)	Reduction (%) ≥1°	Reduction (%) ½°
Vejle	~650	1973-1977	8	10	61	14	7
Roskilde	~500	1974-1978/79	8	11	46	18	18
Frederiksborg	~400	1974-1978/78	1	11	56	22	10
København	~150	1974-1978/79	4	17	72	5	2
Århus	~200	1973/74-1981	10	18	47	22	3

The discharge Q is the product of the current velocity v and the cross section area A: $Q = v \times A$. Since Q is constant along a given stream, an increase in v leads to a decrease in A, i.e., in the water level. The velocity depends on the slope which can be increased by shortcutting, and sometimes also by excavating the stream bottom to a lower level.

A naturally meandering stream over a reach of 1 km typically has a denivellation of 4 m, corresponding to a slope of 0.004, or 4‰. If the stream is regulated to a straight channel, the length may be reduced to 500 m, increasing the slope to 8‰. If such a channel is not maintained, the erosional forces will bring the stream back to the original shape after some years. To prevent this, the slope can be concentrated over broad-crested weirs. Also the reinforcement of the banks with stones or concrete will prevent the re-meandering of the stream.

The maintenance of running waters includes traditional macrophyte control by *cutting* in the stream and on the banks and by *excavation* of sedimented material. The removal of macrophytes and sediment is done mechanically. To reduce costs and the impact of the often-damaging maintenance, more ecological methods have been introduced. The growth of the macrophytes can be reduced by planting shady trees and bushes along the river bank, and a less frequent cutting of the bank vegetation will reduce the admission of light to the stream. Furthermore, the use of herbivores such as grass carps is implemented in some streams.

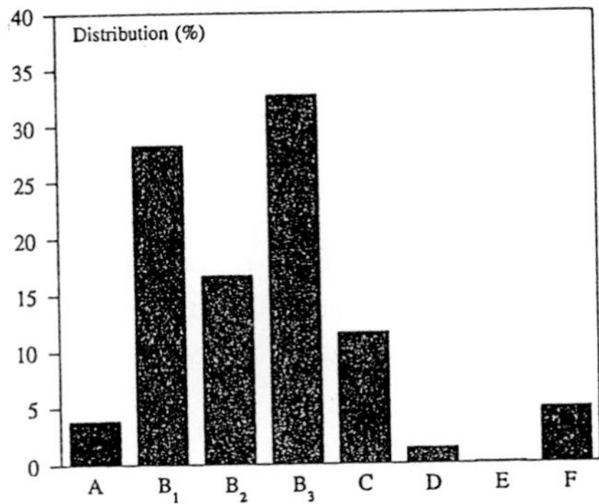

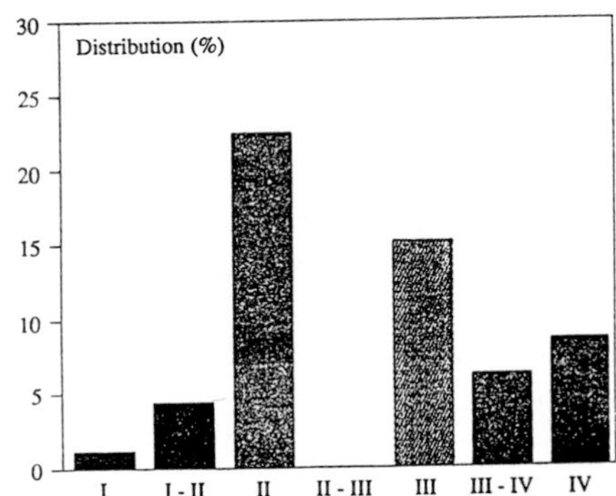

Figure 4.18. (Left) Percentage distribution of the objective types that have been established for Danish watercourses affected by the regional planning. After Anonymous (1990*).

Figure 4.19. (Right) Percentage distribution of the degree of pollution at the counties' biological assessment of watercourses 1989. After Anonymous (1990*).

The cutting of macrophytes changes the biological structure by favouring species with leaves shooting from the base and fast-growing filamentous algae like *Cladophora*. The increased current velocity after macrophyte removal will reduce the biofilm on the remaining substrates, and nitrification/denitrification will be reduced. Also the fauna composition will change: the populations of scrapers will decline due to the reduced biofilm, and the number of filter feeders will fall off because of reduced substrate. Hiding places for fish will become scarce and the fish populations will also decline, especially salmonids.

4.3.9 Recipient Quality Planning and State for Danish Streams

The objectives for Danish running waters are specified in the subdivisions in Table 4.11, and the distribution of the various objectives for the whole of Denmark is shown in Fig. 4.18.

Table 4.12 gives an overview of the changes in state of pollution for streams in a number of Danish counties 1973-1981. The table shows that in most streams no changes were observed during the period, in some the situation improved, but at other stations the state got worse. In 1989 (Fig. 4.19) the situation was still bad: 36% of the streams were in an unacceptable state of pollution (III-IV), and for 30% the recipient quality objective could only be considered to have been achieved if the objective came under the category 'reduced criteria'.

The main reasons for the relatively poor results during the first 20 years under the Danish Environmental Protection Act is (1) the reduced flow in many streams in Eastern Denmark and (2) increased loadings from farms and other diffuse sources - about 200,000 persons are not connected to a sewer system.

4.4 LAKES

Compared to running waters, lakes are less turbulent due to lower current velocities. This fact, together with a lower surface/volume ratio, tends to make the oxygen-supply problems more severe in lakes than in streams. In streams the vegetation has to be attached to a substrate, but in lakes the residence time of the water is so long that free-floating microscopic algae, *phytoplankton*, comprise the major part of the primary production. Primary production can take place in the surface waters regardless of the water depth; therefore, light is less important for the regulation of the production compared with running waters. Instead, the nutrients become the important regulators of production.

Since the early 1900s, lakes have been classified according to their nutrient content. Oligotrophic lakes have a low content of these compounds, whereas eutrophic lakes are rich in nutrients and hypertrophic lakes are extremely rich, a condition often caused by human activities.

4.4.1 The Physics of Lakes

In many other respects, the physics of lakes is different from that of running waters. The lower influence of turbulence creates temperature stratification, causing a physical stabilization of the water masses and vertical gradients in oxygen and nutrient concentrations (Fig. 4.20). Because of a longer residence time, the autochthonous production by far exceeds the allochthonous input, and the production is much more controlled by internal regeneration than by actual external loading. But on a longer time scale the level of nutrients is of course determined by the loading.

The *stratification* of lakes is determined by the temperature regime, the wind action, and the properties of water. Water has its highest density at about 4°C (due to the dipole character of the water molecule), and this property prevents lakes from freezing solid from the bottom. After the final melting of snow the lakes are heated at the surface by the absorption of infrared radiation by the water molecules. When the wind no longer has the power to circulate the water body against a steadily increasing density gradient, stratification starts from the bottom. A *thermocline* is formed at a depth which depends on wind exposure - in small, wind-protected ponds the thermocline may be established at 1 m depth, but in large, open lakes it can be as deep down as 50-100 m.

The thermocline separates the lake water into two layers, an upper *epilimnion* and a lower *hypolimnion*. In late summer and autumn, when the lake starts cooling from the surface, the thermocline moves downwards until the wind can again mix the whole water body. During winter, when ice is forming, a reverse stratification can occur, with 'light' water of 0°C just under the ice and 'heavy' water of 4°C at the bottom of the lake. This *dimictic* (complete mixing in spring and in autumn) is characteristic for the temperate zone. Other stratification patterns occur in other temperature regions (Fig. 4.21).

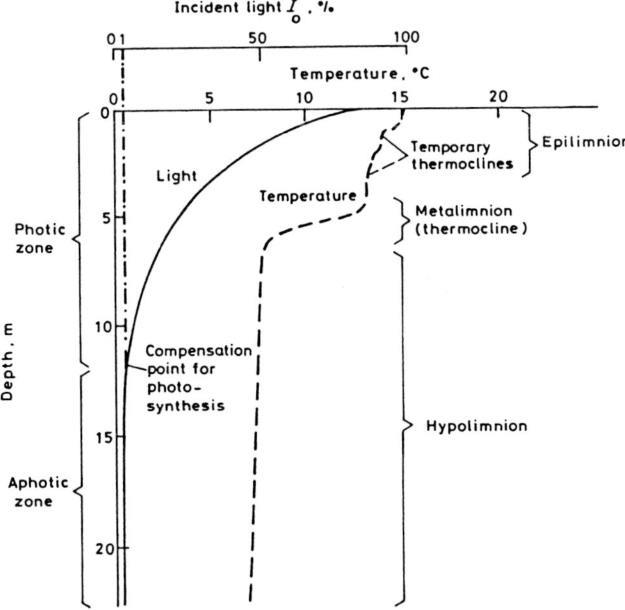

Figure 4.20. Structure of a stratified, temperate lake. The temporary thermoclines are caused by heating on calm days; they are destroyed every night by convective cooling or by wind. The rather low transparency indicates that the lake is eutrophic (high biomass). - After Jørgensen and Vollenweider (1988).

The stratification during the growing season separates the lake effectively into an upper, well-mixed water body, where equilibration with the oxygen in the atmosphere is possible, and a lower zone, where the oxygen consumed can only slowly be replaced by diffusion across the thermocline. Moreover, the amount of oxygen arising from primary production decreases exponentially with water depth, due to light absorption by the water and by its dissolved and particulate components (Fig. 4.22).

The layer where the net production is positive on a diurnal basis is called the *trophogene zone*. It extends down to the level where the incident light has been reduced to about 1% (the *compensation depth*). The layer below which respiration exceeds production is called the *tropholytic zone*.

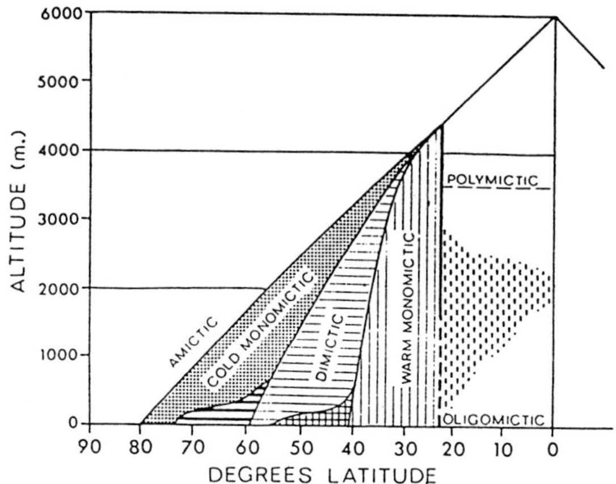

Figure 4.21. Schematic arrangement of thermal lake types by latitude and altitude. The small regions below are transitional regions. The two equatorial types occupy the unshaded areas labelled oligomictic and polymictic, separated by a region of mixed types, mainly variants of the warm monomictic type. - After Wetzel (1983).

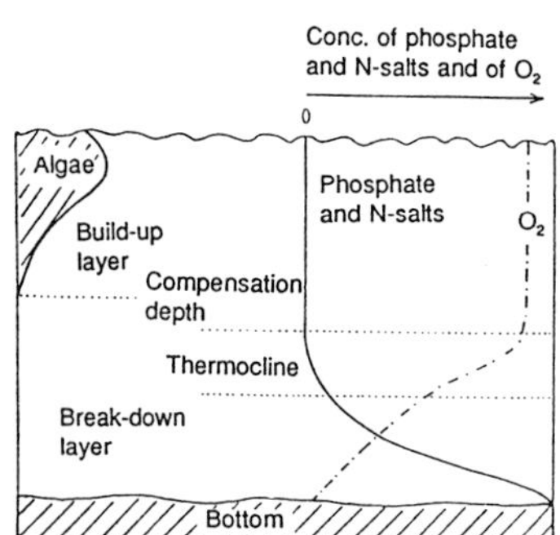

Figure 4.22. The water column in a nutrient-rich lake with a thermocline. The production of plankton algae takes place exclusively above the thermocline where it gives rise to nutrient-salt consumption and oxygen production. Decomposition processes further below, on the other hand, consume oxygen and produce nutrient salts. - After Jensen et al. (1988*).

In eutrophic lakes the compensation depth is above the thermocline, but in oligotrophic lakes it can be in the hypolimnion. This means that with increasing nutrient levels the oxygen-production zone becomes more and more restricted to the surface layers, and the risk of oxygen depletion in the bottom water increases.

This has been known for many years, and it is thus not an ecologically good solution to discharge oxygen-consuming sewage below the thermocline. Although lakes generally have a P/R ratio (i.e., the ratio of total phosphorus concentration to total nitrogen concentration) greater than 1, the stratification means that the ratio varies over the watercolumn in a fashion which is unfavourable for the life at the bottom of the lake.

4.4.2 The Eutrophication Process

With increased loadings of nutrients into a lake, the autotrophic production will increase and be reflected in increased biomass of autotrophic components. The increased food supply to the heterotrophs - bacteria and zooplankton, fish and bottom animals - will also lead to an increase in their biomass. But a larger phytoplankton biomass tends to decrease transparency, thereby shading out the macrophytes (Fig. 4.23). The trophogene zone will decrease, and a maximum of oxygen production will be reached when the transparency depth - or Secchi depth (named after an Italian admiral) - is below 10-15 cm.

During this process the biomass of both autotrophs and heterotrophs increases the oxygen demand, and oxygen depletion in the bottom water becomes more and more severe (Fig. 4.24). Since the oxygen reserve has a final entity in the hypolimnion, the problems increase during the stagnation period (Fig. 4.25). In shallow, non-stratified lakes the oxygen problems are most severe at high temperatures and during the night. A temporary lowering of the atmospheric pressure might release poisonous hydrogen sulfide from the anaerobic sediments and cause instantaneous fish-kills.

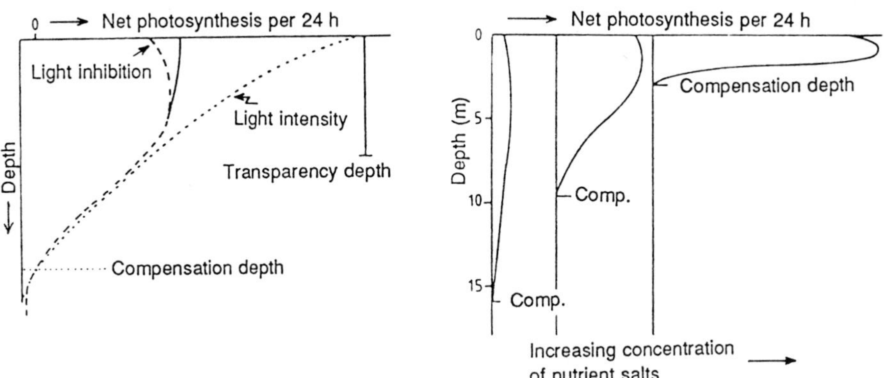

Figure 4.23. Left: Typical photosynthesis profile showing the relation between net photosynthesis of plankton algae and depth. Right: Characteristic photosynthesis profiles in lakes with increasing content of nutrient salts and plankton. The maximal rate of photosynthesis increases but the photic zone becomes narrower because the plankton algae absorb more and more of the light energy. - After Jensen et al. (1988*).

4.4.3 Nitrogen and Phosphorus

In common with all other plants, phytoplankton also has a demand for both phosphorus and nitrogen, in the proportion 7:1 by weight. Due to the relative scarcity of phosphorus in the lithosphere, phosphorus is the potentially most limiting nutrient in freshwater. Compared to terrestrial ecosystems the nutrient circulation is much more 'open' in aquatic systems due to the unidirectional flow of water and the solubility of the nutrients. In standing waters the production of organic matter takes place close to the surface, but the remineralization occurs partly in the sediment, and the nutrients are thereby 'diluted' into the whole water body or locked in the bottom water, and they are easily transported out of the system.

In natural aquatic ecosystems, phosphorus and nitrogen are present in a ratio close to the requirements of the primary production. This is a consequence of an evolutionary adaptation to the availability and a regulation of it by, e.g., phosphate production and nitrogen fixation. But many of our aquatic ecosystems are not in a natural state anymore. The change in the terrestrial environment caused by even primitive agriculture opens up the closed nutrient cycles, and the losses of nutrients to the aquatic systems increase.

The increased losses caused by higher run-off and erosion due to monocultures and reduced vegetation coverage are compensated by fertilization, and the plant production becomes more and more dependent on external nutrient supply. Furthermore, the concentration of population in bigger and bigger towns speeds up the nutrient cycling and creates imbalance between nutrient uptake and nutrient mineralization.

The relative contribution of nitrogen and phosphorus from various point sources and diffuse sources can be differentiated by splitting up a given watershed into parts dominated by agriculture and parts dominated by point sources such as municipal sewage and fishponds. In Table 4.13 such a differentiation is presented; export coefficients for the various areas are stated, as well as the resulting average concentrations in the receiving streams. - The main contributor of nitrogen is agriculture, and the main contributor of phosphorus is municipal sewage and fishponds in the watersheds considered.

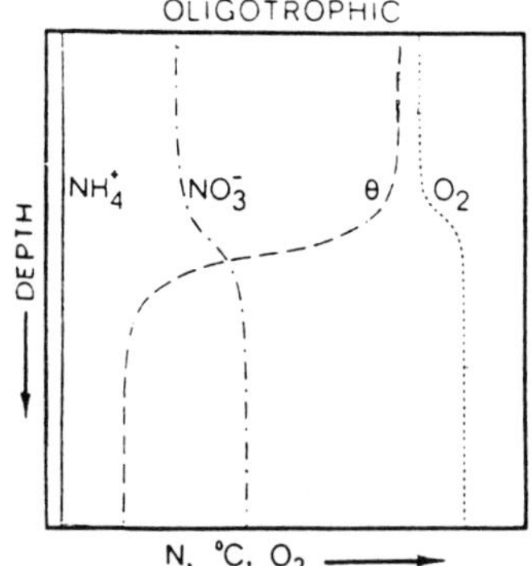

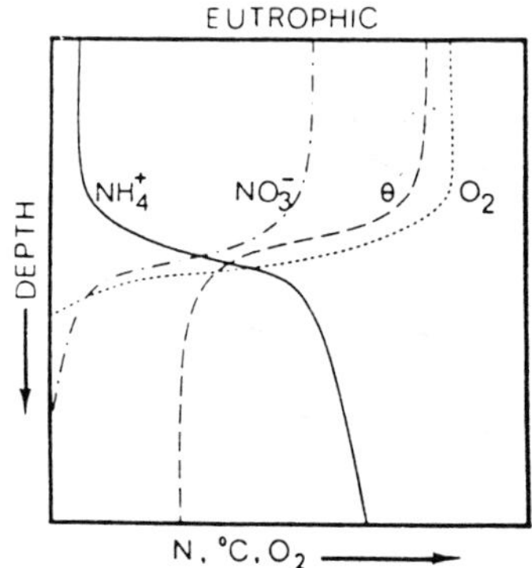

Figure 4.24. Generalized vertical distribution of nitrogen (ammonia and nitrate) in stratified lakes of very low productivity (left) and of high productivity (right). - After Wetzel (1983).

Table 4.13. Run-off and concentrations of nitrogen and phosphorus from various types of areas in Denmark. - After Anonymous (1990*).

	Area coefficient kg ha^{-1} year^{-1}		Concentration weighted by waterflow mg l^{-1}	
Nitrogen:				
reference areas	2.9	1.9	1.9	1.6
cultivated areas:				
without point sources	11.6	9.3	7.1	5.8
with point sources	14.1	12.8	7.9	7.2
with fish farms	13.4	12.6	3.4	3.4
Phosphorus:				
reference areas	0.07	0.05	0.06	0.06
cultivated areas	0.27	0.21	0.16	0.14
fish-farm areas	0.76	0.78	0.17	0.18
waste-water areas	1.46	0.44	1.12	0.33

Table 4.14. Overview of important parameters for Danish lakes. - After Anonymous (1990*).

	mean	median	max.	min.
total phosphorus (mg P l^{-1})	0.302	0.146	10	0.008
total nitrogen (mg N l^{-1})	2.97	2.12	15.9	0.29
chlorophyll a (mg l^{-1})	0.080	0.054	0.601	0.0002
transparency depth (m)	1.21	0.91	6.3	0.2
suspended matter (mg l^{-1})	18	12	130	1

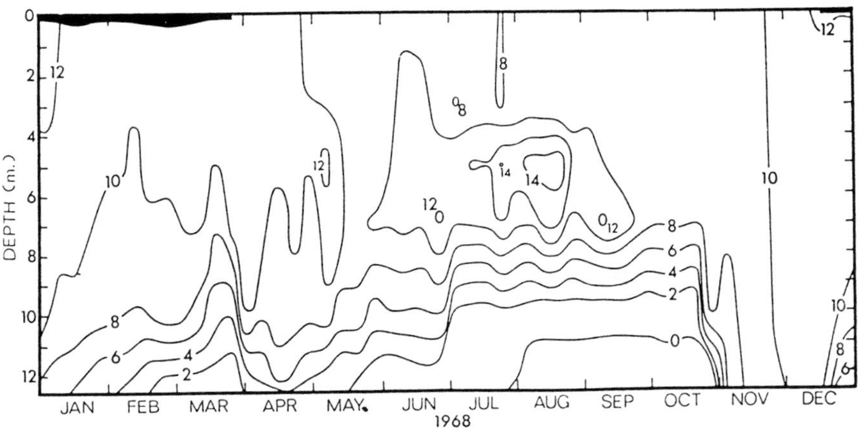

Figure 4.25. Depth-time diagram of isopleths of dissolved oxygen concentrations (in mg l^{-1}) of Lawrence Lake, Michigan, 1968. Ice-cover drawn to scale. - After Wetzel (1983).

If we compare the average concentrations in the streams with those in 350 Danish lakes (Table 4.14), it is obvious that the lakes have lower concentrations than the streams. The reason is the losses of nitrogen and phosphorus by sedimentation and denitrification in the lakes. Lakes are net consumers of N and P, and consequently not all the incoming nutrients to a lake are available for the primary production.

For the study of effects of nutrient loading to lakes, the concept of *mass balance* is essential.

4.4.4 Mass Balances

Generally, a mass balance over the time (t) for a given element in a lake has the form:

$$\frac{dM}{dt} = M_{in} - M_{out} - \sigma M \ , \tag{4.12}$$

where M is the total amount in the lake, M_{in} is the total amount of the element entering the lake per time unit, M_{out} is the total amount leaving the lake via the outlets per time unit, and σ is the sedimentation rate.

Normally, we estimate the amounts in equation (4.12) by

$$\frac{dM}{dt} = Q_{in}C_{in} - Q_{out}C_{out} - \sigma M \ , \tag{4.13}$$

where Q_{in} and Q_{out} are the (measured) incoming and outgoing waterflows, respectively, and C_{in} and C_{out} are the corresponding (measured) concentration in these flows of the element in question. Dividing by the volume V of the lake yields the following equation for the concentration $C = C(t)$ in the lake:

$$\frac{dC}{dt} = \frac{Q_{in}C_{in}}{V} - \frac{Q_{out}C_{out}}{V} - \sigma C \ , \tag{4.14}$$

The ratio $r = Q_{out}/V$ is called the *flushing rate*; it is the number of times the lake volume is replaced per time unit. If we assume that $C(t) = C_{out}$ (only true when the lake is totally mixed), we get:

$$\frac{dC}{dt} = \frac{M_{in}}{V} - rC - \sigma C \ , \tag{4.15}$$

indicating that the change in lake concentration over time is the volumetric load less volumetric outwash and net sedimentation.

If we further assume that the in-lake concentration C_{in} is constant over time, we have a steady-state situation:

$$\frac{M_{in}}{V} - rC - \sigma C = 0 \ , \tag{4.16}$$

or

$$C = \frac{M_{in}}{V(r + \sigma)} \; . \tag{4.17}$$

Since the primary production varies with depth due to light absorption, we normally use the depth-integrated production, expressing it as area-specific production. To relate this to nutrient loading we also use the area specific loading L, and from $V = z\,A$, where z is the average depth and A the surface area, we get:

$$C = \frac{L}{z(r + \sigma)} \; . \tag{4.18}$$

This is the classical *steady-state lake model* developed by R. A. Vollenweider. It expresses the in-lake concentration of an element as a function of area-specific loading, lake depth, flushing rate and sedimentary-loss coefficient. We can calculate L as the sum of loadings from different sources: river discharge, direct point sources, seepage and precipitation. The quantities z and r are found by measurements, mapping of the lake and calculation of its water balance. The estimation of σ is difficult because it requires an estimation of the net burial in the sediment. Alternatively, σ can be replaced in the model by R, the fraction of the loading that is retained in the lake and later washed out by the outlet:

$$R = \frac{C\,V\,r}{L\,A} = \frac{C\,z\,r}{L} \; . \tag{4.19}$$

It follows readily that

$$C = \frac{L\,R}{z\,r} \; . \tag{4.20}$$

Sometimes R denotes the net retention in the sediment, and we get instead:

$$C = \frac{L\,(1-R)}{z\,r} \; . \tag{4.21}$$

In this case, R is simply measured as the ratio (inflow-outflow)/inflow.

4.4.5 Empirical Models

Over a period, many efforts have been made to develop empirical models which can predict the retention of nitrogen and phosphorus in lakes. By using such a model we will be able to predict how the in-lake concentrations of an element is affected by changes in loading, in hydraulic regime and possibly also by changes in morphometry, provided we have a loading estimate and a water balance.

For 94 Danish lakes covering 131 annual mass balances, 21 empirical retention models were tested, expressing the retention of phosphorus R_p as a function of hydraulic load $q_s = Q/A$ or hydraulic residence time $t_w = l/r$ and of average inlet concentration P_i (Table 4.15). The lakes tested with the models represent a range in morphometry, hydrology and loading, as shown in Table 4.16.

Table 4.15. Phosphorus-load models tested with data from Danish lakes (see text.) All models have been reformulated so as to express the retention coefficient r_p in terms of other parameters. For detailed references, see Kristensen et al. (1990*).

1	Kirchner and Dillon (1975)	$r_p = 0.4088 \exp(-0.2899\, q_s) + 0.5912 \exp(-0.01019\, q_s)$
2	Ostrofsky (1978)	$r_p = 0.201 \exp(-0.0425\, q_s) + 0.574 \exp(-0.00949\, q_s)$
3	Vollenweider (1975)	$r_p = 10/(10 + q_s)$
4	Chapra (1975)	$r_p = 16/(16 + q_s)$
5	Chapra (1975)	$r_p = 12.4/(12.4 + q_s)$
6	Dillon and Kirchner (1975)	$r_p = 13.2/(13.2 + q_s)$
7	Ostrofsky (1978)	$r_p = 24/(30 + q_s)$
8	Canfield and Bachmann (1981)	$r_p = 5.3/(5.3 + q_s)$
9	Nürnberg (1984)	$r_p = 15/(18 + q_s)$
10	Reckhow (1979)	$r_p = (11.6 + 0.2\, q_s)/(11.6 + 1.2\, q_s)$
11	Canfield and Bachmann (1981)	$r_p = (2.99 + 1.7\, q_s)/(2.99 + 2.7\, q_s)$
12	Prairie (1988)	$r_p = (0.11 + 0.18\, t_w)/(1 + 0.18\, t_w)$
13	Prairie (1989)	$r_p = (0.25 + 0.18\, t_w)/(1 + 0.18\, t_w)$
14	Canfield and Bachmann (1981)	$r_p = 0.129\, t_w^{0.451}\, P_i^{0.549}(1 + 0.129\, t_w^{0.451}\, P_i^{0.549})$
15	Rognerud et al. (1979)	$r_p = 1 - 0.63 \exp((-0.067\, t_w)$
16	Berge (1987)	$r_p = 1 - 0.436\, t_w^{-0.16}$
17	Vollenweider (1976)	$r_p = 1/(1 + t_w^{-0.5})$
18	OECD (1982), final	$r_p = 1 - 1.55\, P_i^{-0.18}/(1 + t_w^{0.5})^{0.82}$
19	OECD (1982), Nordic	$r_p = 1 - 1.12\, P_i^{-0.08}/(1 + t_w^{0.5})^{0.92}$
20	OECD (1982), shallow	$r_p = 1 - 1.02\, P_i^{-0.12}/(1 + t_w^{0.5})^{0.88}$
21	Frisk et al. (1980, 1981)	$r_p = P_i\, t_w/(30 + P_i\, t_w)$

Table 4.16. Statistical characteristics of the Danish lake data by which the phosphorus models listed in Table 4.15 were tested.

	n	ave.	std.err.	min.	25%	median	75%	max
lake area (km^2)	131	2.4	0.6	0.04	0.2	0.5	1.5	41
mean depth (m)	131	4.0	0.3	0.30	1.6	2.8	5.3	15.4
t_w (years)	131	1.1	0.2	0.004	0.05	0.36	1.35	20
(days)		394		1.5	19	133	493	7300
q_s (m $year^{-1}$)	131	39.3	7.8	0.2	3.8	11.9	35.3	605
L_p (g P $m^{-2} year^{-1}$)	131	13.1	2.5	0.06	1.0	2.5	12.4	217
P_i (µg P l^{-1})	131	415	39	34	164	260	456	2396
P_{lake} (µg P l^{-1})	131	301	35	16	99	162	298	3130
$(P_i - P_{lake})/P_i$	131	0.25	0.04	-2.1	0.02	0.36	0.60	0.87

Of the 21 models tested, 4 stood out as describing things better than the remaining 17. However, the medians of the percentage deviation between observed and calculated R_p values were still large (33-41%). It appeared that in 24% of the investigated lakes a negative R_p was measured, and most of these lakes had an extremely low residence time (less than 19 days); in such a lake a negative R_p can be calculated if

Table 4.17. Morphometrical data and total nitrogen concentrations (yearly basis) for 69 lakes, cf. text. After Kristensen et al. (1990*).

	average	median	std.err.	min.	max.
lake area (km^2)	3.3	0.7	1.0	0.1	41
mean depth (m)	5.1	2.3	0.5	0.6	16
max. depth (m)	8.6	5.0	1.1	1.0	37
residence time (years)	1.2	0.3	0.3	< 0.1	14
influx conc. (mg N l^{-1})	5.6	5.0	0.8	0.6	15
in-lake conc. (mg N l^{-1})	2.8	2.5	0.2	0.5	9

Table 4.18. Nitrogen load, nitrogen loss and denitrification in the 69 lakes, cf. Table 4.17 and text. Percent-loss was calculated for each lake *before* average was taken.

	average	median	n	std.err.
nitrogen load (g N m^{-2} $year^{-1}$)	142	52	69	35
nitrogen loss (g N m^{-2} $year^{-1}$)	29	17	69	4
nitrogen loss (%)	43	41	69	4
denitrification (g N m^{-2} $year^{-1}$)	23	16	58	3
denitrification (%)	33	30	58	3

$$R_p = \frac{C - m_{in}}{m_{in}} . \qquad (4.22)$$

If we use instead

$$R_p = \frac{M_{in}/Q_{in} - M_{out}/Q_{out}}{M_{in}/Q_{in}} , \qquad (4.23)$$

then we get a positive value more in accordance with the R_p-value calculated by the empirical models. In other words: In a lake with a very short residence time, steady state between loading and loss is never achieved, and a systematic error will occur if we use observed in-lake concentrations, the reason being that residence time, inlet concentrations and in-lake concentrations vary over the year.

Corresponding models for the relation between nitrogen loading and in-lake nitrogen concentrations are in principle more difficult to develop, since net losses occur both by sedimentation and by denitrification, whereby nitrate is reduced to gaseous di-nitrogen oxide and nitrogen escaping from the lake. For 69 Danish lakes (see Table 4.17), mass balances allowed calculations of both absolute and relative loss by net sedimentation and by denitrification (Table 4.18). The denitrification is calculated as the difference between total loss and sedimentary loss, calculated by multiplying the sedimentary phosphorus loss by the N/P-ratio in the surface sediment:

$$N_{den} = N_{loss} - P_{loss} \times (N/P)_{surface\ sed.} \quad (4.24)$$

Table 4.18 shows that on average 43% of the nitrogen loading was lost as sedimentation and denitrification; this is a much higher percentage than the 25% lost of the phosphorus loading. The 'extra' loss by denitrification amounted to 77% of the total loss.

Fig. 4.26 shows the relation between average inlet concentration of nitrogen and average in-lake concentration. Lakes with short residence times suffer the smallest losses.

A test was made of 3 different models describing the relation:

$$N_{lake} = 0.45\ N_{in}\ , \quad (4.25)$$

$$N_{lake} = 0.42\ N_{in}\ t_w^{-0.11}\ , \quad (4.26)$$

$$N_{lake} = 0.34\ N_{in}\ t_w^{-0.14}\ z^{0.17}\ , \quad (4.27)$$

where N_{lake} is the annual mean of the in-lake concentration of total nitrogen, N_{in} is the annual mean in the incoming water, t_w is the hydraulic residence time (years), and z is the average depth (m). Compared with the performance of other models (Table 4.19) the deviations between observed and calculated in-lake concentrations were reasonably small for the three models listed above. The reason why the other models underestimated the nitrogen losses is probably that Danish lakes are rather uniform with respect to loading, residence time and depth, whereas the data used to calibrate the other models include data from lakes with smaller loading, longer residence time and greater depths.

The next step in the predictive modelling of a eutrophication response is the development of empirical relations between phytoplankton biomass and nutrient level. A variety of such empirical models have been described in the literature, and they are often quite different due, a.o., to geographical differences. For example, lakes at higher latitudes have relatively more chlorophyll due to lower insolation, and different chlorophyll-extraction procedures may have been used (Fig. 4.27). Therefore, a direct relation between nutrient level and transparency depth might be more appropriate.

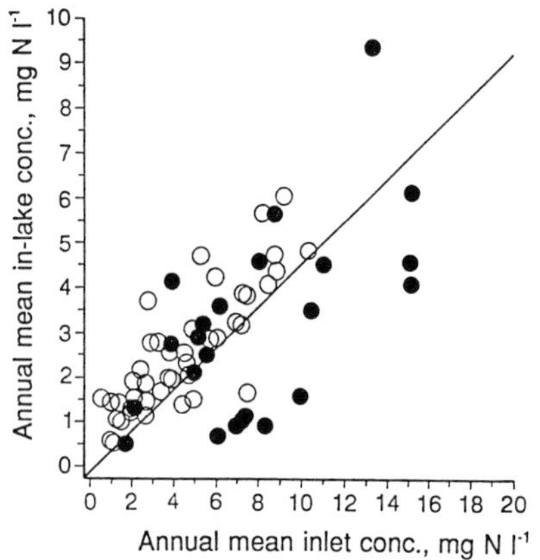

Figure 4.26. The relation between in-lake and inlet concentration of nitrogen, both given annual averages. O: lakes with residence time less than 1 year; ●: lakes with residence ' greater than 1 year. - After Kristensen et al. (1990*).

Table 4.19. Six models of the relation between inlet and in-lake concentrations of nitrogen were tested with data from 98 Danish lakes. The table shows the results, giving the deviations in % of observed values. For additional references, see Kristensen et al. (1990*).

	mean	std.err.	median	P(mean=0)
model (4.25)	-2.3	9.0	17.0	< 0.257
model (4.26)	-4.1	6.5	7.0	< 0.531
model (4.27)	-7.9	6.9	0.3	< 0.802
Lijklema et al. (1989)	-51	9.0	-25.0	< 0.004
Bachmann (1984)	-153	118	94	< 0.200
OECD (1982)	-17.1	8.9	-8.3	< 0.001

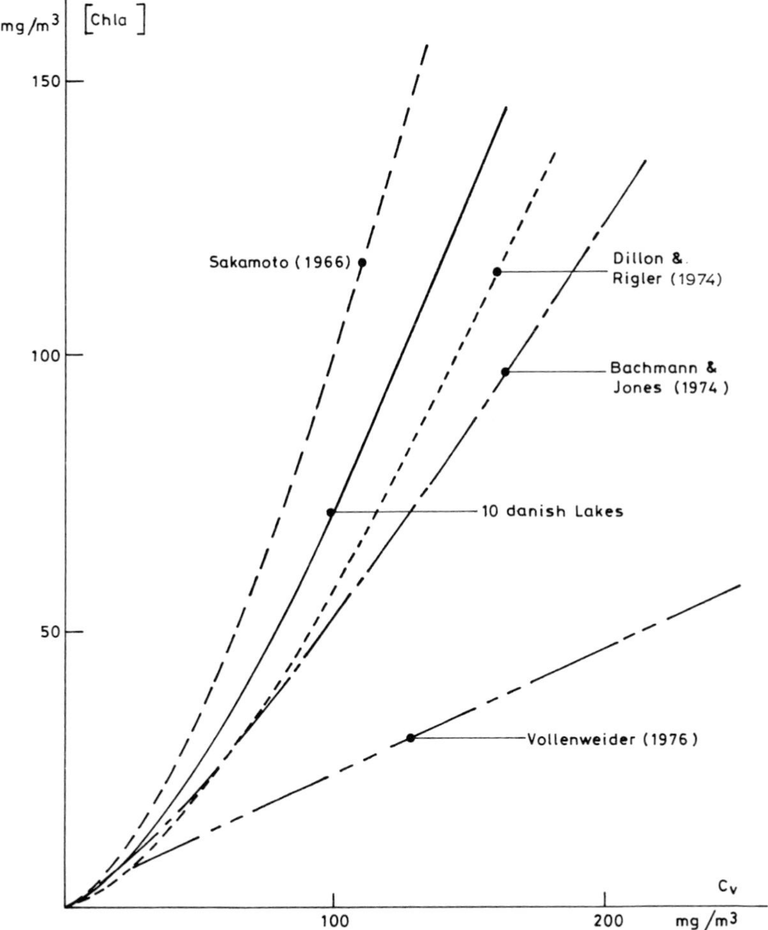

Figure 4.27. Some empirical relations between summer chloryphyll concentration (chla) and annual average phosphorus concentration (C_v). - After Kamp Nielsen (1986).

Table 4.20. Statistics for data from 252 Danish lakes (see text): morphometrical properties and summer averages of total phosphorus concentration, total nitrogen concentration, transparency depth, chlorophyll a concentration, and suspended matter concentration. Figures marked with an asterisk are whole-year averages. - Source: Kristensen et al. (1990*).

	average	median	std.err.	min.	max.
lake area (km^2)	2.3	0.6	0.4	< 0.01	41
mean depth (m)	4.0	2.6	0.2	0.5	15
max. depth (m)	8.7	5.5	0.9	1.0	34
residence time (years)	1.8	0.4	0.3	< 0.01	21
total phosphorus (mg P l^{-1})	0.4	0.2	0.03	0.01	2
* total phosphorus (mg P l^{-1})	0.4	0.2	0.04	0.02	3
total nitrogen (mg N l^{-1})	2.3	2.0	0.09	0.2	9
* total nitrogen (mg N l^{-1})	2.9	2.3	0.11	0.2	10
transparency depth (m)	1.1	0.8	0.06	0.2	5
* transparency depth (m)	1.2	1.0	0.05	0.2	5
chlorophyll a (µg CHL l^{-1})	89	74	5.0	5.0	308
suspended matter (mg l^{-1})	22	18	1.7	3.4	73

For 252 Danish lakes covering 498 measuring years (Table 4.20) the relation shown in Fig. 4.28 was found. The relation is logarithmic because the transparency depth z_{eu} (m) is related to the extinction coefficient n (m^{-1}) by

$$n = 1.7/z_{eu} . \tag{4.28}$$

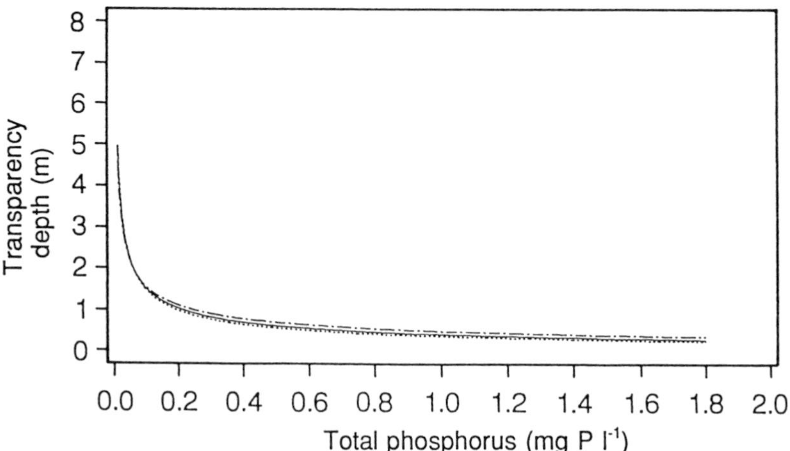

Figure 4.28. The relation between transparency depth z_{eu} and total phosphorus concentration P in a survey of 252 Danish lakes. Solid curve: both z_{eu} and P are summer averages; dotted curve: both z_{eu} and P are annual averages; dot-and-dash curve: z_{eu} is summer average and P is annual average. - After Kristensen et al. (1990*).

Table 4.21. Modelling the relation between average transparency depth (z_{eu}) and phosphorus concentration (P_{lake}); the influence of mean depth (z) is included in three of the models. Equations 1 and 2: summer mean z_{eu} and summer mean P_{lake}; equations 3 and 4: summer mean z_{eu} and annual mean P_{lake}; equations 5 and 6: annual mean z_{eu} and annual mean P_{lake}. Estimates of the model coefficients are supplemented with standard errors. - After Kristensen et al. (1990*).

equation 1:	$z_{eu} = 0.44(\pm0.038)\ P_{lake}^{-0.54(\pm0.031)}$
equation 2:	$z_{eu} = 0.36(\pm0.029)\ P_{lake}^{-0.29(\pm0.028)}\ z^{0.51(\pm0.042)}$
equation 3:	$z_{eu} = 0.39(\pm0.038)\ P_{lake}^{-0.58(\pm0.034)}$
equation 4:	$z_{eu} = 0.34(\pm0.028)\ P_{lake}^{-0.29(\pm0.028)}\ z^{0.55(\pm0.040)}$
equation 5:	$z_{eu} = 0.52(\pm0.042)\ P_{lake}^{-0.48(\pm0.031)}$
equation 6:	$z_{eu} = 0.43(\pm0.026)\ P_{lake}^{-0.20(\pm0.022)}\ z^{0.55(\pm0.030)}$

Table 4.22. Continuation of Table 4.21. Data from 240 lakes were divided into two sets, according to the N:P ratio being either larger than 10 or less than 10. No significant difference between the model coefficients was found. - After Kristensen et al. (1990*).

equation 7:	$z_{eu} = 0.40(\pm0.055)\ P_{lake}^{-0.69(\pm0.064)}$
equation 8:	$z_{eu} = 0.34(\pm0.044)\ P_{lake}^{-0.60(\pm0.041)}$

The extinction coefficient is found by measuring the light attenuation over the depth:

$$I_z = I_o e^{-nz}\ , \tag{4.29}$$

where I_o is the irradiance at depth z, and I_o is the irradiance at the surface. By taking logarithms and rearranging we can rewrite the equation as

$$nz = \ln I_o - \ln I_z\ . \tag{4.30}$$

By inspection of the data material, an influence of the lake depth was found; shallow lakes had generally less transparency depth due to resuspension of sediments. A set of empirical models was developed, relating summer values, annual values, or combinations of the two (Table 4.21).

In a typical Danish shallow lake there is often a distinct nitrogen limitation in late summer, and one would expect improved relationships if the lakes were screened for nitrogen limitation. However, separating the lakes according to the N/P-ratio being above 10 (indicating P-limitation) or below 10 (indicating N-limitation) did not significantly change the relation between total P and transparency depth (see Table 4.22).

Another indicator of a true P-limitation is the low P-concentration in the production period, but again no significant effect of this screening was found (Fig. 4.29).

In another investigation, comparing a number of European lakes with respect to recovery, the screening for N-limitation by both N/P-ratio and lower P concentrations in summer gave a significant difference in response direction (Fig. 4.30).

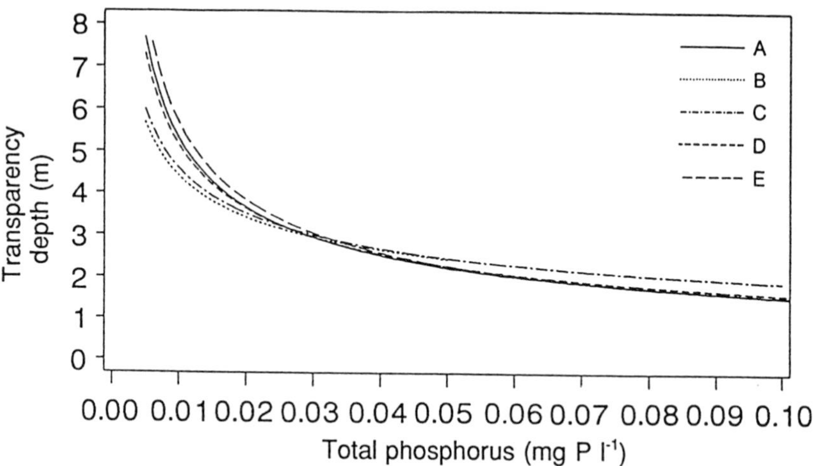

Figure 4.29. The relation between summer-average transparency depth (z_{eu}) and summer-average total-phosphorus concentration (P) by various maximum limits for P, cf. Figure 4.28 and text. A: all observations; B: P < 0.4 mg P l^{-1}; C: P < 0.2 mg P l^{-1}; D: P < 0.1 mg P l^{-1}; E: P < 0.05 mg P l^{-1}. - After Kristensen et al. (1990*).

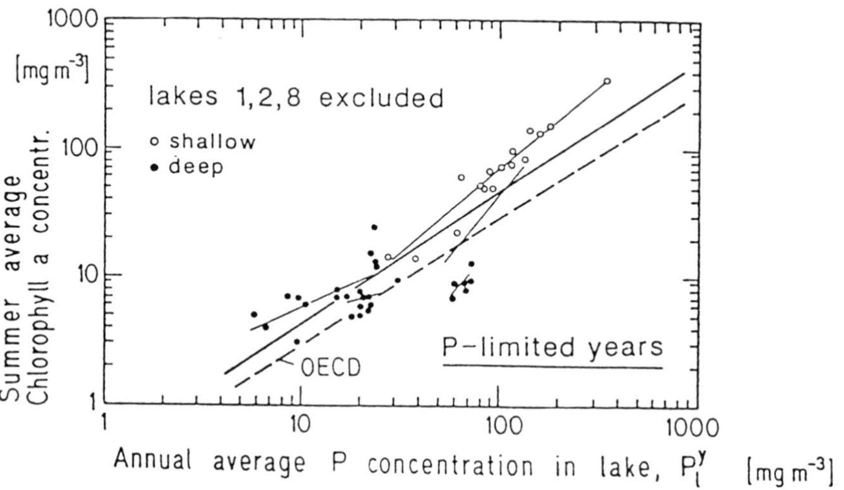

Figure 4.30. Results of a regression analysis of growth-seasonal average chlorophyll-a response to varying P-concentration, performed on data screened for P-limitation to occur. Steering variable is the annual in-lake average P-concentration, P_l^y. - Source: Kamp Nielsen (1989).

Quantitative changes in phytoplankton biomass are accompanied by qualitative changes during the eutrophication process. Bluegreen algae and green algae become more and more dominant with increasing phosphorus level (Fig. 4.31). Especially the bluegreens are a nuisance, since they float to the surface in competition for light. Here they are killed due to their high susceptibility to light inhibition; during their decomposition an unpleasant smell is developed and, more seriously, some of the species are toxic to animals.

Some filamentous bluegreens are able to fix atmospheric nitrogen and reduce it to ammonia in specially developed cells (heterocysts), and it is generally believed that this nitrogen fixation is favoured by low nitrogen levels and low N/P-ratios. But the material from Danish lakes show that total phosphorus was more probably regulating the abundance of both non-N-fixing and N-fixing bluegreens (Fig. 4.32). It is also remarkable that at very high P-concentrations the small green alga becomes dominant.

The competitive power of the bluegreens is low at high light intensities and it has been suggested that a better description of bluegreen-algae abundance could be achieved by correcting the phosphorus dependence by the ratio z_{eu}/z_{mix}, where z_{eu} denotes the *photic depth* (2.3 × transparency depth), and z_{mix} is the *mixing depth* (total depth in non-stratified lakes; epilimnion in stratified lakes). Figure 4.33 suggests that such a relationship holds and that a significant difference exists between deep lakes and shallow lakes, but there is no indication that their relative abundance is decreased at higher phosphorus levels as shown in the Danish material.

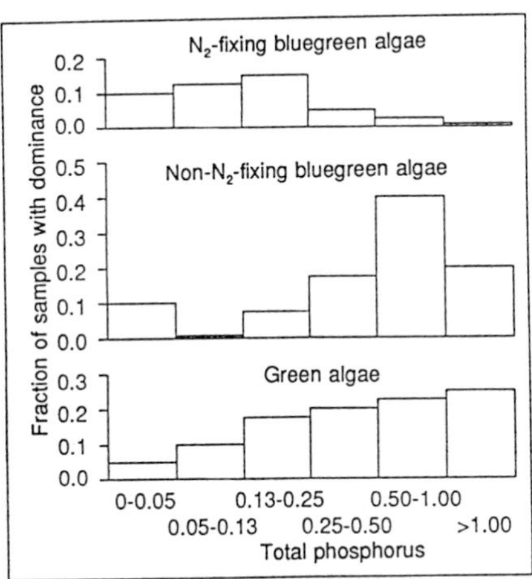

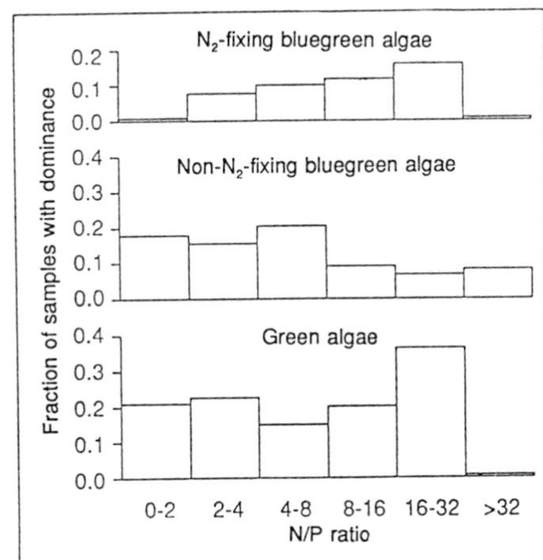

Figure 4.31. (Left) The fraction of samples with dominance of (1) N_2-fixating bluegreen algae, (2) non-N_2-fixating bluegreen algae, and (3) green algae, plotted against average total-phosphorus concentration (May-September). - After Kristensen et al. (1990*).

Figure 4.32. (Right) As Fig. 4.32, plotted against N/P ratio.

Kamp Nielsen

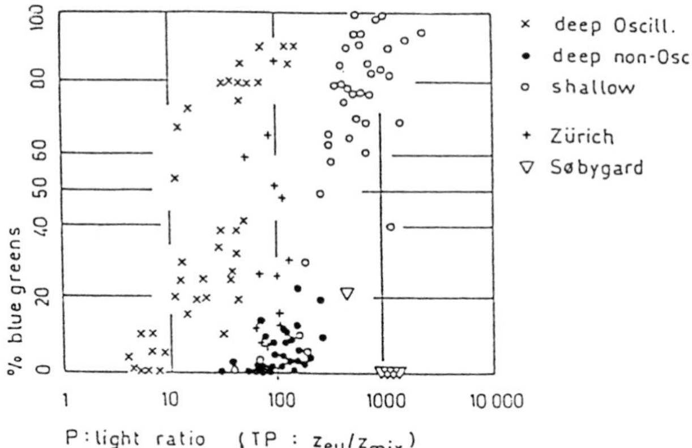

Figure 4.33. Growth-seasonal average share of cyanobacteria in total algal biomass (arcsin transformed) as a function of growth-seasonal P:light ratios a certain time lag before. - Source: Kamp Nielsen (1989).

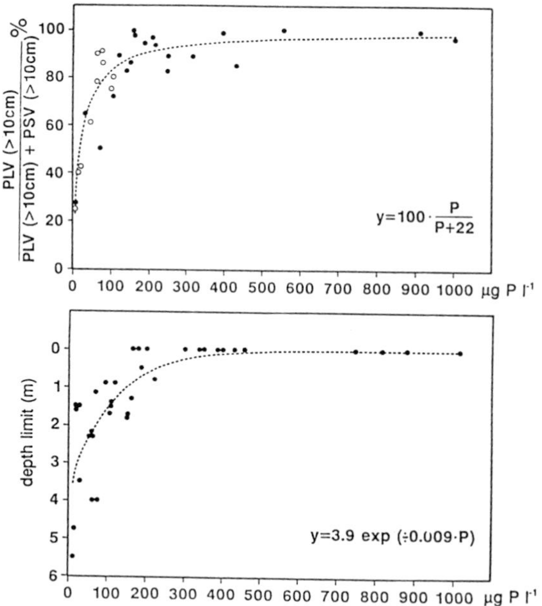

Figure 4.34. (Above) The relation between the ratio PLV:(PLV + PSV) and average total-phosphorus concentration (May-September), where PLV = number of planktivorous fish (roach, rudd, bream) and PSV = number of carnivorous fish (perch, pike, zander), all of size > 10 cm. O: lakes in Southern Sweden; ●: Danish lakes. - After Kristensen et al. (1990[*]).

Figure 4.35. (Below) The relation between depth limit for the distribution of bottom vegetation and summer-average total P concentration in a number of Danish lakes. - After Kristensen et al. (1990[*]).

The next level in the limnic food web is the *zooplankton*. Its qualitative and quantitative composition is governed by both the availability of appropriate and sufficient food and the predation from fish. In oligotrophic lakes species preferring small particles dominate, and in eutrophic lakes crustaceans such as *Daphnia* take over. The larger zooplankton species in the eutrophic lakes are excellent prey for the planktivorous fishes, and they increase their dominance relative to predatory fishes (Fig. 4.34).

An indirect effect of the increased phytoplankton biomass and the resulting decrease in transparency is the outshading of the submersed macrophyte vegetation. Where the emergent vegetation such as *Phragmites* can form a dense vegetation along the lake shores, and where floating plants like water lilies can cover the near-shore lake surface, the submersed plants must reduce their depth distribution (Fig. 4.35).

The coincident disappearence of bluegreen algae and the very strong response in phytoplankton biomass at phosphorus concentrations below 100 µg P/l indicate that this concentration is the level not to be exceeded when reduction in phosphorus loading is considered.

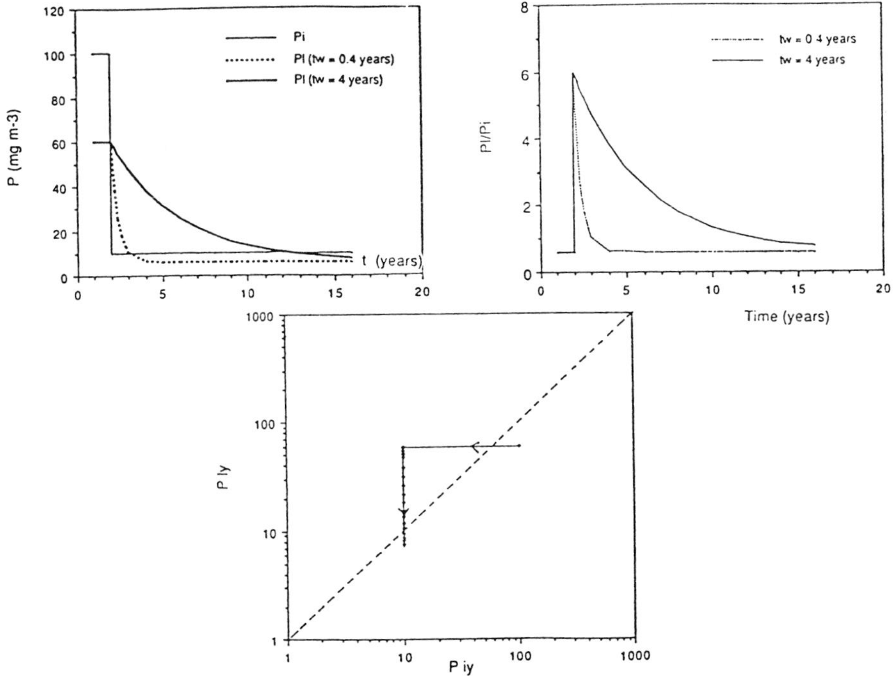

Figure 4.36. The delaying effect of water dilution on the in-lake-P concentration (Pl) following a load reduction, i.e., a drop in the inlet-P concentration (Pi). Top left: The course in time of a reduction in year 2, considering two hypothetical cases with different retention times (tw). Top right: Same situation; plot of Pl/Pi. Below: Same situation; phase plot of Pl versus Pi for tw = 4 years. - Source: Kamp Nielsen (1989).

4.4.6 Recovery of Lakes

When the nutrient loading to a lake is suddenly reduced, the return to equilibrium between the new inlet concentration and the in-lake concentration is delayed due to the dilution effect which depends on hydraulic residence time, and possibly also due to 'sediment memory' or internal loading which is a continued release of nutrients from the sediment. The effect of dilution alone is shown in Fig. 4.36.

That dilution alone is part of the explanation for the delayed response is obvious from Fig. 4.37. From the figure it appears that lakes with long residence times respond almost according to a dilution scheme or even faster, whereas lakes with short residence times have a long recovery period. The reason is that the Danish lakes with short residence times are also the lakes with the highest preceding loading (Fig. 4.38), and they have the biggest pools of sedimentary phosphorus. However, regardless of hydraulic residence time, most lakes do respond and recover within a few years, yet some only after a period of up to 15 years.

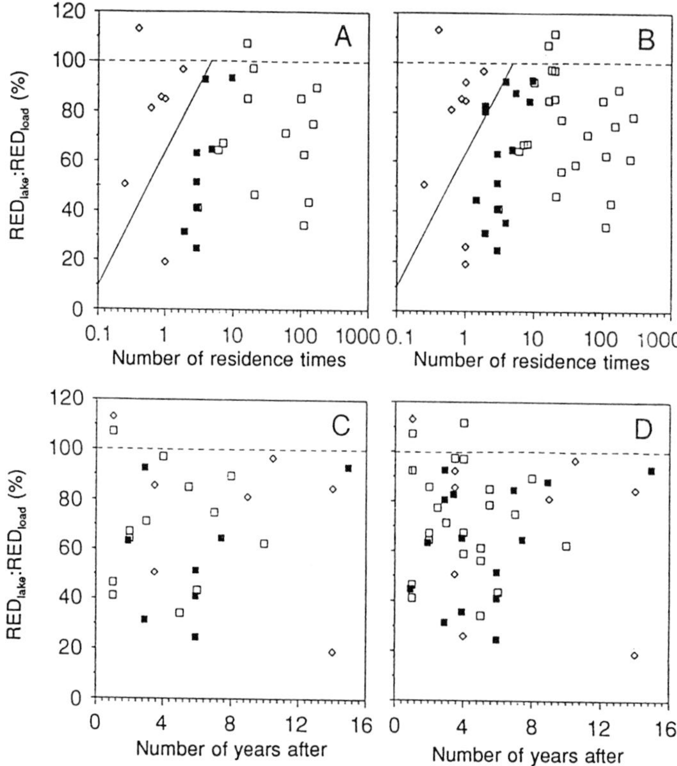

Figure 4.37. The ratio (in %) between reduction in P_{lake} and reduction in P_{load}, plotted against number of residence periods t_w (A and B) and against number of years (C and D) passed since the reduction in load took place. A, C: Danish lakes; B, D: Danish lakes supplemented with data from Cullen and Forsberg (1988). □: $t_w < 0.5$ year; ■: $0.5 < t_w < 2.5$ years; ◊: $t_w > 2.5$ years. - After Kristensen et al. (1990*).

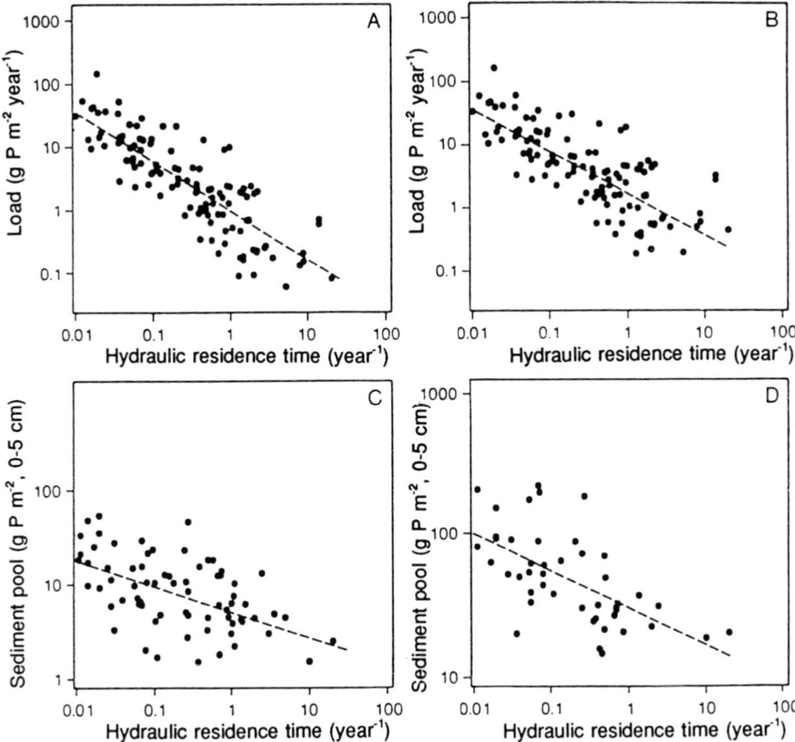

Figure 4.38. Relations between phosphorus load (A, B) and accumulated phosphorus pool in the sediment (C, D), and hydraulic residence time. A: P-load; B: P-load corrected for a difference in P-retention in lakes with different t_w values; C: P-pool 0-5 cm; D: P-pool 0-20 cm. - After Kristensen et al. (1990*).

The recovery patterns for some lakes are shown in Fig. 4.39. For comparison, the dilution response alone is also shown. The lakes recover fast immediately after reduced loading, and a 50% recovery is achieved after 2-4 years, but total recovery may take 10 years or more. Some of the resilience caused by the release from the sediments can be related to the accumulated pools of sedimentary phosphorus (Fig. 4.40), but there is also the phenomenon that in lakes with short residence time the released phosphorus is resedimented, because the residence time during the release period is relatively long. A big amplitude in hydraulic residence time is also a cause for delayed recovery.

In the investigation just mentioned the response in phytoplankton biomass and transparency depth followed the reduction in phosphorus loading (Fig. 4.41), but in some cases resilience in the biological structure occurred. In shallow lakes, where the submersed vegetation had disappeared, the response was absent at the beginning, but the removal of 50% of the planktivorous fish increased the transparency, and a positive feedback was introduced due to the stabilizing effect on the sediment, and an improvement in transparency depth above the expected was observed (Fig. 4.42).

4.5 RESTORATION OF STREAMS AND LAKES

Improving the water quality by reducing the outlet of pollutants is not always enough to reestablish the habitat and its natural biological diversity, and in lakes the recovery process may take too long. In such cases restoration measures may be implemented.

Due to the short residence time, a stream responds almost instantaneously to reduced loading. However, contamination of sediments with heavy metals or toxic organic compounds may require a dredging of these sediments.

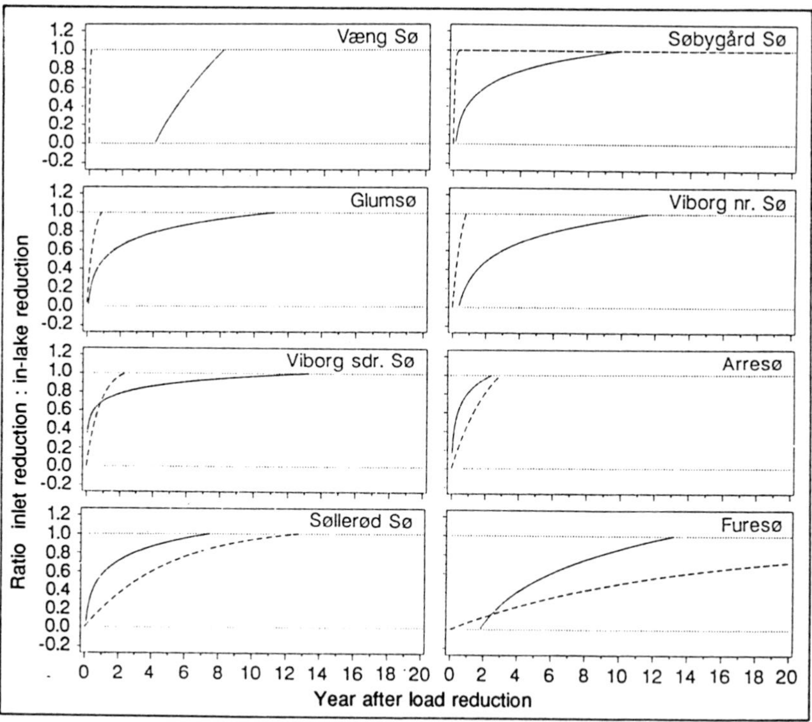

Figure 4.39. The course in time of the ratio of reduction in inlet concentration to reduction in in-lake concentration, as observed in 8 Danish lakes. Solid curve: best fit with an exponential function; dotted curve: best fit with a simple dilution model. - After Kristensen et al. (1990*).

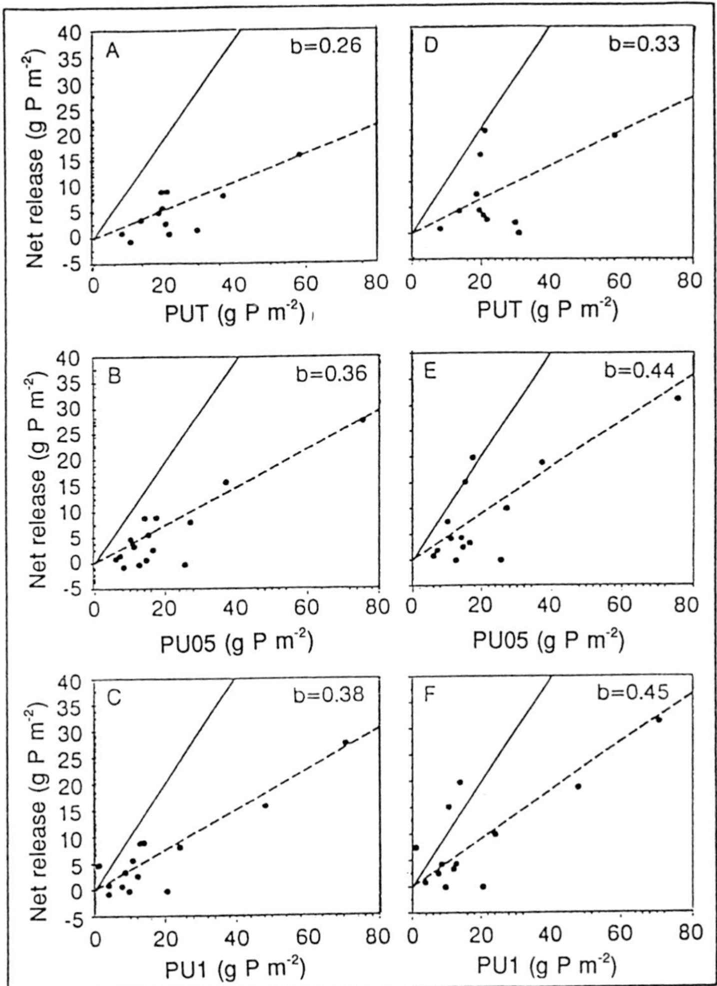

Figure 4.40. The relation between net release of total phosphorus (A, B, C: first 5 years after load reduction; D, E, F: entire known period since load reduction) and P-pool in the upper 10-cm layer of the sediment. A, D: total P-pool; B, E: P-pool > 0.5 mg P g^{-1} DW; C, F: P-pool > 1.0 mg P g^{-1} DW. Solid line: release = pool; dotted line: linear regression of release as a function of pool; b = slope of regression line. - Source: Kamp Nielsen (1991*).

The Danish Watercourse Act provides for public subsidies for habitat improvement in channelized and regulated streams, and modifications of the weedcutting and dredging patterns in the streams are introduced. The natural riffle-pool sequence in streams can be reestablished by replacing weirs with stretches of rocky cobbles; streams confined to concrete pipes can be opened up; the flow-rate can be increased locally by current concentrators; re-meandering can be achieved by weedcutting in a wave pattern with a wavelength of 10 times the stream width, which is the natural sinuosity in Danish streams; hides can be established by means of treetrunks, stones or riparian vegetation; and artificial spawning grounds for salmonids can be made (Fig. 4.43).

In *lakes* the restoration measures can be directed at the symptoms of eutrophication: excessive phytoplankton biomass or, more specifically, excessive growth of bluegreens; and too dense coverage of macrophytes. Or the measures can counteract oxygen depletion during winter and during the summer stratification. In other cases the initiatives are directed at the causes of the eutrophication, i.e., the nutrients. They can be removed from the lake water directly by precipitation or by removal of biomass, or their flushing out of the lake can be enhanced by increased flushing, when the nutrient concentration is high - possibly by siphoning off the hypolimnion.

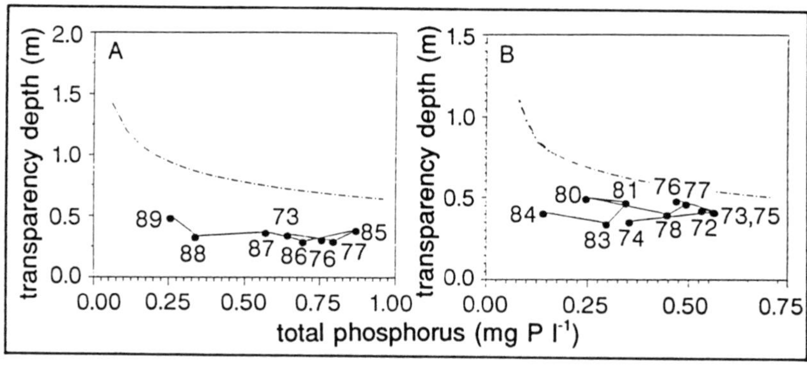

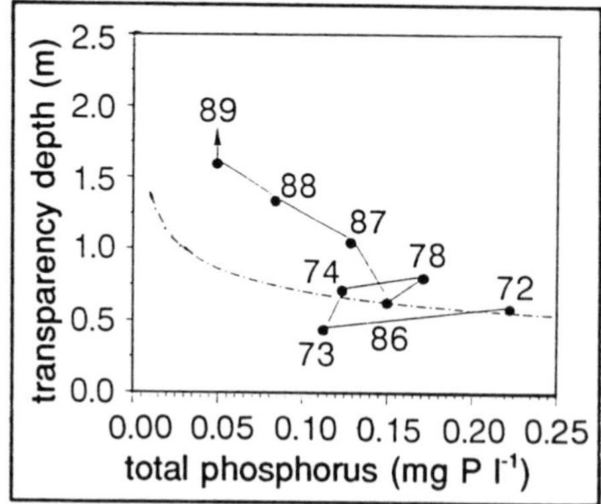

Figure 4.41. (Above) The relation between transparency depth and in-lake phosphorus concentration in the period before and after load reduction (May-September). The dotted curve shows the relation as generally estimated (including depth-correction) for Danish lakes. A: Arresø, Sealand; B: Lyngby Sø, north of Copenhagen. - After Kristensen et al. (1990*).

Figure 4.42. (Below) As Figure 4.41, for Væng Sø, Jutland.

If the delayed recovery is caused by extremely large sediment pools, the sediments can be removed by dredging, or they can be sealed by covering with membranes. More sophisticated techniques include chemical stabilization by pH-regulation and addition of phosphorus-binding agents such as iron. Alternatively the sediment mineralization can be enhanced by adding nitrate (organic matter is used when the nitrate is denitrified), or the sediment can be oxygenated (Fig. 4.44), for example with hydrogen peroxide.

All these restoration measures must be carefully planned, to avoid unwanted results. The removal of phytoplankton by filtration is expensive, and in practice it is not feasible. The prevention of growth of bluegreens by increased circulation has proved useful in reservoirs, but the bluegreens are most likely to be replaced by diatoms, which can cause problems by clogging of filters if the water is used for drinking.

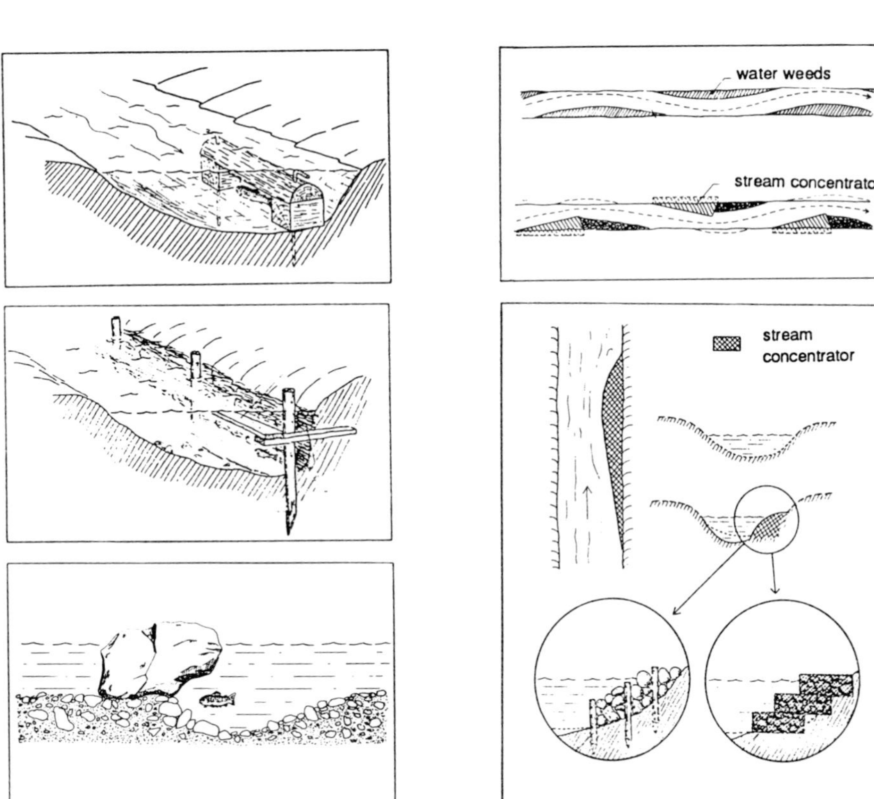

Figure 4.43. Self-explanatory sketches of various watercourse-restoration measures: three ways of establishing fish hides (left), and the siting and design of stream concentrators (right). - Source: Anonymous (1983a*).

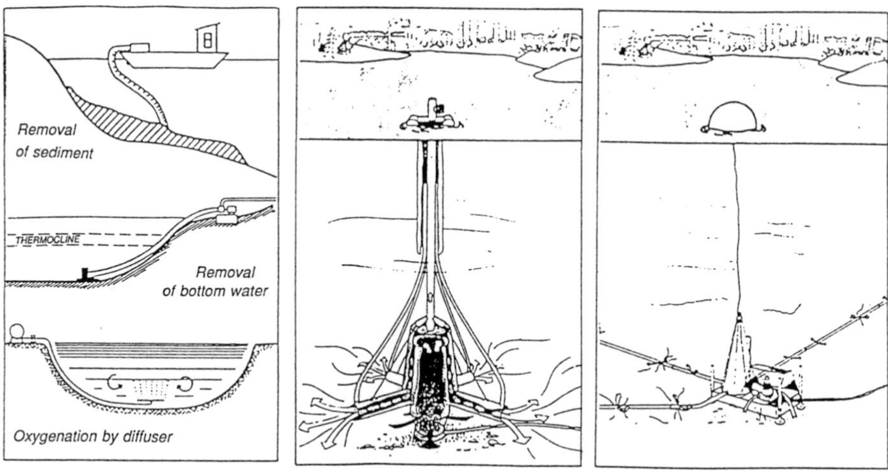

Figure 4.44. Various lake-restoration measures, in particular oxygenation by means of hydrogen peroxide. - Source: Krogsgaard (1987*).

The introduction of *grass carp* in weed control is done by routine in many channels or lakes where weeds are causing problems for navigation. But the grass carp accumulates very little of the nitrogen and phosphorus it takes up when eating the plants; the rest is excreted and pbytoplankton blooms are formed instead. However, the *silver carp* is an obligate planktivore, and the two species in combination are said to be successful controllers in ponds.

The prevention of oxygen depletion in shallow lakes by aeration saves many small lakes during ice-cover periods. In stratified lakes one can aerate so much that destratification occurs, but in such cases it has to be remembered that in the normal stagnation period, there is also an increase in sediment temperature and thereby in oxygen consumption. In some cases such a destratification has increased the oxygen consumption above the aeration capacity, and fish-kills have occurred due to severe oxygen depletion. Where the aeration is done in the hypolimnion only, leaving the thermocline intact, the measure can be applied succesfully, as proved in several instances.

In very deep lakes the aeration has to be done against a high pressure and a resulting oversaturation with nitrogen can cause damage to the fishes, but in such cases the use of pure oxygen may be advantageous. In the Danish Lake Hald such a measure has been implemented for several years with good results, but the method is rather expensive; in spite of a careful administration of the oxygen and saved costs for pumping, the annual costs of oxygen are about 60 000 USD for a lake volume of 3 km^3.

By application of aluminum sulfate to the lake water, phosphorus can be precipitated as aluminum phosphate. This has indeed been practiced in many lakes, but the effect is only temporary. After precipitation the phospate is rapidly redissolved at the sediment surface where pH is lower, and controlling the pH in the whole water body in well-buffered lakes is not an easy matter. Alternatively, the lake water can be pumped into basins where precipitation or adsorption on activated aluminum oxide columns can be performed, but the method is costly. Increased flushing from the hypolimnion has been done in some cases, but if the lakes have an anoxic hypolimnion, the smell of hydrogen sulphide from the siphoned water can be a real nuisance. But the measure is cheap, since there are no running costs.

The removal of the nutrient-rich surface sediments (0.5 to 1 m) has been carried out in some cases. The best known example is Lake Trummen in Sweden, where the upper part of the sediments were dredged and the interstitial water stripped for phosphate and fed back into the lake. The costs were about 800 000 USD for a lake of 1 km^2 surface area. The lake recovered considerably to lower nutrient levels and lower phytoplankton biomass.

The treatment of lake sediments with a mixture of nitrate, iron chloride and lime has been undertaken in a few cases; some with success, some without. The theory behind the treatment is that the nitrate mineralizes the sediment, releasing phosphate and decreasing oxygen demand, while the phosphate is fixed as iron (III) phosphate under pH-control by the lime. Below the sediment surface, however, iron (III) will be reduced as soon as the nitrate is used up, phosphate will be released again, and disastrous effects can occur if the lake is nitrogen-limited prior to the application of nitrate.

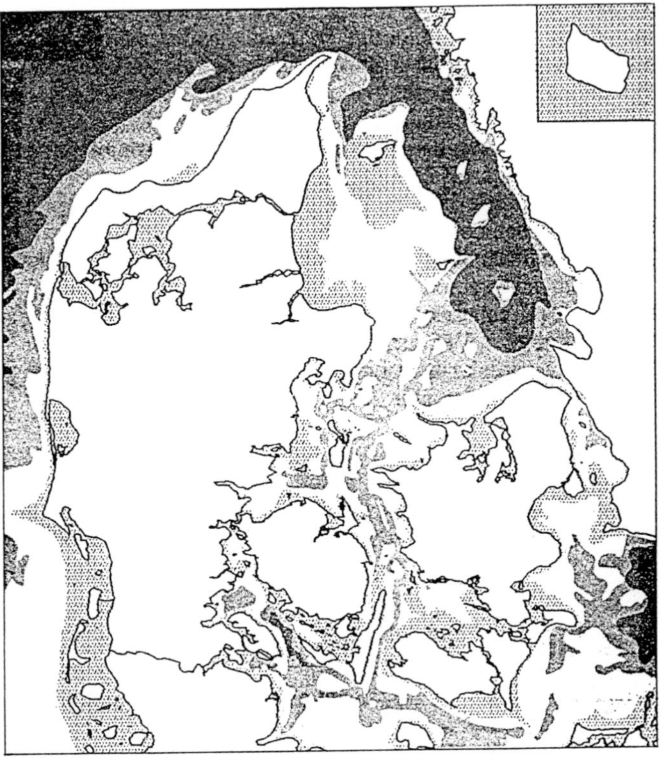

Figure 4.45. Regions of 10 m (grey), 20 m (white), and 30 m depth (dark grey) in Danish waters. - After Anonymous (1990*).

4.6 COASTAL WATERS

Coastal waters include a variety of very different ecosystems: salt marshes, seagrass beds, seaweed systems, mangroves, lagoons, estuaries, sill fjords, bays, coves, and coral reefs. Some of the systems are closed systems, but most of them are much more open than lakes. They have an open boundary to the sea, and they exchange water with the open sea by tidal and wind-driven currents. The connection with the huge volume of water in the sea damps the seasonal and diurnal temperature amplitudes, and the temperature regime is sometimes influenced by oceanic currents moving over long distances.

4.6.1 Hydrography of the Kattegat and the Belt Sea

The Danish coastal waters are shallow, with depths typically lower than 30 m, except that along the Swedish coast a ridge extension of the Norwegian Ridge has depths of 50-100 m (Fig. 4.45).

Originating from run-off into the Baltic Sea, the Danish belts and the Kattegat receive a net flow of about 500 km^3 per year, but the exchange is about double. Winds, aided by the Coriolis force, are pressing saline waters (35 ‰) from the North Sea into the Kattegat where it flows southwards as a bottom current separated from the north-flowing current of brackish water (7-8 ‰) by a halocline.

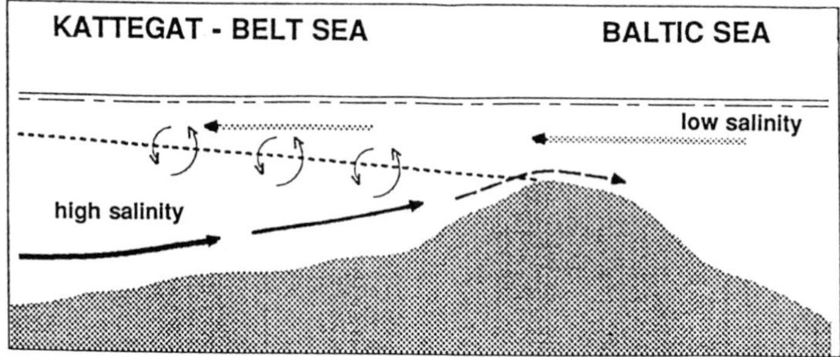

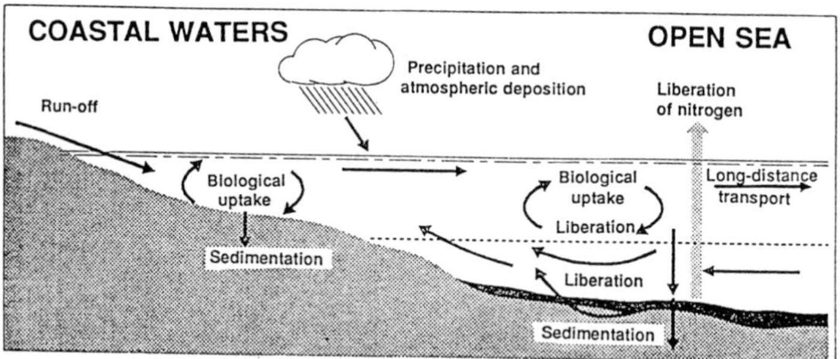

Figure 4.46. (Above) Stratification and salinity in Danish coastal waters. - After Anonymous (1990*).

Figure 4.47. (Below) Rotation of nutrient salts in the sea. - After Anonymous (1990*).

But during the passage through the shallow Kattegat a mixing of the two waterbodies occurs, the halocline moves upwards, and the thickness of the surface layer decreases as it moves north. The sills at Drogen and Darss normally prevent the entry of the highly saline Skagerrak water - only in extreme wind situations is the bottom water pressed over the sills, and the bottom water in the depths at Gotland is replaced by saline and oxygen-rich Skagerrak water (Fig. 4.46).

The halocline represents a strong barrier between surface and bottom water, as the thermocline does in stratified lakes. The stratification is most stable during summer, and very little of the regenerated nutrients from sedimentated phytoplankton returns to the photic layer during the production period. The primary production is left to utilize nutrients regenerated in the surface water. This regeneration can be very efficient through the 'microbial loop', starting with excreted organic matter from the algae that are being utilized by bacteria, which in turn are grazed by a web of micro- and macrozooplankton. The nutrients are thus returned to the algae which in this period become dominated by small forms with high surface/volume ratios.

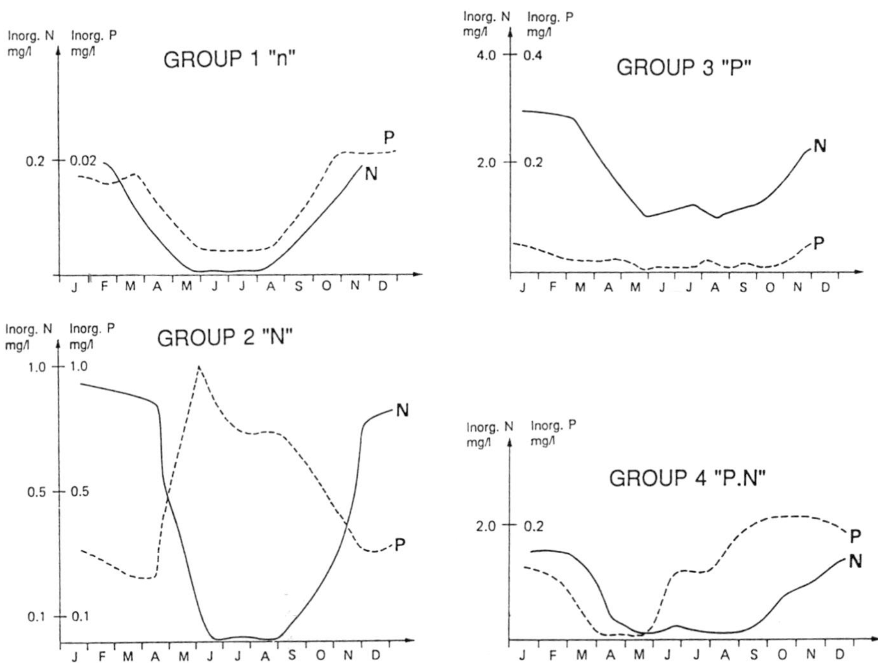

Figure 4.48. Typical annual concentration curves for N and P in four groups of Danish coastal waters. The groups are labeled so as to suggest whether nitrogen or phosphorus is the limiting factor for production during summer months. - Source: Anonymous (1984*).

There is a significant difference between the stratified coastal waters with depths greater than 10-15 m and the shallow, non-stratified waters. In the stratified waters nutrient depletion in the euphotic layer prevails throughout the production period, and the bottom waters are susceptible to oxygen depletion. The shallow waters are richer in nutrients because they are closer to the terrestrial sources and have a more rapid regeneration of nutrients in the sediments (Fig. 4.47). If the nutrient loading is high, also temporary oxygen depletion can occur in this area during quiet periods.

Nutrients are transported to the coastal ecosystems by rivers, diffuse run-off and precipitation, but they are diluted in a big volume, and generally the primary production is lower in the sea than in lakes and terrestrial ecosystems. However, some coastal ecosystems such as salt marshes, sea-grass beds and mangroves are very productive systems, utilizing the benefits from being anchored in a turbulent environment with a steady but small supply of nutrients.

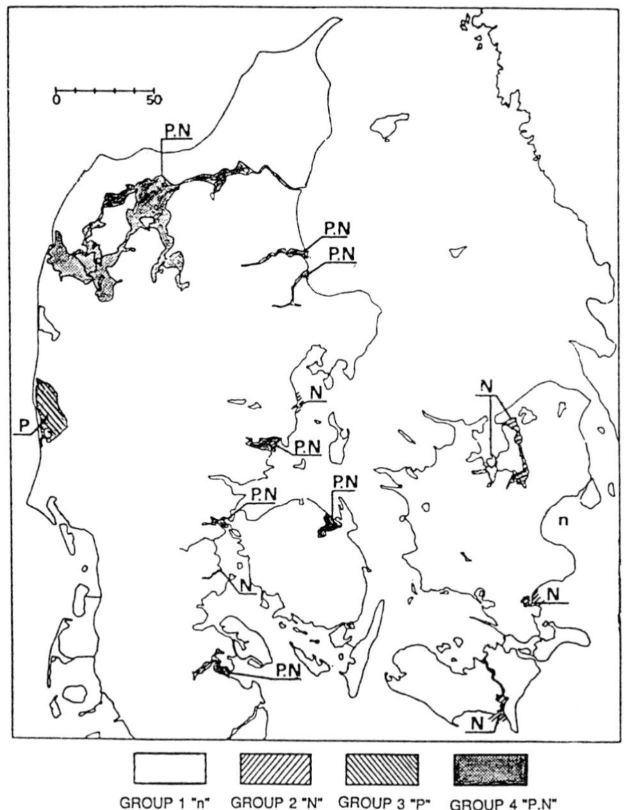

Figure 4.49. Danish coastal waters classified according to N or P limitation, see Fig. 4.48. Group "n" is not shadowed in the figure; all the larger water regions except the North Sea (i.e., the Skagerrak, the Kattegat, the Belt Sea and the Baltic Sea) belong to Group "n". - Source: Anonymous (1984*).

Table 4.23. Annual direct import of nutrient salts into the Danish coastal waters (not including import by sea currents). Some of the figures for Sweden and Germany 1989 are estimated by comparison with Danish conditions. - Source: Anonymous (1990*).

	Nitrogen		Phosphorus	
	1989 tons	81-88 tons	1989 tons	81-88 tons
Watercourses (incl. waste-water)	43000	77000	2120	3000
Direct outlet:				
Municipal installations	9950	9950	2510	2510
Rainwater outlet		220		50
Industry	3000	260	40	40
Aquaculture	300	260	40	40
Denmark (rounded)	56000	90000	5050	5900
Sweden				
Watercourses (incl. waste-water)	22000	40500	*	760
Direct outlet	4400	4800	500	770
Germany				
Watercourses (incl. waste-water)	6600	12500	*	1950
Direct outlet	> 6300	> 6300	*	> 670
Precipitation	44000	48500	450	500
Total (rounded)	139000	203000	*	10500

The run-off from watersheds dominated by drains from agriculture has an N/P ratio of 40-60, whereas the ratio for domestic sewage is about 4. Depending on the dominant sources, different coastal waters achieve different N/P-ratios. But in streams and lakes the nitrogen losses are generally higher than the phosphorus losses due to the 'extra' loss by denitrification, and these 'extra' losses continue through the coastal waters. With increasing oceanic influence the N/P-ratio decreases further, and nitrogen limitation of the primary production becomes the most common limitation.

In Danish coastal waters we find a range from phosphorus almost being in control, to both nitrogen and phosphorus control and to nitrogen control alone (Fig. 4.48). The distribution of the various limitation patterns in the Danish coastal waters is shown in Fig. 4.49.

A typical decreasing N/P-ratio is observed in the Roskilde Fjord (Sealand) and in one of its watersheds, Langvad River. Upstream the river the N/P ratio is about 20; beyond a group of lakes the ratio is reduced to about 10; and at the outlet to the Isefjord and the Kattegat it has decreased further to approximately 5. The decrease becomes even more pronounced when we take into consideration that all the nitrogen is available for the primary production.

4.6.2 The Eutrophication of Coastal Waters

During the past decades the levels of nutrients, especially of nitrogen, have increased in the inner Danish seas (Table 4.23). The increase is largest in the Belt Sea, and here also an increase in the primary production has been observed (Fig. 4.50). The sources of both are local from the surrounding countries (Fig. 4.51), but in certain periods there is also an important contribution from the Jutland current which goes north from the German Bight along the west coast of Jutland into the Skagerrak. The contribution from the outgoing surface water from the Baltic Sea is less significant since only a small proportion of the nitrogen is in the inorganic form. Last, but not least, the contribution from the atmosphere is important, since it makes its major contribution in the late summer, when the needs of the phytoplankton are most severe, and its relative importance is greater than suggested by the annual figures.

The increase in nitrogen levels and primary production has been accompanied by increases in phytoplankton biomass, and in the near coastal waters dramatic changes in the balance between the autotrophic components have occurred. The depth limits for the submersed, higher vegetation has decreased considerably, following the reduction in transparency depth which again relates to nitrogen levels (Fig. 4.52).

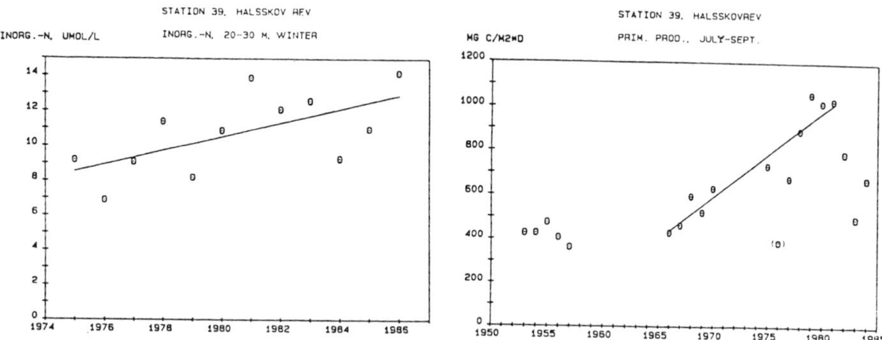

Figure 4.50. (Left) Course of the concentration of nitrogen nutrient salts (NO_3^-, NO_2^-, NH_4^+) in Jan.-March at Halskov by the Belt Sea (west of Sealand) 1975-86; regression coefficient: r = 0.636. (Right) Average production of phytoplankton (mg C m^{-2} day^{-1}) in July-Sept. at Halskov 1953-84; r = 0.941. - Source: Brøgger Jensen (1987*).

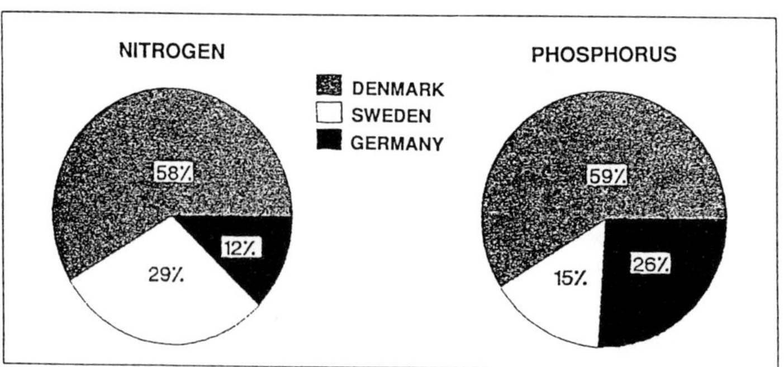

Figure 4.51. Outlet and run-off of nutrient salts to Danish coastal waters 1981-88, distributed between Denmark, Sweden and Germany. - Source: Anonymous (1990*).

A survey of Roskilde Fjord in 1942 showed that eelgrass covered almost the entire ground, while in 1989 only on the fringes of the fjord did a vegetation cover exist. A much more rapid change was observed in Ringkjøbing Fjord (West Jutland) where an increase in summer chlorophyll from 0.5 µg/l to 70 µg/l in the period 1978-1981 removed almost the entire vegetation cover, and approximately 25 000 swans disappeared due to starvation. The development in Nissum Fjord also illustrates the rapid development during the 1970s and the 1980s (Fig. 4.53).

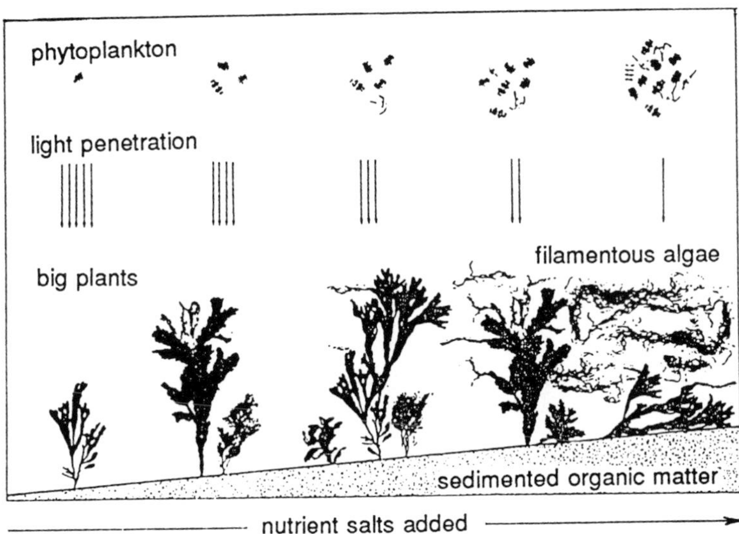

Figure 4.52. Changes in the vegetation in coastal waters by increased import of nutrient salts. - After Anonymous (1990*).

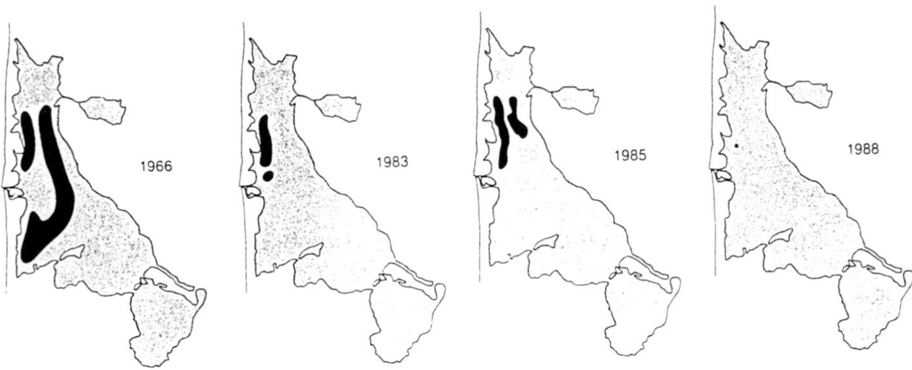

Figure 4.53. Development 1966-88 of the extension of bottom vegetation in Nissum Fjord (West Jutland). - After Anonymous (1990*).

The decreased transparency and increased nitrogen levels favour the development of epiphytic algae on the leaves of rooted macrophytes and macroalgae; also filamentous algae such as *Cladophora* and *Enteromorpha* and free-floating, fast-growing algae like *Ulva* take over the dominance by outshading of the rooted, slow-growing species. The mass development of such filamentous and free-floating algae often creates near-shore oxygen depletion when they decay in accumulations formed by wind and waves.

Many estuaries and bays change rapidly when the rooted vegetation disappears, since the stabilizing effect on the sediment stops and organic matter and nutrients are resuspended in the water column, thereby accelerating the adverse conditions.

Changes within the phytoplankton community due to eutrophication is a well-known phenomenon. Bloom-forming species seem to have increased in abundance during the 1980s, and some of the species are toxic to animals and man. In May-June 1988 the ichthyotoxin-producing *Chrysochromulina polyepis* bloomed all over the northern part of Kattegat and in the Skagerrak and caused fish kills in marine aquacultures.

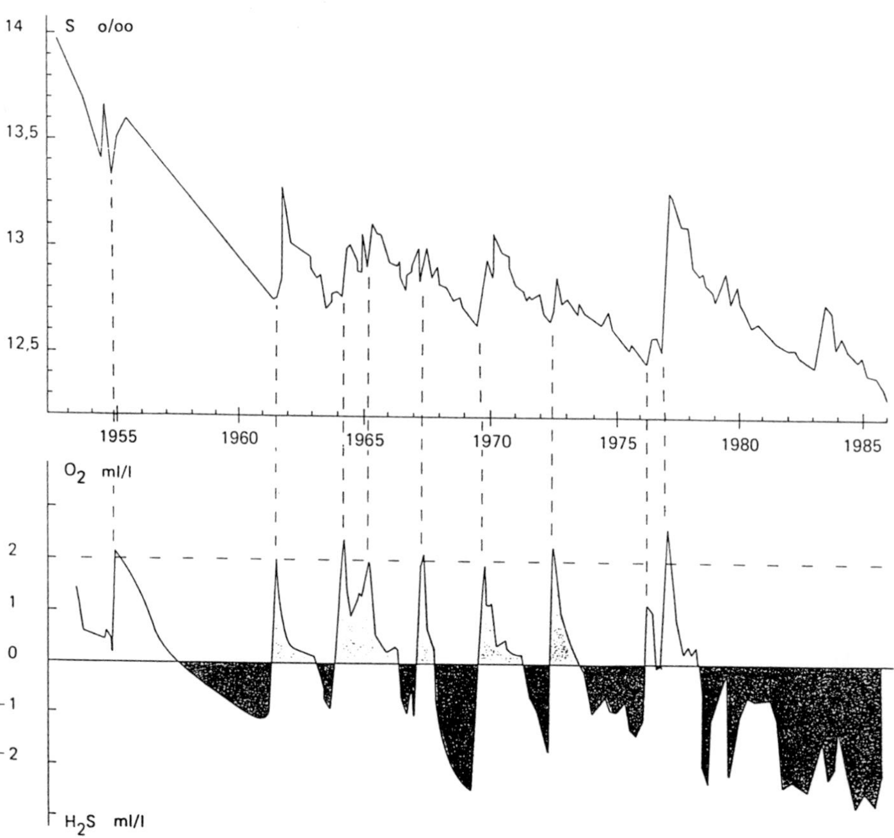

Figure 4.54. The Baltic Sea: variations 1952-86 in salinity (S), oxygen concentration (O_2) and hydrogen sulfide concentration (H_2S), as measured at a depth of 240 m in the Gotland Deep. Vertical lines show points of water renewal. - After Anonymous (1988*).

The PSP (paralytic shellfish poison)-producing *Alexandrium tamarense* is observed every year in Limfjorden, but although it can be deadly poisonous to man if he eats mussels with accumulated toxins, the findings of such mussels have been too low to initiate a ban. On the other hand, every year temporary bans on the fishing of mussels are imposed due to occurrence of *Dinophysis* species producing the DSP (diarrhetic shellfish poison).

4.6.3 Oxygen Depletion and Bottom Fauna

In Danish coastal waters oxygen depletion has been observed since the start of the century in the deep parts of the southern Lillebælt, and an almost permanent oxygen depletion in the stagnant, deep basins of the central Baltic Sea have been known for long (Fig. 4.54). But in 1981 oxygen-depleted areas in Kattegat, the Belt Sea and in the North Sea came as a surprise to everybody; and during the 1980s the situation has been the same every late summer. The extension and the periodicity of the depletion events depend on the wind and the mixing of the waterbody, but oxygen-depletion events in the spring seem to correlate with the winter run-off of nitrogen.

With increased transport of organic material to the sediment, the oxygen demand of the sediment is increasing (Fig. 4.55). The oxygen will not penetrate so deep; burrowing invertebrates will disappear, their active ventilation of the sediment will stop, and the sediment will thus become even more anaerobic. The aerobic layer which oxidizes sulphide formed in the deeper sediments may reach the surface, and a white sheet of sulfide-oxidizing bacteria may be formed, indicating that no invertebrates are able to survive (Fig. 4.56).

If the supply of organic material is increased, both the number of species and the total biomass will also increase at first, but a further increase in supply will lead to a decrease in number and biomass. However, the reduced competition may favour specialist detritivores in certain regions of organic matter supply.

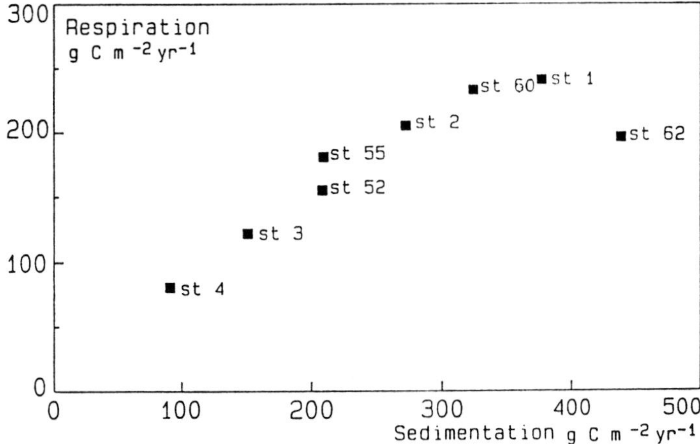

Figure 4.55. Sediment respiration plotted against carbon sedimentation. - Source: Kamp Nielsen (1991).

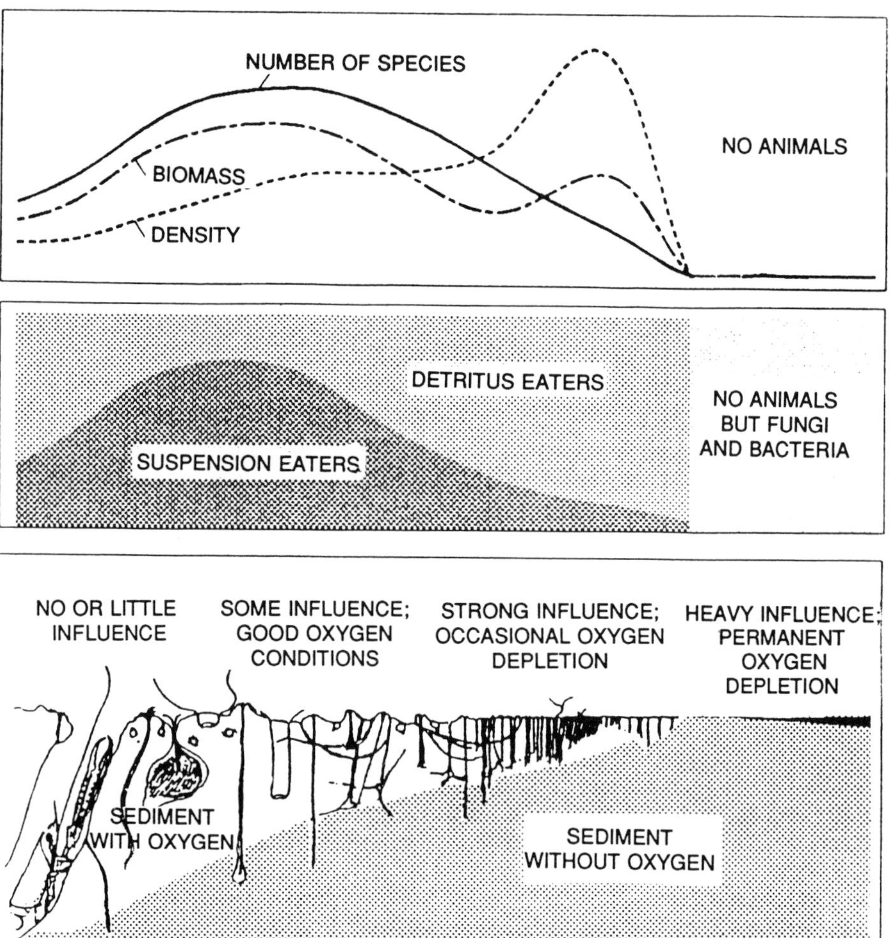

Figure 4.56. Changes in the bottom fauna caused by increasing concentration of organic matter. - After Anonymous (1990*).

The bottom invertebrates are not able to escape a decreasing oxygen concentration, but fish are to some extent able to flee, and only if a large area is depleted, or a fish stock is surrounded by oxygen-depleted water, do virtual fish-kills occur. But due to the reduced food availability, especially bottom-living fish species such as plaice and cod are reduced in abundance, and the catch is going down (Fig. 4.57). The most dramatic change in catch is exhibited by the Norwegian lobster, which lives buried in the soft bottom in the deeper parts of the Kattegat. The reduced oxygen levels at the bottom forces the lobsters to the sediment surface, and at the start of the oxygen depletion the catch by the trawlers can be tremendous.

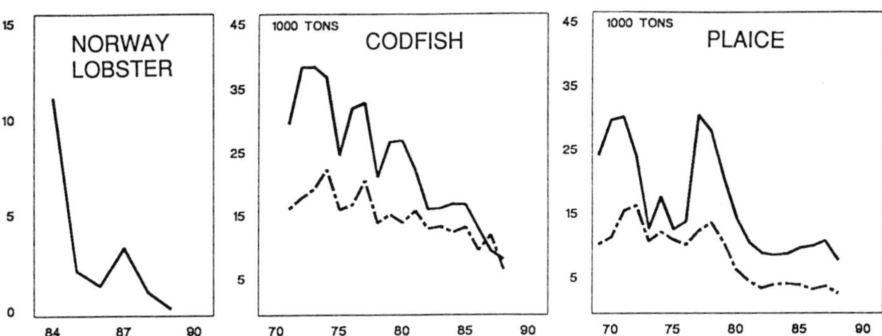

Figure 4.57. Development of spawning populations (solid curves) and catches (dot-and-dash curves) of codfish and plaice and of standardized catch (CPUE) of Norway lobster in the Kattegat. - After Anonymous (1990*).

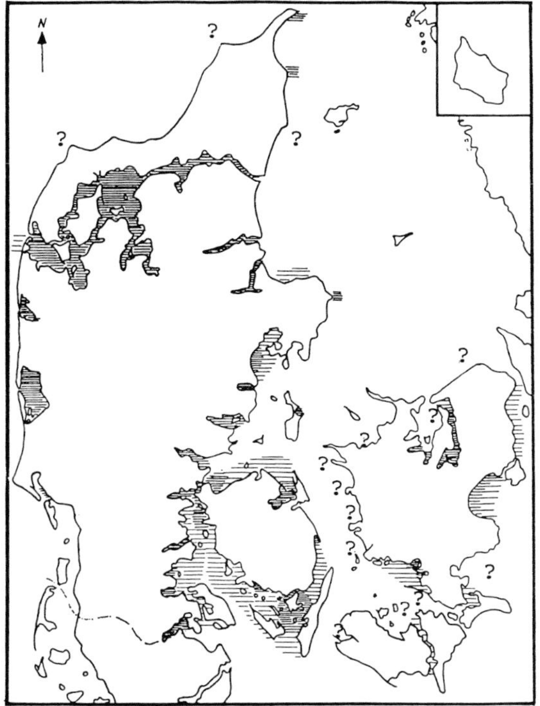

Figure 4.58. Danish coastal areas where the general objectives regarding no or little influence have been judged not fulfilled (dark shade) or threatened (light shade). A "?" indicates that no assessment was made as yet. - Source: Jensen (1987*).

4.6.4 Recipient Quality Planning for Coastal Waters in Denmark

The coastal areas have much more open boundaries, and it has been more difficult to assess the responsibilities for the various areas. Also the requirements of seagoing vessels and equipment has delayed the implementation of the recipient quality planning and surveillance in the marine area. In principle the 6 m depth curve separates the responsibility of the counties, having the responsibility inside the depth curve, and the Ministry of Environment with the responsibility outside. But in practice all bays and fjords which can be confined within straight land to land lines are under county administration (Fig. 4.58). The general, extended, and reduced criteria are also valid for the coastal waters, but some differences exist in the administration due to the open character of the areas.

An area with reduced criteria shall meet the general criteria in the 'conflict front' between the two areas, and similarly shall the extended criteria be met in the 'front' between a general and an extended criteria. The reference for the general criteria can in some cases be found outside the planning area, if it cannot be found inside. But the general development in the open parts of the Kattegat and the North Sea have forced the authorities to move away from the reference practice and to accept a more general and 'soft' description according to which the general objectives are as follows (cf. Table 4.3):

- Phytoplankton appears in moderate quantities only, and there are no excessive occurrences, in particular not of annoying or poisonous algae;
- On soft bottom, the vegetation is dominated by dense populations of eel grass, with a good depth-range. On stone and hard ground, the alga vegetation shows a natural zonation with a good depth-range, and annual algae do not dominate excessively;
- The bottom fauna shows a high diversity; pollution-tolerant species do not dominate;
- The fish fauna consists of common species such as eel, flounder, dab, plaice, codfish, trout; there is no excessive incidence of diseases and the fishes do not taste disagreeably. Seasonally, also herring, garfish and mackerel occur; and on shallow water cutling and flatfish fry;
- Bath-water standards are met.

REFERENCES

Anonymous, 1983*. Forslag til recipientkvalitetsplan og spildevandsplan for Roskilde Fjord og opland. (Reject of recipient-quality plan and waste-water plan for the Roskilde area). Greater Copenhagen Council, Copenhagen, 82 pp.

Anonymous, 1984*. NPO-Redegørelsen. (The NPO Account). National Agency of Environmental Protection, Copenhagen.

Anonymous, 1986*. Miljøforvaltning. (Environmental Management). 4th ed. The Center for Environmental Protection. Royal Veter. and Agric. Univ., Copenhagen.

Anonymous, 1988*. Miljøet of Storebæltsforbindelsen. (The environment and the Storebaelt Bridge). A/S Storebæltsforbindelsen, Copenhagen.

Anonymous, 1990*. Vandmiljø - 90. (Water Environment - 90). Report no. 1 / 1990. National

Agency of Environmental Protection, Copenhagen, 204 pp.

Anonymous (ed.), 1991*. Konsensuskonference: Eksperternes indlæg. (Consensus Conference: Abstracts). Ministry of Education, Copenhagen, 423 pp.

Brøgger Jensen, J., (1987*). Vurdering af vandkvaliteten i de danske kystvande. (Assessment of the water quality in Danish coastal waters). In: Federley (1987*), 373-387.

Federley, B. (ed.), 1987*. Eutrofiering av havs och kustområden. (Eutrophication of sea and coastal water). Proc. 22. Nordic Symposion on Water Research, Laugarvatn.

Jensen, G.E., 1987*. Årsager til og effekter af eutrofieringen i Kattegat og Bælthavet. (Eutro phication in the Kattegat and the Belt Sea: causes and effects). In: Federley (1987*), 87-100.

Jensen, K.S., T. Moth Iversen and C. Lindegaard, 1988*. Ferskvandsøkologi. (Freshwater ecology). Freshwater-Biological Laboratory, Copenhagen University.

Jørgensen, S.E. and R.A. Vollenweider, 1988. Guidelines of Lake Management, I: Principles of Lake Management. ILEC/UN Envir. Progr., 199 pp.

Kamp Nielsen, L., 1986. Modelling of eutrophication processes. In: Frangipane, E.F. (ed.): Lakes Pollution and Recovery. Proc. Internat. EWPCA Congr., 15-18 April 1985, Rome, 61-101.

Kamp Nielsen, L., 1989. The relation between external P-load and in-lake P-concentration. Chap. III in: H. Sas (ed.): Lake Restoration by Reduction of Nutrient Loading. Academia Verlag, Sankt Augustin (Germany).

Kamp Nielsen, L., 1990*. I hvor høj grad tilbageholdes fosfor i de forskellige typer våd- og vandområder? / Tilbageholdelse af fosfor. (Retention of phosphor). In: Anonymous (1991), 31 pp.

Kamp Nielsen, L., 1991. Benthic-pelagic coupling of nutrient metabolism along an estuarine eutrophication gradient. Developm. Hydrobiol. (in press).

Kern-Hansen, U. (ed.), 1983*. Vedligeholdelse og restaurering af vandløb. (Maintenance and restoration of watercourses). National Agency of Environmental Protection / Freshwater Laboratory.

Kristensen, P., J.P. Jensen and E. Jeppesen, 1990*. Eutrofieringsmodeller for søer. (Eutrophication Models for Lakes). NPo Research Report C9, National Agency of Environmental Protection, Copenhagen, 120 pp.

Krogsgaard, J., 1987*. De danske søer. (The Danish lakes). VKI Orientering (Bulletin of the Danish Water Quality Institute) 43, 3-7.

Moth Iversen, T. and C. Lindegaard, 1983*. Biologisk bedømmelse af vandløb forurenet med organisk stof. (Biological assessment of watercourses). Freshwater-Biological Laboratory, Copenhagen University.

Moth Iversen, T., C. Lindegaard, K. Sand-Jensen and J. Thorup, 1989*. Vandløbsøkologi. (Watercourse Ecology). Freshwater-Biological Laboratory, Copenhagen University, 109 pp.

Rasmussen, K. and C. Lindegaard, 1988. Effects of pollution with iron compounds (ochre) on the macroinvertebrate fauna of the river Vidå in South-West Jutland, Denmark. Water Res. 22, 1101-1108.

Wetzel, R.G., 1983. Limnology. 2nd ed. Saunders College Publ., Philadelphia, 760 pp.

5 WATER MANAGEMENT AND WATER RESOURCES

SVEN ERIK JØRGENSEN

5.1 THE PROPERTIES OF WATER

Water is the most abundant chemical compound on Earth (Table 5.1), and it also has several unique properties. Its importance for all life on Earth appears from numerous facts, some of which are:

1. *Our bodies consist of 70% water,* and we need at least 1.5 l per day to survive. We can survive without food for perhaps 80 days, but without water for only a few days.
2. *Water serves as a basic transport medium for several vital nutrients.*
3. *Water removes and dilutes many natural and man-made wastes.*
4. *Water has a great ability to store heat energy and to conduct heat; it also has an extremely high vaporization temperature, compared with its molecular weight.* These thermal properties are major factors of influence on the climatic pattern of the world, e.g., in minimizing sharp changes in temperature on the Earth.
5. *Water has its maximum density at +4°C,* so that solid water, ice, is less dense than liquid water. This is the reason why a water body starts to freeze from the top. If ice were denser than liquid water, then lakes, rivers and oceans would freeze from the bottom up, killing most higher forms of aquatic life.
6. Temperature changes produce characteristic patterns of *water stratification and circulation* which greatly influence aquatic life, cf. Chapter 4.

5.2 THE HYDROLOGICAL CYCLE

Water evaporates from the oceans, rivers, lakes and continents, and gravity pulls it back down as rain. Some of this water falls on the land and sinks or percolates into the soil and ground to form groundwater. Like a sponge, the soil can hold a certain amount of water, but if it rains harder than the maximal percolation rate, water begins to collect in puddles and ditches, and to run off into nearby streams, rivers and lakes. This run-off causes erosion. Eventually, the water runs into the ocean which is the largest water-storage tank. Because of this cycle, water is continually replaced, as indicated in Table 5.2.

Freshwater ecosystems occupy a relatively small portion of the surface of the Earth, in comparison to marine and terrestrial habitats (see Table 5.3). The amount of freshwater, including the glaciers of the Arctic and Antarctic regions, accounts for only 2.4% of the total global amount of water; the remaining 97.6% are the vast amounts of water in the oceans which cover 71% of the surface of the earth. Only a very small part, about 0,01% of the global amount of water, is contained in lakes.

Table 5.1. Water resources and annual water balance of the continents of the world.

Component	Europe	Asia	Africa	N.Amer.	S.Amer.	Austr.	Total
Area (10^6 km^2)	9.8	45	30.3	20.7	17.8	8.7	12.3
Precipitation (km^3)	7165	32,690	20,780	13,910	29,355	64,051	110,000
Total river runoff (km^3)	3110	13,190	4225	5960	10,380	1965	38,830
Underground runoff (km^3)	1065	3410	1465	1740	3740	465	11,885
Infiltration (km^3)	5120	22,910	18,020	9690	22,715	4905	83,360
Evaporation (km^3)	4055	19,500	16,555	7950	18,975	4440	71,475
% underground runoff of total	34	26	35	32	36	24	31

Globally, the water balance is dominated by the fact that more water evaporates from the oceans than is returned via precipitation. The oceanic evaporation supplies 86-88% of the total global evaporation, whereas the area of the oceans amounts to only 71%. Thus, the oceanic evaporation is a regulator of the global water balance (see Fig. 5.1). The difference between the evaporation from the oceans and the precipitation into them is about 41,000 km^3 per year; some 27,000 km^3, however, return to the sea as flood run-off which cannot be tapped; and another 5,000 km^3 flow into the sea in uninhabited areas. This cycle, therefore, leaves 9,000 km^3 of water readily available for human exploitation worldwide. This is a plentiful supply of water. Yet, because of an uneven distribution of the world's population and of usable water, local water shortage is a problem in many regions.

The supply can be increased, either by damming rivers or by mining groundwater. In spite of such efforts, there is no doubt that water is becoming increasingly scarce, as population and industrial and agricultural activities are all expanding. The water withdrawal has increased from 1000 km^3 in 1950 to about 4000 km^3 in 1989. If these figures, and the uneven distribution, are considered in the light of the above amounts, it is understandable that we are facing a water shortage.

5.3 STRUCTURE OF THE HYDROSPHERE

The major components comprising the *structure* of an aquatic ecosystem are the following (after Odum, 1971):

Abiotic Components

1. ***Inorganic substances*** involved in material cycles. The total salinity of surface waters has a composition which is dominated by four major cations, Ca^{2+}, Mg^{2+}, Na^+ and K^+ and four major anions, HCO_3^-, CO_3^{2-}, SO_4^{2-} and Cl^-. Usually, these ions constitute the total ionic salinity of the waters. The specific conductivity is almost proportional to the concentrations of the major ions, and changes of conductivity reflect proportional changes in ionic concentrations.

Three major mechanisms globally control the *salinity* of surface waters: weathering of rocks, atmospheric precipitation and the relation between precipitation and evaporation. Fig. 5.2 gives a diagrammatic representation of the general processes controlling the salinity of surface waters of the world.

Table 5.2. The water cycle.

Water in	is replaced every
Human body	month
The air	12 days
A tree	one week
Rivers	a few days
Lakes	0.1 - 100 years
Oceans	3600 years
Polar ice	15,000 years

Table 5.3. Water of the world.

World Water Reserve		1358.8 mill. km^3
Oceans		1321.3 mill. km^3
Underground Salt Water		4.2 mill. km^3
Freshwater Reserve		33.3 mill. km^3
- in Polar Ice & Glacier		29.1 mill. km^3
- Groundwater		4.1 mill. km^3
- in Rivers and Lakes		0.1 mill. km^3
Reserve in Rivers and Lakes		139,200 km^3
- Atmosphere	9.3%	12,950 km^3
- Rivers	0.9%	1,250 km^3
- Lakes *)	89.8%	125,000 km^3
*) in the Laurentian Great Lakes (Superior, Michigan, Huron, Erie, Ontario): 18.2% or		22,725 km^3

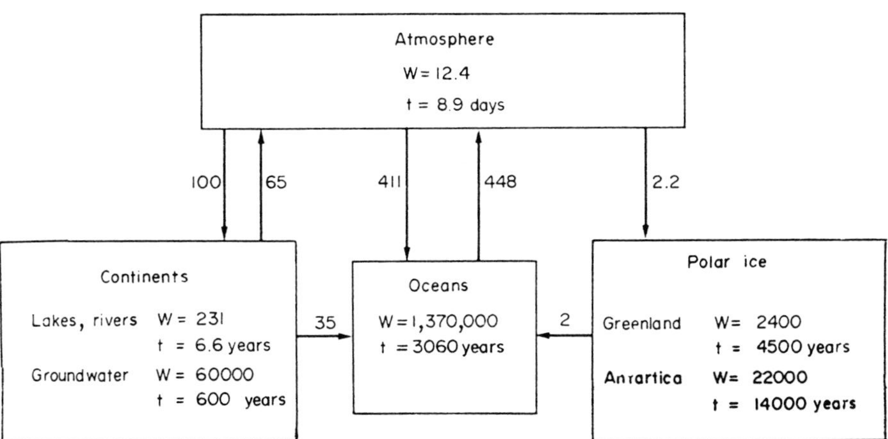

Figure 5.1. The global water cycle. Figures for W (water content in compartment) are given in 1000 km^3, and for fluxes in 1000 km^3 per year; t is the retention time. Notice that the difference between evaporation and precipitation for the oceans corresponds to the total return flow from the continents and the polar ice.

Fresh waters dominated by rock weathering are usually rich in calcium and bicarbonate. Climate, basin-relief, and the composition of rock material have a dominant influence on the composition of water. In the humid tropical areas of South America and Africa, the rainwater has a rich ionic composition. This atmospheric precipitation dominates the salinity, as much as low rainfall and high evaporation do in hot and arid regions.

Nutrients and Trace Elements. The amounts of nitrogen and phosphorus are largely significant for the productivity of lakes and streams. Phosphorus is commonly the limiting factor for productivity, due to the small natural supply of this element (see further on this topic in Chapter 4). These major nutrients and numerous trace elements (e.g., iron, manganese, molybdenum, zinc) are of essential biological importance but do not contribute substantially to the total salinity.

2. ***Organic Components.*** Dissolved carbohydrates, proteins, humic substances, pigments and vitamines comprise the major organic components of water. They are mainly produced by metabolic processes within cells and can play an important role in the aquatic ecosystem as extracellular dissolved organic matter (DOM), released by autolysis or excretion. Thus, the excretion of amino acids by zooplankton may, temporarily, act as a major source of DOM. Free enzymes (exoenzymes) are of importance, too. The phosphorus cycle, e.g., cannot be understood without consideration of free phosphatases.

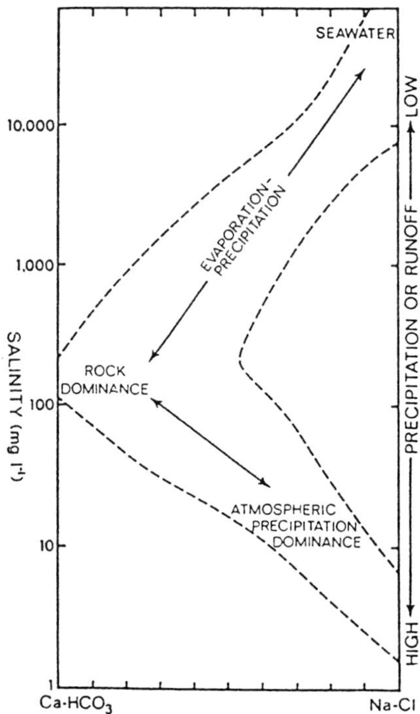

Figure 5.2. Diagrammatic representation of the general processes controlling the salinity of surface waters of the world. - Source: Wetzel (1983).

Biotic Components

3. ***Producers,*** i.e., autotrophic phytoplankton and higher plants (macrophytes), produce biomass from simple inorganic substances.

4. ***Macroconsumers,*** i.e., zooplankton and fishes, feed on other organisms or on particulate organic matter (detritus).

5. ***Microconsumers,*** i.e., heterotrophic organisms, chiefly bacteria and fungi, are responsible for the degradation of the particulate or dissolved organic substrate produced by autotrophic processes or coming from allochthonous sources. Thus, from a trophic point of view, the biomass can be separated in an *autotrophic* component and a *heterotrophic* component. They are metabolically coupled through a food web.

5.4 THE BASIC DIFFERENCE BETWEEN AQUATIC AND TERRESTRIAL ECOSYSTEMS

Aquatic and terrestrial ecosystems have basically the same structure and function, but there is a striking difference: The producers in the *hydrosphere*, i.e., the aquatic ecosystems, mostly belong to the phytoplankton and are almost exclusively unicellular algae. Their life cycle and turnover time (ratio of biomass to production) are measured in hours or days. By contrast, the producers in the *lithosphere*, i.e., the terrestrial ecosystems, are mainly higher plants with a large biomass and a long turnover time; in forests, e.g., the turnover time is measured in years. According to Walter (1976), the difference between structure and function of the hydrosphere and the lithosphere (estimated phyto-biomass) is as follows :

	area (10^6 km^2)	biomass (10^9 t)	annual production (10^9 t)
Lithosphere	149	2,000	150
Hydrosphere	361	2.8	60

The ratio between the biomass of the lithosphere and that of the hydrosphere is 700:1, while for production, the ratio is only 2.5:1. It follows that the specific productivity (productivity per unit biomass) in the aquatic ecosystems is much higher than in the terrestrial ones.

5.5 WASTE WATER

The quality of inland waters, comprising our water resources, depends not only on the amount of waste generated, but also on the pollution abatement that has been put into effect. The contamination loads of inland waters depend on the population density, the per capita gross national product, the effectiveness of decontamination, and the amount of water discharged.

Waste-water technology has progressed rapidly during the last two decades, and today, a wide spectrum of waste-water-treatment methods is available which can meet almost all water-quality criteria. A survey of the waste-water-treatment methods most generally applied is given in Table 5.4, both for industrial and for municipal waste water.

Table 5.4. Survey of generally applied methods of waste-water treatment.

Method	Pollution problem	Efficiency
Mechanical treatment	Suspended matter removal	0.75-0.90
	BOD_5 reduction	0.20-0.35
Biological treatment	BOD_5 reduction	0.70-0.95
Chemical precipitation $Al_2(SO_4)_3$ or $FeCl_3$	Phosphorus removal	0.65-0.95
	Reduction of heavy-metal concentrations	0.40-0.80
	BOD_5 reduction	0.50-0.65
Chemical precipitation $Ca(OH)_2$	Phosphorus removal	0.85-0.95
	Reduction of heavy-metal concentrations	0.80-0.95
	BOD_5 reduction	0.50-0.70
Ammonia stripping	Ammonia removal	0.70-0.95
Nitrification	Ammonium is oxidized to nitrate	0.80-0.95
Active carbon adsorption	COD removal (toxic substances)	0.40-0.95
	BOD_5 reduction	0.40-0.70
Denitrific. after nitrific.	Nitrogen removal	0.70-0.90
Ion exchange	BOD_5 reduction (e.g., proteins)	0.20-0.40
	Phosphorus removal	0.80-0.95
	Nitrogen removal	0.80-0.95
	Reduction of heavy-metal concentrations	0.80-0.95
Chemical oxidation (e.g., with Cl_2)	Oxidation of toxic compounds (e.g., CN^- - N_2)	0.90-0.98
Extraction	Heavy metals and other toxic compounds	0.50-0.95
Reverse osmosis	Removes pollutants efficiently, but is expensive	
Disinfection methods	Reduction of microorganisms	(high)

The specific problem, the method to solve it and the removal efficiency generally experienced are indicated in the table. These indications must, however, be used cautiously, as the efficiency depends on the composition of the waste water, the temperature and the pH.

Table 5.5 summarizes the relation between methods and waste-water-pollution parameters. The efficiencies indicated are the best ones attainable. E.g., the removal of heavy metals by precipitation will require calcium hydroxide to obtain the efficiency shown in the table.

The solution of a waste-water problem often requires a combination of two or several methods. In such a case, the overall efficiency, e, of a n-step treatment can be approximated by use of the following equation:

$$1 - e = (1 - e_1)(1 - e_2)...(1 - e_n), \tag{5.1}$$

where e_i (i=1,2,...,n) are the efficiencies of the individual steps.

Table 5.5. Efficiency matrix, relating pollution parameters to waste-water-treatment methods (with the exception of reverse osmosis).

	Suspended matter	BOD_5	COD	P-total	NH_4^+	N-total	Heavy metals	E. coli	Colour	Turb-idity
Mechanical treatment	0.75-0.90	0.20-0.35	0.20-0.35	0.05-0.10	~0 ~0	0.10-0.25	0.20-0.40	- -	~0	0.80-0.98
Biological treatment*)	-	0.75-0.95	0.65-0.90	0.10-0.20	0.05-0.10	0.10-0.25	0.30-0.65	fair	~0	-
Chemical precipitation	0.80-0.95	0.50-0.75	0.50-0.75	0.80-0.95	~0 ~0	0.10-0.60	0.80-0.98	good 0.70	0.30-0.98	0.80-
Ammonia stripping	~0	~0	~0	~0	0.70-0.96	0.60-0.90	~0	~0	~0	~0
Nitrification	~0	~0	~0	~0	0.80-0.95	0.80-0.95	~0	~0	~0	~0
Active carbon adsorption*)	-	0.40-0.70	0.40-0.95	~0.1	high**)	high**)	0.10-0.70	good	0.70-0.90	0.65 0.90
Denitrification after nitrification	~0	-	-	~0	-	0.70-0.90	~0	good	~0	-
Ion exchange	-	0.20-0.40	0.20-0.50	0.80-0.95	0.80-0.95	0.80-0.95	0.80-0.95	very good	0.60-0.90	0.70-0.90
Chemical oxidation	-	corresponding to oxidation	~0	~0	~0	~0	~0	~0	0.60-0.90	0.50-0.80
Extraction	-	corresponding extraction of toxic compounds	~0	~0	~0	~0	0.50-	~0 0.95	~0	~0
Disinfection	-	much corresp. to applic. of chlorine, ozone, etc.						very high	0.50-0.90	0.30-0.60

*) depends on the composition **)as chloramines

As already mentioned, Tables 5.4 and 5.5 only provide approximate results which must be used with caution. In practice, more precise information will always be required, yet crude estimates such as can be found in the two tables are useful for a first consideration of possible solutions to a specific waste-water-pollution problem.

5.6 WATER RESOURCES

Man cannot exist without water. The demand for water has always been strong, and in most regions of the world the nearest and more obvious sources have already been exploited. Any additional demand will have to be met by exploiting more remote and increasingly less attractive sites. For this reason alone, development costs must rise continuously in the future.

The relationship between the hydraulic cycle and the water demand now and in the near future has already been touched on in Section 5.2.

Most waters have to be purified before they can be used for human consumption. Raw water is extremely variable in quality, and there is no fixed starting point in the treatment process. Many countries have their own standards of acceptable purity for potable water, and these standards vary. *The WHO lays down standards* which are widely applied in developing countries.

Virtually all water may be purified to potable standards, yet some raw waters are so bad as to merit rejection because of the expense involved.

Water from underground sources is generally of a better quality than surface water, but it may be excessively 'hard', and/or it may contain iron and manganese. A full treatment of water comprises pretreatment, coagulation, mixing, flocculation, settling, filtration and sterilization. However, not all waters require the full treatment.

The differences between the two sources, groundwater and surface water, are summarized in Table 5.6.

Pretreatment includes screening, raw-water storage, prechlorination, aeration, algal control and straining.

As *coagulants*, the following are in use: aluminium sulphate, sodium aluminate, and iron salts. Usually, they are applied in combination with coagulant acids, which include lime, sodium carbonate, activated silica and polyelectrolytes. After coagulation, *mixing*, *flocculation* and/or *sedimentation* take place.

For *filtration*, sand filters are widely used, either after coagulation, mixing, flocculation and sedimentation of surface water, or after aeration of groundwater for removal of iron and manganese compounds.

Typical flow diagrams for treatment of groundwater and surface water are shown in Fig. 5.3.

5.7 WATER AND WASTE-WATER MANAGEMENT

Water management is closely linked to waste-water management. Insufficient treatment of waste water can have several negative consequences for the water supply, of which the two most important ones are:

1. Low-quality surface water requires a *more advanced treatment of the raw water* for the production of potable water;

2. After treatment, the waste water is usually discharged to the sea, to avoid a deterioration of the quality of the surface water. Consequently, it is *necessary to use supplementary sources of raw water*, which may be difficult when close to cities or to areas suffering from a water shortage.

Waste-water problems were surveyed in Section 5.5. The present section is devoted to linking these problems with the various water-treatment methods listed in Section 5.6.

The selection of optimal waste-water *and* water treatments is a very complex problem. Quantitative management requires the application of environmental modeling, the principles of which are presented in Chapter 13 of this book. The search for an optimal solution also requires a comprehensive knowledge of the treatment methods available. Furthermore, the problem is complicated by the interdependence of water supply and waste water-disposal.

Good water-management practice, therefore, should consider not only the ecological effects in the recipient, but also the effect on the quality and economy of the water supply. Figure 5.4 illustrates these considerations.

Table 5.6. Characteristics of groundwater and surface water.

Properties	Groundwater	Surface water
Salt concentration	high	low
Iron concentration	high	low
Manganese concentration	high	low
$KMnO_4$ number	low	high
Hardness	high	low
pH	6-8	7-9
Turbidity	low	high
Temperature	low	high
Number of E. coli	0	> 0
Colour	none	yellowish

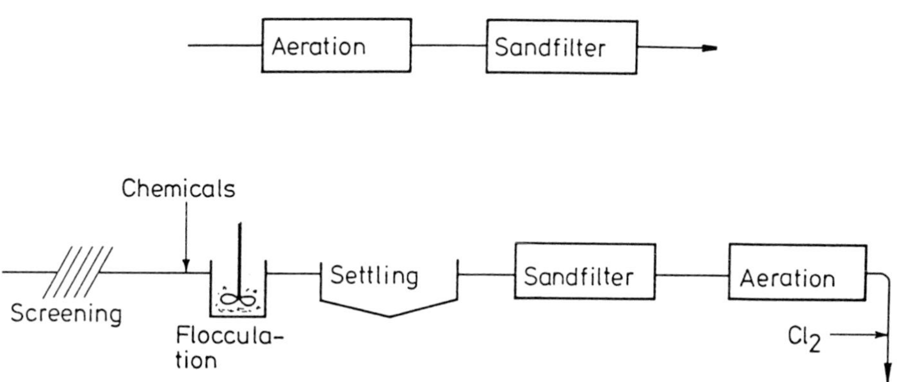

Figure 5.3. Typical treatment of groundwater (above) and of surface water (below).

Effluents fall into the seven groups listed below. Many effluents may, however, to some degree possess the polluting properties of at least two of the seven categories:

1. *Organic residues*, including domestic sewage, effluent from food-processing industries, ensilage, manure heaps and cattle yards, laundries, paper mills, etc. These effluents vary a great deal, yet they have much in common. They all contain complex organic compounds in solution and/or suspension, sometimes together with toxic substances and various salts. Their basic property, however, is that they contain unstable compounds which are readily oxidized and thereby use up the oxygen dissolved in the water. Some of these compounds are more readily decomposed than others; for example, slaughterhouse wastes oxidize rapidly, whereas wood pulp is comparatively stable.

2. *Nutrients*, including ammonia, nitrates, other nitrogen compounds, orthophosphates, other phosphor compounds, silica and sulphates. The main sources are domestic sewage and

effluents from fertilizer manufacture. Discharge of nutrients may cause undesirable eutrophication, as described in Chapter 4; also in Section 5.5, we have already briefly discussed the methods available for nutrient removal.

3. *Poison* in solution occurs in the waste water originating from many industries. The poisons include acids, alkalis, oil, heavy metals and toxic organic compounds, mainly from chemical industries, gas works and use of insecticides.

4. *Inert suspensions* of finely divided matter result from many types of mining and quarrying and from washing processes, such as those of coal and root crops.

5. *Other inorganic agents,* such as salts or reducing agents (e.g., sulphides, sulphites and ferrous salts) occur as constituents of the effluent of several types of industry. Minor discharges of salts are generally harmless to the environment, but reducing compounds use up the oxygen in the receiving body of water, and have the same effect as organic residues. This effect can, however, easily be eliminated by aeration, a process which is related to biological treatment methods.

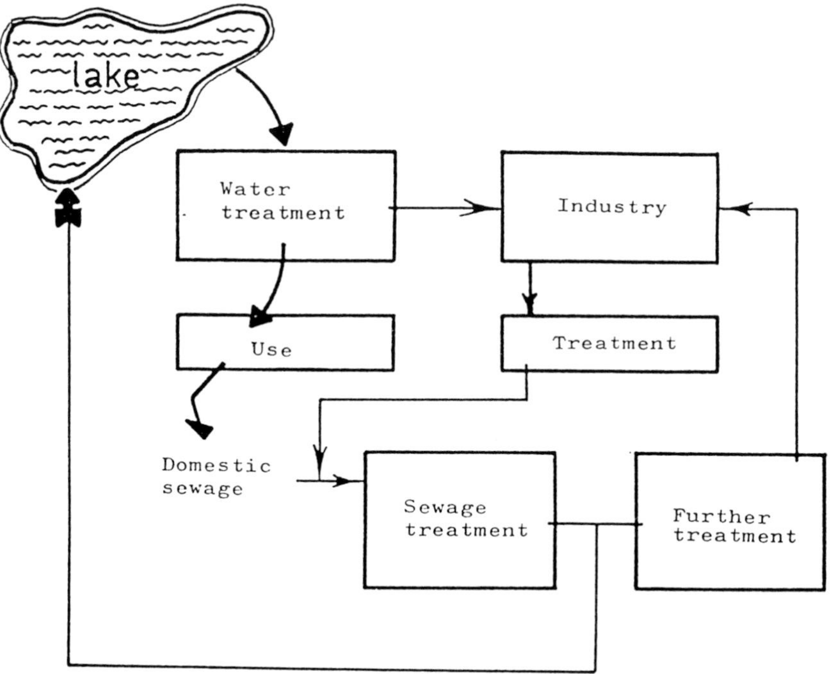

Figure 5.4. An example of good water-management practice, characterized by three features: 1) After an additional treatment, a part of the waste water treated is reclaimed for industrial purposes. 2) The industrial waste water is treated before being discharged into the public sewage system; the sewage treatment chosen pays regards to the lake as well as to the water treatment. 3) 'Non-point' pollution is taken into regard by use of a wetland which can denitrify the nitrogen originating from agricultural use of fertilizers.

Table 5.7. Pollution from urban and agricultural runoff.

Constituent	Urban runoff (Storm water)	Agricultural runoff
Suspended solids (mg/l)	5 - 1200	-
Chemical oxygen demand, COD (mg/l)	20 - 610	-
Biological oxygen demand, BOD (mg/l)	1 - 173	-
Total phosphorus (mg/l)	0.02 - 7.3	1.1 - 0.65
Nitrate nitrogen (mg/l)	-	0.03 - 5.0
Total nitrogen (mg/l)	0.3 - 7.5	0.5 - 6.5
Chlorides (mg/l)	3 - 35	-

6. *Hot water* is produced in many industries where water is used for cooling purposes. In many cases, river water is pumped through the cooling system, and sometimes heated to very high temperatures during part of the process. The methods available to meet this problem are use of a) cooling towers, b) heat exchangers, c) alternative technology, d) an alternative receiving water body which is less susceptible to damage.

7. *Bacteriological contamination* of waters mainly originates from domestic sewage, but food-processing industries, manure heaps and cattle yards also give rise to this type of pollution. Various methods to meet the problem are in use in the production of potable water, for process water in industry, and in the treatment of waste water.

Waste waters emanate from four primary sources: 1) municipal sewage, 2) industrial waste waters, 3) agricultural runoff and 4) storm water and urban runoff. The problems with the municipal sewage are related mainly to organic residues and nutrients, while the second type, industrial waste waters, encompasses the entire spectrum of pollution problems, the discharge of heavy metals and organic compounds being the most serious ones. Here, it is not possible to give a comprehensive review of industrial waste-water problems; for a more detailed discussion, see Jørgensen (1979).

As municipal and industrial waste waters receive treatment, an increasing emphasis is being placed on the pollutional effects of urban and agricultural runoff. The range of pertinent characteristics of these waste waters is given in Table 5.7.

In many places, sewage is continuously being discharged into systems of drains, intended also for the removal of surface runoff from rainstorms and from snow or ice melting. This is called 'combined sewerage'. However, in most modern developments, sewage and runoff are colleted separately in a system of sanitary sewers and storm drains, in order to avoid pollution of water courses by the occasional spillage of sewage and stormwater mixtures. This is called 'separate sewerage'.

The receiving body of water often also serves as an important source of supply for many purposes. It is this multi-purpose use of natural waters that creates the most impelling reasons for a sound water-quality management.

Agricultural pollution problems are related to:

1) the extensive use of natural and industrially produced fertilizers to increase yield,
2) use of pesticides to eliminate damage by pests,
3) waste from domestic animals.

To solve problems 1) and 2) seems possible only by use of sound ecological engineering, as discussed in Chapter 1. Waste-water and solid-waste problems related to 3) are, in principle, not different from municipal- and industrial-waste problems.

REFERENCES

Jørgensen, S.E., 1979. Industrial Waste Water Management. Elsevier, Amsterdam.

Jørgensen, S.E., and Johnsen, I., 1989. Principles of Environmental Science and Technology. Studies in Environmental Science 33. Elsevier, Amsterdam, 627 pp.

Mitsch, W., and Jørgensen, S.E., 1989. Ecological Engineering, An Introduction to Eco-Technology. John Wiley & Sons, New York.

Odum, E.P., 1971. Fundamentals of Ecology. W.B. Saunders Co., Philadelphia, Penn.

Walter, H., 1976. Die ökologischen Systeme der Kontinente (Biogeosphäre). Fischer, Jena.

Wetzel, R.G., 1983. Limnology. 2. ed. Saunders College Publishing Co., Philadelphia, Penn., 760 pp.

6.1 PESTICIDES: LEGISLATION, CONTROL AND CONSUMPTION IN DENMARK

BETTY BÜGEL MOGENSEN

6.1.1 INTRODUCTION

To ensure that the many different chemicals in use will not harm human health or the environment, legislation has been established in Denmark to regulate the import, sale, application, etc. of these products. It is primarily the Act on Chemical Substances and Products that influences the field, but legislation on environmental protection, food, disposal of chemical waste, etc., are of importance too.

6.1.2 ACT ON CHEMICAL SUBSTANCES AND PRODUCTS. DEFINITION OF PESTICIDES

The objective of the Act is to prevent impact on health and on the environment by chemical substances and products. The Act sets up a frame for regulation and gives title to issue statutory orders which set provisions in more detail within the scope of the Act.

The annex of the Act defines what pesticides are by listing all substances and products regarded as pesticides. The list includes:

A. Chemical substances and products for the control of plant diseases, pests and weeds; also products for the control of pests in buildings, feed- and foodstuff storages; and a few other biocides.

B. Repellents. Chemical substances and products intended to prevent damage from pests, rodents and birds, or to repel these animals from places where they are unwanted.

C. Plant growth regulators. Chemical substances and products which, not being plant nutrients or soil conditioners proper, are intended to regulate the growth or development of plants or the ripening of seeds.

6.1.3 STATUTORY ORDER ON CHEMICAL PESTICIDES (No 791)

Approval. Pesticides shall not be sold, imported or applied in Denmark until approval has been granted by the National Agency of Environmental Protection (NAEP).

To make it possible for the NAEP to evaluate a pesticide before approval, a series of data is needed both on the active ingredient(s) and on the product formulated. A particular two-part application form is used for the approval procedure.

Part A of the application form provides the information on the formulated product as it is marketed, including solvents, additives to improve dispersion or penetration into the plants, and the like. Part B gives information on the active ingredient(s). All data must be verified by reports.

As is seen from the application form, pesticides have to be carefullly investigated prior to approval. This includes studies on degradation and break down in soil, water and plants and on the toxicity of the products to animals and plants in the terrestrial as well as in the aquatic environment.

The effect on human health is estimated from the effect on animals. Rats and other rodents are frequently used as models for man.

Table 6.1.1. Simplified presentation of the application form for approval of pesticides.

A Application concerning the formulated product

Composition and mode of action.

Application field, dosing, application rate and -method, efficacy.

Package size and type. Directions for use.

Toxicity by ingestion, by dermal contact and by inhalation. Skin and eye irritation.

Physical, chemical and technical properties.

Inflammability classification. Information about destruction method and method of analysis.

B Application concerning the active ingredient.

Identity of the active ingredient (designation, formula, molecular weight).

Degree of purity (name and quantity of impurities).

Methods for qualitative and quantitative analysis.

Origin and manufacture of the active ingredient.

Physico-chemical properties of the active ingredient.

Acute toxicity: Toxicity by ingestion, by dermal contact and by inhalation. Skin and eye irritation. Sensitization.

Various effects after a short period, and after some time: Subchronic toxicity, chronic toxicity, carcinogenicity, mutagenicity. Reproduction studies, teratogenicity, neurotoxicity.

Toxicity of possible metabolites, break down products and impurities.

Metabolism in animals: Absorption, distribution, transformation and elimination in mammals.

Human toxicity (Experience from production or use).

Absorption, transportation and metabolism in plants: Residues in relevant edible parts of plants and in products of animal origin.

In soil: Transformation, degradation, adsorption, leaching and mobility, accumulation, evaporation.

In water: Degradation, adsorption.

Toxic effect in aquatic organisms: Toxicity to fish, daphnia and algae. Possible bioaccumulation.

Toxic effect in soil organisms: Toxicity to earthworm. Effect on microbiological processes in soil: Respiration, nitrification, ammonification, N-fixation.

Toxic effects in birds. Acute toxicity and reproduction studies.

Effect on bees and other beneficial animals.

Phytotoxicity.

Safety advice, destruction method etc.

Table 6.1.2. Review of some toxicological expressions, and their interconnections.

Expression	Explanation	How	Example
LD_{50}	Acute toxicity, indicating the amount (mg/kg body weight) sufficient to kill 50% of the test animals.	By short-term feeding studies. High doses.	1000 mg/kg body weight.
0-effect level	Indicates the level (the dose) which causes no changes in the test animals despite long-term ingestion (2 years). All internal organs are investigated.	By long-term feeding studies. Lower doses.	100 mg/kg body weight.
ADI-value	The acceptable daily intake for people provided they ingest the substance during a whole life. This value is used when calculating the tolerance for pesticides in food.	The 0-effect value is divided by a safety factor of 100.	1 mg/kg body weight.
Harvest time restrictions	The minimum period from treatment to harvest.	Calculated from degradation curves of residues in relevant crops combined with the tolerance level for the substance.	2 weeks.

The efficacy of the products shall be ensured, amongst other factors to avoid the introduction of unnecessary amounts of pesticides into the environment.

The information about the effect of a pesticide on human health and the environment is evaluated together with the information on application field, rate and method, efficacy, etc.

In approving a pesticide for use on edible crops, information about residues in the crop at different intervals after treatment is considered together with the acceptable daily intake (ADI) of the pesticide.

Typically, the ADI-value is of the order of size of 1/100 of the highest dose which has no effect on animals used in the experiments, even after long-term exposure (0-effect level), cf. Table 6.1.2.

The ADI-value states the acceptable daily intake of a substance through a life time. It is used to establish the tolerance, i.e., an upper limit for the pesticide residue in the edible crop.

To ensure that the tolerance for a product is not exceeded, harvest time restrictions are set, laying down the minimal interval between treatment and harvest of a crop.

Approvals are granted for a period of eight years, except for very toxic or toxic pesticides for which the period is only four years.

Approval cannot be granted for substances or products which present a special risk to health or the environment, or are suspected of presenting such a risk. The NAEP works out criteria for non approval.

Neither can approval be granted if significantly less dangerous substances, products or methods are available in the same field of application.

For one alternative to be preferred to another on these grounds, it is however a condition that the alternative products or methods can be used to the same effect on the target organism without significant economic and practical disadvantages to the user.

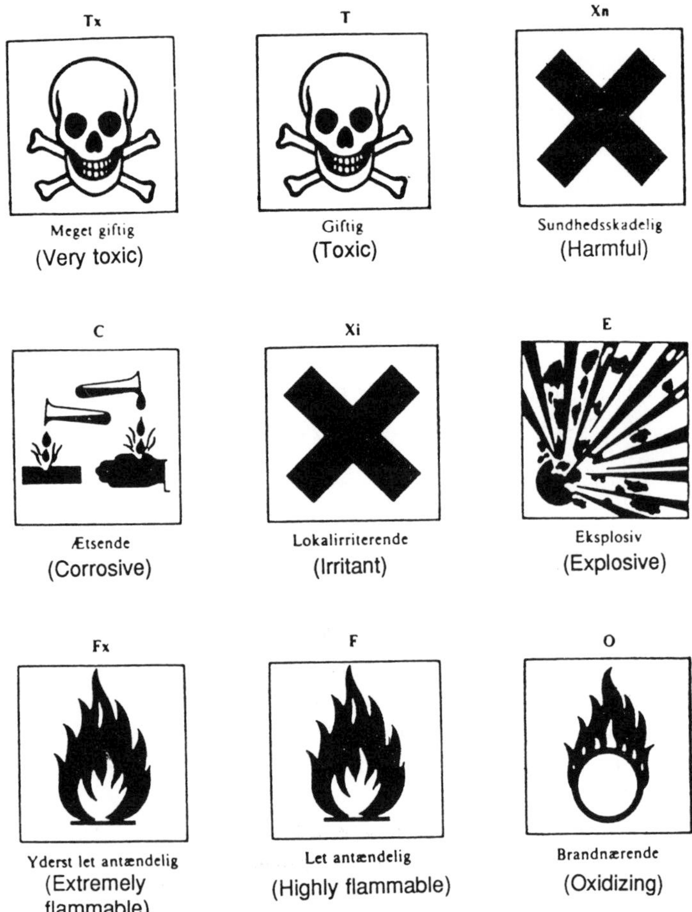

Figure 6.1.1. Danger categories and danger symbols.

6.1.3.1 Classification, Packaging and Labelling

Dangerous pesticides are classified by the NAEP according to the nine danger categories, with pertaining danger symbols as indicated in Fig. 6.1.1.

The packaging shall be strong, and not be able to react with the product it contains. Besides, it shall be designed so that complete or partial emptying can take place in a safe way. Containers fitted with replaceable fastening devices shall be so designed that the packaging can be refastened without loss of content.

The packaging shall be sealed by the manufacturer or importer in such a way that the sealing is broken completely when the packaging is opened for the first time.

The packaging shall bear a label in Danish including the following information:

1) Trade name of the product.
2) Name and address of the holder of the approval.
3) Nature of the product, followed by the phrase: "Covered by Statutory Order on Chemical Pesticides from the Ministry of the Environment".
4) Name and content of each of the active ingredients in the product.
5) Name of each of the very toxic, toxic, harmful or corrosive substances that are contained in the product above a specified concentration.
6) Danger category.
7) Risk indications and safety measures.
8) Legal provisions for use and storage.

Besides this label, the packaging shall be fitted with instructions for proper use of the chemical. Label and instructions for use shall be approved by the NAEP prior to sale.

6.1.3.2 Sales and Storage

The sale of very toxic and of toxic pesticides needs an authorization from the NAEP. Anyone selling very toxic pesticides must keep a record of purchases and sales of such products. The products must be sold only to persons authorized to use them.

Toxic pesticides shall be sold only to the parties mentioned above or to anyone having a commercial interest in use of the product in his own enterprise, or who is engaged in commercial pest control for others. There are no such restrictions on the sale of other pesticides. Harmful and corrosive pesticides shall, however, be stored in such a manner that customers do not have direct access to the products.

Pesticides shall only be sold in the original packaging, and the packing shall not be broken. Likewise, the user shall store the pesticide in the original packaging only.

Very toxic and toxic pesticides shall be stored under lock and key, and any pesticide shall be stored securely out of reach of children and not together with food, feeding stuffs, etc.

Apart from storing the pesticide in this way, it is important never to leave spray liquids etc. prepared from pesticides unattended.

6.1.3.3 Use and Disposal

Very toxic pesticides shall be used only by holders of a special authorization granted by the NAEP and by the assistants to these persons. The holder of the autorization is responsible for the use and has to give the assistants sufficient instructions and supervision. The above-mentioned authorization is granted on special conditions, and only if the applicant has attended a special course approved by the NAEP.

Toxic pesticides can be bought and used by anyone who has a commercial interest in the use of the product, either in his own enterprise or in pest control for others. Very toxic and toxic pesticides shall not be used by persons under the age of 18, and they shall not be used in private gardens, in public grounds or other areas to which the public has access, around institutions for children, along roadsides, etc.

Pesticides hazardous to bees shall bear a special warning label: "hazardous to bees" or "very hazardous to bees". In the case of impact on bee families, the beekeeper can claim for damages from the person responsible for the pesticide treatment. Even if the damage is caused by winddrift to flowering plants in another field there can be a claim.

The user of the pesticide is responsible for the safe disposal of empty packings and of surplus pesticides. The instructions for use for each pesticide shall give information on this disposal.

6.1.4 CONSUMPTION

According to the Statutory Order on Chemical Pesticides, the holder of an approval of a pesticide has to keep a record of the quantity sold of each pesticide and of its value, and he should report the figures to the NAEP every year. This information is the basis for calculating the charge that has to be paid for each pesticide. Besides, it is the basis for the statistics of pesticide sales per year which are published by the NAEP.

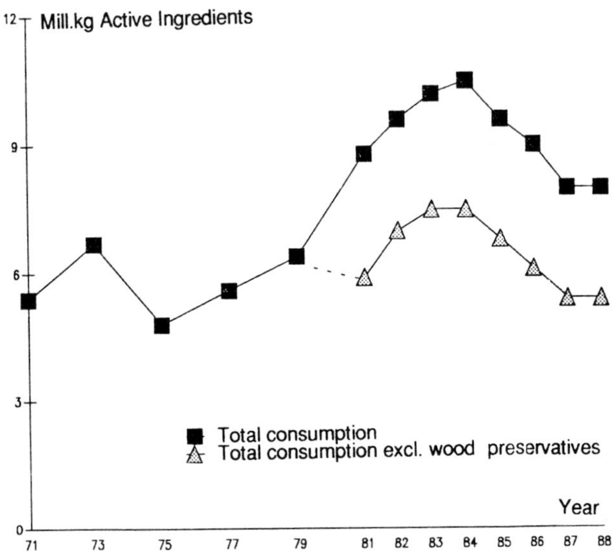

Figure 6.1.2. Pesticide sales/consumption in Denmark 1971-1988.

Figure 6.1.2 shows the development in pesticide sale and consumption for 1971-1988. In 1980 some new groups of chemical products were being considered as pesticides, and as such they appeared in the statistics. Wood preservatives absolutely constitute the greater part among these new products. To make it possible to evaluate the development in consumption, Fig. 6.1.2 includes both the total consumption and the consumption exclusive of wood preservatives.

Fig. 6.1.3 shows the development in consumption of the main agricultural pesticides. The drop in consumption, taken as the amount of active ingredient, illustrates partly a change to more active substances with a lower application rate and partly a drop in intensity of spraying.

For further discussion of the development in the use of insecticides and herbicides, see Sections 6.3 and 6.4 of this chapter.

6.1.5 CONTROL OF RESIDUES IN FOOD AND FEEDSTUFFS. CONCLUSION

Referring to statutory orders from the ministries of health and agriculture, tolerances have been set for pesticide residues in food and feedstuffs, respectively. The actual concentration is controlled by spot-checks carried out by the authorities.

The legislation on pesticides aims at lowering the risk involved with the sale, storage, use, etc. of pesticides. This presentation has focused primarily on the Act on Chemical Substances and products and on the Statutory Order on Chemical Pesticides which constitute the main regulation of these products.

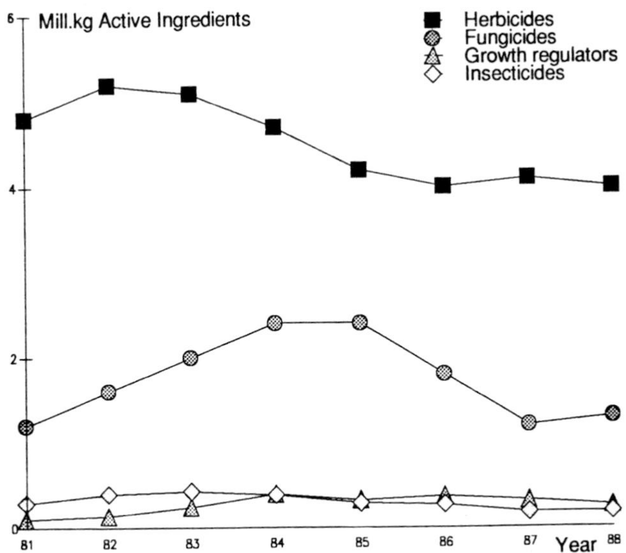

Figure 6.1.3. Consumption of the main agricultural pesticides in Denmark in the period 1971-1988.

APPENDIX: ACTS AND STATUTORY ORDERS

Miljøministeriets lovbekendtgørelse nr. 574 af 26. august 1984 om kemiske stoffer og produkter/Consolidation Act from the Danish Ministry of the Environment No. 574 of August 26, 1987 on Chemical Substances and Products. In Danish and in English.

Miljøministeriets bekendtgørelse nr. 791 af 10. december 1987 om kemiske bekæmpelsesmidler/Statutory Order from the Danish Ministry of the Environment No. 791 of December 10, 1987 on Chemical Pesticides. In Danish and in English.

Landbrugsministeriets bekendtgørelse nr. 65 af 9. februar 1988 om fastsættelse af tilladte størsteindhold af uønskede stoffer og produkter i foderstoffer. In Danish. (Statutory Order from the Danish Ministry of Agriculture No. 65 of February 9, 1988 on the maximal content of undesirable substances and products allowed in feedstuffs).

Miljøministeriets bekendtgørelse nr. 1 af 5. januar 1982 om maksimalgrænseværdier for indhold af bekæmpelsesmidler i levnedsmidler. In Danish. (Statutory Order from the Danish Ministry of the Environment No. 1 of January 5, 1982 on the maximal content of pesticides allowed in food).

Landbrugsministeriets bekendtgørelse nr. 588 af 8. december 1983 om klassificering m.v. af bekæmpelsesmidler (farlighed for bier). In Danish. (Statutory Order from the Danish Ministry of Agriculture No. 588 of December 8, 1983 on classification etc. of pesticides, in particular regarding the danger to bees).

6.2 PESTICIDES: DEGRADATION AND TRANSPORT

ARNE HELWEG

6.2.1 INTRODUCTION

The use of pesticides in agriculture leads to the appearance of these chemicals and their degradation products in crops, soil, air and water. The pesticide may be bound to soil particles, decomposed by soil microorganisms, or leached to drain or groundwater. Pesticides may also be taken up into a crop or evaporated into the atmosphere from where it may be washed out with the precipitation (Fig. 6.2.1).

To protect consumers, 'maximum residue limits' for crops are established. To protect the quality of soil and water and to limit the risk to the environment, the persistence, transport and side effects of a pesticide are determined and evaluated before it is registered for use.

Among the modern chemicals, pesticides were the ones that were first declared environmentally dangerous. In her book 'Silent Spring' (1962), Rachel Carson points to the danger of dispersing chemicals in the environment without evaluating their persistence, accumulation and side effects on non-target organisms. Rachel Carson mainly chose the chlorinated hydrocarbons as examples: DDT, aldrin and dieldrin were widely used in those days.

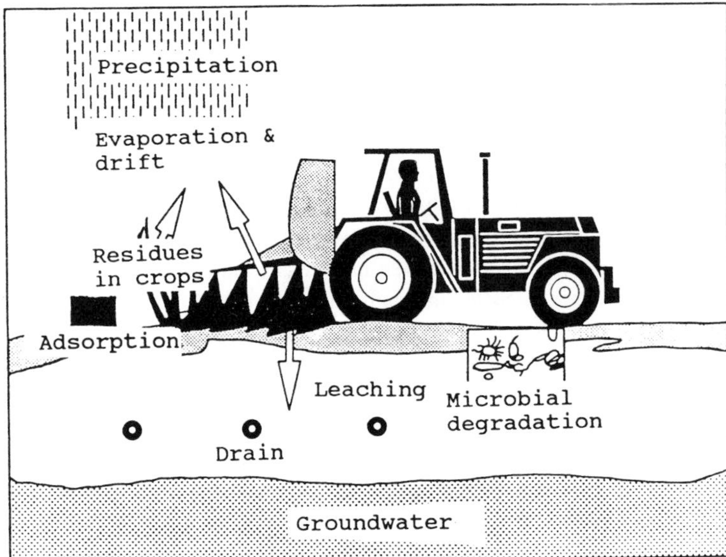

Figure 6.2.1. The use of pesticides has led to the appearance of these chemicals in soil, crops, water and in the air. In the environment the pesticides may be decomposed or transported from one compartment to another.

Table 6.2.1. Examples of pesticides from the first, second and third generations (H = herbicide, I = insecticide, F = fungicide).

First generation:	$NaAsO_2$, (H), $PbHAsO_4$ (I), $CuSO_4$+$Ca(OH)_2$(F), Nicotine (I), Pyrethrum (I), DNOC (H).
Second generation (from 1945):	Chlorinated hydrocarbons (I) e.g., DDT, lindane, dieldrin, aldrin, endrin Organophosphates (I) e.g., parathion, malathion, diazinon Phenoxyacids (H) e.g., 2,4-D, MCPA, dichlorprop Triazines (H) e.g., atrazine, simazine, cyanazine Ethylene bis dithiocarbamates (F) e.g., maneb, zineb, mancozeb
Third generation (from 1975):	Synthetic pyrethroids (I) e.g., cypermethrin, deltamethrin, permethrin Benzimidazoles (F) e.g., benomyl, carbendazim, thiabendazole Sulfonyl ureas (H) e.g., chlorsulfuron, metsulfuron methyl

6.2.2 A BRIEF HISTORY OF PESTICIDES

The use of toxic chemicals against pests and diseases in crops is not a modern invention. Homer mentions the value of burning sulphur as a fumigant, and Pliny (A.D. 79) refers to the use of arsenic compounds against insects.

By the 16th century, also the Chinese applied arsenic compounds as insecticides, and at least 300 years ago nicotine in extracts of tobacco was used for the same purpose. A report from 1828 describes how extracts from Pyrethrum served as an insecticide. About 1850 soap was found useful against aphids, and sulphur was applied as a fungicide.

Bordeaux mixture (copper sulphate, lime and water) was introduced as a fungicide in 1885 and as a herbicide in 1896. About the same time, it was discovered that iron sulphate could kill weeds in cereals, and within the next 10 to 20 years other simple inorganic substances like sodium nitrate, ammonium sulphate and sulphuric acid came into use as herbicides.

The use of pesticides increased in the 1920's and 1930's, and organic chemicals began to substitute for the inorganic ones. Among the organic compounds from that period were petroleum oil and dinitro-ortho-cresol (DNOC). The latter was used both as a selective herbicide in cereals, and for the control of aphid eggs (cf. Hassall, 1969).

Table 6.2.1 shows some examples of early and modern pesticides.

During and just after the Second World War, a second generation of pesticides appeared. They were: the organochlorine insecticides like DDT, lindan, aldrin, endrin and dieldrin; and the organophosphates like parathion, malathion and diazinon. Selective herbicides like the phenoxyacids 2,4-D, MCPA and dichlorprop also came into being. Also the triazine-herbicides, such as atrazine, simazine and cyanazine, as well as the fungicides maneb, zineb and mancozeb, are reckoned among the second-generation pesticides.

A third generation appeared after 1975, and it includes the synthetic pyrethroids like cypermethrin, deltamethrin and permethrin, the benzimidazole fungicides like benomyl, carbendazim and thiabendazole, and the sulfonylurea herbicides chlorsulfuron and metsulfuron methyl. All these agents are highly active yet not very target specific.

New pesticides are developed primarily in the multinational chemical industry. Through extensive synthesis and test programmes, they produce and test thousands of new chemicals against fungi, weeds and insects. When a promising compound has been found, its toxicological and environmental behaviour must be tested before it can be registered.

6.2.3 THE DISTRIBUTION OF PESTICIDES IN THE ENVIRONMENT

6.2.3.1 Pesticides in the Atmosphere and in Precipitation

As shown in Fig. 6.2.1, pesticides may end up in the atmosphere and drift away. Short-distance transport of pesticides in the atmosphere is responsible for the herbicide damage that appears occasionally in gardens and fences near sprayed fields. Such damage due to drifting of herbicides is seen especially where phenoxyherbicides are used in the spring. When spraying is performed under windy conditions, many of the droplets are carried to nearby areas.

Due to drift and to evaporation from sprayed areas, the pesticides may appear also in small concentrations in rainwater. Table 6.2.2 shows the concentrations in rainwater of some herbicides (results from Germany). Concentrations are given in microgrammes per liter, equivalent to mg per m^3 rain-water, collected on an uncropped location in an agricultural area. Especially in the spraying season, pesticide residues were found, but residues of, e.g., mechlorprop were detected in the precipitation several weeks after spraying.

6.2.3.2 Pesticides in Surface Water and Groundwater

During recent years, pesticides have been detected in groundwater, in wells and in drainage and surface water. The concentrations are generally low in relation to the toxicity of the pesticides, but residues of pesticides in drinking water have been declared undesirable and maximum residue limits of 0.1 microgramme per liter (i.e., 1 g per 10.000 m^3) have been established in most EEC-countries.

Table 6.2.2. Herbicides detected in rainwater. The water was sampled from April to August on uncropped land in an agricultural area. - Source: Hurle et al. (1987).

	Concentration (μg/l)		
Atrazine	0.03-0.5	(April to July),	< 0.01 from August
Simazine	0.01-0.2	(April to June),	< 0.01 from July
Mecoprop	0.04-1.4	(April to June),	< 0.04 from July
Dichlorprop	0.02-1.0	(April, May),	< 0.02 from July

Table 6.2.3. Pesticide concentrations in Swedish streams, 1986 - Source: Kreuger (1986).

Pesticide	Maximum concentration	Month
MCPA	3.0	May
Dichlorprop	3.1	July
Atrazine	1.0	May

Table 6.2.4. Pesticide concentrations in groundwater in the USA. - Source: Cohen (1984).

Pesticide	Concentration, µ/l
Aldicarb	1 - 50
Altrazine	0.3 - 3
Carbofuran	1 - 5
Dinoseb	1 - 5
Simazine	1 - 2

Pesticides in surface water. During pesticide treatment, the chemicals may end up in streams and lakes, directly or due to drift. Run off from treated fields into streams and lakes is another route for pesticide contamination of surface water. Drainage water is also in some cases found contaminated with pesticides leached out from the plough layer. Finally, contamination of surface water has been observed to happen during the filling and cleaning of sprayers.

Table 6.2.3 shows the content of some herbicides in Swedish streams in 1986. Note that the highest concentrations, found during the growth period, were 3 microgramme per liter. These results indicate that the contamination may have resulted from drift or from cleaning of sprayers, since only a small amount of drain water will appear during the summer period. German and Norwegian experiments show similar results.

Contamination of groundwater. Pesticides can reach the groundwater either by direct contamination through wells and well borings, by leaching from treated fields, or by leaching from chemical-waste disposals. Several cases per year in Denmark have shown that direct contamination is a serious risk of pollution which is very difficult and costly to remove. To avoid these cases it is important that (1) back-flow valves are installed, (2) tubes for the filling of sprayers are not inserted into the spray tank, and (3) filling and cleaning of sprayers is done at a safe distance from wells and well borings.

To protect groundwater from pesticide contamination, a 'maximum residue limit' has been established in most EEC-countries, as mentioned above. The limit is 0.1 µg per liter for each pesticide, and 0.5 µg per liter for all compounds in total. A concentration of 0.1 µg per liter is equal to 1 g pesticide in 10.000 m^3, or 1 g in a water layer of 1 m on 1 ha. If the pore volume in the groundwater zone is 0.3, a layer of 1 m of plain water is equal to a layer of 3 m in the groundwater zone. Thus 1 g of pesticide leached out from 1 ha is enough to bring the concentration in 3 meter of groundwater to 0.1 µg per liter. Since about 500 - 1.000 g of pesticide per ha is a typical dose, the degradation and adsorption in the soil must be very efficient to avoid groundwater pollution.

Table 6.2.4 shows the concentrations in groundwater in the USA of some pesticides, presumably originating from leaching from agricultural fields. Many of the concentrations shown in the table are well above the European maximum residue limit of 0.1 µg per liter.

In a German monitoring of 206 wells and well borings, the highest pesticide concentrations were: atrazine 0.26 µg per liter, bentazone 0.85 µg per liter, mecoprop 0.37 µg per liter and simazine 0.14 µg per liter. Although these concentrations are low, they are above the limit, but from these values it does not seem unrealistic that the very low residue limit for pesticides in groundwater can be met in most cases.

6.2.3.3 Adsorption and Transport

As shown in Table 6.2.4, small residues of pesticides have been found in groundwater. Thus leaching of pesticides seems to occur. The persistence of pesticides in soil and their adsorption to soil particles is of special importance in evaluating the potential transport of a pesticide in the soil. Surplus of precipitation and soil organic matter content are the important enviromental parameters of leaching.

Adsorption of a pesticide in soil is usually described by the distribution coefficient K_d which is determined by shaking an aqueous solution of the pesticide with soil (e.g., 25 ml of water + 5 g of soil). After shaking for 16 hours, water and soil are separated, residual pesticide in the water is determined and the amount adsorbed to the soil is calculated. Finally, K_d is determined as the ratio of the pesticide concentrations in soil and in water:

$$K_d = \frac{\text{concentration in soil (mg/kg)}}{\text{concentration in water (mg/liter)}}$$

A high K_d value corresponds to a large adsorption and thus to a low risk of leaching.

Adsorption may also be calculated in relation to the content of organic carbon in the soil, termed K_{oc}, to exclude variations from one soil type to another:

$$K_{oc} = \frac{100\ K_d}{\%\ \text{C in the soil}}$$

Table 6.2.5 shows K_d and K_{oc} values for the insecticide parathion and the herbicide MCPA in soil sampled in the ploughlayer, and in subsurface soil. The figures clearly demonstrate the different adsorption properties of the two pesticides and the low adsorption of both compounds in subsoil due to the low content of organic matter in this soil.

Correlation between adsorption and persistence of a pesticide and the risk of leaching of the compound to groundwater have been proposed by Gustafson (1989). He suggests the following function which seems to apply to most pesticides found in groundwater:

$$GUS = \log_{10} t_{½} (4 - \log_{10} K_{oc}) ,$$

Table 6.2.5. Adsorption K_d- and K_{oc}-values of parathion and MCPA in soil from the plough layer and K_d in subsurface soil sampled 1 meter below the surface. - Source: Helweg (1987*).

Soil	% organic carbon	Parathion		MCPA	
		K_d	K_{oc}	K_d	K_{oc}
Plough layer (0-20 cm), sandy clay	1.2	28	2333	0.9	75
Subsoil (80-100 cm)	0.1	1.2	-	0.4	-

where $t_{½}$ = half life of the pesticide (days). A pesticide with a GUS-value above 2.8 is likely to be a leacher, a value between 2.8 and 1.8 indicates possible leaching, whereas at GUS-values below 1.8, leaching is not expected.

6.2.3.4 Pesticides in the Crop

Most pesticides are applied when the crop has already become established. Thus residues of pesticides will often appear in the crop. During plant growth the concentration will decrease, mainly due to dilution and degradation within the plant.

To ensure that the residues do not present a risk to the consumers, a 'maximum residue limit' (MRL) in food is laid down, typically in the range of about 1 mg per kg. Before registration of a certain application pattern for a pesticide, evidence must be given that used in this way the pesticide will not appear in concentrations above the MRL limit.

The MRL is fixed only when it is known which residues will result from 'good agricultural practice' (GAP). If the GAP residue is lower than a value based on toxicological findings, the maximum residue limit is defined to be this GAP residue.

The Danish National Food Institute continuously controls the pesticide residues in Danish food. Various kinds of food are sampled in the market and pesticide residue analysis is carried out, to ensure that the MRL is not exceeded.

The control has shown that, as a rule, the content of pesticides in Danish fruits and vegetables stays under the MRL. Only for 1%-2% of the samples is this value exceeded, and in most cases only slightly.

6.2.4 DEGRADATION OF PESTICIDES

When a pesticide reaches the soil, the chemical is in an environment that can change the molecule. On the surface of the soil and plants, the compound is exposed to sunlight of which especially the UV light is active in the degradation. In the soil chemical degradation may start after contact between the pesticide and the soil liquid, or after adsorption to active surfaces in the soil.

Quantitatively, most important however is the microbiological degradation brought about by enzymes produced by fungi or bacteria in the soil. A typical soil contains 0.5 - 1 billion bacteria and 200 - 2,000 meter of fungi hyphae in one gramme of soil, altogether a biomass of 4 - 8 tons in the plough layer in one ha. The importance of soil microorganisms for degradation is described by Torstensson (1980).

The soil microorganisms are also responsible for the mineralization of straw and root residues, and some of these organisms can produce enzymes which can decompose the xenobiotic pesticides.

Recall that degradation is a series of processes leading to still simpler organic molecules and hopefully ending up in a total mineralization to CO_2, salts and water, in turn inducing the build-up of new microorganisms and organic material in the soil. Pesticide molecules which are not (or only partly) decomposed may end up as residues bound in the organic fraction of the soil.

Fig. 6.2.2 illustrates (a) the process of stepwise degradation of an organic compound, and exemplifies (b) this process by the total mineralization of the pesticide 2,4-D. It is important to know the time for a complete degradation, to make sure that stable degradation products are not left in the environment.

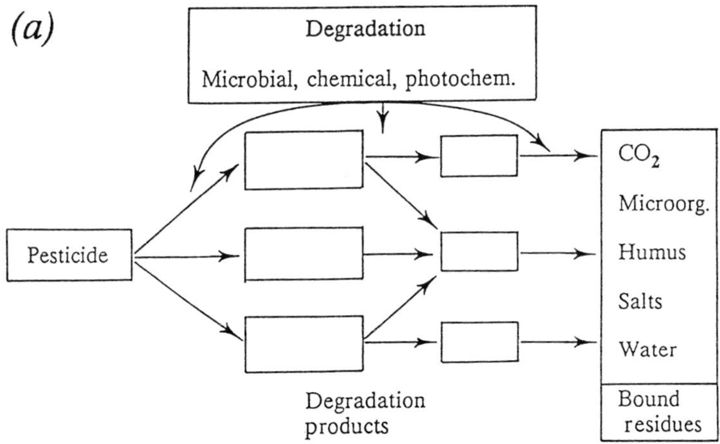

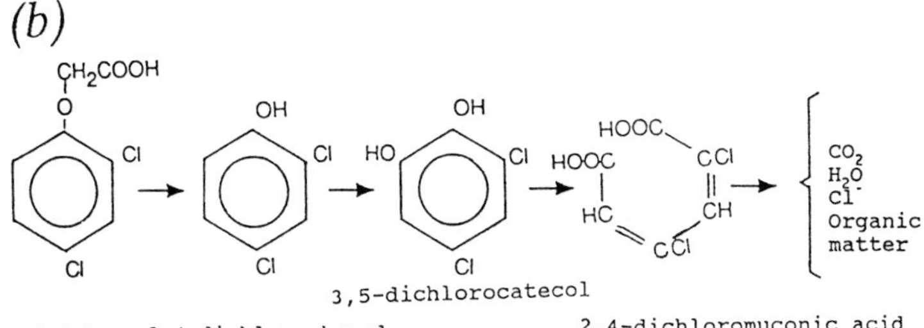

Figure 6.2.2. Degradation of pesticides.

(a) The degradation of a pesticide molecule may result in a total mineralization of the chemical, or in the formation of more stable degradation products, possibly bound residues.

(b) The microbial degradation of the herbicide 2,4-D is fast and ends up in a total mineralization of the molecule into CO_2 , water, chloride and organic matter. - Source: Loos (1975).

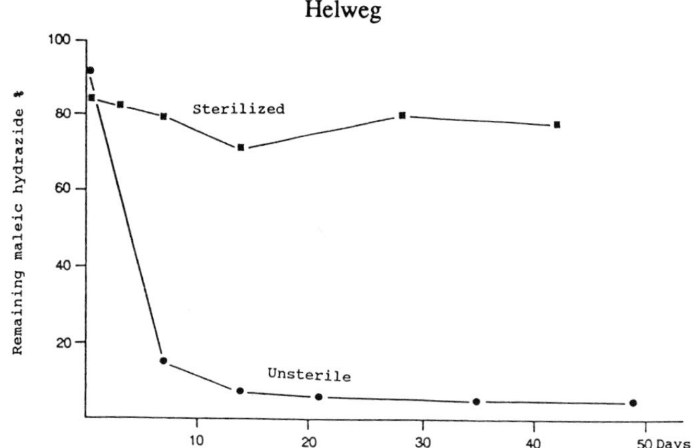

Figure 6.2.3. Degradation of the herbicide maleic hydrazide in soil sterilized by gamma irradiation and in unsterile soil. - Source: Helweg (1983).

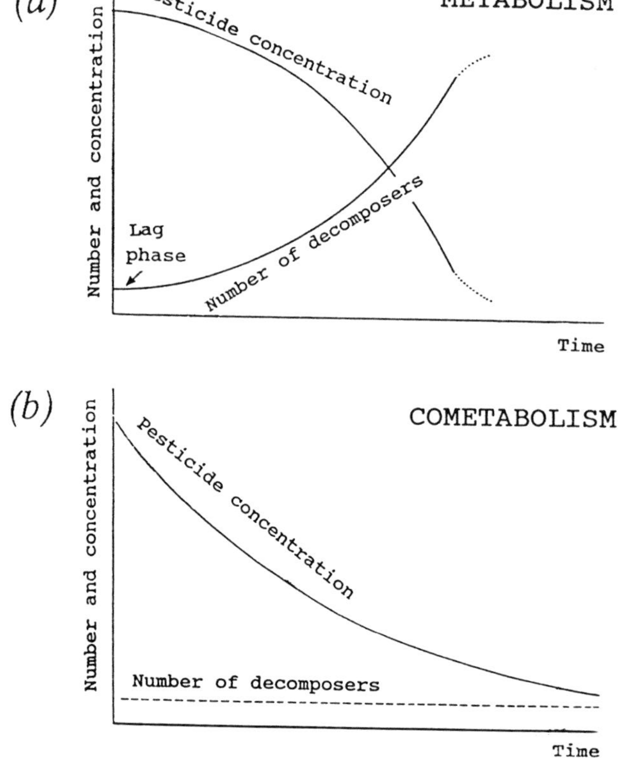

Figure 6.2.4 Degradation of pesticides by (a) metabolism, (b) cometabolism. -Source: Torstensson (1977).

Fig. 6.2.3 shows the influence of soil microorganisms on the degradation of the herbicide maleic hydrazide in soil. The herbicide was added to soil samples of which some were sterilized by gamma irradiation and the rest were left unsterile. The figure shows that if the soil microorganisms are killed, the degradation stops completely, whereas only a small percentage of the herbicide is left in the unsterile soil after 10 - 20 days.

Some pesticides may be metabolized, i.e., utilized for the growth of microorganisms. Other pesticides are 'cometabolized', i.e., just decomposed without leading to increased growth (Horvath, 1972). Degradation by metabolism or by cometabolism gives rise to different degradation patterns.

Fig. 6.2.4, part (a) shows how the concentration of the pesticide and the number of microorganisms may develop during a metabolic degradation. Just after addition of the chemical, only very few microorganisms are able to decompose the pesticide. Since they can proliferate on this new substrate, the number increases, and so does the degradation rate of the pesticide. Pesticides like the phenoxyherbicides MCPA, MCPB, mecoprop and 2,4-D are decomposed in this way, and the decomposing microorganisms are found in quantities from 1 to some few thousands per gramme in untreated soil. The number may increase to several hundred thousands in soil treated with the herbicides (Loos et al., 1979; Ou, 1984). This 'enrichment' of the soil by specific decomposers may prevail for several years since many soil microorganisms can survive in a dormant stage for years.

That the number of decomposing microorganisms and the concentration decrease during a cometabolic degradation is illustrated in Fig. 6.2.4, part (b). The number of decomposers is not influenced by the pesticide and the organisms proliferate on other substrates in the soil. The degradation curve shows the fastest decrease in concentration just after the start. When the concentration drops and the probability of contact between microorganisms (enzymes) and pesticide molecules becomes smaller, the rate of degradation also decreases.

6.2.4.1 Description of the Degradation

The degradation of a great number of pesticides, both in the field and in laboratory experiments, seems to follow degradation patterns similar to those reported for the cometabolic degradation, cf. Fig. 6.2.4, part (b).

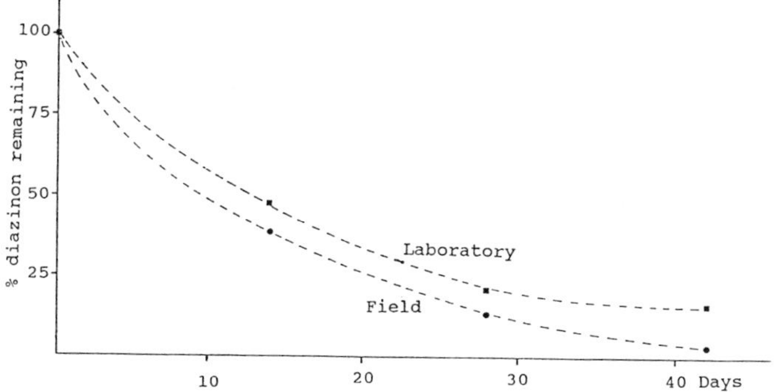

Figure 6.2.5. Degradation of the insecticide diazinon (4 mg per kg) under field and laboratory conditions.

Fig. 6.2.5 shows the degradation of the insecticide diazinon (4 mg kg^{-1}) both in a laboratory experiment and in a field experiment, carried out in May-June in identical soils. Note that the disappearance is faster in the field than in the laboratory experiment. The reason for this is that in the field disappearance of the pesticide is caused by evaporation, leaching and p-hotochemical degradation on the soil surface, together with degradation and adsorption in the soil. In the laboratory experiment, it is mainly degradation and adsorption which are responsible for the disappearance, and although both temperature and moisture are ideal (20°C and water to 80% of field capacity) in the laboratory, this is not enough to lead to a degradation as large as in the field experiment.

The degradation process has been described by Hamaker (1972) for a large number of pesticides. In most cases, the process is fairly well described by first-order reaction kinetics:

$$r = - k c ,$$

wherec= c(t) is the pesticide concentration, r = dc/dt is the degradation rate and k is the rate constant. It follows readily that $c(t) = c(0) \exp(-kt)$, i.e., if $\ln c(t)$ is plotted versus time, this so-called 'degradation curve' turns out to be a straight line, with slope -k .

Fig. 6.2.6 shows the degradation curves for diazinon. The correlation coefficients were 0.998 and 0.981 for the field and the laboratory experiments, respectively. When the slope -k of the line is known, the half life of diazinon (the constant time it takes for half of the amount to disappear) can be found as $t_{½} = (\ln 2)/k$. In this example, the slope is -0.079 and -0.045 respectively. The half lives of the insecticide are thus

0.6931/0.079 = 8.8 days under field conditions,
0.6931/0.045 = 15.4 days in the laboratory.

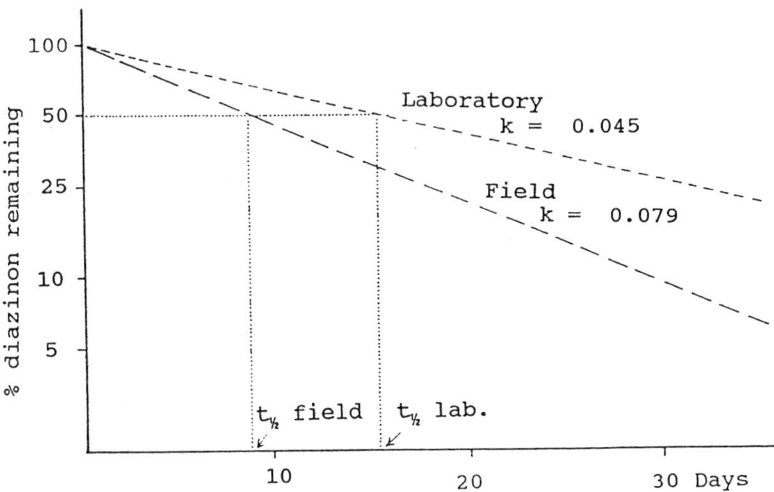

Figure 6.2.6. Degradation of the insecticide diazinon (4 mg per kg) under field and laboratory conditions. Semilogarithmic plot: per cent of remaining diazinon versus time; slope = -k (first order rate constant).

Table 6.2.6. Half lives for 6 herbicides in soil.

Atrazine	4 - 30 weeks
Chlorpropham (CIPC)	1 - 2 weeks
Chlorsulfuron (Glean)	6 - 16 weeks
Dichlobenil	4 - 32 weeks
Maleic hydrazide	1 - 2 weeks
Simazine	4 - 30 weeks

Table 6.2.7 Influence of soil temperature on the half life of the herbicide propyzamide in soil. - Source: Walker (1978).

Temperature	Half life ($t_{1/2}$)
23 °C	29 days
8 °C	120 days
3 °C	245 days

Many degradation processes in nature are, of course, much more complex than in this simple example, but for practical purposes first-order reaction kinetics with a constant half life are often presumed, sometimes even for pesticides which are decomposed by metabolic degradation.

After 4 half lives, about 95% of the pesticide is decomposed, and normally there is no effect left after this time.

Table 6.2.6 shows the half lives of 6 herbicides. It appears from the table that there is a big difference between the most stable herbicide, dichlobenil, with half lives up to 32 weeks, and maleic hydrazide with half lives of 1 - 2 weeks. There is also a big difference between the shortest and the longest half life for each compound, e.g. from 4 to 32 weeks for dichlobenil. The reason for this difference is that environmental conditions such as soil temperature, water content and soil type greatly influence the degradation (half life).

6.2.4.2 Influence of the Soil Environment on Degradation

The persistence of a pesticide may vary considerably from one environment to another. In subsurface soils with low microbial activity, degradation is generally very slow. Under cold, dry or acid conditions, it is also prolonged.

In the Northern part of Europe, the soil temperature varies from below zero in the winter period to above 20°C in summer. Table 6.2.7 shows that the half life for the herbicide propyzamide varies from 29 days at 23°C (summer temperature) to 245 days at 3°C (winter). This illustrates that degradation in the soil is low in winter. Thus, it is possible that if a pesticide which can leach is applied in the autumm, the risk of groundwater pollution is much greater than if the same pesticide were applied in the spring, due to the slow degradation and the water infiltration during the winter.

Table 6.2.8. Degradation of ^{14}C-labelled MCPA and TCA (5 mg per kg) in sandy clay soil from the plough layer and in coarse sandy soil taken 1 m below the soil surface. Number of days until 5% of ^{14}C had been liberated in the form of CO_2 - Source: Helweg (1987*).

	Sandy clay (surface)	coarse sand (subsoil)
MCPA	11 days	100 days
TCA	16 days	300 days

Table 6.2.9. Bacteria and fungi in soil from the plough layer and in subsurface soil. - Sources: Schnürer (1985), Brookes et al. (1985), Wilson and McNabb (1983).

	Bacteria, millions per g	Fungi, meter per g	Biomass in plough layer, kg per g
Plough layer	5000-1000	200-2000	4000-8000
Subsurface	1-10	very few	-

Differences in soil parameters may also influence the degradation rate of pesticides. Of special importance is soil pH, content of clay and organic material, content of nutrients and the composition and activity of the soil biomass.

Table 6.2.8 shows that the degradation of the herbicides MCPA and TCA, labelled with ^{14}C, happens much faster in soil from the plough layer than in soil from 1 meter below the surface (subsoil). The degradation is illustrated by the liberation in the form of CO_2 of an amount of ^{14}C added, and the table shows that 5% of the ^{14}C in soil from the plough layer had been evolved after 11 - 16 days, while it took 100 - 300 days in the subsurface soil.The main reason for the slow degradation in subsurface soil is that the biomass is much smaller in this soil and that the content of nutrients is low. Table 6.2.9 shows the total number of microorganisms in soil from the plough layer and in subsurface soil. It appears from the table that several hundred millions of bacteria can be found in a gramme of surface soil, against 1 to 10 million in the subsurface. Besides, fungi are almost absent in the subsurface soil.

6.2.5 CONCLUSION

Pesticides form an integrated part of modern agriculture. In many countries, most of the cropped area is treated once or several times every year. Due to this extensive use, pesticides can be found widespread in our environment. They also appear in groundwater, rain water and food.

It is essential that a continued surveillance of the environment takes place, to follow the transport and deposition of pesticides. It is also essential that we constantly increase our basic knowledge of the environmental fate and effect of pesticides, so that the consequences of their use can be predicted.

REFERENCES

Brookes, P. C., Powlson, D.S. and Jenkinson, D.S., 1985. The microbial biomass in soil. In: A.H. Fitter (ed.): Ecological Interactions in Soil. Blackwell Scientific Publ., Oxford, 123-125.

Carson, R., 1962. Silent Spring. Houghton-Mifflin Co., Boston, 368 pp.

Cohen, S.Z., Creeger, S.M. Carsel, R.F. and Enfield, C.G., 1984. Potential for pesticide contamination of groundwater resulting from agricultural uses. In: R.F. Kruger and J.N. Seiber (eds.): Treatment and Disposal of Pesticide Wastes. ACS Symposium Series No. 259. Amer. Chemical Society, Washington, DC: 297-325.

Gustafson, D.I., 1989. Groundwater ubiquity score: A simple method for assessing pesticide leachability. Environmental Toxicology and Chemistry, 8: 339-357.

Hamaker, J.W., 1972. Decomposition, Quantitative aspects. In: C.A.I. Goring and J.W. Hamaker (eds.): Organic Chemicals in the Soil Environment. Marcel Dekker, New York: 253-340.

Hassall, K.A., 1969. The historical setting. In: World Crop Protection, Vol. 2, Pesticides. Illife Books Ltd., London 1969: 1-4.

Helweg, A., 1983. Microbial Degradation and Effect of Maleic Hydrazide, Carbendazim and 2-Aminobezimidazole in Soil. Thesis, Royal Veterinary and Agricultural University, 153 pp.

Helweg, A., 1987*: Nedbrydning og adsorption af pesticidkemikalier i jordlag under rodzonen og jordluftens sammensætning ned til 2 meters dybde. (Degradation and absorption of pesticide chemicals in soil below the root zone and the composition of the air in the soil down to 2 meter below the surface). Danish Journal of Plant and Soil Science, S 1881, 78 pp.

Horvath, R. S., 1972. Microbial co-metabolism and the degradation of organic compounds in nature. Bact. Rev., 36: 146-155.

Hurle, K., Giessl, H. und Kirschhoff, J., 1987. Über das Vorkommen einiger ausgewählter Pflanzenschutzmittel im Grundwasser. Proc. Grundwasserbeeinflussung durch Pflanzenschutzmittel, 5. Fachgespräch in Berlin, 21./22. November 1985. Gustav Fischer Verlag: 169-190.

Kreuger, J., 1986*. Undersökning av pesticidrester i svenska vattendrag. (Investigation of pesticide residues in Swedish groundwater). Vattendrag i jordbrukslandskapet, FVH-publikation, 1986-4: 39-45.

Loos M.A., 1975. Phenoxyalkanoic acids In: P.C. Kearney and D.D. Kaufman (eds.): Herbicides, Chemistry, Degradation and Mode of Action. Marcel Dekker Inc. New York. Vol.1: 1-128.

Loos, M.A., Schlosser, I.F. and Mapham, W.R., 1979. Phenoxy herbicide degradation in soils: quantitative studies of 2,4-D and MCPA-degrading microbial populations. Soil Biology and Biochemistry, 11: 377-385.

Ou, L.-T., 1984. 2,4-D degradation and 2,4-D degrading microorganisms in soils. Soil Science, 137: 100-107.

Schnürer, J., 1985. Fungi in Arable Soil. Diss. Report 29, Dept. of Microbiol.,

Swedish Univ. Agric. Sci., Uppsala.

Torstensson, N.T.L., 1977*. Herbiciders inverkan på marken. (The influence of herbicide residues on the soil). Sveriges Skogvårdsforb. Tidskr., 75: 201-211.

Torstensson, N.T.L., 1980. Role of microorganisms in decomposition. In: R.J. Hance (ed.: Interactions Between Herbicides and the Soil. Academic Press, London: 159-178.

Walker, A., 1978. Simulation of herbicide persistence in soil. In: Simulation of Herbicide Persistence in Soil, Symposium at the Weed Science Society of America, 36 pp.

Wilson, J.T. and McNabb, J.F., 1983. Biological transformation of organic pollutants in groundwater, EOS. American Geophysical Union, 64: 505-507.

6.3 ECOLOGICAL ASPECTS OF INSECT PEST CONTROL

JØRGEN EILENBERG, HOLGER PHILIPSEN AND LEIF ØGAARD

6.3.1 INTRODUCTION

Crop protection means conscious interfering with the environment in order to limit the effects of various environmental factors, such as insect pests.

Abusive use of chemicals has been a serious global problem for some time and has led to pollution, poisoning and too high values of toxic residues - and the abuse continues. The consequences of this abuse, be it out of thoughtlessness, of insufficient information or of conscious disregard, have sharpened the conscience of consumers, farmers, farm advisers and politicians to a much higher awareness of 'the reverse side of the coin', so that it is not just the apparent advantages of reduced populations and yield increase which attract the attention.

With this in mind, we shall treat not only the past mistakes and the risks connected with the use of insecticides, but also the efforts which are being made to secure that the impact of treatments is easy on the environment and limited to insect pests. We will also deal with the plant-protection measures which can limit, or even replace, chemical control. Pest control strategies may actually be disregarded if the yield increases turn out to be too costly, all consequences of the treatment taken into consideration.

We will mainly treat subjects which are relevant to Danish conditions, giving both an all-round introduction to the general aspects of pest control and environment, and some detailed examples.

6.3.2 WHAT IS AN INSECT PEST?

In agricultural terms, an insect pest is a population of insects thriving in an environment where we are trying to produce a crop or make plants appear in a certain way. An insect becomes a pest when it appears in such quantities that it has adverse effects, quantitatively or qualitatively, on the crop yield. In most cases, the problems of insect pests are man-made. Above all because we optimize their living conditions, but also because we are less and less apt to accept yield-deteriorating competition from insects and other pests.

It is essential to note that this definition does not imply that insect pests are insects feeding on cultivated plants; it is the quantity of individuals which categorizes them as a pest.

Other animals are harmful because they feed on stored food or because they parasitize on domestic animals or transmit diseases.

From a medical point of view, many species may be regarded as highly nuisible. Some of humanity's worst plagues, such as Malaria, are transmitted by blood-sucking insects.

In the following, we will deal mostly with control measures against insect pests related to plant cultivation, and with the consequences of these measures.

6.3.3 INTERACTION BETWEEN INSECTS AND PLANTS - COEVOLUTION

Some animals, especially insects, are attracted to the plants we cultivate because we grow just one crop on a large area (monoculture), and with a high level of fertilization. When cultivating plants, there is a tendency to regard phytophagous insects which feed on the cultivated plants as insect pests.

It is important to emphasize the coevolution of plants and insects; it can be seen as a continuous competition in which the plants develop defense systems against insect attacks, for instance by producing toxins or by means of developing tough or hairy surfaces. The insects react by specializing in order to become indifferent/immune to the defense systems of the plant. Eventually, this leads to the insect-host plant relationship, and this host specificity means that plant families have their specific 'enemy' - or 'enemies'.

The ways of adaptation are numerous; some insects, for instance, limit their feeding to certain parts of the plant, such as the particularly nutritious buds, young leaves, pollen, etc., or they seek the parts of the plant which offer protection. Sometimes, the plant has only temporarily a nutritious value; thus, the presence of the insect is synchronized with the growth of the plant. This means that the plants do not offer an inexhaustible source of food to the insects. The plant grower must be aware of these interactions, in order to know when the insects are competitors.

All cultivated plants are derived from wild species which host phytophagous insects. The wild plants find some protection in growing among other plant species, i.e., they are difficult to localize (non-apparent) for the insects. When these plants are cultivated, they become easy to localize (apparent) because they are often grown in monocultures, covering large areas. The balance between insect population and plant population is upset in favour of the insects.

The consequences of this cultivation are illustrated by the following figures. In ecosystems (wildlife conditions), plant eaters devour less than 1% of the biomass produced yearly (Edwards and Wratten, 1980), whereas yield losses can reach as much as a gross 5%-30%, the worst being in tropical agriculture.

A matter of particular interest is the ability of the insects to select particularly nourishing parts of the plants, as well as their increased capability to develop on plants in good growth, e.g., as a consequence of fertilizing.

When the interaction between cultured plants and insects develops in favour of too large insect pest populations, it is necessary to take precautions, in order to avoid yield loss. These precautions can either be direct, trying to diminish the population instantly, or they can aim at a long-term solution.

6.3.4 THE USE AND GAIN OF INSECTICIDE APPLICATION

Insecticides have proved to be of invaluable use in our fight against some of mankind's worst diseases: Malaria and Yellow Fever. The application of DDT in Shri Lanka (Ceylon) reduced the number of Malaria victims from 2.8 million in 1946 to a mere 110 in 1961. (After this, however, the fight against Malaria ran into substantial problems.)

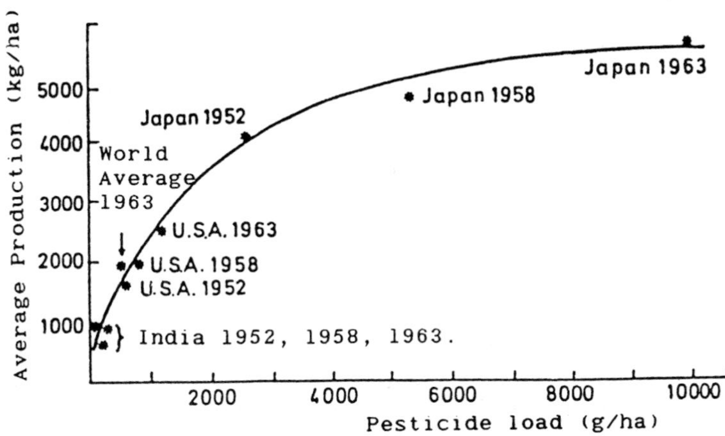

Figure 6.3.1. Average yield per ha plotted against pesticide application in India, USA and Japan in the years 1952, 1958 and 1963. Of course, no causal relation is implied. - Source: Gunn and Stevens (1976).

Also, in most parts of the world, the yield per unit area depends on the extent of plant protection. Fig. 6.3.1 shows the tendency in the results from application of pesticides (not only insecticides).

The total yield increase due to pesticide application for agricultural and horticultural products in Denmark has been estimated as follows:

Insecticides:	0.6 billion Dkr
Herbicides:	1.7 billion Dkr
Fungicides:	1.3 billion Dkr.

(Thonke et. al., 1986*). When split into main crops, the net yields are as shown in Table 6.3.1.

The yield increases per acre are estimated averages because they vary over the years, being strongly dependent on the weather conditions. The need for treatment in main crops is an estimate based on reports to The National Center for Plant Protection. It turned out that 50% of the spring barley area and 70% of the winter wheat area need treatments against aphids. As for oil-seed rape, an estimated 75% of the area is submitted to one treatment and about 40% is treated twice.

According to the statistics for application of marketed pesticides and growth-regulating products, published by the National Laboratory for Control of Chemicals, the application of chemical agents amounted to 10,000 tons in 1983 (and similarly in 1984). Of this total, 75% was applied in connection with plant protection, and the remaining 25% was applied as treatment against flies, parasites in domestic animals, and insect pests in stocks (Nøddegård, 1986*).

Table 6.3.1. Net yield and cost by pest control in Danish agricultural and horticultural crops. - Source: Thonke et al. (1986*).

PEST	treated area (1000 ha)	increased yield hkg/ha	crop value *Dkr/hkg	control costs Dkr/ha	increased yield total 1000 tons	value of incr.yield mill Dkr	total costs of control	net gain in incr. yield
SPRING BARLEY, aphids	500	3.0	135	**60	150	203	30	173
WINTER WHEAT, aphids	210	4.0	140	**60	84	118	13	105
RAPE, 1st pest control	140	1.4	370	250	20	73	35	38
RAPE, 2nd pest control	75	0.8	370	250	6	22	19	3
SUGAR-BEET, aphids (virus)	60	30	30	140	180	54	8	46
RYE, PEAS, FODDER-BEETS, POTATOES, SEEDGRASS, CORN							estimated:	150
VEGETABLES, FRUITS AND BERRIES, OTHERS							estimated:	100
							total:	615

* 1£ = 10.5 Dkr; 1$ = 6.5 Dkr

** Covers only product price: it is assumed that application is made together with other control agents

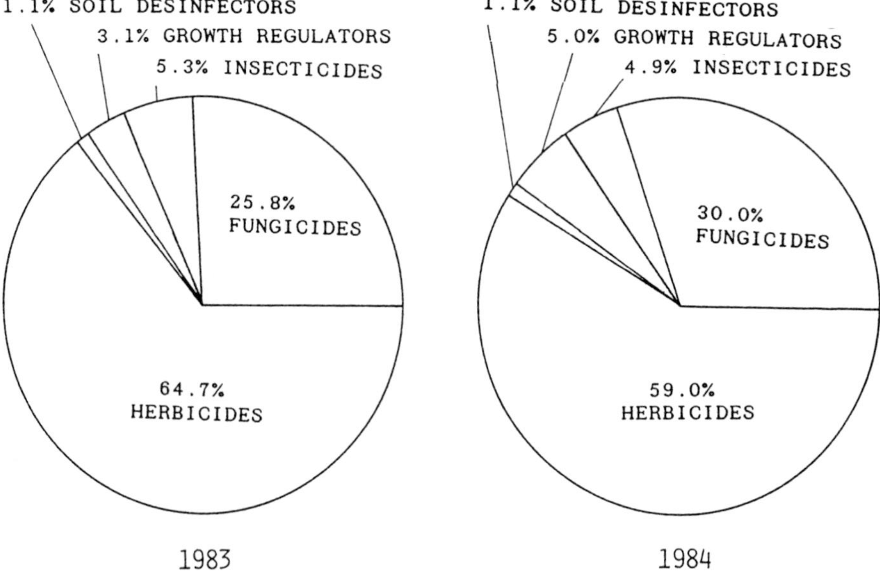

Figure 6.3.2. Relative distribution of the Danish trade in pesticides and growth regulators in 1983 and 1984. - Source: Nøddegaard (1986*).

Fig. 6.3.2 shows the distribution onto specific fields. About 5% of the total consumption are insecticides.

From the mid-1950's and up to the beginning of the 1970's, the use increased by 300%-400% (of the total amount of agents sold). Within the last 10-15 years, the rate of consumption has climbed only moderately where herbicides and fungicides are concerned, and insecticides have remained stable (Fig. 6.3.3).

These statistics, however, are only concerned with tons and kilos and do not take into consideration the variation in the amount used of each agent over the 30 years in question; some products have indeed left the market - or have been banned - and are replaced by others. Figs. 6.3.4, 6.3.5, and 6.3.6 illustrate the fluctuation in the application of insecticides, as well as the fact that a gross statistical analysis based on the total amount is likely to be dominated by agents which must be applied in large quantities.

Fig. 6.3.5 shows the sales rate for Permethrin - one of the synthetic pyrethroids. The increasing sale of pyrethroids indicates a change towards agents which are less toxic to vertebrates, and also towards some highly active products; this will eventually result in decreasing doses per acre, see Table 6.3.2. It has therefore been suggested that the statistical evaluation of the development in pesticide consumption should be based on the calculation of the maximal area that can be treated with the approved amount of each product (Kjølholdt, 1986*). When calculated in this way, the average treatment frequency has mainly decreased within the last years, see Table 6.3.3.

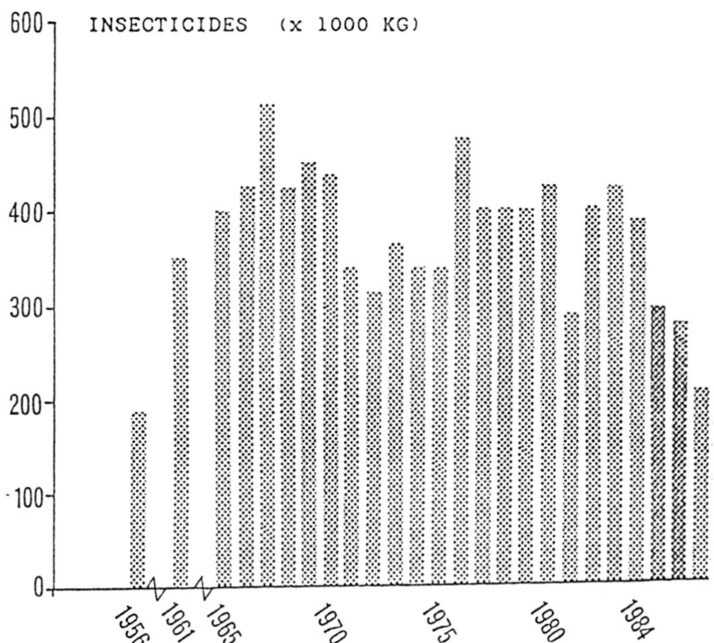

Figure 6.3.3. The Danish trade in insecticides (including agents against mites and snails), tons of active material, 1956-1984. - Source: Nøddegaard (1986*).

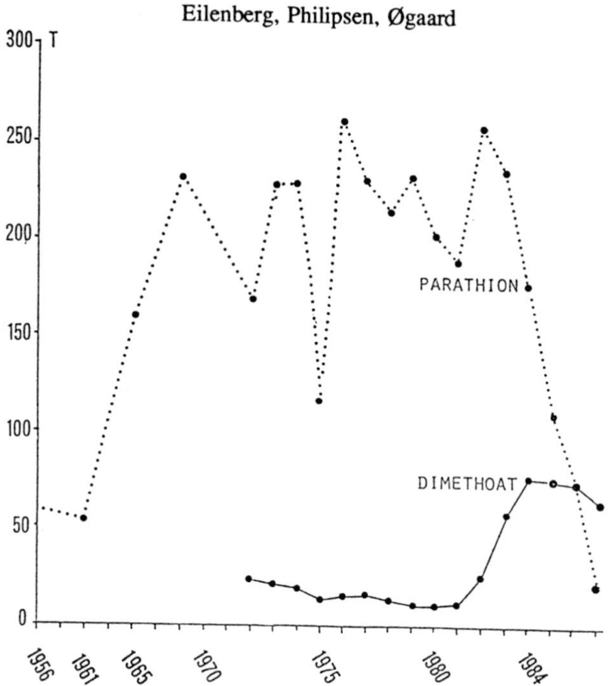

Figure 6.3.4. The Danish trade in insecticides containing dimethoate and parathion (including methyl parathion), tons of active material per year. - Source: Nøddegaard (1986*).

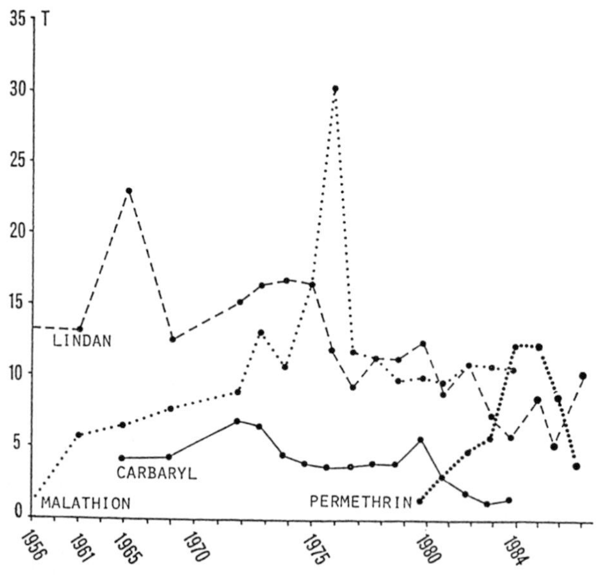

Figure 6.3.5. Insecticides with a Danish trade of less than 15 tons of active material per year. - Source: Nøddegaard (1986*).

Table 6.3.2. Average dosage in Denmark for the main types af pesticides. - Source: Kjølholt (1986*).

	Average dosage, kg/ha			
Pesticide category	1981	1982	1983	1984
Herbicides	1.75	1.63	1.45	1.23
Growth regulators	0.80	0.67	0.60	0.68
Fungicides	1.39	1.03	0.76	0.70
Insecticides	0.42	0.37	0.29	0.23
Total	4.36	3.70	3.10	2.84

6.3.4.1 Routine Treatment

A problem in relation to the agricultural use of pesticides is the uncertainty as to when and if plant protection is necessary. Routine treatment is an answer to this uncertainty, the purpose being maximum protection of the crop, and it does not include an estimate of each application - is it necessary and profitable? Often a yield increase has been obtained, but no knowledge as to which insect pests were in fact controlled.

The reason for carrying out routine treatments is insufficient and inaccurate knowledge of the insect pests, of when they appear, and of their susceptibility to weather conditions and cultivation methods. The result is - this goes for the most 'pest-prone' crops - that treatments have to be frequent and adaptable to the growth and general care of the crops.

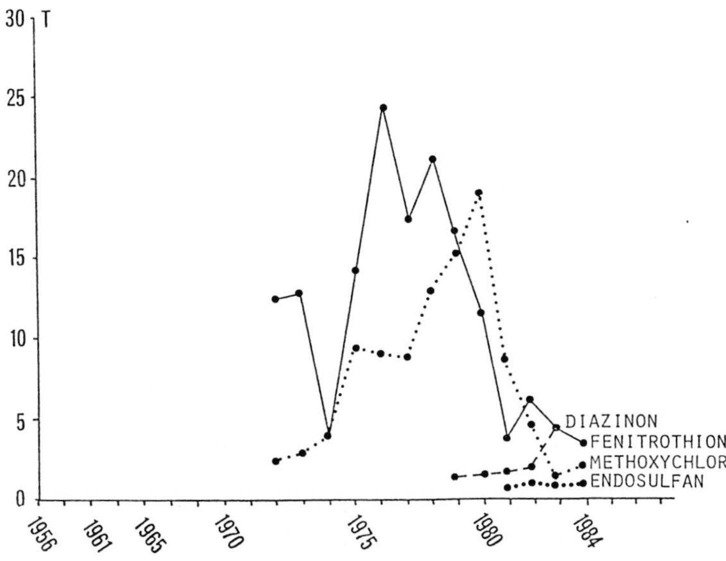

Figure 6.3.6. Insecticides with a Danish trade of less than 5 tons of active material per year. - Source: Nøddegaard (1986*).

Table 6.3.3. Development of (a) quantities of pesticide sold, and (b) frequency of pesticide treatment for farming purposes in Denmark. Target plan numbers refer to the action plan for a reduced consumption of pesticides, initiated by the Danish Minister of the Environment. - Source: Mortensen (1990*).

Pesticide category	Average 1981-85	1986	1987	1988	Target plan for 1990
a. tonnes sold					
Herbicides	4236	3810	3900	3762	3477
Growth regulators	238	360	303	259	179
Fungicides	1779	1682	1124	1082	1334
Insecticides	319	233	158	150	239
Total	6572	6058	5485	5253	5229
b. treatment frequency					
Herbicides	1.27	1.25	1.35	1.43	0.95
Growth regulators	0.14	0.19	0.16	0.14	0.11
Fungicides	0.81	0.63	0.54	0.56	0.61
Insecticides	0.45	0.58	0.46	0.46	0.34
Total	2.67	2.65	2.51	2.59	2.01

Oil-seed rape is an excellent example of such high-frequency-treatment crops, being very susceptible to attacks all through the growth period. Various parts of the plant are attacked: flower buds (blossom beetle), pods (pod midge), seeds (cabbage-seed weevil), stems (cabbage stem weevil), leaves (butterflies and aphids), and roots (cabbage-root flies).

Routine treatment often implies combined treatment with both herbicides (or fungicides) and insecticides. This saves work and may thus have its economic advantages, or it may lead to choosing routine treatment as a plant protection measure.

6.3.5 ECOLOGICAL ASPECTS OF INSECTICIDES

In the years following World War II, chemical control agents began to come into use, and the general opinion was that the problems of insect pests were now solved. This did not come true - and Rachel Carson's book "Silent Spring", published in the USA in 1962, caused a general discussion of the consequences of using chemical agents, in particular DDT. At that time, it had been discovered that DDT was accumulated all through the food chains, with fatal consequences to the predatory birds. Even animals in the arctic and antarctic parts of the world, living far from agricultural land, sometimes carried residues of DDT.

We shall not report the discussion any further, since no one in the industrialized countries can by now have any doubt left that the insecticides have their disadvantages, and that there is a serious drawback to uncritical use. (A recent summary of the ecological effects of actual pesticides in Great Britain since "Silent Spring" is given in Harding (1988)).

It is a bit late to say that these products should have been more properly researched before being marketed. However, the deepened knowledge of the dangers of pesticide application has not been able to limit the use of chemical agents which are acknowledged as noxious to the environment in all parts of the world. This must be due to the fact that the use of chemical agents is a matter of economy, which by far overshadows the ecological aspect. We refer to Sheail (1985) and Weir and Schapiro (1983*) for an account of the situation in the industrialized as well as in the developing countries.

So, where has the discussion taken us? Recognizing the adverse effects of chemical control, the discussion naturally takes up possible alternatives and ways of reducing the present consumption of pesticides. Of course, also agriculturists are preoccupied with the problem.

As already mentioned, chemical agents have solved many problems, and we cannot leave them out completely. However, we still have problems with these agents, such as their toxicity to beneficial and neutral animals and the fact that some of them are accumulated in the food chains. Furthermore, resistance to insecticides has added to the misère. These problems are of a general nature, and there are probably even more effects than we know of so far.

Where reduction of beneficials and the problem of resistance are concerned, they typically occur in connection with insect pests that are hard to control. Instead of a full account of these questions we shall merely give some examples, and then proceed with a description of the adverse effects of chemical control.

6.3.5.1 The Influence of Chemical Agents on Beneficials

With the approval of products for control goes an estimate of their toxic effect on the fauna. In order to come up with comparable results for all products, international standard tests are the present goal for scientists. The IOBC (International Organization for Biological Control) has established a working group, each member of which being responsible for the development and adaptation of a test of toxicity receptivity in a specific group of beneficials.

The first round is carried out in the laboratory, and the tests follow specific directions:

All beneficials are exposed to a surface (glass, leaves, soil or some other material selected according to the biology of the beneficial) which has been treated with a known amount of the pesticide in question. The tests are carried out in a ventilated container, and the beneficials are given suitable food. A watery surface serves as control.

At the end of the test period, the beneficials are compared with the control group, and their performance as predators or parasitoids is examined, for instance according to number of eggs or percentage of parasitization. The pesticides are then classified according to four categories (see Table 6.3.4, legend). Insecticides and acaricides, fungicides and herbicides are tested. Table 6.3.4 shows a summary of some of the results published.

According to the IOBC group, the test is so rigid that a product categorized 'harmless' will in fact be so in the field (Fig. 6.3.7). On the other hand, some pesticides may turn out to be less hazardous on the environment than first proved in the laboratory. At present (1990), directions for final testing have not yet been conceived, but field tests are being carried out in accordance with the guidelines of the working group, and guidelines and methods are published either in the EPPO Bulletin, cf. Anonymous (1988), or as scientific papers, e.g., Samsøe-Petersen (1987).

6.3.5.2 Insecticide Resistance

When applying insecticides one rarely kills off the entire population, and this is not the general idea, either. However, when insecticides are tested, the aim is that their efficiency, i.e., the proportion of insects killed, should be 95%-100%, in order to provide agriculture with the highest possible yield (natural conditions).

If insecticides are applied, but less than 95% of the insects are killed, one will often need to repeat the treatment, and the population is then submitted to a more constant and long-lasting pressure of selection, hence the risk of development of resistance. A similar risk is present when agents of a high residual effect (persistence) are used.

Resistance occurs when some insects, having survived a first encounter with a pesticide, pass on to successive generations a lower degree of sensitivity, which can be accounted for by one or several genes. The entire problem is rather complicated, and we will not go into further detail in this chapter. Let us mention, however, that resistance may wear off if control is abolished for some time: the 'wild ones' are often more competitive than the resistant individuals when there is no pressure of selection from control agents.

Fig. 6.3.8 gives a survey of the number of insect and mite species in which resistance has been detected since pesticides were introduced as a means of plant protection. Evidently, the number is increasing very fast.

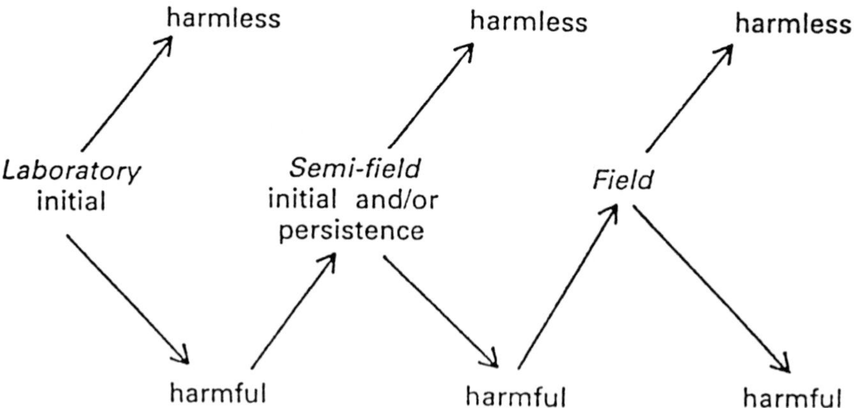

Figure 6.3.7. A sequential procedure for testing the side effects of agents on beneficial arthropods.

Table 6.3.4. Side effects of pesticides on beneficial insects and mites. Survey of results from 6 countries of the fourth joint pesticide testing programme carried out by the IOBC/WPRS-Working Group "Pesticides and Beneficial Organisms". - After Hassan et al. (1988).

Pesticide	Laboratory																									Semi-field								Field	
	Parasites										Predators														Fungus	Initial[c]					Persistence[d]				
											Mites/Spiders					Insects																			
	Trichogramma[a]	*Trichogramma*[b]	*Encarsia*[a]	*Encarsia*[b]	*Aphidius*[a]	*Aphidius*[b]	*Leptomastix*	*Cales*[b]	*Phygadeuon*	*Coccygomimus*	*Phytoseiulus R*	*Amblyseius potent.*	*Typhlodromus pyri*	*Typhlodromus p.* R	*Chiracanthium*	*Chrysoperla*	*Syrphus*	*Harmonia axyridis*	*Semiadalia* 11-not.[a]	*Semiadalia*[b]	*Anthocoris*[a]	*Anthocoris*[b]	*Bembidion*	*Pterostichus*	Verticillium	*Chrysoperla*	*Coccinella*	*Phygadeuon*	*Phytoseiulus*	*Aleochara*	*Trichogramma*	*Encarsia*	*Coccygomimus*	*Amblyseius finl.*	*Typhlodromus pyri*[e]
Asepta Nexion	4	4	4		4	4	4	2	4	4	1	4	4	3	4	4	4	4	4	3	4	4	4	4	2	4	2	4	4	4	4		1	4	
Birlane EC 40	4	4	4	1	4	3	2	2	4	4	4	4	4	4	3	3	4	4	4	3	4	4	1	1	2	1	1	2	4		4	4	1	4	
Dursban Spritzpulver	4	4	4		4	3	4	1	4	4	1	4	4	4	4	4	4	4	4	4	1	4	4	4	1	4	3		4	4	4		3	4	
Ambush C	4	4	4	3	4	4	4	3	4	4	4	4	4	4	3	2	4		4	3	4	4	2	1	1	3	1		4	4	4	–	4	4	4
Basudine Vloeibaar	4	4	4	1	4	4	3	2	4	4	1	4	4	1	4	4	4	1	4	3	1	2	3	4	1	2	1		4	4	2	4	2	4	
Perfekthion	4	4	4		4	4	4	2	4	4	1	4	4	4	2	4	4	4	4	3	3	4	4	2	1	4	4	4	4	4	4		3	4	3
Phosdrine W 10	4	4	4	1	4	3	4	2	4	4	1	4	4	2	3	3	4	1	4	3	1	1	4	1	1	3	4	1	4		2	1	2	4	4
Dimecron 20	4	3	4		4	4	4	1	4	4	3	4	4	4	4	4	4	4	4	3	3	4	3	1	1	4	4		4	1	2		4	4	
Hostathion	4	4	4	3	4	4	4	3	4	4	1	4	4	4	4	4	4	4	4	4	4	4	4	2	2		4	4	4	4	4	4	4	4	
Milgo-E	1	–	2	–	1	–	1	2	1	1	1	1	1	1	1	1	1	1	3		1	–	1	1	1	–	1	–	1		–	–	–	1	–
Rubigan Vloeibaar	2	–	1	–	1	–	1		1	1	1	1	1	1	1	2	1	1	2	–	1	–	1	1		1		–	1	1	–	–	–	3	1
Corbel	4	1	4		2	–	4	2	1	1	1	1	1	1	1	1	1	1	2	–	1	–	3	1	4	1		–	2		1		–	1	–
Ortho-Phaltan 50	1	–	1	–	1	–	1	1	1	1	1	1	1	1	1	3	2	1	3		1	–	1	1	2	1		–	1	1	–	–	–	2	1
Polyram-Combi	4	1	3		1	–	1	1	1	1	4	4	3	4	1	1	3	1	1	–	1	–	1	1	2	–		–	1	1	4		–	4	4
Trimidal EC	3	1	1	–	2	–	1	1	1	1	1	1	1	1	1	1		1	1	–	1	–	1	1	3	–		–	1	1	2	–	–	1	–
Topas	1	–	1	–	1	–	1	1	1	1	1	1	2	1	1	1	2	1	3		1	–	1	1	4	1		–	1		–	–	–	3	1
Tilt	3	1	1	–	1	–	1	1	1	1	1	2	3	3	1	1	2	1	3		1	–	1	1	4	1		–	1		1	–	–	3	–
Gesaprim 50	2	–	1	–	1	–	1	1	1	1	1	1	1	1	1	1	2	1	1	–	1	–	4	1	1	–		–	–	1	–	–	–	3	–
Certrol B	4	1	4		4	1	1	3	1	1	2	4	4	4	1	1		1	1	–	1	–	1	1	3	–		–	–	1	2		–	–	
Fusilade	1	–	2	–	4	2	1	1	1	1	1	1	2	1	1	1	4	1	2	–	1	–	3	1	1	–		–	–		–	–	–	–	–
Roundup	2	–	1	–	1	–	1	1	1	1	1	1	2	1	1	2		1	2	–	1	–	3	1	1	–		–	–		–	–	–	–	–

Laboratory, initial toxicity: 1 = harmless (<50 %), 2 = slightly harmful (50–79 %), 3 = moderately harmful (80–99 %), 4 = harmful (>99 %); Field, Semi-field, initial: 1 = harmless (<25 %), 2 = slightly harmful (25–50 %), 3 = moderately harmful (51–75 %), 4 = harmful (>75 %); Semi-field, persistence: 1 = short lived (<5 days), 2 = slightly pers. (5–15 d), 3 = moderately pers. (16–30 d), 4 = persistent (>30 d); a = Laboratory, vulnerable life stage; b = Laboratory, less vulnerable stage; c = Semi-field, initial; d = persistence; e = Field; R = resistent; – = test not required

Chemo-Resistance in House Flies. The development of resistance in houseflies (Musca domestica) gives a good illustration of the battle one enters when is it a question of being one step ahead of adapting abilities of these animals. It has been established that this 'race' began already one year after DDT was introduced in the fight against house flies.

Fig. 6.3.9 clearly illustrates the course of events, marking the years when resistance was detected towards this or that product. At the moment no product is available towards which the housefly does not carry resistance. Chemical control is therefore adapted so that a certain measure of control is obtained without the development of resistance in the local populations.

The Danish Pest Infectation Laboratory in Copenhagen is continuously working on this problem. Once a year, the laboratory publishes guidelines for the control of houseflies. The 1985 edition recommended ceasing chemical control at regular intervals, in order to help the non-resistant flies in the competition with the resistant ones. For aerosol sprays containing Pyrethrum or Pyrethroids which have immediate, but not a long-term effect, it is recommended that treatments are carried out only once a week. Smear products, designed to kill adult flies, are applied as narrow, vertical lines. This method has the advantage that not all flies come into physical contact with the poison; in this way resistance is prevented from developing too fast because the insect population maintains some heterogeneity.

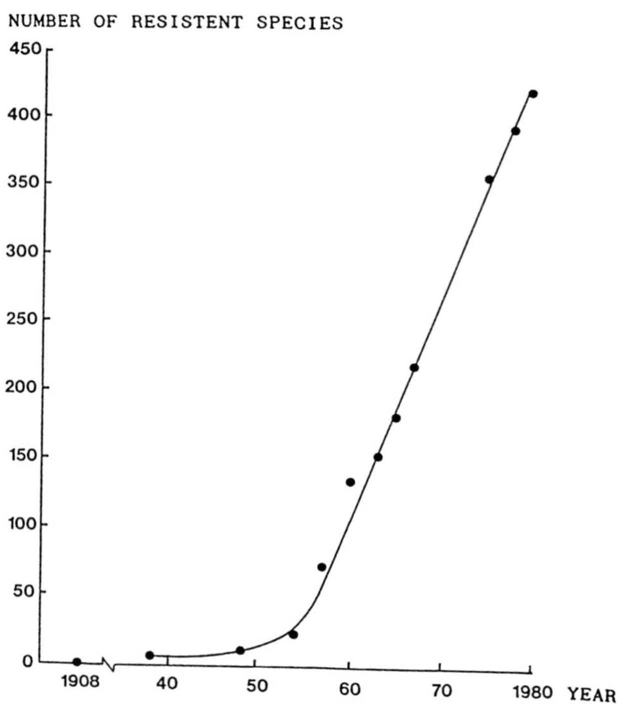

Figure 6.3.8. The number of insect and mite species in which resistance to pesticides has been established. - Source: Beorgiou and Mellen (1983).

As a consequence of all these problems with resistance, larval treatment with growth--regulating agents is becoming predominant, together with the preventive effect of cleaning stables and dung-heaps, thus limiting the possibilities of population growth.

There are various reasons for the rapid development of resistance in Danish house flies towards chemical control agents. Keiding (1976) points out two important features leading to a constant and efficient selection pressure on the populations: (1) the extensive and well-organized control which has been carried out in Denmark, (2) the fact that many farms are situated so far from neighbours that the flies appear as isolated populations.

Fruit Tree Red Spider Mite. The fruit tree red spider mite (Panonychus ulmi) is a serious problem in Danish orchards. One reason is that due to the high number of generations per growing season, the fruit tree spider mite has become resistant towards numerous control agents. Another important reason is that the natural enemies of this mite are seriously affected by insecticides used in the orchards, and this goes for fungicides as well. In addition to this, the natural enemies are being starved because the number of prey is reduced.

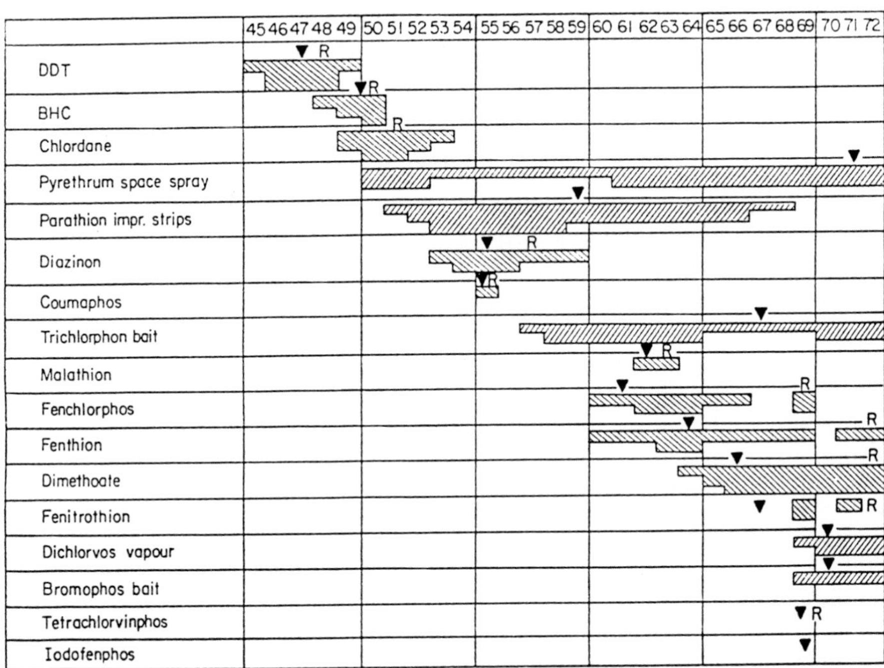

Figure 6.3.9. Application of pesticides to control the house fly (Musca domestica) in Danish farms 1945-1972, as seen in relation to resistance. The width of the hatched band suggests the size of the consumption for each pesticide; a "▼" indicates the first case of resistance reported; an "R" indicates resistance problems causing failure of the control measures. - Source: Keiding (1976).

In several cases it has been proved that herbivores become resistant to pesticides earlier than do carnivores. Some of these cases were explained by the fact that herbivores adapt more easily to 'eating poison', being already equipped with mechanisms to detoxify the secondary plant substances.

The ability in some predators to develop resistance is now being integrated in plant protection. For instance, resistant predatory mites (Typhodromus pyri) are used for controlling the red spider mite (Panonychus ulmi). The carnivore mites are collected in orchards where frequent treatments have taken place, or alternatively they are produced under laboratory conditions, being submitted to the pesticides to which they are to be resistant.

In Denmark, only a small number of problems has been reported concerning resistant insect pests in agricultural crops.

Mechanisms of Resistance. The fact that an agent does not affect some insects may be due to various reasons:

a) the cuticula of the insect is permeable only to a limited degree,
b) the insect is able to accumulate the agent in the body,
c) the insect possesses enzymes which rapidly neutralize or break down the toxin,
d) or the insect is simply immune/indifferent to the agent.

Lack of effect may also be due to the behaviour of the insects which may keep major parts of the population from coming into contact with the agent. Analyses of the genetic background for the resistance have shown that frequently each character is based on one single gene, with examples of dominant, recessive and intermediary heredity. Extensive testings, based mostly on houseflies, have shown that high resistance to a specific agent can be due to a combination of characteristics which, when viewed apart, do not ensure resistance, but when interacting lead to a high degree of resistance.

The biochemical basis of resistance has not yet been fully explored, but it has turned out that the enzymes which act as neutralizers of the pesticides are non-specific (broad range of activity), and that they can be induced (Plapp & Wang, 1983). This implies that sensitive insects possess only a small amount of enzymes, and a higher level of enzymes means a higher level of resistance.

6.3.6 METHODS FOR REDUCING INSECTICIDE CONSUMPTION

We have already discussed several examples of adverse effects due to uncritical application of broad-range pesticides. For this reason, in the field of insect pest control the national research effort in Denmark focuses on developing suitable methods of reducing the insecticide consumption.

Methods which are soft on the environment have been known for some time, and they are gradually being adapted for practical use. As to the industrial sector, the motivation for partaking in the research and development of ecological products is directed by the economic aspects of such a production.

Jackson (1984) states that the production of goal-specific products, such as insect growth regulators (IGR), insect viruses and sex pheromones, may eventually become attractive to the industry. He also points out the possibilities of distributing the agents in such a way that they become selective. For instance, the distribution of micro-capsules implies that only insects which eat them will be affected by the insecticide, whereas predators and parasitoids remain unaffected.

The cooperation between private and public research may reinforce the initiation of the production of certain types of agents which have not as yet been judged profitable. The following sections will deal with these and other methods which can contribute to the reduction of insecticide consumption.

6.3.6.1 Techno-Cultural Measures

The traditional methods of plant growing stimulate population booms which lead to economic damage. Generally speaking, healthy plants are more fit to resist insect pests than are plants in a detrimental state. However, this may mean larger insect populations on well-nourished plants. Dutch experiments (Vereijken, 1979) have demonstrated that nitrate fertilizing of cereals can stimulate aphid populations. The combination of intensified fertilizing and fungicides can lead to healthier plants and thus induce a higher risk of aphid infestation.

Traditional plant growing aims at healthy plants, and likewise research aims at stimulating the means of defense of the plant itself. The use of more or less resistant varieties is based on a cooperation, frequently international, in the field of plant breeding. When combined with other measures of control, even a low level of such resistance can greatly influence the development of insect pests.

Organic farming in particular tries to avoid serious pest attacks by means of crop rotation and mixed crops. Crop rotation works against non-mobile insect pests, such as nematodes. Mixed cropping, for instance, benefits from the fact that the odour from onions sometimes has a repellent effect on insects which are attracted to other crops. Opinions on the actual effect of such methods are strongly divided. The scientific basis is often inadequate when it comes to evaluation of the methods.

Hedges around the fields offer protection to a number of animals, both harmful and beneficial. Intensive spraying and removal of fences, completely or partly, make it hard for the natural enemies to survive when prey is scarce. Example: Ground beetles (carabidae) have a number of potential food resources, and their availability during the ovipositioning of the insect pests is strongly dependant on the possibilities of survival in the period preceeding the ovipositioning.

Unsprayed marginal zones along the hedges can therefore have the effect that beneficials have better possibilities of limiting pest populations. The effect of such marginal zones have been examined (Hald et al., 1988).

6.3.6.2 Prognosis and Forecasting as a Basis of Control Adapted to Needs

It seems obvious to minimize the number of chemical treatments in accordance with the actual situation, meaning that it is essential to obtain information as to whether control should take place at all, and if so, when it should be carried out.

The basis of such a control adapted to needs is extensive knowledge of the biology of every single insect pest. On this basis, methods must be developed which make it possible to predict the size of the insect pest population, so as to estimate the need for control. Later on, the insect pest is to be monitored, and information of importance to the decision-maker, concerning the general state of crops, temperature, precipitation etc., must be made available.

When the insect pest population has grown to a size which may lead to important economic losses, we say that the *damage threshold* has been reached. This means that damage thresholds are established on the basis of both biological and economic facts and evaluations. To provide this fund of knowledge takes a large amount of research. In many cases not even the basic biological facts of the pest insect are known, e.g., the number of generations per year.

Also, experience from other countries may not be applicable to Danish conditions, either because practice differs, or because the insect pest appears in different pathotypes, or because the natural enemies are not the same, etc. A complete and adequate description of the interaction between plant culture, insect pest and natural enemies is just not possible.

It is therefore necessary to choose a quasi-adequate strategy. This implies, for instance, that only the most important insect pests are monitored, and that the investigation is limited to specific parts of the life cycle, such as the survival of larvae. It has turned out to be a reasonably good method of estimating the size of insect pest populations, as a basis of prognoses and forecasting.

Apple farming in Central Europe is an example of an extensive and efficient system involving monitoring and specification of damage thresholds. Various simple census methods have been developed, such as the counting of eggs, larvae and traces of larvae activity. Each grower decides for himself whether control is necessary or not.

The following thresholds have been assessed for the green apple aphid (Aphis pomi) (Anonymous, 1980):

winter months:	5 - 10 eggs per 10 branches, 20 cm each,
before blooming:	10 - 15 aphid colonies per 100 buds
	or 25 - 50 aphids per 100 branches (knock test),
after blooming:	8-10 aphid colonies per 100 fruit rudiments
	or 40 - 50 aphids per 100 branches (knock test),
summer:	8 - 10 aphid colonies per 100 fruit rudiments
	or 50 - 80 aphids per 100 branches (knock test),
end of season:	10 - 15 aphid colonies per 100 fruit rudiments
	or 50 - 80 aphids per 100 branches (knock test).

Note that the damage threshold varies according to the season. Generally, more aphids can be tolerated at the end of the season than in springtime. - Also note that damage thresholds are given as intervals, not as fixed values.

The National Centre for Plant Protection, Lyngby, manages the Danish forecasting and prognosis systems. As a rule, an insect pest is monitored by means of traps which are looked after by the local farmers or by extension officers. The results are combined with information about the weather and soil conditions, last year's figures and so forth; and the prognosis or forecasting for a large area is based on this.

Taken altogether, a control system adapted to needs has several advantages. The strain of insecticides on the environment is somewhat eased, and each treatment is carried out at exactly the right moment. Another point is that the farmer himself will get used to 'keeping an eye on the insects'.

Finally, it should be mentioned that 'control adapted to needs' is not only meant to reduce the amount of chemical treatments. Biocontrol, too, is often based on an estimate of the population sizes.

6.3.6.3 Biocontrol

Biocontrol is an ambivalent notion which is being used in any context but the chemical and techno-cultural ones. In a more narrow sense of the word, biocontrol means control of insect pests by using live organisms:

- parasitoids, such as Ichneumonids,
- predators, such as mites,
- fungi, protozoes, virus, bacteria and nematodes, etc.,
- sterile males.

Biological control has been attempted for more than a hundred years, with varying degrees of success. The basic idea of biocontrol is that it is bound to be ecologically safe since it is based on natural interactions. In some cases, biocontrol has been chosen from lack of alternatives.

Biocontrol by natural enemies can be carried out in three ways:

(1) introducing natural enemies which are not already present,
(2) increasing the population of natural enemies or reinforcing their efficiency,
(3) using natural enemies as a direct measure of control.

Strategies (1) and (2) aim at the establishing of an equilibrium, by which the natural enemies keep the insect pest population at an acceptable level. Once again, let us take a look at the root of the problem with insect pests.

Many plant species originate from other parts of the world, and when introduced into their new environment, various pests often join them, while none of the natural enemies of these pests are brought along.

As to the increase in the populations of the present enemies, studies of the interaction between host and enemy may lead to methods of cultivation which give the natural enemies better possibilities of reducing the insect pest population.

When dealing with natural enemies as control agents, cf. strategy (3), investments in control research and production should be matched by reasonably good prospects of control. This goes for strategies (1) and (2) as well, but here it is likewise possible that the prospect of a permanent solution to an insect pest problem justifies substantial investments once and for all.

As for the means of control belonging to the third strategy, they are sometimes called 'biopesticides' because the way they are used resembles that of the chemical control agents. There are, however, a few things to be aware of where all three strategies are concerned.

Above all, the natural enemy should be easy to propagate, and the product easy to store safely. As to the production of microbiological control agents, it is essential that it can run continuously and independently of possible outbursts of insect pests. Furthermore, the application should be easily adaptable to the usual practice. Biopesticides can usually be applied with ordinary spraying eordinaryquipment, or with accessories which do not call for large investments.

Whether control with natural enemies according to strategy (3) is to be preferred in favour of chemical control depends on a number of variables. The most important ones are the price and the efficiency, together with environmental gentleness. The fact that the natural enemies are indeed soft on the environment has inspired the research tremendously, but competition is tough, so the larger part of this research must be expected to be orientated towards easily marketable products, or to concentrate on the very controversial aspects of chemical control.

Details of Control Methods. *Predators* are often unspecialized when it comes to prey. Numerous beetles (Carabids and Staphylinids) and birds feed on a great variety of insects at all larval stages. It is a well-established fact that predators play an important part in controlling insect pests, but it takes intensive research to determine the exact role of every single predator.

That predators may play an important part in plant protection is illustrated, for instance, by the successful application of predatory mites (Phytoseiulus persimilis) against glasshouse spider mites (Tetranychus urticae) in glasshouses. Gall midges (Aphidoteles aphidimyza), which in their larval stage prey on aphids, are used against aphids where biological control of glasshouse spider mites and glasshouse whiteflies (Trialeurodes vaporariorum) is carried out.

This leads us to the heart of the matter: Once biological control has been introduced, there will be certain limitations as to the choice of means of control. Chemical agents may sometimes be used along with biological methods, but new problems may arise. In glasshouses, thrips are controlled chemically, for instance, in connection with the control of glasshouse spider mites and glasshouse whiteflies. If chemical control is given up in favour of biological control, the thrips may turn into an insect pest. In order to solve this problem, research is aiming at the development of controlling thrips with mites. Leaf miners and aphids, likewise, have become insect pests of considerable importance. Leaf miners can be controlled with Ichneumonids; aphids either with the above-mentioned gall midges, with other species of Ichneumonids, or with the larvae of lacewings.

Parasitoids in their larval stages are characterized by the habit of killing their hosts at some point of their life cycle - in contrast to parasites which do not necessarily kill their hosts.

Fig. 6.3.10 shows the life cycle of a host and a parasitoid. The parasitoid is synchronized with its host, thus ensuring optimal conditions for its offspring.

Ichneumonids are predominant among the various means of biocontrol. Some species of Ichneumonids are already being used, such as the glasshouse whitefly parasite (Encarsia formosa), which is marketed in Denmark for biocontrol of the glasshouse whitefly (Trialeurodes vaporariorum), and the parasitic wasps, Aphidius spp., which serve as periodic control of aphids in greenhouse cultures. In the fields, Trichogrammas can be used against various butterfly species at the egg stages.

It is important to note that predators and parasitoids are suitable for biocontrol only if there is no urgent need to kill off the insect pest immediately. One must also accept a certain level of the pest remaining in the crop. Of the three strategies referred to above, it is only (1) and (2) which are applicable.

Outside Denmark, a number of other species are being used for biological control. An early success in the field was the introduction of the ladybird Rodolia cardinalis for control of a scale, Icerya purchasi. The latter was imported into California where it caused great damage on citrus fruits.

There are several examples of control of 'imported' insect pests by means of natural enemies likewise imported.

Pathogens. Insects are attacked by pathogens, such as viruses, bacteria, fungi, protozoas, rickettsias, etc. Nematodes do not naturally belong here, systematically speaking, but their affinity with insect pathogens as to epidemical appearance is such that the nematodes are frequently categorized along with microbials.

Insect viruses are obligate intra-cellular parasites which enter through oral passage. Most kinds of insect viruses carry the virus particles in an inclusion body which dissolves in the midgut of the insect. The virus particles pass through the walls of the gut epithel and multiply in the cell nuclei of the insect. The most important virus groups are:

Baculovirus		NPV	(Nuclear Polyhedrosis Virus)
	and	GV	(Granulosis Virus)
Cytoplasmatic virus		CPV	

Most insect pathogenic bacteria are facultatively pathogenic, i.e., they are not always pathogenic and they can feed on other media besides insects.

Within the genus Bacillus, several species have a high pathogenecity towards insects. B. popilliae is special by being an obligatory parasite on Scarabaeidae larvae living in soil.

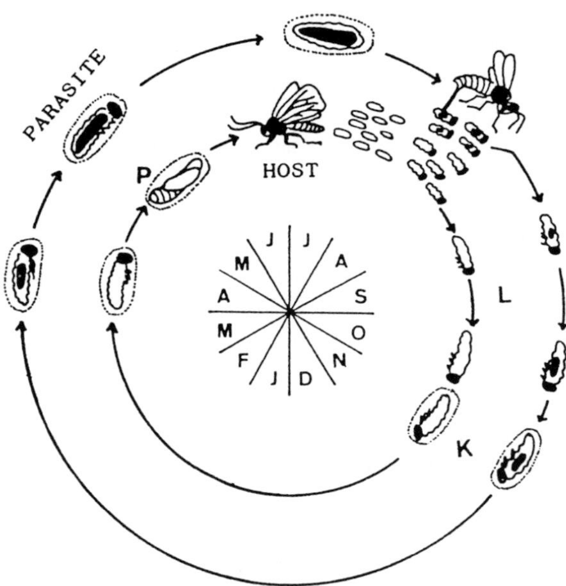

Figure 6.3.10. The life cycle of a parasitoid and its host. The stages of development of the parasitoid are suggested by means of the black figures inside the host larvae in the outer ring, and those of the host itself in the inner ring. L = larval stages, K = cocoons with hibernating larvae, P = pupae in cocoons. - Source: Münster-Swendsen (1977*).

By contrast, B. thuringiensis is relatively non-specific; for instance this bacteria thrives on simple, artificial diets. B. thuringiensis produces toxins which are used in the control of insect larvae (Diptera and Lepidoptera). B. thuringiensis exists in a number of sub-species, distinguished by the kind and the amount of toxins produced; and these properties also qualify them for possible control of specific groups of insects.

Insect pathogenic fungi are likewise obligatory or facultative parasites. Unlike insect viruses and bacteria, fungi invade their host by penetrating cuticula straight after the adhesion and germination of the infective unity. A certain toxin production has been demonstrated, but as a rule, the death of the host is due to the infiltration of the tissue which is devoured by the fungus.

Important groups of insect pathogenic fungi are found in various categories, e.g., the Entomophthora fungi (class: Zygomycetes) and the species Beauveria bassiana and Metarhizium anisopliae (category: Deuteriomycetes). As to the known methods of propagation, they vary according to the species, some being easily propagable on simple, artificial diets, while others, such as certain species of Entomophthorales, are propagable only in the host.

Insect pathogenic protozoas are obligatory parasites, and their infective units (spores) are activated by oral passage. The infiltration of host tissue generally progresses slowly, and this may lead to the death of the host caused by a secondary bacteria attack. The most important of these species belong to the genera Nosema, Vairimorpha, and Amblyospora.

Nematodes. Strictly speaking, nematodes parasitizing on insects are parasitoids, but their affinities with insect pathogens rank them together with these. One point of similarity is the rapid growth of the nematodes, which can cause an epidemic growth within the host population. Nematodes enter orally or through the tracheal system.

The sterile-male method. The idea of this method is to propagate the insect pest in question. Both males and females are sterilized by means of radiation, usually in a late pupal stage. Later, when large numbers of sterile insects are released, outnumbering the natural population by up to a factor of 10, the eggs of the natural population will not be fertilized. The method has its limitations: the propagation must be extensive, and the species must be one that mates only once, to ensure a large majority of unfertilized eggs. Also, the proper dose of radiation must be known in order to sterilize the males without weakening them.

The method has been used for some years in the Netherlands, against onion flies (Delia antiqua) amongst others.

The Practical Use of Biocontrol. As mentioned above, biocontrol by means of predators or parasitoids has been an established praxis in Danish greenhouses for more than a decade. For a description of the methods in use, see Hansen et al. (1984*). In Denmark, microbial control agents have recently been introduced commercially, both outdoors and in greenhouses. Several products are now available: products based on Bacillus thuringiensis against caterpillars and sciarid larvae; the fungus Verticillium lecanii against aphids and white flies; and nematodes (Nevaplectana spp. and Heterorhabditis spp.) against soil insects. In some other countries, the use of microorganisms has become even more extensive and in general, the potential for biological and microbial control seems great.

Table 6.3.5. Survey of the applications of certain organisms for microbiological control of insect pests. - Source: Payne (1988).

Species	Target pest	Country
a) Bacteria		
Bacillus thuringiensis	Lepidoptera, Diptera	Worldwide
Bacillus popilliae	Japanese beetle	USA
b) Nematodes		
Heterorhabditis spp. and *Steinernema* spp.	Vine weevil; other soil-borne pests	Netherlands, USA
c) Fungi		
Beauveria bassiana	Colorado beetle	China, USA
Metarhizium anisopliae	Beetles, bugs	Brazil
Verticillium lecanii	Aphids, whitefly	UK
d) Protozoa		
Nosema locustae	Crickets	USA
e) Baculoviruses		
Cydia pomonella GV[1])	Codling moth	Switzerland
Lymantria dispar NPV[2])	Gypsy moth	USA
Mamestra brassicae NPV	Several lepidoptera	France
Neodiprion sertifer NPV	Pine sawfly	UK, USA, Finland
Orgyia pseudotsugata NPV	Douglas fir tussock moth	USA
Spodoptera littoralis NPV	Cotton leafworm	France

[1]) GV = Granulosis virus (a baculovirus)
[2]) NPV = Nuclear polyhedrosis virus (a baculovirus)

6.3.6.4 Biotechnical Control

Pheromones. Pheromones are substances which enable the insects to communicate with each other. Man's practical use of pheromones largely derives from their usefulness in connection with forecasting, cf. Esbjerg et al. (1983*), Ravn and Harding (1985*). But they have also been used directly for control purposes, viz. as a means of attracting the bark beetle (Ips typographus). In Norway, in years following heavy windfalls and consequently with abundant populations of this beetle, traps were set up and beetles were caught in millions, yet it is doubtful whether the method did actually reduce the beetle population.

Pheromones are also used to confuse the insects by slowly releasing the substances from microcapsules over a large area, thus interfering with the mating process.

Insect growth regulators. Various hormones act in the process of molting, such as molting hormone and juvenile hormone. If the hormonal equilibrium is upset, the insect cannot accomplish its life cycle in a normal way. This fact is exploited in the use of hormone analogues, especially juvenile hormone analogues (JHA). The latter are first and foremost used against insect pests which are harmless in their larval stages, but damaging or nuisable as adult insects. The JHA are increasingly used in the control of house flies; they are mixed with or dispensed in the environment of the larvae.

A similar effect can be obtained by using diflubenzurone or similar inhibitors of chitin synthesis. They affect the ability of the insect to grow a normal cuticula. The new cuticula is weak and many insects die in the process.

Repellents and attractants. As discussed earlier, plants and insects evolve together in a continuous fight, in which, on the one hand, the plants develop repelling and feeding-inhibiting agents in order to prevent attacks, while on the other hand, the insects adapt to these agents, or they are even attracted by them. The possibilities of exploiting the repellents (and attractants + pesticides) for crop protection are being continuously investigated. The agents may be natural extracts, or they may be made synthetically. It is however only in a few cases that the work has gone beyond the experimental phase.

6.3.6.5 Integrated Control

The definition used by FAO and IOBC is as follows: "The control of pests and diseases employing all methods consistent with economic, ecological and toxicological requirements while giving priority to natural limiting factors and economic damage thresholds." (Brader, 1975).

The elements of integrated pest management are shown in Fig. 6.3.11 which comprises all the insect pests in a crop; efforts cannot be limited to just one pest.

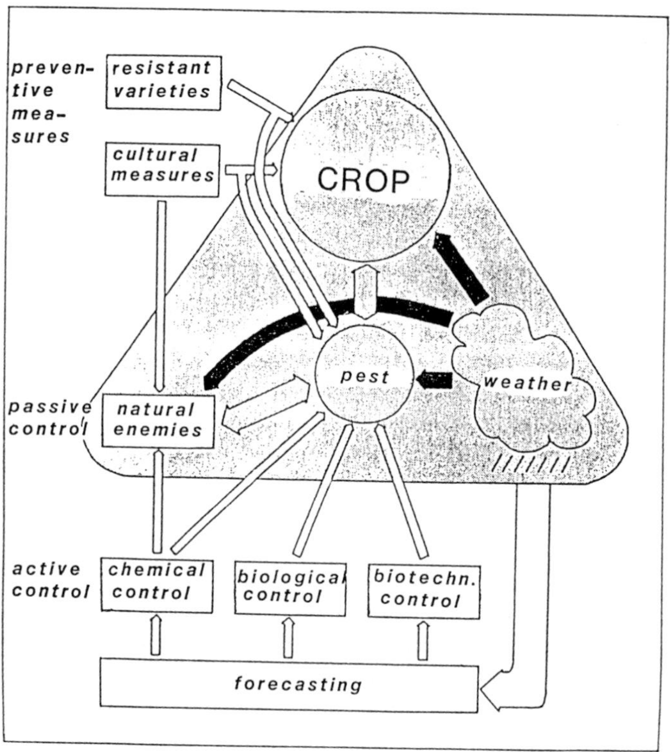

Figure 6.3.11. The elements of integrated pest control. - Source: Esbjerg (1983*).

Within the field of fruit production, attempts have been made over the last 30 years to practice this integrated control. The methods are now extensively applied in West Germany, Switzerland and Italy. The fruit growers themselves survey the insect pests and beneficials, on a solid basis of consultation with extension officers and handbooks. The existing handbooks treat subjects such as (a) Description of the insect pests, their biology and the present damage thresholds (Anonymous, 1980), (b) Methods of monitoring (Anonymous, 1975), and (c) Description of beneficials and their influence on the risk of exceeding the damage thresholds (Anonymous, 1976).

In the field of agriculture, the take-off was slower, but the methods are gaining a world-wide foothold. Within the IOBC, a working group has been established to work with arable farming systems for integrated crop production. The group has suggested the following definition for integrated systems in agriculture: An integrated production system consists of one or several farms which make use of mainly techno-cultural or biological systems, with chemicals as supplementary agents. The main objectives are (A) to minimize the exploitation of limited resources, (B) to balance yield and income against ecological, environmental and sociological objectives. All decisions must be compatible with the cost of efficiency (Vereijken et al., 1986).

As yet, the results in the field of agriculture are limited, but preliminary evaluations of Dutch and German experiments show good results which can compete with other systems. Yield is generally the same, but the expenses for means of production are lower, and a positive influence on the environment is visible, such as an increase in the number of earth worms and of some natural enemies (El Titi, 1986; Vereijken, 1986). Both authors stress the importance of constantly expanding knowledge, if the yield from integrated plant protection is to be maintained. These systems work only if each omission of treatment or change of practice is based on thorough knowledge of all the consequences.

From the summary description given above, it is clear that to get to integrated crop production via integrated control will take extensive knowledge - also from other fields besides plant protection and ecology.

6.3.7 THE RISKS OF MICROBIAL CONTROL

Whatever risks are related to biocontrol of insect pests, they will depend on whether predators and parasitoids, or microbiological agents are chosen as control measure.

As to the parasites and predators, there is no apparent risk of adverse effects. However, imported species should go through ecological screening in order to avoid undesirable pests, other parasites or plant diseases, cf. De Bach (1964). The use of insect pathogens, though, demands great care in handling, both in production and in application.

Environmental Risks. It is important to note that the interaction between insects and microorganisms is an integrated part of the environment, and that initially, only microorganisms which fit in should be introduced as means of control of insect pests. This implies that they are already there, just not in sufficient numbers, or that they are present, but not yet in an active stage - for instance as resting spores.

There are examples of Nature producing a surplus of pathogenic entities, in comparison to what is actually needed for control (Øgaard, 1983*). Under natural conditions remainders of insect pathogens are also present in the crop. Thomas (1975) found between 4,600 and 33,000,000 NPV polyhedras of insect virus per gramme of cabbage. This example shows that human beings are periodically exposed to massive doses of insect pathogens, yet no effect whatsoever has been proved. However, this is no reason for skipping the security tests. It does say a lot about the risk being low, but it also indicates the need to carry out security tests based on other criteria than those for insecticides.

As to the effect on invertebrates, some broad-range microorganisms (B. thuringiensis, and certain fungi) may also infect and kill insect pests other than those aimed at.

Risks of Production. Whether the propagation takes place in vivo or in vitro, a genetic change of characteristics might be the result over a couple of generations. Such changes mostly mean reduced efficiency towards the initial host; but a change in host range is also a possible consequence.

Whatever the method of propagation, other microorganisms may breed in the same medium and contaminate it. The final test of the product should therefore be one of purity, and of the characteristics of the active organism in question.

A third element of risk is the exposure of staff to unnaturally high doses of pathogens. Allergy is a possible consequence of such exposure.

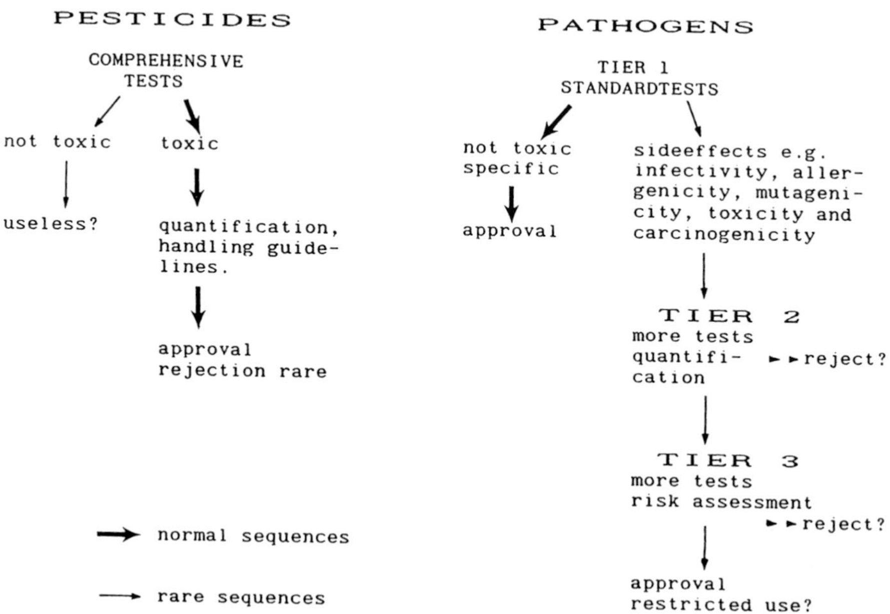

Figure 6.3.12. A simplified comparative survey of security tests: chemical pesticides versus insect pathogens.

Security Tests for Pathogens. Insecticides are thoroughly tested before being marketed. These tests are designed to eliminate those that seem too poisonous.

This is not the case with insect pathogens. These are not poisonous, but alive, so the tests must instead comprise infectivity and cancer effects (Fig. 6.3.12). Step-by-step tests might facilitate the registration procedure: some results would be generally valid for sy-stematic groups, such as several stocks of one microorganism, or several species within one genus.

The most alarming secondary effects are observed in the testing of B. thuringiensis exotoxin which is proved toxic to higher animals when injected in high doses.

At present, there is no legal authority in Denmark for the registration of insect pathogens, except for those that have been genetically manipulated; these shall be approved according to the gene-technology legislation. In the EEC, however, a common regulation of the registration of (unmodified) microbial control agents is expected within a few years.

6.3.8 CONCLUSION CONCERNING MICROBIAL CONTROL

The application of microbiological control agents is bound to have effects on the environment. The negative consequences will be secondary effects, maybe lethal effects for a few species or groups of invertebrates. If these effects can be limited for certain, they are acceptable. As to the actual risks, such as the effect on higher animals and humans, they seem to be very few.

The insect pathogens used outside Denmark have of course been submitted to a number of security tests in order to be proved free of risks. Producers of macrobiological pest control agents are eager to inform their customers about the positive outcome of such tests.

*

To sum up the conclusion:
- Chemical insect-pest control has proved to have undesirable and unacceptable effects on the environment.
- Forecasting and prognosis have been able to reduce the amount of insecticides used in certain crops effectively.
- Techno-cultural, biotechnical and biological methods have obvious environmental advantages.

REFERENCES

Anonymous, 1975. Die Klopfmethode. IOBC/WPRS, Wageningen, 142 pp.

Anonymous, 1976. Nützlinge in Apfelanlagen. IOBC/WPRS, Wageningen, 242 pp.

Anonymous, 1988. List of EPPD Guidelines for Biological Evaluation of Pesticides. Bulletin OEPP, 18: 595-850.

Anonymous, 1990*. Fugleføde i kornmarker - insekter og vilde planter. (Bird-feed in Corn Fields - Insects and Wild Plants). National Environment Research Institute, Project No. 123, Copenhagen.

Carson, R., 1962. Silent Spring. (Danish Edition: Det tavse forår, Gyldendal 1963).

DeBach, P., 1964. Biological Control of Insect Pests and Weeds. Chapman and Hall, London, 844 pp.

Edwards, P.J. and Wratten, S.S., 1980. Ecology of Insect-Plant interactions. Studies in Biology vol. 121. Edward Arnold, London, 60 pp.

El Titi, A., 1986. Design and preliminary results of the Lautenbach Project/West Germany. Bulletin SROP/WPRS, 9: 16-22.

Esbjerg, P., 1983*. Integreret bekæmpelse - principper og definitioner. (Integrated control - principles and definitions). Tidsskr. Planteavl, 87: 357-364.

Esbjerg, P., Jørgensen, J., Nielsen, J.K., Philipsen, H., Zethner, O., and Øgaard, L., 1983*. Afsluttende rapport om Forskningsrådenes initiativ: Integreret bekæmpelse af skadedyr. (Conclusive report of the Research Council program 'Integrated pest control'). Tidsskr. Planteavl, 87: 303-355.

Fuxa, J.R., 1989. Fate of released Entomopathogens with reference to risk assessment of genetically engineered microorganisms. Bull. of Ent. Soc. Am., 1989: 12-24.

Georghiou, G.P. and Mellon, R.B., 1983. Pesticide resistance in time and space. In: Georghiou and Saito (1989): 1-46.

Georghiu, G.P. and Saito, T. (eds.), 1983. Pest Resistance to Pesticides. Plenum Press, New York, 809 pp.

Gunn, D.L. and Stevens, J.G.R. (eds.), 1976. Pesticides and Human Welfare. Oxford University Press, Oxford, 278 pp.

Hald, A.B., Overgaard-Nielsen, B., Samsøe-Petersen, L., Hansen, K., Elmegaard, N. and Kjølholt, L., 1988*. Sprøjtefri randzoner i kornmarker. (Unsprayed Borders of Corn Fields). National Environment Research Institute, Project No. 103.

Hansen, L.S., Pedersen, O.C. and Reitzel, J., 1983*. Skadedyr og nyttedyr. Håndbog om biologisk bekæmpelse i drivhuset. (Harmful and Useful Insects. A Manual of Biological Control at Greenhouse Level.) De Danske Haveselskaber (The Danish Garden Society), Copenhagen, 110 pp.

Harding, D.J.L. (ed.), 1988. Britain since 'Silent Spring'. Proc. Symp., Cambridge, UK, 131 pp.

Hassan, S.A., 1989. Testing methods and the concept of the IOBC/WPRS working group. In: Jepson (1987): 1-18.

Hassan, S.A., Bigler, F., Bogenschütz, H., Brown, J.G., Firth, S.I., Huang, P., Ledieu, M.S., Naton, E., Oomen, P.A., Overmeer, W.P.J., Rieckmann, W., Samsøe-Pedersen, L., Viggiani, G. and Vanzon, A.Q., 1983. Results of the Second Joint Pesticide Testing Programme by the IOBC/WPRS - Working Group 'Pesticides and Beneficial Arthropods'. Zeitschr. angew. Entomol., 95: 151-158.

Hassan, S.A. et al. (see preceding ref.), 1988. Results of the Fourth Joint Pesticide Testing Programme by the IOBC/WPRS - Working Group 'Pesticides and Beneficial Organisms'. J. Appl. Entomol., 105: 321-329.

Holm, E. (ed.), 1977*. Biologisk bekæmpelse af skadedyr. (Biological Pest Control). Kaskelot, Gedved DK, 144 pp.

Jackson, G.J., 1984. Present trends in pesticide development regarding safety to beneficial organisms. British Crop Protection Conference - Pest and Diseases, vol. 1: 387-394.

Jepson, P.C. (ed.), 1989. Pesticides and Non-Target Invertebrates. Intercept, Wimborne Dorset, 240 pp.

Keiding, J., 1976. Development of resistance to pyrethroid in field populations of Danish houseflies. Pesticide Science, 7: 283-291.

Kjølholt, J., 1986*. Udviklingstendenser i landbrugets anvendelse af pesticider 1981-1984. (Trends in agricultural application of pesticides 1981-1984). Ugeskr. Jordbr., 131: 133-136.

Kurstak, E. (ed.), 1982. Microbial and Viral Pesticides. M. Dekker, New York, 720 pp.

Maramorosch, K. (ed.), 1987. Biotechnology in Invertebrate Pathology. Academic Press, New York, 511 pp.

Mortensen, L., 1990*. Status for handlingsplanen til nedsættelse af pesticidforbruget. (Actual state of the action plan for reduced pesticide consumption). In: 7. Danish Plant Protection Conference: Pests and Diseases. Danish Ministry of Agriculture: 9-14.

Münster-Swendsen, M., 1977*. Naturlige fjender. (Natural enemies.) In: Holm, E. (ed.): Biologisk bekæmpelse af skadedyr. (Biological Pest Control). Kaskelot, Gedved DK: 62-65.

Nøddegaard, E., 1986*. Udvikling i forbruget af pesticider og vækstregulerende midler 1956-1984. In: Nøddegaard et al. (1986).

Nøddegaard, E., Jacobsen, J., Thonke, K.E. and Jørgensen, L.N. (eds.), 1986*. Pesticider. Forbrug, fordele, ulemper, fremtidsperspektiver. (Pesticides: Consumption, Advantages, Drawbacks, Future Perspectives). Report S 1820, National Plant Breeding Experiments, 269 pp.

Payne, C.C., 1988. Prospects for biological control. In: Harding (1988): 103-116.

Plapp, F.W. and Wang, T.C., 1983. Genetic origins of insecticide resistance. In: Georhgiu and Saito (1983): 47-70.

Ravn, H.P. and Harding, S., 1985*. Barkbillestrategi. (Strategy of the bark bug). Ugeskr. Jordbr., 130: 1318-1324.

Samsøe-Petersen, L., 1987. Laboratory methods for testing side-effects of pesticides on the rove beetle Aleochara bilineata - adults. Entomophaga, 32: 73-81.

Sheail, J., 1985. Pesticides and Nature Conservation, The British Experience 1950-1975. Clarendon Press, Oxford, 276 pp.

Summers, M., Engler, R., Falcon, L.A. and Vail, P. (eds.), 1975. Baculovirus for Insect Pest Control: Safety Considerations. American Society for Microbiology, Washington, 186 pp.

Thomas, E.D., 1975. Normal virus level and virus level added for control. In: Summers et al. (1975): 87-89.

Thonke, K.E., Jørgensen, L.N. and Jacobsen, J., 1986*. Nettomerudbytte ved pesticidan vendelse. (Net-yield increase by application of pesticides). In: Nøddegaard et al. (1986): 37-75.

Vereijken, P.H., 1979. Feeding and multiplication of three cereal aphid species and their effect on yield of winter wheat. Centrum voor Landbouwpublikaties en Landbouw-documentatie, Wageningen: 58.

Vereijken, P.H., 1986. Design and some preliminary results of the experimental farm 'Development of Farming Systems' at Nagele, Netherlands. Bulletin SROP/WPRS, 9: 23-34.

Vereijken, P.H., Edwards C., El Titi, A., Fougeroux, A. and Way, M., 1986. IOBC/WPRS. The Management of Arable Farming Systems for Integrated Crop Protection. Bulletin SPROP/WPRS, 9: 1-15.

Weir, D. and Shapiro, M., 1983*. Giftcirklen. Farlige pesticider i det globale miljø. (The Poison Circle. Dangerous Pesticides in the Global Environment). Mellemfolkeligt Samvirke, Copenhagen, 111 pp.

Øgaard, L., 1983*. Muligheder for anvendelse af insektvirus til biologisk bekæmpelse af skadelige insekter. (Possibilities of applying insect virus in biological pest control). Tidsskr. Planteavl, 87: 407-415.

Øgaard, L., Eilenberg, J. and Bolet, B., 1984*. Mikrobiologisk skadedyrsbekæmpelse. Muligheder i Danmark. (Microbiological insect pest control: possibilities in Denmark). Ugeskr. Jordbr., 129: 195-202.

6.4 ECOLOGICAL ASPECTS OF CHEMICAL WEED CONTROL

JENS CARL STREIBIG

6.4.1 INTRODUCTION

Through the history of agriculture, weeding has been man's lot. Although the farmer knows which plants on his land are weeds, some formal definition for non-farmers is pertinent, in order to put weeds in their proper perspective. One of the most common definitions of weeds is: *Weeds are plants growing where they are not wanted.* Today, however, in the light of the development of resistant biotypes of weed species, formerly susceptible to herbicides, and the ever on-going development of herbicide-resistant crops, a more optimistic definition, wisely suggested by Emmerson, could be: "*A weed is a plant whose virtues have not yet been discovered*".

For more than 7 millennia, human beings have changed the original vegetation by cultivating crops in monoculture. During this period, the prevailing weed-control methods have been relatively static. Even at present, hand weeding is the most important means of control in many parts of the world, where agriculture is dependent upon an army of professional hand weeders.

Real changes in weed control methods have taken place only in the last 200 to 300 years; for example, agricultural implements have been made in order to lessen the manual burden of hand weeding. Radical changes in the weed-control methods in the developed world, however, only happened during the last 40-50 years. In this period, more than 200 chemical compounds have been made commercially available to agriculture.

6.4.2 WEEDS

Weed species are pioneers that increase the diversity of agricultural ecosystems by utilizing the environmental potential especially developed by human beings for crop production. These pioneer species form the first plant community of a disturbance brought about by harrowing, ploughing, etc., and hence they pave the way for new colonizing species, competitively superior to the pioneers, to gain foothold.

Table 6.4.1. Weeds of the world. - Source: Holm (1976).

206 species important to man, in 59 plant families
80 species of primary importance
126 species of secondary importance

The presence of weeds on arable land, therefore, is the first step in a succession towards plant communities in equilibrium with the prevailing climate and soil conditions. If land is abandoned, the presence of specific weed species is just an episode, although an important and necessary one, in a succession for more stable plant communities.

In relation to the crops, weeds are successful competitors in that they are a nuisance to man's ability to grow crops. Therefore, they must be controlled to secure yield.

Worldwide, more than 200 species are considered economically important (Table 6.4.1), but only 80% are of primary importance. Worldwide, they reduce crop growth, block waterways and irrigation systems, and some are even poisonous to man and animals. The remaining species are of minor importance, yet they can be troublesome in specific crops and under specific climatic conditions.

Of the weed species included in Table 6.4.1, 50% belong to only 5 families, the most important ones being *Poaceae*, *Cyperaceae* and *Asteraceae*. No doubt, the world's worst weed is *Cyperus rotundus*, a sedge native to India, but now reported from more countries, regions and localities than any other weed. Noxious weeds of the temperate regions of Northern Europe are *Avena fatua* and *Chenopodium album*, already in prehistoric time two cosmopolitans and probably the two most successful colonizers amongst non-cultivated plants (Holm et al., 1977).

In Denmark, more than 200 different weed species have been found on agricultural land, but only two, *Chenopodium album* and *Avena fatua*, are of primary importance worldwide. Regionally, in Northern Europe and around the Great Lakes in North America, *Elymus repens*, with a circumpolar distribution, is an important weed.

The natural environment for most weed species is unstable habitats. For example, 25% of the most common weeds in Denmark come from sea shores and sand dunes, 20% from lake and river banks, and 5% from hillsides and forests. The remaining 50% are aliens introduced by humans or otherwise; they now have been growing in arable land long enough to be naturalized and are considered an integral part of the 'natural' flora. The weeds in our fields are thus no more 'natural' than are our crops. Several valuable crops, e.g., rye and oats, were considered noxious weeds in the ancient days of agriculture. During the long evolutionary history of agriculture, those former weeds have acquired domestic attributes and are today important crops. On the other hand, ancient crop species, e.g., *Spergula arvensis*, have now gained foothold as weeds and are interfering with modern day's crop growing.

The common weed species are perfectly fit to grow in the fields, as this unstable environment resembles their natural habitats. Most crops in Northern Europe are harvested each year and crops replace each other in rotational systems. Therefore, most weeds are annuals or at least they mimic annual phenology when growing among annual crops. Even though the most common weeds in temperate regions are annuals, the terms annual and perennial have little or no meaning outside the temperate zones. On a worldwide basis, a little less than 60% are annuals.

In contrast to fungi and insect pests that attack crops in an epidemic way, weeds, with some few exceptions, cannot fly and must therefore be present in the field as seeds or vegetative propagules.

The most important factor in maintaining diversity of the weed flora and the level of weed infestation is the seed reservoir in the soil. This seed bank may contain thousands of viable seeds that tend to offset the effects of radical environmental changes brought about by man. A large proportion of viable seeds in soil belongs to the most common weeds.

Many successful weed species are inbreeders which produce stable duplicates of readily adapted genotypes. A comparative study of the degree of polyploidy of weeds and species from the 'natural' angiosperm flora has shown that weeds are more often polyploids than are species growing outside agricultural land.

6.4.2.1 Harmful and Beneficial Effects of Weeds

The harmful effects of weeds are difficult to judge on the basis of crop loss alone and must be looked at in relation to other pests. The yield loss encountered by weeds depends on the competitive ability of the crop and numerous other factors. On a worldwide basis, the total yield loss in major crops is equally divided between weeds, insect pests and plant diseases.

The harmful effect of poisonous weeds for man and animal cannot easily be summarised. Poisonous weeds kill or injure livestock worth more than A$ 100 million every year in Australia, and in Afghanistan 3,000-4,000 people died in one year from eating wheat flour contaminated with a poisonous *Heliotropium spp.* Also *Senecio spp.*, contaminating feedstuff and food for human consumption, can cause serious illness.

One way to illustrate the harmful effect of weeds on crop growth has been given by Holm (1976):

"In many places of the world the size of a man's holding is governed not by his ability to buy land, but by how much he and his family can plant before they must start weeding."

This measure of the importance of weeds in the world is probably one of the best ways to express the effect of weeds on world food production.

Notwithstanding, one and the same weed can be a curse during cropping periods but a blessing at other times. Weeds can protect against soil erosion and provide valuable diets for animals in the non-cropping season. In some traditional farming systems of the tropics, weeds are effectively reducing soil erosion, preserving soil moisture, fixing nitrogen and also maintaining a balance between insect pests and their predators. In some places farmers only weed during early crop growth so that subsequent weed flushes can provide a desirable dense cover under the crop to avoid soil erosion hazards.

6.4.3 A BRIEF HISTORY OF CHEMICAL WEED CONTROL

In 1896, a French wine grower sprayed $CuSO_4$+CaO to control diseases on his vine. He observed a beneficial side effect in that a weed, *Sinapis arvensis*, died on being exposed to the spray. One year later another French grower discovered the herbicidal activity of H_2SO_4 that could selectively control some weeds without injuring the crops.

These discoveries were, in fact, among the first successful chemical weed control methods, and until recently H_2SO_4 has been used in many parts of Europe. Several other inorganic compounds were introduced as herbicides for a shorter period of time. The first organic herbicide, DNOC, was patented by George Truffaut and K. Pastac in 1932, to be used as a selective herbicide in cereals.

The rapid development of modern chemical substances was initiated by the need for increasing food production during World War II. The shortage of food in the UK made agricultural researchers take advantage of previous discoveries of substances called auxins which stimulate plant growth, primarily by promoting cell elongation. Independently, workers at Jealott's Hill Research Station and workers at Rothamstead Experimental Station were studying chlorinated phenoxyacetic acids, and both groups reported remarkable herbicidal activity. The substances appeared to act like an over-dose of auxin in the target weeds, but did not harm the cereal crop. With the return of peace the original findings, together with new ones based on independent work in the USA, were published.

The phenoxyacetic acids are fundamentally different from the other organic compounds, for example DNOC; they are systemic in that they have to be translocated in the plant to exert their action. Soon after the release of MCPA and 2,4-D a trichloro-phenoxyacetic acid, 2,4,5-T, was also released and a new era of weed control had begun. Within a few years, screening systems to test chemical substances were set up by various chemical companies, and they formed the basis for a rapid development of new herbicides to control specific weed problems in important crops.

In principle, the screening systems for new herbicide molecules have not changed much since the end of World War II. The chemical companies still screen thousands of molecules in a laborious random empirical screening process before a commercial viable compound is released. Today random screening is used together with other strategies, for example analogue synthesis by linking together molecules of known herbicidal activity. Over the years, the costs of developing a new herbicide have increased dramatically and are now about DM 180 million, of which 30% is used in ecotoxicological research.

The range of new herbicides has given the farmer a safety factor in growing crops. To some extent it has also freed him of past crop rotation and fallow systems, partly implemented to cope with noxious weeds. Today the farmer can chemically 'weed' the unwanted plants on his land and within certain limits he is able to grow crops in demand without being too restricted by crop rotation, etc. This development has, however, produced some unintentional side effects, agriculturally and ecologically, which were not thought of during the earlier years of herbicide use.

6.4.4 THE HERBICIDES

In contrast to fungicides and insecticides, herbicides are designed to kill green plants. Hence, the use of herbicides for selective purposes is in several respects different from that of other pesticides. For all chemical substances, the axiom by Paracelsus, published in his Drey Bücher 1564, still applies:

"Was ist das nit Gifft ist: alle Ding sind Gifft und nichts ohn Gifft. Allein die Dosis macht das ein Ding kein Gifft ist."

Paracelsus (1494-1541).

The essence of this axiom is that, whatever the chemical substance, it is the dose of a compound administered that determines whether it is not poisonous. His philosophy was that all substances are poisonous.

6.4.4.1 Herbicide Selectivity and Mode of Action

The recommended dose rate of herbicides in crops is a balance between the tolerance of crops and the susceptibility of weeds. The selectivity of herbicides is quite easily assessed by the screening systems developed by the chemical industry.

Fig. 6.4.1 shows herbicide dose-response curves for two herbicides. At high dose rates both herbicides kill the plants. At moderate dose rates the intrinsic selectivity of the compounds implies that less of herbicide A than of B is required to obtain the same effect. The selective properties of the two herbicides are most easily seen in the mid-region. Such selectivity studies are carried out in greenhouse and field experiments, giving a first indication of whether a new compound can be used for selective purposes.

The causes for selectivity in Fig. 6.4.1 are much more difficult to unravel, and in earlier days the exact mode or site of action of many compounds was only discover-ed several years after their release. This state of affairs has changed dramatically during the last 10 to 15 years. The development of herbicide-resistant biotypes of formerly susceptible weed species has had spin-off effects on plant breeding of crops and on the interest in mode of action research, cf. Section 6.4.5.2 below.

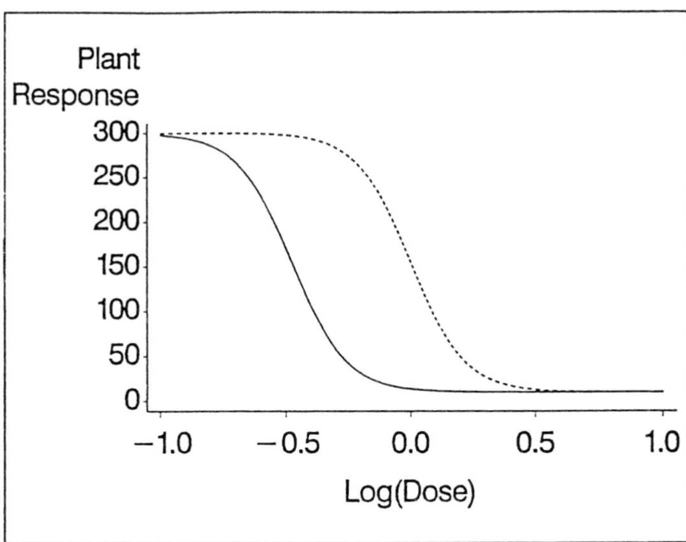

Figure 6.4.1. Dose-response curves for two herbicides, A (solid line) and B (broken line). Herbicide A is more potent than B. At small doses neither A nor B affect plant growth; at very high doses both A and B kill the test plant. The selectivity properties of the two herbicides stand out at intermediate doses.

With the exception of some early herbicides such as DNOC and dinoseb, most herbicides affect metabolic pathways of plants which do not exist in animals. DNOC and dinoseb uncouple the oxidative phosphorylation in the mitochondria in both plants and animals and are therefore toxic to man.

At present, more than 50% of all commercially available herbicides exert their primary mode of action by blocking the electron flow from photosystem II to I in the photosynthesis. The phenoxy acids act like auxins in the plants but cannot be degraded to the same extent as the natural auxins. And since the concentration of auxin is crucial for its action, the phenoxy acids disturb the delicate balance of growth substances with fatal consequences for the plant.

New groups of herbicides which affect the synthesis of branched or aromatic amino acids, a unique synthesis in the Plant Kingdom, have been developed in the last 15 to 20 years.

The acute toxicity of most herbicides is relatively low. Therefore their ecological effects are often of a secondary nature.

6.4.4.2 Herbicide Use

The use of herbicides in various crops worldwide is shown in Table 6.4.2, and the trends in global pesticide consumption in Table 6.4.3. The most demanding crops are maize, soybeans and wheat which are also the major crops of North America. In the early days of chemical crop protection herbicides only accounted for 5% of total pesticide use but now they account for about 50%.

Herbicides are used in various ways depending upon their intrinsic selectivity to crops. They can be sprayed either before the crops are sown or have emerged or after crop emergence. The particular pattern of use for a herbicide is important for understanding its effects on the flora and fauna.

Some herbicides are so-called ‘soil acting compounds’, primarily absorbed by the root system. Another group of herbicides are the foliage-applied compounds which exert their effect after being absorbed by aerial plant parts. Within this group we can roughly distinguish between the systemic compounds which are translocated from their site of uptake to their site of action, and the contact herbicides which have a limited mobility in the plants and therefore must exert their action at their site of uptake.

For example, simazine is a distinct soil-acting herbicide: it cannot for any practical purpose be absorbed by the foliage. To a certain extent, the same applies to atrazine. Distinct foliage-applied herbicides are paraquat and diquat which are strongly adsorbed to the soil colloids and thus immobilized, preventing uptake by the roots. Another notable foliage herbicide, highly mobile in all parts of the plant, is glyphosate. In the soil, glyphosate behaves similarly to anorganic phosphorous. Paraquat, diquat and glyphosate can therefore only be used to control weeds after they have emerged.

While most foliage-applied herbicides affect only the plants that are exposed directly to the spray, the soil-acting herbicides exert their activity in the soil for a much longer period of time. For the latter group of compounds, only the amount of herbicide available in the soil water is taken up by the plant, and thus the interaction between the herbicide and the soil must be taken into account.

Table 6.4.2. Herbicide market in 1985. Unit: 1 million US dollars.

Crop	USA	Western Europe	Japan, Far East	Other Areas	Total	%
Maize	1034	118	18	225	1395	22
Wheat	148	439	28	176	791	12
Rice	60	23	334	90	507	8
Sorghum	79	8	3	12	102	2
Other corn crops	40	245	17	115	417	7
Soybeans	1095	13	21	219	1348	21
Cotton	125	7	13	143	288	5
Sugar beet	24	204	5	54	287	5
Sugar canes	15	-	14	119	148	2
Perenn.s + permanent grass land	51	12	9	44	116	2
Horticultural crops	142	193	71	81	487	8
Other crops	101	8	131	129	445	7
Total	2914	1346	664	1407	6331	100

Table 6.4.3. Developing trends in the global consumption of pesticides.

	Average value of Pesticides Billion US$ (1984)	Fungicides + Insecticides %	Herbicides %
1950	?	95	5
1980	11.0	56	44
1985	13.1	52	48
1990 (expected)	15.0	52	48

Table 6.4.4. Adsorption (K_d) and biological effect (ED_{50}) of two herbicides in identical Danish soils. ED_{50} is the dose required to reduce test plant dry matter by 50% relative to untreated control. (CEC: Cation Exchange Capacity in meq/100 g soil). - Source: Streibig and Haas (1983*).

Soil	Organic matter %	Clay %	CEC	Simazine		Chloridazon	
				K_d	ED_{50}	K_d	ED_{50}
Moraine sand	2	7	11	1.3	0.1	1.3	0.3
Loamy sand	12	12	26	7.4	0.8	5.9	1.3
Sandy clay loam	23	19	82	18	2.4	23	5.8

Table 6.4.4 shows the relationship between some soil factors and the adsorption of some herbicides expressed by a partition coefficient, K_d, i.e., the ratio of (1) the amount of herbicide adsorbed to the soil colloids and (2) the amount in the soil solution. Within certain limits, the partition coefficient tends to be constant. It follows that the amount of plant-available herbicide in the soil water can be considered linearly related to the dose applied, provided the soil moisture content is constant. Apart from this, the partition coefficient is a complex function of the chemical and physical properties of the soil and the herbicide.

Another important aspect of a soil-acting herbicide is its fate in the soil. The ideal soil-acting herbicide is a compound that persists in the soil for a certain period of time, until the crop can compete with the weeds, and then it disappears by degradation. From an agronomic point of view, the persistence of a herbicide can be defined as the time span necessary after spraying before a susceptible crop may be planted. The persistence is not always closely related to the degradation process; for example, the above-mentioned herbicides paraquat, diquat and glyphosate all have a persistence of virtually zero in the soil, but this is because they are immobilized by strong adsorption to the soil colloids. Their actual degradation is often slow because the adsorption also protects them from chemical and microbiological attacks.

The degradation of a herbicide is in general determined by its soil partition coefficient, the soil moisture and the soil temperature. At recommended dose rates for selective purposes, simazine and atrazine have an agricultural persistence of almost a full growing period in Western Europe. Some sulfonylureas have a quite short persistence under humid conditions, but it can extend to a considerable period of time in more arid regions.

For an overall assessment of the most important factors governing the degradation of pesticides, see Section 6.2 of this book.

6.4.5 HERBICIDE IMPACT ON THE AGROECOSYSTEM

The most direct assessment of the impact of herbicide use is probably mirrored by the composition of the weed flora before and after the introduction of modern herbicides. The composition of the weed flora is dependent on the agricultural system, such as cropping pattern, climate, soil, etc. Therefore it is virtually impossible to give a clear-cut picture of the role of herbicides *per se* in the agroecosystem. To a great extent we must base our judgments on circumstantial evidence.

6.4.5.1 Herbicides and the Weed Flora

In Denmark we are in the unique situation of having weed surveys from the turn of this century and up to the present. Four surveys were conducted in 1911-15, 1944-45, 1964-70 and 1986-89. Results from the last survey are not yet (1990) fully accessible, but the three first surveys can give an indication of changes of the Danish weed flora for the last 60 years. Below we shall summarize some of the most important trends of the findings; for a detailed description see Streibig (1979), Haas and Streibig (1982), Andreasen et al. (1989, 1991).

As two of the surveys were done before the advent of modern herbicides, we can look at the changes in the distribution of weed species with different life cycles. Table 6.4.5 shows that changes in the distribution of annual and perennial weed species were already in progress well before the introduction of herbicides; during the entire period 1910-1970, the proportion of annuals has increased, probably by more intensive soil cultivation etc. The long-term effects of herbicide treatment after World War II may have enhanced this trend, further increasing the number of annuals and diminishing the number of perennials. In other parts of the world with a warmer climate, perennials such as *Cyperus Rotundus* and *Cynodon dactylon* have become noxious weeds, probably because competition from other weeds has been removed by herbicides.

When trying to detect the influence of herbicides on the distribution of weed species on arable land over this relatively long period, we have to keep in mind that several other agronomic factors have been operating too, some of the major ones even parallel to the increased use of herbicides. Among these agronomic changes, let us just mention the changes in the land use, the application of fertilizer, and the changes in crop-rotation systems (Table 6.4.6).

The consumption of herbicides has increased considerably during the last decades (Table 6.4.6). Until recently, a major part of this increase has been due to cereal herbicides, mainly phenoxyacetic or propionic acids such as MCPA, dichlorprop and mecoprop.

The increase in herbicide use parallelled that of fertilizer use and to a certain extent also the increase in area under cereal crops (Table 6.4.6). Such a development is common in developed countries with a climate and an agricultural system similar to ours.

Table 6.4.5. Changes in the proportions of annual and perennial weeds in crops of different longevity in Danish farmland between 1911 and 1964. - Source: Haas and Streibig (1982).

Crop type	Period	Annuals %	Perennials %
Spring cereals	1911 - 1915	76	24
	1944 - 1945	88	12
	1964 - 1969	92	8
Winter cereals	1911 - 1915	77	23
	1967 - 1968	83	17
Grass leys	1911 - 1915	45	55
	1969	53	47

Table 6.4.6. Cereal area, nitrogen consumption and purchase of herbicides in Denmark. - Source: Haas (1989), modified.

	1950	1960	1970	1980	1985
Spring cereals in 1000 ha	1038	1206	1617	1629	1084
Winter cereals in 1000 ha	239	239	122	187	514
Cereals, % of farming area	48	53	65	69	61
N per ha, average of farming area	63	84	145	194	198
Herbicides, tons of active ingred.	-	1162	3794	4914	4244

In conjunction with this development, liming and draining of land have severely reduced the importance of calcifuge weeds favoring acid soils (*Rumex acetocella*, *Scleranthus annuus*) and species favoring water-logged soils (*Juncus bufonius* and *Mentha arvensis*). The rapid growth of mechanization, too, has had an impact. In later years, crop rotation, previously an important method of weed control, has almost ceased to exist in some areas.

We can now grow, e.g., cereals in continuous monoculture without fearing severe attacks of diseases and pests and flushes of troublesome weeds. Analysis of the survey data from the 1960's has demonstrated that the composition of a weed flora is closely related to the crop. Annual crops tend to promote a flush of weeds different from that in perennial crops. A subtle difference was detected even between summer annual crops (e.g., spring barley) and winter annual crops (e.g., winter wheat). Similar trends were also found for the last survey during 1986-1989. In assessing the impact of crops on the resulting weed flora, we have to remember that any crop has its own 'history' in terms of different soil preparation, fertilization etc, which, of course, all affect the establishment of a particular weed flora.

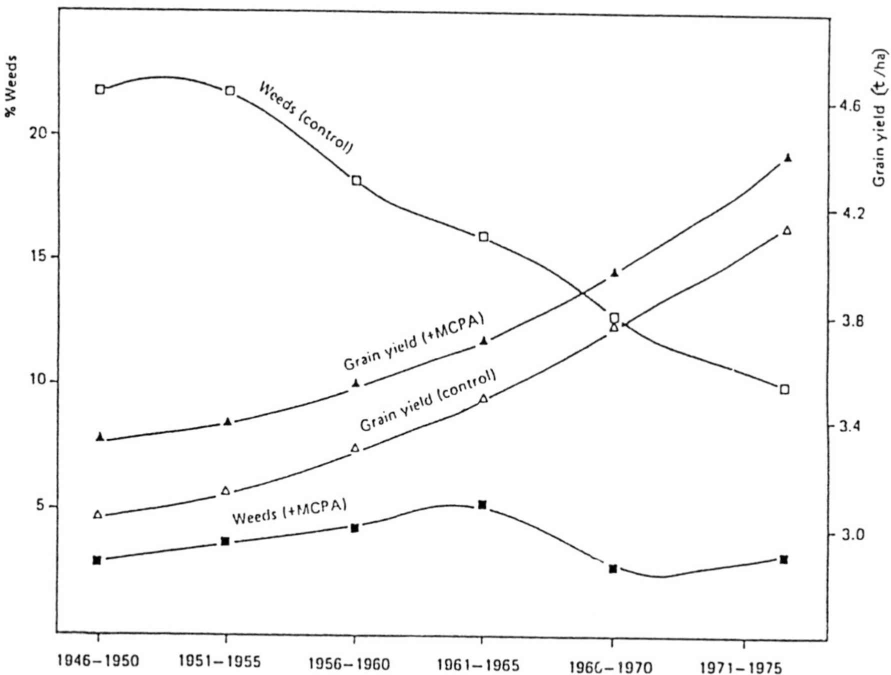

Figure 6.4.2. Effect of MCPA on grain yield and weed infestation level. Data from all Danish field trials (>4000 experiments) with MCPA in spring cereals 1946-75. Weed infestation is expressed as % fresh weight of weed, in relation to total vegetation (fresh weight of crop + weed) in several subsamples of 0.25 m^2 per plot. The experiments were placed within the normal crop rotation system. The control plots were not sprayed in the year of the experiments but had been sprayed in previous years. - Source: Haas and Streibig (1982).

The general trend in spring cereal yield since the introduction of MCPA is shown in Fig. 6.4.2. Note that there has been a marked decrease in the amount of weeds in control plots not treated in the experimental year, whereas the amount of weeds in treated plots has been fairly stable during the period. At the same time, the crop yield has increased both in treated and untreated plots, almost at the same rate.

But other factors are operating too. Increase in crop yield also reflects a better crop stand and increased use of fertilizer, and thus a stronger competitive pressure upon the weed flora. No doubt, some of the decrease of weeds in untreated plots was caused by herbicide use in previous years. German long-term experiments with various weed-control methods clearly support this view.

Intensive use of herbicides is accompanied by a dramatic decrease in the soil seed bank (Table 6.4.7). It is often asserted that depletion of the soil seed bank leads to a decrease in the diversity of the weed flora. Hard data on this subject are scarce. A small survey on 11 farms in southern Germany has been carried out, and it did not reveal any relationship between the size of the soil seed bank and the number of weed species.

Turning to the on-going Danish survey, the picture of the changes in the flora is even more pronounced than previously (Andreasen et al., 1989*). Generally, the frequencies of weeds were higher 20 years ago than they are now, which probably parallels the trend in the soil seed bank mentioned above. This trend was not so obvious in previous surveys, probably because the soil seed bank offsets rapid environmental changes brought about by herbicide use and other agricultural methods. A preliminary comparison between the number of weed species recorded has shown no difference between the 1964-1970 and the 1986-1989 surveys: in both surveys about 200 species were found.

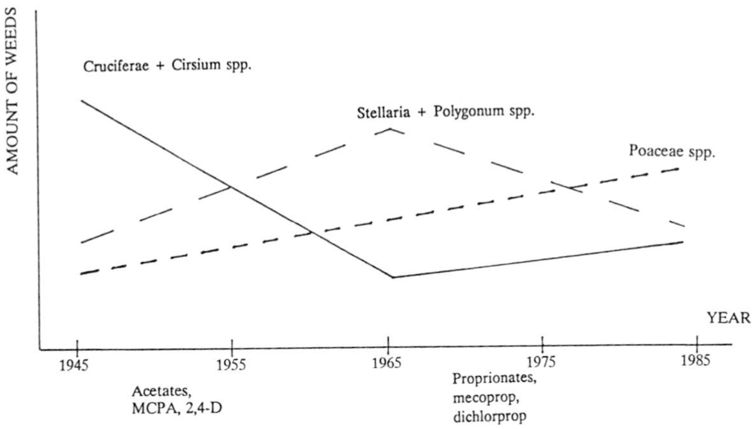

Figure 6.4.3. Changes in some groups of weeds. Around 1965 the phenoxy-proprionic acids were introduced. Their selectivity spectrum is slightly different from that of the herbicides previously used, and they caused some changes in the composition of the weed flora. Up to 1985 the grass weeds increased in importance because very few herbicides could be used selectively in major crops. - Source: Thorup (1982).

Table 6.4.7. Effects on the seed bank of long-term weed control. - Source: Hurle (1986).

Conditions	Seed bank (seeds m^{-1})	Reduction (%)
12 years spring cereals		
untreated	43 800	
herbicides	23 400	47
harrow	37 800	14
16 years cereals		
untreated	39 300	
intensive control	24 360	38
16 years root crops		
hoeing (1-2 times)	96 720	
intensive control	32 750	66
6 years winter wheat		
hand hoeing (once)	10 800	
herbicide 1	6 000	44
herbicide 2	6 000	44
herbicide 2+3	5 200	52
herbicide 1+2+3	2 900	73

Although the surveys give a reasonably good picture of the general trends, the effect of herbicidal compounds with different spectrums of selectivity cannot be detected. An assessment of the qualitative importance of certain groups of weeds after World War II has shown that species susceptible to phenoxyacetic herbicides decreased in importance whereas more tolerant weeds increased until the mid-1960's, see Fig. 6.4.3. Notable exceptions were species with a large production of seeds, such as *Chenopodium album* (Haas and Streibig, 1982).

During the entire period grasses gradually increased. Here, this trend in the weed flora is associated with the use of phenoxyacetic acids and phenoxy-propionic acids. The phenoxyacetic acids are able to control some broad-leaf weeds and thus give rise to swift changes in the weed flora. *Stellaria* and *Polygonum* species are fairly tolerant to MCPA and to a certain extent to 2,4-D. Around 1965, the phenoxy-propionic acids, mecoprop and dichlorprop were introduced and provided good control of *Stellaria* and some *Polygonum* species. The only group of weeds left unaffected was the grasses; they became more important as their fellow weeds were annihilated, see Fig. 6.4.3.

Evidently, grasses have become a major problem on arable land, not only in Denmark but in all developed countries, partly because we have not had effective herbicides to control them. The most important grass weed in Northern Europe is *Elymus repens*. About 10% of all herbicides applied in the late 1970's were used to control this noxious species.

The problem with grass weeds has, of course, triggered the development of new grass herbicides some of which can now be used selectively, even in some monocot crops.

6.4.5.2 Herbicide Resistance in Plants

For the last ten years there has been an increasing concern about the development of herbicide-resistant biotypes in formerly susceptible weed species. Early warnings came already in the mid-1950's when resistant or tolerant biotypes of common weeds were found in Hawaiian sugarcane fields. But this was soon forgotten, perhaps because weeds have a relatively long life cycle compared to insects and fungi, resistant strains of which were developed already in the early days of insecticide and fungicide use. Today we must face the fact that about 150 biotypes of weed species have acquired resistance and/or tolerance to commonly used herbicides. Table 6.4.8 shows some examples of herbicide-resistant weeds in Europe.

The terms herbicide resistance and/or tolerance are often used indiscriminately without any formal definition of the plausible mechanisms involved. In the literature on selective herbicides, weed species tolerating fairly high dose rates are frequently termed resistant. In most cases, these species have not acquired resistance *per se* but have always been tolerant to the recommended agricultural dose rates.

In the present context we may give a brief definition of resistance/tolerance; it is a state in which certain biotypes of a usually susceptible species are left unaffected by a herbicide, even at high dose rates. A tolerant biotype manifests itself by the decrease in susceptibility relative to the 'wild type': it is only partly affected by dose rates that would kill the wild type. Purely resistant biotypes are not affected at all, even at very high dose rates and perhaps even if the herbicide reaches its primary site of action (Fig. 6.4.4).

The most well-known mechanism of resistance in weeds is found among the group of *s*-triazines inhibiting the photosynthesis by blocking the transfer of electrons from photosystem II to photosystem I. In the resistant biotypes, an interchange of only one amino acid at the normal binding site for *s*-triazines is enough to prevent the herbicide from acting. So even if the compound reaches its site of action it does not affect the photosynthesis. Apparently, this particular way of developing resistance only implies mutation in one gene.

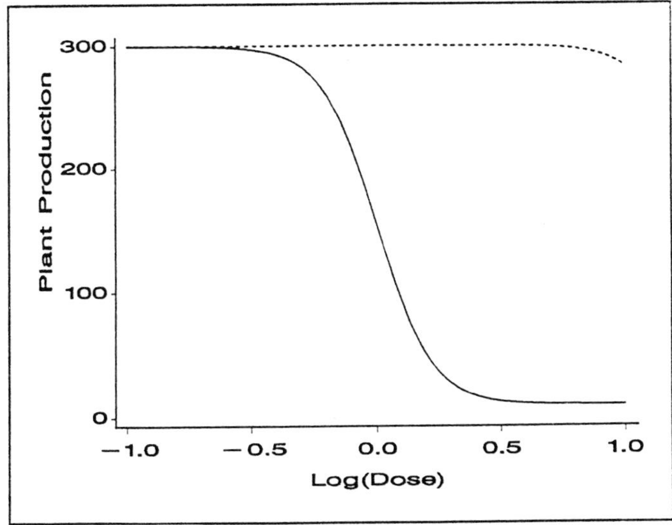

Figure 6.4.4. Dose-response curves of a sensitive wild type (solid line) and a resistant/tolerant biotype within the same weed species, selected by continuous use of the herbicide.

Table 6.4.8. Examples of herbicide-resistant weeds in Europe from the late 1980's. - Source: Olofsdotter and Haas (1990*).

Herbicide	Species	Crop	Country
Triazines	*Chenopodium album*	Maize	Belgium
		Orchards	Spain
			France
			Yugoslavia
	Solanum nigrum	Maize	Belgium
		Orchards	Spain
	Senecio vulgaris	Non-crops	Belgium
		Maize	Denmark
		Orchards	England
	Poa annua	Orchards	Belgium
		Nurseries	England
	Polygonum lapatifolium		Holland
	Polygonum convolvulus		Holland
	Galinsoga ssp.		Holland
Chlortoluron	*Alopecurus myos.*		England
Propanil	*Echinoclea crus-galli*	Rice	Greece
Paraquat	*Poa annua*	Orchards	England
Mecoprop	*Stellaria media*		England

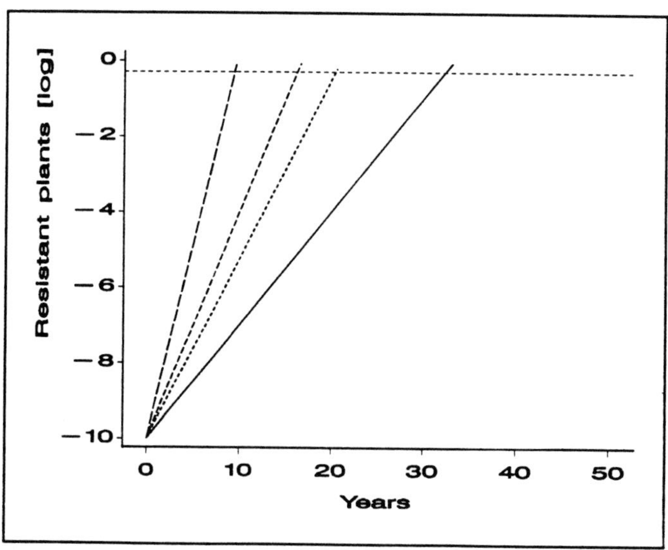

Figure 6.4.5. Theoretical development of herbicide-resistant strains of a weed. The initial proportions of resistant types in the population is 10^{-10}, average seed dormancy is 5 years and relative competitive ability 0.5 . From left to right: selection pressure s = 10%, 20%, 30%, and 100%.

The change at the herbicide binding site, however, makes the photosynthetic capture of CO_2 less effective relative to the 'wild type', and numerous experiments have shown that when the selection pressure is eased, the resistant biotypes are competitively inferior to the 'wild types'. Discovery of the mechanism governing s-triazine resistance has been given a theoretical basis which appears to quantify the observations found in the field. The proportion of resistant types in a natural population (N_n) being subject to continuous spraying with a herbicide is

$$N_n = N_o\left(1 + \frac{k\,s}{h}\right),$$

where N_0 denotes the proportion of resistant plants in a natural population just before the herbicide was introduced in the ecosystem; k is the competitive ability of resistant biotypes, s is the selection pressure imposed by the herbicide, also called the effective kill; h denotes the average proportion of dormant seeds in the soil; and n is the number of years of herbicide use. The implication of the above equation is that, all other things being equal, the higher the selection pressure, the more rapidly the selection for resistant plants works (Fig. 6.4.5).

Another notable hypothesis claims that the farmer only realises the development of a resistant biotype when about 30% of the whole weed population has become resistant. The most rapidly developing resistance amongst weeds has been found with soil-acting herbicides with a long persistence in the soil.

Hidden in the weed flora lies a potential genetic material which makes possible the development of resistant or tolerant biotypes. This ability has already expressed itself in the winter-wheat growing areas of the USA and Canada. Biotypes resistant to sulfonylurea and imidazolinone herbicides have been recorded after only three years of spraying. In the UK there has been a considerable recent expansion in the occurrence of *Alopecurus myosuroides*, partially resistant to chlortoluron.

6.4.5.3 Herbicides and the Fauna

With some few exceptions, commercially available herbicides do not affect the fauna *per se*, but continuous use of a herbicide does change the weed flora and thus causes unintentional secondary side effects.

This applies to animals living in the arable land, because the weeds act as a host for insects and as an important food resource for some animals.

The classical example is the decline of the grey partridge in the UK and in Denmark, associated with chick mortality because of lack of a suitable diet of insects. For their first weeks, partridge chicks are dependent on insects, whereas later in life they mainly feed on common weeds. The use of herbicides has been made responsible for the decline of grey partridge populations, but it cannot be the only cause. Nesting facilities also play an important role. The partridge prefers nesting along hedgerows and dikes which have decreased in numbers parallel to the increase in herbicide use. Consequently, the uniformity of the agricultural landscape without good nesting facilities for the partridge may operate in the same direction as does herbicide use.

6.4.6 NEW TRENDS IN WEED CONTROL

The success of modern agriculture in terms of yield has been overwhelming but has also had some unwanted influence on the agroecosystem. The first attempt to quantify the need for herbicide use in cereals to save chemicals was in fact triggered by the environmental concern of the public, let alone the first oil crisis in the early 1970's.

Before that time, herbicides were sprayed in a routine manner to keep weed infestation down. But, among other things, the prices of herbicides went up quite dramatically and the farmers were concerned about the considerable costs of chemical weed control. That was the time in Europe when we began to think seriously about thresholds for weeds. Since then much research has shown that it may pay to use economic thresholds for weeds in certain crops. Today, economic thresholds are an integral part of cereal growing in Northern Europe and may be a useful tool in reducing herbicide use.

Because of environmental concern for pesticide use in modern agriculture, a Danish Parliament's Action Plan of 1986 aims at a 50% reduction in the use of pesticides within a period of 10 years, taking the average pesticide consumption 1981-85 as reference, cf. Haas (1989).

In order to implement this Action Plan, it was necessary to find objective ways of defining the reduction in herbicide use relative to the reference years. This is now done by means of an index of frequency of treatment. Briefly, this index is based on the recommended dose of a herbicide: if the recommended dose is 2 kg of active ingredients ha^{-1}, then the use of this amount corresponds to an index value of 1.00. This way of monitoring pesticide consumption stems from the fact that in the early 1980's, certain new, biologically highly potent compounds were released, with recommended dose rates of, say, 4 g of active ingredients ha^{-1}. This should be compared with older herbicides doing the same job at recommended dose rates of 1 to 2 kg ha^{-1}. Since a dose of 4 g of the new compound is just as biologically active as is a dose of 1 to 2 kg of the old one, a comparison directly by weights would be without meaning.

Biological control of weeds is based on the introduction of insects and diseases that attack the weeds. As a management tool, biological control of weeds is an environmentally desirable approach because it reduces the risks of undesirable impacts on other vegetation and of chemical contamination of primary produce. Biological control is well suited for weed species which are capable of invading undisturbed native vegetation and difficult to control by conventional means. Biological control has had some success in Australia and the USA where it has been used to control alien weeds on public and range land (Combellack, 1989). In the intensive agriculture of Northern Europe with a diverse weed flora, the biological control methods probably have limited value.

6.4.7 OUTLOOK FOR THE FUTURE

Future weed control strategies are likely to be based on an integration of efficient utilization of herbicides and non-chemical control techniques. The various options to achieve a balance between minimizing environmental risks and maintaining yield level are numerous in modern agriculture.

Until recently the arsenal of herbicides with favorable ecotoxicological properties was increasing every year. This state of affairs will probably slow down in the future because the costs of developing a new compound will preclude the rate of release of novel compounds in the market place experienced in the past.

If biotechnology justifies the expectations of some biotechnologists, a new era of weed control will emerge. Biotechnology may provide mankind with a feeling of delightful enthusiasm about possibilities without end. Resistant crops, formerly sensitive to environmentally acceptable herbicides, will be produced and novel compounds will be made available to the market, together with gene-engineered resistant crops. Within a short period, the industry will be able to provide the farmers with 'weed control packages', i.e., crop seeds and herbicides which fit one another like a key in the right lock.

Although the alleged 'Brave New World' of weed control may be just around the corner, we must temper our expectations with history. Whatever changes we make to fight the weeds, Nature always has surprises in stock. What man can do with the genes in the laboratory, Nature can do better.

6.4.8 CONCLUDING REMARKS

Herbicides have an impact on the delicate balance between weeds and crops. The herbicides have eased the infestation of weeds, and together with other agronomic factors they have changed the weed flora; new species have shown up, others have disappeared from arable land. These changes in the weed flora have in turn changed the composition of the fauna, due to secondary effects. Compared with the weed-control methods which have been employed for millennia, the application of herbicides is quite new, and it is likely that the changes in the weed flora brought about by the herbicides are just beginning to emerge.

Besides this ecological effect, the introduction of herbicides has greatly influenced the socio-economic side of agriculture and society. For the last 50 years the herbicides have given the farmers a safety factor in growing crops and have led to a redistribution of labour. In the past, 95% of the population did the weeding for themselves (and for those few engaged outside agriculture). Today, a mere 5% of the population do all the weeding. Once kept busy weeding, this labour force can now produce commodities and services for the consumer. Perhaps this is the most important ecological aspect of modern chemical weed control.

REFERENCES

Alrieri, M.A. and Liebman, M. (eds.), 1988. Weed Management in Agroecosystems: Ecological Approaches. CRC Press, Boca Raton, Florida, 354 pp.

Andreasen, C., Haas, H. and Streibig, J.C., 1989*. Floraændringer, foreløbig status. (Preliminary Report on Changes in the Weed Flora). 6. Danske Planteværnskonference/Ukrudt 1989: 125-133.

Andreasen, C., Streibig, J.C. and Haas, H., 1991. Soil properties affecting 37 weed species in Denmark. Journal of Applied Ecology (submitted).

Auld, B.A., Menz, K.M. and Tisdell, C.A., 1987. Weed Control Economics. Academic Press, London, 177 pp.

Combellack, J.H., 1989. The importance of weeds and the advantages and disadvantages of herbicide use. Plant Protection Quarterly, 4: 14-32.

Haas, H., 1989. Danish experience in initiating and implementing a policy to reduce herbicide use. Plant Protection Quarterly, 4: 38-44.

Haas, H. and Streibig, J.C., 1982. Changing patterns of weed distribution as a result of herbicide use and other agronomic factors. In: H.M. LeBaron and J. Gressel (eds.): Herbicide Resistance in Plants. John Wiley & Sons, New York: 57-79.

Haas, H. and Streibig, J.C., 1989. Herbicide-resistant weeds - threat or challenge?. In: R. Cavalloro and G. Noyé (eds.): Importance and Perspectives on Herbicide-Resistant Weeds, A.A. Balkema, Rotterdam: 7-16.

Holm, L.G., 1976. The importance of weeds in world food production. In: 1976 British Crop Protection Conference, Weeds: 754-769.

Holm, L.G., Plucknett, D.L., Pancho, J.V. and Herberger, J.P., 1977. The World's Worst Weeds, Distribution and Biology. The Univ. Press of Hawaii, Honolulu, 609 pp.

Hurle, K., 1988. How to handle weeds? - Biological and economic aspects. Ecological Bulletin, 39: 63-68.

LeBaron, H.M. and Gressel J. (eds.), 1982. Herbicide Resistance in Plants. John Wiley & Sons, New York, 441 pp.

Olofsdotter, M., and Haas, H., 1990*. Herbicidresistens i ukrudt og afgrøder. (Herbicide resistance in weeds and crops). 7. Danish Crop Protection Conf. 1990, Weeds: 117-130.

Radosevich, S.R. and Holt, J.S., 1984. Weed Ecology. Implications for Vegetation Management. John Wiley & Sons, New York, 265 pp.

Streibig, J.C., 1979. Numerical methods illustrating the phytosociology of crops in relations to weed flora. Journal of Applied Ecology, 16: 577-584.

Streibig, J.C., 1988. Weeds - the pioneer flora of arable land. Ecological Bull., 39: 59-62.

Streibig, J.C., and Haas, H., 1983*: Kemisk ukrudtsbekæmpelse - anvendt biologi. (Chemical Weed Control - Applied Biology). Landhusholdningsselskabets Forlag, Copenhagen, 144 pp.

Thorup, S., 1982. Personal communication.

ACKNOWLEDGMENT

I wish to thank Heinrich Haas for valuable suggestions and improvements of the text, and for the encouragement and advice he has given me during the preparation of this chapter.

7 GENE-TECHNOLOGY

EBBA LUND

7.1 INTRODUCTION

The various methods covered by the term 'gene-technology' have only been known for less than 20 years. Their importance in the development of research and production has, however, proved to be much more extensive than was initially conceivable. Very soon, discussions on our right to tamper with the work of the Creator by transgressing the species barrier began in the general debate, whereas natural science by and large found it acceptable and useful to obtain such new knowledge on biology and to utilize it. Risk assessments have introduced national and international rules for this field.

Around 1984, risk assessment for research and production by new methods seems to have reached a point where, though regulations for such work are still needed, special problems are not envisaged. So far, no examples of unexpected properties due to gene-technology have been found; neither have harmful side effects been proven.

From the time when the development continues with release into the environment of genetically modified micro-organisms, plants or animals, a new situation, however, arises with respect to risk assessment. It is difficult to know what problems may arise, and to make general rules. As pointed out in the OECD publication of 1986, "Recombinant DNA Safety Consideration", it is necessary to decide from case to case and step-wise from the laboratory via greenhouse to first small-scale and then large-scale field tests.

7.2 THE DEVELOPMENT OF MOLECULAR BIOLOGY

The techniques of molecular biology have helped in giving us an enormous increase in our understanding of the function of cells and the genetic and biochemical steering mechanisms at cellular level.

This knowledge was first exploited in medical research and the production of medicines, while research in plants has been more stagnant over a number of years. In later years, however, biotechnological research in agriculture has increased, and one result is that many projects have started with more or less direct relation to the agricultural sector and consequently to food production. It is now assumed that the most important development by means of the new techniques will occur within agriculture.

In trying to establish important steps on the road from genetic and molecular biotechnology to gene-technology, the following events can be pointed out:

1871 It is reported that the sperm cell contains nucleic acid.

1943 Nucleic acid turns out to be a substance which can transmit hereditary properties in bacteria.

1953 It is stated that the DNA molecule is constructed as a double helix with a certain structure. In the same year it is shown that 20, and only 20, amino acids form peptide chains, which again form proteins.

1958 It is shown how one DNA molecule becomes two. Enzymes necessary for this synthesis are found. Hereditary properties depend on the sequence of the bases of the DNA strands.

1959 An enzyme is found that has the ability of forming RNA on the surface of a single strand of DNA.

1960 Discovery of messenger RNA, which transmits the genetic code and translates it into protein.

1965 It is understood that DNA is not always attached to chromosomes, but may be found as plasmids in the cell.

1967 Finding of the enzyme DNA ligase, which can glue DNA strands together.

1970 Finding of an enzyme that can cut at an exact location of a DNA strand (restriction enzymes from bacteria).

1972 Utilization of ligase and restriction enzymes for the production of recombinant DNA molecules.

1973 Foreign DNA is transferred into plasmid DNA, after which the plasmid is introduced into a bacterium. In principle it is now possible to transmit quite foreign hereditary properties into bacteria.

1973 First worries about gene-technology.

1974-1975 Meetings and discussions in England and the US.

1976 The first suggested rules for DNA work in the US.

1977 The first commercial gene splicing companies.

1978 The first human hormone produced by gene splicing (somatostatin).

1979 Less strict rules in the US.

1980 First production on industrial scale is launched (insulin in California).

1981 Utilization of yeast and coli bacteria in gene splicing research no longer needs notification in the US.

1982 Super-mice with rat or human genes are produced. Insulin produced by gene splicing is marketed. Splicing in plant cells succeeds. Relaxation of US regulations.

1984 First permit for small-scale field tests with bacteria in the US.

1986 OECD's report on Recombinant DNA Safety Considerations.

The basic idea of gene-technology is to transmit genes from one cell to another in such a way that the gene, also in its new situation, is able to produce the protein to which the gene has the key.

Nucleic acid is built of long strands consisting of sugar, phosphate and 4 different nitrogen-containing bases. The nucleic acid is constructed in exactly the same way, both in bacteria, plants, animals and humans.

In order to form a protein, a number of complicated reactions must take place. The first step is to make a nucleic acid copy of the 'gene' similar to the original with small differences. The copying process is called 'transcription' - and the copy is called a *messenger RNA* (m-RNA). There are small protein factories in the cell called ribosomes, which direct the reading of m-RNA. The sequence of bases determines which amino acid is formed and fastened at the end of the growing protein chain. Chains seem to be nature's solution to complicated steering processes. The process is called 'translation', and the result is a protein.

Gene splicing usually consists of 3 components:

1. *Donor DNA* from animals, humans, plants, yeast, bacteria or other living creatures. It may also be synthetic.

2. *Vector DNA*. Usually a vector, i.e. a means of transportation, is needed to bring the gene into a new cell. Such a vector may be a plasmid or a virus. Recombinant DNA molecules are produced outside living cells by putting together pieces of DNA so that they can be brought into a living cell and multiply there. The gene-splicing or r-DNA technique thus is a technique that allows production of a recombination of 1 and 2, but for multiplication the r-DNA molecule must be brought into

3. a *recipient* or host cell. The host cell may be bacteria, yeast or cells in culture. Cells in whole organisms, such as plants and animals, are also becoming of interest as host cells.

If the operation has succeeded, the r-DNA molecule will cause the gene(s) coming from the donor DNA to be expressed, i.e., to produce its protein. As all nucleic acids are constructed in an identical manner, in principle only the right enzymes (obtained from bacteria) are needed to move genes about, but this does not mean that all attempts are successful. It has been pointed out that such processes take place in nature all the time. Other people consider species barriers as absolute realities that are to be respected. Many ecological and ethical problems are discussed on this basis.

7.3 SOME DEFINITIONS

The term *biotechnology* is often used nowadays for the new technology, but in essence all industrial production that utilizes micro-organisms (bacteria, yeast, fungi, etc.), e.g., production of beer, dairy products, bread, antibiotics and much more, is biotechnology. For a technique in which a genetic operation has been performed prior to production, the term 'new biotechnology' would be proper.

Terms such as 'genetic engineering' and 'gene manipulation' cover planned changes in the genetic construction. This could be *gene splicing* or, with a different term, *recombinant DNA*, as described in the previous passage, but it could also be other methods. A very wide term such as 'genetically modified organisms' is also used in many connections.

It may seem pedantic to be so much concerned about which term to use, but where national or international rules, recommendations or even laws are concerned, it is of great importance to employ the same terminology and to understand the same thing by the various terms.

While the OECD and other organizations have used the concise term 'recombinant DNA technology', 'genetically modified' has been used within the EC and elsewhere. This seems to have been done deliberately, as it will render possible a later agreement on the limits of the definition and a change of the meaning of the word. The definition 'genetically modified' does not, however, cover such techniques as have been employed in plant and animal breeding for a long period and with sufficient safety.

Cell hybrids. A cell hybrid may contain the almost complete genetic material from the cells in question, but hybrid cells may also occur which contain only some elements from the cells in question. In any case the situation is different from gene splicing, where single genes are transferred to another cell in a very specific way.

Hybridoma cells and production of monoclonal antibodies. Production of cell hybrids in order to produce good antibodies is one very important use of cell hybridization; it has already gained great diagnostic value and in the future will probably also be employed therapeutically.

An organism, whether animal or human, reacts to contact with foreign proteins (and some other substances) by forming antibodies against them. A certain type of small white blood cells, the lymphocytes, produce the antibodies. The antigens, which stimulate the production of antibodies, are rarely or never pure substances, and even if each lymphocyte only produces one particular antibody, there are so many lymphocytes, each starting its own production, that blood serum will contain a broad mixture of antibodies against the antigens introduced. Antibodies are not produced continuously after the contact, and if, e.g., such an antiserum is to be produced in a different animal, it will never be quite similar to the first production.

If cells are grown in a culture, normal cells will only divide a certain number of times, e.g., one hundred times, and then stop multiplying. If they continue to grow in a bottle when properly fed, they are in fact no longer normal. The suspicion arises that they may have turned into a kind of cancer cell. Cancer cells may grow in culture for years; in principle, they can live eternally and keep growing unless a technical mishap occurs.

In 1975, Koehler and Milstein showed that if hybrid cells are made of 1) small lymphocytes which already produce antibodies but have a short life, together with 2) fast-growing leucaemia cells which have eternal life, a hybrid *clone* can be selected which produces a certain type of antibodies (i.e. monoclonal) forever. It is quite a laborious task to reach this goal, but the advantages are immense.

The word clone is stolen from botany and means a group originating from one single unit, here one single cell. It is now used in molecular biology. One 'clones' when cultivating from a 'cloned' cell. Even though in essence it only means that many cells have been cultivated from one specific cell, the word is now used in a way which suggests that the very transfer of genes has taken place.

Within plant breeding, hybrid formation is of great importance, regardless of whether old or new techniques are being employed.

7.4 GENERAL EXAMPLES OF RESULTS OBTAINED BY GENE-TECHNOLOGY

Much present-day research within cell biology, immunology, virology and many other fields is performed by means of methods of gene splicing. Perhaps half of all basic and derived research is performed by means of such methods. Often monoclonal antibodies are used as well. Development work may, e.g., lead to production of drugs and may aim at developing methods for use on a large scale. The following *example*, taken at random, shows how complicated these matters are becoming.

In many cells proteins are produced which are of importance for the development and growth of various blood cells pertaining to the immune response of the body (colony-stimulating factors). Normally, the cells contain very little of these substances, which may be important in order to activate the proper defense cells.

It is now possible to make DNA copies of those m-RNA molecules that correspond to the proteins wanted, to control that they really do correspond to the desired genes, and to make them work. These artificial genes are then transferred into a rather complicated plasmid, originating from a common type E.coli plasmid.

This plasmid has received various gene segments by splicing, in order to stabilise it and to enable it to produce foreign proteins. The plasmid contains the genes of the original plasmid, determining its ability to multiply and to ensure antibiotic resistance. Further, it contains many segments of cells from various higher animal species, namely some from a monkey virus, rendering it capable of making many copies, various segments from human adenovirus, and certain segments of mouse immunoglobulin gene and a mouse gene, coding for an enzyme. This Harlequin of a plasmid is now functioning well and may be used as a vector for many different transportations of DNA-segments.

The task of choosing the right producing cells and then purifying the products is enormous. While without gene splicing, only 4-6 microgrammes of the desired substances can be produced from 40 l cell material, it is now possible to get amounts measured in milligrammes of very active, pure substances. Similar advantages, enabling obtaining sufficient amounts of substances for research, have proved very important in virology. Today much is understood about the conversion of cell functions for virus production. The functions can now be properly studied, and drug production methods may have been found, too.

Many results are of interest for basic research only, and many experiments lead nowhere, as they fail on the way. The right gene may have been found, but cannot be put into place. Or it has been possible to integrate the gene into a virus or plasmid, but it has not been possible to transfer these into cells. Or this has been possible, too, but there is no translation for protein production. Or, even if this has succeeded, but the capacity to do so is lost after a while. There are long and narrow roads to a stable production of desirable and well-defined products, and these are, of course, a prerogative for production.

Another example of a successful production by means of gene splicing is a product called TNF (human tumour necrosis factor). The substance, a protein, was purified and examined. There was not very much of it until it was produced in cultures of leucaemia cells. By studying m-RNA of the amino-acid chain of the protein, a c-DNA copy was produced. It was then possible to transfer the DNA segment in plasmids into coli bacteria.

The substance TNF destroys tumour cells, seemingly without attacking normal cells. The US FDA (United States Food and Drug Administration) has permitted this product to be employed in the treatment of a cancer patient in a major New York hospital. The problem is that the animal tests and clinical tests usually required have not yet been completed. A 'compassionate exemption' was granted. This is an exemption that is possible in the US, when normal procedures would take too long, but where important tests have been performed. This also happened in connection with the treatment of AIDS patients with new drugs.

From Japan we learned (in June 1985) about a quite different model. A virus vector was developed which should be able to transfer foreign genes, e.g., genes from alpha-interferon from humans, into silkworms. The virus employed is an insect virus, a baculo virus, which has the characteristic - important in this case - that it is not contagious for wild insects. A plasmid was linked and cut so that it became a hybrid plasmid supplied with various characteristics. Then the interferon gene was transferred into the plasmid, and the plasmid into the silkworm. There was no difference between the interferon produced in human cells and in silkworm cells, and the concentration was up to 100 times higher than in a mouse system.

7.5 A SURVEY OF THE APPLICATIONS OF GENE SPLICING

Research results obtained by means of gene splicing cover almost the entire field of the construction and functions of normal and diseased cells. The applied use can be divided according to the character of the host organism. Thus there is applied microbiology and application in plants, animals and humans.

This section lists some categories of gene-technological production and application, essentially without touching upon the questions of risk assessment or ethics which will be discussed later.

7.5.1 Applied Microbiology

1) *Drugs.* The first commercially exploited fields are within the medical industry. Various substances for human and veterinary use have been produced from cloned micro-organisms, namely hormones, blood factors, antibiotics and vaccines. Compared to the conventional approach, these productions have advantages with respect to purity, safety, economy and otherwise. Other substances could not be produced by conventional means, e.g., growth hormones and certain vaccines.

2) *Diagnostic reagents.* Nucleic-acid probes have been developed for the determination of hereditary defects, for diagnosing infectious diseases or cancer. Probes for forensic tests should be mentioned, too. The production of such reagents will not in itself give rise to any safety problems, but their application may lead to ethical problems (see later).

3) By means of cloned organisms, better fodder utilization, feedstuff production or preparation of additives for the food industry may be obtained.

4) Various forms of combating pollution may be improved by means of organisms enhanced by gene-technology.

5) Biological pest and pathogen control may be developed. Protection of the environment by means of spliced organisms may be a possibility.

6) Genetically modified micro-organisms may be developed which may function directly linked to plants or animals.

7.5.2. Gene Splicing Applied in Plants

The genetic modification of plants, for both research and development, has developed faster than anticipated.

Considerable technical difficulties have arisen in connection with attempts at genetic modifications of cereals, but otherwise there is a considerable development of research and production in plants.

Research is being done on:

1) Herbicide resistance.

2) Disease resistance.

3) Increased tolerance to all kinds of external factors such as salt, draught, cold and heat.

4) Methods are being investigated to enable the plants to fix nitrogen.

5) Plants are being developed which are enhanced quantitatively or qualitatively with respect to protein production or to the production of single amino acids.

7.5.3. Application of Gene-Splicing Methods in Animals and Humans

1) *Gene therapy.* A very large number of hereditary defects exist, some of which cause incurable diseases in humans. Some are caused by a defect in a single gene and that gene is known. If it becomes possible to replace such genes with non-defective genes in body cells, e.g., blood cells, a sophisticated cure has been developed which would not cause hereditary changes, as gametes are not affected. Such therapy is the object of much research, but so far no example of successful use of such a sophisticated cure is known.

2) *Transgenic transfers.* Within veterinary medicine and in research laboratories there is a desire to perform research where genes, e.g., for the production of growth hormones and others, are transferred to other animals with the object of producing a larger and/or better type of domestic animal or a new prize-winning parrot or whatever.

It has turned out to be difficult to transfer new genes into gametes or small embryos in such a manner that they are well controlled by the whole organism. The principles may however be utilized for better and more precise animal breeding than by the conventional methods.

The first examples of such a gene transfer concerned the production of genetically stable giant mice of considerably increased size by transferring a growth hormone gene from a rat or human cell. Transfer of resistance factors and many other things may also be of interest. Even the transfer of new genes to domestic animals so that, e.g., milk may contain all kinds of additives is envisaged. Only our imagination sets a limit to the possibilities.

The Danish Parliament discountenanced transgenic experiments with higher animals, so that such experiments would be acceptable for banana flies, but not for mice for support from the special biotechnology programme. This is regrettable for research, because transgenic research is necessary, for instance, in order to explore and understand gene regulation.

7.6 RISK ASSESSMENT

Since 1975, when researchers put forward conjectural risks to be debated which might be associated with gene-technology, the possible risks have been discussed in many countries.

Most countries of the western world followed the suggestions of the National Institutes of Health, USA, as guidelines. These guidelines soon became far less restrictive than they were at first. The reason for this was that much experience was gained and more and more experts participated in the assessments, but especially the fact that not even in experiments in the laboratory designed to provoke new and unexpected characteristics did these appear after gene splicing.

The significantly increased knowledge of genes and their function contributed to the considerably decreasing concern amongst experts. Both in WHO and OECD meetings and others it was concluded that no new combinations were constructed due to gene-technology which could develop dangerous products which were not known from the components used for transferring the genes.

From about 1984 there has, however, been the new development that genetically modified micro-organisms are desired to be deliberately released to serve a function in agriculture and in the environment. This development gives new aspects of risk assessment. It is imaginable that a genetically changed organism released into the environment may have unintended effects.

Risk assessment consists of a calculation of the probability of the occurrence of a harmful effect and an assessment of the consequences of such damage. When attempting to calculate the probability of a harmful effect, the strange and difficult situation arises that there is no standard of comparison as such hazards have never occurred. This means that one is referred to subjective assessments between two extremes: 1. Since a harmful effect has never occurred, there is nothing to worry about. 2. Clearly there is no way of assessing the matter and thus one should refrain from using the new methods. But the issues are so important that we are forced to take a stand.

Risks to the environment, nature and health are not in themselves a consequence of using gene-technology, but would depend on the character of the organisms and genes used. A risk assessment should, therefore, concentrate on the organisms or products produced and not the technique employed.

7.6.1 Pathogens

A definition of the term 'pathogen' is not as simple as it may seem: it is not just 'an organism that causes disease'. Whether a disease actually develops, depends on many other factors than the organism itself, its ability to survive and its virulence. It depends on socio-economic circumstances and the ability of the organism to spread. It also depends on whether transmission of infection between various species is possible, especially transmission from other species to humans (zoonozes). Thus, the question of pathogenicity may end up by being a politico-economic question, and it may depend on the legislation of each country.

In most countries, the classification of pathogens has been done on the basis of rules as expressed in "Classification of etiological agents on the basis of hazards", 4th ed., Dept. of Health, Education and Welfare, Publ. No. (NIH) 75-790, 1974. It has been used unmodified as Appendix B in "Guidelines for Research Involving Recombinant DNA Molecules", National Institute of Health, 1986. Unfortunately, the lists have not been updated, but the principles have stood the test. The WHO has set similar criteria with a grouping into four classes. Referring to the fact that the term 'pathogen' is not absolute, the organisms have not been listed, but it has been left to each country to group the pathogens according to local circumstances (climatic, social, economic and other factors).

According to the environmental authorities of the USA, a pathogen is an organism which can cause infectious disease (in humans) or which produces substances harmful to humans. In the U.K., pathogens are only such micro-organisms as can cause infection and disease in a healthy laboratory worker. Toxin production belongs to another law. Organisms which are in fact harmful to other animal species are registered according to their potential for causing disease in humans. Also the British rules are divided into four classes, covering (1) organisms pathogenic to humans, (2) hazardous to laboratory staff, (3) transmittable to the society outside the laboratory, and (4) rules to ensure good prophylaxis and treatment being available.

These examples have been given to stress how difficult definitions can be. There are different rules in different countries. The EC Commission is presently (1990) working on a draft directive, Kom (529), concerning biological agents causing deterioration of health, such as, e.g., pathogen micro-organisms, and on gene-technology potentially hazardous to health. Much research is being done to find factors of pathogenicity, both in order to learn about their functions and in order to be able to remove them, e.g., to produce vaccines.

From a gene-technology point of view, it is interesting that these classifications according to pathogenecity actually have nothing to do with gene-technology.

7.6.2 Physical Containment

Safety and discipline at work are fields that are not yet covered by the Danish regulations for gene-technology. Several countries, e.g., West Germany and USA, attach great importance to the training in microbiological techniques and the responsibility of the supervisor. It is, of course, important to have good, appropriately organized laboratories and equipment that make it easier to work safely. The greatest efficiency and safety, however, is ensured by sufficient training in safety techniques for microbiology, and by working with sufficient discipline and obeying rules for good microbiological techniques.

Physical security measures may support good microbiological techniques, but they cannot replace it. The US guidelines emphasize that not everything can be covered by rules, and they recommend people to use their heads. With regard to design and equipment, laboratories are classified into four groups according to the potential danger of the organisms concerned.

7.6.3 Biological Containment

At an early stage of the classification of gene-technological work, it was suggested that it should be possible to work within principles for biological containment, i.e. within systems where the host organism cannot survive and multiply outside the laboratory or fermenting tank and where vectors cannot be established in other cells. Such a host-vector system can be more or less biologically contained. The higher the degree of biological containment that can be ensured, the less physical containment is required.

7.6.4 GILSP (Good Industrial Large Scale Practice)

Within the OECD's efforts regarding security for recombinant DNA work, it has been suggested that basically it should be possible to work with the principles for biological containment even on an industrial scale and thus save time and money for companies as well as authorities. The basic ideas are shown in Table 7.1. The Danish authorities have been rather reluctant to carry the idea through so far, as they wish to be able to control the amount of organisms escaping from a production irrespective of its type. The Association of Biotechnological Industries in Denmark argues that the OECD's recommendations should be followed and points to suitable GILSP hosts. The OECD group are continuing their work on the issue. It is estimated that more than 90 per cent of industrial production could follow GILSP rules.

Table 7.1. Suggested criteria for r-DNA GILSP (Good Industrial Large Scale Practice) Micro-Organisms.

Host Organism	r-DNA Engineered Organism	Vector/Insert
- Non-pathogenic	- Non-pathogenic and free from known harmful sequences	- Well characterised
- No adventitious agents	- As safe in industrial setting as host organism, but with limited survival without adverse consequences in the environment	- Limited in size as much as possible to perform the intended function; should not increase the stability of the construct in the environment (unless that is a requirement of the intended function)
- Extended history of safe industrial use; *or*		- Should be poorly mobilisable
- Built-in environmental limitations permitting optimal growth in industrial setting but limited survival without adverse consequences in the environment		- Should not transfer any resistance markers to micro-organisms not known to acquire them naturally (if such acquisition could compromise use of drug to control disease agents)

7.6.5 Deliberate Release

If a micro-organism, a plant or an animal is to be released into the environment or used in agriculture, the situation is quite different from industrial production, where it is not intended to let anything escape, or where this will at least only happen if the organism is considered totally safe.

In the case of deliberate or planned release, the objective is to establish the organism in the environment with a certain function. Will this result in ecological imbalance? In reality it may not be possible to assess the character of a potential problem beforehand, and much care must be taken. Ecological conditions must be studied carefully, and so must anything known about the transfer of non-modified organisms. In 1986 the OECD recommended that decisions should be made case by case and step-wise from the laboratory to final production.

Various countries have different attitudes towards release. In Eastern and Southern Europe, for instance, so far there have been no special rules, but a number of countries have special committees and rules, and Denmark has an exceptional law stating that release is prohibited. As the Danish minister of the environment may grant exemption, the difference between Denmark and the countries with special committees is more formal than real.

Release can be classified into 4 types:

1. Deliberate or planned release is, in the Danish law, defined as release with a function in agriculture or in the environment. This justifies concern for adverse or harmful influence on

the environment. E.g., it is imaginable that a natural organism might be ousted.

2. A different situation may arise if production of food or feedstuffs (e.g., silage) takes place in such a manner that organisms are released into the environment without intention (incidental release).

3. Due to accident or less suitable production/research procedures, organisms may escape into the environment although this is not desired (accidental release). Procedures in research and production must be such that this risk is minimized; it is not reasonable to assume that cloned organisms will behave differently from non-cloned ones.

4. Finally, organisms from systems with good biological containment, i.e., without the ability to multiply in the environment or to transmit genes to other organisms, may be released. This should be of no practical consequence (see GILSP).

The real problems of release thus concern cases 1 and 2. The problem that might arise in case 2 do not seem to be very carefully treated in the various countries. Heated products from dairies, breweries and other fermenting industries ought not give rise to any problems, even if the product contains gene-spliced organisms, as these have been killed, but regarding both feedstuffs and additives a development of products that contain living organisms can be envisaged. The development probably points towards the use of gene-spliced organisms, e.g., in the production of silage, additives, etc., and in that case it may become necessary to decide on their presence in the environment.

So far, however, it is case 1, the actual release, that constitutes the main problem. Obviously, the approach must vary according to whether a virus, bacteria, plants or animals are concerned. We shall briefly discuss the first three of these four situations.

Virus. The ability of a virus to penetrate into cells and become an integrated part of a suitable host cell can be exploited in gene-technology in various ways. If new genes have been added to baculovirus, which is an insect virus, it may be used for pest control. Such experiments are being done, e.g., in the UK. The risk to be borne in mind would then be that these insect viruses may be too good at establishing themselves in the environment, and that harmful genetic changes might occur.

Another field where gene-technology has been useful is the production of vaccines by removing genes for harmful properties, so that the result is a safe, live, non-pathogenic vaccine. This has been done successfully with Aujetzsky virus (swine herpes virus). Environment organisations in the USA argued that this was a release, while the American Ministry of Agriculture decided that it was no different from the use of other live vaccines (e.g., against polio, measles, etc.).

Bacteria. The greatest potential problems concerning release are considered to be those concerning bacteria. In several countries (e.g., West Germany and Australia) a statement is required as to why an applicant wants to conduct a certain project and whether there are any alternatives. The authorities of other countries (e.g., Denmark) do not consider themselves in the right to ask such questions. It is, however, widely agreed that international regulations for harmonizing release experiments must be laid down.

At present, risk assessment of the release of cloned micro-organisms is attempted on the basis of 5 questions: 1) Can a released micro-organism survive? 2) Can it multiply? 3) Can it spread from where it was attempted to be put to use? 4) Can genetic material be transferred to other organisms? 5) Can the original or other organisms which have received the new gene become dangerous?

Plants. Besides micro-organisms, a field of vivid current interest regarding release is plants. The possibilities and actual experiments with the release of modified plants have developed much faster than most people imagined possible. This involves, for instance, resistance against disease or herbicides, enrichment of plant protein, experiments with nitrogen fixation and much more.

In trying to find more concrete solutions with maybe less risky experiments, the USA's Food and Drug Administration came first with suggesting the introduction of the term 'Good Development Practice' (GDP), which should be used in connection with 'small-scale field tests'; it could also be termed 'controlled release'. The OECD amongst others is currently working on a set of rules for such controlled release, as it is considered that acceptance of such a concept regarding micro-organisms and plants would mean a considerable reduction of administration and control. The idea is that after tests in the laboratory and in a closed greenhouse it should be possible to proceed to small field tests, if, e.g., spreading from the place of experiment is prevented (by preventing seed formation, dispersal, etc.); in reality this equals biological containment for the field in question.

Analyzing the first Danish release experiment with resistant sugar beets, this does not seem to be a release in the sense of the law. The law speaks about release with a function in the environment, but the 'disarmed' sugar beets are already prevented from establishing themselves. It is, however, a small-scale field test under controlled conditions (GDP).

This special case, and the entire discussion as to what may in some cases be achieved due to the GDP principle, does not mean that the long way of evaluation step by step and from case to case can be cut short. So far, there is no other way to effect a risk assessment for deliberate release.

7.7 ETHICAL PROBLEMS

When we talk about ethics, we usually mean something related to responsibilities towards other human beings. We may have different opinions as to whether humans are anything more than the most highly developed animal, but as such we have an ethical and moral responsibility towards the other animals, plants and the ecological balance.

Even if people, especially from the Western World, have assumed the right to exploit the resources of the Earth, there must be a level where we say stop. Also in the field of gene-technology, where we have come closer to shortcuts to evolution than elsewhere, we must be aware of our responsibility to the rest of nature; for the sake of man as well as of nature. This is why it is so necessary that we try to decide on ethical questions concerning the environment. Such questions are, e.g., for certain parts of the agricultural sector, far more difficult to distinguish from risk assessments than for laboratory work and industrial production 'indoors'.

The harmful effects we fear are eradication of species, e.g., by means of pesticides, and limitation of the natural diversity by one-sided breeding of some few characteristics. If such a development is carried too far, maybe we will only discover our losses too late. Both common sense and a sense of responsibility point in the same direction: that we must preserve our natural resources.

The long-term harmful effects in ecology are far more serious than a local effect due to, e.g., pesticide residues. These worries should not, however, hinder considerate employment of modern methods for the improvement of our cultured plants and domesticated animals.

It is remarkable that ethical questions are nowhere mentioned in Danish legislation on gene-technology in the environment. The same observation can be made in other countries as well.

In the field of application covering transgenic transfers in animals and application of gene-technology methods in humans, ethical problems may arise, although developments are only on their threshold. It is likely that people generally have no qualms where bacteria are concerned, but what about earthworms? Do the problems start with higher animals? Or do ethical problems arise only when it becomes possible to change genes in humans for repair or improvement?

In many cases, the very production of gene-spliced DNA segments hardly presents any ethical problems, but the area around the use of DNA probes may become ethically very difficult. This is, e.g., the case in embryo diagnostics, or in a possible future situation where a 'gene chart' would be a prerogative to, say, employment or insurance.

7.8 INVENTORS' RIGHTS AND PATENTS

Most countries want to have a clear legislation to ensure inventors' rights for researchers and companies, in spite of public insight into projects and production within gene-technology.

The ensuring of rights through patents for plants and animals has not previously been practiced. Since Pasteur in the last century, it has, however, been possible to obtain patents for micro-organisms and the use of micro-organisms, without generally giving thought to the fact that this might be something basically different from patenting a method for the production of, e.g., an enzyme. For many years, there has also been examples where the employment of cell cultures for the production of, e.g., vaccines may be patented.

Most countries recognize (e.g., through the European Patent Convention of 1973) that patents may be awarded to any invention 1) than can be used industrially, 2) that is new, 3) that contains a certain invention as one step in the production. Discoveries and abstract ideas (e.g., mathematical methods) cannot be patented, and neither can computer programmes or medical or surgical methods. Products for therapeutic or diagnostic use may, however, be patented.

It has not been possible to obtain patents for variants of plants or animals or biological methods for producing them, but this is now changing in several countries.

With very little ado, the European conventions have been altered so that plants may now be patented. Patent rights have been awarded for the cultivation of an alfalfa variation, which has been enhanced with regard to protein production by means of gene-technology. In Denmark micro-organisms can be patented, but not plants or animals. An EC directive will, however, probably alter this. A directive on patents is being drafted.

An important change in the attitude to patents for animals happened last year when the US

Supreme Court decided that a mouse variant, which had been made especially prone to develop tumours by cloning, was patentable. Hereafter, the American patent authorities find that anything can be patented that meets the ordinary criteria for patents. Many other patents are expected to follow, but efforts are also meing made to change this basis politically.

The general rule seems to be that patents have nothing to do with ethics, but at least in Nordic patent legislation it is possible to reject a patent application if the use of the invention would offend the public sense of morals or 'public order'.

An important problem in connection with the patenting of living material is that it cannot be sufficiently described for others to do likewise. This is a basic patent requirement. For this reason, deposit systems have been tried, but such systems make it difficult to defend the patent. If another party can obtain a sample, how can abuse be controlled? And what about spread? Animals can escape and seeds can spread.

If patents have not caused legal or practical problems before, it is easy to imagine how they will develop in the case of animals and plants. It is said that if it should prove impossible to ensure patent protection, one must think up a different system. From several quarters it is deemed unethical to patent live material, i.e., nature itself. Others point to the increase of problems of the poor countries compared to the rich ones, which may now have acquired patents on the basis of species that were imported from the Third World in the first place, but this discussion cannot be continued here.

7.9 GLOSSARY

Aerobic - employed for a process requiring free oxygen.

Anaerobic - employed for a process which cannot take place in the presence of free oxygen.

Asilomar - the name of a conference centre in California. It became internationally known because of the meeting in 1975, where the first voluntary rules for gene-technology were accepted. Paul Berg arranged the meeting.

Bacillus subtilis - a common soil bacterium, which is important as a degrading bacterium for organic matter. Industrially, it is employed for production of viral enzymes and antibiotics, and in gene-technology as a host cell, because it grows well even on a large scale, and the desired gene products (proteins) can relatively easily be separated from the bacterial matter.

Baculovirus - a DNA virus almost exclusively known as an insect virus. After cloning it can work as a biological pesticide.

Bacteriophage (bacterial virus) - a virus that eats bacteria (Greek: phagein = to eat). Numerous types of phages exist, larger and smaller, DNA-viruses or RNA-viruses. A phage can multiply in a suitable bacterium which is then destroyed, or it may form an integrated part of the chromosome of the bacterium. In this stage the bacterium consequently is genetically altered and is called lysogenic, because the situation may become changed so that new phages are formed and the bacterium is destroyed.

Base pair copying is the way in which a double strand of nucleic acid can be formed by adding nucleotides. For structural reasons an adenine (A) is always placed at the thymine

(T) of the first strand if it is in a DNA molecule, and at the uracile (U) if it is an RNA molecule. Correspondingly, guanine (G) is placed at the cytidine (C), and thus a new strand is formed. By splitting a DNA double strand it becomes possible to add new nucleotides so that two new double strands are formed, which are identical to each other and to the original double strand. In this way genetic stability is preserved at cell divisions.

Biological containment: see containment.

Biotechnology has been defined in various ways, like 'the use of scientific and engineering principles to treat materials by means of biological methods for production and functions'. By 'scientific and engineering principles' are then understood microbiology, biochemistry, genetics and biochemical and chemical production methods. By 'biological methods' are understood the use of micro-organisms, enzymes and animal and plant cells. Both processes employ the biological methods directly, but also preparatory methods and further treatment of the product obtained. By 'products' are understood, e.g., industrial production of food, drinks, pharmaceutical products, biochemical products and metal extractions. By 'functions' are understood, e.g., water purification and treatment of domestic and industrial waste water. The production (but not the use) of drugs is included in the public health area. Agriculture is in general not considered biotechnology, but the manufacturing of the raw materials can be. Production of pesticides and the use of gene-technology methods in micro-organisms, plants and animals are also considered as biotechnology. - Source: OECD (1982).

Chromosome - the threadlike structures in a cell which contain DNA protein, i.e., the genetic material. The name is derived from cromo, dye, because the chromosomes were found as banded structures after staining.

Clone originally meant a plant group from one individual (Greek: clon = seed or twig). The word is now employed for a cell which is 'renewed' by introducing new DNA as part of the genome. A cell clone thus becomes such a cell population which arose from a single cell, with new genetic material introduced.

To clone has, in gene-technology, become synonymous with introducing new genetic material and succeeding in making this cell grow and multiply.

Containment. By physical containment is understood the employment of good microbiological technique and in addition such methods and equipment which to a suitable degree prevent the release of active material from the working area. By biological containment is understood the use of vectors and host organisms which do not survive or become established causing infection of new host organisms in the environment, or in, e.g., humans. The higher the degree of biological containment obtainable, i.e., the less the ability to survive outside the laboratory, the lower the degree of physical containment necessary. By employing biologically contained systems, important practical, economic and safety advantages may be obtained.

DNA (desoxy ribonucleic acid) - a nucleic acid (from nucleus), is a substance of chains of nucleotides. DNA nucleotides consist of 4 different bases containing nitrogen, sugar (desoxy ribose) with 5 carbons, and phosphate. The genome of the cell consists of helix-shaped double chains of DNA, and in this structure the genetic code of the cell is contained.

E.coli, or Escherichia coli, are rod-shaped non-sporogenous bacteria. The number of coliform bacteria is large. They form a majority of the normal bacterial flora of the intestinal tract, but pathogenic strains exist that can cause diarrhea. The strain E.coli K12 is of special importance in gene-technology, because it does not establish itself in the normal intestinal tract. For this reason and because its genetics is well known, it is suitable for genetic engineering.

Enzyme - an organic catalyst. The word is derived from the Greek word for sourdough: zymé. Enzymes are proteins. The living cell contains a large number of enzymes without which the living cells could not function. Certain enzymes are the necessary components in gene-technology.

Eukaryote - a cell with a nucleus. All organisms are eukaryotes except bacteria and bluegreen algae. These are prokaryotes and have no organized nucleus.

Fermentation - this notion was originally employed for the degradation of sugar to alcohol by means of yeast enzymes. Today it is used about any enzymatic process such as, e.g., the production of antibiotics.

Gene - the unit of a chromosome which controls a single heritable property. The conception 'gene' was introduced before it was known that the chemical structure of a gene was a sequence of DNA. A chromosome of a colibacterium contains 4 million base-pairs and more than 1000 genes. Cells of higher animals and plants may contain many chromosomes and a very high number of genes.

Genome - the complete sequence of genes containing the genetic code of the cells.

Gene therapy - change of the genome of a cell by means of gene-technology with the purpose of repairing gene defects, i.e., in order to cure disease. The change is non-genetic if somatic cells (cells of the body) are changed, e.g., blood cells. If ovae or sperm cells or small embryos are changed correspondingly, a new situation arises; then a successful gene therapy would give genetic changes.

Hybrid - an individual or a cell, formed as a cross between two or more cells of different character.

Ligase (DNA-ligase) - an enzyme which can seal a binding between nucleotides in a DNA molecule.

m-RNA, messenger RNA - such nucleic acid that brings the genetic information from the DNA to the ribosomes. Here the message is translated to protein.

Mutant - a permanent change in a gene, a chromosome or in parts of a chromosome.

NIH, National Institutes of Health - the US public health institutes have important federal functions and support research projects.

Nuclease - an enzyme which can degrade nucleic acid.

Nucleotide - the building stone of nucleic acids. It consists of phosphate, a pentose (sugar) and a nitrogen-containing base (see base pair copying).

Plasmid - DNA-containing structure in bacteria, yeasts and probably many other cells. This DNA does not form part of chromosomes, and it consists of circular double-stranded DNA. Often the material is enough to code for 5-150 average sized proteins. Some plasmids can be transferred to other cells and integration with chromosomal DNA can also take place.

Polymerase - enzyme which can form nucleic acids out of nucleotides.

Restriction endonuclease. An endonuclease is an enzyme which can degrade a nucleic acid by opening inside a double-strand. This is contrary to exonuclease which attacks at the end of such a molecule. The term 'restriction' refers to the capacity of the enzyme to destroy foreign nucleic acids which have entered into the cell. Several hundreds of restriction nucleases are known. Each attacks a certain sequence of nucleotides at a certain point. This is the important condition for splicing identical sequences from unlike DNA pieces.

Ribosome - the small bodies consisting of RNA and proteins found in the cytoplasm. They are about 20 million parts of a mm. The ribosomes are the location for the formation of protein employing aminoacids and the code from mRNA.

Transgenic transfer - transfer of genes from one species to another. The term is employed in particular for the transfer between higher animals.

Yeast - unicellular organisms with a nucleus. Systematically they belong to the fungi. In gene-technology it is often saccharomyces types (beer and bread yeast) that are employed.

REFERENCES

Anonymous, 1988a. Engineered Organisms in the Environment. First Internat. Conf. on the Release of Genetically Engineered Micro-Organisms (Regem 1), Cardiff.

Anonymous, 1988b. The Laws of Life. In: Development Dialogue 1-2. Dag Hammarskjöld Foundation, Uppsala.

Bishop, D.H.L., 1988. The release into the environment of genetically engineered viruses, vaccines, and viral pesticides. TREE 3(4) TIBTECH 6(4), 12-15.

Bishop, D.H.L., Entwhistle, P.F., Cameron, I.R., Allen, C.J., and Possee, R.D., 1988. Field Trials of Genetically-engineered Baculovirus Insecticides. In: Sussman, Collins, Skinner and Stewart-Tull (eds.): Proceedings of the First International Conference on the Release of Genetically-engineered Micro-organisms. Academic Press.

Commission of the European Communities, 1988a. Proposal for a Council Directive on the Contained Use of Genetically Modified Micro-Organisms. COM(88)160 final. Published in the Official Journal of European Communities, 28 July 1988.

Commission of the European Communities, 1988b. Proposal for a Council Directive on the Deliberate Release to the Environment of Genetically Modified Organisms. COM(88)-160 final. Published in the Official Journal of the European Communities, 28 July 1988.

Council of the National Academy of Sciences, 1987. Introduction of Recombinant DNA-Engineered Organisms into the Environment: Key Issues. Report prepared by the Committee on the Introduction of Genetically Engineered Organisms into the Environment. National Academy Press, Washington, D.C.

Deutscher Bundestag, 1987. Enquete-Kommission des Deutschen Bundestages. Chancen und Risiken der Gentechnologie. (Report of the Commission of Enquiry on Prospects and Risks of Genetic Engineering). Bundestag Drucksache 10/6775.

Dickman, S., 1989. Pink petunias sow controversy in West Germany. Nature, 338: 194.

Din, N., Gausing, K. and Thode-Andersen, S., 1988*. Genteknologi og dansk lovgivning. (Gene-technology and the Danish legislation). Forskningsdirektoratet, Copenhagen.

Forskningsrådsnämnden, 1988*. Djuren och gentekniken. (The animals and gene technology). Källa 30, Stockholm.

Interdepartmental Committee on Biotechnology, 1986. A Plain Man's Guide to Biotech nology Support and Regulations in the UK. The Laboratory of the Government Chemist, Department of Trade and Industry.

Jensen, O., Molin, S., Pedersen, J.L. and Simonsen, H.B., 1988*. Etik og bioteknologi. (Ethics and biotechnology). Teknologinævnet, Copenhagen.

Joyce, D., 1988. Patent on mouse breaks new ground. New Scientist, 118(1609): 23, 21 April 1988.

Kingsman, S.M., Kingsman, A.J., 1988. Genetic Engineering: An Introduction to Gene Analysis and Exploitation in Eukaryotes. Blackwell, Oxford.

Lund, E., 1986*. Gensplejsning. (Gene-splicing). Hekla, Copenhagen, 164 pp.

National Research Council USA, 1987. Agricultural Biotechnology. Nat. Acad. Press.

Nordisk Ministerråd, 1988*. Bioteknologiska uppfinningar och immaterialrätten i Norden. (Biotechnological inventions and the Nordic legislation concerning immaterials. Nordic Council of Ministers, Stockholm.

OECD, 1986. Safety considerations in recombinant DNA-technique. Office of Technology Assessment: New developments in biotechnology 3: Field-Testing of Engineered Organisms.

Saunders, V.A., Saunders, J.R., 1987. Microbial Genetics Applied to Biotechnology. Croom Helm.

Tiedje, J.M., Colwell, R.K., Grossman, Y.L., Hodson, R.E., Lenski, R.E., Mack, R.N., and Regal, P.J., 1989. The planned introduction of genetically engineered organisms: ecological considerations and recommendations. Ecology, 70: 297-315.

US Congress Office of Technology Assessment, 1988. New Developments in Biotech nology. 3: Field Testing Engineered Organisms: Genetic and Ecological Issues.

Watson, J.D., Hopkins, N.H., Roberts, J.W., Steitz, J.A., Winer, A.M., 1987. Molecular Biology of the Gene. 4th Ed. Addison-Wesley.

8 COUNTRYSIDE PLANNING

JØRGEN PRIMDAHL

8.1 INTRODUCTION

In this chapter, the overall public efforts to regulate

- rural land use,
- natural resource exploitation (excluding oil and natural gas), and
- landscape change

will be termed *countryside planning*. Countryside planning is thus broadly defined as comprising planning legislation on the one hand and the administration of detailed provisions on the other. In between lies the actual task of plan making. It is this part of practical planning work that will be emphasized in the following.

Rather than controlling development, the aim of planning is much more to *guide* countryside change. Such planning comprises but few means for actively influencing development, means which are above all found within the context of nature conservation and the maintenance of recreation facilities. On the other hand, the planning authorities dispose of a number of legal means of adjusting current or impending changes. So in relation to investments and other initiatives, planning is predominantly *reactive* and *defensive*. Despite their chiefly passive role, planners may adopt a strategic attitude to the future of the countryside. The prerequisite for such strategies is knowledge of actual trends in countryside change.

8.1.1 Countryside Change

Depending on prospective and prevailing normative ideas, countryside changes can be perceived and evaluated in various ways. Most often, these changes have to be obvious and therefore sometimes serious, before they lead to revisions of planning types and strategies (Primdahl, 1987[*]). An instance of predominant notions of the future from the growth-obsessed 1960's is given in Fig. 8.1.

Changes of landscape, land use and resource exploitation bear special relevance to the elements of current planning efforts.

The last type, *natural resource exploitation*, deals firstly with the exploitation of *freshwater resources*, where pollution of groundwater from former refuse dumps and agricultural operation are two major problems, cf. Chapter 4 and others. To the extent that contamination of clean drinking water can be called 'consumption', it is obviously here that the great challenge of reducing future consumption lies. Equally, the protection of major aquifers will be an important planning objective.

Extraction of raw materials is the other main resource issue that is subject to public planning. The increasing demand for special deposits, such as plastic clay for the ceramic industry, or chalk for the Finnish paper industry makes this type of planning increasingly important. Creating planning strategies related to technological development and a more deliberate landscape reconstruction of excavation sites are two essential tasks of planning (Algreen-Ussing, 1988*).

Where *land-use changes* in Denmark are concerned, a decline of urban growth and an increase in abandoned agricultural land have been characteristic features of the main trends in recent years. During the period 1978-1982, the area consumed for urban expansion declined from about 6,100 ha/year to 3,700 ha/year (Anonymous, 1982*). The other important trend is the increase in planting or abandoning of agricultural land. A survey has pointed out that about 0.5% of the total area in rotation was taken out of use within a 5-year period (1981-86). This was a representative survey, and converted into figures for the country as a whole, it equals a total of approx. 13,000 ha (Jensen and Koch, 1986*). This figure is expected to rise considerably if the forecasts on reduction of EC subvention arrangements hold true. A debate presentation issued by the Danish Ministry of the Environment mentions a gross 10%-20% of the area in culture within a period of 20 years (Anonymous, 1985*). If such becomes the case, a major part of the area will be afforested. Whether or not this takes place, future changes of land use promise to be quite comprehensive in comparison with the post-war period. This makes great demands on planning strategies for areas which change most rapidly, in effect, the urban fringe and marginal agricultural areas.

Landscape may be defined as "a heterogeneous land area composed of a cluster of interacting ecosystems that is repeated in a similar form throughout" (Forman and Godron, 1986, p. 11). A survey of small biotopes (field roads, hedges, bogs, ponds, etc.) in various East-Danish locations has shown the dynamism of the Danish agricultural landscape (Agger and Brandt, 1988). From 1884 to 1981, biotopes have been registered by means of maps at 7 different points in time. In the total of 1566 registered small biotopes, only 142 were 'unchanged'; i.e., the same type of biotope was registered at a minimum of every other one of the 7 maps, including the start and end points. The rest had disappeared (709), had changed biotope type (265), were new (192), or had arisen and disappeared again (258). As for countryside planning, the prevalence of wildlife and facilities for recreation in these 'interacting ecosystems' are of special interest. With few regional exceptions, it is a general trend that conditions for both wildlife and recreational facilities have deteriorated along with the intensification of agricultural use (Agger et al., 1986*; Biotopgruppen, 1986*; Jensen, 1982*). In addition, urban development, and especially the associated traffic systems, tend to impair the immediate access to the countryside (Primdahl, 1986*).

8.2 COUNTRYSIDE PLANNING IN DENMARK

In Denmark, countryside planning is practiced partly as an ingredient of the comprehensive planning system and partly as one of a number of sectorial types of planning. Each of the latter works more or less independently, whereas a certain integration of sectorial views takes place in the comprehensive planning system.

In general, the five sectors shown in Fig. 8.2: *raw materials*, *water supply*, *water protection*, *agriculture*, and *nature conservation*, are included under the heading of countryside planning. Moreover, urban development (and thus urban planning) has a great impact on the countryside; in the same way, waste and recycling planning is becoming more important. This section will deal with the Danish planning system, first in retrospect and then in a review of the existing system emphasizing comprehensive physical planning.

8.2.1 Background

For a great many years, physical planning in Denmark was, with one exception, synonymous with urban planning. From 1939 to the mid-seventies this planning mainly consisted of inter-municipal town development planning (regional and urban development planning), and in the preparation and administration of master plans and town-planning ordinances. The former plan types have since been abandoned, whereas the town plans have been replaced by others (Eyben, 1978*; Svensson, 1981).

The ***Fingerplan*** of 1948 for the Copenhagen Metropolitan Area is an example of a plan produced without a legal foundation (Egnsplankontoret, 1947*). This plan had a great impact on urban development in the Copenhagen area. The major part of the outer urban area is actually located in the five fingers, though the 'webs' - the green agricultural and recreational areas between the town ribbons - have grown thinner and more filled up with highways and power lines than was intended in the original plan. The Fingerplan is a classic in planning literature. It is based on the original and simple idea of locating urban growth in narrow ribbons along efficient transport lines with easy access to the countryside and has lent

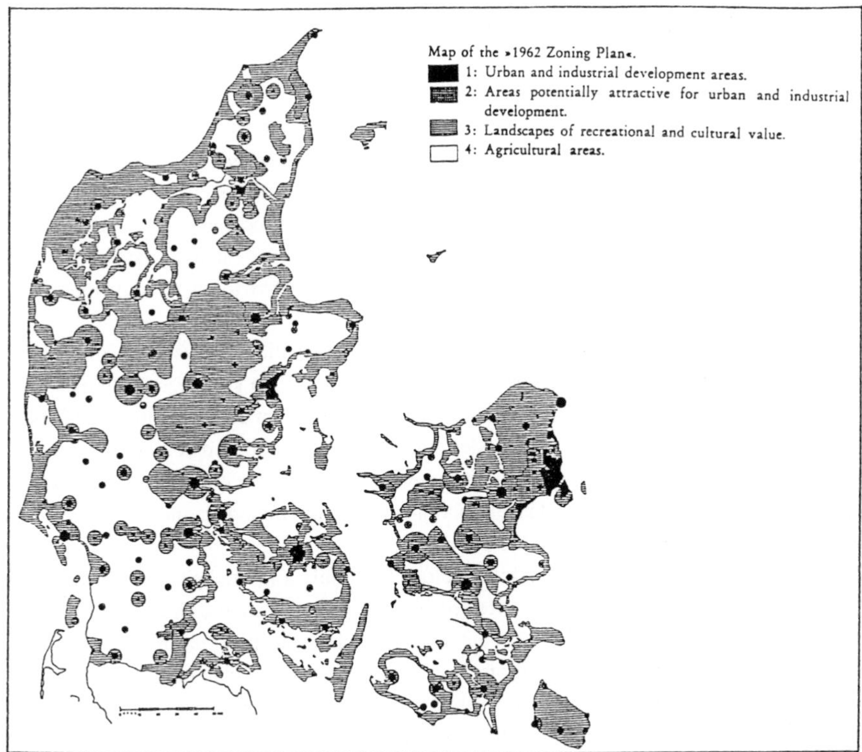

Figure 8.1. The 1962 Zoning Plan. - Source: Humlum (1966*), p. 488.

inspiration to many other urban plans. The southern finger (Køge Bay) was developed in the 1960's according to a large, comprehensive plan based on specific legislation in 1960.

Another instance of legally unfounded planning in Denmark is ***The 1962 Zoning Plan***, which subdivided the whole country into four zones (Fig. 8.1). The planning proposal was prepared by the so-called Government Committee on Planning (Landsplanudvalget) and it clearly demonstrates the predominant values and views of the future among planners of the early 1960's. There was a firm belief in the probability of rapid urban growth along with a large increase in the recreational needs of the city dwellers, and a concurrent decrease in the importance of agriculture. Zones 1 and 2, existing and potential urban areas, made up 18% of the total area against the corresponding figure today of 6%, which comprises the urban zone as well as existing and designated summer-house areas. Conservation and recreational areas of high priority (most of which were farm land) made up 43%, while the remaining area (zone 4), termed agricultural areas, equalled 39% of the total. The land interests of agriculture were not included in the planning deliberations; agricultural areas were merely seen as remainder areas.

The 1962 Zoning Plan was never approved; a major planning reform bill put to parliament the following year, along with amendments to the agricultural legislation, failed in a mandatory referendum. So the plan had no direct effect, but it had an indirect impact by initiating a general debate on Danish development strategies (Landsplanudvalget, 1964*; Humlum, 1966*). Furthermore, the zone plan initiated a long debate for and against establishing *nature parks*, as a strategy in nature-conservancy work. Today Denmark is one of the few industrialized countries without national parks.

In one field, plans for the countryside were carried through at an early stage, namely ***conservation plans***. These conservation plans, introduced in the 1930's served as strategies for the bringing of future *conservation cases*. Furthermore, the plans were important as general indications of areas worthy of conservation which the local authorities should not - and often had agreed not to - allow to be affected by urban development because of their conservation values. In general, these plans were directed primarily at the development of urban and summer-house areas.

Seen from the point of view of the countryside, conservation values only entered into considerations as to where to locate (or rather: *not* to locate) urban growth and summer-house areas. In addition, the planning content was determined by urban considerations, such as the reciprocal location of dwellings and trades, the relations between dwellings, institutions, commercial centres, and transportation, and interests associated with these. Considerations such as protecting the best arable land, economizing on raw materials and protecting water resources was not incorporated into the planning.

Finally, it is important to understand that before 1970 only a limited part of the total urban and summer-house development was affected by planning provisions. One main reason for this was that the obligation of the local authorities to carry out planning was rather limited and could often be circumvented. Another serious limitation to planning was the lack of efficient legal means to prevent scattered urban growth in the countryside. It was not until the late 1960's that scattered urban growth and related public expenditures for infrastructure (roads, sewage, water supply, schools) was regarded as a substantial problem by the parliament. At that point planning practice was brought up to date and equipped with the necessary means for enforcement through radical legal amendments. On the other hand, the very fact that Danish planning was modernized so comparatively late explains why the newly introduced system was so advanced, compared to that of other countries. For example, this reform required far-reaching decentralization, coupled with extensive plan obligations and public participation. A thorough description of the physical planning system and its background is found in Eyben (1978*).

8.2.2 The Present Planning System

The cornerstone of today's planning system in Denmark was laid down in 1969 as the *Urban and Rural Zones' Act.* According to this act, the entire country was divided into three zones: (1) the *urban zone* within the borders of which urban development can take place, (2) *summer-house areas* within which new summer cottages must be located, and (3) the *rural zone* where construction must not take place without specific permission, with the exception of construction related to the primary sectors, above all agriculture. In rural zones, planning permission can be refused *without* compensation to the owner, and transfer from a rural zone can take place only when concurrent with planning. In this way, an end was put to scattered urban growth.

In comparison with legislation in other countries, the Urban and Rural Zones' Act is interesting in that urban development itself is secured through a coupling with the taxation system; assessment for taxes on real estate will rise steeply upon a change of zone designation. The owner thus has an economic incentive to develop or to sell his land in the case that it becomes part of the urban zone. Since 1982, the option of compulsory purchase for urban development purposes has existed, but it is rarely used.

SECTOR / LEVEL	RAW MATERIALS	WATER CATCHMENT	WATER QUALITY	AGRICULTURE	CONSERVATION	COMPREHENSIVE PHYSICAL PLANNING
CENTRAL	National supply pl Extraction pl. for the territorial sea	Guidance/approval Test cases	Guidance/approval Test cases	Soil classific. Guidance/ approval Administration	Guidance/approval Test cases	Guidance/approval National planning directives
REGIONAL (county councils)	Exploitation pl. Digging pl. Renovation pl.	Water catchment pl. Administration	Water quality pl. Administration	Agricultural pl.	Conservation pl. Administration	Regional planning - rural areas - urban development - urban renewal
LOCAL (municipal councils)		Water supply pl. Administration	Waste water pl. Administration			municipal planning - rural areas - urban development - urban renewal Development planning
LEGISLATURE	Raw Material Act	Water Supply Act	Environmental Protection Act Watercourses Act Ochre Act	Agricultural Holdings Act Land Consolidation Act	Conservation of Nature Act	National and Regional Planning Act Municipal Planning Act Urban and Rural Zones Act

Figure 8.2. The overall Danish planning system for the countryside.

The *Nature Conservation Act* was also revised in 1969, after several years of preliminaries. Among the most important amendments were the expansion of public accessibility rights to include woods larger than 5 ha (where there is public access to the wood) and the provision on *landscape analyses*.

During the following 10 years, all the laws mentioned in Fig. 8.2 were created or expanded. A comprehensive planning practice was developed for each of the three political-administrative levels, and an extensive system of sectorial plans was introduced. Furthermore, the conservation plan commission was abolished, and the nature conservation work was transferred to the county authorities. By 1978 we had the outline of todays' system.

8.2.3 Comprehensive Physical Planning

When the most essential planning acts, *The National and Regional Planning Act* (there is a separate act for the Copenhagen Metropolitan area) and *The Municipal Planning Act*, were approved, nothing was adopted concerning the countryside, apart from provisions concerning the extraction of raw materials. A few years later, in the context of introducing sectorial plans for the countryside, the planning acts were expanded to include the whole countryside. Except for various urban issues, the above acts make the following demands as to the *content* of the topics to be dealt with in planning:

- Urban development in a broad sense
- Summer-house development and location of recreational sites
- Utilization of land for raw material extraction
- Quality of surface waters
- Use and protection of freshwater resources
- Identification of areas reserved for agricultural purposes
- Protection of nature conservation interests

These issues must be dealt with both in the *regional plans* elaborated at the county level and in the *municipal plans*, concerned with the local level. However, water issues are addressed in regional plans only. Both plans are traditional land-use plans, containing provisions for the area development of the whole county or municipality, respectively.

In relation to the countryside, regional plans are the most important ones, as most economic and legal means of plan implementation are managed by the county authorities. A closer description of the origin, construction as to content, and practical implementation of these regional plans will be given in the next section. Apart from the two plan types mentioned, the comprehensive planning system consists of all-embracing national plan directives, and, at the other end, detailed development plans.

The *national plan directives* are central directives which are binding on the lower planning levels; for instance, relating to area reservations for the extension of the natural gas network and interim suspension of hotel development along the coast lines. Actual national planning does not take place.

At the most detailed level we find the *development plans*. They are legally binding both on citizens and on public authorities. A development plan involves comparatively narrow compulsory provisions, and since 1977 the municipalities have worked out approximately 1000 such local plans per annum. In Denmark, there are few minimum requirements as to on which topics the plans must take a stand - contrary to, for example, the Swedish system which is characterized by extensive use of standards. On the other hand, local plans may, if so desired by the municipalities, contain detailed provisions for the site, including: overall use; property size and delimitation; traffic; density, use, location, and appearance of buildings; existing and proposed vegetation and terrain; other site-related issues. However, most of these regulatory possibilities cannot be applied to agricultural areas, and thus development planning in Denmark, the only type of in-depth land-use planning, is of limited interest to the countryside. In later years, there has been a move, especially in the planning profession, to have legislation amended so as to facilitate detailed planning in agricultural areas.

It is a general feature of the comprehensive plans that they are brought into use only *if and when* other changes take place. Thus, the actual plans do not comprise means of action, and in principle they have no bearing on 'present, lawful use', as stated in the standard wording of the development plans. The fact that planning is mostly reactive implies, among other things, that municipalities have to find an equilibrium between the supply of detailed planned sites, and the local demand for plots. If there is a shortage in supply, construction processes are delayed, and the municipality's chance of leaving its stamp on an individual urban development area is reduced. Once a developer turns up and is knocking at the door, a great many municipalities find it hard to work out conditions for the detailed use and design of the sites.

On the other hand, reserving very large areas is also undesirable because such areas remain a part of the urban zone for too long without development. This will affect farmers who wish to maintain intensive agricultural production for as long as possible. In addition, excessively large area reservations make it difficult or impossible for the municipality to direct urban growth chronologically, in accordance with plans.

In the long run, too small and too large undeveloped urban zoned areas will undermine the credibility of the planning. Here is the point at which land speculation takes over, and this is in the interest of nobody but the speculators.

8.3 SECTORIAL PLANNING

While the binding guide-lines on urban plans and development in general are laid down in the comprehensive plans, the sectorial plans provide the most essential data for the considerations of resource economy and landscape values which are involved in this urban growth. This is indicated by the horizontal arrows in Fig. 8.2. Setting up an order of priority is a prerequisite when these considerations are made. Such orders of priority or *evaluations* are established for each sector individually, and later a mutual balancing of priorities takes place. This section will deal briefly with the individual types of sectorial plans, emphasizing issues for internal evaluations.

8.3.1 Raw Materials Plans

Raw materials planning can be divided into a superior section, comprising an entire county, and a detailed one covering an individual excavation area. The most important resources embraced by this sectorial planning in Denmark are gravel, clay and chalk, and the major planning effort is made by the county autorities, as described below.

The superior section of county planning consists in elaborating *exploitation plans*, the most important elements of which are: mapping raw materials; identifying areas of interest; laying down policies insuring 'resource economical' use of raw material deposits; selecting a plan period; specifying the needs for raw materials within the county; preparing further mapping; and finally, formulating superior requirements on the final treatment, i.e., the reconstruction of the site after excavation.

The detailed raw materials plan consists of the preparation of *digging plans* and *renovation plans*. The former are guidelines for the order and procedure of excavating the individual areas. Before starting it has to be decided how to renovate the site when the excavation is concluded. The excavation plan is closely linked with the renovation plan which shows the design and use of the area after digging.

When excavation *does not penetrate the groundwater level*, the area is typically returned to agricultural use. One important exception is urban development areas. Here, the general policy of 'resource economical' exploitation may have implied that conditional approval of urban development in a given direction requires that the raw materials be exploited before this development makes such action impossible. In that case, the renovation plan is designed in anticipation of the urban development. Several examples of attractive districts located on former excavation areas are to be found in Denmark.

As a consequence of the general raw-materials policy of fully exploiting valuable deposits, permits for excavation beyond the groundwater table are often granted, provided that this will not endanger important water-catchment interests. Such areas are typically renovated as natural habitats and/or recreational sites.

From a landscape-ecological viewpoint, it is interesting that a large part of the minor wetlands in the countryside are areas created by extraction of raw materials in earlier days, e.g., marl digging or peat cutting. In this way, raw-material extraction has meant - and may continue to mean - a more heterogeneous landscape. Fig. 8.3 shows an example of a proposed natural habitat and recreational site on a chalk-exploitation area.

8.3.2 Water-Catchment Plans

Planning serves two practical purposes. Firstly, it establishes the administrative framework for the granting of catchment permits. Secondly, the water-catchment plans constitute an important basis for municipal water-supply planning.

In 1977, the Ministry of the Environment set up a general order of priority for water resources, in which first priority was given to water for household use, the second place to environmentally justifiable discharge of rivers and water levels in lakes; satisfying the demand for industrial and agricultural water was given third priority. In an actual, local situation, all these priorities can be departed from, but in any given circumstance this requires a general review of the consequences. Part of the planning objective is to accomplish this evaluation.

Based on forecasts of expected demand and accessible resources, above all groundwater resources, the water-catchment plans establish provisions for *the actual order of priority and allocation of the available resources* to supply the consumers of the county. A critical point in this planning is (as in similar planning) providing tolerably reliable prognoses.

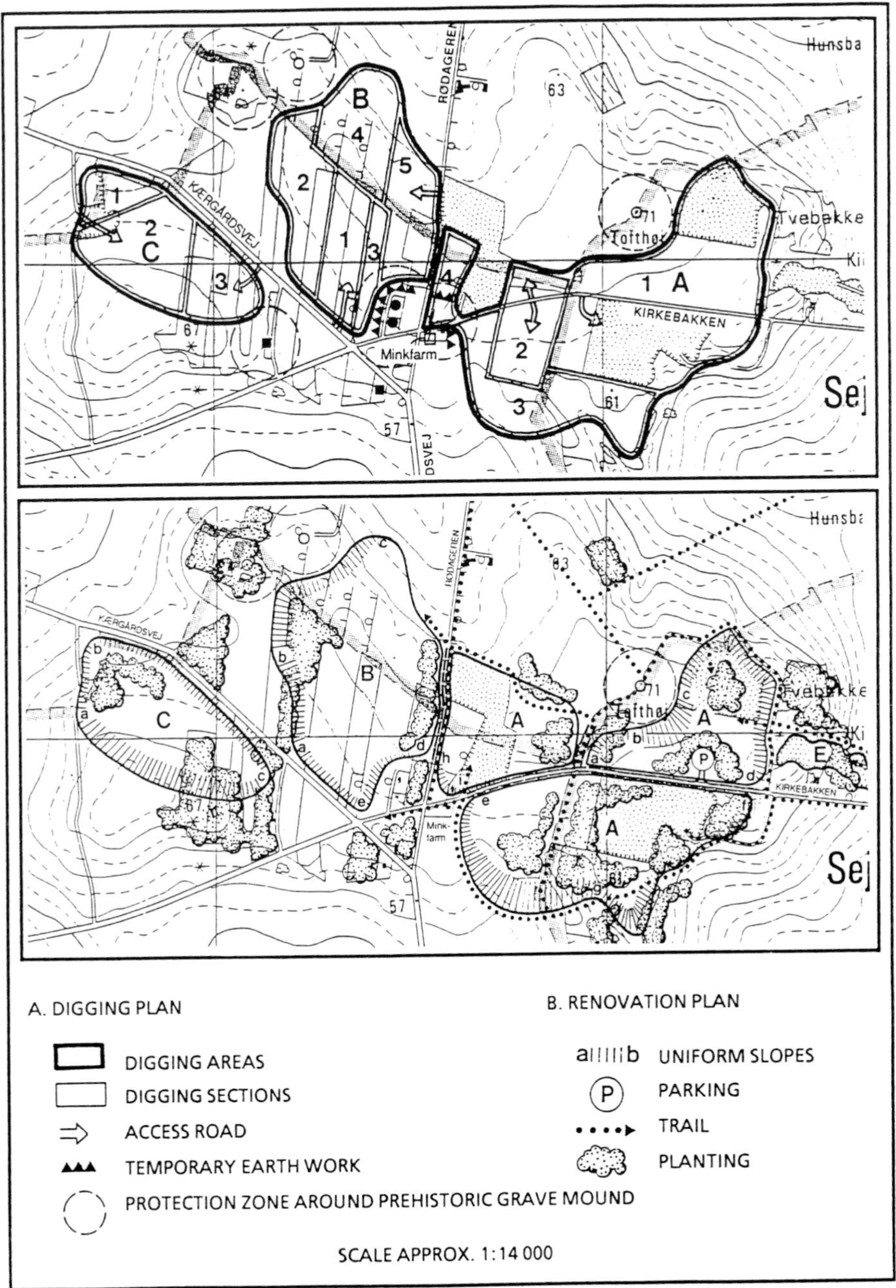

Figure 8.3. Part of a digging plan and renovation plan for a chalk exploitation area South of Aalborg. (Plan prepared by Sv. Allan Jensen, Planning Consultants for Aalborg County).

Table 8.1. The eight soil types shown in the classification maps and their relative share of the total agricultural area.

soil type	% of total agricultural area
1. coarse sand	24
2. fine sand	9
3. clayey sand	28
4. sandy sand	25
5. clay	-
6. heavy clay or silt	7
7. organic soils	-
8. atypic soils	7

Withdrawal of the state subsidies for establishing irrigation plants and raising the consumer price for drinking water are examples from the past years which have undermined such prognoses. Another planning problem is assessing the influence of water catchment on the groundwater and surface-water flow, and subsequently establishing priorities between environmental and economic considerations. This is indeed a classic problem of environmental management, and in this case it is further intensified by the fact that climatic changes create greatly fluctuating groundwater levels. One of several possible solutions to this problem is to grant *conditional permits* and supplement them with monitoring of the environmental impact of the catchment. Such a solution has been adopted on the island of Samsø (Thomsen, 1982*).

8.3.3 Water-Quality Plans

This plan type, like the previous one, serves two practical purposes. Firstly, it constitutes a foundation for granting discharge permits; secondly, the plan is a precondition for the preparation of municipal waste-water plans. The central part of water-quality plans is the stated *objectives* for the ecological state of rivers, lakes and coastal areas. The objectives for the individual waters are formulated from an assessment of the existing conditions and sources of pollution, as seen in relation to the background conditions.

A closer review of water-quality plans is given in Chapter 4. Let it merely be stated here that water-quality planning, along with water-catchment planning, has an important co-ordinating role in relation to the rest of countryside planning. The same can be said for urban development where, by tradition, water supply and waste-water discharge are important issues. It also applies to raw-materials planning because the most important gravel deposits are normally located in substantial water-catchment areas; this is why the exploitation of gravel below the groundwater level is so widespread.

Finally, a position on the exploitation and protection of a water resource is essential in relation to the two sectorial plans reviewed next: the agriculture plans and the conservation plans. It is not possible to zone agricultural land in regions with sandy soils without knowing where permits for irrigation should be granted or refused. Equally, water quality and quantity is crucial to the wildlife in many rivers and lakes, and in a similar way, the groundwater level in general determines the location and size of the wetlands at any point in time.

8.3.4 Agriculture Plans

So far, the most important task of agricultural planning in Denmark has been to evaluate agricultural areas, so that the most valuable ones are protected and allowed to develop comparatively freely. *Protection* concerns withdrawal for other land use, above all urban development. These *free-development conditions* primarily imply avoiding limitations on agricultural operations founded on other considerations, such as environmental and nature conservation. The purpose is to warrant the financial investments made by agriculture. In sum, this means that the indicated primary agricultural areas should not be affected by external changes, while changes from within, for the development of agriculture itself, can only be impeded to a limited extent.

The most important information for this evaluation has been the *National Soil Classification* of 1978. Other variables may also be involved, such as structural conditions or levels of investment and production; but as in all counties, the soil classification forms the most important data. In addition, this classification still plays a certain role in the administrative decisions of the Ministry of Agriculture. In the soil classification, the total agricultural area is subdivided in 8 soil types (see Table 8.1).

Departing from this classification, 'reliability of culture' is estimated from the water available during the growing season. So soil types 1, 2, and 3 are marked as safe for growing only if irrigation is possible. This possibility is to some extent determined by the above-mentioned water-planning process. The agricultural area is then subdivided according to cultivation value, which is done slightly differently in the various counties. In Viborg county, which will serve as a case in the follow-ing section, the subdivision made up to now discriminates between: 1. *particularly valuable*, 2. *valuable*, and 3. *remaining agricultural areas.* Furthermore, the river valleys in this county have been sorted out into so-called (4) 'culture meadows', more than 50% of the area in rotation, and (5) natural meadows, less than 50% in rotation.

8.3.5 Conservation Plans

Unlike the other types of sectorial plans mentioned, conservation plans have a long tradition in Denmark. From the late 1930's up to the 1970's, more than 30 con-servation plans for various parts of the country were approved. Above all, these plans were aimed at urban and summer-house development, but at the same time they lacked efficient legal means, apart from those inherent in the introduction of conservation orders. (Conservation orders are specific sets of rules, for instance a ban on development or a ban on ploughing on a specified stretch of meadow. The use of conservation orders is possible in Denmark only with compensation, typically 200-800 US$ per ha agricultural land.)

This type of conservation planning ceased in 1975, only to be reintroduced three years later in a new form.

Conservation planning involves mapping, analysing and evaluating the conservation values of the county. These values, somewhat misleadingly termed 'interests', concern: geological, biological, cultural, aesthetic, and recreational issues. For each of these issues, a map of valuable areas in the county is produced, and on this basis high-priority areas for nature conservation are identified.

8.4 CASE: COUNTRYSIDE PLANNING IN VIBORG COUNTY

An overview of the countryside planning system has already been given. As mentioned earlier, horizontal cohesion is secured (i.e., intersectorial co-ordination by comprehensive plans), with the regional level being the most important in the case of guiding countryside change.

Relevant questions are: (A) How is such a regional plan designed? (B) What is the course of the process? (C) How is the plan implemented?

In order to illustrate these questions, we shall make use of an actual case: regional planning in Viborg County. In reviewing it, the description will be limited to land use, i.e., to what is called land resources in the plan, focusing particularly on nature conservation interests, agricultural land use interests, and their relationships.

8.4.1 The Plan

The present regional plan, in which much weight has been attached to the countryside compared with the plans of many other counties, was elaborated in 1980-1985 and finally approved in 1987. Land-use questions are dealt with in a special paragraph which comprises land, landscape, and environmental issues. Viborg County has chosen to regard raw-material extraction as a provisory land use.

The plan is a typical zoning plan, according to which the countryside area of the county is divided into 6 proper zones: (1) primary agricultural land, (2) primary agricultural land with particularly many natural areas, (3) other agricultural areas, (4) other agricultural areas with particularly many natural areas, (5) primary natural areas with some agricultural areas, and (6) primary natural areas. To this must be added the designation of so-called (7) dispersal corridors. These are corridors in the agricultural landscapes, where biotopes of varying size such as water courses, lakes and ponds, bogs, heaths, commons, hedges and the continuity among them must be protected. An enlarged part of this zoning plan is shown in Fig. 8.4.

The land-use and landscape changes in these zones are covered by *objectives*, regarding environmental protection, multiple use of the land, reduced land consumption for urban development and infrastructure, and protection of raw materials with a view to future use.

Furthermore, the zones are associated with a series of *provisions*, which are legally binding on the decisions of the county and the municipality. According to these, agriculture is given the highest priority in zone 1, whereas nature conservation has the highest priority in zone 6. Zones 2 and 5 also have great agricultural and conservation values, respectively, but both functions play a part in these zones. Zones 3 and 4 are a kind of 'intermediate' zone, and according to planning pro-visions, *this is where urban development should take place*, whereas urban development does not take place in zone 6 and should be avoided in 1, 2, 5, and 7. In other words: in zones 1 and 2, the agricultural occupation should be protected and secured against the possibility of deve-lopment, while landscape protection is particularly important within zones 5, 6, and 7. Some implications of this will be reviewed in the paragraph on implementation below.

Now to the question: how did this plan come into existence?

8.4.2 The Planning Process

The plan was created by sector-wise identification of agricultural interests and conservation values. These identifications are professional evaluations undertaken by each sector separately (see Fig. 8.5).

The agricultural interests were defined and identified primarily on the basis of the national

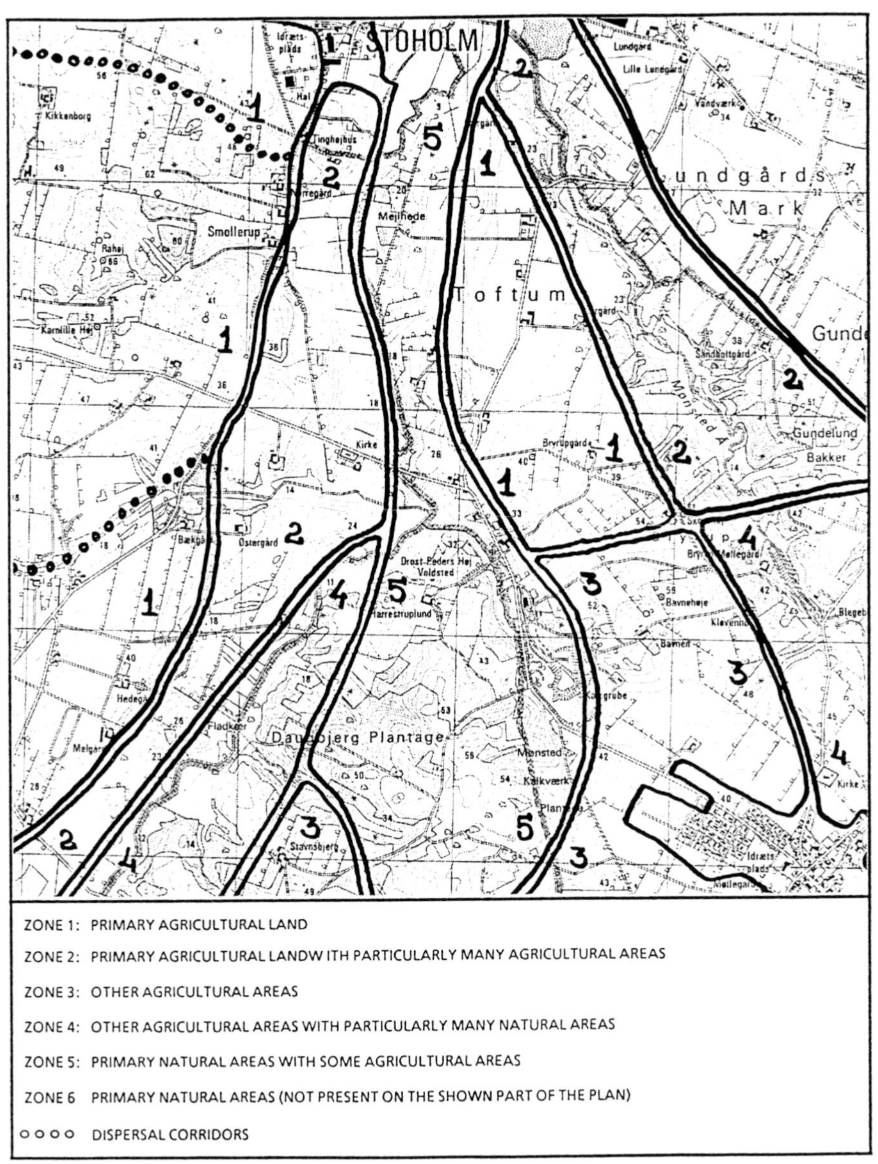

Figure 8.4. Enlarged part of the structure plan for Viborg County. Scale: 1:25 000.

soil classifications, supplemented with estimates on irrigation requirements and facilities. The actual irrigation possibilities depended partly on hydrological conditions and partly on the possibilities of granting permits, which in turn is mainly determined by the priority of water resources determined by water-catchment planning. Finally, some rough estimates on structural conditions, such as level of investment and composition of production, were included when the most valuable agricultural areas were pointed out. Local agricultural advisors contributed their detailed knowledge of the area during the actual identification and evaluation of areas.

The conservation values are, above all, associated with the degree of landscape heterogeneity, as it appears in topographical maps (scale: 1:25 000), with the exception of a few particular landscape types. For example, the heath at Kongenshus Memorial Park, which is given a high conservation value, must be described as homogeneous as to landscape, but it also contains some rare plant communities and wildlife.

Initial identification of the values in the county took place through overlays of maps showing various areas of high value seen from geological, biological, historical, aesthetical, and recreational perspectives. Through this process, a rough map of conservation values was prepared. In actual practice, the more detailed delimitation of the individual areas was carried out by means of topographical maps (scale: 1:25 000) maps. As a first result, maps were produced showing 'major natural areas', and also biological, geological and historical values and recreation interests.

The two sectors produced their individual drafts, to be utilized partly for further sectorial planning work (the agriculture planning work is not yet complete, whereas the conservation plan was finally in 1990), and partly for regional planning. During the process of regional planning, the different orders of priority have been balanced interrelatedly in a so-called 'comprehensive balancing of interests' process (Fig. 8.5).

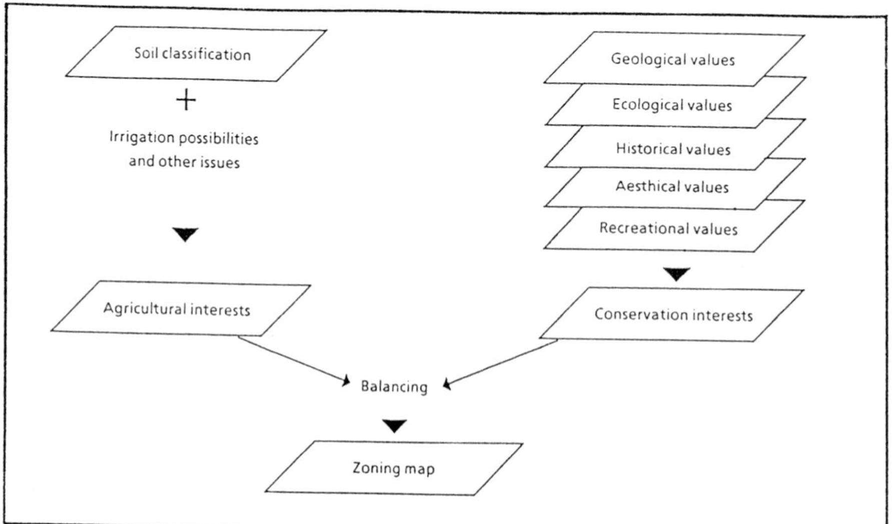

Figure 8.5. The evaluation process employed in the Viborg case.

8.4.3 Implementation

Now, what happens to the plan after approval? Is it forgotten by the politicians the very day after the last county council meeting? Is it kept on the planner's bookshelves, only to be used when the planner entertains visiting students or others from outside? Or is it in use frequently - and if so: to what purpose and with what effects? In other words: how is the plan implemented?

First, the plan *is* being used in practice. It serves as: (1) a guideline for the plan-making process carried through by other authorities and levels; (2) a framework for the daily decisions to be made by the county and municipal administrations; (3) a strategy for public economic activities, including the passing of conservation cases, selection of landscape management programs, construction of trails, parking areas, camping sites, marinas and other recreational facilities; and (4) a source of information useful to all those involved in countryside change and protection, not least the general public.

Next, how does the use of the plan actually affect countryside change - does it mean anything?

Yes it does! Although there is limited knowledge on the outcome of the planning process, it is evident that the countryside would develop quite differently without a plan like the one in question. A few examples based on an ongoing research project on implementation will illustrate this.

The reason why there has has been little if any urban or summer-house development within highly protected areas, i.e., areas which were designated as protected about ten years ago in the first regional plan, is not that these areas are unattractive to developers. It is because the municipalities, responsible for local development planning, respect - or are told to respect - these areas with reference to the plan. The same way with conservation orders. They are also passed according to the plans, in the sense that conservation areas are located within areas zoned for nature protection. However, this does not mean that failures in implementation do not occur. In fact, indications of such failures are quite common when the prime agricultural protection policy is reviewed, although systematic findings still have to be published.

Finally, one may go a step further and ask if the total planning process, including planning proper and implementation, as described above, is carried out in the best possible way, given the actual political and economical constraints. This is hardly the case, because the planning process relates to changing circumstances in an obsolete and somewhat irrational way. I will return to this in the final section.

8.5 EVALUATION IN COUNTRYSIDE PLANNING

Evaluation in planning can be defined as the process of obtaining, organizing and weighing information on the consequences, or impacts, of alternatives (McAllister, 1980). Every planning situation is bound to hold *at least* two alternatives which must be evaluated: 'something is done' (action, permitting or preventing action); or 'nothing is done', that is, 'solving' the problem without any use of planning guidelines. So evaluation is a central concept in the literature, and applied evaluation methods - formal or more intuitive ones - are essential characteristics of any planning process.

Good reviews of evaluation methods in relation to countryside planning, and to environmental planning in general, are found in McAllister (1980) and in O'Riordan and Turner (1983). The former characterizes evaluation in relation to what he describes as 'the evaluation dilemma'. This dilemma consists of the fact that on the one hand, we analyse the consequences of a planning decision by dividing it into many manageable components that can be studied independently, and on the other hand, we still yearn for a means of synthesizing the impacts or acquiring an integrated view of the implications of a plan under consideration.

"There are two general ways of approaching the dilemma: one informal, the other formal. The informal approach tends to be qualitative and holistic; using this approach the individual simply studies the detailed impact information until a holistic view emerges in the mind. The formal approach is quantitative and additive; it seeks to solve the dilemma by use of an equation that can transform the many bits of information into a single score that presumably measures how the welfare of society would be affected by a plan."

(McAllister, 1980, p. 184).

Both approaches mentioned are schematic. Even in the most 'technical' planning process, a need for qualitatively based decisions will arise, just as an apparently purely qualitatively process may require some quantitative analysis. The dilemma is not merely a 'macro' one: it exists within every discipline and school of planning and even within every specific planning process. Countryside planning is no exception in this respect, although qualitative oriented analysis has traditionally dominated. This is obvious from the above-mentioned books, and it also appears clearly from a brief Danish review of six different types of landscape analysis (Stahlschmidt, 1983*), as well as from the following description of three classical schools in physical planning.

8.5.1 McHarg's Ecological Planning Method

The ecological planning method - Ian McHarg thus named his ideas on landscape planning in the book "Design with Nature" (McHarg, 1969). The fundamental notion behind the method is that ecological analyses and values associated with ecology should play a major role in planning. To show how this may be done, McHarg gives examples from his practical planning work on the East Coast of the U.S. A brief outline of one of these will be given here to illustrate his method. The example is based on the proposition that any place is the sum of natural processes, and these processes constitute social values (McHarg, 1969; pp.103-116).

Staten Island, south of Manhattan, New York City, is taken as a case area. The evaluation problem is phrased: which lands are intrinsically suitable for *conservation*, for active and for passive recreation; which are most suitable for *commerce and industry*; and which for *residential land use*?

The questions are answered by mapping, interpreting and evaluating basic data on climate, geology, hydrology, soil, plant ecology, wildlife, and land use. For each potential use mentioned above, a series of maps is produced, showing different issues of relevance (Fig. 8.6). Each map shows the areas of interest on a five-stage scale; the darker the tone, the higher is the value. For *conservation*, three maps out of a total of twelve such 'interest maps' show: beach quality, geologic-feature value, and scenic value. Now, the individual maps are overlaid, and the same principle applies: the darker the areas, the higher is the *total* conservation value. Recreation and urbanization suitabilities is treated in the same way. In the end, a total evaluation of Staten Island with regard to these three uses and their overlapping values results.

In another example, the 'intrinsic' landscape values and opportunities for various land uses are evaluated against environmental impacts of the individual uses. This so-called *land-suitability* analysis has, like the 'overlay' example, been applied to a region of several thousand square kilometers in size (McHarg, 1969; pp. 127-151).

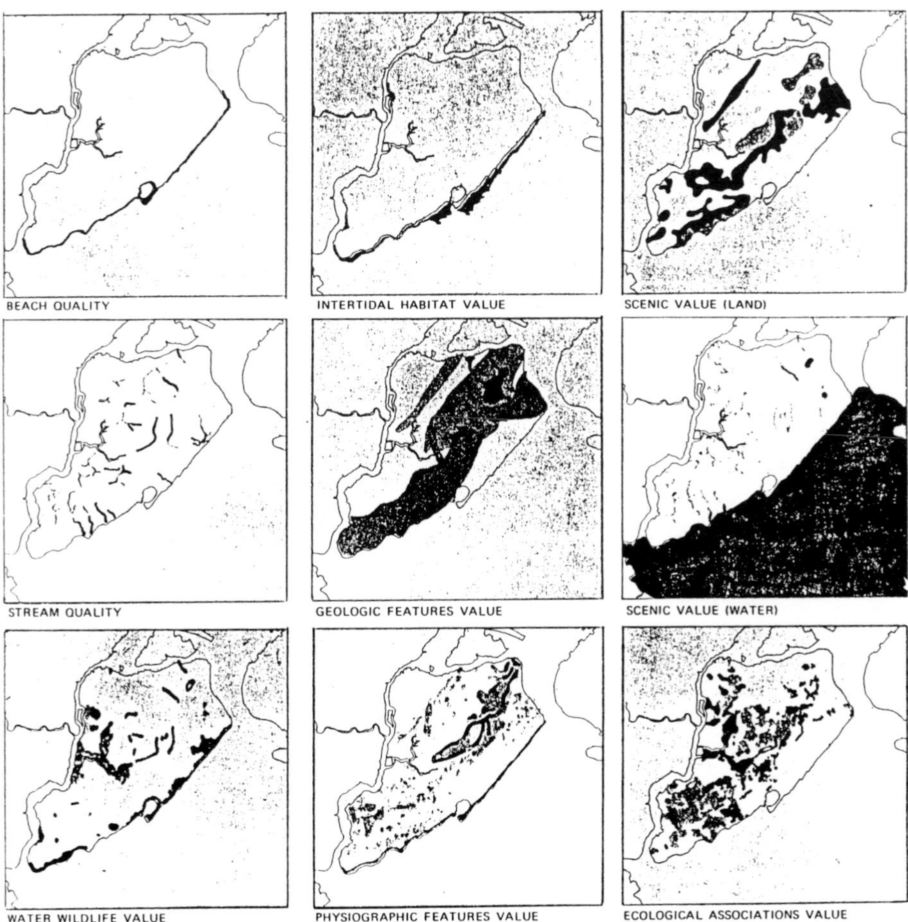

Figure 8.6. Nine maps (out of twelve) from a case described in McHarg (1969, p. 111). Each map illustrates a 'conservation interest' on Staten Island, New York; the darker the area, the higher is the conservation value. The individual maps can be overlaid, resulting in a composite map which shows the over-all conservation interests.

McHarg's ideas and techniques have come into widespread use. In Denmark, for instance, suitabilities for urbanization have been modelled on his land-suitability analysis (Olsen and Stahlschmidt, 1975*). Similarly, the landscape analysis based on 'intrinsic values' and the principle of overlays have been used in the regional analyses mentioned in Section 8.4.

Discussion. McHarg made a great contribution to the field by pointing out the ecological and environmental aspects of physical planning and indicating concrete methods for evaluating the landscape. But it is a shortcoming of the ecological planning method that the social processes *causing* land-use changes do not play any major part in the analyses. Furthermore, when the method is applied on a regional level, there is the hazard of favouring single uses within larger areas, and thus a risk of *segregation* of land-use functions rather than integration. This means that planning based on this method may contribute to enhancing existing (maybe undesired) trends towards monotonization of the landscape on the local level. And the tendency to reinforce segregation instead of preventing it is, actually, one of the main problems in Danish countryside planning.

8.5.2 Lynch's Spatial and Visual Analysis

Suppose the following planning problem arises: How can recreational opportunities - particularly recreational accessibility and visual quality - be improved within a given area? The analytical frameworks developed by Kevin Lynch provide useful tools for solving such a problem.

Through a study of people's images of their city, Lynch developed a method by which it is possible to describe the quality - or rather - the 'image quality' of a place (Lynch, 1960). Although three American cities were used to test the method, it has proved useful in landscape analysis as well. (See, e.g., Andersson (1974*) for a demonstration of the method applied to a rural landscape.) In a later book, "Managing the Sense of a Region" (Lynch, 1976), Lynch takes up landscape issues, although the work is dealing more with policy analysis than with evaluation methodology.

The 'legibility' (the term used by Lynch) of a landscape, i.e., how it can be grasped visually, depends on *identity*, *structure*, and *meaning*. What makes this landscape different from others? Or, according to the landscape definition (Section 8.1.1): What makes this land a landscape? How is it organized spatially? What are the practical and emotional meanings of the landscape as a whole, and of its various elements?

Essentially, these questions are answered by classifying the physical form of the landscape into five types of elements:

- ***Paths***. Channels used or potentially usable for movement. The landscape is experienced by moving along the paths and other landscape elements are arranged and related to the paths.
- ***Edges***. Visual - and usually functional - boundaries in the landscape, not used for movement: an edge of a wood, a slope, a hedgerow, a town border, etc.. These are important organizers of our environment.
- ***Districts***. Areas within the landscape which have a common character, identified from the inside as well as from the outside. These are the places you are going from, through, or to, when describing a trip to others or to yourself.

- ***Nodes***. Strategic spots in the landscape which an observer can enter; a place where it is easy to arrange meetings, where it makes sense to locate facilities, etc.
- ***Landmarks***. Like nodes, these are points of reference, but landmarks are external points; you cannot enter them. Tall buildings, single outstanding trees, prehistoric monuments, TV-masts etc. The 300 m-tall TV2-masts are examples of important landmarks in the Danish countryside.

These elements are useful concepts in describing the visual characteristics of a landscape. It is important to realize, however, that the elements are abstractions in the mind of the observer (or signs on a map reflecting them). They do not give an objective illustration of the physical landscape. In fact, the image map differs from a topographical map by showing what has been judged significant, and indirectly, what lacks significance. Therefore, an image map is an essential source of information, although a subjective one, when identifying areas that need protection or improvement.

Such landscape images are constructed by planners and others with appropriate training. As Lynch points out, the outcome of such analysis can be strongly improved when supplemented by interviews with and observations by users of the landscape.

Fig. 8.7 shows some of the analytical maps prepared in a visual study of the island Martha's Vineyard. These maps were produced through a combination of 'expert judgment' and interviews with users (Vineyard Open Land Foundation, 1973).

Discussion. The image analysis rougly outlined above provides a tool for evaluating important qualities of a place, qualities which are predominantly of a visual nature. This is both a merit and a disadvantage of the method. It is a merit because visual characteristics, which are so often overlooked in political decisions, are of great importance to how people orient themselves and how they enjoy moving through or staying at a place. It is a shortcoming of the method that it does not deal directly with symbolic and functional qualities. A TV-mast like the ones mentioned above, located by a highly centralized decision, without any local participation, may have a negative value associated with it by the local population, whereas a tall windmill financed and located by the local community may be viewed positively. Both the TV-mast and the windmill will be mapped as significant landmarks, but symbolic values cannot be understood by simply analysing the visual characteristics of the objects.

8.5.3 Alexander's Pattern Language

The third approach can hardly be termed an evaluation method, because the handling of information is an inseparable part of the total planning process. Stating the problem, identifying and evaluating alternatives, and implementing the plan comprise one process, integrated by the use of what is termed a pattern language.

The basic theory behind the *pattern language* and one comprehensive example of the language are published in separate books (Alexander et al., 1975a and 1977). However, the most useful book, if one wishes to learn about the language as a whole, is "The Oregon Experiment" (Alexander et al., 1975b). This book shows in detail how the language has been utilized in the planning of an American university campus.

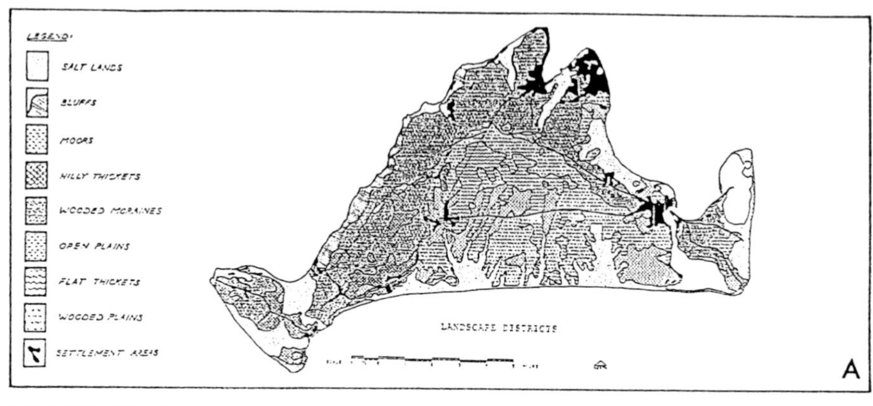

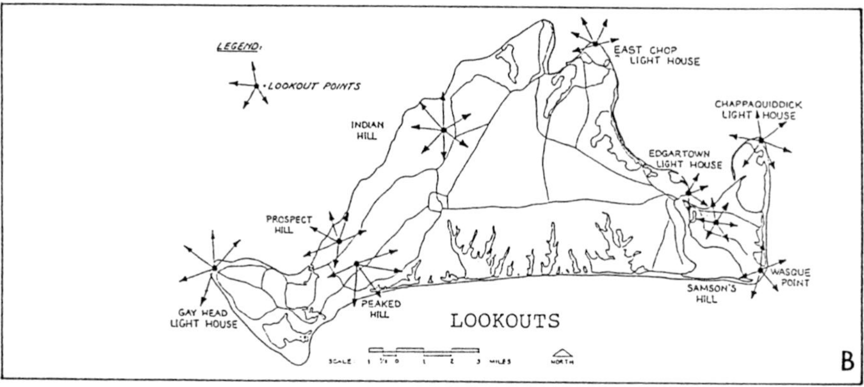

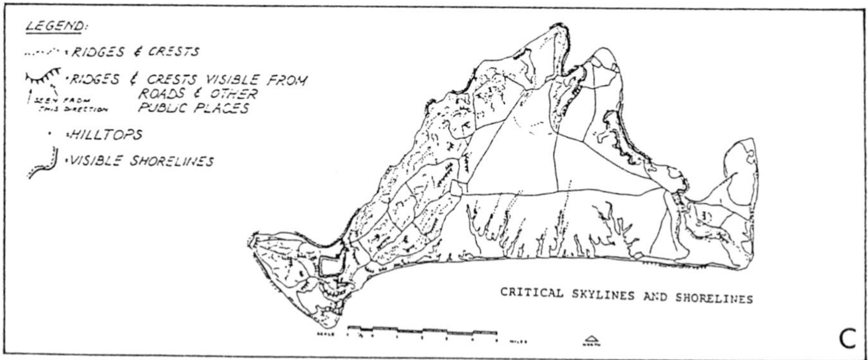

Figure 8.7. Three maps from one of Lynch's own analyses, a visual study of an island (Martha's Vineyard). Map A shows the districts based on landscape type; Map B shows important nodes and paths, here: viewpoints and roads; and Map C shows the predominant edges and landmarks, here: ridges, crests, shorelines and hilltops. In some cases, the individual element may have two or more of the characteristics. - Source: Vineyard Open Land Foundation (1973, pp. 11, 44, 46).

According to Alexander and his collaborators, one of the basic ideas behind the pattern language is that the traditional master plan approach is inadequate for change guidance. Master plans are often too rigid; they alienate the users because the future appears fixed, and decision makers cannot visualize the implications of the plan.

As a whole, the pattern-language approach consists of six overall principles: (1) *organic order*, (2) *participation*, (3) *piecemeal growth*, (4) *patterns*, (5) *diagnosis*, and (6) *co-ordination*. This presentation is limited to two of the principles, those of patterns and diagnosis.

Patterns. While the five other principles basically form the rules for using the pattern language, the patterns form the substance. They are concrete instructions on how to solve specific problems, from planning the overall urban structure of a region to designing windows in individual buildings. But they are more than just technical directions.

A pattern consists of a statement and a detailed description of a concrete planning problem and its relation to other problems. In addition, a pattern description always comprises a form of instruction on how the problem is solved. A couple of examples may give a clearer understanding of what a pattern is.

The *first example* deals with a classical problem in detailed, physical planning: how to locate buildings within a given site so that the building process will improve the totality rather than deteriorating it. This pattern, called *site repair*, is related to a number of other patterns such as 'tree places' (what trees and where to plant them), 'south facing outdoors', and 'positive outdoor space'. The 'solution-part' of the pattern is cited below:

> "On no account place buildings in the places which are most beautiful. In fact, do the opposite. Consider the site and its buildings as a single living eco-system. Leave those areas that are the most precious, beautiful, comfortable, and healthy as they are, and build new structures in those parts of the site which are least pleasant now."
>
> (Alexander et al., 1977, p. 551).

Does this seem commonplace and over-simplified? If so, consider the following two points. First, the principle behind locating buildings and constructions in the countryside - like marinas, camp grounds, etc. - is usually the reverse: every constructor, private or public, searches for the most attractive location on the *present site*. If the most beautiful place is preserved, then the second most beautiful is sought. But it makes a lot more sense to think in terms of the site as whole. If the problem is to locate a new marina in town X, and there are a number of practical options available, why not follow the pattern and select the place which actually needs some change?

The second point to be made about this type of 'evaluation' has to do with the doctrinaire way of stating the solution, which may seem too generalized. The principle of *always* selecting the ugliest place may actually be debatable. However, this is one of the purposes of formulating the patterns: they must be so concrete and simplified that laymen can participate in the decision process. In the Oregon process, for instance, the planning team developed a pattern, 'small parking lots' which said that no parking lot may hold more than 8-12 cars. One may argue: why eight to twelve, why not fifteen to twenty - and that's exactly the idea. The common way to deal with such problems is by wordings such as: there must be a suffient number of parking lots built, each of a suffient size in relation to the area. Who can disagree (and that means who can agree) on such a provision?

The *second example* deals with a planning problem at the regional level: how to locate urban development in relation to farmland. Alexander refers to a specific plan mentioned in McHarg's Design With Nature, namely a plan for urban development on a hilly part of the Philadelphia region. This pattern called agricultural valleys has a form similar to the pattern above: It is simple and explicit and has an encouraging effect on public participation.

> "Preserve all agricultural valleys as farmland and protect this land from any development which would destroy or lock up the unique fertility of the soil. Even when valleys are not cultivated now, protect them for farms and parks and wilds."
>
> (Alexander et al., 1977).

Diagnosis is the other principle which should be touched upon here. The purpose of making a diagnosis is to direct the use of patterns so that all the individual decisions related to the patterns work together. A diagnosis map tells basically what is wrong, and what is working well within the area in question. In the *Oregon Experiment* a diagnosis map showed which areas were functioning well according to the patterns, which ones needed repair, and which were dead. The map also showed where new patterns were required. Together with the development of patterns, diagnosis forms the basic tool for the formulation of a framework for decisions and acts related to environmental change.

Discussion. Although the pattern language has not been applied to Danish countryside planning, I believe that it has great potential as a planning approach. The main argument to support this is a rather evident one: patterns are already used to a wide extent in the planning process, but they are used implicitly. The pattern language offers a method to make the process of development and use of patterns explicit, which makes the planning process more transparent, more democratic, and more efficient in terms of goal achievement and value protection. It is also a more flexible way to deal with a distant and uncertain future, compared to the traditional master plan. Finally, the pattern language offers a solution to a traditional problem in planning: it makes knowledge accumulation possible. Since the patterns are no longer kept in the heads of the planners but are actually printed, discussed and revised, the planners (and others involved) will be much better able to benefit from the experience of others than they are by traditional master planning.

All this does not mean that the pattern language is without weaknesses. To develop and maintain the patterns is a time-consuming process, and users will have to participate actively. This implies that the approach does not apply to centralized planning situations.

8.6 THE COUNTRYSIDE OF TOMORROW

Having described countryside planning, its background and practice, and having shortly reviewed some of the methodological tools available, we shall now try to look ahead. Great alterations are taking place, not only in the Danish countryside, but throughout Europe as well.

"It is now a well-established fact that the rural areas of industrialised countries of Europe are undergoing the most significant and profound changes since the industrialisation process itself began in the 18th and 19th centuries".

(Hall 1988, p. 202).

The words are by David Hall, director of the British Town and Country Planning Association, and the question which will be addressed in this last paragraph is: how do these trends relate to countryside planning in the future? Is it geared to tackle the problems to come, or will the present planning system force us to be "...steering with yesterday's compass"? (O'Riordan, 1988).

I believe a need exists for new planning policies and new planning methods. First, integrated planning policies on the European Community (EC) level will be increasingly needed, because this is where the most important decisions are made, with reference to countryside change. Second, the need to be able to guide countryside change by planning on the local level becomes still more apparent. The alternative to local planning regulations would be more and more uncoordinated administrative decisions, resulting in a mess that nobody can have an interest in.

8.6.1 The European Landscape

The Common Agricultural Policy (CAP) within the EC is one of the key factors in the changing European landscape. It has been so in the past, and it will probably be even more important in the years to come. Not only is the CAP causing more and more political problems related to the EC budget, but it has also been partly responsible for the severe environmental and landscape problems that agricultural regions are currently facing. Thus, solutions that can reduce the cost of the CAP, as well as policies that incorporate environmental and landscape considerations, have been demanded (European Community, 1985; Conrad, 1987; Green, 1986)

Incorporation of environmental and landscape concerns could be done in two distinctly different ways. The first is based on segregation. According to this approach, agricultural policies are limited to agricultural production, i.e., to intervention prices, export refunds, set-aside programs, guarantee thresholds, quotas, and others - all oriented towards the agro-economic system within the EC countries.

Besides these, another set of policies dealing with environmental and landscape protection has been designed. This is on the whole the approach which is being applied currently. In the long run, this policy leads to segregation of the European landscape in regions where agro-business is developing. The North Atlantic countries and the big deltas in the Mediterranean would most probably fall into this category. Other regions, primarily great parts of the Mediterranean countries, would be marginalized and afforested. Some of the policies incorporate planning decisions on the national or the regional levels. Thus, in Denmark some of the areas to become afforested will be identified through the planning authorities on the county level.

The alternative approach is quite different. Here agricultural and environmental/landscape policies are integrated. The reduction of budget problems, and of surplus production which causes much of the costs, is not separated from improvement and/or protection of environmental and landscape values.

How such policies can be designed still remains to been seen, and obviously there are no simple solutions to be found. *Price policies, tax-policies* and *quota systems* should all be designed to cover the production and the protection perspective simultaneously. *Increasing organic farming* and *planning focusing on the common agricultural landscape* (as opposed to the present emphasis on remote, preserved areas appearing more or less as landscape museums) could supplement such policies (Primdahl, 1990).

However, the EC-level is hardly appropriate for the making of any concrete physical plans. This is due to the lack of two important prerequisites in the plan-making process: some degree of political consensus on goals/values and operational knowledge. Within the EC, policy making is based on political compromises and general statistics.

8.6.2 The Local Landscape

No matter how policies that affect landscape are designed on the EC-level, protection and change of the local landscape remains a challenge to countryside planning in Denmark. As mentioned in Section 8.2, countryside planning in Denmark does not include the common local landscape. Local plans are prepared for raw-material extraction, outstanding recreational sites, preserved areas and the like. But no local planning takes place which concerns the rapidly changing agricultural landscape that often provides near and attractive recreational opportunities to the urban population, and often contains important wildlife habitats. Thus, present planning activity occurs to a large extent independently of local needs for guiding change.

What issues local contryside planning ought to cover is a matter of professional, political and ideological controversy. This chapter is mainly built on the view that detailed planning regulation of agricultural production is impossible, as well as undesirable. The market is a much better means of regulation when we talk about how, what, when, and where to produce. However, this does not mean that the market is the best guidance as to how, what, when, and where *not to produce*. In fact, the market only deals with the 'not-problem' in a very narrow sense, that is, from the economic or rentability point of view.

Protecting resource and landscape values may only be done through some sort of planning which guides but does not initiate change. Other, more active local planning issues are dealing with public access (and public access limitations as well), *landscape restoration* for areas which need improvement, and *afforestation* - to mention only some tasks of immediate importance; the regional planning task in these cases would be identification of the landscapes where change is needed or where it is undesirable. The detailed design of the actual changes, as well as the detailed regulations for protection should - ideally - take place on the local level. The types of evaluations developed by McHarg, Lynch and Alexander would be helpful in preparing such local plans.

REFERENCES

Agger, P., Andersen, S.S., Brandt, J., Nielsen, T.S., Pedersen, S., Tvevad, A., Larsen, K.S. and Ettrup, H., 1986*. Morænelandskabets marginaljorder. Marginaljorder og miljøinteresser. (Marginal farmland in Danish moraine landscapes). Ministry of the Environment, Project Investigations. Summary Report No. VIII a. Dept. of Forests and Nature, Copenhagen.

Agger, P. and Brandt, J., 1988. Dynamics of small biotopes in Danish agricultural landscapes. Ecology, 1(4): 227-240.

Alexander, C., Ishikawa, S. and Silverstein, M., 1975. The Timeless Way of Building. Oxford University Press, New York, 567 pp.

Alexander, C., Ishikawa, S. and Silverstein, M., 1977. A Pattern Language. Oxford University Press, New York, 1171 pp.

Alexander, C., Silverstein, M., Angel, S., Ishikawa, S. and Abrams, D., 1975. The Oregon Experiment. Oxford University Press, New York, 190 pp.

Algreen-Ussing, G., 1987*. Perspektiver i råstofforvaltningen. Synspunkter på en dansk naturudnyttelse i de kommende år. (Perspectives in the management of raw materials). Ministry of the Environment, Dept. of Forests and Nature, Copenhagen.

Andersson, S.-I., 1974*. Struktur, Identitet og Skala. (Structure, Identity and Scale.). Dept. of Rural and Landscape Architecture, Academy of Fine Arts, Copenhagen, 8 pp.

Anonymous, 1982*. Landskabsplanlægning 1983-2000, Byarealet. (National Planning 1983-2000, Urban Land). Planstyrelsen, Ministry of the Environment, Skovlunde.

Anonymous, 1985*. Miljøinteresser og marginaljorder. Et debatoplæg. (Environmental interests and marginal land. Discussion paper). Ministry of the Environment, Copenhagen, 89 pp.

Biotopgruppen, 1986*. Udviklingen i agerlandets småbiotoper i Østdanmark. (Development of small biotopes in the East Danish agricultural landscape). Dept. of Geography, Social Analysis and Computer Science: Research Report No. 48. Roskilde Universitetscenter, Roskilde.

Danmarks Statistik, 1986*. Statistisk Årbog. (Statistical Yearbook). 90. ed., Copenhagen, 510 pp.

Egnsplankontoret, 1947*. Skitseforslag til Egnsplan for Storkøbenhavn. (Regional Plan Proposal for Greater Copenhagen). Bureau of Regional Planning, Copenhagen.

European Community, 1985. A Future for Community Agriculture. Commission Guidelines No. 34, Brussels, 27 pp.

Eyben, W.E.v. (ed.), 1978*. Dansk Miljøret, Vol. 1-5. (Environmental Law). Akademisk Forlag, Copenhagen.

Forman, R.T.T. and Godron, M., 1986. Landscape Ecology. J. Wiley, New York, 620 pp.

Green, B., 1986. Agriculture and the environment. A review of major issues in the UK. Land Use Policy, July: 193-204.

Hall, D., 1988. Future of rural areas: a European perspective. Town and Country Planning, 57: 202-204.

Humlum, J., 1966*. Landsplanlægningsproblemer. Med skitse til en landsplanlægning i Danmark. (National planning problems. Proposal for a Danish national plan). Munksgaard, Copenhagen.

Jensen, K.E., 1982*. Landbrugsarealer, landskabeligt og rekreativt. (Agricultural areas, landscape and recreation). Dept. of Rural and Town Planning, RVAU, Copenhagen.

Jensen, F.S. and Koch, N.E., 1986*. Landbrugeren og de marginale jorder - en spørgeskemaundersøgelse. (The agriculturer and the marginal areas: a survey). Summary Report III, Ministry of the Environment, Dept. of Forests and Nature, Copenhagen.

Landsplanudvalget, 1964*. Zoneplankommentarer. (Comments on the 1962 Zoning plan). Secretariat of the National Planning Committee, Copenhagen, 104 pp.

Lynch, K., 1960. The Image of the City. MIT Press, Cambridge, Mass., 194 pp.

Lynch, K., 1976. Managing the Sense of a Region. MIT Press, Cambridge, Mass., 221 pp.

McAllister, D.M., 1980. Evaluation in Environmental Planning. MIT Press, Cambridge, Mass., 308 pp.

McHarg, I., 1969. Design with Nature. Doubleday/Natural History Press, Garden City, 198 pp.

Nielsen, V., Brix, B., Koester, V. and Plougmann, O., 1973*. Naturfredningsloven. Alm. fremstilling og kommentarer. (The Nature Conservation Act, general account and comments). G.E.C. Gads Forlag, Copenhagen, 600 pp.

Olsen I.A. and Stahlschmidt, P., 1975*. Egnethedsanalyse for Skovbo Kommune. (Landscape assessment in Skovbo). Landskab, 6: 111-117.

O'Riordan, T. and Turner, R.K. (eds.), 1983. An Annotated Reader in Environmental Planning and Management. Urban and Regional Planning Series, vol. 30. Pergamon Press, Oxford, 459 pp.

O'Riordan, T., 1988. Steering change with yesterday's compass. Town and Country Planning, 57: 209-211.

Primdahl, J., 1986*. Friluftsliv mellem land og by. (Outdoor recreation between the country and the city). Centring, 7: 220-231.

Primdahl, J., 1987*. Det åbne lands planlægning - og virkelighed. (Countryside planning - and reality). In: Bramsnæs et.al. (eds.): Sådan ligger landet. Danish Town Planning Laboratory, Copenhagen: 46-57.

Primdahl, J., 1990. Heterogeneity in agriculture and landscape. From segregation to integration. Urban and Landscape Planning, 18: 221-228.

Svensson, O. (ed.), 1981. Dansk Byplanguide/Danish Town Planning Guide. (In Danish and English). The National Agency for Physical Planning and the Danish Town Planning Institute, Copenhagen, 116 pp.

Thomsen, R., 1982*. Administration af vandindvindingen. (The administration of water catchment). Ugeskr. f. Jordbr., 14: 294-298.

Vineyard Open Land Foundation, 1973. Looking at the Vineyard. W.Tisbury, Mass., 75 pp.

ACKNOWLEDGMENT

I wish to thank Sally Kratz Richman and Finn Kjærsdam for critical comments and useful suggestions.

9 ENVIRONMENTAL ECONOMICS

SØREN KJELDSEN-KRAGH

9.1 THE DIFFERENT AREAS OF ENVIRONMENTAL ECONOMICS

Environmental economics deals with a broad spectrum of problems. Three main problems present themselves in environmental economics, namely: pollution problems, problems concerning the management of natural areas, and problems concerning prosperity.

Pollution economics includes economic problems with respect to the prevention as well as the control of pollution. Natural-area economics deals with the economic considerations which must be taken into account when dealing with the conservation or expansion of our natural areas. What are the advantages of natural areas, how are these advantages assessed, and what are the expenses connected therewith? Problems concerning prosperity deal, among other things, with food quality, including the formulation of a nutrition policy. How do we ensure that our food is 'clean' and 'healthy', does not cause illness and meets public nutritive standards? Another problem is the survival of the rural districts. Can they survive, and if so - how can this be ensured?

All these areas have one thing in common: they do not appear in our national economic. This is due to the fact that the national accounts only deal with economic values and not, for instance, esthetic values, recreational values, or values connected with greater prosperity. The environmental area is characterized by not having a price mechanism in this field. Hence, the price mechanism cannot be applied to considerations as to what actions should be taken and the form of the relevant measures but rather the issue must be solved by so-called cost-benefit analyses, through which it is attempted to assess both advantages and expenses in terms of money. Pollution economics deals specifically with the assessment of the consequences of a number of 'negative effects', whereas natural-area economics deals specifically with the value assessment of a number of 'positive effects'.

In the following, these considerations will mainly concentrate on pollution economics. Within the other areas, the problems are so closely connected that most deliberations on pollution economics also can be applied to them.

9.2 WHAT DOES ECONOMIC THEORY TELL US?

It is not the aim of this chapter to summarize the very extensive economic literature on environmental problems. For a survey of these issues, the reader is referred to general works, such as Førsund and Strøm (1988), Fisher (1981), Tietenberg (1989), or Hahn (1989).

Economists' views of environmental problems are based on the work of A.C. Pigou (1946). Expressed in modern terms, Pigou's central thesis was that pollution problems arise because enterprises' private costs, which form the basis for their actions and investments, do not correspond to the social costs. If an enterprise pollutes, the social cost will exceed the private cost by the cost incurred in preventing the pollution. It follows that a socially efficient production structure cannot be obtained[1]. A solution to this problem is to work out the marginal social economic costs and the marginal private costs and then levy taxes on the enterprises corresponding to the differences between them.

This main idea has been carried on in work which introduces pollution problems into a general economic equilibrium model, see e.g., Mäler (1974). As pollution problems are general and as the control of these problems influences the entire economy, it has been thought obvious to proceed from more partial models to general models. The model used by Mäler is one of the Arrow-Debreu type which is a decentralized model with a price mechanism in markets with complete competition. We have a production function for the enterprise and a utility function for the household and, furthermore, we have full knowledge of the consequences of the pollution and the cost connected with the control of this pollution. If we introduce some more or less plausible assumptions concerning the appearance of the production and utility functions, it can be concluded that by using a set of taxes on goods and services the pollution problems can be solved. We obtain a solution in the sense that we can achieve a state of equilibrium which at the same time is a socially efficient state.

Thus, the conclusion is that it is possible to solve pollution problems through a system of levying taxes on enterprises. If we assume that interpersonal utility comparisons can be made, or that the income and capital distribution is unchanged, then economic theory readily infers that it is possible to find an optimal level of pollution.

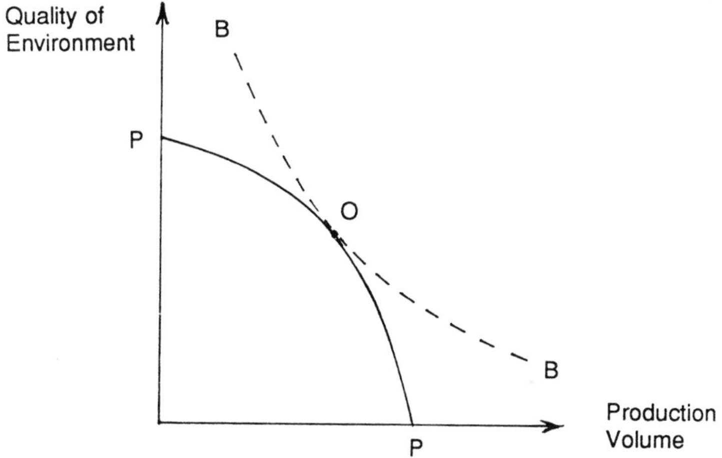

Figure 9.1. The scale of the production and the quality of the environment plotted against each other.

---

[1]The production structure is *efficient* if the maximal consumption of goods and services is attained by means of a given set of production factors.

In the following these two questions will be elucidated: Is it possible to find an optimal level of pollution? Is the application of a tax system the best method in environmental policies?

It is no longer assumed that we always have full knowledge of the economic consequences of pollution or full knowledge of the costs connected with pollution control.

9.3 IS IT POSSIBLE TO FIND THE OPTIMAL LEVEL OF POLLUTION?

The resources which are applied in pollution control could alternatively be applied to the production of goods and services. Our welfare depends both on the amount of goods and services and on the quality of our environment. It is therefore relevant to ask if it is possible to find an optimal level of pollution.

In the following we will analyze the situation first from a total perspective and then from the perspective of the individual enterprise.

9.3.1 Seen from a total perspective

In Fig. 9.1 the scale of the production and the quality of the environment are plotted against each other.

The curve PP is a production possibility boundary in the sense that the curve illustrates the production correlations between the attainable environmental quality and the attainable production scale. The curve BB shows those combinations of environment and production which give the public the same welfare.

If we know the relation between the possibilities of combining different production scopes with different environmental qualities (the curve PP), and if we know the public preference structure concerning the choice between the scale and composition of production, on the one hand, and the environmental quality, on the other (the curve BB), it is easy to find the optimal combination between production and environment. The best possible welfare is obtained at the point O, where the two curves are tangential.

In the above, the connection between production and environment is looked at from a total-society perspective. By making a simple optimization based on a known production possibility boundary and a known societal indifference curve we have, however, eliminated the most central questions.

1) Connections between Production and Environment

In the short run it is fair to consider production and environmental quality as replaceable goods.

In the longer run, such a simple consideration is no longer valid. This can be illustrated by several examples.

It is discussed in earnest whether air pollution can cause climatic changes, even though no agreement has been reached as to what these changes will be. Nordhaus (1982) has linked climatic models with economic models. He finds that a doubling of the amount of carbon dioxide in the atmosphere can have noticeable consequences for the global national product.

Nordhaus estimates the consequences to be between a drop of 12 per cent and an increase of 5 per cent in the world's national product, depending on the consequences of pollution on the weather.

The fact that a better environment means better places of work and a better quality of our recreational time can, of course, also influence the productivity and creativity in production.

Efforts to improve the environment can provide an individual country with knowledge of the development of environmental protection systems, pollution preventive measures and more environmentally sound production methods which can be advantageous for both employment and foreign exchange conditions. These arguments are valid under conditions with unemployment and balance of payments problems.

There is also a positive connection the other way around. The larger the growth in production, the sooner the new environmentally acceptable machines and production processes will be used in trade and industry. This may cause less pollution.

2) Environmental Quality Is a Multidimensional Quantity

By talking about a connection between production and environmental quality, we implicitly presuppose that environmental quality is a clear and well-defined quantity. That is not the case, however. The environment is a quantity composed of numerous dimensions which it is difficult - not to say impossible - to balance. We have pollution of soil, water, and air. We have working environments, we have esthetic values etc.

Within each of these areas it does not suffice only to have technical statements: that the air has a sulphur-dioxide content of n per cent, or that the noise level is m decibels, or that the nitrate content in the ground soil is at a given level. We have to determine the pathogenic and growth-inhibiting consequences. Here we reach a large number of scientific questions which are far from clarified. It can often be agreed that a certain degree of pollution has some consequences, but how great are the consequences? This is the point at which disagreements occur.

3) Public Preference Structure

The individual countries' priorities regarding production and environment depend on the material standard of living and the character of the environment in an individual country. The fact that rich countries attach a greater importance to the environment than poorer countries - even within a relatively homogenous area such as the European Community - may cause problems when these countries have to cooperate on issues which can only be resolved jointly.

Within an individual country, the weighing up of production against the environment will be individual. Apart from personal preferences, the individual person's income and capital situation will be decisive. Furthermore, the various sections of the population will benefit in different degrees from the pollution-preventive measures and will suffer in different degrees from the consequences on production and employment.

The question of whether it is fair to work with social indifference curves can certainly not be answered in the affirmative. Even if it could, there still remains the question of attaining knowledge of the population's preferences.

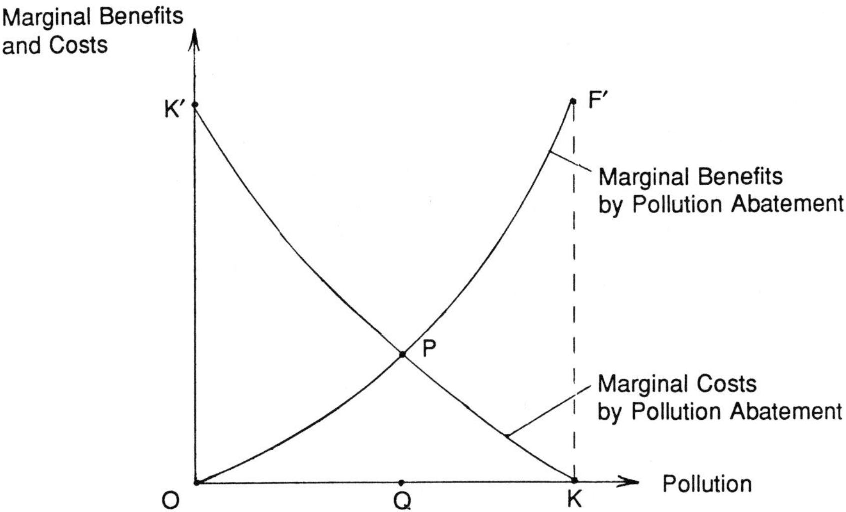

Figure 9.2. Marginal costs and pollution. Note that the curves may have other shapes, and they do not necessarily have to start at O nor stop at K on the horizontal axis.

9.3.2 From the Perspective of the Individual Enterprise

At the macroeconomic level it is hence not possible to attain the fixing of an optimal level of pollution. The question is whether the problem can be solved by starting with the pollution which takes place in connection with an individual enterprise.

Assume that we could make a cost-benefit analysis for every pollution economic problem, for example a case of discharge of waste water from an enterprise. Such an analysis is shown in Fig. 9.2.

OK is the total extent of the pollution. Every time the pollution is reduced by one unit, the enterprise will incur costs in compliance with the curve KK′. Should the enterprise not pollute at all, the cost would be the area KOK′.

The economic loss at the last pollution unit is KF′. The total loss at the pollution level OK is thus the area KOF′.

By moving successively from K to the left, more and more rigorous pollution preventive measures are taken which will cause an increase in cost to the enterprise. At the same time, the total advantages increase as the consequences of the pollution are eliminated (the marginal costs are diminishing, however).

At Q we reach an optimal point as the last amount of money of the cost of pollution prevention corresponds to the last attained profit gained by limiting the consequences of the pollution.

The cost of limiting the pollution from OK to OQ is KQP (the area below the marginal cost curve) and the advantages by limiting the pollution are KQPF′ (the area below the marginal advantage curve by pollution prevention). The net advantage is therefore the difference between KQPF′ and KQP, that is, KPF′.

If the curves in Fig. 9.2 were known for all the pollution-causing activities and if it could be assumed that the curves for the individual enterprises were independent from each other, we would have the solution to what would be the optimal level of pollution in society and at the same time we could determine how high the cost of pollution prevention ought to be.

However, the curves for the individual enterprises are often interdependent. A number of more or less partial analyses cannot solve the problem. Furthermore, in practice it is often impossible to determine especially the curve for marginal advantages in particular. Not only do we have to know the scientific consequences of increased pollution; we also have to know the economically relevant damaging effects (on people, nature, and objects), and finally we have to determine the price of these damages and nuisances.[2]

9.3.3 Conclusion

Hence, we must conclude that in practice it is usually not possible to find the optimal level of pollution. This is true whether the problems are seen from a total perspective or from the perspective of an enterprise.

Even though it is not usually possible to find the optimal level of pollution, it is still necessary to plan a number of environmental measures as we wish to some extent or other to stop the nuisances which are a consequence of the deterioration of the environment. When assessing the extent and type of these measures, we must consider, on the one hand, the type and extent of the nuisance and on the other, the cost of the protective measures.[3]

The problem can be viewed in two ways. If we have determined how much we will spend on pollution prevention efforts, the purpose must be to carry out the most effective pollution effort with the aid of the given instruments. On the contrary, if we have set ourselves specific aims, the purpose must be to solve the tasks as inexpensively as possible.

9.4 MEANS OF CONTROL IN POLLUTION PREVENTION

A reduction of pollution can be achieved either through administrative or through economic means of control. The various means of control will only be mentioned briefly here.

The administrative means of control can be divided into three categories: *Physical planning and localization, public waste-water purification and public waste treatment, and requirements presented to enterprises*. Through the localization policy it is possible to concentrate

[2]Uncertainty may be introduced in Figure 9.2 by placing a band around each curve. With respect to the marginal benefits in particular, there is reason to believe that the width of the band is quite large. The wider the band, the more uncertain the analysis, and the less instruction we get.

[3]The Danish Environmental Protection Act, Section 1, Subsection 3 states: The scope and nature of anti-pollution measures shall consider, on the one hand, the character of the physical environment and effects of pollution thereon, and on the other, the benefit derived by society as a result of the activities mentioned in Section 2 of this Act, and the costs of anti-pollution measures.

some of the environmental problems geographically. Collective purification and waste treatment installations which enterprises are compelled to use are usually more cost-effective, due to economies of scale, than individual installations at the individual enterprises. Finally, various requirements may be made on the individual enterprise: for instance, a system of approvals or orders and injunctions (fixed terms for discharge, technology, etc.) or a system of standards which have to be followed (discharge standards, product standards).

The economic means of control may consist of a tax system and/or a grant system. Taxes may be imposed on discharges as a motivation for the enterprises to purify or treat the waste. Taxes may be imposed on raw materials and semi-products, machinery, and finished goods in order to restrict the use of certain means of production and of certain finished goods.

Likewise, the aim of the grants may vary: for instance direct state grants for environmental investments, tax incentives in the shape of especially favourable rules for write-off, environmental investments or cheap government loans.

The administrative means of control act as quantitative and qualitative restrictions on the enterprises. The economic means of control act as an incentive for the enterprises to act in accordance with the best interests of society.

If we look at Fig. 9.2, the administrative means of control can be regarded as a control on the amount of pollution, while the economic means of control involve price regulation. If the curves in Fig. 9.2 are known, it would be fair to assume that quantity and price control produce the same result. Either administrative directives reducing the pollution to OQ should be introduced or a tax per pollution unit corresponding to QP should be imposed[4].

9.5 DEFINITION OF THE OBJECTIVE

Whether we choose administrative or economic means of control, we have to consider the objective of the interventions and the future consequences thereof.

9.5.1 What are the Criteria for the Scope of the Order or the Size of the Tax?

Should we aim at a tax (order) which ensures that the individual producers' marginal costs of controlling the discharge are identical?

Should we aim at a tax (order) which is differentiated according to how much damage is caused to nature? The same discharge may easily have different effects on the environment in different cases (the recipient conditions are different).

Should our aim be to ensure that the quality of the environment is the same in different places? The idea is that the risk of causing a nuisance or disease as a consequence of pollution should be the same regardless of where the person lives. This means that the environmental requirements should be even more stringent in densely populated areas where the level of pollution frequently is higher, e.g., pollution from car exhaust gasses or the discharge of sulphur from oil-burners.

---

[4]If we introduce uncertainty by placing a band around the curves, quantity and price control will only accidentally produce the same result.

If the environmental quality is to be the same in different places, this leads to the conclusion that the requirements must be different regionally. This can obviously influence the geographical pattern of industry and settlement.

9.5.2 What Consideration Should be Given to Foreign Environmental Requirements?

If our domestic requirements are higher than the requirements abroad, it may reduce our competitiveness. Conversely, an individual country may impose less stringent environmental requirements to attract investment from abroad. If we wish to place the producers in the various countries on an equal footing, the requirements imposed on the enterprises' pollution-restricting activities must be identical in the various countries.

However, if we view the quality of the environment from the consumers' point of view on an equal level with other goods, many things point to the advantage of different requirements with respect to additional discharges according to the amount of pollution in the various countries. This means that countries where the quality of the environment is poorer will be especially careful regarding further pollution. The demands on the enterprises in the individual countries will thus vary according to the state of the environment in the individual country. The environmental requirements will also vary with the size of real income. Poorer countries will place less importance on the environment than the richer countries.

The consumers' viewpoint should have a priority over the producers' viewpoint. This means that international cooperation must ensure that the differences in environmental requirements are solely dictated by differences in the quality of the environment in the different countries, at the same time assuming that the different countries' inhabitants' trade off between environmental quality and production is identical. If the differences in the requirements on the enterprises are larger or smaller than the differences in environmental quality, which can be ascertained, it is a matter of inexpedient competition distortion.[5]

9.5.3 To What Extent Should We Differentiate Between Already Existing and New Enterprises?

Generally, there will be a tendency to impose lower taxes and milder orders on already established installations. How large can these differences be without distorting the competitiveness? Part of the usual cost of construction for new projected enterprises will contain costs which will help restrict damage to the environment. These costs are not usually considered as environmental investments.

In practice, it has been common to subsidize environmental investments undertaken by already existing enterprises. This is often very inefficient.

Giving state grants to environmental investments is at variance with the 'polluter pays' principle. When grants are given anyway, it is from a point of view of reason.

Already established enterprises will incur, at short notice, a number of additional costs

---

[5]However, an international coordination of pollution control is necessary simply because pollution does not recognize national borders. As a large part of, say, the Danish air pollution and the pollution of Danish waters originate from other countries, a strong Danish effort to control pollution will be more or less worthless for Denmark if other countries do not adopt regulatory measures.

which up till then they have not had to consider. Grants are given to alleviate the economic consequences. The grants, which can be shaped individually following application, can take into consideration the individual enterprise's special conditions. The grants thereby become selective and in principle consider factors other than the purely environmental. Of course, the arrangement may also be of a more general nature.

For older enterprises in particular, environmental investments can be a considerable strain compared to newer enterprises, not to mention those enterprises that are only established after the introduction of environmental requirements. As a principle, all enterprises can be required to live up to the same standards regardless of age, and the grant can then be differentiated according to age so that the enterprises established or investments made subsequent to the introduction of the environmental requirement receive no or very small grants.

Additionally, Danish enterprises may be in an inferior position concerning international competition if environmental grants are given abroad but not in Denmark.

Summing up the above, it can be said that economically it would be better for society if different standards were applied to older enterprises, new enterprises and not yet established enterprises instead of giving differentiated grants which especially consider older enterprises, as it is possible to attain a less expensive solution to the pollution problem through differentiated standards (see further below, Section 9.6, a)[6].

It is difficult to make a general statement regarding how large the differences in the standards for already existing and new enterprises should be. If there is little difference, newly established enterprises which are on a very large scale compared to old enterprises may end up polluting more in absolute terms than the older enterprises.

9.6 ADVANTAGES OF TAX INSTRUMENTS

If the marginal cost curve of pollution control is known (see Fig. 9.2) it could be assumed that administrative control and economic control would produce the same result. This is not the case, however. If the choice lies between administrative control and economic control, there are significant factors that speak for economic control. The advantages of these are as follows:

(a) Pollution restriction is made with the least cost to society, when the conditions vary from enterprise to enterprise. This is illustrated in Fig. 9.3, where we have two enterprises with

[6]A combination of taxes or administrative directives, on the one hand, and grants for environmental investments, on the other, may moreover result in overinvestment in environmental installations. In a system of taxes and grants for environmental investments there is clearly a risk of overinvesting unless these taxes and environmental grants are carefully adjusted. If this is not the case, it is relevant to ask whether it would be sufficient solely to have differentiated standards or a differentiated tax system. If there are administrative directives which are expected to remain fixed in the future, grants for environmental investments ought not to result in overinvestment in environmental protection. If, on the other hand, the rules and regulations are expected to be tightened at a future date, a temporary overinvestment is plausible if the purifying capacity is to a large extent connected with the choice of environmental investment.

different marginal cost curves. By imposing a tax of O_1P on emitted pollution per unit, enterprise 1 will pollute O_1Q_1 while enterprise 2 will pollute O_2Q_2. The total amount of pollution $O_1Q_1 + O_2Q_2$ could be attained by administratively ordering the enterprises to limit their pollution O_1K_1 and O_2K_2 by the same per cent.

There will be the same amount of pollution in the two cases but the cost will be larger in the latter case using administrative orders.

(b) The taxes make it advantageous for the enterprises to make running adjustments towards more environmentally sound techniques and thus save on Government imposed taxes.

(c) Decisions on the use of techniques, raw materials and semi-products will be made by the individual enterprise as each enterprise ultimately has the best knowledge of its own state of affairs and each enterprise will therefore be anxious to reduce its costs as much as possible.

Even though it is clear that there are many benefits to price regulation, quantity control through administrative orders is the dominant method used in practice.

9.7 PROBLEMS CONNECTED WITH TAX INSTRUMENTS

Tax control is not used to any large extent as there are a number of problems connected to this means of control.

(a) If we wish to secure a given level of pollution through economic means of control, it is necessary to know the marginal cost curves regarding pollution control.

Even if we know the marginal cost curve, however, it is not possible - through one uniform tax rate - to attain a given pollution control effort from the enterprises as we also have to consider the time dimension. If we wish to restrict the pollution within a certain period, we can choose a system of two tax rates. One rate before making the environmental investment and another after the investment has been made.

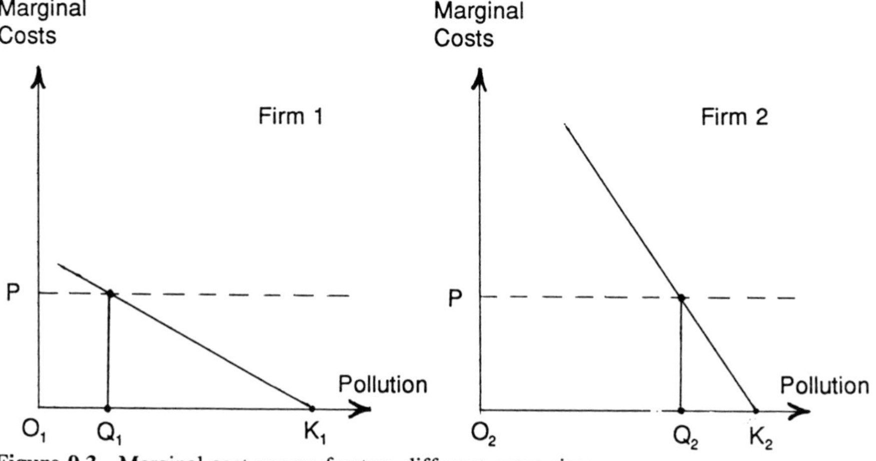

Figure 9.3. Marginal cost curves for two different enterprises.

If we want to avoid a differentiated tax system, we might instead order the enterprises to reduce their pollution within a certain time-limit and at the same time impose a previously published tax on pollution from the enterprise emitted after the lapse of the time-limit, cf. Ricketts and Webb (1978).

(b) If we do not know the marginal cost curve, it is difficult to apply economic means of control. When imposing a tax it is uncertain which pollution control effort will be attained.

It takes an extensive effort to work out the marginal cost curve for the representative enterprise, especially if the cost conditions vary considerably from enterprise to enterprise. Moreover, such calculations will, under any circumstances, be very time consuming and hence delay the efforts to fight pollution.

It has been stated that even if the marginal cost curve is not known, we can vary the tax rate as a means of judging which consequences it will have on pollution.

The difficulty in this is that the enterprises will probably be reluctant to make environmental investments as long as the level of the taxes is not fixed. The nature and extent of the environmental investment will, in most cases, depend on the level of the taxes. The higher the requirements, the larger and more comprehensive the environmental installations will be. If the enterprise has invested in an installation it will often be difficult in practice to alter the existing installation in order to adhere to more stringent environmental requirements.

As long as the taxes have not settled at their final level, the enterprises will decline to make any environmental investments at all. The result of this is that the public authority does not receive the information concerning the tax level necessary to produce the desired limitation of the pollution.

If the enterprise invests without knowing the final tax level, there is a large risk that the investment will not be optimal. This will strain the enterprise until it is reasonable to renew the installations.[7]

Thus we can conclude that applying a tax system may incur very large 'information costs', cf. Walker and Storey (1977).

(c) If we know the marginal cost curve for the representative enterprise, there is a basis for applying one tax rate if the aim is a uniform limitation of the pollution.

If the recipient conditions and the population concentrations vary from area to area, it might be necessary to reduce the pollution to different degrees to attain the same environmental quality.

This logically leads to a zoning of a country with different taxes in the different zones. In order to make such a zoning, we have to have models showing how the pollution is distributed geographically.

It is obvious that the more differentiated the environmental conditions are from place to place, the more divisions must be made. If we get to a point where one or very few

---

[7]We can also conclude from these considerations that it is to be recommended that the public authorities only rarely alter the level of the taxes or the administrative orders. It is furthermore recommendable that the enterprises - other things being equal - invest in technology which is adaptable to increased environmental requirements.

enterprises form a zone, it might be administratively advantageous to apply administrative orders instead of a highly differentiated tax system.

(d) If there are economies of scale at collective purification plants, which have been set up, for instance, in connection with the establishment of industrial areas (physical planning), it would not be rational to promote private purification plants through taxes. In this case it would be correct to order the enterprises, etc., to be connected to the collective plant. Whether a tax is imposed at the same time is a purely financial question unless the tax is aimed at promoting a 'pre-cleaning process' at the enterprise.

(e) If several dangerous substances are contained in the discharge, a tax on 'waste water' will not solve the problems if the composition of dangerous substances varies to a high extent from discharge to discharge. If taxes are to be imposed in cases like this, they must be differentiated according to the quality of the waste water.

(f) Naturally, it is not reasonable to apply a tax system if the waste is so dangerous that it should be either destroyed or processed. In that case, administrative regulations would be the obvious means of control.

(g) When choosing means of control, the administrative problems and costs should be taken into consideration.

Generally, it can be said that control through directives is easier to administer than control through taxes. If, for instance, there are only few enterprises polluting within the area in question and the enterprises are spread out geographically, it would be natural to regulate through orders instead of taxes.

Even though there are many polluters, it can be practical to apply administrative orders if in practice there is only one way of reducing the pollution. Examples are the sulphur content in oil and the lead content in petrol. It makes more sense to impose limitations on the maximum sulphur content in oil and lead content in petrol than to impose taxes on the consumers' and producers' emission of sulphurous smoke or leaded exhaust gases.

9.8 CONCLUSION ON ADMINISTRATIVE VERSUS ECONOMIC INSTRUMENTS

To the extent that no administrative or other considerations speak against economic control, this should be preferred to administrative control.

In practice, there will often be a large number of considerations, as mentioned above, which speak for administrative control. Therefore, this means of control is almost always chosen.

However, there are two considerations which cause special concern in the application of administrative orders.

First, where the cost conditions vary in the various enterprises, administrative orders will result in a considerably more expensive solution to the pollution problems than when applying a tax system. Surveys from other countries all point to administrative orders resulting in much more expensive solutions than taxes.

A solution to this problem would be to introduce a system of negotiable pollution rights. Every enterprise will be allowed to emit pollution of a certain type and scope corresponding to the average norm. Those enterprises that have the possibility of reducing their pollution cheaply will then have an economic incentive to do so, provided that the difference between the permissible and the actual emission can be sold to enterprises which would incur very large expenses in order to reduce their emission to the level required. It would be a condition for such a system to work that the conditions of the enterprises' pollution are very uniform, both regarding the nature of the pollution and the recipient conditions.

The other concern regarding administrative control is that it may give rise to an extensive system of advance approvals. Prior to implementing a new production process or introducing a new product, it is required that the production methods and products are approved. Advance approvals of production methods are inherent in the wish for technological evaluation.

It does not take much imagination to envisage what this might mean for Danish trade and industry in the shape of lack of flexibility and development opportunities, especially as such advance approvals will, in practice, take a long time to administer. Not only do they require a number of studies and investigations but also a political weighing up of risks and counter-considerations.

This can easily mean that the development opportunities for innovative and dynamic enterprises will be impeded, as it is well known that many products go through different phases: an introductory phase, a growth phase, and a stagnation phase. The competitiveness depends on the ability of the enterprise to introduce a new product quickly. The adaptability of the enterprises regarding new products and processes is impeded. Advance approvals may prove especially hampering for small and medium-size enterprises like the Danish which are competitive precisely by being adaptable. However, if the administration is ordered to make decisions very quickly, obviously the inconveniences may be somewhat reduced.

If the different countries apply uniform rules for approvals which apply to both domestic and foreign products and if the time-limits on obtaining approvals are the same everywhere, the risk of distortion of competition will be reduced.

9.9 NOT ALL ENVIRONMENTAL PROBLEMS CAN BE SOLVED AT ONCE

There is hardly any doubt that we will have to focus on environmental problems in the future. Partly because some problems will increase and partly because the interest in the environment in general will increase.

As it is not possible to solve all environmental problems at once, it is important to fix an order of priority for the tasks on the national level.

As the resources set aside for the protection of the environment increase, it will become necessary to make an order of priority. If this is neglected, there is a large risk that the resources applied to environmental protection will not be used effectively.

The question is therefore whether we have the instruments which indicate the areas that should receive special attention. Where is the greatest need for analyses of pollution problems? In what area is there a special need - based on the knowledge we have today - for us to intervene?

Such an instrument could be found by piecing together all the information we have today in a economic-ecological model. Such a model should show, firstly, how physical production influences the environment (pollution), secondly, how there are flows from the ecological system to the economic system (raw material deliveries), thirdly, the physical flows within the economic system (input-output relations), and fourthly, the flows within the environment (purely ecological relations).

The basis of such a model exists today in the shape of an economic input-output model. The task is then to link the ecological system to this model, cf. Kneese et al. (1970).

The indication of the priorities of different tasks is, however, only a provisional guideline. The model shows physical flows. Prices and costs are not considered.

The purpose of the model is to obtain a total view of the pollution problems in order to point out areas in which further research and further measures are necessary.

The Utopian aim that we can strive for is to supplement the physical flows in the economic-ecological system with a flow chart of the corresponding prices. These prices will, in the ecological part of the system, be based on the economic consequences of the pollution, the economic consequences of the draining of natural resources, and the economic costs of the purification measures. As there are not markets for all these products, we cannot obtain a market price. But we have to work with shadow prices which to a certain extent are politically determined.

On the basis of the economic-ecological model, we can find the areas where we ought to start by making further analyses of the cost-benefit type. In connection with task priorities, we must pay special attention to the pollution that causes irreversible damage to society, that is, damage which cannot be corrected and restored.

If a source of pollution does irreversible damage to the environment, we should - all other things being equal - intervene as soon as possible. On the contrary, if natural areas are being destroyed by the construction of a new road, the planning of the road should be delayed as long as possible in order to have enough time to clarify the problems concerning the value of the natural areas in question.

9.10 HOW TO ENSURE A FAIR ANALYSIS OF THE INDIVIDUAL ENVIRONMENTAL PROBLEM?

As shown above, cost-benefit analyses can provide us with an instrument which can ensure rational decisions.

There are, however, two main problems in connection with the application of the cost-benefit method. Firstly, there is the problem of our lack of knowledge of the curves which form part of the cost-benefit analysis. This problem has already been touched upon. Secondly, cost-benefit analyses tend to be partial analyses. This means that it can be difficult to see the real problems.

9.10.1 Lack of Knowledge of the Curves

A cost-benefit analysis requires knowledge both of the marginal cost curve and the marginal benefit curve.[8] Let us look closer and more systematically at the problems that arise in this connection.

1⁰. The Marginal Cost Curve

Knowledge of the relevant cost curve requires a number of investigations which are not without obstacles.

Firstly, we have to be aware that pollution-restrictive measures can either consist of preventive measures or of subsequent treatment measures. In practice, there are several areas in which to apply preventive measures and in many cases there will also be several ways to apply subsequent treatment measures. Prevention of pollution may, for instance, be by recycling waste, transforming waste into harmless products, use of new machinery, use of new production technology, or use of other raw materials than before. The costs of all these options must be calculated in order to find the cost curve with the lowest level.

Secondly, the marginal cost curve may vary greatly from enterprise to enterprise within the same industry. It is often very expensive to install treatment plants in older enterprises, while the expenses are often considerably lower in newer enterprises. If we use taxes as a means of control, it is sufficient to know the marginal cost curve for the representative enterprise. If we use administrative orders, it may be valuable to know the marginal cost curves for the different types of enterprise. In both cases, the analyses become more difficult to make, the more the industrial structures vary.

2⁰. The Marginal Benefit Curve

The problem of working out the marginal benefit curve is almost always larger than the problem of working out the marginal cost curve, as there are five types of problems which arise. Let us consider emission of polluting substances. Firstly, we have to know the extent of the emission. Secondly, we have to consider the consequences of the emission on the environment. The recipient conditions may vary greatly from place to place and therefore a given pollution may be more or less damaging according to the state of the environment to begin with.

Thirdly, we have to know which chemical, biological, and climatic processes take place following this emission. Fourthly, we must clarify the physical and medical consequences of the emission. Fifthly and finally, we have to assess these physical and medical consequences. In a large number of cases, this may lead to, among other things, situations in which we may have to consider the value of a human life.

9.10.2 What Can Be Done to Overcome the Problems?

1⁰. Not Everything Can Be Settled Quantitatively

It is easier to make a decision when all aspects of a case can be quantified in money. Therefore, there is pressure on public officials and other experts to quantify as much as possible. This quantification, in areas which are difficult to quantify, often involves political decisions.

In order to avoid the pressure to quantify in a way which is sometimes more harmful than

---

[8]A cost-effectiveness analysis requires knowledge of the marginal cost curves for the different procedures through which the problems may be solved.

helpful, we could try to inform the politicians of these difficulties. In conclusion we could point to the important conditions which are not quantified and which apart from the quantified aspects ought to form part of the total decision.

We could - in order to satisfy the wishes of the politicians and mass media for concrete figures - make more calculations giving the aspects that are very hard to quantify different values.

2⁰. Introducing Uncertainty

We can introduce uncertainty concerning the areas which are difficult to quantify by - as mentioned above - fixing several alternative values.

Because of our lack of knowledge, there will also be an uncertainty in the aspects which in principle can be quantified. This uncertainty can be introduced into the analysis by placing a band around the marginal-cost and marginal-benefit curves in Fig. 9.2 above, and thereby determining an area within which it is relevant to discuss the matter.

3⁰. Often We Should Start with Cost-Effectiveness Analyses

Of course, the uncertainty can be so great and hence the bands around the curves in Fig. 9.2 so wide that the analysis becomes rather meaningless. Normally, the uncertainty around the marginal benefit curve will be considerably greater than that around the marginal cost curve. This is because the problems of value assessment and the uncertainty due to lack of or limited knowledge are especially connected with the marginal benefit curve.

If the uncertainty - especially regarding the marginal-benefit curve - is great, it is not possible to make a reasonable cost-benefit analysis. In that case, we must limit the work to a cost-effectiveness analysis.

Cost-effectiveness analyses are easier to approach than the cost-benefit analyses as the former is contained in the latter. Generally, it can therefore be said that it is a good idea to start with the cost-effectiveness analysis and then later to see how far it is possible to carry out the cost-benefit analysis.

4⁰. Attempts at Determining Values Reasonably

As already mentioned above, the determination of values is often very problematic when there is no market with prices. Attempts can be made to reach a better basis for the decisions through separate analyses. Some examples are mentioned in the following.

How do people value the benefits of a good environment, e.g., fresh air or scenic surroundings? It has been said that the value of these benefits can be assessed by people's willingness to pay for them. This requires a number of interviews of a representative section of the population. There are problems in such a procedure. Are people capable of grasping the problem? Is there a tendency when stating the amount we are willing to pay to overestimate or underestimate the real willingness to pay?

How much nuisance does the noise from one of the main thoroughfares into Copenhagen cause? We could try to compare the prices of houses on the road to the prices of similar houses elsewhere. The difference in price should then be the price of the nuisance caused by the noise. In such an analysis it is essential that everything else is equal, that is, that the two sets of houses are equal in every way apart from the noise problem.

In the USA, the degree of pollution may vary from city to city. To illustrate people's assessment of this, we could make an analysis of the differences in wages for the same work in different cities. If all other things are equal and if there is full mobility in the labour market, then the higher wages in the most polluted cities should be a kind of compensation for the nuisance caused by the increased pollution.

What is the future of small communities? What is the value of the advantage that many people still think is connected with living in so-called 'communities'. Farming still plays a major part in small communities. So the difference in income between farming and urban occupations may be an expression of this estimation of value. The analysis should be extended in this case as the all-other-things-equal-condition is not fulfilled. That people are willing to accept lower wages in agriculture may be due to the advantage connected with being your own employer.

As we have seen, there are major problems in determining the price of the benefits of a good environment. This leads to the thought that it might be reasonable to introduce a number of further indicators of welfare besides the national product. Or the national product could be corrected with respect to the cost connected with pollution control and restoration of pollution-caused damages.

5⁰. Monetary and Employment Considerations Should Not Play a Major Part

To what extent should foreign exchange and employment effects be part of the analysis or are only the production (i.e., the 'purely' cost-related) effects interesting? The economic situation of the country determines this.

If the country has problems of unemployment and the balance of payments it may seem reasonable to include the effects of the environmental planning on the problem.

In principle, general imbalance problems ought to be solved through general means such as income policy, changes in the exchange rate, etc. The question is whether these business cycle policy instruments are applicable in practice within the timespan the economy is influenced by the environmental project. If the general means can solve our imbalance problems, we should not include considerations of employment or exchange rates in the environmental projects. If, however, the general means do not apply - so that we are in a deadlock in relation to economic policy - it may be relevant to let these considerations of employment and exchange rates play a certain part.

9.10.3 The Analyses Must Not Become Too Partial

When formulating the problem, it is important not to confine the scope of the problem so much that a number of alternative methods are excluded.

For example within the area of energy planning it is natural to include environmental issues from the start. By determining to burn coal in the power plants there is a known environmental consequence (among others, pollution) which could have been avoided by using other sources of energy, for instance natural gas. By making decisions in stages, we risk ending up with a solution which is not expedient from an overall point of view.

There is also a problem of priorities in connection with implementing recycling projects. Politically it should be considered how much Government support in total will be given to these projects. Then the task is to select the most profitable projects. This requires that all practicable projects are known from the start. Calculations must be made for each of these projects to show the rate of return, in order to implement the most profitable projects first.

If one project has been chosen in advance without considering the other projects it can easily result in a misallocation of resources.

It can therefore be concluded that it is important right from the start to have a broad approach to the problem that is to be solved so that no possible solutions are precluded beforehand.

It is essential for the politicians and the public to know the formulation of the problem and the conditions forming the basis of the analysis. Is the formulation of the problem comprehensive and satisfactory? Could the problem have been formulated in another way and might that have produced a different result? Where in the analysis have the conditions been chosen that are decisive for the results of the analysis? These questions must be stated in the conclusion of the analysis. They are essential to the users of the analysis.

9.10.4 Conclusion

As shown, there are large problems involved in working out good environmental analyses. These difficulties must not deter us. Political decisions on environmental issues shall and will be made whether the analyses are made or not. Therefore it is important to contribute to making the basis of those decisions as substantial as is at all possible.

REFERENCES

Fisher, A.C., 1981. Resource and Environmental Economics. Cambridge Univ. Press, Cambridge, 256 pp.

Førsund, F.R. and Strøm, S., 1988. Environmental Economics and Management: Pollution and Natural Resources. Chapman and Hall, London, 308 pp. (Norvegian edition: Miljø- og Ressursekonomi. Oslo 1980, 391 pp.).

Hahn, R.W., 1989. A Primer on Environmental Policy Design. Harwood Acad. Publ., New York, 135 pp.

Kneese, A.V., Ayres, R.U. and d'Arge, R.C., 1970. Economics and the Environment. A Materials Balance Approach. Johns Hopkins, Baltimore and London, 132 pp.

Mäler, K.-G., 1974. Environmental Economics. Resources Future, Baltimore, 267 pp.

Nordhaus, W., 1982. How fast should we graze the global common? Amer. Econ. Rev., 72: 242-246.

Pigou, A.C., 1946. The Economics of Welfare. 2. ed. Macmillan, London.

Ricketts, M. and Webb, M.G., 1978. Pricing and Standards in the Control of Pollution. Scand. J. Econ., 80: 53-61.

Tietenberg, T., 1989. Environmental and Natural Resource Economics. 2. ed. Scott, Foresman & Co., Glenville Ill., 559 pp.

Walker, M. and Storey, D.J., 1977. The Standards and Price Approach to Pollution Control: Problems of Iteration. Scand. J. Econ., 79: 99-109.

10 DANISH ENVIRONMENTAL LAW

HELGE WULFF

10.1 INTRODUCTION

Environmental law is a part of the legal system which regulates Man's use of and influence on his physical environment.

Environmental law serves *many purposes:* Pollution control; the conservation of landscapes, areas of scenic beauty and wild animals and plants; control of the use of natural resources: the arable soil, water, wood and raw materials in the subsoil. Some include in environmental law legislation aiming at better and healthier urban areas, at establish recreational areas, and even at improving farm structures and road system.

In this chapter I will limit myself to dealing with pollution control and the control of land use (mostly in the open spaces) in order to conserve nature and regulate the use of natural resources.

I also limit myself to explaining the *principles* of the law. This is partly owing to considerations of space, and partly to the fact that the Danish Government in 1988 decided that the laws on planning, nature conservancy, water, and pollution control should be amended and simplified. The new legislation will probably take effect some time in 1991. At present (spring 1990) the details thereof are not known.

Pollution and environmental problems have existed throughout most of human history. Obviously, this has also been the case in Denmark. For centuries, the law has tried to solve conflicts between neighbours concerning water rights, etc.

However, the problems became more serious in the last century as the country became more densely populated, the towns grew, and industrialization began.

In order to solve the environmental problems which arose from this situation, new laws were passed, such as a public health legislation and a legislation concerning the pollution of streams. However, the legislation did not keep pace with the development. Therefore, the problems had to be solved in other ways: through judge-made neighbour law, ease-ments, and the rule of torts. I will deal first with these three elements of environmental law, after which I will review the written legislation that has gradually made its appearance during the last 20-30 years, and finally I will make a few general statements about Danish environmental law.

10.2 THE JUDGE-MADE LAW

For more than 100 years, the courts have stated that a landowner cannot use his land in a manner which *interferes substantially* with his neighbours' use and enjoyment of their properties.

The neighbours can *institute legal proceedings* in order to obtain the court's judgment to the effect that the *nuisance must be reduced* or to receive *compensation* for the damage that has been caused. This is a *case law*, which has been created by the courts outside the written law. It is very much like the common law of private nuisance as known in British and American law.

In the various cases the courts have judged whether the neighbours have suffered a *substantial nuisance* at a level above that which those concerned in the case in question or neighbours in general could be expected to suffer. In many cases, the courts have reviewed what the neighbours could be expected to suffer, considering the *nature of the neighbourhood* or the situation of the property. Such decisions were not based on whether the act causing nuisance or the victimized neighbour arrived first. However, if the neighbours have for a long time passively accepted the nuisance, the court might not take action against the nuisance or at least only award compensation to the victims.

We have a vast number of court decisions in this field. They deal with *widely different subjects*: noise pollution from airfields, machine shops and orphanages, smoke pollution from factories and plants, groundwater pollution, etc. There are also decisions concerning noise, flies, and odors from barns and stables, mink and poultry farms or regarding sand drifts over horticultural enterprises.

Not all these cases are concerned with important environmental problems. Often they deal with ‘a minor daily pollution’ in the immediate vicinity which can, however, seem quite as important to the individual citizen as the major environmental risks.

The importance of the judge-made neighbour law is *gradually declining*. The planning legislation and the Environmental Protection Act will contribute to the reduction of the number of conflicts. Should conflicts arise, the victimized neighbours will probably not seek compensation through slow and expensive court proceedings. Instead they will use the more simple process of contacting the authorities, requesting that they intervene in the form of an order or prohibition pursuant to the Environmental Protection Act or the administrative provisions based on this Act. If the neighbours use this process, they will not receive compensation for the nuisance and inconvenience they have suffered, as the Act does not provide for such compensation. However, it seems that the neighbours prefer to seek the help of the administrative authorities instead of bringing their case to court. They seem more interested in eliminating the nuisance than in receiving com-pensation - at least if no actual financial loss has been incurred.

Even if the judge-made neighbour law is losing some of its importance, some of its principles are applied in the administration of the Environmental Protection Act.

10.3 EASEMENTS

In some cases, landowners have tried to solve environmental problems through private agreements, especially when the issue is to make sure that residential areas are kept free from activities that are damaging to the environment. When a land developer platted his subdivision into lots and blocks, he very often imposed certain limitations on the lots in the development. These limitations are called *easements*.

Sometimes the easements prohibit "arrangements which through odors, smoke, noise, unpleasant sights, etc., can be a nuisance to the surrounding residents". Sometimes the easements reserve the area for single family dwellings, thus forbidding factories, farming, etc. In many cases, the easements simply forbid the landowners in the area to conduct business in any form. These easements can pertain to anything from factories, workshops, and haulage contractors to restaurants, boarding houses, sports grounds, and schools.

Who *enforces* an easement? It is indicated in the agreement (i.e., the title deed) which creates the easement who is entitled to take proceedings if the easement is violated. Sometimes, all the landowners of the development can take proceedings. In many cases, the municipal council is also indicated in the agreement. If an easement is violated, those entitled to take proceedings must do so in court by bringing an action against the negligent landowner.

Since the introduction of the Municipal Planning Act of 1975, limitations on the use of land are usually imposed by the *'local plans'*, as mentioned below, not by easements. However, existing easements are still valid and are considered of such importance that the law states that they can always be enforced by the municipal council even if the agreement does not specifically mention the council as entitled to take proceedings.

10.4 THE LAW OF TORTS

Very often, the pollution from an enterprise is not only a nuisance and inconvenience to its surroundings, it might also cause the neighbourhood a direct pecuniary loss. Groundwater used as drinking water may be polluted because of a leaky oiltank or because chemicals have been buried in the ground. A water stream can be polluted by a farmer's discharge of liquid manure, silage juice, or leftover herbicides. The stream can also accidentally receive excessive amounts of toxins from an industrial enterprise. All this may result in mortalities in fish-pond farms or the ruin of crops. If the polluter does not voluntarily offer compensation for the damage he has caused, it will be necessary to institute legal proceedings.

Such cases will, of course, arise from time to time and they are settled by the courts according to Danish tort law which states that a person who intentionally or through negligence causes a pecuniary loss to another person shall usually pay damages. Often the cases also involve criminal liability according to the Environmental Protection Act or other provisions.

10.5 LEGISLATION ON POLLUTION CONTROL

10.5.1 The Environmental Protection Act and Other Statutes

The most important Danish act on pollution control is the Environmental Protection Act but additional provisions can be found in a number of other acts, for instance, the Act on the Protection of the Marine Environment, the Act on the Disposal of Oil and Chemical Waste, The Act on Restricted Sulphur Content in Fuel, the Act on Restricted Lead Content, etc., in Motor Fuel and the Act on Chemical Substances and Products, etc. The acts dealt with below in Section 10.6 concerning land use of open spaces are also instrumental in preventing the emergence of pollution problems.

The background for the Environmental Protection Act is well known: During the 1960's the industrial world became concerned about the increase in pollution as a result of urban growth, industrialization and increased production.

In many countries, new legislation was implemented to prevent pollution and the destruction of nature: In the USA, the Clean Air Act of 1963, the National Environmental Policy Act of 1969 and an act on water pollution of 1972. In France, legislation concerning water was introduced in 1964 and 1973 and a nature conservancy act was made in 1976. In Denmark, a nature conservation act and a planning reform were implemented in 1969. An environmental reform was introduced in 1973. That reform in-cluded the present Environmental Protection Act which took effect on October 1st, 1974.

The Environmental Protection Act has since been amended several times and it must be assumed that it will change considerably as a result of the present law reform, which is mentioned above.

10.5.2 The Environmental Protection Act: Objects and Principles

The *objects* of the Act are first and foremost to prevent and combat pollution of air, water, and soil, as well as noise nuisances, and to establish environmental regulations based on considerations of hygiene. The Act also aims at safeguarding those physical qualities of the environment which are essential to the hygienic and recreational aspects of human life and at maintaining the diversity of plants and animals. Accordingly, the Act concerns people's 'physical' environment, not their places of work or their homes.

By *'pollution'* the Act refers to the emission of solid, liquid, or gazeous substances, vibrations and noise, but not nuisances in the form of light, the use of ionizing rays and radioactivity. Other statutes deal with these items.

The administration of the Environmental Protection Act is based on various *principles*.

Most important is the internationally recognized *'The polluter pays' principle*: Any person who proposes to commence an activity which might cause pollution shall take the necessary precautions at his own cost. The Act also mentions two other principles which can be said to stem from the 'polluter pays' principle:

According to the *'localization principle'*, an enterprise shall be located at a site with the least risk of pollution.

According to the *'pollution restriction principle'* any enterprise shall adopt the necessary measures and plan its operations with a view to avoiding pollution to the greatest possible extent.

It is evident from these principles that an enterprise cannot claim compensation if it suffers losses through orders or prohibitions issued by the environmental authorities with the aim of reducing the pollution from the enterprise.

At one time, the Environmental Protection Act also contained an *'interest weighing principle'* according to which decisions in cases concerning approvals, exemptions, and intervention should be weighed with a view, on the one hand, to the harm caused by the pollution and, on the other, to the expense necessary to eliminate the pollution and the importance of the enterprise to the community. This principle was removed from the Act in 1986 in order to emphasize that the authorities should only consider the effects of the enterprise on the environment.

Fortunately, the *principles of administrative law* oblige the authorities to allow minor deviations from the usual environmental requirements if the enterprise would otherwise be put to too great expense through pollution-control measures. The enterprise's im-portance to society can also constitute a reason for deviations from the usual environ-mental require-ments. To a certain extent, you have to suffer pollution from power plants and airports.

10.5.3 The Authorities of the Environmental Protection Act

The Act is an example of the modern organization of the authorities in environmental legislation (see Section 10.7.4).

The *municipal councils* deal with most of the individual cases: Approvals, licences for waste disposal, intervention against polluting enterprises, etc. Certain cases are dealt with by the *county councils*, especially if they pertain to municipal plants and installations. Both councils have planning powers, see below. The municipal councils supervise that the law is complied with and the county councils supervise the condition of the waters.

The Act falls under the Danish *Ministry of the Environment.* The Danish Minister for the Environment is responsible for the entire sphere of environmental issues, he draws up bills and orders and has the right to decide to take over certain decisions. A special division in the Ministry: *The National Agency of Environmental Protection*, deals with the daily administration of the Act, including the drawing up of procedural circulars and guidelines (see Section 10.7.5), the agency decides on complaints against the municipal and county councils' decisions in individual cases.

Certain decisions of The National Agency of Environmental Protection can further be appealed to the so-called *Environmental Appeal Board* that consists of experts and vocational representatives. Such appeals are possible in cases concerning heavily polluting enterprises (see below). Certain actions for damages are settled by special *'land boards'*.

In connection with the projected law reform, various changes in the organization of the authorities of the Environmental Protection Act are contemplated.

10.5.4 Pollution of Soil and Subsoil

It is illegal to *bury liquids or solid substances* that are likely to pollute the groundwater and to discharge these substances into the soil or subsoil through percolation systems, borings or other installations. The prohibition does not include ordinary *manure spreading* (see, however, Section 10.5.8).

It is also illegal to bury *containers* of liquids and solid substances likely to pollute the groundwater. This includes, among other things, oil tanks, collection tanks for domestic waste water, etc. The law makes an exception, however, in the case of sealed containers used exclusively for liquid manure, slurry, or silage effluent. Furthermore, ministerial orders provide for certain exceptions concerning the establishment of percolation systems and the like on isolated properties, the burying of oil tanks, etc.

10.5.5 Pollution of Surface Water

Polluting substances *must not be discharged into watercourses* lakes or the sea or be stored so close to such waters as to cause danger that the substances may enter them.

The prohibition does not include waste-water plants that were lawfully constructed or permitted *prior to 1974,* but the authorities have the right to demand that the discharge should stop and the property be connected to a common waste-water plant.

The prohibition does not include - at least not according to the present legislation - *ochre pollution.* Neither does it prevent the pollution of a stream by discharge of *surplus manure* from manuring of fields (see further in Section 10.5.8).

Streams are the main recipients of waste water and the discharge may be permitted on certain conditions, e.g., that the water has undergone a *special treatment* or has passed through a *municipal sewage system.* Sewage treatment works are constructed according to sewage plans drawn up by the municipal councils.

In the *regional plans*, there are guidelines concerning the use of water resources and the quality and use of streams, lakes and coastal areas. These guidelines determine the construction of waste-water plants and the issue of licences to discharge waste water. There are also guidelines for the use of water resources.

10.5.6 Heavily Polluting Enterprises

Enterprises, plants or activities which are included in an annex to the act shall *not be established or commenced without prior approval* from the authorities. Enterprises, etc., which were established prior to October lst, 1974 do not require approval unless they are extended or modified in a way which increases the pollution they may cause.

The *annex* today includes the majority of Danish industries and a number of other plants and enterprises, including large pig and cattle farms, fur farms and poultry farms.

The proposed law reform *considers reducing the number of enterprises* included in the annex by 1/3 or 1/2. The approval procedure takes much time and there are other means of control. Pig-, cattle-, poultry- and fur farms are among the enterprises proposed for elimination from the annex. As to the categories which will remain in the annex after the reform, it is the intention to *examine all enterprises* which have not yet been approved because they were established prior to October lst, 1974.

The approval of an enterprise provides a certain *protection* for the *first eight years.* During this period, the authorities are not allowed to take measures against the pollution unless it is considerable and

a) new information about the harmful effect of the pollution has come to light, or

b) the enterprise causes environmental damage which was not foreseen at the time of the approval, or

c) the pollution considerably exceeds the terms of the approval.

Eight years after the date of the approval, the authorities can, in all cases, modify the terms of the approval for reasons of environmental protection or if better cleaning measures or less polluting production measures have been developed. After the eight years, the authorities can also modify the terms of the approval for reasons of environmental protection or if better cleaning procedures or less polluting production methods have been developed.

Enterprises, etc., *which have not been approved* because they were started before 1974, can receive an order to remedy the pollution if it is considerable.

10.5.7 Other Enterprises and Activities

Pursuant to the Environmental Protection Act, the so-called order of *'Environmental Regulation'* has been drawn up; this is administered by the municipal councils and contains rules concerning various sanitary conditions.

The regulation also authorizes *intervention against enterprises of categories which are not included in the annex*, if they cause unhygienic conditions and nuisances to a considerable extent.

A similar rule applies to public and private building and construction works, public enterprises and institutions, including hospitals and schools, and noise pollution from sports clubs and other organized recreational activities.

Keeping livestock on a large scale is illegal in urban areas with mainly aggregate housing.

10.5.8 Pollution from Animal Husbandry, etc.

Pursuant to the Environmental Protection Act, a special ministerial order has been drawn up with the purpose of restricting pollution and nuisance from the production, storage, and use of animal manure and silage, etc.

This order pertains to both farms with a *predominantly animal production* and farms with a *predominantly plant production* that either have a smaller stock of animals or receive manure from other farms.

The background for the order is the fact that in Denmark, as in other Western industrialized countries, there is increasing concern about the effect of intensively worked farms on the environment, especially the pollution of water sources and groundwater *with nitrogen from manure*. The Danish Parliament - 'Folketinget' - has called for an increased effort to be made in the fight against agricultural pollution, especially through the so-called 'NPO-Programme of Action' of 1985 and 'The Aquatic Environment Programme of Action' of 1987.

This order is also administered by the *municipal councils* that regularly supervise that it is complied with. *Violation* of the provisions has led to a number of criminal cases.

The order includes rules and regulations concerning the position and construction of *barns, manure heaps, etc.*, and concerning the *storing* of manure, silage, etc. Field dump heaps and silaging of liquid releasing crops in field stacks are prohibited.

Most farms with animal husbandry are also obliged to have a certain *storage capacity* for manure unless there exists a written agreement about storage on another property.

There are detailed rules concerning the *spreading of animal manure* in the fields which also state that the amount of manure spread must not exceed what the manuring requirement dictates, just as *limits* have been set as to the *amount of manure* which can be spread per acre per year on the land. Should the farm produce such large amounts of manure that the rules cannot apply, the farmer must enter an agreement with another farmer in the neighbourhood who can dispose of it.

Another order prescribes *plans for rotating crops* on most farms and also plans stating a farm's need for nitrogen and phosphorus fertilizer. 65% of a farm's adjoining lands shall, moreover, consist of *'green fields'*, that is, grassland laid out in certain crops, for instance, winter crops, maize, beets and outdoor vegetables, etc.

10.6 LAND USE CONTROL IN THE OPEN SPACES

10.6.1 Planning Legislation

a. Zoning

One of the most important problems of environmental law has been to prevent *scattered and random building* of dwellings, weekend cottages, industrial enterprises, etc., etc., all over the open spaces.

Experience in other countries shows that it is necessary in modern society to prevent an impractical extension of urban areas, with much too great distances between homes and places of work and public institutions, and excessive demands on society for new roads, bus lines, water supplies, waste-water plants, etc. It is also necessary to place industries reasonably near major roads, railways and water supply, and last but not least, it is important to avoid the environmental conflicts and the destruction of nature in which an unregulated development in the countryside can result.

The zoning law solves this problem by dividing the whole country into *urban zones, summer-house areas*, and *rural zones*. Urban zones and summer-house areas are zoned by local plans according to regional and municipal plans and it is in these areas that future residential areas, summer houses, and industrial areas are built.

The *rural zones*, on the other hand, are kept free from this sort of development. In the rural zones it is necessary to obtain the county council's - in some cases the municipal council's - permission to develop and build and to alter the use of existing buildings and land without buildings. This rule does not apply if the building or the land is intended for agricultural purposes.

The zoning law is administered in such a way that no building or other development of open spaces takes place contrary to the intentions of the regional and municipal plans, which are mentioned below.

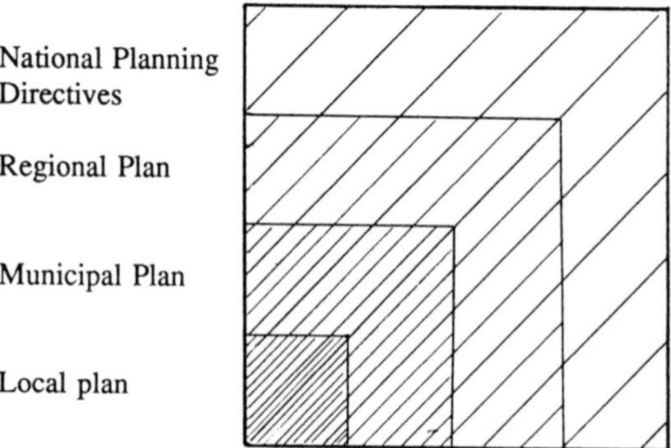

Figure 10.1. The planning system.

b. National Planning

The Act on *National and Regional Planning* prescribes the implementation of a national planning.

It is not the intention to work out an actual national plan. The national planning results, in effect, in *national planning directives* from the Government. These directives have not been comprehensive political guidelines for the future planning and land use control - which perhaps was the original intention. The national planning directives have, to a large extent, prescribed land reservations, e.g., in connection with the establishment of the pipeline network for the natural-gas supply; some directives are concerned with very concrete measures such as the location of short-wave transmitters, very polluting enterprises, TV masts for the Danish Channel Two, and storage areas for waste products.

The Government's general political attitude concerning planning issues is primarily expressed in *annual statements* from the Minister for the Environment to the Parliament. The statements are printed and published.

c. Regional Planning

Furthermore, the Act prescribes that the county councils draw up *renal plans* for each region in the country.

The regional plans have been subject to public debate in connection with the local elections in 1978. The regional plans and any proposed amendments must, when they have been adopted by the county councils, be approved by the Ministry of the Environment (see further Section 10.7.5).

The plans must be brought up to date regularly. The first regional plans were adopted in 1978-80. In 1989, the '3rd generation' has been forwarded to the Minister for approval.

A regional plan must show an *overall survey* of the use of the county's area. The survey must contain guidelines to a division of the *area into the various uses*: Urban areas, important centres, major traffic installations and public institutions, areas for summer houses, recreational areas, farming areas, gravel pits, nature reserves, or new forest areas.

The plan also consists of directives concerning the *quality of the water* in streams and lakes, etc., as well as the use of water resources (see Section 10.5.5).

The *location* of enterprises and plants that can put an especially heavy strain on the environment must be carefully considered (airports and airfields, waste-treatment plants, cement works, fertilizer plants, etc., etc.; see Section 10.7.2. on the EIA assessment).

The different interests must be *weighed against* each other according to the overall view. This is why the regional planning - and the municipal planning mentioned below - are described as *'synthesis planning'*, whose purpose is to solve conflicts between the different interests of area.

The National and Regional Planning Act specifically lays down that the use of areas should be determined in such a way as to *prevent pollution* of air, water, and soil.

It should therefore be attempted to solve noise problems by locating airfields, motor tracks, steel rolling mills, and certain other industries, at a sufficient distance from housing and recreational areas. Furthermore, it would seem reasonable to locate smelly and air-polluting enterprises (i.e., water-treatment plants and fertilizer plants) at a suitable distance from residential areas, hospitals, childrens' and old people's homes, etc. Heavily polluting enterprises (see Section 10.5.6) should, as a general rule, be concentrated in industrial areas.

Environmental considerations must, however, be weighed against the necessity of situating enterprises within easy access to roads, existing railway stations, ports, and ground-water resources.

Naturally, waterworks should not be located close to refuse dumps or holiday-house areas with percolation installations, which might pollute the groundwater.

In connection with *the present law reform*, it is being considered to limit the sphere of application of the regional plans. Henceforth, they shall only comprise the open spaces, and installations and measures which exceed the municipal boundaries, while it will be the task of the municipal councils alone to plan the urban areas.

d. Municipal Plans

Whereas the regional plans are overall surveys, the municipal plans are the result of a *more detailed planning*. The rules and regulations concerning these can at present be found in the Municipal Planning Act which, in its preamble, prescribes that the purpose of the act is to *prevent the pollution* of air, water and soil and noise pollution. Obviously, this purpose will not be fundamentally changed during the present legislative work.

According to the Municipal Planning Act, each municipal council in the country is under the obligation to produce a *municipal plan* covering the whole area of the municipality. The plan is *drawn up* based on a complete evaluation of the municipality's natural resources, its economic situation and the goals which the municipal council sets for the future demographic and industrial development within the municipality. The plan shall both determine the long-term development of the municipality and set out more a short-term and precise framework for local planning (see below).

The whole country is covered by the municipal plans. The local councils are under the obligation to *revise* the plans every four years and the second generation of the municipal plans for the entire country is due in 1993 at the latest.

The consideration mentioned above regarding a regional planning also apply to municipal planning. The municipal council must also respect *standards* concerning air and noise pollution and guidelines for the location of refuse dumps, etc., which are issued by The National Agency of Environmental Protection. The Ministry of the Environment has also issued a number of *instructions* concerning the planning procedure.

The municipal plans must also consider the sector planning and the municipal sewage plans (see Section 10.5.5).

e. Local Plans

Within the framework of the municipal plans the municipal council may draw up more detailed 'local plans'.

In some cases, the local council is even *under obligation* to draw up local plans. This is especially the case if the matter concerns a major development scheme, a major installation, or a major building scheme. When deciding whether the project is a *'major' project*, it is not enough to consider the scale of the project. It must also be considered if the project will have such an effect on the neighbourhood that it is reasonable to seek the opinion of the local residents, who have a right to express their views on a proposal for a local plan during the planning procedure.

A local plan can comprise a *large area*, for instance, when a new residential or industrial area is laid out. The local plan can then ensure that the area is developed in such a way that pollution and nuisances are avoided as much as possible. A local plan can also comprise a *much smaller area*, for instance, when an industrial enterprise extends its building with a new machine shop. During the planning procedure, the municipal council weighs the wishes of the enterprise against the neighbours' fear of increased air or noise pollution.

The law prescribes in detail what a local plan can comprise, i.e., the size and use of the individual building sites, the location, use and construction of the individual buildings, the location of roads, paths and wires, the conservation of special landscape features in connection with a development, the regulation of fencing and hedging and the protection of housing areas against road and street noise.

Municipal and local plans must not be in conflict with regional plans and national plan directives, and local plans must not be in conflict with municipal plans.

f. Sector Planning of County Councils

The county councils have drawn up sector plans: concerning the quality of streams and lakes, the use of water resources, the location of especially polluting installations and enterprises, the conservation of the landscape and sites of scenic beauty, the layout of recreational areas, the extraction of raw materials, the preservation of valuable farmland, etc., etc. The sector plans are meant to help the county councils and the municipal councils in drawing up regional and municipal plans (see Section 10.7.3 on the future sector planning of the county councils).

g. Legal Effects of Regional, Municipal, and Local Plans

Regional and municipal plans are *not directly binding* on the citizens. The *regional plans* are meant as guidelines for the county councils' and municipal counties' development schemes and for their discretionary decisions according to the zoning, nature conservation, and the water legislation, etc. The regional plans also constitute the framework of the municipal and local plans.

In principle, the municipal council must apply the municipal plans when it draws up development schemes and local plans, and when it grants licences and permits.

Should a municipal plan lay out an area within an urban zone or summer-house area for housing purposes, the municipal council can object to the building of factories and workshops in the area. Conversely, the municipal council can object to the building of bungalows in urban zones laid out for industrial purposes.

In contrast to the regional and municipal plans, the *local plans* are directly binding on the owners. Violation of the provisions of the plan may render the offender liable to penalties and he is obliged to reestablish the former state of the area, even if it means demolishing a house which he has built against the provisions of the plan.

10.6.2 Legislation on the Conservation of Landscapes and Areas of Scenic Beauty

The *purpose* of the Nature Conservation Act is to protect the Danish nature and landscapes and to give people an opportunity to enjoy the open spaces.

The classic means of realizing these purposes are decisions made by a local nature-conservancy board; decisions which are called in Danish 'fredningsbestemmelser' - *'conservation decisions'*.

The nature-conservancy board consists of a judge, who is the chairman, a member appointed by the municipal council and a member appointed by the county council. In the future, the authority to make preservation decisions will probably be transferred to the county council (see Section 10.7.4).

A conservation decision may *transfer* land to public authorities, for instance, with the purpose of creating a recreational area, but in most cases the conservation decision only submits the land in question to an *easement*.

The most frequent conservation decisions are *'status quo' easements* according to which an area must be preserved in its present state. The easements prohibit building, putting up masts, gravel digging, tall growth, drainage systems, etc. Some 'status quo' easements preserve areas of special scenic value, for instance, Dollerup Bakker, Raabjerg Mile, Hjerl Hede, Svannike Bakker and hundreds of other large or small areas. Many conservation easements protect the surroundings of a body of water, for instance the lakes in the north of Zealand and the lakes at Hald, Stubbe and Roerbaek in Jutland.

Conservation easements can also be used as a means of opening up areas that are of interest to the public for *outdoor activities*.

All over the country, efforts are being made to create *nature reserves*. This has happened, e.g., at Tystrup-Bavelse and in Mols Bjerge, and can be achieved through regional plans and conservation planning. Nature reserves can be created through conservation decisions combined with a restrictive administration of the legislation on zoning, raw materials, etc.

The conservation decision is a kind of *expropriation* (see Section 10.7.1). If it means the transfer of an area, the owner is entitled to a *compensation* corresponding to the market value of the area. If the conservation decision is an easement, the compensation corresponds to the relative reduction in the market value which it brings about.

10.6.3 Water Law

Legislation concerning fresh water consists today primarily of the Watercourse Act, the Water Supply Act, the Act on Fresh Water Fishing and some provisions in the Nature Conservation Act and the Environmental Protection Act. (I have already dealt with the Environmental Protecting Act, and I will not go into the provisions of the Act on Freshwater Fishing).

The present legislation can be expected to be significantly amended by the ongoing law reform. Therefore, I shall only mention a few rules which I assume will continue to exist in the future:

a. As a principal rule, nobody may *abstract groundwater or surface water* or establish new wells or drilling for water *without a licence* from the county council (sometimes the municipal council), which examines whether the water is suitable for drinking, for irrigation of crops or other purposes, and if the abstraction of water in any other way may have environmentally unfortunate consequences.

b. When a county council issues a licence to abstract groundwater or water from a water course, it may, according to provisions in the Environmental Protection Act, lay out certain *protection areas*. Within these areas it may be forbidden to use cesspools with WC effluent or - in the case of abstraction of surface water - to carry on industrial enterprises, institutions or camping sites.

c. The authorities can *close down* existing wells and water plants if a water shortage occurs, if the installations are injurious to health or if the authorities find that an area with many small wells and water plants should have a common water-supply system, for instance, because it would be expedient to allow houses nearby to have waste-water cesspools.

d. Streams and lakes are of inestimable importance to an active outdoor life. Therefore, the *public has a right to sail*, without the use of engines, on streams and lakes (unless there is only one riparian).

e. Drainage and ditching in ochre areas can be made conditional on the establishment of *ochre purification plants* which are eligible for public grants and subsidies. If a landowner wishes to drain his land and lead the drain water to a watercourse on his neighbour's land, he must have his neighbour's permission and a licence from the municipal or county council.

f. *Special regulations* are laid out for the most important water courses. These prescribe, among other things, how the stream must be *maintained* by the authorities. Other water courses must be maintained by the riparians.

g. As a rule, the *present condition* of streams and lakes must not be changed by regulation, pipe laying, filling in, etc.

h. In recent years, it has been under consideration whether to protect streams and lakes against pollution by laying out *protective zones* by the streams. The ongoing legislative work suggests a cultivation-free border of 2 m along all streams of high environmental quality.

10.6.4 Forest Legislation

The most important rules on forests are to be found in the Forestry Act of 1989, whose purpose is to *preserve and protect the Danish forest area.* In administering the act, emphasis is put on both the production value of the forest and the importance of the forest to the landscape, outdoor life, etc.

According to the act, most forest land in Denmark is submitted to restrictions which *oblige the owners to preserve their forests.* The land must be *used for forestry only* and not be turned into farmland, building sites, gravel pits, etc. The land must be covered with trees, which form or, within a certain time span will form, a *close high forest.*

However, the forest authorities may *issue licences* to use forest land for purposes other than forestry.

The *choice of tree species* is normally free. However, grants can be obtained to promote the growth of deciduous trees, as the areas of deciduous trees in general and beech tree areas in particular are declining.

In the regional plans, special *'afforestation areas'* are laid out. In these areas both public and private landowners can plant trees. The Government Forestry Service may acquire land for this purpose, either in the free market or by expropriation.

The Danish forestry policy and the common agriculture policy of the EEC both *promote the afforestation* of private farmland. According to a special act which implements the EEC-policy on this point, farmers may obtain grants to afforest their land.

Public forests and most private forests are *open to the public*. As to the private forests, this only applies to visits in daytime - by foot and only on the roads. Bicycles, riding on horseback, the use of motor vehicles, etc., are forbidden without the owner's consent.

10.6.5 Legislation on Raw Materials

According to the Raw Materials Act, the exploitation of stone, gravel, sand, clay, lime, chalk, and other natural underground deposits on land and in the territorial waters, as a general rule, demand a special *licence* from the authorities. The law does not comprise oil, salt, and natural gas, etc., which can only be extracted on the basis of a concession granted according to a special act.

The aim of the Raw Materials Act is to ensure that raw materials are not extracted unless a number of *considerations* have been taken into account. Extraction might be favoured in the light of the building and construction trade's need for materials, employment considerations, and the possible income from exports. These advantages must, however, be *weighed against* the disadvantages in the form of destruction of the landscape and scenic beauty, groundwater pollution, the risk of destroying the coast, noise pollution in connection with transport and operation of machines, dust pollution in connection with processing and storage, etc., etc.

It must be taken into consideration that some *resources are limited.*

According to the law, *industrial exploitation* of raw materials requires a licence from the county council. Such a licence is issued following a *weighing of considerations* as stated above and the sector planning of the county council. The licence is usually issued for only *ten years*. The licence may contain special terms and conditions to ensure a *subsequent treatment* of the area in order to avoid lasting damage to the landscape or to prevent pollution.

Extraction of raw materials from the territorial waters will not be dealt with here.

10.6.6 Other Legislation

A number of provisions in various acts protect the beaches, the moors, salt meadows and salt marshes, the dunes of Western Jutland, ancient monuments, wild game, mammals and birds, rare plants, geological formations, etc., etc. There are also provisions dealing with public access to beaches and uncultivated land.

10.7 GENERAL VIEWS ON DANISH ENVIRONMENTAL LAW

10.7.1 Property Rights and Environmental Law

Until well into this century, it was widely held that any interferences with property rights by the government were basically wrong and should therefore be limited and well-founded, and that the landowners were entitled to compensation for any losses the intervention might cause.

Naturally, the landowners have been opposed to far-reaching regulations of their property rights. This was clearly expressed in 1963 when a comprehensive reform of the planning legislation was rejected in a referendum. It should also be mentioned that the agricultural sector would not accept the environmental reform of 1973 and has systematically been opposed to many of the reforms of Danish environmental law.

This seems in keeping with the *Danish Constitution* (Section 73) which states that property rights are inviolable and that no person is obliged to cede his property unless it is for the common good and then only according to the law and upon receiving a full compensation.

Such a compulsory cession is called *an expropriation*. It may include the *total transfer* of an area to the authorities, but it may simply consist of a few *limitations* of the owner's property rights, such as when a landowner is obliged to accept a sewage pipe or a public path on his property.

If Section 73 of the Danish Constitution should be taken literally, any limitations on property rights should be considered as an 'expropriation'. In that case, it would hardly be possible to carry through an effective environmental legislation. For instance, society could hardly afford to pay full compensation for the losses which the building restrictions in the rural zones have caused the landowners. It would also be difficult to order a polluting enterprise to stop or limit its activities, if society were compelled to pay compensation for the losses which it causes the owners of the enterprise by this action.

However, it is quite clear that Section 73 of the Danish constitution does not comprise all limitations imposed by society on property rights. Even when the constitution was written almost 130 years ago, legislation existed regarding leaseholds, farm structures and forests which restricted the landowners' and forest owners' use of their land without this being considered expropriation.

The question is simply where to *draw the line* between expropriation and *regulation without compensation.* This problem exists also in other countries with written constitutions. In the USA, it corresponds to the problem of drawing the line between a 'taking' and the use of 'police power'.

In order to solve this problem, in Danish law one must consider several factors:

First of all, a restriction on property rights is usually not considered as an expropriation, if (like the duty to preserve a forest) it concerns *all or most properties of a certain category.*

The *impact* of the regulation is important. If you deprive a person of all property rights to his land, e.g., in order to construct a road or a water supply plant, it would be considered as an expropriation.

The *purpose* of the regulation is also important and on this point the views of the legislature have changed considerably over the years:

If the purpose was *town planning*, Parliament originally felt that landowners were entitled to a compensation for the limitations imposed on their land by the town plan. The Town Planning Act of 1925 remained without effect because of the compensation provisions of the law. Thirteen years would pass before it was considered justified - in 1938 - to work out a new legislation which, in principle, did not compensate landowners for the restrictions which by a town plan made upon their building possibilities. This has been followed up in the provisions in local plans of the modern Municipal Planning Act.

A similar development can be traced for the legislation on *land use in the open spaces*:

Previously, the intention was to prevent the scattered and random building of houses in the open country through the Nature Conservation Act. From 1961 it was, as a general rule, necessary to obtain a building permit from The Nature Conservancy Board to build houses outside towns and urban areas. However, if a building permit was refused, the landowner was considered entitled to a compensation for lost building opportunities, which sometimes meant a lot of money. As a result, the law remained without effect. This state of affairs was not corrected until the passing of the Zoning Act of 1969.

There has also been a change of attitude in the legislation on *raw materials.*

For many years it has been considered desirable to control the extraction of raw materials.

However, if the authorities wished to intervene against undesirable gravel digging or the like, they usually had to resort to conservation easements, and in that case the landowners were entitled to compensation for the loss of income incurred by not being able to exploit the deposits of raw materials on their land. Not until the Raw Materials Act of 1972 did we get provisions which prohibit, without compensation, the extraction of raw materials without permission from the authorities.

How the views have changed can perhaps most clearly be seen when you consider *'the polluter pays' principle* of the Environmental Protection Act. This principle is based on a totally different line of reasoning from Section 73 of the constitution. According to the constitution, society must compensate the landowner for any loss incurred by limitations of his property rights, even if they are dictated by 'the common good'. According to 'the polluter pays' principle, an owner is obliged, at his own expense, to adapt the use of his property to the common good.

The final decision as to where to draw the line between expropriation and regulation without compensation rests with the courts. But these have almost never found an act of Parliament on this issue to be unconstitutional, and it is hardly likely that landowners - based on the provisions of the Danish constitution - can obtain the aid of the courts to hinder legislation on pollution control and control of land use, which the popularly elected political authorities deem desirable.

10.7.2 The Internationalization of Environmental Law

Many environmental problems cannot be solved by the individual countries but more effectively so through international cooperation. This is, for instance, true concerning the pollution of the oceans and the air pollution from major industrial areas, and the protection of migratory birds.

Therefore a certain 'internationalization' of environmental law is taking place. Parts of our environmental legislation are the result of international cooperation.

Denmark has ratified several *international conventions* concerning, among other things, pollution of the oceans, air pollution, and preservation of nature and bird life (e.g., the so-called Ramsar Convention of 1977 which is the basis of the preservation of Danish wetlands).

But it is *the environmental policy of the EC* that is gaining the largest influence on Danish environmental legislation.

Originally, environmental protection *did not play a large part* in EC policies and this issue was not mentioned at all in the Treaty of Rome. However, during the 1970's the EC Council of Ministers gradually formulated a common environmental policy which was reflected in 'action programmes'. These were meant as guidelines both for the individual countries' efforts regarding environmental policies and for the drawing up of common EC rules (directives).

In 1986, the Treaty of Rome was amended on various points, and an *article on EC environmental policy was incorporated in the Treaty.* According to this article, the Common Market must seek to preserve, protect, and improve the quality of the environment, contribute to human health, and ensure that the resources of nature are applied carefully and sensibly. Furthermore, it is laid down that the EC environmental policy must be based on the *principles of preventive measures, restoration of environmental damages at the source,* and the *'polluter pays' principle*, mentioned above.

The EC environmental policy is carried out through a number of different measures, extending from *financial aid* to research and development projects to *directives*, of which the Council of Ministers has issued a considerable number in recent years. The citizens of a member country are bound by these directives when that nation has carried out the directives by new legislation or administrative regulations. In Denmark, the directives have been implemented in the form of orders and circulars pursuant to the Environmental Protection Act and the Water Supplies Act.

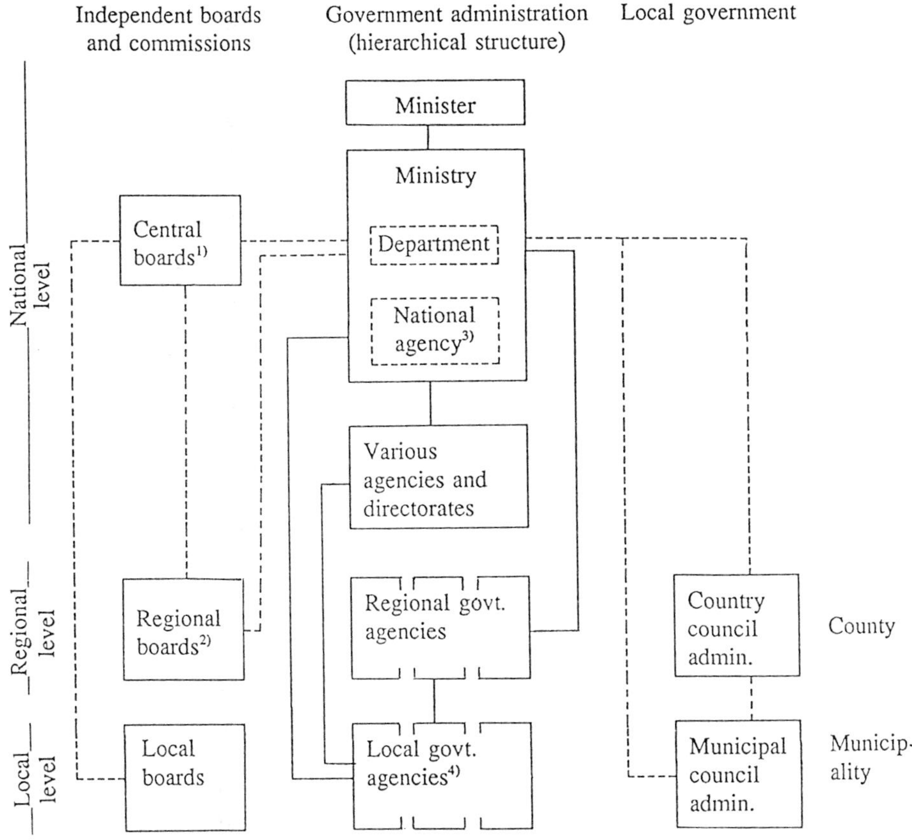

[1] The Environmental Appeal Board
[2] nature conservancy boards; land boards
[3] The National Agency of Environmental Protection; The National Agency of Physical Planning; The National Forest and Nature Agency
[4] the police; state forest districts

Figure 10.2. The organisation of the Danish administration.

The directives have dealt with issues as different as the quality of drinking water, groundwater pollution, protection of the aquatic environment, air pollution from motor vehicles, noise and vibrations, pesticide control, and the protection of birds.

An EC-directive of 1985 lays down that when carrying out certain major public and private projects, a special assessment of the installation's impact on the environment shall be made ('Environmental Impact Assessment' = EIA, cf. Chapter 12). The idea probably stems from the National Environmental Policy Act of the United States. It has also been applied by other nations, at least by France, since 1976. In Denmark, the need for a special EIA assessment is not clear, as projects are usually considered according to a number of statutes with a view to evaluating their environmental consequences.

However, the Regional Planning Act now states that the county council shall make an assessment of the environmental consequences of major installations when it draws up a regional plan.

Finally, it should be mentioned that *the EC's socio-structural policy* regarding agriculture also contains environmental policy elements. According to an EC regulation of 1985, aid can be granted to farmers who wish to limit pollution on their farms and improve the environment on their land. Farmers can also obtain aid for the planting of forests and farming in environmentally sensitive areas.

10.7.3 Rules and Regulations

As in other countries, the Danish environmental legislation now consists of a very comprehensive set of rules: A large number of *statutes* and a vast number of *administrative orders, circulars, and guidelines.* Under the Environmental Protection Act alone, more than 100 orders and guidelines have been issued.

The different statutes have authorized the working out of a large number special *sector plans*, which contribute to the regional and municipal planning. The plans were made according to detailed rules of procedure (see Section 10.6.1, f).

This whole system of rules and plans has, to some extent, made the environmental law and legislation very *confusing* for the citizens, enterprises, and the authorities that have to apply them. Hereby, the environmental legislation has evidently become a less useful (and also unnecessarily costly) means of carrying out the environmental policy.

Probably all of the Western world has seen efforts to *simplify legislation and administrative provisions* during the last decades. Also the Danish Government will attempt to cut down on the large member of provisions and plans during the coming reforms of the legislation and to concentrate it in a few very simple laws in order to promote clarity and avoid dealing with trifling matters. The rules concerning the sector planning of the county councils have already been simplified and it is under consideration to stop setting out rules for this planning altogether.

However, one can hardly doubt that the environmental legislation will always consist of an extensive set of rules and regulations which will be complicated and sometimes comprehensible only to specialists. Naturally, this makes it even more important to clear up the tangle of rules every once in a while.

10.7.4 The Authorities

Environmental legislation used to be divided up between a number of widely different authorities who each administered their area of the legislation. This made it difficult to coordinate the pollution prevention and the efforts to protect the environment.

Centrally the environmental legislation was divided between several ministries. *Locally* the legislation was administered by a confusion of different authorities: municipalities, county councils, land boards, nature conservancy boards, town development committees, health committees, etc., etc.

During the 1970's this system was gradually considerably simplified.

At the *central level* two very important changes were made.

Firstly, the legislation on zoning and planning, forests, pollution control, water courses, water supply, and raw materials was *concentrated* under one ministry: The Ministry of the Environment.

Secondly, the Ministry of the Environment was divided into one *'department'* and *several agencies*, today numbering three: The National Agency of Environmental Protection, the National Agency of Physical Planning, and the National Forest and Nature Agency. The National Agency of Environmental Protection is responsible for the Environmental Protection Act and the Water Law. The National Agency for Physical Planning is responsible for the planning legislation. The National Forest and Nature Agency is responsible for the Forestry Act, the management of Government forests, the Nature Conservation Act and the legislation on raw materials.

The agencies of the ministry take care of the day-to-day administration at the central level, including decisions on complaints against county council and municipal decisions, and the drawing up of guidelines to other authorities (see Section 10.5.3). The Ministry's department deals with the more important tasks in the form of providing secretarial services to the minister, coordinating functions, decisions in major appeal cases of a more principal nature, etc., and the drawing up of bills, orders, etc.

At *the local level* the authority to decide individual cases (issue licences, approvals, etc.) is placed with the municipal councils or the county councils. Many decisions made in individual cases include a weighing of many considerations - urban development, pollution, conservation interests and a landowner's personal interests. This weighing of interests is considered to be of a political nature and should therefore come within the jurisdiction of the popularly elected political authorities and not within the sphere of councils and boards that to some extent are independent of the political authorities.

The decisions of municipal and county councils can usually be *appealed* to one of the agencies under the Ministry of the Environment, see below.

The planning and control of compliance with the law also fall under the jurisdiction of the county councils and municipalities.

Even after the law reforms of the 1970's, there remain a number of *independent councils and boards*, for instance, the Environmental Appeal Board mentioned above, as well as nature-conservancy boards, that make many decisions pursuant to the Nature Conservation Act. The reason has probably been a perhaps not quite unfounded fear that the municipal councils would not put as high a priority on nature-conservation interests as on other interests they have to consider.

The ongoing law reform retains the idea that individual cases fall under municipal and county councils. It is also based on the idea that the county councils primarily should have jurisdiction in open spaces. The county councils should then take over the work of the nature-conservation board and become the only authority dealing with watercourses. To the extent that complaints will be allowed at all (Section 10.7.7), the relevant authorities should be the agencies of the Ministry of the Environment.

10.7.5 The Control of the Administrative System

How can Parliament and Government control the subordinate authorities' administration of the law to make sure that they apply their powers in compliance with the intention of the law and the environmental policy of the government?

Parliament can hold the minister politically responsible for the administration of matters under his jurisdiction. Standing parliamentary committees - for instance the Committee for the Environment and Physical Planning - also follow the developments in the country and can demand a statement from the minister on problems they consider important.

The Minister for the Environment has various means of controlling agencies, counties and municipalities.

First of all, through *circulars* the minister can give county councils and municipalities binding instructions for the administration of the law, and indicate to what extent these authorities may grant exemptions, licences, permits and approvals and on which terms.

Secondly, the minister can issue *guidelines* which are not binding and which are aimed at both authorities and citizens. This means of control is, e.g., used in the field of pollution control, where a very large number of guidelines has been drawn up. They have formed a significant basis for the authorities' administration of the Environmental Protection Act.

The most important guidelines are concerned with standards regarding external noise from enterprises, waste water, and air pollution from enterprises, etc., etc. They are drawn up as a combination of emission and immission standards.

Many guidelines have been drawn up to help county councils and municipalities in making regional, municipal, and local plans.

Furthermore, in most laws the Ministry of the Environment is the *appeal authority* in cases decided by county and municipal councils but, as is made clear in Section 10.7.7, this means of control will probably not be so significant in the future.

In certain cases, the minister has the right to make the decision himself in a case which would otherwise have been settled by an agency, a county council or municipal council (*'Call in'*). Finally, the minister can control the physical planning of the county councils' and local councils' planning sphere through *national planning directives* and by *approving* the regional plans which, as already mentioned, are determinative for the county councils' and municipal councils' more detailed planning and administration.

Perhaps the coming law reform will revoke the minister's authority to approve regional plans and instead give the minister the right to *veto* a plan. This amendment springs from the wish to decentralize the planning as much as possible.

10.7.6 Instruments of Environmental Law

a. Legal instruments

Of course, the most important legal instrument is *the statute.*

However, to a large extent, modern statutes leave a good part of the regulation of the citizens' conduct to administrative authorities and limit themselves to marking out the framework for the activities of the administration. This means that the Minister for the Environment can issue rules of law by *ministerial orders* (bekendtgørelser) which are legally binding on the citizens. Not least within the field of pollution, the rules have to be changed frequently concurrently with the obtaining of new knowledge. Therefore, it is desirable not to be bound by the laborious legislative procedure.

County councils and municipal councils can work out *plans* for land use, etc., as has been described in the previous sections.

When the law forbids a certain activity, for instance the construction of buildings in a rural zone or the discharge of waste water into streams, etc., the county councils and municipalities have far-reaching powers to grant the necessary *exemptions, licences and permits*, and to *dictate the terms* which are deemed necessary in each individual case. In this connection, it is relevant to mention the Environmental Protection Act's provision which forbids commencing heavily polluting enterprises without previous *approval.*

When dealing with applications for licences and approvals, the authorities most often adhere to the *circulars and guidelines* which are mentioned in Section 10.6.5. By reading these, the applicants will be able to see which standards and guidelines form the basis for the authorities' decisions.

Finally, the authorities are, in many cases, entitled to place certain obligations on the citizens in the form of concrete *orders and* prohibitions. As examples can be mentioned conservation decisions, municipal orders to improve waste-water plants, and land expropriations for the establishment of waterworks and recreational areas.

One last legal means of control within the environmental legislation should be mentioned: *Agreements.* The environmental authorities can make management agreements with a farmer about the tending and care of an area submitted to a conservation easement, etc. They can buy areas in the free market with a view to planting forest and establishing recreational areas. (In this connection the authorities are entitled to submit areas they wish to procure to a right of preemption). The ongoing legislative work might give the authorities the right to enter into agreements with industrial enterprises regarding a reduction of their pollution in return for financial aid. Similar agreements are known, for instance, in France.

b. Non-Legal Means of Control

Financial means of control are also used to implement environmental policy such as *aid* in the installation of ochre purification plants, the planting of deciduous forest, and the reduction of pollution from a farm or an enterprise. It is also contemplated to levy *environmental duties* if the pollution exceeds a certain limit.

The environmental authorities can implement an environmental policy by managing enterprises and plants themselves. The local authorities manage *waterworks and waste-water plants*, just as the National Forest and Nature Agency manage the *state-owned forests and plantations*, etc., with a view to public visits, etc.

A more detailed description of non-legal means of control and an evaluation of whether legal or non-legal means of control should be applied to implement the environmental policy is not within the framework of this chapter.

10.7.7 The Citizen and Environmental Law

Modern environmental legislation often allows the citizens to participate in the working out of plans and projects. Many projects - e.g., for the construction of a road or a water-supply plant - are not decided upon unless all interested parties have had the opportunity *to advance their opinion.*

Moreover, the planning legislation prescribes that county councils and local councils shall create a *public debate* about the aim and contents of the regional and municipal plans. Proposals to the local plans must be published in order to inform citizens and enterprises and give them an opportunity to raise objections.

In return for this 'citizen participation', the planning legislation has to a large extent *cut off the citizens' right of appeal* against the authorities' decisions - not just the final plans - but also individual decisions.

As part of the ongoing law reform, the rules concerning publicity about plans, projects, and decisions will probably be further elaborated but at the same time the citizens' *right of appeal will be limited to important issues.* The reason given for this is that the right of appeal prolongs the decision-making process and incurs public expense. It is a matter of opinion whether this is an adequate reason for abolishing the citizen's right to appeal to a higher authority when he feels that he has received a wrong decision from an agency or municipal council.

10.7.8 Public Confidence in Environmental Law

In recent years, the public sometimes has shown a certain distrust of the environmental legislative system. Many people have held the view that the sentences for violating the law are too mild and that it can be difficult to make the authorities intervene energetically against a polluting enterprise with a large number of employees and a production which is important for the region. The courts and the municipal councils are sometimes reluctant to order the demolishing of a valuable building which is built contrary to the provisions of a local plan. The situation is, of course, especially unpleasant, if the building is constructed in good faith according to an illegal permit from the municipal council.

An effort is now being made to raise the level of fines so that it no longer pays to violate the law and so that any environmental damage or economic gain is considered aggravating circumstances. Through various law amendments, attempts have been made to make legalization a more frequent course of action than it has been up to now and to make it possible to sentence members of regional and municipal councils who take part in violations of the environmental legislatition.

There is without doubt an increasing public demand that effective measures be taken against violations of the environmental legislation. It is therefore to be hoped that all these measures will be fruitful.

REFERENCES: SOME DANISH LITERATURE ON ENVIRONMENTAL LAW

Andersen, B., and Christiansen, O., 1988*. Kommuneplanloven, 3. udgave. (The Act on Local Planning). Jurist- og Økonomforbundets Forlag, Copenhagen.

Bjerring, J., and Møller, G., 1987*. Miljøbeskyttelsesloven. (The Environmental Protection Act). Jurist- og Økonomforbundets Forlag, Copenhagen.

Basse, E.M., 1987*. Erhvervsmiljøret. (Enviromental Business Law). Gad, Copenhagen.

Herslund, B., Holmboe, E. and Brix, B., 1979*. Råstofloven. (The Raw Materials Act). Juristforbundets Forlag, Copenhagen.

Illum, K., 1976*. Dansk Tingsret (3. omarb. udgave v. V. Carstensen). (Danish Law of Property). Juristforbundets Forlag, Copenhagen.

Nørby Jensen, P. and Wulff, H., 1981*. Hvad må min nabo? (My neighbour's rights). Gad, Copenhagen.

Anonymous, 198?*: Karnovs Lovsamling, inkl. kommentarer. (The Karnov Statute Book). Karnov, Copenhagen.

Miljøministeriet, 1987*. Økonomiske styringsmidler i miljøpolitikken. (Financial Means of Control in Environmental Policies). The Ministry of the Environment, Copenhagen.

Miljøstyrelsen, 1986*. Muligheden for at anvende afgifter som supplerende styringsmiddel/finansiering af nye foranstaltninger på miljøområdet. (The Possibility of Using Duties as a Means of Control/for Financing New Measures within the Environmental Sphere). National Agency of Environmental Protection (Miljøstyrelsen), Copenhagen.

Nielsen, V. et al., 1973*. Naturfredningsloven, almindelig fremstilling og kommentar. (The Nature Conservation Act, common version and comments). Gad, Copenhagen.

Revsbæk, K., 1986*. Planer og forvaltningsret. (Planning and Administrative Law). Gad, Copenhagen.

Stagetorn, M., 1978*. Nabo-ret. (The Law Relating to Adjoining Properties). Berlingske Forlag, Copenhagen.

Tolstrup, F. and Barfod, J., 1975*. Vandløbs- og vandforsyningslovgivningen (Ældre lovgivning). (Watercourse and Water Supply Legislation). Juristforbundets Forlag, Copenhagen.

von Eyben, W.E., 1977-78*. Dansk Miljøret 1-5. (Danish Environmental Law, vol. 1-5). Akademisk Forlag, Copenhagen.

von Eyben, W.E. et al., 1986*. Miljørettens Grundbog. (Basic Environmental Law). Akademisk Forlag, Copenhagen.

Wulff, H., 1979*. Landboret. (Agricultural Land Law). DSR Forlag/RVAU, Copenhagen.

Wulff, H., 1970*. Skovloven (Ældre lov). (The Forestry Act). Ministry of Agriculture, Copenhagen.

In the agencies of the Danish Ministry for the Environment, it may be possible to obtain statutes, reports, etc., concerning environmental problems, translated into English.

11 ECOLOGICAL ASPECTS

SVEN ERIK JØRGENSEN

11.1 HOW TO CONSIDER THE ECOLOGICAL ASPECTS?

Environmental problems are caused by man's emission of mass and energy from society into nature, i.e., to the ecosystems. To reduce the discharge to zero is not possible - from either a technological or an economical point of view. It is, therefore, relevant to attempt to answer the following questions:

- *which effects on the ecosystems are caused by different levels of emissions?*
- *which types and quantities of emissions are tolerable?*

The fact that an ecosystem is a very complex system renders it difficult to answer these questions. *Models* make it feasible to survey complex systems, and such models are, therefore, a powerful tool in environmental management. But, as discussed in Chapter 13, good environmental models are constructed from a good knowledge of the problem and the (eco)system, not the other way around. Therefore, it is urgently needed for the environmental management to know the reactions of the ecosystems to changes of the man-made impact on them.

The problem may be reformulated in the following way: One must know the relations between the 'forcing functions', i.e., the impacts on the ecosystem, and the 'state variables', i.e., the variables describing the state of the system. Fig. 11.1 illustrates such a relation between a forcing function and a state variable. In most cases, the relation is nonlinear.

A quantity termed the *ecological buffer capacity*, ß, is used to describe the ability of the ecosystem to meet small changes in the forcing functions with small changes in the state variables. The ecological buffer capacity is defined by the expression

$$\beta = \frac{\Delta(\text{forcing function})}{\Delta(\text{state variable})} . \qquad (11.1)$$

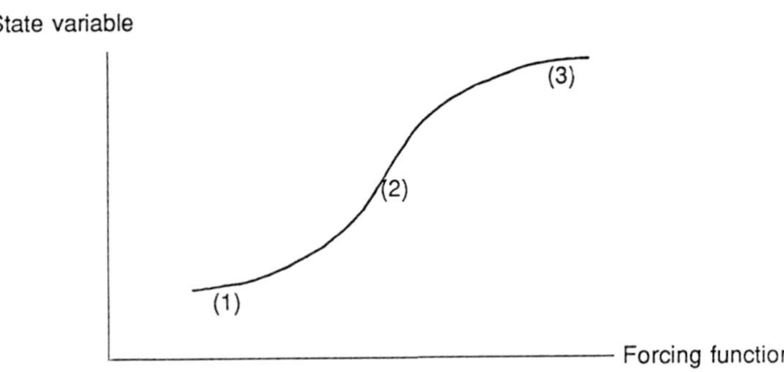

Figure 11.1. A relationship between a forcing function and a state variable is shown. At points 1 and 3, the ecological buffer capacity is high; at point 2, it is low.

Table 11.1. The hierarchy of regulation/feed-back mechanisms in ecosystems.

[1]	Regulation of rates, e.g., for the uptake of a nutrient by algae.
[2]	Feed-back regulation of rates, e.g., by a high nutrient concentration in algae which will slow down the uptake.
[3]	Adaptation of process rates, e.g., by changing the dependence of nutrient uptake rate on temperature.
[4]	Adaptation of species to new conditions, e.g., adaptation of insects to DDT.
[5]	Shift in species composition. Species better fitted to new conditions will be more dominant.
[6]	A more pronounced shift in species composition, causing a shift in the structure of the ecosystem.
[7]	Change in the genetic pool available for selection.

Because there is a large number of forcing functions and of state variables, there are also many buffer capacities. The environmental manager should have a good knowledge of the various buffer capacities and, in general, of the relations between impacts and ecosystem conditions. An overview of an ecosystem's properties is necessary if one wishes to understand the ecosystem's reactions to changes in the man-controlled forcing functions.

In this chapter we intend to give an overview of the most important ecosystem properties in this respect. The chapter focuses on the following topics: the feed-back mechanisms of the ecosystems; the possibilities for adaptation; the basic conditions for life; diversity and ecological development; the stability of an ecosystem and its relationship with structure. The above-mentioned concept of ecological buffer capacity will be treated in some detail.

11.2 FEED-BACKS IN ECOSYSTEMS

Ecosystems have a hierarchy of feed-back mechanisms, cf. Table 11.1. These mechanisms are able to regulate the influence of forcing functions, to *maintain the proper functioning of the system*. The many processes in the ecosystem will, in the first instance, try to minimize the effects of changes imposed on the system. For instance, an increase in a nutrient concentration will be reduced by uptake in plants. We can speak about a 'Le Chatelier's Principle of Ecology': the ecological processes will proceed in the direction that minimizes the effects of the changes imposed on the system from outside. These processes react promptly, to guarantee a fast regulation.

However, many of the processes are able not only to regulate, but also to do it faster, the larger the imposed changes are.

As an example, let us consider the uptake rate of a nutrient in a plant. Such a rate may often be described by a so-called Michaëlis-Menten expression:

$$\mu = \mu' \frac{N_s}{k_m + N_s}, \tag{11.2}$$

where μ is the uptake rate, μ' is the maximum uptake rate (a species-dependent constant), N_s is the concentration of dissolved nutrient, and k_m is the so-called 'half-saturation constant'. For $N_s \ll k_m$, the uptake rate is seen to be approximately proportional to the nutrient concentration. On the other hand: for $N_s \gg k_m$, the uptake rate approaches μ' and thus becomes independent of N_s, and the regulation becomes less effective. (At the intermediate value $N_s = k_m$, (11.2) yields $\mu = 0.5\ \mu'$, which explains the notion 'half-saturation constant').

Adaptation may then be the next answer to the regulation. Adaptation means that the organisms change: they become more fitted to handle the new situation. In the nutrient-uptake example it may be described, e.g., by an increase in the half-saturation constant.

If the organisms in question cannot cope with the new conditions, even after possible adaptations, other species may take over, perhaps some which are better equipped to the conditions. Or it may even happen that new foodwebs take over, to ensure a proper regulation (cf. Table 11.1). Still further, a regulation may be based on the evolution of the species composition, i.e., on a selection of the best-fitted species in the ecosystem.

A good knowledge of the regulation mechanisms is crucial in ecological modelling, in the application of ecotechnology, and in the entire field of environmental management. The following section is devoted to a further presentation of some of these important regulation mechanisms, and to what extent they are able to maintain the functions of the ecosystem.

11.3 ADAPTATION AND THE ECOLOGICAL NICHE

Past environments act as a filter through which combinations of characters have passed on the way to the present. *Organisms appear to be adapted or fitted to the present environment only because present environments tend to be similar to past ones.* Organisms are not designed for their present or future environment: they are consequences of their past environment, and therefore they are adapted by it.

By definition, the individuals best fitted in a population are those that leave the largest number of descendants. Fitness is, however, a relative, not an absolute term. It is the proportionate contribution made to future generations by an individual, which determines its fitness. And those individuals that leave the largest proportion of descendants in a population have the greatest influence on the heritable characteristics of that population.

The individuals that make up a population of a species are not identical. They vary in response to the many environmental factors such as temperature, pH, composition of media and so on. The individuals that are better fitted to the present conditions will produce more descendants, and thereby the population will become better adapted. This process - by which new genes are not 'tested', only the present ones - may be called adaptation. The entire process, where adaptation is working hand in hand with a steadily changing genetic pool, including new sexual recombinations of genes, is termed evolution. It involves even the emergence of new species.

We are now in a position to consider, even if briefly, a concept which is central to much ecological thinking: the *ecological niche*. When defining this concept we shall take our stand with Hutchinson (1957, 1969).

Organisms of any given species can survive, grow, reproduce and maintain a viable population within certain temperature limits. This range of temperature is the species' ecological niche in one dimension, the dimension being in this case the one connected with temperature. The ecological niche is an n-dimensional concept, n being the number of factors influencing the species in question.

11.4 CONDITIONS FOR LIFE

The life-building processes require the presence of the elements that are characteristic to the biosphere. On the other hand, the composition of the biosphere is closely related to the biological functions of the elements.

The high concentrations of C, H and O in the biosphere are due to the composition of organic compounds. The nitrogen concentration results from the presence of proteins, including enzymes and polypeptides, and of nucleotides. Phosphorus is used as a matrix material in the form of calcium compounds, in phospate esters and in ATP (adenosine triphospate), which is involved in all energetically coupled reactions.

ATP is an energy-rich compound, because of its relatively large negative free energy of hydrolysis, denoted ΔG:

$$\begin{aligned} H_2O + ATP &\rightarrow ADP + P + \Delta G_{high} , \\ H_2O + ADP &\rightarrow AMP + P + \Delta G_{high} . \end{aligned} \tag{11.3}$$

AMP is not a high-energy compound, since we have

$$AMP \rightarrow A + P + \Delta G_{low} . \tag{11.4}$$

These processes do not actually occur in living cells, but ATP participates, directly or indirectly, in group transfer reactions. A simple example will illustrate this point:

$$ATP + glucose \rightarrow ADP + glucose\text{-}P . \tag{11.5}$$

Whenever food components are decomposed by a living organism, the energy released by the process is either used as heat or stored in the form of a number of ATP molecules.

As it is for ATP, it is possible to indicate a function for other elements needed by living organisms - a function related to the biochemistry of each of the organisms.

The biochemical pattern of the organism determines the relative need for a number of elements of the biosphere (in the order of 20-25), while the remaining 65-70 elements are more or less toxic. Some elements needed by some species are toxic to others, even in very small concentrations. This does not imply that a particular species requires a fixed composition of elements. The composition may vary within certain limits.

It is known, for example, that algae species may contain from 0.5 to 2.5 g phosphorus per 100 g of dry matter, with an average of about 1 g. A high phosphorus concentration indicates that a 'luxury' uptake has taken place.

Table 11.2. Dissolved oxygen (ppm) in fresh, brackish and sea water at different temperatures and at different chlorinities (%). Values are amount of saturation.

°C	0%	0.2%	0.4%	0.6%	0.8%	1.0%	1.2%	1.4%	1.6%	1.8%	2.0%
1	14.24	13.87	13.54	13.22	12.91	12.58	12.29	11.99	11.70	11.42	11.15
2	13.74	13.50	13.18	12.88	12.56	12.26	11.98	11.69	11.40	11.13	10.86
3	13.45	13.14	12.84	12.55	12.25	11.96	11.68	11.39	11.12	10.85	10.59
4	13.09	12.79	12.51	12.22	11.93	11.65	11.38	11.10	10.83	10.59	10.34
5	12.75	12.45	12.17	11.91	11.63	11.36	11.09	10.83	10.57	10.33	10.10
6	12.44	12.15	11.86	11.60	11.33	11.07	10.82	10.56	10.32	10.09	9.86
7	12.13	11.85	11.58	11.32	11.06	10.82	10.56	10.32	10.07	9.84	9.63
8	11.85	11.56	11.29	11.05	10.80	10.56	10.32	10.07	9.84	9.61	9.40
9	11.56	11.29	11.02	10.77	10.54	10.30	10.08	9.84	9.61	9.40	9.20
10	11.29	11.03	10.77	10.53	10.30	10.07	9.84	9.61	9.40	9.20	9.00
11	11.05	10.77	10.53	10.29	10.06	9.84	9.63	9.41	9.20	9.00	8.80
12	10.80	10.53	10.29	10.06	9.84	9.63	9.41	9.21	9.00	8.80	8.61
13	10.56	10.30	10.07	9.84	9.63	9.41	9.21	9.01	8.81	8.61	8.42
14	10.33	10.07	9.86	9.63	9.41	9.21	9.01	8.81	8.62	8.44	8.25
15	10.10	9.86	9.64	9.43	9.23	9.03	8.83	8.64	8.44	8.27	8.09
16	9.89	9.66	9.44	9.24	9.03	8.84	8.64	8.47	8.28	8.11	7.94
17	9.67	9.46	9.26	9.05	8.85	8.65	8.47	8.30	8.11	7.94	7.78
18	9.47	9.27	9.07	8.87	8.67	8.48	8.31	8.14	7.97	7.79	7.64
19	9.28	9.08	8.88	8.68	8.50	8.31	8.15	7.98	7.80	7.65	7.49
20	9.11	8.90	8.70	8.51	8.32	8.15	7.99	7.84	7.66	7.51	7.36
21	8.93	8.72	8.54	8.35	8.17	7.99	7.84	7.69	7.52	7.38	7.23
22	8.75	8.55	8.38	8.19	8.02	7.85	7.69	7.54	7.39	7.25	7.11
23	8.60	8.40	8.22	8.04	7.87	7.71	7.55	7.41	7.26	7.12	6.99
24	8.44	8.25	8.07	7.89	7.72	7.56	7.42	7.28	7.13	6.99	6.86
25	8.27	8.09	7.92	7.75	7.58	7.44	7.29	7.15	7.01	6.88	6.85
26	8.12	7.94	7.78	7.62	7.45	7.31	7.16	7.03	6.89	6.86	6.63
27	7.98	7.79	7.64	7.49	7.32	7.18	7.03	6.91	6.78	6.65	6.52
28	7.84	7.65	7.51	7.36	7.19	7.06	6.92	6.79	6.66	6.53	6.40
29	7.69	7.52	7.38	7.23	7.08	6.95	6.82	6.68	6.55	6.42	6.29
30	7.56	7.39	7.25	7.12	6.96	6.83	6.70	6.58	6.45	6.32	6.19

Animals require oxygen for respiration, and there is a pronouncedly close relationship between oxygen concentration and growth rate (or mortality). Oxygen has a relatively low solubility in water (see Table 11.2). A low oxygen concentration in an aquatic ecosystem has frequently caused the destruction of fish, due to the discharge of otherwise harmless organic material which is being biologically decomposed by microorganisms. Through the breakdown of the organic components, oxygen is consumed, and the oxygen concentration in the water becomes critically low. This is especially dangerous at high temperature, where the biological degradation is fast and the oxygen solubility low (Table 11.2).

Examples of limiting oxygen concentrations for aquatic organisms are given in Table 11.3.

The relation between nutrient concentration and growth has long been known for crop yields. Fig. 11.2 illustrates the so-called

Liebig's minimum law: *If a nutrient is at a minimum relative to its use for growth, there is a linear relation between the concentration of the nutrient and the (biomass)-growth rate.*

If the nutrient concentration becomes so high that the supply of another factor is now at a minimum, further addition of the nutrient will no longer influence growth (see Fig. 11.2).

In arid climates, primary production (i.e., the amount of solar energy stored by green plants) is strongly correlated with precipitation, as shown in Fig. 11.3. Obviously, it is water which is 'the limiting factor' in this case. Among many possible limiting factors, the most important ones are: various nutrients, water, and temperature.

The relation between nutrient concentration and growth is described by the Michaëlis-Menten function, cf. equation (11.2). In general, this function is well suited to describe the rate of a biochemical reaction as a function of substrate concentration:

$$v = \frac{k\, s}{k_m + s}, \tag{11.6}$$

where v = the rate of the process (e.g., a growth rate)
s = the substrate concentration
k = a constant, viz. the maximum rate
k_m = the so-called 'half-saturation constant' .

In most cases, the situation in nature is not so simple, because two or more nutrients may interact. This can sometimes be described fairly well by a product of two Michaëlis-Menten factors, one for each nutrient:

$$v = \frac{k_1\, N_1}{k_{m1} + N_1}\,\frac{k_2\, N_2}{k_{m2} + N_2} = K_r\,\frac{N_1}{k_{m1} + N_1}\,\frac{N_2}{k_{m2} + N_2}, \tag{11.7}$$

where v = the growth rate
N_1 and N_2 = the nutrient concentrations
$K_r = k_1 k_2$ = the overall maximum rate
k_{m1} and k_{m2} = half-saturation constants .

However, Equation (11.7) often limits growth too much and is in disagreement with many observations (Park et al., 1978). The following equation seems to overcome some of these difficulties:

$$v = K_r\, \mathrm{Min}\left(\frac{N_1}{k_{m1} + N_1}, \frac{N_2}{k_{m2} + N_2}\right). \tag{11.8}$$

Table 11.3. Examples of limiting oxygen concentrations for aquatic organisms.

Organism	Temperature, °C	mg O_2/l
Brown trout	6 - 24	1.3 - 2.9
Coho salmon	16 - 24	1.3 - 2.0
Rainbow trout	11 - 20	1.1 - 3.7
Worms (*Nereis grubei* and *Capitella capitata*)	22 - 26	1.5 - 3.0
Amphipod (*Hyglella azteca*)	-	0.7 -

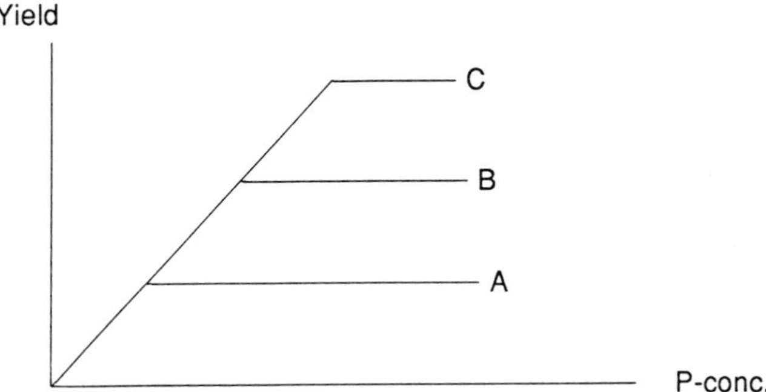

Figure 11.2. Illustration of Liebig's law. The yield is plotted against the phosphorus concentration. To begin with, there is an almost linear relationship between the two, but at a certain concentration value of P , some other component will become the limiting factor, and higher P concentrations will not make the yield increase. In this case study, the three levels A, B and C correspond to three different potassium concentrations.

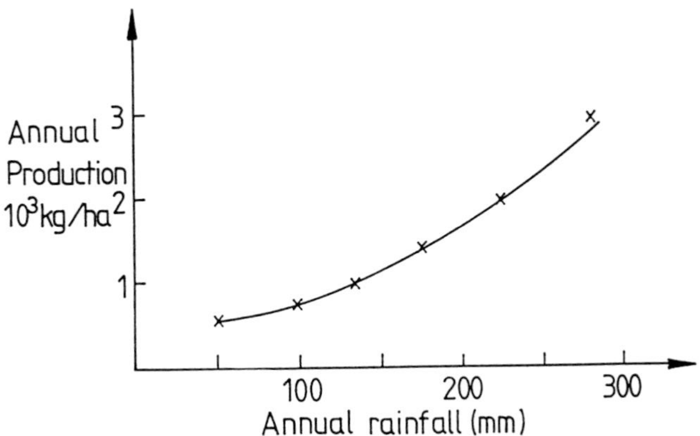

Figure 11.3. A strong correlation is shown between annual rainfall and primary production along a precipitation gradient in a desert region (South West Africa).

Table 11.4. Concentration of ammonia + ammonium (NH_3 + NH_4^+), assuming an ammonia (NH_3) concentration of 0.025 mg l^{-1}.

C°	pH = 7.0	pH = 7.5	pH = 8.0	pH = 8.5	pH = 9.0	pH = 9.5
5	19.6	6.3	2	0.65	0.22	0.088
10	12.4	4.3	1.37	0.45	0.16	0.068
15	9.4	5.9	0.93	0.31	0.12	0.054
20	6.3	2	0.65	0.22	0.088	0.045
25	4.4	1.4	0.47	0.17	0.069	0.039
30	3.1	1	0.33	0.12	0.056	0.035

Table 11.5. The influence of temperature on environmental processes.

A. $v(T) = v(20°C) \times k^{T-20}$

Process	k
Nitrification	1.07 - 1.10
NH_4^+ — NO_2^-	1.08
NO_2^- — NO_3^-	1.06
Org-N — NH_4^+	1.08
Benthic oxygen uptake	1.065
Degradation of organic matter in water	1.02 - 1.09
Reaeration of streams	1.008 - 1.026
Respiration og zooplankton	1.05

B. $v(T) = K \times v(T-10°)$

Proces	K
Respiration of communities	1.7 - 3.5 (2.5)
Respiration of freshwater fish	2.18 - 3.28 (2.4)
Sulphate reduction in sediment	3.4 - 3.9
Excretion of NH_4^+ from zooplankton	2.0 - 4.3
Excretion of total nitrogen from zooplankton	1.5 - 2.5
Oxygen uptake of sediment	3.2
Respiration of zooplankton	1.77 - 3.28

The relationship between nutrient discharge and its effect on an ecosystem is illustrated in Chapter 5. If the nutrient concentration in a lake is increased, the growth of algae will be enhanced. As a result, oxygen is produced through photosynthesis:

$$6\ CO_2 + 6\ H_2O \rightarrow C_6H_{12}O_6 + 6\ O_2\ . \tag{11.9}$$

However, the extra amount of organic matter produced by this process will sooner or later decompose, thereby causing a deficit of oxygen. For further details, see Chapter 5.

While nutrients are necessary for plant growth, they may produce a deterioration in life conditions for other forms of life. Ammonia is extremely toxic to fish, whereas the ionized form, ammonium, is harmless. The relation between ammonium and ammonia depends on pH:

$$NH_4^+ \leftrightarrow NH_3 + H^+ , \tag{11.10}$$

$$pH = pK + \log([NH_3]/[NH_4^+]) , \tag{11.11}$$

where pK = -log K, and K denotes the equilibrium constant for the process (11.10).

Therefore, the pH value as well as the total concentration of ammonium and ammonia are important for the survival of the fish (see Table 11.4).

Because of the mechanism just described, the situation can become very critical in hypereutrophic lakes during the summer, when photosynthesis is most pronounced. The pH increases when the acidic component CO_2 is removed or reduced by the process (11.10).

In distilled water at 25°C, pK is about 9.3, but it increases with increasing salinity. Therefore, the concentrations given in Table 11.4 are higher in sea water.

Also the temperature is of great importance to life in an ecosystem. The influence of of the temperature on some biotic processes is illustrated in Table 11.5.

The amount of solar energy intercepting a unit of the Earth's surface varies markedly with the latitude, for two reasons. First, at a high latitude, a sunbeam hits the surface of the Earth at a small angle, and its light energy is spread out over a large surface area. Second, a beam that intercepts the atmosphere at a small angle must penetrate a thicker blanket of air; hence, more solar energy is reflected by particles in the atmosphere and radiated back into space. Both these effects also imply the well-known fact that average annual temperatures tend to decrease with increasing latitude (Table 11.6). The poles are cold and the trophics are generally warm.

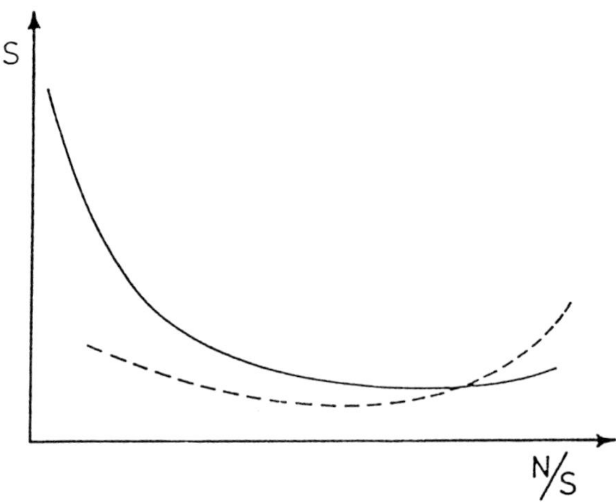

Figure 11.4. Relationship between the number S of species and the number N of individuals per species. Environmental stress tends to flatten out the curve, as indicated by the dotted line.

Table 11.6. Average annual temperature (°C).

Latitude	Year	January	July	Range
90°N	-22.7	-41.1	-1.1	40.0
80°N	-18.3	-32.2	2.0	34.2
70°N	-10.7	-26.3	7.3	33.6
60°N	-1.1	-16.1	14.1	30.2
50°N	5.8	-7.1	18.1	25.2
40°N	14.1	5.0	24.0	19.0
30°N	20.4	14.5	27.3	12.8
20°N	25.3	21.8	28.0	6.2
10°N	26.7	25.8	27.2	1.4
Equator	26.2	26.4	25.6	0.8
10°S	25.3	26.3	23.9	2.4
20°S	22.9	25.4	20.0	5.4
30°S	16.6	21.9	14.7	7.2
40°S	11.9	15.6	9.0	6.6
50°S	5.8	8.1	3.4	4.7
60°S	-3.4	2.1	-9.1	11.2
70°S	-13.6	-3.5	-23.0	19.5
80°S	-27.0	-10.8	-39.5	28.7
90°S	-33.1	-13.5	-47.8	34.3

In terrestrial ecosystems, climate is by far the most important determinant of the gross primary productivity, i.e., the amount of solar energy that plants are able to capture as chemical energy. Table 11.7 shows the net primary productivity and the world net primary production for the major ecosystems.

11.5 SPECIES DIVERSITY AND THE DEVELOPMENT OF ECOSYSTEMS

Out of thousands of species that might be present in an ecosystem, only a few exert a major controlling influence by virtue of their numbers, size, production or other activities. Intracommunity classification, therefore, goes beyond the taxonomic listing and attempts to evaluate the actual importance of organisms in the community.

Three types of indices are used to describe the organization in an ecosystem:

1. *indices of dominance,*
2. *indices of similarity,*
3. *indices of diversity.*

Some of the most commonly used indices in the three groups are listed in Table 11.8.

Table 11.7. Net primary productivity and world net primary production for the major ecosystems.

	Area (10^6 km^2)	Net primary productivity per unit area (dry g/m^2/yr) normal range	mean	World net primary production (10^6 dry tons/yr)
Lake and stream	2	100 - 1500	500	1.0
Swamp and marsh	2	800 - 4000	2000	4.0
Tropical forest	20	1000 - 5000	2000	40.0
Temperate forest	18	600 - 2500	1300	23.4
Boreal forest	12	400 - 2000	800	9.6
Woodland and shrubland	7	200 - 1200	600	4.2
Savanna	15	200 - 2000	700	10.5
Temperate grassland	9	150 - 1500	500	4.5
Tundra and alpine	8	10 - 400	140	1.1
Desert scrub	18	10 - 250	70	1.3
Extreme desert, rock and ice	24	0 - 10	3	0.1
Agricultural land	14	100 - 4000	650	9.1
Total land	149		730	109.0
Open ocean	332	2 - 400	125	1.5
Continental shelf	27	200 - 600	350	9.5
Attached algae and estuaries	2	500 - 4000	2000	4.0
Total ocean	361		155	55.0
Total for Earth	510		320	164.0

Species diversity tends to be low in physically controlled ecosystems and high in biologically controlled ecosystems. But this rule is *not* always valid, it is merely a tendency. There may be a relationship between the stability of an ecosystem and its diversity, but the detailed relationship still has to be discovered, cf. the next section.

The general relationship between species and numbers of individuals is shown in Fig. 11.4. Stress will tend to flatten out the curve, as indicated in the figure by the dotted line.

Two broad approaches to analyzing species diversity in different situations use comparisons based on, respectively,

1. *diversity indices,* cf. Table 11.8, and
2. the shapes, patterns and equations of *species abundance curves.*

It is essential to recognize that species diversity has a number of components which may respond differently to external and internal factors of importance to environmental conditions.

Areas with a very predictable and stable climate tend to support fewer different plant-life forms that do regions with a more erratic climate (see Fig. 11.5).

The index of diversity most widely used is the *Shannon index.* It is normally distributed so that routine statistical methods can be used to test for significance of differences between means. Further, the Shannon index is reasonably independent of the sample size.

Table 11.8. Some useful indices of species structure in a community.

A. Index of dominance (c) , cf. Simpson (1949)

$c = \Sigma(n_i/N)^2$, where n_i = importance value for each species (number of individuals, biomass, production, or similar)
N = total of importance values, $N = \Sigma n_i$.

B. Index of similarity (S) between two samples, cf. Sørensen (1948); for a related index of '% difference', see E.P. Odum (1950)

$S = 2C/(A+B)$, where A = number of species in sample A
B = number of species in sample B
C = number of species common to both samples.

Note: Index of dissimilarity = 1 - S.

C. Indices of species diversity

(1) Three species richness or variety indices (d), cf. Margalef (1958) (d_1), Menhinick (1964) (d_2), and H.T. Odum, Cantlon and Kornicker (1960) (d_3), respectively.

$d_1 = (S-1)/(\log N)$ $\quad d_2 = S/N^{1/2}$ $\quad d_3 =$ S per 1000 individuals

where S = number of species
N = number of individuals, etc.

(2) Evenness index (e), cf. Pielou (1966); for another type of 'equitability' index, see Lloyd and Ghelardi (1964)

$e = H/(\log S)$, where H = Shannon index (see below)
S = number of species.

(3) Shannon index of general diversity (H), cf. Shannon and Weaver (1963), and also Margalef (1968)

$H = -\Sigma P_i \log P_i$, where $P_i = n_i/N$
= importance probability for each species
n_i = importance value for each species
N = total of importance values, $N = \Sigma n_i$.

A higher diversity means longer foodchains, more cases of symbiosis and greater possibilities of negative feedback control which will reduce oscillations and hence increase stability (see, however, the discussion in the next section). For these reasons, the ecologist has a general interest in the concept of diversity; in any measure of diversity, he will see an indicator of the possibilities for constructing feedback systems (Margalef, 1968).

Diversity indices are useful in evaluating man-made stress on the ecosystems, as illustrated in Figs. 11.6 and 11.7.

Usually, ecosystems are very difficult to manipulate experimentally. For this reason, ecologists have for long been particularly interested in islands, because they constitute some of the finest 'natural' ecological experiments.

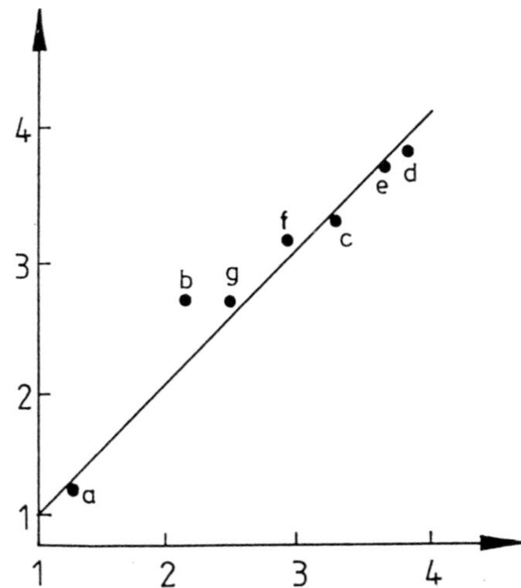

Figure 11.5. Rainfall unpredictability, an indicator of 'climate diversity', plotted against plant-life form diversity. Both diversities were computed as Shannon indices. (a): Tropical rain forest, (b): Subtropical forest, (c): Deciduous forest, (d): Mediterranean scrub, (e): Desert, (f): Steppe, (g): Arctic tundra. - Sources: May (1975) and others.

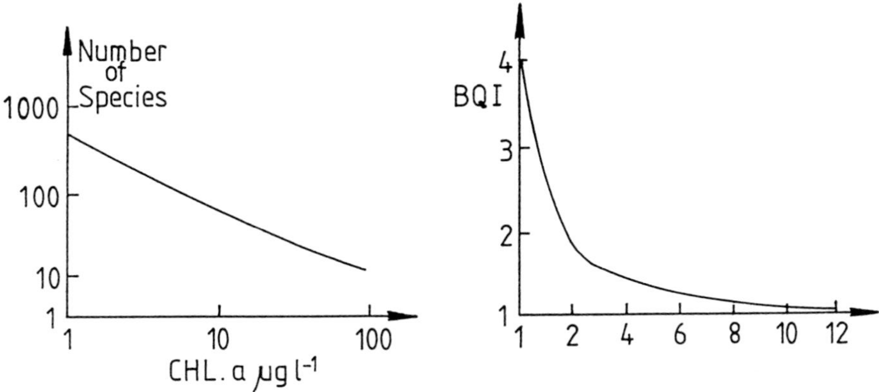

Figure 11.6. Swedish lakes. - In a number of Swedish lakes, Weiderholm (1980) obtained the relationship shown in the curve to the left between number of species and eutrophication, measured as chlorophyll loss, µg l^{-1}. In another survey, Ahl and Weiderholm (1977) found the relationship shown in the curve to the right between BQI and total phosphorus concentration divided by depth. BQI (benthic quality index) is a diversity index for the benthic fauna; it is defined as $BQI = (k_o n_o + k_1 n_2 + ... + k_5 n_5)/N$, where k_i is a 'quality indicator' for each of the six species, n_i the number of individuals in the group, and $N = n_o + n_1 + ... + n_5$ is the total number of individuals.

Table 11.9. Estimated z-values (see Equation (11.9) and text) for various terrestrial plants and animals on different island groups. - Source: MacArthur and Wilson (1967).

Flora or fauna	Island group	z
Carabid beetles	West Indies	0.34
Amphibians and reptiles	West Indies	0.30
Birds	West Indies	0.24
Birds	East Indies	0.28
Birds	Gulf of Guinea	0.49
Birds	East Central Pacific	0.30
Land plants	Galapagos Islands	0.33
Land Vertebrates	Islands of Lake Michigan	0.24
Ants	Melanesia	0.30

Through studies of islands, it has been found that the larger islands generally support more species of plants and animals than do the smaller ones. In several cases, a tenfold increase in area turned out to correspond to an approximate doubling of the number of species.

More precisely, *a relation has been put up between the number of species, S, and the area A of the island*; under the assumption that we limit ourselves to considering a specific taxa and a fairly homogeneous archipelago, the relation is:

$$S = C A^z , \tag{11.12}$$

where C and z are constants that vary between taxa and from region to region; z generally ranges from about 0.24 to about 0.34. Table 11.9 gives some estimated z-values.

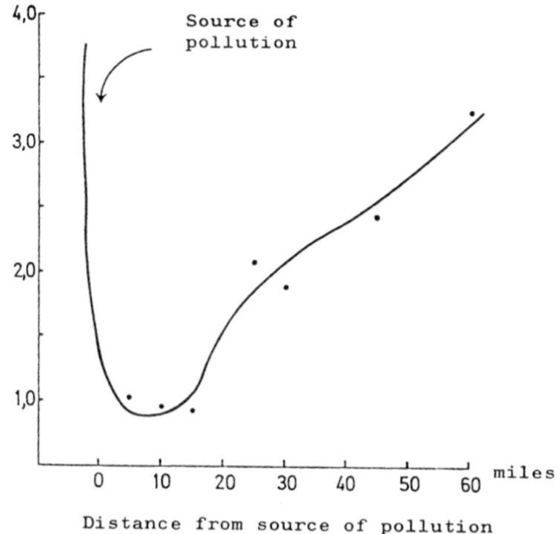

Figure 11.7. Shannon index (H) plotted versus distance from the point (at origo) where a discharge of waste water takes place.

Table 11.10. Ecological succession.

Properties	Early stages	Late or mature stage
A Energetics		
P/R	>>1 or <<1	Close to 1
P/B	High	Low
Yield	High	Low
Entropy	High	Low
Exergy	Low	High
Information	Low	High
B Structure		
Total biomass	Small	Large
Inorganic nutrients	Extrabiotic	Intrabiotic
Diversity, ecological	Low	High
Diversity, biological	Low	High
Patterns	Poorly organized	Well organized
Niche specialization	Broad	Narrow
Size of organisms	Small	Large
Life cycles	Simple	Complex
Mineral cycles	Open	Closed
Nutrient exchange rate	Rapid	Slow
C Selection and homoeostatis		
Internal symbiosis	Undeveloped	Developed
Stability (resistance to ext. perturb.s)	Poor	Good
Ecological buffer capacity	Low	High
Feedback control	Poor	Good
Growth form	Rapid growth	Feedback controlled growth

The number of species and their relative abundance are by no means the only factors involved in community diversity. Arrangement patterns also play a role, concerning the community function and stability. Many different kinds of arrangement in the standing crop of organisms contribute to the pattern diversity in a community. The arrangement may, e.g., follow specific (1) *horizontal zonation* patterns, (2) *stratification* patterns, (3) *reproductive* patterns (parent/offspring relations), (4) *social* patterns (flocks, herds etc.), (5) *periodicity* patterns, and (6) *stochastic* patterns (results of random forces).

There seems to be no doubt that a relationship exists between, on one hand, the diversity in space and species and, on the other, the ecosystem stability, in the broadest sense of the word. However, a reliable quantitative ecosystem theory which includes such a relationship has not yet been put forward. Still, an examination of the diversity is often useful in providing information about the ecological conditions, although such information is qualitative and cannot give a quantitative assessment of the environmental impact.

To understand fully the concept of diversity, we must know also the related concept of *ecotone*. An ecotone is a transition zone between two or more diverse communities, for example, between forest and grassland, or between a fjord and the open sea. The ecotonal community commonly contains many of the organisms of both overlapping communities, as well as organisms which are characteristic of the ecotone and restricted to it.

Often, the number of species and the population density of some of the species are greater in the ecotone than in the communities flanking it. The tendency of increased variety and density at community junctions is known as the 'edge effect'.

The ecological succession process includes a series of changes, e.g., in adaptation and in diversity. Ecological investigations and, more recently, functional considerations have led to the results presented in Table 11.10 which is based on the work of Odum and Pinkerton (1955), Lotka (1925), Margalef (1963, 1968) and Jørgensen and Mejer (1977), Jørgensen et al. (1979). The concept of ecological buffer capacity is included in the table; it will be discussed in the last section of this chapter. All the other concepts referred to in the table have been defined already. Trends are emphasized by contrasting the situation at the early developmental stages of the ecosystem with that at later stages, 'early' and 'late' referring to the time after a substantial change in the ecological conditions has occurred. The time required for the transition from one stage to the next may vary with climatic, physiographic and ecosystem factors. However, the changes will usually occur more rapidly when the ecosystem is far from being stabilized.

One of the characteristic trends to be expected in the development of an ecosystem is that the P/R *ratio* (P = gross production, R = respiration) *approaches* 1 , *and that the* P/B *ratio* (B = biomass) *decreases*. This is illustrated in Fig. 11.8, based on data from Cooke (1967), respectively on results presented by Kira and Shidei (1967).

Balanced ecosystems represent the mature stage, and although there is a pronounced difference in production and respiration in the ecosystems in these parts of the diagrams in Figs. 11.8, they both have a P/R ratio approaching 1 . The production in a coral reef is almost 1000 times larger than that in a desert.

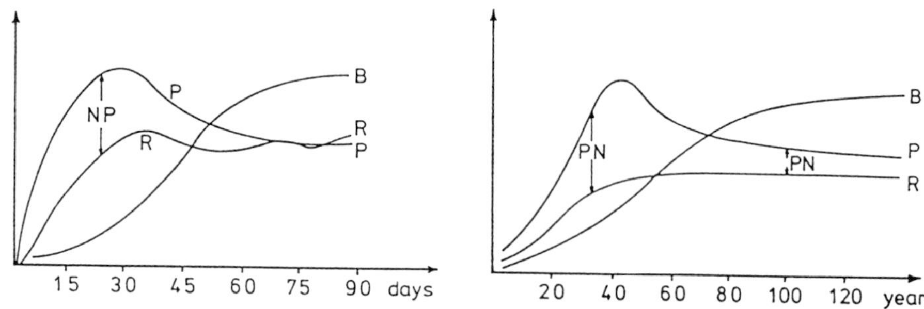

Figure 11.8. Microcosmos succession (left) and forest succession (right). P = gross production, NP = net production, R = respiration and B = biomass are plotted against time.

Figs. 11.9 and 11.10 show some characteristic observations of succession patterns in ecosystems. The figures demonstrate the trends to be expected from Table 11.10. The changes referred to in the two diagrams and in Table 11.10 are all brought about by biological processes within the ecosystem. Geological and human forces acting on the system can reverse the trends, in which case the ecosystem will have to start again from the very beginning.

Eutrophication of a lake is a good example of this mechanism: the high nutrient concentration pushes the system back to a simpler state, with a high P/R ratio and little diversity. Such a change renders the system more able to to cope with the high nutrient concentration by increasing the production and thereby removing more of the nutrient dissolved in the water. In other words:

The structure of the ecosystem is changed in accordance with changing environmental factors. (In ecological modeling, these factors are often labeled 'the forcing functions').

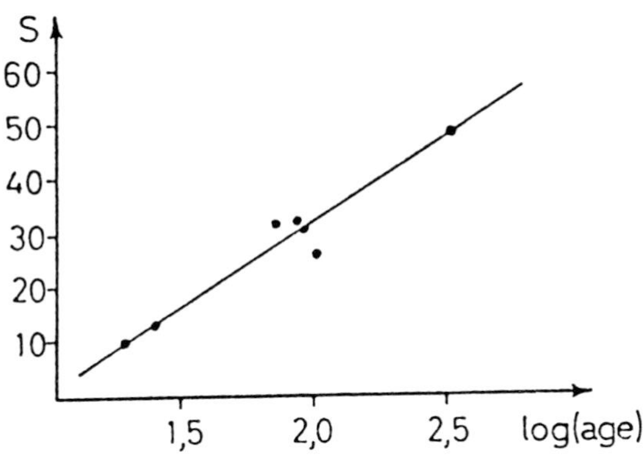

Figure 11.9. Number of plant species, *S*, in a pond, plotted against the logarithm of the age (in years). - Source: Godwin (1923).

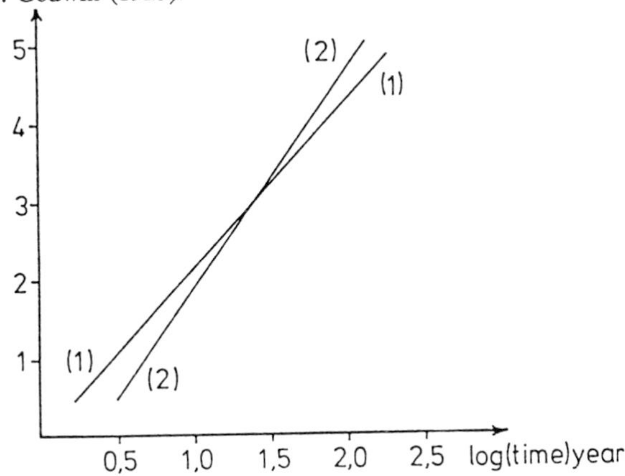

Figure 11.10. Succession in a bird community. (1) Number of pairs per ha, and (2) number of species per 10 ha, both follow the same pattern. - Source: Johnston and Odum (1956).

In an eutrophic lake, the nutrient concentration is high, and consequently, the ecosystem will change its structure so as to be able, in the long term, to reduce the nutrient concentration. Recent studies of land sediment, and theoretical considerations as well, indicate that lakes can progress, and do progress, to more ologotrophic conditions when the nutrient input ceases (Mackereth, 1965; Cowgill and Hutchinson, 1964; Harrison, 1962; Jørgensen, 1976; Jørgensen and Mejer, 1977; see also Chapter 5).

Apparently, there is a *conflict between the strategies of man and of nature*. Agriculture and forestry aims at the highest possible production, while nature attempts to achieve the maximal support of a complex ecosystem structure, with P/R close to 1 and a net production close to zero. However, the problem is not that simple, since man is dependent not only on food, fibres and wool, but also on the oxygen concentration in the atmosphere, the climate buffer, and clean air and clean water, for many purposes.

Until recently, man has taken it for granted that nutrient cycling, water purification and other protective functions of self-maintaining ecosystems can work independently of environmental manipulations, such as the discharge of pollutants or changes of an ecological structure (e.g., forest to arable land). This point of view is becoming untenable.

The most pleasant landscape to live in, from an aesthetic point of view, and ecologically the safest, is a landscape which contains a variety of crops, forests, lakes, etc. In other words, it seems to be essential for man to plan for the landscape to have *a large pattern diversity*, and to allow for the exchange between different types of ecosystems. Thus, the preservation of natural areas is not a luxury for society, but a capital investment of crucial importance to our civilization and to our life on Earth.

11.6 STABILITY AND STRUCTURE

Stability of ecosystem communities is of great importance in environmental management. When it is considered what will be the reaction to specified changes in impact on the ecosystem, the question is not only: How will the ecosystem react? - but rather: How is the stability of the ecosystem possibly affected?

Stability is a wide concept, with several different meanings. It is, therefore, important to apply the word 'stability' only after it has been defined a bit more concisely. We shall do so by defining four different ways of understanding it:

Resilience: the speed at which a community returns to its former state after having been perturbed and displaced from that state.

Resistance: the ability of the system to avoid displacement in the first place.

Local stability: the tendency of the system to return to its original state, or close to it, after having been subjected to a small perturbation.

Global stability: the tendency of the system to return to its original state, even after having been subjected to a large perturbation.

Yet another concept will be mentioned in the next section, i.e., that of *'ecological buffer capacity'*; it can be viewed as a quantification of the resistance concept, recognizing that displacement cannot be totally avoided, but that the question is how small a displacement will be the reaction of the system to a given perturbation.

The relation between the various stability concepts and the structure of the ecosystems has been widely discussed in the ecological literature. Elton (1958) and MacArthur (1955) proposed that increased complexity of the system, i.e., more components and feed-back mechanisms, lead to an increased stability. This statement was based on the following general observations:

1) Simple laboratory communities consisting of two or a few species are very unstable.
2) Islands, usually possessing only a few species (Section 11.5), are more vulnerable to invading species than is the species-rich continent.
3) Crop monocultures are vulnerable to invasion and destruction by pests.

However, May (1972, 1975) has shown that such a simple relation between complexity and stability does not hold true, generally. On the contrary, the use of foodweb models has revealed that there is tendency that a reduction of the number of feed-back mechanisms (see below) will stabilize the community.

The connection between stability and complexity is, in general, much more complex than proposed by Elton and MacArthur. It has, for instance, been observed that an oligotrophic lake is more stable when many species are present, whereas a very hypertrophic lake is more stable when only a few species are present (Jørgensen, 1983).

May (1972, 1975) explored mathematically the relationship between community stability and complexity. His considerations, as well as numerous investigations of food-web models and of real ecosystem communities, all indicate that the relationship sought for between complexity and stability is quite complicated.

11.7 ECOLOGICAL BUFFER CAPACITY

The ecologist working with environmental problems is concerned with the response of the system to changes in the external factors. Fig. 11.11 shows the response of Lake Fure (Sealand, DK) to an increased phosphorus loading. During the period 1945-1973, the loading increased almost linearly with time. However, as appears from the figure, the phosphorus concentration in the water remained almost unchanged for the first two decades, mainly because the phosphorus added was stored in the sediment by the following chain of processes:

$$\text{soluble P in water} \rightarrow \text{uptake by algae} \rightarrow \text{settling} \rightarrow \text{P in sediment.}$$

Although some of the phosphorus in the sediment was released back into the water, a substantial part was stored in the sediment. This exemplifies the following general principle:

An ecosystem tends to minimize changes caused by external sources. However, this 'buffer capacity' is finite, and once the capacity is used up, the changes become more pronounced.

The course of the response thus parallels the change in pH caused by the addition of acids or alkalies to a buffer mixture.

Of course, it is very important to recognize the response of ecosystems to changes in external factors, such as an increased discharge of pollutants.

The response is, however, very rarely proportional to the external factor. If such a proportionality is assumed when predicting the ecosystem response, the prediction would often be completely wrong, and an environmental impact might be tolerated which was too high. If, for example, the response to increased P loading in Lake Fure observed in 1950-56 was used to forecast the situation in the following years, it would have predicted that the removal of P from the waste water would not be required - but today it is indeed so. Of course, the problem of lake management is much more complicated than this simple example (and also Fig. 11.11) might suggest (Jørgensen, 1980), as many different processes are involved. Still, these observations point to the essentially non-linear global response of the ecosystems, which can be clarified by means of the concept of buffer capacity.

The ecological buffer capacity is the reciprocal sensitivity of the state variable in question (Halfon, 1976):

$$\text{sensitivity of state variable} = \frac{d(\text{state variable})}{d(\text{external factor})} \; . \tag{11.13}$$

As it is often problematic to measure differential coefficients directly, the ecological buffer capacity is found as (Jørgensen et al., 1977):

$$\beta = \frac{\Delta(\text{external variable})}{\Delta(\text{internal variable})} \; . \tag{11.14}$$

An ecosystem has many buffer capacities. E.g., the buffer capacity related to the changes in soluble phosphorus caused by an increased P discharge can be defined as

$$\beta_P = \frac{\Delta\text{P-loading}}{\Delta\text{P-soluble}} = \frac{\Delta\text{P-total}}{\Delta\text{P-soluble}} \; . \tag{11.15}$$

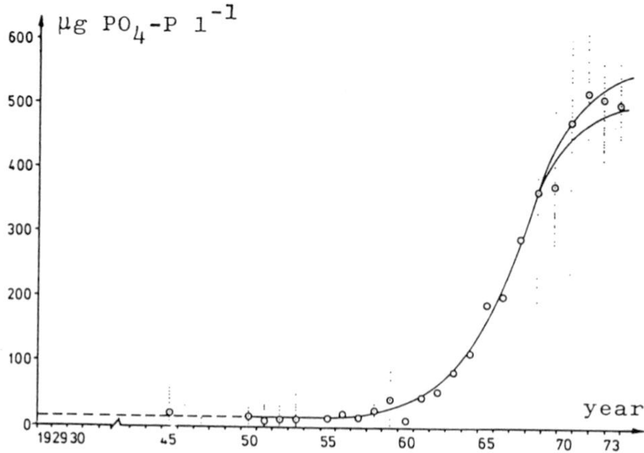

Figure 11.11. The phosphorus concentration in Lake Fure plotted against time (years). During the period considered, the phosphorus loading increased considerably.

The change in the total phosphorus concentration is measured by the increased discharge of P. This follows from the law of mass conservation: all the phosphorus (mainly soluble) which is fed into the lake must indeed be present in one form or another. But due to the buffer capacity, or rather, to the many processes involving phosphorus, the concentration of soluble P in the lake will increase less than would be expected from the input, because the system will minimize the direct effect of an increased input of soluble phosphorus.

A definition similar to (11.15) can be put forward for the buffer capacity in response to a change in temperature. It is difficult to compare changes in temperature with changes in concentration of phytoplankton or zooplankton, so we would like the buffer capacity be dimensionless, as it is in the case of (11.15), and we, therefore, define it as the ratio between the relative changes in temperature and phytoplankton, respectively:

$$\beta_{T\text{-rel}} = \frac{\Delta \text{Temp}}{\text{Temp}} : \frac{\Delta \text{Phyt}}{\text{Phyt}} , \tag{11.16}$$

where Temp and Phyt denote the temperature and the phytoplankton concentration, respectively.

The concept of ecological buffer capacity was examined by Jørgensen et al. (1979). Using ecological models, they set up the following conjecture:

The ecosystem will respond to changes in external factors, such as the nutrient input, the irradiance and climatic changes of temperature, by developing a structure with the best possible ability to meet perturbations. It can be shown that an ecosystem (e.g., a lake) with little diversity has a larger buffer capacity at a high nutrient-input level than a more complex ecosystem has; this explains why many eutrophic lakes have a low diversity. It was also found that complex ecosystems have a very high buffer capacity for temnperature changes, and that species with a more flexible temperature-regulation system contribute more to the buffer capacity in question than do species that are less well suited to changes in the temperature pattern.

Table 11.11. Ecosystem reactions and ecological buffer capacities.

Change in external variable	Ecosystem reactions	Increased buffer capacity
P-loading increased	Lower diversity. Species with lower specific surface, and thereby slower nutrient uptake	β_P
Temperature	Species with other temperature. Optimum take over	$\beta_{T\text{-rel}}$
Increased conc. of toxic substances	Some species become extinguished. Less susceptible species become more dominant	$\beta_{TOX} = \frac{\Delta \text{ toxic subst.}}{\Delta \text{ biomass}}$
Increased BOD_5	Some species become extinguished. Species less susceptible to low oxygen concentrations become more dominant	$\beta_{BOD} = \frac{\Delta \text{ BOD}}{\Delta \text{ biomass}}$

From these considerations, it seems that ecosystems possess, not only a buffer capacity which minimizes changes in the system caused by external factors, but also the ability to change their structure so as to maximize the buffer capacity which has to meet the changes actually taking place.

However, like the buffer capacity, the ability of the ecosystem to adapt its structure to a new situation is also finite. Drastic changes in an ecosystem cannot under any circumstances be tolerated, as we consider a simplification of an ecosystem (in terms of reduced diversity) to be an ecological deterioration. Also, a decreased complexity of the ecosystem may lead to an increase in the buffer capacity for input of nutrients or other pollutants, but at the same time, the buffer capacity for temperature or other climatic changes decreases, making the ecosystem more vulnerable to natural changes in its external factors.

We conclude the chapter by listing, in Table 11.11, some ecosystem reactions to changes in external factors, which can be interpreted in terms of the ecological buffer-capacity concept.

REFERENCES

Ahl, T. and Weiderholm, T., 1977. Svenska vattenkvalitetskriterier. Eutrofierande ämnen. (Swedish water quality criteria. Eutrophication). SNV PM, Stockholm, pg. 918.

Cooke, G.D., 1967. The pattern of autotrophic succession in laboratory microecosystems. Bioscience, 17: 717-721.

Cowgill, U.M. and Hutchinson, G.E., 1964. Cultural eutrophication in Lago Montesori during Roman antiquity. Proc. Int. Assoc. Theor. Appl. Limnol., 15(2): 644-645.

Elton, C.S., 1958. The Ecology of Invasions by Animals and Plants. Methuen & Co., London.

Godwin, H., 1923. Dispersal of pond floras. J. Ecol., 11: 160-164.

Halfon, E., 1976. Relative stability of ecosystem linear models. Ecol. Modelling, 2: 279-296.

Harrison, A.D., 1962. Hydrobiological studies of all saline and acid still waters in Western Cape Province. Trans. Roy. Soc., South Africa, 36: 213.

Hutchinson, G.E., 1957. Concluding remarks. Cold Spring Harbor Symposia on Quantitative Biology, 22: 3-26.

Hutchinson, G.E., 1969. The Ecological Theater and the Evolutionary Play. Yale University Press, New Haven, 139 pp.

Johnston, D.W. and Odum, E.P., 1956. Breeding bird populations in relation to plant succession on the Piedmont of Georgia. Ecology, 37: 50-62.

Jørgensen, S.E., 1976. A eutrophication model for a lake. J. Ecol. Modelling, 2: 147-165.

Jørgensen, S.E., 1980. Lake Management. Pergamon Press, London, 180 pp.

Jørgensen, S.E., Bengtsson, L., Mejer, J.F. and Friis, M., 1979. A case study of lake modelling. Södra Bergundasjön. ISEM Journal.

Jørgensen, S.E., and Mejer, H.F., 1977. Ecological buffer capacity. J. Ecol. Modelling, 3: 39-61.

Kira, T. and Shidei, T., 1967. Primary productionand turnover of organic matter in different forest ecosystems of the western Pacific. Japanese J. Ecol., 17: 70-87.

Lloyd, M. and Ghelardi, R.J., 1964. A table for calculating the equitability component of species diversity. J. Anim. Ecol., 33: 421-425.

Lotka, A., 1925. Elements of Physical Biology. Williams and Wilkins, Baltimore. [Reissued as: Elements of Mathematical Biology. Dover Publ., New York, 1956].

MacArthur, R.H., 1955. Fluctuations of animal populations, and a measure of community stability. Ecology, 36: 533-536.

MacArthur, R.H., and Wilson, E.O., 1967. The Theory of Island Biogeography. Princeton Univ. Press, Princeton, Mass.

Mackereth, F.J.H., 1965. Chemical investigations of lake sediments and their interpretation. Proc. Roy. Soc., London, Ser. B., 161: 295-309.

Margalef, R., 1958. Information theory in ecology. Gen. Syst., 3: 36-71.

Margalef, R., 1963. Successions of populations. Adv. Frontiers of Plant Sci. (Inst. Adv. Sci. and Culture, New Delhi, India), 2: 137-188.

Margalef, R., 1968. Perspectives in Ecological Theory. Univ. of Chicago Press, Chicago, Ill., 122 pp.

May, R.M., 1972. Will a large complex system be stable? Nature, 238: 413-414.

May, R.M., 1975. Stability and Complexity in Model Ecosystems, 2. ed. Princeton Univ. Press, Princeton.

Menhinick, E.F., 1964. A comparison of some species diversity indices applied to samples of field insects. Ecology, 45: 859-861.

Odum, E.P., 1950. Bird populations of the Highlands (North Carolina) Plateau in relation to plant succession and avian invasion. Ecology, 31: 587-605.

Odum, H.T., 1956. Primary production in flowing waters. Limnol. Oceanogr., 1: 102-117.

Odum, H.T., Cantlon, J.E. and Kornicker, L.S., 1960. An organizational hierarchy postulate for the interpretation of species-individuals distribution, species entropy and ecosystem evolution and the meaning of a species-variety index. Ecology, 41: 395-399.

Odum, H.T., and Pinkerton, R.C., 1955. Times speed regulator, the optimum efficiency for maximum output in physical and biological systems. Amer. Sci., 43: 331-343.

Park, R.A. et al., 1978. The aquatic ecosystem model MS. CLEANER. Proc. Int. Conf. Ecol. Modelling, 28/8-2/9 1978, Copenhagen (ISEM), p. 579 ff.

Pielou, E.C., 1966. Species-diversity and pattern diversity in the study of ecological succession. J. Theoret. Biol., 10: 370-383.

Shannon, C.E., and Weaver, W., 1963. The Mathematical Theory of Communication. Univ. of Illinois Press, Urbana, 117 pp.

Simpson, E.H., 1949. Measurement of diversity. Nature, 163: 688.

Sørensen, T., 1948. A method of establishing groups of equal amplitude in plant society based on similarity of species content. Kgl. Danske Vidsk. Selskab. (Royal Danish Academy of Science).

Weiderholm, T., 1980. Use of benthos in lake monitoring. J. Water Pollut. Control Fed., 52: 537.

12 ENVIRONMENTAL IMPACT ASSESSMENT

SVEN ERIK JØRGENSEN

12.1 WHAT IS E.I.A.?

In the 1970's, the simulation models of the 'Club of Rome' propounded an almost apocalyptic view of impending global disaster. Probably, these models represent the most important single influence in fostering public concern for the effects of continued economic growth upon our physical environment.

Correspondingly, the so-called Brundtland report has, during the 1980's, created an equal interest and concern about the maintenance of what is sustainable growth. The resulting global view of this report is the narrow relationship between ecology and economy. Economical growth should be feasible, but only if it does not irreversibly effect the environment. We need global economic growth to be able to give the global population of more than 5 billion people a life of quality, but if the economic growth takes place on the cost of the environment it is not acceptable, and we must find new ways, i.e., make better planning and develop a new, non-polluting technology.

Many countries, both in the developed and in the developing world, now have recognized that major development projects may have a harmful environmental impact. It is in this broader context of concern that *Environmental Impact Assessment* (EIA) was evolved and has been applied since the mid-1970's.

Before the first green wave in the late 1960's, projects were assessed mainly on grounds of technical and economic feasibility. Environmental, social and health impacts were rarely examined explicitly or rigorously. Even when included, the assessment usually took the form of a mere cost-benefit analysis.

For example, the Aswan High Dam (Egypt) proved to have deleterious secondary effects, such as a decrease in agriculture productivity and in fishery in the Delta of the Nile. EIA had not been applied before the realization of this project, which might never have been realized if a proper EIA had been carried out before the final decision was taken.

There is no generally accepted definition of EIA. However, a combination of Anonymous (1978) and Heer and Hagerty (1977) will be proposed and used in this chapter:

EIA is an assessment of all the relevant environmental effects which would result from a project under consideration. As far as possible, the assessment should establish quantitative values for selected environmental components, indicating the quality of the environment before, during and after the action. In this sense, EIA means a systematic examination of the likely environmental consequences of projects, programmes, plans and policies proposed. The results of the assessment, which are assembled in a document known as an *environmental impact statement* (EIS), are intended to provide decision-makers with a balanced appraisal of the environmental, social and health implications of alternative courses of action. The EIS is one contribution to the information base upon which a decision is made.

EIA aims at logical and rational decision-making. It is agreed upon that in general, EIA should be concerned with the identification, measurement, interpretation and communication of environmental impacts of the action proposed. Attemps should be made to reduce the potential adverse impacts and to identify alternative sites and processes. EIA is intended to be an objective exercise with no decision-making components. There are, however, a number of ways in which EIA can improve the efficiency of decision-making, but to be efficient, EIA should be implemented at an early stage of the project planning and design. EIA must be an integral component of the entire project, not something which is utilized *after* the design phase has been completed. This means that EIA should give a continous feed-back to project designs at an early stage, to help choosing the solutions which emphasize the benefits and minimize the harmful effects.

Once alternatives, including of course the 'no action' alternative, have been selected to be subject to EIA, the main activities in EIA may be summarized as follows:

1. Impact identification.
2. Impact prediction and measurement.
3. Impact interpretation and evaluation.
4. Identification of monotoring requirements and mitigating measures.
5. Communication of impact information to users, to the public and to decision makers.

12.2 E.I.A. METHODS

Methods are structural mechanisms for the identification, collection and organization of environmental impact data. Methods include means by which information is presented in a variety of visual formats, for interpretation by decision-makers and by representatives of the public. The prediction techniques are concerned with predicting future states of specific environmental components, such as the concentrations of specific air pollutants.

The main types of EIA methods are:

1. *Application of Checklists.*
2. *Application of Environmental Quality Index.*
3. *Overlay Mapping.*
4. *Network Diagrams.*
5. *Systems Diagram.*
6. *Simulation Models.*

The last method is the most important and most quantitative one, and it is treated separately in Chapter 13. The five other methods are presented briefly in this chapter.

12.2.1 Checklists

The checklist was one of the first EIA methods to be applied, and it is still in general use, although in many different forms. Of these, the simplest one is merely *a list of environmental factors* to be considered. Hopefully, this ascertains that no particular significant environmental factor is omitted. Such lists do not give any guidance as to how impacts on the factors in question should be assessed.

Table 12.1. 'Threshold of concern' worksheet with sample elements, criteria, thresholds of concern, and impact data. - Source: Sassaman (1981).

Element	Criteria	Threshold of Concern (TOC)	Alternative 1 no action Impact+ duration	Impact >TOC?	Alternative 2 median investment Impact+ duration	Impact >TOC?	Alternative 3 high investment Impact+ duration	Impact >TOC?
Air quality	State guidelines	3	4 C	Yes	4 C	Yes	4 C	Yes
Economics	Efficiency (benefit -cost ratio)	1:1	3:1	No	4:1	No	4,5:1	No
Employment	10^3 private sector jobs	Present level	9 C	No	9.5 C	No	10 C	No
	Forest service manpower requirements	Present + 10%	400 C	No	440 C	No	500 C	Yes
Range resources	10^3 animal unit months provided	Present level	5 C	No	5 C	No	3 C	Yes
Recreation	10^3 dispersed camping sites	5	2.8 C	Yes	5 C	No	6 C	No
	Winter sports (10^6 visitor days)	1	0.7 C	Yes	1 C	No	2 C	No
Threatened/ endangered wildlife species	Number of spotted owls (pairs)	35	50 D	No	35 D	No	20 D	Yes
Water quality	State water quality standards	3	3 C	No	3 C	No	4 C	Yes
Wildlife	Viewing deer and elk	25% decrease in population	10% C	No	10% C	No	30% C	Yes

Descriptive checklists give a certain guidance on impact assessment. For each factor on the list, information on measurements and predictive techniques is provided. However, neither simple nor descriptive checklists will enable the user to determine which impacts are important and which are not.

Scaling checklists incorporate 'Thresholds of Concern', i.e., they attempt to state the importance of impacts in a manner which is useful to decision-makers. A scaling checklist is a list of environmental elements or resources, such as water quality and wildlife habitat, accompanied by criteria which express the desirable values of these resources.

Table 12.1 shows such a scaling checklist; the environmental features are listed in the left-hand column. The criteria applied for water quality are state-water-quality standards, and in the case of an endangered species, the criterion is the number of pairs of the species. Similarly, a 'Threshold of Concern' (TOC) value is selected for each criterion. In the case of the spotted owl (see Table 12.1), the TOC-value selected is 35 pairs. In the case of economics, the TOC for the criterion 'benefit/cost ratio' is 1.1.

The TOC for each environmental element can be conceived as the point at which those assessing a proposal become concerned with the impact of a particular activity. Any impact which causes a criterion to exceed its TOC is considered significant to decision-makers. The TOC may represent an objective to be achieved, or a limit not to be exceeded.

Table 12.2. Sections from a questionnaire checklist for developing countries. - Source: Anonymous (1980).

Terrestrial ecosystems

(a) Are there any terrestrial ecosystems of the types listed below which, by nature of their size, abundance or type, could be classified as significant or unique?

- Forest? Yes____ No____ Unk.____
- Savanna? Yes____ No____ Unk.____
- Grassland? Yes____ No____ Unk.____
- Desert? Yes____ No____ Unk.____

(b) Are these ecosystems

- Pristine? Yes____ No____ Unk.____
- Moderately degraded? Yes____ No____ Unk.____
- Severely degraded? Yes____ No____ Unk.____

(c) Are there present trends towards alteration of these ecosystems through cutting, burning etc. to produce agricultural, industrial, or urban land? Yes____ No____ Unk.____

(d) Does the local population use use these ecosystems to obtain non-domesticated

- Food plants? Yes____ No____ Unk.____
- Medicinal plants? Yes____ No____ Unk.____
- Wood products? Yes____ No____ Unk.____
- Fibre? Yes____ No____ Unk.____
- Fur? Yes____ No____ Unk.____
- Food Animals? Yes____ No____ Unk.____

(e) Will the project require clearing or alteration of:

- Small areas of land in these ecosystems? Yes____ No____ Unk.____
- Moderate areas of land in these ecosystems? Yes____ No____ Unk.____
- Large areas of land in these ecosystems? Yes____ No____ Unk.____

(f) Does the project rely on any raw materials (wood, fibre) from these ecosystems? Yes____ No____ Unk.____

(g) Will the project cause increased population growth in the area, bringing about increased stress on these ecosystems? Yes____ No____ Unk.____

Estimated impact on terrestrial ecosystems: ND..HA..MA..LA..O..LB..MB..HB

Disease vectors

(a) Are there known disease problems in the project area transmitted through vector species such as mosquitos, flies, snails, etc.? Yes____ No____ Unk.____

(b) Are these vector species associated with:

- Aquatic habitats? Yes____ No____ Unk.____
- Forest habitats? Yes____ No____ Unk.____
- Agricultural lands? Yes____ No____ Unk.____
- Degraded habitats? Yes____ No____ Unk.____
- Human settlements? Yes____ No____ Unk.____

(c) Will the project:

- Increase vector habitat? Yes____ No____ Unk.____
- Decrease vector habitat? Yes____ No____ Unk.____
- Provide opportunity for vector control? Yes____ No____ Unk.____

(d) Will the project workforce be a possible source of introduction of disease vectors not currently found in the project area? Yes____ No____ Unk.____

(e) Will increased access to and commerce with the project area be a possible source of disease vectors not presently occurring in the project area? Yes____ No____ Unk.____

(f) Will the project provide opportunities for vector control through improved standards of living? Yes____ No____ Unk.____

Estimated impact on disease vectors: ND..HA..MA..LA..O..LB..MB..HB

ND = not determinable	O = low or insignificant
HA = high adverse	LB = low benefit
MA = medium adverse	MB = medium benefit
LA = low adverse	HB = high benefit

The example presented in Table 12.1 shows a TOC worksheet for three alternative strategies for the harvest of an overmature stand of trees on a productive site. The alternative strategies consist of the 'no action' strategy and two strategies involving median and high investments in road and harvesting systems.

Only two of the many other characteristics of impacts are considered in this checklist (Table 12.1), namely time dimension and reversibility. The following scale is used:

A. 1 year or less.
B. 1-10 years.
C. 10-50 years.
D. irreversible.

The implication of each alternative strategy can be appreciated by examining the number of criteria which exceed the TOC for the alternative in question. Alternative 2 in Table 12.1 has less impacts of concern than alternatives 1 and 3. Alternatives 1 and 3 would result in 3 and 6 of such impacts, respectively. This suggests that alternative 2 should be chosen.

Questionnaire checklists are exemplified in Table 12.2. This type was developed by US Agency of International Development (USAID) for assessing rural development projects in developing countries. Whenever sufficient evidence was not available, the mark 'Unk.' (=unknown) should be applied.

The relative significance of those impacts identified as important has still not been resolved, neither in this checklist nor in the scaling checklist.

12.2.2 Environmental Quality Index (EQI)

The first step in this procedure is to determine the environmental parameters that can be measured, for example, the concentration of dissolved oxygen in a river, or the concentration of particulate matter in the air. A number of environmental parameters are selected to provide a representative and comprehensive picture of possible environmental impacts. The impacts of alternatives may be expressed in terms of predicted changes in the same parameters. Systematic comparisons of the various levels of environmental parameters are carried out by setting up a *utility function*, U(X), where X represents an environmental parameter. The utility function U(X) is measured on a scale from 0 to 1, 1 representing the highest utility.

Fig. 12.1. shows a typical relationship between a utility function and an environmental parameter, in this case the oxygen concentration in a river. A concentration of oxygen at 80% saturation corresponds to a utility value of 0.5.

A suitable relationship between the utility function and an environmental parameter may be found in one of the following ways:

1) U(X) represents a probability; for instance, if X is the oxygen concentration in a river, U(X) could be the probability to find salmon in the river at this oxygen contentration.
2) U(X) represents an actual measure of environmental quality related to the parameter X; for instance, U(X) could be the number of salmons actually found at the oxygen concentration X, divided by the number found at 100% saturation.
3) U(X) represents an index, in accordance with the public opinion or the opinion by a group of experts about various levels of the environmental parameter, X.

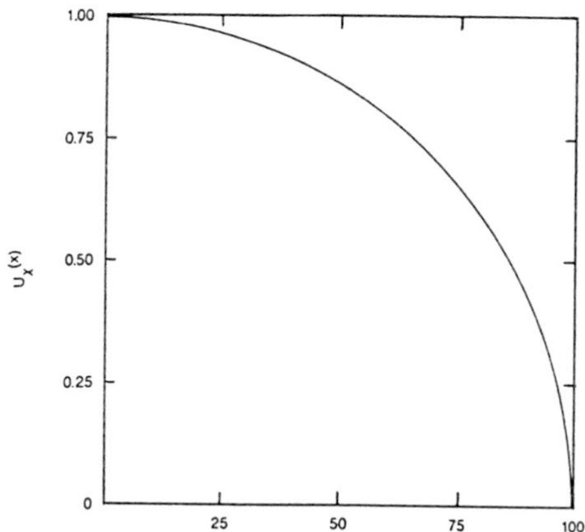

Figure 12.1. Utility function for percentage loss of salmon from a river where less than 100,000 adult salmons return to spawn. - Source: Keeney and Robilliard (1977).

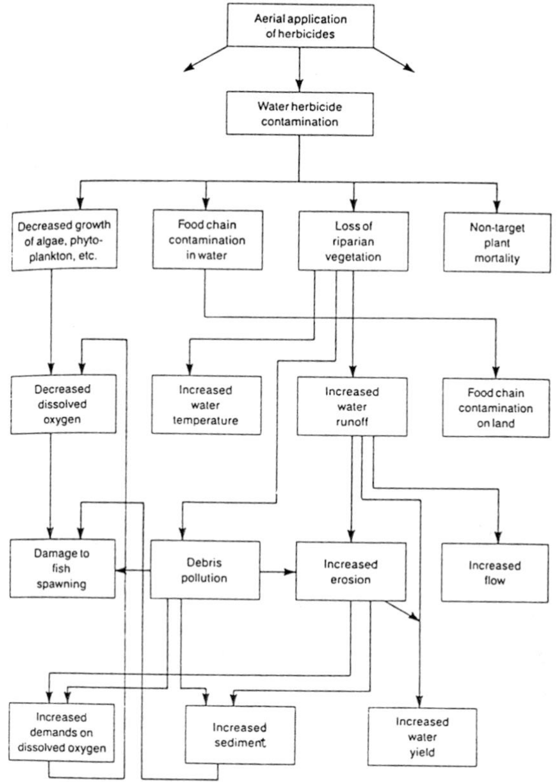

Figure 12.2. Section of the IMPACT network. - Source: Thor et al. (1978).

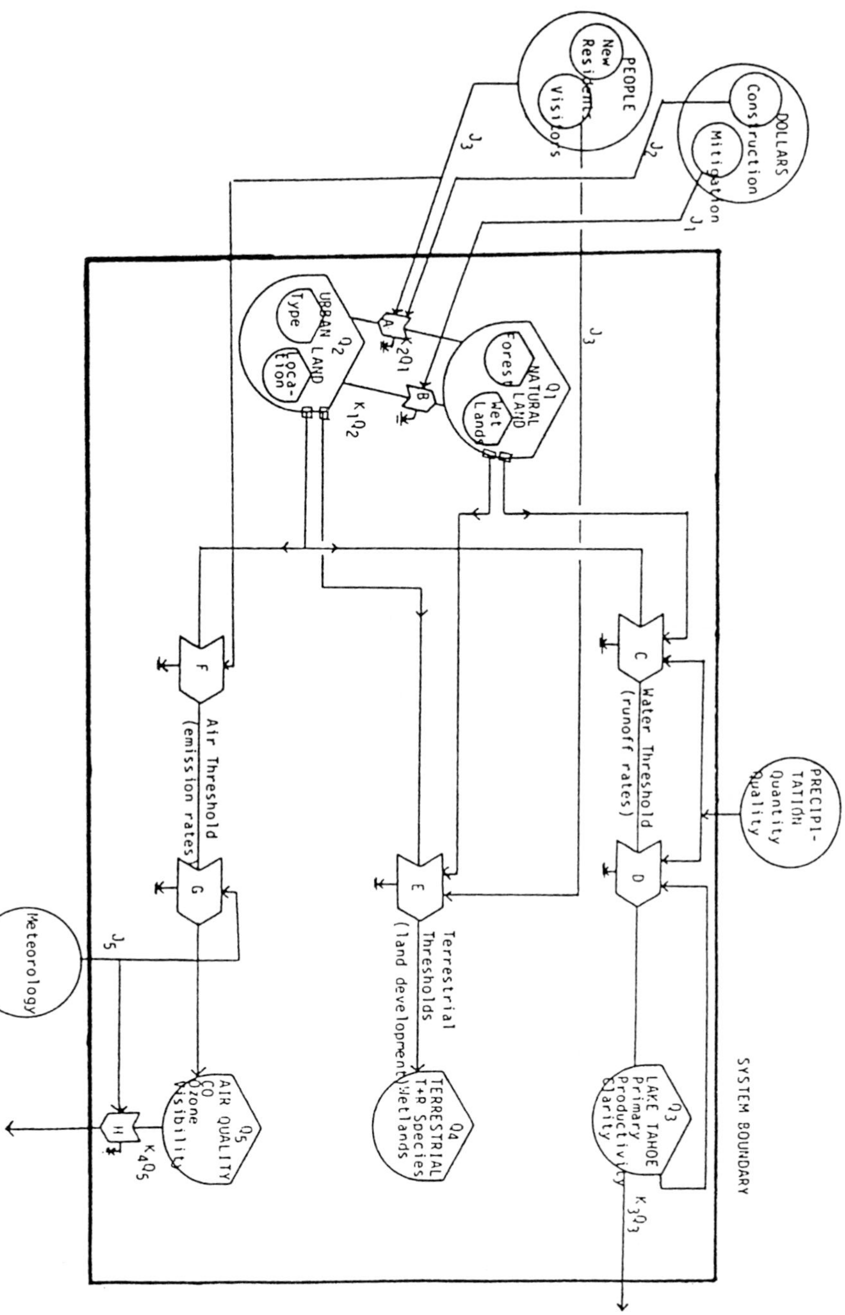

Figure 12.3. Threshold-carrying capacity model of the Lake Tahoe basin. The interactions are described in Table 12.3.

Table 12.3. Verbal description of the carrying capacity model in Fig. 12.3.

SYSTEM INPUTS AND STATE VARIABLES

People-related inputs	Natural inputs	State variables
J_1 Mitigation dollars	J_4 Precipitation	Q_1 Amount and location of natural land
J_2 Urban development dollars	J_5 Meteorological conditions	Q_2 Amount, type and location of urban land
J_3 People		Q_3 Lake Tahoe
		Q_4 Terrestrial environmental quality
		Q_5 Air quality

INTERNAL MODELS

Combine information on:	To determine:
A. Population activity (J_3), development dollars (J_2), and natural land (Q_1)	Additions to the amount of urban land (Q_2)
B. Mitigation expenditures (J_1), urban land development (Q_2)	Additions to the amount of natural land (Q_1)
C. Land development (Q_1 and Q_2), and precipitation quantity and quality (J_4)	Runoff quantity and quality
D. Runoff quantity and quality, precipitation quantity and quality (J_4), and the hydrological/biological/chemical character of Lake Tahoe (Q_3)	Water quality of Lake Tahoe
E. Land development (Q_1 and Q_2) and population activity (J_3)	Wildlife populations and wetland characteristics (Q_4)
F. Urban land development (Q_2) and population activity	Emission rates (transportation models)
G. Emission rates and meteorological conditions (J_5)	Air quality (Q_5) (air dispersion models)
H. Meteorological conditions (J_5) and air quality (Q_5)	Export of air pollutants (air mass stability measures)

DIFFERENTIAL EQUATIONS

$$dQ_1/dt = K_1\ Q_2\ J_1 - K_2\ Q_1\ J_2\ J_3$$

$$dQ_2/dt = K_2\ Q_1\ J_1\ J_3 - K_1\ Q_2\ J_1$$

$$dQ_3/dt = Q_1\ Q_2\ J_4\ [C]\ [D] - K_3\ Q_3$$

$$dQ_4/dt = Q_1\ Q_2\ J_3\ [E]$$

$$dQ_5/dt = Q_2\ J_2\ J_5\ [F]\ [G] - K_4\ Q_5\ J_5\ [H]R$$

Once utility functions U_i have been established for the individual environmental parameters X_i (i=1,2,...,n), they can be combined into an overall environmental quality index, EIQ. Each parameter is given a scaling value, k_i, which reflects the relative importance of different parameters, as perceived by the decision-makers, and the EIQ is found from the following equation:

$$EIQ = \sum_{i=1}^{n} k_i \, U_i(X_i) \, . \tag{12.1}$$

Equation (12.1) assumes the parameters X_i to be environmentally independent of each other. Usually, this is not the case, and a more complex formula is then required for the computation of the EIQ.

12.2.3 Overlay Mapping

This method was first used manually. A transparent overlay sheet is prepared as a base map, showing the location of the project and the boundaries of the area to be considered in the impact assessment. The map shows the actual environmental characteristics of the area likely to be affected by a project, according to experts. The 'degree' of the impact can be shown by the intensity of shading on the overlay.

Today, the hand-made overlay maps have almost completely been replaced by computerized maps. The technique is useful to facilitate comparisons of various alternatives. Overlay mapping is an excellent tool for showing the spatial dimensions of impacts, but is less successful in dealing with other impact characteristics, such as probability, time and reversibility.

12.2.4 Network

A network consists of a number of linked impacts, known to result from a variety of alternative plans. Fig. 12.2 illustrates a network diagram constructed during the Saguling dam (Indonesia) EIA-study. The figure demonstrates the potential impacts during the operational period of the dam. Such a network diagram gives an excellent overview of the possible linkages between actions and impacts, being able to show as well the primary as the secondary, tertiary or higher-order impacts.

12.2.5 Systems Diagram

A systems diagram is the first step towards the construction of an environmental model, see Chapter 13. It is also called a conceptual diagram, and it illustrates how the forcing functions (variables), including those that are man-controlled, influence the ecosystem, i.e., the state variables and among these, in particular, the environmental quality variables.

Fig. 12.3 gives an example, taken from Gilliland (1983). The model has been applied to state the carrying capacity of the Lake Tahoe Basin. The so-called energy circuit language, developed by H.T.Odum, has been applied in this case. This language is particularly well suited to give an overview of the relations between the forcing functions (impacts) and the environmental quality variables (state variables). Table 12.3 explains the symbols used in Fig. 12.3 and presents the differential equations used in the model.

The development of a conceptual model is often the first step in a series of models. If it is possible to quantify the relations, it is recommendable to construct a mathematical model, see Chapter 13, but this will require an access to good, i.e., precise and reliable data. If a quantification is not possible, due to lack of data, it is still of importance to construct a conceptual diagram. It will give an overview of the problem and the linkages between the possible impacts and the environmental quality factors.

REFERENCES

Anonymous, 1978. The Selection of Projects for EIA. Battelle Institute, Commission of the European Communities Environment and Consumer Protection Services, Brussels.

Anonymous, 1980. Environmental Design Considerations for Rural Development Projects. US Agency for International Development, Washington D.C.

Gilliland, M.W., 1983. Models for evaluating human carrying capacity: a case study of the Lake Tahoe basin, California-Nevada. In: S.E. Jørgensen and W.J. Mitsch (eds.): Application of Ecological Modeling in Environmental Management, Part B. Elsevier, Amsterdam.

Heer, J.E. and Hagerty, D.J., 1977. Environmental Assessment and Statements. Van Nostrand Reinhold, New York.

Keeney, R.L., and Robilliard, G.A., 1977. Assessing and evaluating environmental impacts at proposed nuclear power plant sites. J. Envir. Econ. Managem., 4: 153-166.

Sassaman, R.W., 1981. Threshold of concern: a technique for evaluation environmental impacts and amenity values. J. Forestry, 79: 84-86.

Thor, E.C., Elsner, G.H., Travis, M.R. and O'Loughlin, K.M., 1978. Forest environmental impact analysis - a new approach. J. Forestry, 76: 723-725.

13 ENVIRONMENTAL MANAGEMENT MODELLING

SVEN ERIK JØRGENSEN

13.1 MODELLING IN ENVIRONMENTAL MANAGEMENT

Models can be considered a synthesis of different elements of knowledge of a system. The quality of models is, therefore, very dependent on the quality of our knowledge elements and on the data available. If our knowledge and data on a given problem related to a system are poor, it must not be expected that the model can fill the holes in our knowledge, nor that it can repair on a poor data set. On the other hand, models do have the ability to provide new knowledge about the reactions and properties of the entire system. The model represents a synthesis of knowledge and data, and as such, it can provide results, particularly about the system properties.

Traditionally, science has considered the analysis of problems to be rather more important than the synthesis of existing knowledge. The emergence of the very complex environmental problems has provoked a development of ecological and environmental modelling as a powerful synthezising tool, putting the system reactions and properties in focus.

Models are a synthezising tool in the first hand, but it should not be forgotten that models may also be used to analyse the properties of the entire system, on the system level. For this reason, we use models in environmental management not only to overview the problems, but also to reveal the reactions of the entire system to the impact from emissions.

The use of models as such is not new; they have served for centuries as simplified pictures of reality and helped to solve problems. For example, Newton's laws may be considered models of the impact of gravity on bodies. Models, even when used as a synthezising tool, will of course not contain *all* features of the real system - only the real system itself does so. But it is of importance that we extract the knowledge which is *essential* in the context of the problem to be solved or described.

Correspondingly, an environmental model should contain exactly those features which are of interest for the management, or regarding a scientific problem that we wish to solve. This statement is of particular importance for environmental management models, as they can very easily become too complex to be developed for practical use.

Models may be either of a physical or of a mathematical nature. Physical models contain the main components of the real system, and it is attempted to observe the processes and reactions of the complex system - an ecosystem - by use of observations in the simpler system - the physical model. If we want to study, e.g., the interactions between a toxic substance and a system of plants, insects and soil in nature, we may construct a simplified system which contains these components; making our observations on the simpler system, we facilitate the provision and interpretation of data, yet it is hoped that the interpretation holds for the real system as well. Physical models are often referred to as 'microcosmos', as they contain all the major components of the larger system, but on a smaller scale.

This chapter focuses almost entirely on mathematical models, based on a mathematical formulation of the processes most important for the problem considered.

The field of environmental modelling has developed very rapidly during the last decade, due essentially to two factors:

1. The development of computer technology, which has made possible the handling of very complex mathematical systems.

2. A general understanding of pollution problem, including the problems related to the application of ecology in this context.

An overview of the applications of models in environmental management is presented in Fig. 13.1. Emissions from the man-made or man-controlled systems to the environment (the ecosystems) interfere with the living organisms and may change the reactions, the function or even the structure of the entire system. Complete elimination of all emissions is impossible for the pre-industrial man, and with a global human population of more than 5 billions to feed. But if we can properly relate an emission to its ecological implications in the environment, we will be able to give recommendations concerning the emissions we have to eliminate or reduce, and how much they have to be reduced, to guarantee no or almost no adverse effect.

The idea behind the use of models is to come up with the best possible estimation of the relation between emissions and their ecological consequences, by synthezising all the knowledge - or the most important parts of this knowledge - to a degree where one is able to overview the problem in focus.

Applying a model may be considered one possible performance of EIA, environmental impact assesssment (see Chapter 12). However, it is the most advanced and the most quantative EIA method available, and consequently also the most data-demanding one. With this in mind, we should try to apply models in environmental management whenever possible, but if data are too scarce or too costly, the other methods of EIA should be used instead.

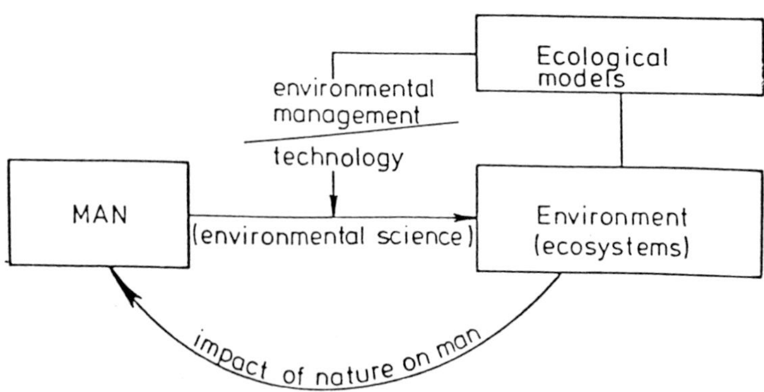

Figure 13.1. Relations between environmental science, ecology, ecological modelling and environmental management and technology.

The recommendations resulting from an environmental model may be in the form of suggestions, either of emission limitations or of legislation on the type of emission in question. What happens next is of course a political decision - although the model may give a rather clear advice - in particular because there is always economy involved in such decisions. It is possible in some instances to construct *ecological-economic* models which consider also the economy of the problem, but such models are not yet sufficiently well developed to give reliable guidelines, at least they have not done so in more than a few cases. But it is to be expected that the ecological-economic models will develop rapidly and will be used much more widely in environmental management within the next decade.

The difficult part of modelling is not the mathematical formulations, nor is it the translation of the mathematics into a computer language. The introduction of personal computers and readily applicable software has made it much easier to handle these steps of modelling. The more difficult part is to provide the necessary knowledge, in particular to judge which components and processes should be included in the model and which should be left out.

Generally speaking, an ecologist, an environmental scientist or an environmental engineer with a certain knowledge of mathematics and computer science is better fit to construct ecological and environmental models than a mathematician with a certain knowledge of ecology and environmental science. However, the very best development of environmental models is carried out by a *team* representing all the relevant disciplines, such as ecology, environmental engineering, mathematics and computer science.

13.2 MODELLING ELEMENTS

In its mathematical formulation, an environmental model has five components:

1. ***Forcing functions*** or *external variables* are functions/variables of an external nature that influence the state of the ecosystem. In a management context, the problem to be solved can often be reformulated as follows: consider certain forcing functions which describe an environmental impact; if these forcing functions are varied, what will be the influence on the state of the ecosystem? The model is used to predict the changes in the ecosystem when forcing functions are varied during time. The man-controlled forcing functions are termed the *control functions*. In ecotoxicological models, e.g, the control functions typically would describe the input of toxic substances from society to the ecosystems; other forcing functions of interest in this case could be the climatic variables, because they influence the biotic and abiotic components and the process rates.

2. ***State variables***, as the name indicates, describe the state of the ecosystem. The selection of the proper state variable is crucial for the model structure, yet in many cases the choice is obvious. If, for instance, we want to model the bioaccumulation of a toxic substance, the state variables should be the various species biomasses in the most important foodchains and their concentrations of certain substances. When a model is used in a management context, the values of the state variables predicted by changing the forcing functions can be considered the results of the model; in fact, the very nature of the model is to relate the state variables directly to the forcing functions.

3. ***Mathematical equations*** are used to represent the biological, chemical and physical processes. They express the relation between forcing functions and state variables. The same type of process may be found in many different environmental contexts, and therefore, the same equations can be used in different connections and in different models. This does not imply, however, that the same process should always be formulated by use of the same equation. First of all, the influence of other factors may imply that some other equation is better fit to describe the process considered. Furthermore, the number of details that we need or want to include in the model may be different, due to a difference in complexity of the system or/and of the problem. Some modellers refer to the description and the mathematical formulation of such processes as 'submodels'.

4. ***Parameters*** are the coefficients in the mathematical representation of processes. They may be considered constant for a specific ecosystem or part of an ecosystem. In causal models, the parameter usually has a scientific definition, e.g., the excretion rate of cadmium from a fish. In the literature, many parameters are indicated not by a precise value but merely by some range; but even that is of great value to the parameter estimation. Jørgensen et al. (1979, 1990) provide a comprehensive collection of values/ranges of parameters used in ecology and environmental science.

5. ***Universal constants***, such as the gas constant, atomic weights of the elements or various biochemical process rates, are also used in most models.

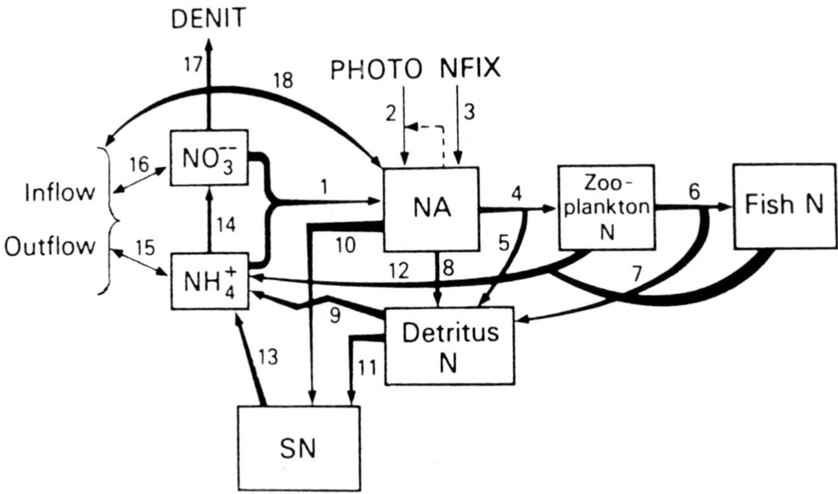

Figure 13.2. The conceptual diagram of a nitrogen cycle in an aquatic ecosystem is shown. The processes are: 1) uptake of nitrate and ammonium by algae, 2) photosynthesis, 3) nitrogen fixation, 4) grazing with loss of undigested matter, 5), 6) and 7) are predation and loss of undigested matter, 8) mortality, 9) mineralization, 10) settling of algae, 11) settling of detritus, 12) excretion of ammonium from zooplankton, 13) release of nitrogen from the sediment, 14) nitrification, 15), 16) and 18) input/output, and 17) denitrification.

Models can be defined as formal expressions in mathematical terms of the essential elements of a problem. The formulation of a model only happens at a later stage of the work with the problem; when the problem is first recognized, it is often expressed verbally. This may be looked at an essential preliminary step in the modelling procedure which we shall treat in more detail in the next section. The verbal model is, however, difficult to visualize and it is, therefore, conveniently translated into a *conceptual diagram* which contains the state variables, the forcing function and the mathematical formulation of their interrelationships.

Fig. 13.2 shows a conceptual diagram of the nitrogen cycle in a lake. The state variables are nitrate, ammonium (which in the un-ionized form ammonia is toxic to fish), nitrogen in phytoplankton, nitrogen in zooplankton, nitrogen in fish, nitrogen in sediment and nitrogen in detritus.

The forcing functions are: the water inflow and outflow, the concentration of nitrogen components in the in- and outflow, the solar radiation (indicated by the arrow PHOTO) and the temperature; the latter is not shown on the diagram, but it influences all process rates.

The arrows in the diagram illustrate the processes; these are formulated by use of mathematical expressions (differential equations) in the mathematical part of the model. Three important steps in the modelling procedure should be defined in this section; they are calibration, verification and validation.

Calibration means attempting at the best accordance possible between computed and observed data, by systematically variating selected parameters. The calibration may be carried out by the so-called trial-and-error method, or by use of software developed to find the parameter values which give the best fit between observed and computed values. In a few cases, calibration may be unnecessary; this is the case for some static (time-independent) models, and for simple models containing only a few parameters which are well defined or are measured directly.

Verification is a test of the *internal logic* of the model. Typical question in the verification phase are: Does the model react as expected? Is the model long-term stable? Does the model follow the law of mass conservation? In general terms, verification is a subjective assessment of the behaviour of the model. The verification will go on during the building of the model, until the calibration phase described above.

Validation must be distinguished from verification. The validation consists of an objective test of how well the model output fit the data. The selection of possible objective tests depend on the scope of the model. The standard deviation between model predictions and observations is often used as an indicator; a comparison of observed and predicted minimum or maximum values of a particularly important state variable is another possibility. If several state variables are included in the validation, they may be given different weights.

Further details on these important steps in modelling are given in the next section, where the entire modelling procedure is discussed.

13.3 THE MODELLING PROCEDURE

In this section a tentative modelling procedure is presented. The author of this chapter has used the procedure successfully several times and can strongly recommend to follow it carefully, through all the steps. Other scientists in the field have published procedures slightly different from the one described below, but a detailed examination of the differences will reveal that they are only minor. The most important steps of modelling are included in virtually all the recommended modelling procedures.

The primary focus of all research, and indeed of environmental management, is to define the problem properly. This is the only way to ensure that limited resources are appropriately allocated instead of being dispersed into irrelevant activities.

The first modelling step, therefore, is to put up a ***definition*** of the problem. Necessarily, the definition is bounded by the constituents of *space, time and subsystems*. Since the bounding of the problem in space and time is usually rather easy, it is also more explicit than the identification of the subsystems to be incorporated in the model.

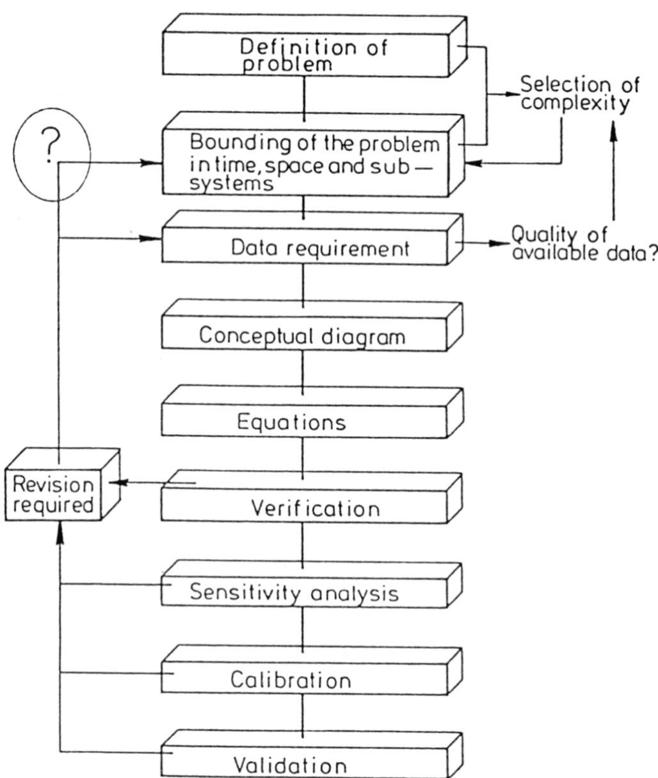

Figure 13.3. A tentative modelling procedure. - Reproduced from Jørgensen (1988).

Fig. 13.3 shows the procedure presented by the author (Jørgensen, 1988), but it is important

Fig. 13.3 shows the procedure presented by the author (Jørgensen, 1988), but it is important to emphasize that this procedure is unlikely to be suitable in a first attempt: there is no need to aim at perfection in one step. The procedure should be considered an iterative process, and the main requirement is to get started (Jeffers, 1978).

At least in the first instance, it is difficult to determine the optimal number of subsystems to be included in the model, when the aim is an acceptable level of accuracy in view of the scope of the model. In many cases it become necessary, at a later stage, either due to lack of data to accept a lower level than intended at the start, or to provide additional data for the improvement of the model.

Many times it has been argued that a more complex model should be able to more accurately account for the reactions of the real system, but this is not necessary true. Some additional factors must be introduced into these considerations. A more complex model will also contain more parameters, and when the number of model parameters is increasing, there will also be an increasing uncertainty. The reason is that the parameters have to be estimated, either by more observations in the field, by laboratory experiments or by calibrations which are again based on field measurements. Parameter estimations are never error-free, and the errors are carried along into the model, thereby contributing to the total level of uncertainty of the model.

The problem of selecting the right degree of model *complexity* is of particular interest for modelling in environmental management.

A first approach to the data requirement can be given at this stage, but it may most likely be changed at a later stage, when experience with the verification, calibration , sensitivity analysis and validation has been gained. To a certain extent, modelling is to be considered an iterative procedure.

In principle, data for all the selected state variables must be available, and it is only in a few cases acceptable to omit the measuring of selected state variables, as the success of the calibration and validation is closely linked to the *quality and quantity of the data.*

Once the *model complexity* has been decided for, at least regarding the first modelling attempt, it is now possible *to conceptualize the model.* This is typically done in the form of a diagram, like the one shown in Fig. 13.2. Such a diagram helps recalling which state variables, forcing function and processes are required in the model.

The next step is to formulate the processes more precisely as ***mathematical equations***. For many processes, several equations are at hand to describe what happens, and it may be crucial for the reliability of the results of the final model that the right equation is selected for the case considered.

Once the system of mathematical equations is put up, the ***verification*** can be carried out. As we have pointed out in Section 13.2, this is an important step which is, unfortunately, omitted by some modellers. It can be recommended at this stage to attempt to answer at least the following questions:

1. Is the model *long-term stable*? To investigate this, the model is run on the computer for a long period, assuming the same annual variations in the forcing functions, and it is observed whether or not the state variables are maintained at approximately the same levels. During the beginning of the period, the state variables will depend on the initial values they are

given, so the model should be run also with initial values corresponding to the long-term values of the state variables.

2. Does the model *react* as expected? For instance, if the input of toxic substances is increased, we would expect a higher concentration of the toxic substance in the top-carnivorous organisms. If this does not happen, it indicates that some formulation may be wrong and should be corrected.

In general, it is a good idea to 'play' with the model in this phase. Through such exercise, the modeller gets acquainted with the model and observes how it responds to pertubations, i.e., to small changes in the parameters or the initial values. It is important that the modeller acquires a good 'feeling' for the reactions of the model to such changes.

After the verification follows a closer look at the model's response to perturbations, viz. the ***sensitivity analysis*** through which the modeller obtains an overview of the most *sensitive components of the model.* The analysis attempts at providing a measure of the sensitivity of the important state variables to changes in the parameters, the forcing functions or the initial values, to the inclusion of submodels, etc. For example, if a modeller wants to simulate the toxic-substance concentration in a carnivorous insect, assuming a certain scheme of insecticide application, then he will obviously consider this state variable as the most important one, supplied with the toxic substance concentration in plants and herbivorous insects; and the sensitivity analysis must concentrate on the response of these variables to various perturbations of the model input.

In practical modelling, the sensitivity analysis is carried out by changing the parameter, the forcing function or the submodel and observing the response in the selected state variables. A more formal definition of the sensitivity of, say, a state variable x with respect to a parameter P, goes:

$$S = \frac{\Delta x}{x} : \frac{\Delta P}{P}, \tag{13.1}$$

i.e., the the sensitivity is the ratio between the *relative* change in x and the corresponding relative change in the parameter. The definition is similar to that of 'elasticity', a concept frequently used in, a.o., economics.

When carrying out the sensitivity analysis, the relative change in a parameter value is chosen with a view to the uncertainty of the parameter. If the modeller estimates the relative uncertainty to be, say, about 50%, he will typically apply changes of ± 10% and ±50% in the parameter in question, and record the resulting changes in the state variable(s). Often it is necessary to determine the sensitivity at two or more levels of parameter changes, as the relation between a parameter and a state variable is rarely linear.

A sensitivity analysis of *submodels* (process equations) can also be carried out. It consists of deleting the submodel equations in the model, or changing them into an alternative (possibly more detailed) submodel, whereupon the resulting changes in the state variable(s) are recorded. Such results may be used to make structural changes of the model. For instance, if the sensitivity analysis shows that it is crucial for the model results to use a more detailed submodel, this knowledge speaks in favor of changing the model correspondingly.

From these considerations it follows that decisions regarding the complexity and the structure of the model should work hand in hand with the sensitivity analysis, cf. the 'feed back loop' from sensitivity analysis to data requirements in Fig. 13.3. This is in accordance with the concept of 'order of model', as presented by Halfon et al. (1979).

A sensitivity analysis of the forcing functions gives an impression of their relative importance and tells us which accuracy is required of the forcing function data.

The scope of the ***calibration*** is to improve the parameter estimation. Some of the parameters frequently used in causal ecological models can be found in the literature, not necessarily stated as 'precise' constants but perhaps rather as approximate values or indicated by ranges (intervals). If an approximate value cannot be found in the literature, one must use one of the estimation methods presented in Jørgensen (1988, 1990).

Even when all the parameters have been bounded within intervals, either from the literature or by estimation methods, it is usually better to calibrate the model. Several sets of parameters are tested by the calibration, and the various model output of state variables are compared with observations of the same state variables. The parameter set, which leads to the model output most in accordance with the measured values, is chosen.

The need for the calibration is emphasized by the following characteristics of ecological models and their parameters:

1. Parameters are rarely known by exact values; and as a rule, parameter values from the literature are subject to some uncertainty.

2. All environmental models are simplifications of nature. The most important components and processes may be included, but the model structure does not account for all the details. To a certain extent, the influence of some components and processes of minor importance can be taken into account by the calibration. This leads to parameters values slightly different from the unknown, 'true' ones in nature, but the difference may partly account for the influence from the details that were omitted.

3. By far, most models in environmental management are *lumped* models, i.e., one parameter represents an average value for several species. As each species has its own characteristic parameter value, the variation in the species composition within time will inevitably lead to a corresponding variation in the average parameter used in the model.

A calibration cannot be carried out randomly if more than a couple of parameters have been selected for calibration. For instance, if ten parameters have to be calibrated, and the uncertainty pattern justifies ten values of the parameters to be tested, it is required to run the model 10^{10} times, which is of course an impossible task. Instead, the modeller may learn about the behaviour of the model by varying one or two parameters at the time and observing the response of the crucial state variables. In some cases, the model can be split up into a number of submodels which can be calibrated more or less independently of each other. Although the calibration described is to some extent based on systematics, it is still a trial-and-error procedure. However, procedures for automatic calibration are available.

In the trial-and-error calibration, the modeller more or less intuitively sets up a number of calibration criteria. For instance, he may want to simulate rather accurately the minimum oxygen concentration for a stream model, and/or the time at which the minimum occurs. When he is satisfied with these model results, he may want to go on to simulate properly the shape of the curve showing oxygen concentration as a function of time, and so on. To achieve these objectives, the model is calibrated step by step along the process.

If an automatic calibration procedure is applied, it is necessary to formulate objective criteria for the calibration. A useful function in this situation is the following which is related to the expression for calculating the standard deviation:

$$Y = \sqrt{\frac{1}{n}\sum_x \left(\frac{x_c - x_m}{x_{m,a}}\right)^2} \qquad (13.2)$$

where x_c is the value of a state variable computed in the model, x_m is the corresponding value measured, $x_{m,a}$ is the average of the values mesured, and n is the number of values measured/computed. The value of Y is computed during the automatic calibration and followed as the model parameters are varied, the goal of the calibration being to obtain the lowest possible Y-value.

In may cases, however, it is only for two or three state variables that the modeller is interested in a good accordance between model output and observations, while he cares less about other state variables. If so, he may choose specific weights for the various state variables, to account for the emphasis he puts on each state variable in the model. For example, consider a model for the effect of an insecticide, and assume that the modeller is much more interested in modelling the toxic substance concentration in the carnivorous insects than those in plants, herbivorous insects and soil; therefore, hey may choose, say, a weight of ten for the first state variable and only one for each of the three others.

If a proper calibration turns out to be impossible, the reason it not necessarily that the model is incorrect or inadequate. It could also be due to a low quality of the data set. The quality of the data is crucial for the calibration. Just as crucial is the condition that *the observations reflect the dynamics of the system*. If it is the objective of the model to give a good description of one or a few state variables, the data have to be able to show their dynamics; in particular, the data-observation frequency must take them into regard. Unfortunately, this rule has often been violated in modelling.

It it highly recommendable that the dynamics of *all* state variables is considered before the data collection program is laid down in detail. Some state variables may have a very pronounced dynamics in a specific period, e.g., in spring; and it may be a great advantage to have a particularly dense data collection in this period. Jørgensen et al. (1981) show how a dense data collection program in a certain period can be applied to give an additional certainty in the determination of some important parameters.

Based on these considerations, we can put up the following principles for the calibration of a model, typically in environmental chemistry:

1. Find *as many parameters as possible from the literature*; even a *wide* range for a parameter should be considered valuable, as approximate initial guesses for all parameters are urgently needed.
2. If some parameters cannot be found in the literature, as is usually the case, use the *estimation methods* described above, or determine the parameters by experiments in situ or in the laboratory.
3. A *sensitivity analysis* should be carried out, determining which parameters it is most important to know with a high accuracy.

4. The use of a *dense data collection program* for the most important state variables should be considered, to provide precise estimates of the crucial parameters.
5. Only at this stage, the *calibration* should be carried out, using the data which have not yet been applied. The most important parameters are selected, and the calibration is limited to these; it should involve no more than 8-10 parameters. In the first hand, calibration is done by trial-and-error, thereby also testing the model's reaction to changes in the parameters. Afterwards, an automatic calibration procedure may 'polish' the parameter estimation.
6. Next, the calibrated model is subjected to a *second sensitivity analysis,* the results of which may differ from the those of the first one.
7. Even a *second calibration* is perhaps carried out for the most important parameters, most important, using the results of the second sensitivity analysis and both the above-mentioned calibration methods.

The calibration now completed should always be followed by a *validation*. In this step, the modeller tests the model against a data set which is independent of all data previously used, observing how well the model simulations fit to this data set.

However, it must be emphasized that the validation confirms the model behaviour only under the range of conditions represented by the data available. For this reason, it is preferable to obtain new data from a period in which other conditions prevail than when data were collected for the calibration. For instance, when a model of the fate and effect of toxic substances is tested, the calibration data and the validation data should have different levels of toxic substance impact on the ecosystem.

If an ideal validation cannot be obtained, it is still important to validate the model which may still be used as a management tool, provided the modeller points out the open questions of the model to the manager. As experience is gained by using the model, the number of open questions may be reduced. A simple model is often better than no model at all, provided its shortcomings are carefully presented by the modeller.

The method of validation depends on the objectives of the model. A comparison between observed data and computed data, e.g., by use of the objective function (13.2), is an obvious test, but often it is insufficient, as it may fail to involve *all* the main objectives of the model, merely testing the general ability of the model to give a fair description of the state variables of the ecosystem. It is, therefore, necessary to translate the main objectives of the model into a few validation criteria. No general formulation is at hand: the criteria are individual for the model and the modeller. For instance, if we are concerned with the maximum concentration of a toxic substance in carnivorous insects, it would be useful to compare the measured and computed maximum concentrations at this level in the food chain.

The above discussion can be summarized as follows:

1. *Validation* is *always* required, to get a picture of the reliability of the model.
2. Attempts should be made to get data for the validation, which are *entirely different from those used in the calibration*. Also, it is important to have data from a *wide range of forcing functions*, as defined by the objectives of the model.
3. The validation criteria are formulated on basis of *the objectives of the model* and *the quality of the available data.*

Table 13.1. Classification of Models (pairs of model types).

Model type	Characterization
Research models	Used as a research tool
Management models	Used as a management tool
Deterministic models	Predictions by 'exact' values
Stochastic models	Predictions by confidence intervals
Compartment models	The variables defining the system are quantified by means of time-dependent differential equations
Matrix models	Time-dependent difference equations (possibly matrices) are used in the mathematical formulation
Reductionistic models	Include as many relevant details as possible
Holistic models	Use general principles
Static models	The variables defining the system do not depend on time
Dynamic models	The variables defining the system are a function of time (directly or indirectly)
Distributed models	The parameters are functions of time and space
Lumped models	Within certain prescribed spatial locations and time limits, the parameters are considered constants
Linear models	Only first-degree equations occur
Non-linear models	One or several equations are non-linear
Causal models	Inputs, states and outputs are causally interrelated
Black box models	The input disturbances affect only the output responses. No causality is required

13.4 TYPES OF MODELS

It is useful to outline the various types of models and to discuss briefly the selection of model types. For a more comprehensive treatment of this topic, see Jørgensen (1988).

A number of 'pairs of models' is listed in Table 13.1.

The first pair, distinguishing between *scientific and management models*, is based on the application point-of-view.

The next pair is: *stochastic and deterministic models*. A stochastic model contains stochastic input disturbances and/or random measurement errors. If they are both assumed to be zero, the stochastic model reduces into a deterministic model, provided the parameters are not estimated in terms of statistical distributions. A deterministic model assumes that the future response of the system is completely determined by the present state and future inputs. Until now, stochastic models have rarely been applied in environmental management.

The third pair in Table 13.1 is *compartment and matrix models*, to some extent equivalent to the distinction between *continuous and discrete models*. (We do not, as do some modellers, by the term 'compartment' simply understand the 'box' in the conceptual diagram). Both types of models are applied in environmental management, although the use of compartment models is by far the most pronounced.

The classification *reductionistic* and *holistic* models is based upon a difference in the scientific ideas behind the model. The reductionistic modeller will attempt to incorporate as many details of the system as possible, to be able to capture its behaviour. He believes that the properties of the system are the sum of the details. The holistic modeller, on the other side, wants the model to include properties of the ecosystem working *as a system*, by use of general principles. In this case, the properties of the system are not merely seen as the sum of all the details considered, but the holistic modeller presumes that the system posseses some additional properties because the subsystems are working together, as an entity. Both types of models occur in environmental management, but in order to get an overview of the very complex problems he is tackling, the environmental modeller will most often have to take a holistic view at things.

A large number of problems in environmental management may be attacked by means of a *dynamic model*, in which differential or difference equations are used to describe the system response to external factors. Differential equations represent continous changes of state in time, while difference equations use discrete time steps.

Consider an *autonomous* dynamic model, i.e., a model whose parameters do not depend directly on time. A *steady state* of the model system is a set of values of the state variables for which all the derivatives are zero. When finding the steady states of a system, one has to provisorily reduce the dynamic model to a *static model* consisting of the algebraic equations that arise when all the state variable derivatives are set equal to zero, and to solve this problem. On the other hand, the full dynamic model is necessary for determining the behaviour of the system 'near' a steady state, i.e., the *stability* properties of the steady state in question.

Some autonomous dynamic systems have no steady state, but instead they may show *limit cycles* or some other type of systematic asymptotic behaviour. Obviously, in such a case a dynamic model is necessary for an appropriate description of the system. A linear system can have a steady state, but not a limit cycle or similar, which is only possible when the model is non-linear.

As stated in Table 13.1, a static model is characterized by all variables and parameters being independent of time. The advantage of the static model is its potential for simplifying subsequent computational effort through the elimination of one of the independent variables, time, in the model relationship. However, this simplification in most cases renders the model too crude.

A *distributed model* accounts for variations of variables both in time and space. A typical example is an advection-diffusion model for the transport along a stream of a substance dissolved in the water. The model may include variations in three directions, i.e., not only along the stream, but also perpendicur to it, vertically and horizontally. However, on the basis of prior observations, the analyst may judge that gradients of dissolved material in one or two directions are minor and may be excluded from the model, or taken into account only by partitioning the state variable(s) in a few sectors/compartments along these directions, thus reducing the model to a *lumped* parameter model. Typically, the distributed model is based on *partial differential equations,* while the corresponding lumped model uses ordinary differential equations.

A *causal* or *internally descriptive model* implies a characterization or a theoretical deduction of how inputs are connected to states, and how states are connected to each other and to the outputs of the system. In contrast, a *black box model* only reflects what changes the input will effect in the output response, and does so in terms of equations and functions chosen 'empirically', with no attempt to justify the equations theoretically. In other words, the causal model provides a proper description of the internal mechanisms of the process behaviour, while the black box model only deals with what is measurable: the input and the output, and connects them in an ad-hoc type of way, e.g., by a statistical analysis.

In a case where his knowledge about the processes is rather limited, the modeller may prefer to use a black box description which has, however, the disadvantage that the application of it is limited to the ecosystem considered, or at least to a narrow class of ecosystems similar to the one considered. If a general applicability is wanted, one must set up a causal model. Of the two types of models, the causal is the more widely used in environmental management, mainly because it gives the user a better understanding of the functioning of the system, including the chemical, physical and biological reactions involved.

Table 13.2 shows another classification of models. The three types of models listed differ by the choice of components used as state variables. If the model aims at describing a number of individuals, species or classes of species, we speak of a *biodemographic model.* A model which describes the energy flows is termed *bioenergetic*, the state variables typically being expressed in kW or kW per unit of volume or area. Finally, a *biogeochemical* model focuses on the flow of material, and the state variables, typically, are indicated as kg, or as kg per unit of volume or area.

Table 13.2. Identification of Models.

Model type	Organization	Pattern	Measurements	Examples
Biodemographic	Conservation of species or genetic information	Life cycles	Number of individuals or species	Fig. 13.4
Bioenergetic	Conservation of energy	Energy flow	Energy	Fig. 13.5
Biogeochemical	Conservation of mass	Element cycles	Mass or concentrations	Figs. 13.2, 6, 7, 8 and 9.

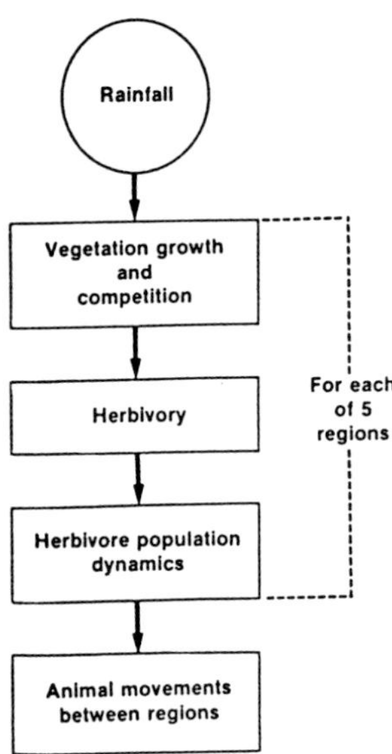

Figure 13.4. A model for the management of a national park in Africa. The sequence of calculations for one iteration of the system model is shown.

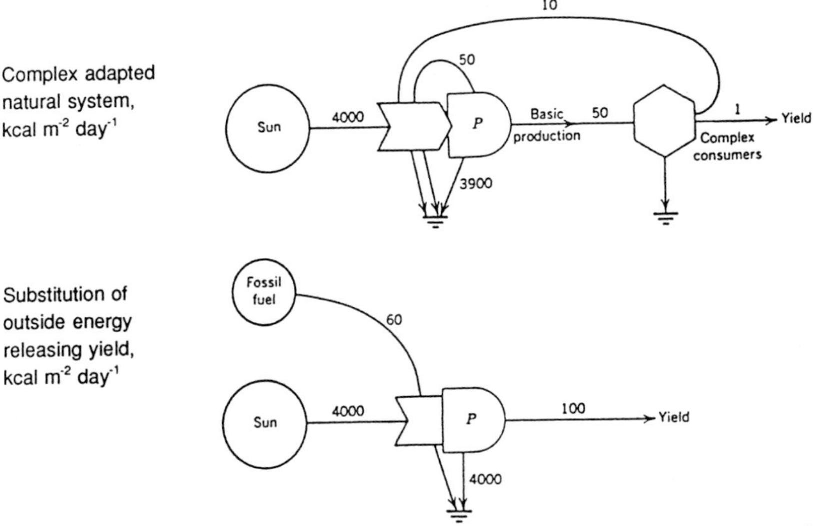

Figure 13.5. Comparison of a complex natural system adapted to maximize its basic production through the the works of its diversified organization of consumer species with the same system after fossil-fuel supported works of man have eliminated the natural species and substituted industrial services for the services of those natural species, releasing the same basic production to yield. (Figures are for plant production only.)

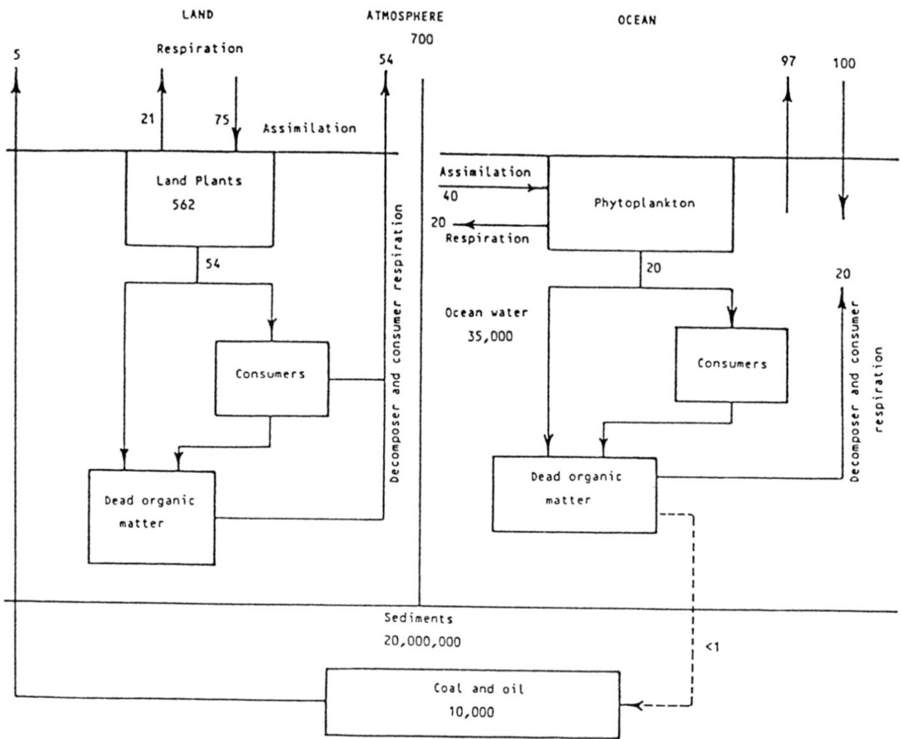

Figure 13.6. The global carbon cycle. Values in compartments are in 10^9 tons and in fluxes, 10^9 tons/year.

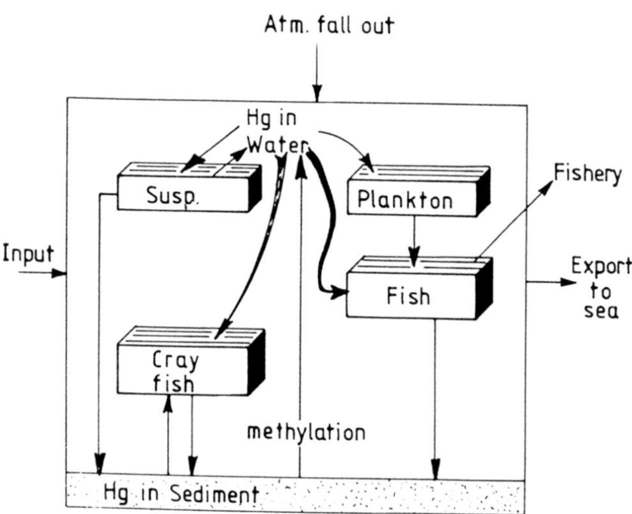

Figure 13.7. Mercury distribution in an aquatic ecosystem.

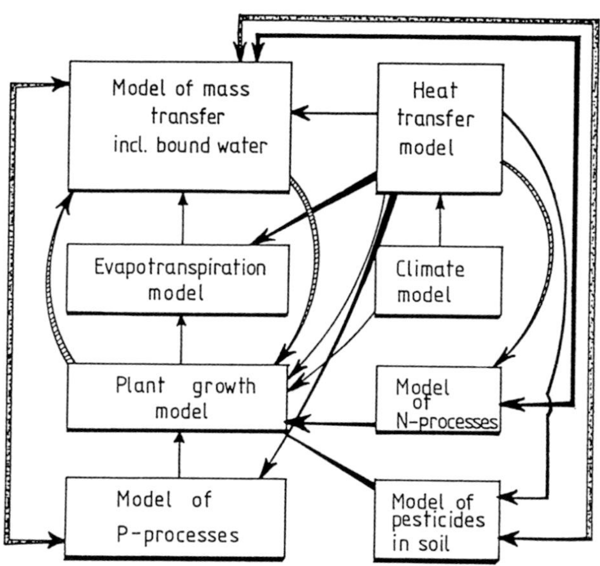

Figure 13.8. The linking of eight submodels, to form an overall agricultural-environmental crop production model. Relations are indicated by arrows, showing all instances where output from one submodel is used in another.

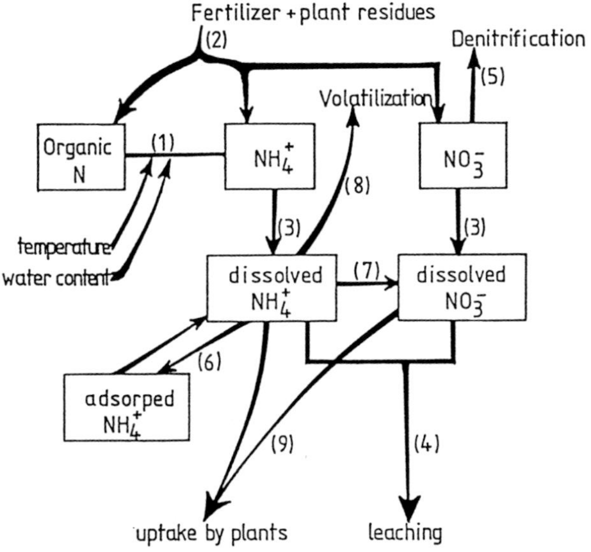

Figure 13.9. Model of nitrogen soil processes.

The six figures following Table 13.2 illustrate various models and model types from the field of environmental management modeling.

Fig. 13.4 shows the basic features of a model which has been applied for the management of a national park in Africa. The model attempts at predicting the fate of various populations as influenced by possible environmental impacts. The model is biodemographic, deterministic, compartment, holistic, dynamic, lumped, non-linear, and causal.

Fig. 13.5 displays the energy flow in primitive agriculture as well as in modern, energy-based agriculture. The model uses the energy-circuit language developed by H.T. Odum. This model is bioenergetic, deterministic, compartment, holistic, static, lumped, linear, and causal.

Fig. 13.6 illustrates the global carbon cycle. It has been applied to predict the so-called greenhouse effect (see Chapter 3) as influenced by man's use of fossil fuel. The model is biogeochemical, deterministic, compartment, holistic, static, lumped, non-linear, and causal.

Fig. 13.7 shows a conceptual diagram for a model predicting the mercury distribution in an aquatic ecosystem. The model is biogeochemical, deterministic, compartment, holistic, dynamic, lumped, nonlinear, and causal.

Fig. 13.8 is a conceptual diagram illustrating how various submodels are linked to form an overall agricultural-environmental management model. This model relates the climatic conditions, the use of fertilizers and pesticides, and the plant growth to each other. The model output is supposed to be, on one side the yield, on the other side the losses of fertilizers and pesticides to the environment. Therefore, the model can be used to find an ecological-economic optimum for the use of fertilizers and pesticides. The submodels of this very comprehensive model have been developed, but there is no experience as yet concerning the use of the full model in agricultural-environmental management. However, extensive research is carried out to develop improvements, and it is hoped that within the next decade, it will be possible to introduce a wider use of the total model.

Fig. 13.9 illustrates a model of the nitrogen processes in the soil. It can be used as a submodel in Fig. 13.8. This model is biogeochemical, deterministic, compartment, holistic, dynamic, nonlinear, and causal.

Additional information about most of the models shown in Figs. 13.4-13.9 can be found in Jørgensen (1988).

13.5 CONCLUSIONS

Models are used more and more widely as a powerful, synthesizing tool in environmental management. During the last decades, several useful models have been developed; they have been properly calibrated and validated, and they have been put to work in actual environmental management. Even validations of prognoses have been carried out. Due to a better knowledge of the environmental and ecological processes and due to an extensive development in computer science, it is to be expected that models will be more and more used in environmental management in the years to come.

It is a task for specialists to develop the models, but it is also important that everybody dealing with environmental mar .gement knows the existence of this tool and appreciates its advantages as well as its shortcomings.

REFERENCES

Halfon, E., Unbehauen, H. and Schmid, C., 1979. Model order estimation and system identification theory to the modeling of ^{32}P kinetics within the trophogenic zone of a small lake. Ecol. Modelling, 6: 1-22.

Jeffers, J.N.R., 1978. An Introduction to System Analysis: with ecological applications. Edward Arnold, London, 198 pp.

Jørgensen, S.E. (ed.), 1979. Handbook of Environmental Data and Ecological Parameters. Int. Society of Ecological Modelling, Copenhagen.

Jørgensen, S.E., 1988. Fundamentals of Ecological Modelling. 2. ed. Elsevier, Amsterdam-New York-Tokyo, 389 pp.

Jørgensen, S.E., 1990. Modelling in Ecotoxicology. Elsevier, Amsterdam-New York-Tokyo, 354 pp.

Jørgensen, S.E., Jørgensen, L.A., Kamp Nielsen, L. and Mejer, H.F., 1981. Parameter estimation in eutrophication modelling. Ecol. Modelling, 13: 111-129.

Jørgensen, S.E., Nors Nielsen, S. and Jørgensen, L.A., 1990. Handbook of Ecological Parameters and Ecotoxicology. Elsevier, Amsterdam-New York-Tokyo.

INDEX